T0236270

Processing
Creative Coding and Computational Art

Ira Greenberg

DESIGNER TO DESIGNER™

an Apress® company

Processing: Creative Coding and Computational Art

ISBN-13: 978-1-4842-2025-2

ISBN-10: 1-4842-2025-0

DOI 10.1007/978-1-4302-0310-0

Trademarked names may appear in this book. Rather than use a trademark symbol with every occurrence of a trademarked name, we use the names only in an editorial fashion and to the benefit of the trademark owner, with no intention of infringement of the trademark.

Distributed to the book trade worldwide by Springer-Verlag New York, Inc., 233 Spring Street, 6th Floor, New York, NY 10013. Phone 1-800-SPRINGER, fax 201-348-4505, e-mail orders-ny@springer-sbm.com, or visit www.springeronline.com.

For information on translations, please contact Apress directly at 2855 Telegraph Avenue, Suite 600, Berkeley, CA 94705. Phone 510-549-5930, fax 510-549-5939, e-mail info@apress.com, or visit www.apress.com.

The information in this book is distributed on an "as is" basis, without warranty. Although every precaution has been taken in the preparation of this work, neither the author(s) nor Apress shall have any liability to any person or entity with respect to any loss or damage caused or alleged to be caused directly or indirectly by the information contained in this work.

The source code for this book is freely available to readers at www.friendsofed.com in the Downloads section.

Credits

Lead Editor Chris Mills	**Assistant Production Director** Kari Brooks-Copony
Technical Editor Charles E. Brown	**Production Editor** Ellie Fountain
Technical Reviewers Carole Katz, Mark Napier	**Compositor** Dina Quan
Editorial Board Steve Anglin, Ewan Buckingham, Gary Cornell, Jason Gilmore, Jonathan Gennick, Jonathan Hassell, James Huddleston, Chris Mills, Matthew Moodie, Jeff Pepper, Dominic Shakeshaft, Matt Wade	**Artist** Milne Design Services, LLC **Proofreaders** Linda Seifert and Nancy Sixsmith
Project Manager Sofia Marchant	**Indexer** John Collin
Copy Edit Manager Nicole Flores	**Interior and Cover Designer** Kurt Krames
Copy Editor Damon Larson	**Manufacturing Director** Tom Debolski

To Robin, Ian, and Sophie.

CONTENTS AT A GLANCE

CONTENTS

CONTENTS

CONTENTS

FOREWORD

If you are like me (and the fact that you are holding a Processing book in your hands indicates there's a fair chance that you are), then a quick flip through the pages of this book, glancing at the many illustrations, should be enough to set your heart beating just a little bit faster, and start seeds of ideas sprouting in your head.

Processing is a richly visual language, which is pretty obvious if you've performed the aforementioned page flipping. It has its roots in a language called Design by Numbers, developed by Professor John Maeda at MIT, and was in fact created by two of Maeda's students, Ben Fry and Casey Reas. Whereas most languages are built to create serious applications, Processing almost seems to have been created to just have fun with. The language has been used to create various data visualization and installation art pieces, but most often you just see people playing with it, creating complex and beautiful pictures and animations. As a matter of fact, you don't even make Processing applications; you make sketches—which go in your sketchbook. This aspect of the language has drawn many creative coders who blur the boundaries between programming and art.

Many like to draw a comparison between Processing and Adobe (née Macromedia) Flash, a commercial program often used to create graphically rich, often purely experimental animations using ActionScript, an easy-to-learn programming language. Indeed, many of the people using Processing started out programming in Flash, and switched to take advantage of the superior speed and performance, additional commands, and flexibility of Processing. Although Flash has gained a lot over the years in terms of performance and capabilities, Processing remains the tool of choice for many artist-coders.

Processing has grown quite a bit over the years. It's an evolving language, added onto by various plug-ins and contributions from a dedicated community. It's deceivingly simple, allowing you to get started quickly, but it provides an incredible amount of depth for those who care to peek beneath the surface.

Although there are various online resources, Processing has lacked a printed book of any sort. This book fills that gap, and then some. In the tradition of the language, this book covers both the artistic and the programming aspects of Processing. And if you are stronger on the art side than the code side, fear not. The author leads you into it gently, giving you just the bits you need to get started. On the other hand, when you are ready to dive in deep, there's more than enough material to keep you up late at night coding.

So take another flip through the book for inspiration, take a deep breath, get comfortable, and dive in, just like I'll be doing as soon as I finish writing this!

Keith Peters, April 2007

ABOUT THE AUTHOR

Photo by Robin McLennan

With an eclectic background combining elements of painting and programming, **Ira Greenberg** has been a painter, 2D and 3D animator, print designer, web and interactive designer/developer, programmer, art director, creative director, managing director, art professor, and now author. He holds a BFA from Cornell University and an MFA from the University of Pennsylvania.

Ira has steadily exhibited his work, consulted within industry, and lectured widely throughout his career. He was affiliated with the Flywheel Gallery in Piermont, New York, and the Bowery Gallery in New York City. He was a managing director and creative director for H2O Associates in New York's Silicon Alley, where he helped build a new media division during the golden days of the dot-com boom and then bust— barely parachuting back to safety in the ivory tower. Since then, he has been inciting students to create inspirational new media art; lecturing; and holding residencies at numerous institutions, including Seton Hall University; Monmouth University; University of California, Santa Barbara; Kutztown University; Moravian College; Northampton Community College's Digital Art Institute; Lafayette College; Lehigh University; the Art Institute of Seattle; Studio Art Centers International (in Florence, Italy); and the City and Guilds of London Art School.

Currently, Ira is Associate Professor at Miami University (Ohio), where he has a joint appointment within the School of Fine Arts and Interactive Media Studies program. He is also an affiliate member of the Department of Computer Science and Systems Analysis. His research interests include aesthetics and computation, expressive programming, emergent forms, net-based art, artificial intelligence, physical computing, and computer art pedagogy (and anything else that tickles his fancy). During the last few years, he has been torturing defenseless art students with trigonometry, algorithms, and object-oriented programming, and is excited to spread this passion to the rest of the world.

Ira lives in charming Oxford, Ohio with his wife, Robin; his son, Ian; his daughter, Sophie; their squirrel-obsessed dog, Heidi; and their night prowler cat, Moonshadow.

ABOUT THE TECH REVIEWERS

Carole Katz holds an AB in English and American Literature from Brown University. Her career as a graphic designer and technical communicator has spanned more than 20 years, including stints at small nonprofits, design firms, government agencies, and multinational corporations. Beginning with PageMaker 1 and MacDraw in the mid-1980s, Carole has used many types of software in a variety of design disciplines, including corporate identity, technical illustration, book design, and cartography. She is currently a freelance graphic designer, and lives with her family in Oxford, Ohio.

Mark Napier, painter turned digital artist, is one of the early pioneers of Internet art. Through such works as *The Shredder*, *Digital Landfill*, and *Feed*, he explores the potential of a new medium in a worldwide public space and as an engaging interactive experience. Drawing on his experience as a software developer, Napier explores the software interface as an expressive form, and invites the visitor to participate in the work. His online studio, www.potatoland.org, is an open playground of interactive artwork. Napier has created a wide range of projects that appropriate the data of the Web, transforming content into abstraction, text into graphics, and information into art. His works have been included in many leading exhibitions of digital art, including the Whitney Museum of American Art Biennial Exhibition, the Whitney's Data Dynamics exhibition, the San Francisco Museum of Modern Art's (SFMOMA) 010101: Art in Technological Times, and ZKM's (Center for Art and Media in Karlsruhe, Germany) net_condition exhibition. He has been a recipient of grants from Creative Capital, NYFA, and the Greenwall Foundation, and has been commissioned to create artwork by SFMOMA, the Whitney Museum, and the Guggenheim.

ACKNOWLEDGMENTS

I am very fortunate to know and work with so many kind, smart, and generous people. Here are just a few who have helped make this book possible:

Advisors, colleagues, and reviewers: Fred Green, Andres Wanner, Paul Fishwick, Paul Catanese, Mary Flanagan, Laura Mandell, Scott Crass, Mike Zmuda, and David Wicks for showing an interest when it really, really mattered; technical reviewers Carole Katz, Mark Napier, and Charles E. Brown for helping me simplify, clarify, and rectify—the book is far better because of your combined wisdom; my wonderful colleagues and students at Miami University, in the Department of Art and Interactive Media Studies program—especially Mike McCollum, Jim Coyle, Bettina Fabos, Glenn Platt, Peg Faimon, and dele jegede—for tolerating such a looooong journey and my perpetual "when the book is finished" response.

The wonderful people at friends of ED: Production editor Ellie Fountain for always responding kindly to my neurotic, 11th-hour requests; copy editor Damon Larson for his patience and precision in helping me craft actual grammatical sentences; project manager Sofia Marchant for keeping the book (and me) from slipping into the procrastinator's abyss—I couldn't have pulled this off without you! Lead editor and heavy metal warrior Chris Mills for believing in a first-time author and providing constant support and sage advice throughout the entire process. I appreciate this opportunity more than you know, Chris!

The wonderful Processing community—especially Ben Fry and Casey Reas for giving me something to actually write about. I know I am just one of many who owe you a world of thanks for selflessly creating this amazing tool/medium/environment/language/revolution.

My incredible mentors, friends, and family: Petra T. D. Chu, for all your generosity and support over the years; Tom Shillea, Bruce Wall, and Sherman Finch for helping plant the "creative coding" seed; Bill Hudders for sticking around even after I put down the paintbrush; Roger Braimon for keeping me from taking anything too seriously; Jim and Nancy for moving 700 miles to join us in a cornfield; Paula and Stu for giving me (and my Quadra 950) our first shot; my uncles Ron and Ed and their respective wonderful families for fostering my early interest in science and technology and the belief that I could do it "my way"; Bill and Rae Ann, for lovingly supporting the west coast surf and burrito operations; Ellen, Sarah, Danny, Ethan, Jack, Anne, Miles, Shelley, Connor, and Matthew for all your kindness and love over so many years; my genius brother Eric, for keeping me humble and bailing me out on (way) more than one occasion—you're a real hero; my parents, Hilary and Jerry, for tolerating (and even supporting) years of artistic indulgence and always, always being there for me; my delightfully mischievous and beautiful children, Ian and Sophie, for letting daddy stare at his laptop all day and night, while having their own screen time severely limited; and most importantly my brilliant and infinitely kind wife, Robin, for being a constant source of encouragement and peaceful joy in my life. I love you bel!

INTRODUCTION

Welcome to *Processing: Creative Coding and Computational Art*. You're well on your way to becoming a Processing guru! All right, maybe it will take a bit more reading, but with Processing, you'll be cranking out creative code sooner than you think. Best of all, you'll be creating as you learn. Processing is the first full-featured programming language and environment to be created by artists for artists. It grew out of the legendary MIT Media Lab, led by two grad students, Casey Reas and Ben Fry, who wanted to find a better way to write code that supported and even inspired the creative process. They also wanted to develop an accessible, affordable, and powerful open source tool; so they decided to make the software available for *free*.

Casey and Ben began developing Processing in the fall of 2001, releasing early alpha versions of the software soon after. In April 2005, they released the beta version for Processing 1.0. To date, over 125,000 people have had downloaded the Processing software, and Ben and Casey had been awarded a Prix Ars Electronica Golden Nica, the electronic/cyber-arts version of an Oscar. In addition, many leading universities around the world have begun including Processing in their digital arts curriculum, including Parsons School of Design; Bandung Institute of Technology, Indonesia; UCLA; Yale; NYU; Helsinki University; Royal Danish Academy of Fine Arts, Copenhagen; School of the Art Institute of Chicago; Miami University of Ohio; University of Washington; and Elisava School of Design, Barcelona (and many, many others).

Yet, in spite of all of Processing's phenomenal success, its story is really just beginning. As of this writing, version 1.0 of the software is on the brink of being released, as are the first few books on the subject. There are even people (as shocking as this sounds) who still haven't heard of Processing. So rest assured, it's still not too late to claim Processing pioneer status. Processing has a very bright future, and I'm excited to be able to introduce you to creative coding with this amazing language.

Impetus for writing the book

If you're anything like me (and I suspect you are since you're reading this book), you are a creatively driven individual—meaning that you do give a damn about how things look, sound, feel, and so on, besides just how they function. I suspect you also learn best in a nontraditional way. Well, if this describes you at all, you've picked up the right book. If, on the other hand, you pride yourself on your robotic ability to tune out sensory data and follow linear directions, then (1) keep reading, (2) make art, and (3) buy multiple copies of this book.

My own interest in writing code evolved organically out of my work as a painter and designer over a long period (a well-timed, nonserious illness also contributed). I graduated with my MFA in painting in 1992, and got a teaching job right out of grad school. However, I soon realized that I wasn't ready to teach (or hold a job for that matter), and landed up quitting within a couple of months (my folks weren't too pleased at the time). Fortunately, an uncle of mine (the previous black sheep in the family) stepped in and suggested I look into computer graphics. With nothing to lose, I rented a Mac 2ci, borrowed some software, and locked myself away for a couple of months.

I eventually developed some basic skills in digital imaging, page layout, and vector-based drawing. I also began studying graphic design, which, despite my two overpriced degrees in painting, I knew next to nothing about. Equipped with my new (very shaky) skills, I put together some samples and went looking for work. Over the next few years, I got involved in a number of startups (most quickly imploded), as well as my own freelance design business. The work included print, CD-ROM/kiosks, 2D and 3D animation, video, broadcast, and eventually web design. Throughout this period, I also continued to paint and show my work, and began teaching again as well.

My paintings at the time were perceptually-based—which means I looked at stuff as I painted. I worked originally from the landscape, which eventually became just trees, and then a single tree, and finally branches and leaves. The paintings ultimately became purely abstract fields of color and marks. This transformation in the painting took a couple of years, and throughout this period I worked as a designer and multimedia developer. I was dealing with a fair amount of code in my multimedia work, but I still didn't really know how to program, although I had gotten really adept at hacking existing code. I suspect this may sound familiar to some readers.

Then I got ill and was laid up, which turned out to be the perfect opportunity to learn how to program. I'll never forget the first program I hacked out, based on the pattern structure in one of my field paintings. The program wasn't pretty, but I was able to translate the color field pattern in the painting to code and generate a screen-based approximation of the painting. But the really exciting thing (or disturbing thing, depending upon your perspective) happened when I was able to generate hundreds of painting variations by simply changing some of the values in the program. I remember excitedly showing what I had done to some of my more purist artist friends—who've since stopped calling.

It wasn't long before I was completely hooked on programming and was using it as a primary creative medium. I also began covering it more and more in my design courses, eventually developing a semester-long class on creative coding for artists. This book grows directly out of this experience of teaching programming to art students.

Intended audience

This book presents an introduction to programming using the Processing language and is intended as an entry-level programming book—no prior programming experience is required. I do assume, though, that you have some experience working with graphics application software (such as Adobe Photoshop) and of course some design, art, or visualization interests—which although not necessary to read the book, makes life more interesting. I *don't* expect you to "be good at" or even like math, but I'd like you to at least be open to the remote possibility that math doesn't have to suck—more on this shortly.

Coding as an organic, creative, and cathartic process

When I tell people I write code as my main artistic medium, they smile politely and quickly change the subject, or they tell me about their job-seeking cousin who makes videos using iMovie. For nonprogrammers, code is a mysterious and intimidating construct that gets grouped into the category of things too complicated, geeky, or time-consuming to be worth learning. At the other extreme, for some professional programmers, code is seen only as a tool to solve a technical problem—certainly not a creative medium.

There is another path—a path perhaps harder to maneuver, but ultimately more rewarding than either the path of avoidance or detachment—a holistic "middle" way. This is the path the book promotes; it presents the practice of coding as an art form/art practice, rather than simply a means to an end. Although there are times when a project is scoped out, and we are simply trying to implement it, most of the time as artists, we are trying to find our way in the process of creating a project. This approach of finding and searching is one of the things that makes the artist's journey distinctive and allows new unexpected solutions to be found. It is possible to do this in coding as well, and the Processing language facilitates and encourages such a "creative coding" approach.

"I'm an artist—I don't do math"

Early on in school we're put into little camps: the good spellers/readers, the mathletes, the artsy crowd, the jocks, and so on. These labels stick to us throughout our lives, most often limiting us rather than providing any positive guidance. Of course, the other *less* positive labels (poor speller, bad at math, tone deaf, etc.) also stick, and maybe with even more force. From a purely utilitarian standpoint, these labels are efficient, allowing administrators and computers to schedule and route us through the system. From a humanistic standpoint, these labels greatly reduce our true capabilities and complexity down to a few keywords. And worst of all, people start believing these limited views about themselves.

A favorite lecture I give to my art students is on trigonometry. Just saying the word *trigonometry* makes many of the art students squirm in their seats, thinking "is he serious?" When I was an art student, I would have reacted the same way. And I remember studying trig in high school and not getting its relevance *at all*. Also, lacking discipline, I wasn't very capable of just taking my trig medicine like a good patient. So basically, I've had to teach myself trigonometry again. However, what I got this time was how absolutely fascinating and relevant trig (and math in general) is, especially for visually modeling organic motion and other natural phenomena—from the gentle rolling waves of the ocean, to a complex swarm, to the curvilinear structure of a seashell. Math really can be an expressive and creative medium (but perhaps not in high school). Finally, and likely most reassuring to some readers, playing with math in Processing is pretty darn easy—no proofs or cramming required.

Toward a left/right brain integration

I once had a teacher who said something to the effect that there is significance in the things that bore us, and ultimately these are the things that we should study. I thought at the time that he was being annoyingly pretentious. However, I've come to recognize something important in his suggestion. I don't necessarily think we need to study all the things that bore us. But I do think that at times, the feeling of boredom may be as much a defense mechanism as it is a real indicator of how we truly feel about something. I've become aware of the feeling of boredom in my own process, and notice it usually occurring when there is fear or anxiety about the work I'm doing (or the pressure I'm putting on myself). However, when I push through the boredom and get into a flow, I'm usually fine. I've heard many artists talk about the difficulty they have in getting started in their studios, spending too much time procrastinating. I think procrastination also relates to this notion of boredom as defense mechanism. My (unproven) hypothesis is that we sometimes feel boredom when we're stretching our brains, almost like a muscular reflex. The boredom is the brain's attempt to maintain the status quo. However, making art is never about the status quo.

Dealing with subjects like programming and math also seems to generate the sensation of boredom in people. Some people find it uncomfortable to think too intensely about analytical abstractions. I don't think this phenomenon has anything to do with one's innate intelligence; it just seems we each develop cognitive patterns that are hard to change, especially as we get older. As I've learned programming over the years, I've experienced a lot of these boredom sensations. At times, I've even (theatrically) wondered how far can I stretch my brain without going bonkers. I think it is especially scary for some of us to develop the less-dominant sides of our minds (or personalities). As artists, that is often (but certainly not always) the left side of our brain (the analytical side). However, I firmly believe that we will be more self-actualized if we can achieve a left/right brain integration. I even conjecture that the world would be a better place if more people perceived their reality through an integrated mind—so make code art and save the world!

Well, enough of my blathering. Let's start Processing!

Setting up Processing

If you haven't already downloaded Processing, you should do so now. You'll (obviously) need a working copy of the software/language to follow the tutorials throughout the book. To download the latest version, go to http://processing.org/download/index. html.

If you're not sure which version to download, keep reading.

> As of this writing, the latest downloadable version of the software is 0124 BETA, released February 4, 2007. It's possible, by the time you're reading this, that the release number has changed, as the developers are in the process of stabilizing the current beta release as version 1.0. Any changes made to the language between beta release 0124 and version 1.0 should be very minor and primarily focused on debugging existing functionality. For more information about the different releases, check out http://processing.org/download/revisions.txt.

Since Processing is a Java application, any platform that can run Java can theoretically run Processing. However, Processing is only officially released for Windows, Mac OS X, and Linux, and the software is only extensively tested on Windows and OS X. Linux users are somewhat on their own. Here's what the Processing site says in regard to Linux users:

> For the Linux version, you guys can support yourselves. If you're enough of a hacker weenie to get a Linux box set up, you oughta know what's going on. For lack of time, we won't be testing extensively under Linux, but would be really happy to hear about any bugs or issues you might run into . . . so we can fix them.

For more details about platform support, please check out http://processing.org/ reference/environment/platforms.html#supported.

In selecting a version to download, Mac and Linux users have only one choice; Windows users have two choices: Processing with or without Java. The recommendation is to download Processing with Java. However, the without-Java version is available if download size is an issue and you know you have Java installed. If you're not sure whether you have Java installed, and/or the idea of changing your PATH variable gives you the willies, please download Processing with Java. If you still want to download them separately, here's a link (but remember, you've been warned): http://java.sun.com/javase/downloads/ index.jsp.

OS X users already have Java installed, thanks to the good people at Apple.

Regarding Java, the most current version available on Windows is Java SE 6 (the SE stands for Standard Edition). On OS X, Java releases typically lag behind, and the most current version is J2SE 5 (the names are also annoyingly a little different). The most current version on Linux is also J2SE 5. If all this isn't confusing enough, Processing only supports J2SE 1.4

and earlier (yes, J2SE 5 and Java SE 6 come after J2SE 1.4). Version 1.4 is the version that comes bundled with Processing's Windows installer, and it is also the default installation in OS X. The reason Java versioning numbers go from 1.4 to 5 is because Sun, in their wisdom, decided to drop the "1." from the names—if you really care why, you can read about it here: http://java.sun.com/j2se/1.5.0/docs/relnotes/version-5.0.html.

What all this means to Processing users is that you can't use any new Java syntax specified in releases after 1.4 within the Processing development environment. (Syntax is essentially the grammar you use when you write code—which you'll learn all about in Chapter 3.) For the latest information on the tempestuous love affair between Processing and Java, please see http://processing.org/faq.html#java.

Web capability

Java's capabilities also extend to the browser environment, allowing Java programs (applets) to be run in Java-enabled browsers, similar to the way Flash programs run within the browser. Processing takes advantage of this capability, allowing Processing sketches that you create within the Processing development environment to be exported as standard Java applets that run within the browser.

One of the factors in Processing's quickly spreading popularity is its web presence. Processing's online home, http://processing.org/, has single-handedly put Processing on the map; the many awards and accolades bestowed upon its creators, Casey Reas and Ben Fry, haven't hurt either. One of the main reasons people continue to go to the Processing site is to visit the Processing Exhibition space (http://processing.org/exhibition/index.html), which has a simple "Add a link" feature, allowing Processors to add a link to their own Processing work. The fact that Processing sketches can be exported as Java applets is the reason this online gallery is possible.

Because Processing has been a web-based initiative, its documentation was also written in HTML and designed to take advantage of the browser environment. The Java API (application programming interface) is also HTML-based. HTML allows both Processing and Java's documentation to have embedded hyperlinks throughout, providing easy linking between related structures and concepts. The Processing API is the main language documentation for the Processing language, and can be found online at http://processing.org/reference/index.html. The Java API most useful with regard to Processing (there are a couple different ones) can be found at http://java.sun.com/j2se/1.4.2/docs/api/index.html.

Aside from the Processing API, there are two other helpful areas on the Processing site worth noting: Learning/Examples (http://processing.org/learning/index.html) and Discourse (http://processing.org/discourse/yabb_beta/YaBB.cgi). The Learning/Examples section includes numerous examples of simple Processing sketches, covering a wide variety of graphics programming topics. This section, like most of the Processing site, is an evolving archive and a great place to study well-written snippets of code as you begin learning. The Discourse section of the site includes message boards on a wide range of subjects, covering all things Processing. You'll even get replies from Casey and Ben, as well as other master Processing coders—a number of whom are well-known code artists and Processing teachers.

Hopefully by now you've successfully downloaded the Processing software. Now, let's install it and fire it up.

Launching the application

- **OS X**: After downloading the software, launch the Stuffit X archive (.sitx), which will create a Processing 0124 folder. Within the folder you'll see the Processing program icon.

- **Windows**: After downloading the software, extract the ZIP archive (.zip), which will create a Processing 0124 folder. Within the folder you'll see the Processing program icon.

To test that Processing is working, double-click the Processing program icon to launch the application. A window similar to the one shown in Figure 1 should open.

Figure 1. The Processing application interface

Processing comes with a bunch of cool code examples. Next, let's load the BrownianMotion example into the Processing application. You can access the example, and many others, through Processing's File menu, as follows:

Select File ➤ Sketchbook ➤ Examples ➤ Motion ➤ BrownianMotion from the top menu bar.

You should see a bunch of code fill the text-editor section of the Processing window, as shown in Figure 2.

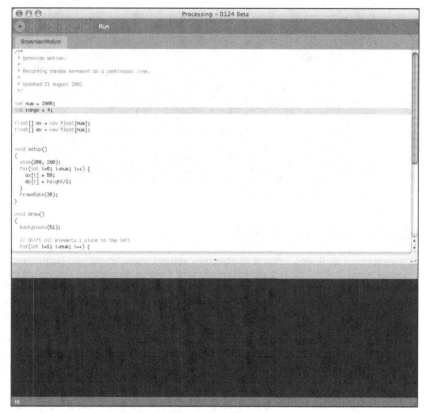

Figure 2. The Processing application interface with a loaded sketch

To launch the sketch, click the right-facing run arrow (on the left of the brown toolbar at the top of the Processing window—it looks like a VCR play button), or press Cmd+R (OS X) or Ctrl+R (Windows).

If you were successful, a 200-pixel-by-200-pixel display window with a dark gray back-ground should have popped open, showing a white scribbly line meandering around the window (see Figure 3). Congratulations! You've just run your first Processing sketch. I rec-ommend trying some of the other examples to get a taste of what Processing can do and to familiarize yourself a little with Processing's simple yet elegant interface.

Figure 3. Screenshot of BrownianMotion sketch

How to use this book

I created this book with a couple of objectives in mind. Based on my own creative experiences working with code and application software, I wanted to present a conceptual introduction to code as a primary creative medium, including some history and theory on the subject. Based on my experiences in the digital art classroom, I wanted to provide an artist-friendly, introductory text on general programming theory and basic graphics programming. Lastly, based on my experience of working with a number of programming languages (especially ActionScript and Java), I wanted to introduce readers to an exciting new approach to creative coding with the Processing language and environment. Accomplishing all this required a fairly ambitious table of contents, which this book has.

> In addition to the 800+ pages within the book, there are an additional 142 pages of "bonus" material online, at www.friendsofed.com/book.html?isbn=159059617X.
>
> The bonus material is divided into Chapter 14 and Appendix C. Chapter 14 covers Processing's Java mode, as well as some advanced 3D topics. Appendix C provides a tutorial on how to use the Processing core library in "pure" Java projects—outside of the Processing environment.

In navigating all this material, I offer some suggestions to readers:

- Don't feel that you have to approach the book linearly, progressing consecutively through each chapter, or even finishing individual chapters before moving ahead. I don't think people naturally operate this way, especially not creative people. I tend to read about 20 books at a time, moving through them in some crazy fractal pattern. Perhaps my approach is too extreme, but beginning on page one of a book like this and progressing until the last page seems even more extreme. I suggest taking a grazing approach, searching for that choice patch of info to sink your brain into.

- Read stuff over and over until it sticks. I do this all the time. I often get multiple books on the same subject and read the same material presented in different ways to help me understand the material. I don't do this to memorize, but to grasp the concept.

- Don't worry about memorizing stuff you can look up. Eventually the stuff that you use a lot will get lodged in your brain naturally.

- Try to break/twist/improve my code examples. Then e-mail me your improved examples—maybe I'll use one in another book; of course I'd give you credit.

- Always keep a copy of the book in the bathroom—it's the best place to read guilt-free when the sun's still out.

Give us some feedback!

We'd love to hear from you, even if it's just to request future books, ask about friends of ED, or tell us how much you loved *Processing: Creative Coding and Computational Art*.

If you have questions about issues not directly related to the book, the best place for these inquiries is the friends of ED support forums, at http://friendsofed.infopop.net/2/OpenTopic. Here you'll find a wide variety of fellow readers, plus dedicated forum moderators from friends of ED.

Please direct all questions about this book to support@friendsofed.com, and include the last four digits of this book's ISBN (617x) in the subject of your e-mail. If the dedicated support team can't solve your problem, your question will be forwarded to the book's editors and author. You can also e-mail Ira Greenberg directly at processing@iragreenberg.com.

Layout conventions

To keep this book as clear and easy to follow as possible, the following text conventions are used throughout:

- Important words or concepts are normally highlighted on their first appearance in **bold type**.
- Code is presented in fixed-width font.

- New or changed code is normally presented in **`bold fixed-width font`**.
- Pseudocode and variable input are written in *`italic fixed-width font`*.
- Menu commands are written in the form Menu ➤ Submenu ➤ Submenu.
- When I want to draw your attention to something, I highlight it like this:

> *Ahem, don't say I didn't warn you.*

- Sometimes code won't fit on a single line in a book. Where this happens, I use an arrow like this: ➥

```
This is a very, very long section of code that should be written ➥
all on the same line without a break.
```

PART ONE **THEORY OF PROCESSING AND COMPUTATIONAL ART**

The creative process doesn't exist in a vacuum—it's a highly integrated activity reflecting history, aesthetic theory, and often the technological breakthroughs of the day. This was certainly the case during the Renaissance, when artists, engineers, scientists, and thinkers all came together to create truly remarkable works of art and engineering. Over the last few decades, we've been experiencing our own Renaissance with the proliferation of digital technology—creating radically new ways for people to work, play, communicate, and be creative. Processing was born directly out of these exciting developments.

In Part 1 of the book, I'll look at some of the history and theory behind Processing, computational art, and computer graphics technology. I'll also discuss some of the challenges and exciting possibilities inherent in working with such a new and evolving medium. You'll learn about a number of pioneers in the computational art field, and also take a tour of the Processing environment. Finally, you'll explore some of the fundamental concepts and structures involved in graphics programming.

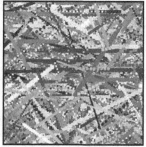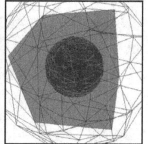

1 CODE ART

Ask the average person what they think computer art is, and they'll likely mention the types of imaging effects we associate with Photoshop or maybe a blockbuster 3D animated film like Shrek. I still remember the first time I cloned an eyeball with Photoshop; it was totally thrilling. I also remember getting a copy of Strata Studio Pro and creating my first perfect 3D metal sphere (you know, the one with the highly reflective ship plate texture map). However, once we get a little more experience under our belts and have tried every freakin' filter we can get our hands on, the "gee whiz" factor subsides, and we are stuck with the same problem that all artists and designers experience—the empty white page or canvas. Of course, each year I have many students who believe that they have found the perfect combination of filters that will produce remarkable and original works of art—without the need to exert too much effort (or leave their game consoles for very long). In the end, though, the stylistic footprints left behind by these filters is unavoidable. That is not to imply that the filters are the problem; I couldn't do my job without the genius of Photoshop. It is the approach to using them that is the problem, or the belief that all that power will make the process of creating art any easier.

The fact that these filters are so captivating and that my students are drawn to them is significant, and I don't think it is only because they are a quick fix. I think what we see in those amazing filters, as we do when we stare at a cool seashell or a dramatic sunset, is algorithmic beauty. Now, I can hear some of you beginning to moan when you read a phrase like that, but I promise you I won't lapse into too many pages of new age touchy-feeliness.

For me, algorithmic beauty is just an apparent mathematical pattern that we find engaging. It can be a passage in music, a strange coincidence of events, a crystal, or, yes, even a Photoshop filter. We see a pattern of forces at work, creating something uncommon, yet familiar at the same time. When we can predict the patterning too readily, and in a sense crack the code, the effect tends to wear off, and we have almost the opposite reaction to awe; we feel cheated or at least unimpressed—thus my disdain at spotting too many filters. The really cool and mysterious thing is that in some sense, in detecting beauty, our brains seem to be doing a strange type of intuitive math, where we are measuring intervals, comparing ratios, and computing some kind of algorithmic aesthetic solution.

I experienced an example of this when I was in grad school studying painting. A bunch of us were eating breakfast at the quintessential greasy spoon in center city, Philadelphia. Somebody had found this pretty cheesy visual literacy quiz. The idea was to look at a series of diagrams and pictures and say which one worked the best. There were about ten separate questions on the page, and everyone at the table took the test independently, between forkfuls of grease heaven. Surprisingly, we all got the same exact answers. Now it could have been due to the common grease we were ingesting, or sheer coincidence, but I like to think we all got the same answers because we all shared a common visual algorithmic literacy. The test wasn't about what we liked, but which images worked best. Had the test instead been about which images were better works of art, not only would none of us have agreed, but we most likely would have been thrown out of the restaurant for disorderly conduct. The decision whether an image, object, or design "works" from an aesthetic standpoint may be as close to a quantifiable measure as you can (or probably should) bring to a piece of art.

The problem with a Photoshop filter is its limited range of expressive possibility. Each filter has a rational consistency, which is absolutely necessary for generating predictable results and overall reliability. But the rationality built into the tool makes it hard to find new solutions. Coding allows you much greater freedom to build in levels of control, and also levels of randomization and even irrational processes that don't always work but can lead to exciting, unexpected results.

Using Processing, it doesn't take too long playing with some code to generate truly evocative images and visual experiences, gain some insight into how a program like Photoshop works, and go way beyond any preprogrammed filters.

Aesthetics + Computation

Aesthetics + Computation is the name of the now famous research group at MIT's Media Lab, where Casey Reas and Ben Fry, the creators of the Processing language, worked as grad students under John Maeda. However, interest in aesthetics and computation goes back way before 1996, when Maeda began teaching at MIT.

If we're a bit flexible in how we translate the term "computation," we can go really way back—as far back, in fact, to when people first learned to count and draw (ironically, skills that some would argue are in sharp decline today because of computers). The term **computation**, according to www.dictionary.com, means "the procedure of calculating; determining something by mathematical or logical methods." If you take the term **mathematical** out of the definition (already I can feel some readers' comfort levels increasing), the definition could pretty much account for most human decisions. For example, I have a faculty meeting coming up. Therefore, I need to remember to bring my sketchpad to the meeting to be able to draw annoying caricatures of my colleagues so that I don't fall asleep. See, a perfect example of aesthetics + computation.

Serious interest in aesthetics + computation as an integrated activity is evident in all cultures and is manifest in many of the objects, structures, and technologies of the times in which they were created. Regardless of whether the technology is an engraving stick, a loom, a plow, or a supercomputer, the impulse to work and play in an integrated left-/right-brain way is universally evident, and the technical innovations of the day most often coincide with parallel developments in aesthetics. Early astrological and calendar systems, across many cultures, combined observed empirical data with richly expressive, mythological narratives as a way of interpreting and ultimately preserving and disseminating the data. Weavings, textiles, engravings, mandalas, and graphs from cultures around the world employ complex algorithmic patterns based upon mathematical principles, yet most often are not developed by mathematicians (see Figures 1-1 through 1-4). Rather, these developments seem to reflect a universal human impulse to integrate right-brain and left-brain activities, combining qualitative notions of aesthetic beauty with analytical systems for structuring visual data.

Figure 1-1. Ur game board, found in grave, 2600 BC

Figure 1-2. Replica of the Aztec stone of the sun, from the original found in the city formerly known as Tenochtitlán

1

Figure 1-3. Example of ancient art of Kolam, southern India, 1970s

Figure 1-4. Tibetan monks making a temporary "sand mandala" in the Kitzbühel City Hall, Austria

Renaissance biographer Giorgio Vasari tells us that the Florentine architect Filippo Brunelleschi (1337–1446) took up painting to apply his newly developed theory of perspective, based upon Greek geometry. Additionally, other major Renaissance painters including Piero della Francesca, Albrecht Dürer, and Leonardo da Vinci not only experimented and applied principles of geometry in their work, but published treatises on mathematics. Dürer even developed several drawing machines that could be used to teach perspective. Especially during the European Renaissance, the division separating art and science blurred to the point that many of its greatest practitioners made nearly equal contributions to each.

Interestingly (or maybe sadly), it may be one of the unique aspects of our contemporary culture that the need for professional hyperspecialization has made left-/right-brain integration more difficult and rare. The amount of training and specialized information we each feel we need to develop "competency," and ultimately, success, in our fields forces a vocational myopia, which then reinforces many of our erroneous assumptions: "I'm not good at math," "I can't draw," and so on. The situation isn't helped when we create totally inscrutable private vocabularies around our fields (especially the most technical ones), making them practically inaccessible to outsiders. This is certainly the case in computing, and especially programming. I think one of John Maeda's hopes in creating the Aesthetics + Computation group at MIT, and the reason he created the programming language Design by Numbers (DBN; the precursor to Processing), was to reveal the aesthetic beauty and power of computation (and math) to artists and designers. By using a really simplified programming language and approaching programming instruction in a straightforward and creatively centered way, he hoped artists would feel free to begin to express themselves through this fascinating medium and challenge some of their unproductive assumptions (such as "artists don't do math").

I think Maeda believes, as I do, that the core expressive element of computing is not at the software application level, using sliders, spinners, dialog boxes, and filters; but at the lower level of computation, most accessible through direct programming. I like to think of programming as the material level of computing, the place to get, at least metaphorically, your hands dirty. Casey Reas and Ben Fry, Maeda's students, understood this vision and built Processing as an extension of (or at least homage to) DBN, adding the features of a powerful programming language while retaining DBN's ease of use to facilitate its application as an expressive creative medium.

Computer art history

The history of computer art goes back further than most people realize. However, before diving into computer art, it's helpful to create some historical context by examining just a little computing history. There are many places to begin the story of computing; we could go back 4,000 years to the ancient Egyptians and Babylonians and the origins of mathematics. I suspect of interest to some readers would be the Egyptian Ahmes Papyrus, which contains some of the first known written equations for, among other things, the formula for beer—one approach to keeping students interested in math. We could then methodically move through the entire history of mathematics, looking at the Babylonian Salamis tablet, or counting board, circa 300 BC; the Roman hand abacus (see Figure 1-5) a little later; and then the *suan pan*, or Chinese abacus, getting us to around 1200 AD. We could then jump 400 years to 1614 and John Napier, the Scottish supergenius who developed logarithms (which allow multiplication and division to be handled like simple addition and subtraction), as well as a system of using metal plates for performing multiplication and division. For this, Napier gets credited with developing the earliest known attempt at a mechanical means of calculation. Building upon Napier's work, Edmund Gunter gets credited in 1620 with developing the second most important geek tool of all time, the slide rule (see Figure 1-6). Leaping ahead 200 years or so to the 1830s, we come across a very significant moment in computing history and some extremely interesting characters: Charles Babbage, Ada Lovelace, and the Analytical Engine.

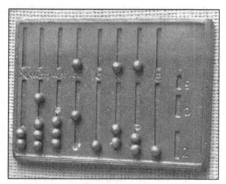

Figure 1-5. Reconstruction of a Roman abacus

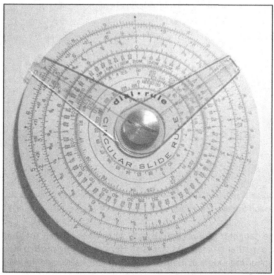

Figure 1-6. Pickett circular slide rule with two cursors

Babbage was a professor of mathematics at Cambridge, who interestingly held the same Lucasian chair as Newton, which is now held by present day supergenius Stephen Hawking— not a bad lineage. Babbage was an obsessive classifier, regularly measuring and collecting all the relevant (by his standards) data he came across, such as the heartbeats of farm animals, the rate at which a man could saw wood, and even the frequency and cause of broken windows around town. He supposedly went so far as to bake himself in an oven for a couple of minutes to figure out the amount of heat that the human body could withstand. Babbage was also a vehement hater of street musicians (not sure why).

Babbage believed, perhaps naively but brilliantly, that his obsessive data analysis would lead to a sort of empirical truth about, well, everything. Babbage designed a complex calculating machine called the Analytical Engine (see Figure 1-7). It was designed as a steam run, automatic, programmable, universal machine capable of solving nearly any algebraic function. Amazingly, Babbage's design included almost all the logical features of a modern-day computer. Unfortunately, as with many visionaries, his wild ambition for the engine was ultimately beyond the reality of its actualization, and it was never completed.

Figure 1-7. The London Science Museum's replica difference engine, built from Babbage's design

Ada Lovelace, the daughter of poet Lord Byron, who never actually met her famous father, was raised to be a mathematician and scientist. Her controlling mother was determined to rid her of any inherited poetical tendencies from her estranged famous husband (she divorced Byron shortly after her daughter's birth). This plan of course failed, and Lovelace's fertile imagination remained intact, along with her phenomenal analytical talents, making her a great exemplar of the power of an integrated mind. The story goes that Lovelace eventually heard about Babbage's analytical engine at a dinner party in 1834, and was quite taken by the idea. She saw many potential applications for the powerful engine, when most everyone else did not, including the wild possibility of having the machine compose music and even generate graphics. Babbage and Lovelace developed a correspondence, and she eventually wrote a document to Babbage suggesting a plan to have the engine calculate Bernoulli numbers. There is no simple way to explain Bernoulli numbers, so I'll just say that they are quite significant in mathematics—here's a link if you're interested: http://en.wikipedia.org/wiki/Bernoulli_numbers. The plan, or algorithm, that Lovelace wrote to Babbage is now regarded as the first computer program—100 years before the invention of the computer! (How cool is that?)

In spite of Babbage and Lovelace's prescient work, computing history went nowhere for nearly 100 years. It wasn't until the mid-1930s that German engineer Konrad Zuse developed the Z1 (see Figure 1-8) and got credited with developing the first computer.

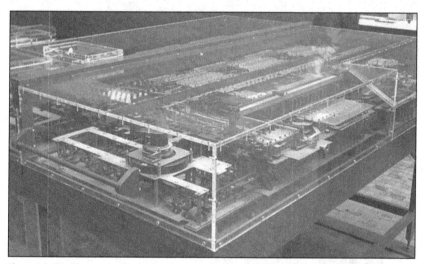

Figure 1-8. The Z1 was a mechanical computer created by Konrad Zuse in 1937. A reproduction of this machine (pictured) is currently housed in the Deutsches Technikmuseum Berlin.

Between the '30s and mid-'40s—thanks in part to the very unfortunate need for things like firing tables and atomic bomb calculations—numerous modifications were made to the Z1, and other significant computer initiatives were begun, including John Atanasoff's ABC computer, the Mark 1 at Harvard, and the ENIAC at Penn (see Figure 1-9). These initial machines were very difficult to program, and the Mark 1 and the ENIAC were absolutely enormous. The Mark 1 was 51 inches long, 8 feet high, and contained 17,486 vacuum tubes. The ENIAC weighed in at 30 tons and used so much power that it was said to cause the lights of Philadelphia to flicker.

Figure 1-9. The ENIAC

Finally in 1951, the first general-purpose computer, the UNIVAC, was developed, with a relatively easy-to-use programming language, including some programming standards. The UNIVAC was used by the Census Bureau in 1951, and famously predicted Eisenhower's victory in 1952. The programming language the UNIVAC used was developed by the amazing Grace Murray Hopper (see Figure 1-10), the first woman to be awarded the rank of rear admiral.

Figure 1-10.
Commodore Grace M. Hopper

As an aside, it's worth observing that computer programming, which has gotten the stigma as a male-dominated pursuit, had two brilliant women as its founding pioneers. Contemporary artist Mary Flanagan addresses this issue in a very interesting way with her RAPUNSEL project, which I'll elaborate upon a little later.

Admiral Hopper is, among many other distinctions, also attributed with coining the term "software bug," when she actually found a dead moth in one of the Mark 2 computers, preventing it from working. She had programmed the Mark 1 at Harvard in the very early '40s, and also developed the first compiler. Compilers are used to convert the mnemonic code that a programmer writes into machine code. Machine code is a binary system composed of zeros and ones that is, in a sense, the native language the computer speaks. Mnemonic code is a higher-level system of symbols and natural language-like constructs, which we use to program the computer with. For example, as it is near lunchtime I am beginning to think "I'm getting hungry." Converting these words into binary machine code, I get the following:

010010010010011101101101001000000110011101100101011101000111010001101001001011011100110011001110010000000110100001110101011011100110011101110110010011111001

I don't know about you, but I find it a bit (no pun intended) easier to understand the symbolic code "I'm getting hungry," rather than the 144 zeros or ones in the binary code.

As computers have evolved, and the problems we throw at them (such as art making) have steadily increased in complexity, the mnemonic codes, or programming languages, that we've developed have steadily gotten higher-level. **Higher-level** means moving the symbolic abstraction of the language further away from the underlying binary machine code and nearer to our natural language—and ultimately (hopefully) nearer to how people think. This idea of creating higher-level symbolic abstractions away from the zeros and ones, allowing the coder to think more naturally and thus gain programming literacy more easily, has led directly to the development of languages like Processing.

It didn't take very long for some pioneering artists to see the expressive potential and fascination in computers. As early as 1956, just five years after the UNIVAC was developed, artists began experimenting with computing as an expressive medium. Of course, computers were inaccessible to most artists in the late '50s. According to Jasia Reichardt in her book *The Computer in Art*, there were no computers in any art departments or art colleges by the end of the 1960s. Although at a few places, notably Ohio State, artists had access to the university computer, as well as some technical staff. Jasia then goes on to state in her 1971 book, "one can assume that there are probably no more than about 1,000 people in the world working with computer graphics for purposes other than the practical ones."

Dividing computer graphics pioneers along practical vs. nonpractical applications in 1971 struck me as amusing. I'd argue that anyone dabbling in this black science back then was pioneering very experimental applied applications at best. I think this same erroneous distinction between applied vs. fine art continues to linger within the digital arts today, as many "hybrid" types (myself included) have struggled to define their places in universities, galleries, and industry. Fortunately, there were times in history when scientists, artists, philosophers, engineers, and so forth were all seen as integrated creative practitioners—not divided solely by their perceived utilitarian value in the marketplace. And there seems to be a growing recognition in industry, thanks in part to companies like Apple, that creativity and design are good for business. Universities are also recognizing and responding to students' interests in blurring old delimiting disciplinary and curriculum boundaries, and digital media and the electronic arts are at the center of this movement. The recent dramatic and swelling popularity of Processing is a testament to this contemporary renaissance.

Code artists

In concluding this chapter, I've included some brief biographies of 12 code/electronic artists, many of whom are still practicing, exhibiting, and teaching. Some have worked as fine and applied artists throughout their careers, many with traditional materials, which in most cases has informed the digital work. All of these artists apply computation and technology to their creative practice in a formally rigorous way, utilizing code and algorithmic approaches. Their work is not solely a commentary on technology, nor illustrated or simply facilitated by it, but is rather *of* it. I also want to preface this list by stating that I have left out at least as many worthy individuals as I have included. I have tried to include those individuals who represent a wide range of approaches and whose work most directly informs the varied directions artists are pursuing with Processing. Following the biographies is a list of additional noteworthy artists with links to their work.

Ben Laposky, 1914–2000

Both mathematician and artist, Ben Laposky was a pioneer among computer art pioneers. He created the first electronic abstract images in 1950 by using an electronic analog device called a cathode ray tube oscilloscope. To put Laposky's pioneering role in some context, it wasn't until 1960 (ten years later) that the term "computer graphics" was first coined by William Fetter, a graphic designer at Boeing. Laposky created images of beautiful mathematical curves he named "oscillons." The curves were based on the basic waveforms utilized in analog computers. Analog computers, now mostly unknown, were utilized as early as the 1920s and were capable of very fast, complex calculations. They used continuous variations in voltage, allowing real-time calculations, as opposed to distinct finite signals, which are employed in digital computers. To learn more about analog computers, check out http://en.wikipedia.org/wiki/Analog_computer. By the 1940s, analog computers began to be replaced by digital computers, which were more affordable to produce and more universal as general-purpose tools. I'll discuss more about the type of waveforms Laposky generated later in the book, including how to generate some of them. To capture the curves, Laposky photographed the images directly off the display with high-speed film. What I find striking about his images is their elegant simplicity and organic quality, in contrast to the technical means from which they arose. Beyond Laposky's pioneering technical virtuosity is his steadfast focus on the aesthetic quality of his work. This combined focus on the technical and aesthetic is an important enduring legacy that unites all the artists mentioned in this chapter. To learn more about Laposky and view some images of his work, check out www.dam.org/laposky/index.htm and www.atariarchives.org/artist/sec6.php.

John Whitney Sr., 1918–1995

John Whitney's work involved photography, film, and eventually also music. In the 1940s, he began to study images in motion, along with his brother James. This interest would remain with him the rest of his long career and eventually involve the integration of motion and sound. Whitney combined a very successful career in commercial film and television with his more personal and experimental investigations. He even produced the title sequence for Hitchcock's *Vertigo*. By the 1960s, Whitney had formed a company, Motion Graphics, to produce commercials, at which he pioneered early computer-based animation and typography with a mechanical analog computer that he invented. Whitney gained wide recognition for his work with the analog computer, as well as for a sample reel entitled "Catalog," which showcased his innovative motion work. Between 1966 and 1969, Whitney got to work with powerful digital computers as the first artist in residency at IBM. From this period through the '70s, he continued to push the complexity of his work, creating numerous experimental films and documentaries while also refining his focus to achieve what he called "harmonic progression." Throughout his entire career, Whitney remained an innovator, eventually developing a computerized instrument that allowed him to compose visuals and music in real time. Additional information on Whitney, including images, can be viewed at www.siggraph.org/artdesign/profile/whitney/nowhitney.html and http://en.wikipedia.org/wiki/John_Whitney_(animator).

Herbert W. Franke, b.1927

Franke is a brilliant generalist, with formal training in physics, mathematics, chemistry, psychology, and philosophy. He is a widely published author—his works include seven science fiction titles, essays, articles, and scripts on subjects as wide ranging as physics, theoretical chemistry, scientific photography, visual perceptions, art and technology, futurology, and speleology (the scientific study of caves). His early work paralleled Loposky's, utilizing oscilloscopes to generate images based on waveforms. Since 1962, Franke has remained active in "experimental aesthetics," lecturing and creating new work in the field. He cofounded the Ars Electronica Festival in 1979, arguably the most prestigious international electronic arts festival in the world, held annually in Linz, Austria. In 2005, for their work on Processing, Casey and Ben won a Golden Nica—the festival's top prize. Franke has remained on the bleeding edge of emerging technology throughout his career, and beginning in the mid '90s began developing algorithmic animations using the Mathematica software system. In 2002, he released a book on the subject, entitled *Animation with Mathematica*. To learn more about Franke (in English), see http://en.wikipedia.org/wiki/Herbert_W._Franke and www.dam.org/franke/index.htm; to learn more about him in German, see www.zi.biologie.uni-muenchen.de/~franke/.

Lillian Schwartz, b. 1927

Lillian Schwartz has been a central and pioneering figure in the history of computer art, making broad and significant contributions in computer-generated art and computer-aided art analysis. Her work and research have led to advances in graphics, film, video, animation, special effects, virtual reality, and multimedia. She gained prominence in the late '60s when one of her kinetic sculptures, *Proxima Centauri*, was included in the groundbreaking 1968 Machine Exhibition at the Museum of Modern Art (MoMA), New York. She is also the first artist to have a piece of computer art acquired by the MoMA. In addition to the MoMA, her work has been exhibited at and is owned by the Metropolitan Museum of Art, the Whitney Museum of American Art, the Moderna Museet (Stockholm), Centre Beaubourg (Paris), the Stedelijk Museum of Art (Amsterdam), and the Grand Palais Museum (Paris). Her films have been shown and won awards at the Venice Biennale, Zagreb, Cannes, and the National Academy of Television Arts and Sciences; and she has been nominated for and received Emmy awards. Like many of the early pioneers, Schwartz has made substantial contributions within industry, academia, and the art world. She was a consultant at AT&T Bell Laboratories, IBM's Thomas J. Watson Research Laboratory, and Lucent Technologies Bell Labs Innovations. Her research has led to advances in the under-standing of visual and color perception, sound, perspective, historic preservation, and applications of the computer in the philosophy of art—using computation to investigate the creative process. She has taught in both fine art and computer science departments throughout the United States, as well as internationally. Schwartz has received numerous awards, including Computerworld Smithsonian awards in three categories. She has also been the subject of articles, books, and television news and documentary programs, and is the coauthor of *The Computer Artist's Handbook* (together with Laurens R. Schwartz). To learn more about Schwartz and see images of her work, go to her personal website, www.lillian.com/.

Harold Cohen, b. 1928

Cohen, probably more than anyone else, made a wide and dramatic migration from the traditional arts to computer art. He was a celebrated painter in the '60s, including repre-senting Great Britain in the Venice Biennial in 1966. In 1968, he moved to Southern California as a visiting faculty at the University of California, San Diego. He soon became interested in artificial intelligence, and in 1971 was invited to spend two years at the Artificial Intelligence Laboratory of Stanford University as a guest scholar. Since then, his work has focused on the integration of artificial intelligence with the visual artist's creative process. Over three decades, Cohen developed an expert drawing system, a rule-based software program capable of simulating aspects of human creativity and intelligence. He named the system he developed AARON. AARON is capable of creating original works of art on its own. Although all the work AARON produces is stylistically similar, the range of subject matter, composition, and color is not. What is so surprising about AARON, and I believe what makes it groundbreaking, is that the work it produces is representational. Most algorithmic systems generate abstract or color field–oriented images. AARON cre-ates, in a sense, freehand drawn images of people, still lifes, and landscapes. Cohen's (and AARON's) work has been shown around the world, including in the Los Angeles County Museum, Documenta 6, the San Francisco MoMA, the Stedelijk Museum in Amsterdam, the Brooklyn Museum, the Tate Gallery in London, and the IBM Gallery in New York. Cohen has a permanent exhibit in the Computer Museum in Boston, and represented the United States in the Japan World Fair in 1985. In 2000, artificial intelligence entrepreneur and inventor Ray Kurzweil licensed the code to AARON and created a screen saver version of the software, which he hosts at his Kurzweil CyberArt Technologies website (www. kurzweilcyberart.com/). Cohen continues to push his work and process, developing even more naturalistic and organic representational images based on machine intelligence algorithms. To learn more about Cohen and to see images of his (and AARON's) work, check out www.kurzweilcyberart.com/aaron/hi_cohenbio.html and www.viewingspace. com/genetics_culture/pages_genetics_culture/gc_w05/cohen_h.htm. Here's an interesting blog entry he wrote about "creative" programming: http://grandtextauto. gatech.edu/2003/06/17/harold-cohen-on-artist-programmers/.

Roman Verostko, b. 1929

Roman Verotsko has had a long, distinguished, multifaceted career. For 16 years, beginning in 1952, he lived as a Benedictine monk. Toward the end of this monastic period, he was sent to New York to develop himself as an artist, with the goal of bringing this experience and training back to the abbey. While in New York, he received an MFA from Pratt and then took graduate courses in Art History at both Columbia and New York University. Eventually struggling with his beliefs in revelation and the dogmas of the church, he left the monastic life in 1968 and took a faculty position at Minneapolis College of Art and Design, where he remained throughout his academic career. Verostko spent the first 30 years of his artistic life painting. This early work dealt with the search for an internal dynamic force in a work of art. He wrote the following about his process:

> Through this process, in a kind of spiritual quest—one has to empty the self of "thinking," be entirely present to the moment, and strive to be one with one's world. To be one with the brush, the crayon, the panel, the universe—in a free flowing gesture was indeed the goal. Being most "free" was also being most "joined."

In 1970, he received a Bush Fellowship grant, which provided him the opportunity to work with Gyorgy Kepes at the Center for Advanced Visual Studies at MIT. At the time, Verostko's interest in computer technology related more to how artists could humanize the emerging medium than how it could be applied directly to the creative practice; it would be 14 years (1984) before Verostko began utilizing computer code within his own creative practice. Eventually, code would become his primary creative medium, extending (rather than supplanting) his earlier interests in spiritual practice and painting.

Verostko was influenced by artists such as Mondrian, Kandinsky, and Malevich in his pursuit to uncover the underlying unity of nature, based on an integration of opposing forces within the image. He developed a software/hardware system he called "Hodos." Hodos generates both screen-based and physical images created with brushes mounted on a pen plotter's drawing arm. Verostko's algorithms control the range of expression of the system, allowing for his personal style and interest in opposing forces to emerge. In 1995, Verostko and a group of artists including Jean-Pierre Hébert and Ken Musgrave formed an informal group they named "the Algorists," for those artists who use their own algorithms for creating art objects. Verostko has received numerous awards and recognition for his work including the Golden Plotter (first prize, 1994), Gladbeck (Germany), and Prix Ars Electronica (honorary mention, 1993). Verostko maintains an excellent site about his work and life at www.verostko.com/.

George Legrady, b. 1950

Chronologically, Legrady represents a generation of digital artists born between the earliest pioneers—Laposky, Whitney, Franke, and Schwartz, who depended upon (and often were) scientists and technical experts—and the current generation of digital artists in their 30s and 40s, who grew up with the ease and convenience of personal home computing. Paralleling this is Legrady's own personal story. He is a two-time immigrant, born in Budapest in 1950, who fled to Montreal in 1956 during the Hungarian uprising, and then eventually settled in California in 1981. This recurring theme of being between or crossing generations, space, cultures, and even time runs throughout his work. Trained originally as a classical musician, Legrady's musical interests eventually crossed over, and in 1969 he worked as a rock and roll keyboard player. A product of the counterculture revolution of the '60s, Legrady created socially conscious documentaries in the 1970s and '80s on the Cree Indians of northern Quebec, communist iconography of central Europe, and hand-painted advertising billboards in China. In 1981, Legrady began working with digital artist pioneer Harold Cohen (whose bio is included in the preceding text), experimenting with computer code as a creative medium. By the mid-'80s, Legrady, then an assistant professor at the University of Southern California, began to receive recognition and awards for his digital work, which at the time consisted of digital prints. In the following decade and through the present, Legrady's work has become more site-specific and computationally intensive, involving interactive and algorithmically-based installations. For example, his well-known piece *Pockets Full of Memories* involves an interactive space with large-scale projections. Here's an excerpt about the piece, taken directly from Legrady's site (http://www.mat.ucsb.edu/~g.legrady/glWeb/Projects/pfom2/pfom2.html):

> *"Pockets Full of Memories" is an interactive installation that consists of a data collection station where the public takes a digital image of an object, adds descriptive keywords, and rates its properties using a touchscreen. The data accumulates through-out the length of the exhibition. The Kohonen self-organizing map algorithm is used to organize the data, moving the images of the objects into an ordered state according to similarities defined by the contributors' semantic descriptions.*

George Legrady is Professor of Interactive Media, with joint appointments in the Media Arts and Technology program and the department of Art at UC Santa Barbara. Additional information about the artist and his work can be found at www.georgelegrady.com/.

Mark Napier, b. 1961

Napier originally studied engineering before switching to studio art. He graduated with a BFA from Syracuse University and began his art career as a painter. A self-taught programmer, he supported himself as a software engineer, developing database systems and web-based tools for the financial industry. In 1995, he merged these two pursuits, ending his painting career and focusing his creative work exclusively, at the time, on Internet-based art. In recent years, some of his work has expanded into gallery and museum settings. Napier pioneered innovative and boldly conceptual web-based pieces such as *Shredder* (www.potatoland.org/shredder/shredder.html), *Digital Landfill* (www.potatoland.org/

landfill/), and *Feed* (www.potatoland.org/feed/). These projects, while technically sophisticated and finely crafted, purposefully revealed the limitations, political implications, and chaos of the Web. *Shredder* is an alternate browser that constructs web pages, not as ordered predictable pages, but in Napier's words, "as a chaotic, irrational, raucous collage." Besides the implicit politics and software engineering in pieces like *Shredder* and another browser he developed called *riot*, one perceives an interest in the visual. These algorithmically-generated pieces are chaotic—at times boisterous, but always aesthetically engaging, informed by a trained painter's eye. It is these opposing forces of the raw and the refined that give Napier's pieces their distinctive energy and appeal. Napier's work is in numerous major collections, including the Guggenheim in New York. He's also had work commissioned by both the Whitney Museum of American Art and the San Francisco Museum of Modern Art. His work has been shown widely, including at the Whitney Biennial (2001), Ars Electronica, the Kitchen, ZKM net_condition, the Walker's AEN show, and many other venues and festivals around the world. Additional information, images, and code can be found on Napier's personal site, http://potatoland.org/.

John F. Simon Jr., b. 1963

John Simon combines a highly refined visual aesthetic with industrial grade coding skills. He graduated from Brown in 1985 with degrees in studio art and geology, and then received two more advanced degrees in earth and planetary science from Washington University in St. Louis, and an MFA in computer art from the School of Visual Arts in New York. His dual interests in analytical systems and aesthetics is almost always apparent in his work. For example, in his *"art appliances" software and LCD panels, 1998–2004*, Simon sets up algorithmically-based, complex software systems that examine abstraction vs. realism, color theory, viewer perception, and other traditional painting concerns. The work often has art historical connections and references (e.g., to Bauhaus, Klee, Kandinsky, Mondrian, and Lewitt). Beyond Simon's impressive software engineering skills and art historical knowledge is a subtle, often poetic, aesthetic sensibility; many of his pieces are beautiful objects. The work, both in concept and execution, is precise and economical. Simon extends his work from the Web to handheld devices to wall-mounted integrated hardware/software systems that he builds. He also produces software-driven laser-cut Plexiglas objects. Simon is redefining how artists exist in the marketplace, pioneering the sale of affordable works of art directly from his site, at http://numeral.com/.

John Maeda, b. 1966

John Maeda is currently the E. Rudge and Nancy Allen Professor of Media Arts and Sciences at MIT. He is also one of the most well-known designers and digital arts pioneers in the world, awarded in 2001 both the US and Japan's top design career honor: the National Design Award and the Mainichi Design Prize—not bad for someone who recently turned 40. Maeda's work and teaching have had a profound impact on the digital design landscape and, perhaps more than anyone else, Maeda has influenced the present generation of code artists. Between 1996 and 2003, he directed the Aesthetics + Computation Group (ACG) at MIT, which conducted research into the application of computer code and computation as a primary creative medium. A number of Maeda's students have become leading designers/artists and (creative) technologists, including Golan Levin, Jared

Schiffman, and of course Casey Reas and Ben Fry. ACG was an outgrowth of an earlier research group at MIT called the Visual Language Workshop (VLW), created in 1973. VLW was created by Muriel Cooper and Ron MacNeil. Muriel Cooper was a renowned designer, like Maeda, who became interested in applying artificial intelligence to the traditional design process. In 2003, Maeda changed directions, transforming ACG into the Physical Language Workshop (PLW), a design-oriented group that according to the site overview, http://plw.media.mit.edu/, "designs tools for creating digital content in a networked environment, and the means by which the content can be leveraged as creative capital within an experimental online micro-economy that we call OpenAtelier." For Maeda, PLW was a return to the core ideas in Muriel Cooper's VLW.

In addition, Maeda codirects SIMPLICITY, a new media lab–wide research initiative aimed at redefining users' relationships with technology in their daily lives. This statement on the SIMPLICITY site says it all: "How do you make something powerful, but simple to operate at the same time? This is the challenge." Maeda's extraordinary range of talents and his critical approach to the development and implementation of technology in our daily lives have contributed to him being included in *Esquire*'s 1999 list of the 21 most important people of the 21st century. Here are some links to learn more about Maeda and view his work: www.maedastudio.com/index.php, www.media.mit.edu/people/bio_maeda.html, and http://weblogs.media.mit.edu/SIMPLICITY/.

Mary Flanagan, b. 1969

Mary Flanagan is an artist, producer, designer, technologist, activist, writer, and theorist, and her work reflects an integration of all these interests. Her multidimensional projects are created primarily for the Net or installation, and thematically involve the influence of technology—net.culture, computer gaming, and mundane technological tools—on our daily lives. Flanagan offers a fresh, alternative voice, inspiring through her work underrepresented populations to cross the digital divide. Prior to her academic appointments, Flanagan spent a number of years working at Human Code, an Austin-based software developer. Although she was a highly regarded and award-winning producer and designer within the gaming industry, she was frustrated by the lack of titles being developed for girls and minorities, so she left the industry for academia to pursue her social activist/artistic vision. Two projects she has since developed directly address this concern. *The Adventures of Josie True* (www.maryflanagan.com/josie/) is the first web-based adventure game for girls. The game's characters include Josie, an 11-year-old Chinese-American girl; a female African-American aviator called Bessie Coleman; and Josie's science teacher, Ms. Trombone, who is also an inventor. Flanagan is also involved in the development of a collaborative and highly ambitious project: RAPUNSEL (www.maryflanagan.com/rapunsel/). The RAPUNSEL project team is made up of a number of leading computer scientists, artists, and educational theorists who are researching and building a software environment to teach programming concepts to kids. Ultimately, RAPUNSEL will become a multiuser 3D game to teach middle school girls computer programming. Flanagan's work has been exhibited internationally at museums, festivals, and galleries, including the Guggenheim, the Whitney Museum of American Art, SIGGRAPH, the Banff Centre, the Moving Image Centre in New Zealand, the Central Fine Arts Gallery in New York, Artists Space in New York, the University of Arizona, the University of Colorado, Boulder, and many other international venues. Her essays on digital art, cyberculture, and gaming have appeared in periodicals such as *Art Journal*, *Wide Angle*, *Intelligent Agent*, *Convergence*, and *Culture Machine*, as well as several books. She has received funding by the National Science Foundation, the Pacific Cultural Foundation, and the National Endowment for the Arts. Flanagan teaches in the Department of Film and Media Studies at Hunter College, New York. Her research group and lab at Hunter is called tiltFactor. Visit it online at www.tiltfactor.org/.

Casey Reas, b. 1972

Casey Reas is a renowned designer/artist, lecturer, thinker, and of course one half of the Processing design/development team. He was a student of John Maeda's at the MIT media lab, where he and Ben Fry helped develop the DBN programming language/environment. Processing was, to a degree, a natural outgrowth of DBN. Reas originally studied design at the University of Cincinnati before attending MIT, and was one of the founding professors at Interaction Design Institute Ivrea. At Ivrea, Reas worked with an international student body to develop a new arts pedagogy. It was during this period in Ivrea that he and Fry initiated Processing. Reas's work is software-based—code and coding are his primary medium. However, he manifests his code-based work in a variety of executions, including kinetic, reactive, and printed pieces. Some of his most recent work employs ideas explored in conceptual and minimal artworks, such as the wall drawings of Sol LeWitt. In a commission he received in 2004 from the Whitney, entitled {*Software*} *Structures*, Reas explored the relationship between conceptual art and software art. For the project, Reas created three unique descriptive structures that merely described relationships between elements in the pieces. He purposely left the structures general, without any code notation, to allow other coders to implement the pieces in different programming languages. Three other leading code artists—Jared Tarbell of Levitated (http://levitated.net/), Robert Hodgin of Flight404 (http://flight404.com/), and William Ngan of Metaphorical.net (http://metaphorical.net/)—created the 26 code implementations. The project can be viewed at http://artport.whitney.org/commissions/softwarestructures/. When Reas is not lecturing around the world and developing Processing, he teaches as an assistant professor in the department of Design/Media Arts at UCLA. Reas is represented by bitforms gallery in New York, (www.bitforms.com), the BANK gallery in Los Angeles (www.bank-art.com/index.html), and the [DAM] in Berlin (http://dam.org/). His work can be viewed online at http://reas.com/.

Jared Tarbell, b. 1973

Jared Tarbell's code art is sensuously analytical, combining gorgeous tonal subtleties and implicit complex mathematical structures. This fine integration of aesthetic and analytical concerns sets his work apart. He gained prominence with his early ActionScript work and his inclusion in the friends of ED *Flash Math Creativity* books. In recent years, Tarbell has been creating with Processing, and the increased low-level capabilities of Processing and Java have allowed him to create even more organic, complex, expressive work. Most of this work reflects his interest in visualization and emergent behavior, as well as his commitment to open source development; he freely distributes his source code in modifiable form. Jared holds a BS in computer science from New Mexico State University, is a frequent lecturer at international conferences, and is a contributing author to another friends of ED book, *New Masters of Flash, Volume 3*. He maintains the websites Levitated (http://levitated.net/) and Complexification (http://complexification.net/), where his work can be viewed, and in the case of Complexification, purchased directly from the site.

Ben Fry, b. 1975

Ben Fry, along with Jared Tarbell, represents a generation of young artists who explore computational processes and structures as fundamental creative modalities. He's also of course the cocreator of Processing. Born the same year as the Altair 8800 was introduced, Fry and his generation never knew a time without personal computers. By the time Fry et al. were entering elementary school, the Macintosh computer was emerging, issuing in a revolution in desktop computer graphics. This generation was able to develop a fluency in computing that would have been impossible for previous generations (especially for artists). I think this fluency (and comfort) with computing is evident in Fry's work, which is less about the phenomena of computation and more about advanced and poetic applications of it.

Fry earned his undergraduate degree from Carnegie Mellon, double majoring in graphic design and computer science, and his PhD from MIT (Media Lab), studying under John Maeda and alongside Casey Reas in ACG. On the online title page of his PhD dissertation, he proposes, "To gain better understanding of data, fields such as information visualization, data mining and graphic design . . . be brought together as part of a singular process titled Computational Information Design."

Much of Fry's work deals with visualizing large data sets, including the human genome. After completing his PhD, he worked at the Eli & Edythe Broad Institute of MIT & Harvard, developing tools for the visualization of genetic data. His personal work also deals with visualization. For example, his well-known and visually engaging piece *Valence* is custom software he wrote about "building representations that explore the structures and relationships inside very large sets of information." You can read more about the piece at http://acg.media.mit.edu/people/fry/valence/index.html. Fry's work has been shown in galleries and museums throughout the world, including the Whitney Biennial, the Cooper Hewitt Design Triennial, the MoMA in New York, and the Ars Electronica in Linz, Austria. His work has also appeared in the feature films *Minority Report* and *The Hulk*, and in print publications, including the journal *Nature*, *New York* magazine, and *Seed*. Fry has been the recipient of numerous awards, including the Golden Nica from the Prix Ars Electronica in 2005 for his work on Processing with Casey Reas, and a Rockefeller Foundation New Media fellowship. He was also included in the "The I.D. Forty: Forty Designers Under 30 Years of Age." Fry currently holds the Nierenberg Chair of Design for the Carnegie Mellon School of Design. When he's not winning awards, helping students at CMU, or creating visualizations, he can be found answering users' questions on the Processing discourse board. You can see more information about Fry and view his work at http://benfry.com/.

And many more . . .

While I have included some wonderful and very noteworthy code art pioneers, there are many others of equal distinction I was forced to omit because of space concerns. I actually struggled quite a bit with this section. The following are some of these prominent folks with links to their work. I'm sorry I wasn't able to include more.

- **Charles Csuri**: www.siggraph.org/artdesign/profile/csuri/
- **Joshua Davis**: www.joshuadavis.com/
- **Andy Deck**: http://artcontext.org/
- **Amy Franceschini**: www.futurefarmers.com/
- **Ken Goldberg**: www.ieor.berkeley.edu/~goldberg/index-flash.html
- **Jean-Pierre Hébert**: http://hebert.kitp.ucsb.edu/studio.html
- **John Klima**: www.cityarts.com/
- **Mario Klingemann**: www.quasimondo.com/
- **Ruth Leavitt**: http://dam.org/leavitt/index.htm
- **Golan Levin**: www.flong.com/
- **Manfred Mohr**: www.emohr.com/
- **Colin Moock**: www.moock.org/
- **Ken Musgrave**: www.kenmusgrave.com/
- **Yugo Nakamura**: www.yugop.com/
- **William Ngan**: http://metaphorical.net/
- **Josh Nimoy**: www.jtnimoy.com/
- **Josh On**: www.futurefarmers.com/josh/
- **Robert Penner**: www.robertpenner.com/index2.html
- **Ken Perlin**: http://mrl.nyu.edu/~perlin/
- **Keith Peters**: www.bit-101.com/
- **Amit Pitaru**: http://pitaru.com/
- **Paul Prudence**: www.transphormetic.com
- **Daniel Rozin**: http://smoothware.com/danny/
- **Karsten Schmidt**: www.toxi.co.uk/
- **Manny Tan**: www.uncontrol.com/
- **Martin Wattenberg**: www.bewitched.com/
- **Marius Watz**: www.unlekker.net/
- **Mark Wilson**: http://mgwilson.com/

Summary

I wanted to create some code art historical context in this chapter and also hopefully provide some inspiring role models. As you progress as a coder, you'll want to study the work/code of others, and this list is a great place to begin. I think you'll find, as I have, that the "creative coding" community is made up of a wonderful group of generous, intelligent, highly creative people. Proof of this can be seen daily on the Processing Discourse board (http://processing.org/discourse/yabb_beta/YaBB.cgi), where a devoted cadre of code-helper zealots—JohnG, st33d, seltar, TomC, mflux, metaphorz, arielm, fjen, blprnt, flight404, shiffman, toxi, fry, REAS, and many more—stand ready to assist new and experienced coders alike. Thanks to all of you! This book has benefited immeasurably because of your generosity and combined wisdom.

2 CREATIVE CODING

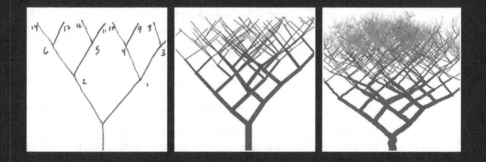

I have a friend, Mark K., who was a web developer who had artistic yearnings (don't they all). I met him a number of years ago when he enrolled in a 3D animation course I was teaching. Mark worked for a sizable, very businessy type company that will remain name-less, doing pretty dull programming. Mostly he was working on legacy code—stuff other people had written—and trying to keep things together with band-aids and string. On top of this, his company was outsourcing most of the interesting development work overseas, and Mark also had the fun job of trying to coordinate video conferences at all hours of the night (big time difference), while integrating their code (in a programming language/development environment he wasn't too familiar with) back into the company's legacy spaghetti (disorganized and poorly structured) code. Is it any surprise Mark was pretty sour on coding and dreamed about painting rainbows and unicorns in the Elysian Fields? Well, actually it was more like working in the game industry. We met at the perfect time.

While Mark was losing his passion for coding, I was losing my passion for pretty much everything else. I was dreading teaching the 3D course at the time, an area just a few years prior I had been passionately involved in. However, my spirits lifted on the first day of class when I met Mark. As a first day ice-breaker, I usually have each student tell me a little about themselves. When Mark described his programming background, I immediately imagined us having these long, intense discussions about the joys and intricacies of coding. Of course this fantasy was shot down quickly as Mark continued to explain his interest of eventually entering the game or animation industry and his waning interest in program-ming. A little disappointed, I summoned encouragement for his new interest and ambition and settled in for a long semester. In the end, the semester turned out to be great. Mark discovered an innate gift and interest in design, and the discussions I originally imagined having with Mark did indeed happen, but of course in a different and actually far more interesting way. Mark and I also developed a real friendship that continues to this day.

One of the subjects that Mark and I often discussed was the intuitive vs. analytical nature of coding. Mark had been formally trained as a programmer and thus had developed a "look before you leap" approach to coding that spilled into his other creative work as well. He was trained to analyze a problem, develop a plan, and then implement it. I on the other hand, trained as a fine artist, was taught to let go of the need to understand everything, and to learn to find structure and meaning in the process. Obviously, the utilitarian aspects of programming and the pretty much complete lack of utility of painting contributed to the approaches adopted in our training. At this point, I was mostly coding little graphics experiments with ActionScript. I would sit on the couch with the TV on, the laptop burn-ing my legs (PowerBook G4), snacks of course, and tweak code until cool things started happening. Eventually one of my convoluted, incomprehensible equations would start yielding something I liked. Then I'd do a "save as" and keep tweaking until I found some-thing else. I was able to hack out tons of art, watch bad reality TV, and still IM Mark dur-ing renderings. Mark was always amazed that I could approach programming that way. He just couldn't see it as an intuitive medium. We eventually tried some collaboration, but would often get stuck in our planning vs. implementing discussions. In time, though, we both began to learn from one another. I began planning some stuff before attacking by the seat of my pants, and Mark began to "throw some dung against the side of the barn." I really began to see the virtue in Mark's analytical approach when my projects began to get more complex and I started developing larger applications and reusable classes (which I'll cover a bit later). I hope Mark was able to learn from me as well, which seems to be the case, as he eventually landed an art director's position, and also has begun to enjoy coding again—with Processing, of course.

I think what was reinforced for me through my collaboration with Mark was the idea that to be really effective, you need to approach a problem both analytically and intuitively or even holistically. It is relatively easy to understand how to approach a painting or even design problem intuitively. As children, most of us scribbled with crayons and learned to make things without much planning. We learned to express ourselves with marks and gestures and weren't too self-conscious about making a mess. Our experiences in math class may have been quite different, as problems got framed by Boolean logic—the answer is either true or false. How you were feeling during the process of solving the problem had little bearing on the answer. When a non-expert looks at a design or painting, especially a representational image, they believe they can understand it (of course, whether they really can is a whole other issue). When that same non-expert looks at a page of computer code, it seems totally inaccessible and very likely overwhelming. They are used to looking at pictures and gestures, for which there doesn't seem to be a right or wrong answer. Looking at code seems like really hard work, and based on those early experiences in math classes, maybe even scary hard work. You do certainly need to put in some amount of effort to learn to decipher the code. But the same thing applies to being able to read a painting or design. It's just that many people believe that just because they have eyes, they can intuitively understand the visual formal language—the underlying pictorial structure—in a painting or design. But seeing, of course—especially seeing critically—involves the brain as well. Now I could very easily lapse into many pages of the most vitriolic prose about the current plague upon our nation because of rampant visual illiteracy, blah, blah, blah . . . but my editor will surely put the kibosh on that. So let me sum it up by stating that in my humble opinion it is much, much, harder to learn a foreign language than it is to learn a programming language, and having taught both painting and programming, it is much, much, much harder to (really) learn to paint or even draw a figure than it is to gain basic fluency in programming.

If you haven't thrown the book at the wall yet, a logical next question might be—especially if you are totally new to programming—"Exactly how much do I need to know before I can begin to start hacking out some art on my couch, and of course what snacks do you recommend?" Well, obviously, unlike drawing, you can't just grab the tool and begin scribbling. Well, if you start with some sample code (which Processing responds quite well to), you can, and that is one valid approach to learning to code. However, I think a much more efficient path, and I guess the main reason for the book, is to quickly (with minimal stress) develop a base coding literacy that will optimize your hack-per-minute efficiency—which translates into making more good art. Regarding snacks, I'm a big fan of Newman's organic stuff, especially the mint Newman-O's. (Yuummm!)

For many years, I tried the steal/tweak/pray coding approach, especially with JavaScript. However, there was always this fear and guilt in the back of my mind: the code will break, somebody will find out exactly how little I know, and I really can't take credit for this. Usually, freelance deadlines beat those feelings back. But using appropriated code that I didn't totally understand to make art for myself didn't feel as good. Also, as a professor I hate being asked questions I don't know the answer to. Of course, this happens practically every day when you have bright, talented students—which I've mostly been blessed to have—and are teaching emerging technology. Teaching Flash for many years, I would get asked practically every ActionScript question imaginable, and I eventually got really tired of BSing my way through half-assed answers. I eventually decided to formally train myself in programming. I got a mountain of books on programming languages (mostly Java and

ActionScript), object-oriented programming, and basic math (mostly algebra and trig), and I took the leap. It was based on this experience that I first got interested in writing a book on creative coding.

I spent many long, lonely nights with those books, especially the Java API (application programming interface—basically a description of the language's rules and tools). Over time I've come to realize that most programming how-to books are excellent for teaching you how to program if you already have a basic understanding of programming. The Java API, although indispensable to me now, was pretty scary, inscrutable, and downright frustrating back then. When I eventually began teaching entire semester courses on creative programming, I really learned a lot about how non-technical people learn technical stuff, and most importantly how to make it engaging. I knew from my own experiences that code was a powerful creative medium, but how to convince my wide-eyed art students was another thing altogether, and I knew most sane people wouldn't do what I did—tackling this scary stuff on their own. I should also point out that besides being obsessive compulsive, I was a science student prior to being an art student, so I had developed some tolerance and coping strategies for studying dense, unfriendly stuff. This book is a tribute to all my coding students who taught me along the way how to be a better teacher and (most importantly) what to do to keep them from dropping my classes.

The origin of Processing

Since around 1945 (or 1834 if you go back to Ada Lovelace's letter to Charles Babbage), many, many programming languages have been developed—in fact, more, I think than most people would guess. Unless you are deep in the computer science world, you maybe have heard of at most five to ten different programming languages. According to a somewhat comprehensive language list at http://people.ku.edu/~nkinners/LangList/Extras/langlist.htm, more than 2,500 languages have been developed. My guess is that the number is actually much higher. Interestingly, at the time of this writing, Processing isn't on the list. This might be due to the list not being properly maintained or because some purists might not see Processing as a separate language. *What*? Well, rest assured, I sent an e-mail telling them all about Processing. But there is a valid argument to be made that Processing is not technically a language, but more of a programming environment—what is commonly referred to as an IDE, or integrated development environment. I'll try to make this argument and then I'll refute it. I love arguing with myself. However, before I get into more Processing nuts and bolts, a more conceptual over-the-hood discussion about Processing and its forebear, DBN, will be helpful, or at least (I hope) mildly interesting.

Processing grew out of research in the Aesthetics + Computation group at the MIT Media Lab in around 2001. Prior to that, John Maeda, the group's famous leader, with the aid of some of his students, developed DBN. DBN was a very simple programming language and environment, begun in around 1999. Casey Reas and Ben Fry also participated in the development of DBN. Processing can be thought of as the very advanced, production-grade child of DBN. DBN was usable on the Web or as a stand-alone application, and was designed to massively simplify the coding process for visual artists. Unlike Processing, DBN didn't have much application outside of the classroom, as the screen output was limited to about 1.5 by 1.5 inches and there was no color. Yet many of the basic processes we expect in a programming language were there, including the ability to set and recall values, create customized commands, and run loops. It even had some basic networking and event behavior (mouse and keyboard detection). If you're interested to learn more, as of this writing, the DBN site can still be found at: http://dbn.media.mit.edu/. DBN was developed to simplify the massive complexity involved in graphics programming. Later on in the book, I will provide some sample code illustrating the minutiae and verbosity of code needed to generate the simplest graphics, even in a high-level language like Java. By "high-level," I mean a language that is supposed to be easier to work in than a low-level language. You can think of the lowest-level language as zeros and ones. DBN was in a sense a reaction to this problem, and it went, some would argue, overboard in addressing it. Processing, having the benefit of standing on the shoulders of DBN, as well as being a second go-around for Ben and Casey, cleverly addressed this problem by providing a multimodal approach, allowing some users to work in a very high-level way—like in DBN— while other codeheads (myself included) could work in pure Java and still others could work with a hybrid approach. This totally inspired design, providing *choice*, is I believe what makes Processing a very special and cutting-edge tool/environment/language. Today, Processing, free from the confines of the Media Lab, is supported by Ben and Casey, with a growing cadre of devoted (some might say obsessed) "Processors" around the world.

Programming language comparisons

Now for some nuts and bolts. If you get a little lost in this section, don't panic; it will become clearer in time. Also, it is not critical info to get started coding. If you really hate it, just skip it. But I strongly recommend coming back to it eventually. I put it here in the beginning of the book because I do think it is important.

The argument to be made that Processing is not actually a programming language, but rather a programming environment, is based on the fact that Processing is built on top of the Java programming language. Of course, parts of Java itself were created with other programming languages as well (C and C++), so what's the point? The point is that when you run Processing, you are actually running a Java program. Processing allows you to write much simpler code than you would need to write if you were working in pure Java. It also allows you to **structure** your code in a **function-based** (procedural), **non–object-oriented** style. But once you **compile** your code, the output is converted to **Java class files**— indistinguishable from any other Java program—and the class files are **interpreted** within the **Java Virtual Machine** as your program runs. Now don't freak out! I know I just dropped a bunch of terms you may not be familiar with. We'll take it slow, and deal with each term, one at a time. Again, my recommendation is to read this stuff and not get too stressed. If it's really bugging you out, skip it and return to it later; you'll still be a good person. I promise, in time, it will all be clear (or at least clearer).

If you have some prior programming experience with another language, or if you're thinking, "Why should I learn Processing instead of another language?" the Processing site includes a good comparison and contrast of a competitive set of languages to Processing (http://processing.org/reference/compare/index.html). Of course, I don't really think these languages compete in any real sense, as each has its own strengths and weaknesses. Additionally, if this coding thing sticks for you, it is very likely that you will learn some if not most of these languages in the future. It actually gets pretty easy to learn a new programming language after you grasp basic programming theory. As I mentioned earlier, learning a programming language is much easier than learning a verbal or natural language. Now let's tackle some of the new terms I just threw at you and look at just a little processing code.

First, what does it mean to "structure" your code?

Here is a simple Processing program that draws a black rectangle on a white background; it's not too ground-breaking, but it is a nice rectangle (see Figure 2-1 for an image of the rectangle that the code produces).

```
size(400, 400);
background(255);
noStroke();
fill(0);
rect(width/4, height/4, width/2, height/2);
```

Figure 2-1. Rectangle created using an unstructured coding approach

A program this simple wouldn't necessitate structuring your code any further. So, at this point, if all you need to make are single squares, you're done. Congratulations! However, imagine instead of having 5 lines of code, you had 50, or 500, or 5,000? It becomes very difficult to understand and maintain a program when it reaches a certain scale. There are ways of structuring your code, kind of like using paragraphs to organize a chapter, that make a large program more manageable. In addition, there are structural ways of simplifying your program, reducing redundant lines of code, and ultimately increasing your coding efficiency and possibly the program's performance (these are all good things).

Function-based (procedural) vs. object-oriented structure

There are a number of ways of structuring your code—I'll discuss two ways it's done in Processing. The first way uses functions (also referred to as procedures, or subroutines— different words essentially describing the same technique). Functions are reusable blocks of code that work like processing machines, which you call when you need them. The second way uses an object-oriented approach, a far more ambitious and abstract approach that models a programming problem using concepts from the real world. In object-oriented programming (OOP), the code is divided into smaller (and independent) blocks of code called objects.

Before I describe and contrast each of these approaches in more detail, it is worth stating that Processing allows you to structure a program using either a function-based, object-oriented, or hybrid approach. In fact, if you want to, you can avoid structure altogether. This amazing flexibility, accommodating different types of coders with varied experience levels, is one of the features that makes Processing such a unique environment. Later in the book, I will go into a much more detailed explanation of this material (I hear your heart fluttering with delight), but for now I'll just describe them in very broad strokes.

Let's go back to the simple five-line program. This program executes from top to bottom. You could test this by moving the fill(0); line below the rect(width/4, height/4, width/2, height/2); line.

```
size(400, 400);
background(255);
noStroke();
rect(width/4, height/4, width/2, height/2);
fill(0);
```

You wouldn't see anything if you now ran this program—can you guess why? It's because the color used by the program to draw the rectangle starts out as white, the same color as the background (255 equals white), and is only changed to black (0 equals black) after the rectangle is drawn. So you are actually drawing a white rectangle on a white back-ground. Now, imagine that you have 5,000 lines of code—wouldn't it be easier to not have to put every line in an exact sequential order to get the program to run properly? Isn't the whole digital thing about not having to be so sequentially linear? Function-based, or procedural, programming can help solve this problem by breaking a program up into reusable code structures that you call as you need them. These blocks are called **functions** (as opposed to objects in OOP); you can think of them as independent processing units waiting for action. Functions are explicitly called when they are needed and can optionally be passed values, which the functions can act upon. Calling a function can be considered the entry point of a function. Once called, a function can either end when it completes its job, or optionally return values. For example, if I wrote a program to keep attendance in my classes (something I've never done very consistently), I might create a function that simply assigned a value of present or absent for each student on a specific date. Then in class, I could call the function and pass in the value present or absent for each student. I wouldn't need the function to return any value. On the other hand, if I wanted to find out which students were absent on a specific day, I might create another function that when called would return the actual names of the students who were absent.

Let's make the current rectangle drawing program a little more complicated. Don't worry about trying to memorize or even understand the code for now. It is the theory that is most important. Here's the program structured using functions:

```
void setup(){
  size(400, 400);
  background(255);
  noStroke();
  float myColor = getRandomColor();
  fill(myColor);
  rect(width/4, height/4, width/2, height/2);
}
float getRandomColor(){
  return random(255);
}
```

The program still draws a rectangle on the white background, but instead of the rectangle always being black, the program calculates a random value between white and black for the fill color of the rectangle. The line return random(255); generates and returns a random number between 0 and 255. 0 equals black and 255 equals white, and anything in between equals a variation of gray. You'll notice the program now has these strange brackets,{ (open) and } (closed). These are called **curly braces**, and they are used to group the lines of code needed by the function to do its job. You'll also notice that the program is broken into two groups of code: void setup(){...} and float getRandomColor(){...}. These groups are both functions. The lines void setup(){...} and float getRandomColor(){...} are the function declarations. It is a good idea to use a verb in the name to describe what the function does. That way, it is easy to understand what that function's job is when reviewing the code. Also, a function is followed by open and closed parentheses. This is the place where any arguments (values) the function will need to do its job are included—commonly referred to as "passing arguments." Even if no arguments are required, as in the preceding case, you still need to include the parentheses.

There is another very common programming structure called a **variable**, which I'll discuss in detail a little later in the book. A variable is simply a location in memory that will hold a piece of data. For instance, in the left part of the expression float myColor = getRandomColor();, float myColor is a variable, to which a numeric value can be assigned. The word "float" just specifies the type of numeric value the variable can hold.

The line float myColor = getRandomColor(); is a function call. Actually, the right part of the expression, getRandomColor();, is the function call, and the left part of the expression (float myColor =) simply assigns the value that the function call returns to the myColor variable. Here's where things get a little interesting. When the getRandomColor() function is called, it takes over—before the line below the function call (fill(myColor);) is dealt with, the code inside the actual getRandomColor() function is run. Only when the function called finishes will the code below the function call be run. Inside the getRandomColor() function, one of Processing's built-in functions, random(), is called. Once the random() function does its job, it returns a number back to where the getRandomColor() function was called from, and this returned value is assigned to the variable float myColor. I realize this may seem a bit overwhelming if this is your first time dealing with coding; I promise it will make (more) sense over time.

OOP was developed later than function-based or procedural programming, and was designed to try to improve on some of procedural programming's perceived limitations. In a general sense, OOP was designed to allow the types of modules that functions introduced to become larger, more complex, and more independent entities. OOP facilitates code reuse—which will become more important as you get more experienced—and enforces certain programming rules. OOP is a much more complex approach to programming that delves into very interesting but quite challenging abstractions. I will cover OOP in Chapter 8, although I include a brief overview of it in the next chapter, which focuses on code grammar. OOP is such a big subject that it would be worthwhile to devote an entire book to creative OOP with processing—maybe if I'm still standing when I'm done writing this one . . .

If you're interested, here is a Processing OOP version of the little rectangle program, with some comments—the descriptions following the two forward slashes (//). I am not going to do a full analysis of the program here, as I'll be covering these concepts in painstaking detail later in the book.

```
// Processing Object-Oriented approach: Create a rectangle
void setup(){
  // set display window to 400 x 400
  size(400, 400);
  // set background color to light gray
  background(225);

  //instantiate a MyRect object and assign it to the reference ➡
    variable rectangle1
  MyRect rectangle1 = new MyRect(width/8, height/8, width/4, ➡
    height/4, 200, -1);

  /* call drawRect() method using MyRect object reference, rectangle1
     calls the method using  dot syntax (literally
     the period between the object and the method call).*/
  rectangle1.drawRect();
}

// MyRect class definition
class MyRect {

  // public instance fields - each MyRect object will have
  // their own set of these properties
  float x, y, wdth, ht;
  int fillCol, strokeCol;

  /*constructor - called when the object is instantiated, using the new
     operator. the parameter list between the parentheses needs to match
     the argument list in the instantiation call */
  MyRect(float x, float y, float wdth, float ht, int fillCol, ➡
    int strokeCol){
  // initialize instance fields - assignment happens form
  // right to left, e.g. the value of x is assigned to the
  // instance property this.x
    this.x = x;
```

```
        this.y = y;
        this.wdth = wdth;
        this.ht = ht;
        this.fillCol = fillCol;

        /* check for stroke - if the last argument passed to the
           constructor is not -1 then use that value to set the
           stroke color. If it is -1, don't draw a stroke */
        if (strokeCol!=-1){
          this.strokeCol = strokeCol;
          stroke(strokeCol);
        }
        else {
          noStroke();
        }
    }

    //drawRect method
      void drawRect(){
        //assign fill color
        fill(fillCol);
        // draw rectangle
        rect(x, y, wdth, ht);
      }
    }
```

The other terms I threw at you earlier were "class files," "compile," "interpret," and "Java Virtual Machine," which I'll define as I introduce Java and describe Processing's special relationship to it.

Java

I want to cover a little of Java's history (sorry), but I think you may find it somewhat interesting, especially as a lesson in the virtue of happy mistakes. I actually cover happy coding mistakes a little later on as well. Java's history is also relevant in regard to a deeper understanding of Processing. Have I convinced you? Hope so.

Java, originally named Oak, was developed in the early 1990s as a language to be used to program devices other than personal computers—things like microwave ovens with embedded processors—not terribly sexy stuff, but as you'll see, pretty visionary. However, appliance manufacturers didn't embrace the idea. So to save face, the Sun engineers went back to their drawing boards and came up with a plan to remarket Oak as a language to control "set-top boxes" for interactive TV. But alas, the cable companies passed on that idea as well. Things were not looking good for Oak. To make matters even worse, it was discovered that the name "Oak" had already been trademarked by another technology company. Before I tell you how Java was reborn out of this very inauspicious beginning, let me explain the basic problem the Sun engineers were trying to address in the design of Oak in the first place. Then you can try to guess (if it is not already obvious) what saved Java.

Without getting too geeky, the main objective in the design of Oak was to develop a relatively simple-to-program, high-level, universal programming language. The really key word here is "universal." A proprietary technology (and a refusal by companies to respect and adhere to standards) creates a difficult landscape to work in. This problem is not limited to the computer industry. A number of years ago my wife and I invested in a water filter system that attaches directly to our kitchen faucet. Over the years we've moved a lot, dragging our filter with us. In almost every new home, we've had to contact the filter company to request yet another odd-sized adapter (we've got a quite a collection by now). Lack of standardization has up until recently been especially frustrating and difficult for web designers, who were forced to develop multiple sites, limit design concepts, and create crazy workarounds to ensure that their sites worked across all the different web browsers (this is no longer so much of a problem because of the advent of web standards, better development practices, and better and more consistent support for those standards across browsers).

One of the benefits of a program like Flash is a universal Flash player that ensures consistent content delivery across different platforms (operating systems and web browsers). The history of Flash, originally called FutureSplash Animator, arguably would have been quite different had Java not a few years earlier pioneered the concept of a portable, universal language.

So the emergence of the Internet saved Java. Java's now well-known slogan, "Write once, run anywhere," turned out to be the perfect strategy for the Internet. And by 1996, Java was also embedded in Netscape's browser, ushering in a revolution in online multimedia-based content and development. Interestingly, in the ten years since this development, Flash has far surpassed Java as the online multimedia-based (front-end) content tool of choice, and Java has moved to the back end of the Web—to the server side. Java is also widely used on mobile and wireless devices, such as PDAs and cell phones. With the development of Processing, Java is again being used for online content creation. So arguably, Processing has saved (or at least resurrected) the Java applet. Although unlike Flash, which is used to enhance/develop entire websites, Processing (currently) is being used primarily for aesthetic exploration. Of course, as more Processing tools and code libraries are developed, this could change. OK, so that's a nice story, but how do Java and Processing work?

Java is considered both a compiled and interpreted language. Unfortunately, the terms "compiled" and "interpreted" don't quite mean the same thing in programming as in general parlance. To compile, in computer-speak, is to convert a (usually high-level) programming language into something lower level. Remember, a computer likes zeros and ones (the lowest-level language), but most people find it frustrating to communicate in binary code. It is easier to write programs in the same natural language we speak (the highest-level language), but a spoken language is extremely complex and would demand tons of processing to be able to interpret it. Therefore, in the design of a programming language, there is a trade-off between ease of use and performance.

Java was designed with this trade-off in mind. Sun's Java compiler, javac (Processing actually uses a similar open source compiler, developed by IBM, called jikes), converts a programmer's code (the stuff we write) into a middle-level language called bytecode (that the compiler writes). This bytecode (also known as class files) is universal, meaning that I can take my class files compiled on my Mac and run them on a Windows machine, as long as the Windows machine has a Java Virtual Machine (JVM). As most operating systems and browsers have a JVM, I can use my class files in any of these environments, regardless of where they were written. Thus, you can see the power of Java's "Write once, run anywhere" strategy.

In Java's early days, it was considerably slower than non-interpreted languages like C or C++, which don't use a middle compilation state (the bytecode). These languages compile directly to machine code specific to the native underlying system. Thus, these languages are highly efficient, but not easily portable. If you write a program in C++ on a Mac, it will only run on a Mac. You have to literally go in and change some of your code to create a second version of your program (referred to as porting your program) if you want it to run on a different platform. Today, based on certain advances in compilers, such as "just-in-time" compilers (in which some of the Java bytecode is compiled to native machine language instructions during runtime), Java's speed is comparable to lower-level, non-interpreted languages like C and C++. This gap continues to narrow, or become insignificant, as computers continue to get faster. So Java's strategy seems to be really paying off.

Processing has all the benefits of Java with a much simpler and optimized environment for creative coding. As an example, following is the original five-line rectangle drawing program written in Processing. I've also written the same program as a Java applet.

Here's the original Processing program:

```
size(400, 400);
background(255);
noStroke();
fill(0);
rect(width/4, height/4, width/2, height/2);
```

Here's the same program as a Java applet:

```
import java.awt.*;
import java.applet.*;

public class MyStage2 extends Applet{
  public void init(){
    setSize(new Dimension(400, 400));
    setBackground(Color.white);
  }
  public void paint(Graphics g) {
    g.setColor(Color.black);
    g.fillRect(getSize().width/4, getSize().height/4, ➥
      getSize().height/2, getSize().height/2);
  }
}
```

The Java applet requires about twice as much code as the Processing sketch. However, as you write more complex programs in Processing, the number of required lines of code to write the same program in pure Java begins to increase exponentially. So if Processing is essentially Java, how does it do the same thing with less code? It does it by using a software framework that does a lot of the extra (non-creatively oriented) work under the hood, leaving you to just concentrate on the fun stuff.

A framework is just a concept for bundling precompiled code together for use in developing a related family of programs. From a programmer's standpoint, a good framework allows you to write less code and focus more on the higher-level concerns of your program. Java relies on many frameworks. For example, Java's Collections framework allows different types of groupings of objects (collections) to be manipulated in a uniform way, and, as Sun says, "independently of the details of their representation." This is a huge advantage to a coder, who now only has to learn one approach (a single pattern) to getting or setting a value within a collection of objects, even though internally these collections may use very different implementations. The Processing framework does a similar thing, but in the area of creating and manipulating graphics and images. Graphics programming is complex, and using pure Java involves ascending a pretty steep learning curve. In addition, after learning how to create some graphics (shapes and text), you would still need to learn a whole new set of procedures for working with images, not to mention video, animation, and so on. Using the Processing framework, these disparate and complex operations are standardized into a uniform and simplified set of commands.

Procedural OOP ("poop") approach

I suspect by now, if you've stuck through this chapter, you're in need of a little diversion, so a short story might be refreshing. A number of years ago I was preparing for a show of my paintings. I was very excited about the show, as I was only a few years out of grad school and had this romantic vision of being discovered, and picked up by a major New York gallery. The fact that my show (actually a two-person show with my friend David) was at a small cooperative gallery in Piermont, New York, didn't seem to have any effect on my fantasy. In preparing for the show, I stretched up a number of large, impressive looking canvases on which to create my "serious" work. Besides preparing for my show, I also had a brain-numbing job doing mostly print production work for an aesthetically bankrupt (though not at all financially bankrupt) corporation. My one fun indulgence was a Thursday night drawing group I frequented in Manhattan.

When I first moved to New York City, I looked up an old professor who invited me to a weekly drawing group at his studio. I was of course thrilled and went to my first session expecting to bask in all the intense aura of professional, established New York artists at work, but instead found a party-like atmosphere with free-flowing wine, loud music, and continuous conversation. In time, I became quite accustomed to this new approach and had a great time listening to the older artists tell stories about the good old days, and of course we did make art.

So each week I would go to the drawing group, crank out a bunch of work, come back to my studio, and pile the work in the corner. During the days, when I wasn't slogging through Quark at the mind-numbing job, I painted my "serious work." This went on for nearly a year, until I began final preparations for my show. When it got down to selecting the actual paintings to put in the show, I had a major revelation (it actually felt more like a kick in the head). My serious work, well, kind of sucked. It was self-conscious and forced. I was pretty desperate and had no time to create new work, so I went to the corner with my "non-serious" work piled high from the Thursday night drawing parties and started rifling through the pile. I was shocked—the work was really interesting and fresh, but also accomplished in its own way. The work had spontaneity and energy, but it also had structure and clarity. The "serious" day painting that I thought was my real work was actually something else altogether. In retrospect, although the work was self-conscious and forced, the discipline of doing the serious painting contributed to my skills and technique, allowing me to let go on Thursday night to really express myself. It was this combination of discipline and freedom that I attribute to the quality of the work. I ended up only putting the Thursday night work in the show, and got a very positive response. Of course I didn't get famous, but I certainly kicked butt in Piermont.

So what the heck does that story have to do with Processing? Well, when it comes to writing creative software, there are a number of ways to approach it. There is the "serious" way and there is the Thursday night party way. It is not so much a specific set of techniques I'm talking about, but rather an attitude. Some programming languages and environments demand a highly structured and rigid approach that doesn't favor spontaneous expressive shifts. OOP, which is a beautiful construct that I will go into later in the book, requires planning and a well-thought-out plan; Without such a plan, a "by the seat of your pants" OOP approach can lead to piles and piles of code and excess complexity, taking you away from self-expression and burying you in pure digital craft, or worse—damage control. The other extreme, pure gut hacking of unstructured spaghetti code, can yield fast effects and little teasers, but it becomes overwhelmingly difficult to carry a creative impulse through to a more realized form. So there needs to be a middle way, combining structure with fast prototyping capabilities. This yin/yang approach is possible in Processing, which provides a fast, loose, procedural coding environment with a highly structured and powerful object-oriented backbone. That is not to say there aren't pitfalls to working in such a flexible environment, in which it's easy to develop nasty hacking habits. My recommendation, and the way I've structured the upcoming tutorial sections in the book, is to begin coding with passion. Don't let the fear of doing it *right* or learning everything first get in the way of expressing yourself, but at the same time, study the language (first Processing and then eventually Java) and OOP; it will ultimately empower you to create larger, more expressive works.

Algorithms aren't as scary as they sound

1. Buy a new copy of *Processing: Creative Coding and Computational Art*.

2. Open the book to page 1.

3. Begin reading at the top of page 1.

4. Stop reading at the bottom of the last page of the book.

5. Write a glowing review of the book on Amazon.com.

6. Go to step 1.

These six steps constitute an algorithm. They are not a computer program—they are just specific directions on how to achieve something. The term *algorithm* comes from Abu Abdullah Muhammad bin Musa al-Khwarizmi (referred to just as al-Khwarizmi), a Persian supergenius (with a really long name) from the early part of the ninth century. We get the word *algorithm* from the al-Khwarizmi part of his name. al-Khwarizmi worked near Baghdad as a scientist, mathematician, astronomer/astrologer, and author. He is also commonly referred to as the father of algebra. You may have first been introduced to the word *algorithm* in a math class in high school, but you may have been daydreaming at the time (or, if you're anything like me, drawing a less-than-flattering picture of your math teacher). Algorithms are fundamental to mathematics, but they are also essential to pretty much any other planned activity. If you go to Google and type define:algorithm, as of this writing, 28 definitions come up. One definition I like in particular, from http://images.rbs. org/appendices/d_glossary_geometric.shtml, is "A step-by-step procedure used for solving a problem." I like this definition because it is so incredibly simple and universal, and can be applied to practically any problem. The only thing I might add to the definition is the limit on the number of steps. My new definition is "A *finite* step-by-step procedure used for solving a problem." When you're dealing with programming—or really, any task— an infinite number of steps is almost always a bad thing. For example, in the preceding algorithm I wrote, experienced coders probably saw a major logic problem; the algorithm never ends. Intellectually this might be an interesting idea, like a hall of mirrors endlessly reflecting one another, but in programming we call this an infinite loop. Loops are central to programming, but we usually want them to end when some condition is met. For example:

1. Buy a new copy of *Processing: Creative Coding and Computational Art*.

2. Open the book to page 1.

3. Begin reading at the top of page 1.

4. Stop reading at the bottom of the last page of the book.

5. Write a glowing review of the book on Amazon.com.

6. If Ira's still not a millionaire, go to step 1.

7. Stop following this algorithm (and thank you)!

The logic in the algorithm will no longer generate an infinite loop. Instead, at step 6, only if the condition is not met (alas, I'm still not a millionaire) does the algorithm repeat. But eventually the condition will be met, step 6 will be skipped, and step 7 will end the loop. Unless there is some specific direction to go somewhere else (e.g., go to step 1), the program keeps executing from top to bottom. This is why the program falls through step 6 when the condition is no longer met and executes line 7, ending the loop.

Computers are inherently dumb machines. They are super-quick at processing data and have awesome memories, but they have no innate intelligence. For example, if I asked a computer to hold a 1,000-pound weight over its head (just assume computers have arms), it would eventually destroy itself by dropping the weight on its head when its arms gave out. Why? Because computers are perfect literalists; they do only and exactly as they are told, without any assumption, reflection, or self-awareness. Unless I instructed the computer to put the weight down when it felt its arms getting tired, it wouldn't do it. One of the difficulties in learning to code is not that we have to think so brilliantly, but rather that we have to think so mind-numbingly literally—without the benefit of emotion, assumption, or intuition. For example, if I want to ensure that you will continue reading this book, I could tell you that you *must* keep reading this book. However, because people are intelligent and not robotic literalists, the majority of you will likely tell me to go to hell. Generally speaking, if we want human beings to do something, we need to make an appeal with a more complex strategy, taking into account feelings, social conventions, personal history, favorite baked goods, and so forth.

Humans are excellent at intuiting. We can meet someone for the first time and within a couple of minutes build a complex initial profile of the person; not that all these assumptions hold up—but it's amazing, with so little data, that any do. We seem to be able to remember subtle general patterns of behavior that let us build composite types. Psychologists have named this organizing function *gestalt*. Gestalt is also commonly defined as the sum of the parts being greater than the individual parts. For example, when you show someone a picture of Elvis, they don't think "two eyes, a nose, lips, sideburns, sequins, etc." They don't even think "man" or "human being"—they think, "It's Elvis!" The gestalt allows our minds to generalize object-oriented models based on our memories and sensory data. The gestalt makes us highly efficient at processing vast amounts of complex information without going insane. Imagine if we were constantly aware of all the sensory data surrounding us? However, this amazing organizing ability we have can also cause major problems when we think our limited mental models reflect all of reality. Teaching drawing for many years, I felt my hardest job was convincing the students to let go of the way they thought they saw the world, to be able to learn to see it again freshly and expand their perceptual paradigm. When people first start out learning to program, they typically make some common intuitive assumptions because of the gestalt. These types of assumptions, which work more or less in the real world, fail miserably when applied to programming. Computers innately lack an internal gestalt to discern the whole from the parts. They are essentially just dumb (although ridiculously powerful) calculators. If computers have any intelligence at all, it is at the software level. Software—operating systems, programming languages, and applications—to some degree create a gestalt-like reality in the computer, the so-called spirit in the machine. Thus, perhaps the passion people feel for their machines is really a connection to the spirit imbued within the machine (the software)—which of course is the human presence.

Here's a concrete example that illustrates how our sophisticated brains can get us into trouble when we first start writing code. An exercise I always cover early in my creative coding class is how to generate a simple moving object programmatically (meaning using code). The problem is pretty simple: Create a small rectangle—we'll name her "recty" (she's a female polygon). Make recty move around the screen and have her bounce off the edges of the frame, never letting any part of her go out the frame.

The first challenge students generally encounter in this problem if they have no programming experience is simply moving recty. For this example, let's assume that recty is already on the screen in a frame and has an x property. This means that recty's x position (her horizontal position) on the frame can be set and retrieved by using her x property. Also assume that recty's registration point—a point or pixel on recty that the x property is measured from—is in her top-left corner, and there is also a variable named speed that controls how fast recty moves. I'll assign a value of 3 to the speed variable using the expression speed = 3, and I'll also start a loop running that continues to update the frame (and recty's position). I'll be covering all this stuff in more detail later on, so it's OK to be a little out of breath at this point—but just avoid operating any heavy machinery.

To move recty, most new coders try this first: `recty.x = speed`, which I think makes perfect sense because they're assigning speed to recty's x property. Unfortunately, this expression doesn't get recty moving; although something else happens—recty gets moved to the left edge of the screen (to 3 pixels to the right of the left edge of the frame) and stays there, because `recty.x = speed` doesn't increment recty's x position by speed, but rather assigns the value of speed (which is 3) to recty's x position—putting her at that point in the frame. The loop keeps running and keeps assigning 3 to recty.x, so she doesn't move (poor recty), even though the frame is being refreshed continuously. So why do people do this (besides just to annoy their teachers)? I think it's because it is so easy for us to understand how to move that we don't waste any brain cells thinking about it.

Let's imagine you and I were standing across a room from one another and I'd like you to come join me on my side of the room. More than likely, I'd just say "please come over here." Your brain would fill in all the details on how to pull this off, which it would then communicate to your body and you'd begin walking across the room, most likely in a direct path toward me. Even though I didn't tell you a rate or direction to move, you'd know exactly what to do. Of course, my one-year-old daughter would probably not respond to the same verbal cue. However, if I held up a shiny object from across the room, she'd likely begin crawling over to me, also in a straight path no less. One of our challenges in programming is thinking beneath our intelligence. Although moving across a room may seem like a really simple task, there are a tremendous number of assumptions and calculations we make to achieve it, not to mention some pretty insane physics. When we model even simple behavior on the computer, we need to account for these assumptions—which is difficult. The correct solution to the movement problem is the following expression:

```
recty.x = recty.x + speed
```

Now this expression often looks a little confusing to people in the beginning. Why would something be equal to itself? It seems illogical. First of all, in programming, the symbol = doesn't mean *equals*, but rather *assignment*. The symbol == means *equals*—I know this seems weird. It might help if I write in English what's going on in the expression recty.x = recty.x + speed: "Add the value of the variable speed to recty's current x property, then assign that value back to recty's x property, and then do it again and again. . ." Thus, after each loop cycle, recty's x property will increment by 3. By writing the logic out as an algorithm, you can better understand what's happening. In this case, recty.x keeps increasing each loop cycle of the program, moving her across the screen. Will recty stop when she hits the end of the frame? Nope, we didn't tell her to. In fact, recty would continue moving until we quit the program, but of course you won't see her, because she's out of the frame. If this is still unclear, don't worry at all. This is difficult stuff to begin to get your head around. Another trick to help you understand this stuff is to do the calculations manually. For example

- Remember speed equals 3.
- Start recty.x out at 0.
- First, loop recty.x = recty.x +speed.
- Now recty.x equals 3.
- Second, loop recty.x = recty.x +speed.
- Now, recty.x equals 6.
- Third, loop recty.x = recty.x +speed.
- Now recty.x equals 9.
- See the pattern.

I hope that helps; it will come in time if it's still a bit fuzzy. If you're anything like me, It just takes some time to restart the brain after years of turpentine exposure and bad TV. When you get stuck on a programming problem, it really does help to write out a simple algorithm. Later on, when you begin cranking out thousands of lines of dense code, creating algorithmic roadmaps before you start coding might even eventually begin to feel like conceptual brainstorming or preliminary sketching—of course, by then you will also be a certifiable geek.

Happy coding mistakes

After my diatribe about algorithms, how can a coding mistake be seen as happy? Well, I don't mean "computer bug" when I write "mistake." A bug is usually not happy. Bugs are when stuff happens that is not very interesting and usually annoying. Bugs are the things in software—such as missing semicolons, misspelled variable names, or infinite loops—that can drive you insane and make you try to physically impale your keyboard. Happy coding mistakes, on the other hand, are nonfatal things that happen, often revealing unforeseen possibilities. As a painter, it took me a long time to be comfortable with my mistakes (which were many). I wanted to control the paint—which of course is pretty much impossible. In time, I began to realize that the so-called mistakes I was making were often the best parts of the paintings. This phenomenon occurs in all creative pursuits, as somehow our unconscious mind seems to assert itself when we least expect it. Arguably, this is also where our inspiration lies. I think more experienced artists just learn how to better utilize this capability as well as gain the ability to more selectively recognize the happy accidents from the bugs. Coding is a creative process, and thus code art can benefit from these happy mistakes. However, because the process of coding involves many more rigid rules than painting, it is not as easy to understand the concept of happy coding mistakes. In addition, when starting out coding, it is easy to get caught up in the technical aspects or craft of coding and lose sight of its power as an expressive medium.

There is a macho aspect to coding, as well as to painting. You begin to feel powerful and capable of describing all kinds of interesting behaviors; plus, you have access to a secret language that most people don't understand. Coding can become like a giant, multidimensional crossword puzzle, and you can easily get consumed in these really dense, abstract worlds—losing site of expressive possibilities or what you need to say (in an artistic sense). You need craft in coding; the more mastery you have of your medium, the wider the scope or range of your work. You also need a creative vision; without it, coding can become an analytical quagmire. I can't say that I always navigate clear of the quagmire myself, as I often get caught in trying to solve these endless, albeit interesting, technical problems. But when I let myself play with the code and let things happen that are not completely in my control, I often have more fun and even experience the same kind of (warning; new-agey phrase coming) transcendent feeling I get when I am in the flow of painting. I also think the work is more original and expressive. Ultimately, I think it is about finding flow in the coding process that takes you to new places and allows you to turn your so-called mistakes into new and fertile investigations.

OK, let's assume you buy some of this; a logical question for a new coder to ask is "How do you begin to find or embrace happy coding mistakes when you don't even know the fundamentals (or basic craft) of programming?" I think the answer is to always try to find the time to play at whatever level you are at. This is a really important approach that teachers are sometimes lousy at implementing. It is easy to get caught up in teaching the pursuit of mastery, focusing on achievement goals for students and checking off the requisite material covered. The school system reinforces this approach with standardized testing, creating crammers and compartmentalizers who separate work and play, craft from art. Is it any wonder that many of us (especially creative types) felt bored and frustrated in the traditional classroom, especially in subjects that required methodical drilling or rote memorization (like math)? Sadly, as we get older, we eventually label these subjects as the problem, not the non-integrated teaching approaches. My experience in the classroom has been that I find most people receptive to learning anything when it's taught effectively. And my vision of effective teaching always involves finding a way of integrating aspects of play and work into the learning process. Before I launch into yet another whiny soliloquy, I'll sum it up with the following: real code art (whatever the heck that means) can be made at any level—by a newbie coder learning the basics or a seventh-degree Java black belt—and happy coding mistakes help us see the expressive possibilities at whatever level we are at.

Before I end this chapter, I think it might be helpful to illustrate this point with a short example of how I approach happy coding mistakes in my own process.

Algorithmic tree

I used to paint a lot of trees. Originally, I painted the entire landscape, but gradually over time, I found myself zooming in closer on the trees, until one summer, I painted an entire series of large paintings based on part of one tree. It is interesting watching your neighbors' reactions as you spend more and more time standing in your backyard, staring up at the same tree.

So in honor of my favorite tree, I thought I'd illustrate some creative coding by generating a tree with code. Let me also preface this by saying that you shouldn't try to follow this code unless you already know how to program; it may seem totally overwhelming. My main point here is to reveal my creative process, not to teach the code; the rest of the book is for that. Feel free to run this sketch and make changes to the code to see what happens. If you get any really cool results, I hope you'll e-mail me some screenshots.

In considering the problem, I decided to think about trees some and to break the problem down into simple parts. In a moment of brilliant clarity, I concluded that trees have a trunk, branches, and leaves. OK, I know I can probably make a trunk (think straight vertical line). Branches could be a little harder, and leaves, well, probably too hard (actually too much work). Branches, I concluded, could be simplified as a thin trunk, splitting off to another series of thinner trunks, splitting off to another series of thinner trunks, and so on. Thus, it seemed branches could be made from a single branch machine, in a fractal progression (huh?). By fractal progression, I mean the branches are self-similar and repeat. Each branch's ending point is a starting point for more branches, with a decreasing scale. Thus, the tree thickness decreases from trunk to branch—which seemed pretty consistent with real trees. I decided to put the leaves on hold for now. I was ready for a little sketch of my branch plan (see Figure 2-2).

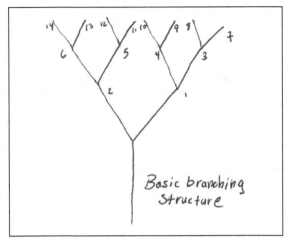

Figure 2-2. Initial schematic sketch of tree branching structure.
The numbers represent the algorithmic branching order.

The drawing is a basic symmetrical tree structure in a purely schematic form. Between each branch is a node. I added some numbers for the nodes to think a little how the computer would sequentially draw the structure. So I was now ready for an algorithm that would help me write code to generate the tree form. Again, the tree trunk was just going to be a line, so I figured I'd come back to it. Here's the branching algorithm:

1. Draw two or more opposing diagonal branches from the top of the trunk.

2. At the ends of these branches, continue adding two or more opposing diagonal, slightly thinner branches.

3. Go back to step two until a specific limit is reached.

The algorithm seemed simple enough, and I noticed that it could possibly loop back on itself—or even call itself. We call such an approach in programming **recursion**, where a function calls itself. Recursion is a somewhat advanced concept, even though it is not that difficult to implement. Recursion will lead to an infinite loop (a bad thing) unless some explicit limit is set. For example, I could tell the program to run until one of the branches touched the top of the frame, or until there are 700 branches on the tree, and so on.

After a couple of well-placed slaps to my head, I finally got the basic branching code written (please note that this code fragment will not run in Processing yet):

```
void branch(Point2D.Float[] pts){
    int stemCount=2;
    if (counter2<branchLimit){
        for (int j=0; j<stemCount; j++){
            line(pts[counter2].x, pts[counter2].y, ➡
              pts[counter2].x+xg, pts[counter2].y-yg);
            pts[counter+1] = new Point2D.Float(pts[counter2].x+xg, ➡
```

```
        pts[counter2].y-yg);
            xg*=-1;
        counter++;
    }
    counter2++;
    branch(pts);
    }
}
```

2

I don't want to spend too much time on the code here, as lots of coding is coming up in subsequent chapters. I'll just give a quick overview of how the function works. If you feel overwhelmed at any point, just skip the code parts. In Chapter 3, I'll begin with a very gentle introduction to the fundamentals of coding, so don't panic. What I'm really interested in illustrating is a creative process using code.

The branch function expects an array, of type Point2D.Float, as an argument (the stuff between the parentheses at the top of the function). An array just holds a bunch of values, as opposed to a variable, which only holds a single value. I chose to use Java's Point2D.Float class because it has built-in x and y properties and can handle real numbers (as opposed to only integers). The stemCount variable controls how many branches each subsequent branch gets. I hard-coded it to 2 just for now. The for loop draws the diagonal lines and updates the pts array with the new branch locations. The variable xg controls whether the branches lean left or right. By continuously multiplying xg by −1, it keeps toggling the branches from right to left—not terribly organic, but efficient. The counters keep track of stuff, and then I recursively call the same function, passing in the updated pts array. At this point, you are probably either like "Cool, that makes sense," or "Is it too late to return this book? This guy is nuts!" Well, I may be nuts, but I don't expect most of you to be able to follow this code. However, hearing some of these terms over and over will help with the "stick in your brain" part. What is really much more important and interesting is how to turn this cold schematic diagram into a tree (see Figure 2-3).

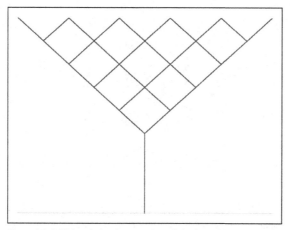

Figure 2-3. Initial code implementation of the branching algorithm

After being somewhat satisfied with the branch algorithm, I started playing with the code. The first thing I did was add some random functions that moved the branches in slightly different places. The random functions contribute to the happy mistakes. Sometimes, I'll put in values that are outside of a reasonable range just to see what happens. Already this started looking better (see Figure 2-4).

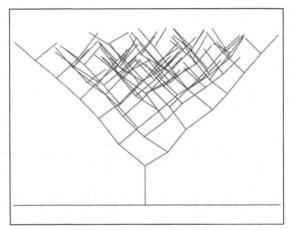

Figure 2-4. Randomness added to the branch structure

Next, I added thickness (using the radius variable) to give the tree some form. Beginning with a larger radius value—not really a radius, but more like thickness—for the trunk, I decremented the radius variable slowly each time the function ran, letting the branches slowly attenuate. This began looking a little more tree-like, as you can see in Figure 2-5.

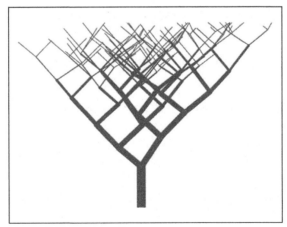

Figure 2-5. Stroke weight variation begins to create a more realistic-looking tree.

The overall movement was good, but the tree seemed too stiff, so I wrote a little redrawing function that added some waviness to the main trunk, and I set this up as a random value. Using randomness is really helpful for generating organic-esque type effects. One of the potential pitfalls of using code as a creative medium is its inherent precision, since it's ultimately based on math. In the real world, "stuff" (friction, gravity, our ineptitude, etc.) intervenes between intention and implementation—the happy accidents. Adding randomness is one (easy) way to introduce some happy chaos into an otherwise highly predictable process (see Figure 2-6). Normally when I use random values, I set a base number that I add to the random part. For example, if I were creating a random number of branches, and I used a random function, such as random(12), I would get a number returned between 0 and 12. However, if I needed a minimum of two branches, I would change the expression to "2+random(10)"—this way, I would get a random number between 2 and 12. Processing has a handy random function that allows you to pass two arguments, as in random(2, 12), which does the same thing.

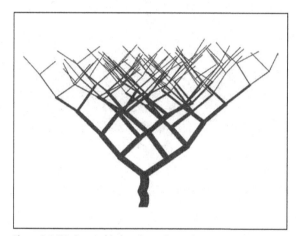

Figure 2-6. Waviness added to the main trunk

Things were beginning to look pretty good, but I still needed to deal with those darn leaves. Then, a really happy coding accident happened. As I began to play with the code, setting weird numbers in the functions, I found a way of generating leaves by really upping the number of iterations and using a couple of conditional statements (if and else) that would at specific times in the branch-creation cycle decrement or increment certain values. Then I added some color the same way, and finally used a similar wavy function for each branch, like I used on the trunk. Figure 2-7 shows a couple of finished trees.

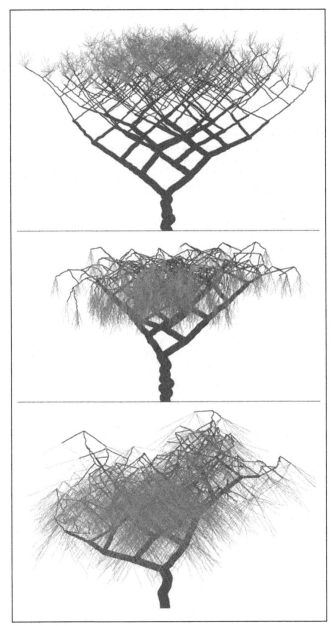

Figure 2-7. Some finished trees

Obviously, there are a lot of things I could still do with the tree code, but hopefully one of you will eventually take the code and improve upon it. I hope I was able to illustrate in this example how you can play with the code and even find stuff in the process of coding. Yes, there is some thinking involved, but there is also a lot of play and discovery. I've included the entire tree program following, with code comments for your hacking pleasure. If you want to try running this, launch Processing and type (or paste) the code into the Processing text editor.

```
/*
algorithmic tree sketch
Ira greenberg, August, 2005
*/

/* import Handy Java class with
   public x and y float props */
import java.awt.geom.Point2D;

// declare/define global variables
int counter;
int counter2;
float xg = 58;
float yg = 46;
int trunkSegments = int(random(7))+5;
int nodeLimit = 20000;
Point2D.Float[]pts = new Point2D.Float[nodeLimit];
int branchLimit = 620;
float trunkLength = int(random(50))+130;
float[]lean2 = new float[trunkSegments+1];
float radius = 26;

// initialize sketch
void setup(){
  size(900, 600);
  background(255);
  stroke(30, 10, 5);

  // create tree turnk
  trunk();
}

void trunk(){
  //draw trunk
  for (int i=0; i<trunkSegments; i++){
    float lean = myRand(22);
    strokeWeight(radius+12);
    line(width/2+lean2[i], height-(trunkLength/trunkSegments)*i, ➡
      width/2+lean, height-(trunkLength/trunkSegments)*(i+1));
    lean2[i+1] = lean;
  }
```

```
                  // set inital branch point from top of trunk
                  pts[0] = new Point2D.Float(width/2+lean2[trunkSegments], ➡
                    height-trunkLength);

                  //create branches
                  branch(pts);
                }

                //main function that draws branches and leaves
                void branch(Point2D.Float[]pts){
                  int stemCount=2;

                  // global variable branchLimit controls complexity of tree
                  if (counter2<branchLimit){
                     //set branch thickness
                     strokeWeight(radius);

                     // some conditionals change branches as
                     // they get further away from the trunk
                     if(counter2<200){
                       yg-=random(.354);
                       xg-=random(.625);

                       if (radius>2) {
                         radius*=.931;
                       }

                     } else if(counter2>=200){
                         // at top of tree branches get thinner and more numerous
                         stemCount = 2+(int)(Math.random()*15);
                         // leave color
                         stroke(random(60), 50+random(90), random(20), 230);

                         yg-=myRand(.65);
                         xg+=random(1.5);

                         radius*=(.91);
                     }
                     for (int j=0; j<stemCount; j++){
                       // randomize branch positions
                       float xx= myRand(30);
                       float yy= myRand(40);

                       /* commented out line below generates straight branches
                       line(pts[counter2].x, pts[counter2].y, pts[counter2].x+xg+xx,➡
                         pts[counter2].y-yg+yy);
                       */
```

```
        // generates organic looking branches
        orgLine(pts[counter2].x, pts[counter2].y, ➥
          pts[counter2].x+xg+xx, pts[counter2].y-yg+yy);

        /* fill up pts array to be passed back
           recursively to branch function */
         pts[counter+1] = new Point2D.Float(pts[counter2].x+xg+xx, ➥
           pts[counter2].y-yg+yy);

        // alternate branches left and right
        xg*=-1;

        // keep track of nodes
        counter++;
      }

    // keeps track of branches
    counter2++;

    //recursive call
    branch(pts);
    }
  }

// generates organic-looking branches
void  orgLine (float x1, float y1, float x2, float y2){

  int sections = 8;

  float xd = x2-x1;
  float yd = y2-y1;

  float twist;
  float[]twist2 = new float[sections+1];

 for (int i =0; i<sections; i++){
   twist = myRand(5);
   line(x1+xd/sections*i+twist2[i], y1+yd/sections*i, ➥
     x1+xd/sections*(i+1)+twist, y1+yd/sections*(i+1));
   twist2[i+1] = twist;
 }
}

//generate a random val between (-n, n)
float myRand(float val){
  return random(val)+random(-val);
}
```

2

Summary

In this chapter, I introduced creative coding as an approach to programming that integrates both analytical and creative processes. Using my friend Mark as an example, I described some of the stereotypes and biases that can make this cross-brain integration so challenging—a problem often (and sadly) reinforced in the classroom, which helped motivate me to teach creative coding and eventually write this book.

I gave a very top-view description about how Processing works, built on top of the Java programming language, and I described some ways of structuring your code, including procedural and object-oriented approaches—both utilized within Processing. I tried to demystify the term "algorithm" and show the relationship between an algorithm and its implementation in code. I also discussed the challenge of learning to think like a "dumb" machine.

Finally, I covered the important role of happy accidents in the creative coding process, and I illustrated the point with an algorithmic tree example. In the next chapter, you'll begin to explore the actual nuts and bolts of coding.

3 CODE GRAMMAR 101

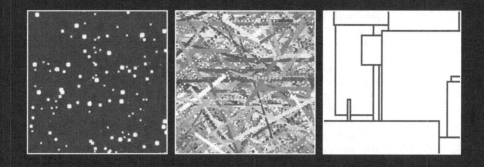

This is where the techie stuff really begins! Hopefully, in the last two chapters you've gotten some context and maybe even inspiration and are ready to dive right in. This chapter looks at the nuts and bolts of programming in general. I make the assumption that you have no experience with coding at all, so for those of you coming to Processing from another language, you may want to skim this chapter. In Chapter 4, I cover the basics of graphics coding, and in Chapter 5, I discuss the details of the Processing environment.

For new coders, my recommendation is to read this chapter at least once, but to not worry about retaining all this info before continuing on. The material will sink in as you begin programming, and you can refer back to this chapter from time to time as a reference. Most of what I cover in this chapter is general programming theory and basic syntax and semantics using Processing and to some degree Java. By syntax, I mean the way language is put together to form actual statements, functions, classes, and so on. Semantics refers to the actual meaning of the code we write. Most of what I cover here, especially the theoretical stuff, is applicable to other languages besides Processing, but of course each language has its own syntax, so the actual code will look different. Without further ado, I present: Coding . . . really, really simplified.

Structure and abstraction

There are a couple of ways to think about structure in coding. On the simplest level, you can think of structure in terms of the syntax you use to write a single line of code. For example, `ball.x = width-ball.width;`. On the other end of the spectrum, structure can involve applying complex rules and protocols for integrating large, convoluted software systems. Fortunately for your needs, most of the structural issues will be pretty straightforward. You will use basic syntactic structure to order a program, not unlike how you would structure any written document, using punctuation, sentence structures, paragraphs, and so on. In coding, there are some other more abstract notions of structure that I will discuss as well.

Our brains like some sense of order—although the range of chaotic tolerance among different people's brains seems pretty wide (as my office usually attests to). When a program gets overly complicated, it becomes hard to keep track of what's going on. This often becomes an especially vexing problem when you take a break from a project and then pick it up some time later. There are a number of structures or abstractions commonly used in coding to help order the process. The two major programming approaches I will cover are **procedural programming** and **object-oriented programming (OOP)**. I introduced and defined both briefly in Chapter 2. Procedural programming relies on reusable blocks of code that work like processing machines, which you call when you need them. These reusable blocks of code are referred to as **functions**. The second approach, OOP, is a far more ambitious and abstract approach that models a programming problem using concepts from the real world. For example, if you were writing an object-oriented program to generate a virtual garden, you would create code structures, called **classes**, to organize your program. The classes might each describe a garden concept from the real world: leaf, vine, flower, sunlight, water, and so forth.

Your first program

In most programming books, the first program written is called "Hello World" (see Figure 3-1). This spectacular program spits back the words "Hello World" to the screen— yawn! Needless to say, I find this program extremely boring and also think it sets the wrong tone for an entire book on creative coding. I for one need more encouragement and inspiration before attempting to learn something as scary and potentially boring as programming. Thus in breaking with tradition, which this book is all about, the first program you write will be entitled "Hello Earth." Here it is:

```
/*
Program Title: "Hello Earth"
Program Description: Blue circle on black background
By Ira Greenberg, August 5, 2005
Comments: Our first Processing program- yippee!
*/
size(200, 200);
background(0);
// keep stroke from showing up around circle
noStroke();
fill(80, 220, 255);
ellipse(100, 100, 100, 100);
print("Hello Earth!");
```

If you haven't done so yet, download Processing from http://processing.org/download/index.html. I recommend selecting the standard download option. The installer will create a Processing directory. Within this directory, you'll find the Processing application icon. Launch it, and type the "Hello Earth" sketch code into Processing's text editor (the big, white area in the middle of the application); then press the right-facing arrow in the circle, at the top of the application.

Figure 3-1. Your first Hello Earth program

Congratulations! OK, so maybe it wasn't a huge improvement to "Hello World," but you got to make a pretty, blue circle. Let's look at the program line by line.

/* and */ are block comment tags, used to comment out multiple lines of information so that it is ignored by the compiler. // can be used to comment out a single line. It is typical at the top of a program to put some info about what your program does, who created it, the creation date, and any other special notes. This is not required, but most people put something up there. In fact, some people put a lot of stuff up there, including specific code usage rights. How much you include up there doesn't really matter because it won't affect how your program functions. However, novellas, mission statements, and manifestos should probably be put other places. Here are some more examples of comments:

```
// this  is a valid comment

/* this is a valid comment */

/*
this is a valid comment
*/

// this
// is also
// a valid
// comment
```

After the comments, I skipped a line. This is called whitespace. Whitespace in Processing and Java is disregarded, as it is in many other programming languages. You can put as much whitespace as you like to help you visually organize your code. The next line in the program, size(200, 200); is a function call (I spoke about functions in Chapter 2—functions are reusable blocks of code that you call when you need them). You know this because of the parentheses after the word size. As stated in Chapter 2, a function call . . . well . . . calls a function—in this case, a function named size. The numbers within the parentheses are called arguments—things that are passed to the function, which the function expects to receive and makes use of. In this case, the numbers represent the width and height of the sketch window. When more than one argument is passed to a function, as in size(200, 200);, commas are used to separate the individual arguments. There is no limit to the number of arguments you can pass to a function, as long as the function has the same number of parameters to receive the arguments. In addition, they must be sent to the function in the same order that the function expects to receive them. In the case of the function calls in the Hello Earth example, the functions I called are built into the Processing language, and thus you can't see the actual function definitions. I'll be discussing functions in much greater detail later on in this chapter. For now, let's keep moving.

At the end of the size(200, 200); call, you should notice a semicolon. Semicolons in coding are like periods in normal human language. They let the compiler know where the end of the statement is. A **statement** is simply a command to the program to do something. In Processing, failure to include a semicolon results in a compiler error—an error message comes up on the bar in the message area of the Processing editor window that says Expecting SEMI . . .. Fortunately, the Processing/Java compiler is smart and keeps you from making too big a goof-up. If you happened to try this, just put the semicolon back, and the program should compile fine. You'll notice almost all the rest of the lines of the program have the same basic structure, each calling a function. As I mentioned previously, the line // keeps a stroke from showing up around the circle is a single-line comment.

The line noStroke(); is a function call that doesn't pass any arguments. noStroke() affects how things are painted to the screen. The function call disables a stroke or outline from being rendered on a shape. I'll be covering Processing's drawing and painting functions a lot in future chapters. The line print("Hello Earth!"); is a call to the print() function that expects an argument of type String. In this case, you passed in your "Hello Earth!" argument. You should have seen the words Hello Earth come up in the black text area at the bottom of the Processing editor window. String is a type of data in Processing (or most any program) for referencing groups of characters. print() is an important function that you'll use all the time in Processing to help you debug your code. Processing has an alternate version, println(), which does the same thing as print(), but adds a return after printing the string argument within the parentheses. For example, if you run the following code:

```
print("hello");
print("earth");
```

the output will be as follows:

helloearth

If you use the println() version, as follows:

```
println("hello");
println("earth");
```

the output will look like this:

hello
earth

The rest of the function calls in the program, Background(0), fill(80, 220, 255), and ellipse(100, 100, 100, 100), set the background color, set the shape fill color, and create the circle, respectively. I will be covering these and other Processing graphics functions in more depth beginning in Chapter 6.

Curly braces

Another important and widely used syntactical structural element is the curly brace: { }. Curly braces, which always work in balanced pairs (an open and closed pair), are used to structure blocks of code. Following are some code examples that show the use of curly braces.

Here's a conditional if...else example:

```
if (thisBook == bestSeller) {
  sleepWellAtNight();
} else {
  addMorePictures();
}
```

Here's a function example:

```
void sleepWellAtNight() {
  println("one sheep, two sheep...");
}
```

Here's a for loop example:

```
for (int i = 0; i < totalPictures; i++) {
  makeSomeInterestingPictures();
}
```

You'll be looking at a lot more examples that make use of curly braces shortly. You'll notice that I structured the blocks of code between the curly braces using indentations. Indenting is not necessary for the code to work, but it is the conventional way to write blocks of code. Indenting makes it easier for other coders to read your code. In the examples in this book, each indentation is created by hitting the spacebar twice.

Dot syntax

The last syntactical structure you'll see in Processing is the dot (.) It looks like a period (and it technically is a period), but it's referred to as a dot; it's the same dot in .com. The dot is an advanced syntactic structure used in OOP.

As I mentioned earlier, there are two approaches to structuring a program in Processing: procedural programming and OOP. Procedural programming uses functions to organize a program. You just saw an example of a function in sleepWellAtNight. When you need to use a function, you explicitly call it—for example, sleepWellAtNight()—pretty simple.

In OOP, you build much more complex structures called classes. To use a class, you create instances of it, known as **objects**. Classes contain properties and methods. You can think of the properties as the traits of the object and the methods as actions you perform on/with the traits. For example, if you create a class called Cat, some of the properties might be color, weight, and markings, and a method might be getBreed(). You use the dot syntax as a way to connect an object with its properties and/or methods. For example, if you create an object myCat from the Cat class, the object can call the getBreed() method using dot syntax, like this:

```
String breedName = myCat.getBreed();
```

Since the getBreed() method would return the name of a breed, you call the method as part of an assignment statement so that the returned named will get assigned to the variable breedName. I'll be covering OOP in much more detail in Chapter 8.

Naming conventions

Perhaps you noticed that a bunch of the fictitious names I used in the examples were combinations of multiple words—for example, sleepWellAtNight() and getBreed(). This is referred to as camelback notation. It is common to use it in case-sensitive environments. By capitalizing the initial character of the multiple words, you can read them more easily. Notice that the initial letter of the first word isn't capitalized. Camelback notation is not required, but highly recommended. However, there are some required naming rules.

Legal names can only contain letters, underscores, numbers, and the dollar sign. The initial character must be a letter, underscore, or dollar sign—not a number. I recommend only using a letter as your initial character. Following the initial letter, it's fine to use numbers. It's also strongly suggested that you use names that are descriptive. For example, which is easier to understand: getAge() or abdi()?

The names you define are called **identifiers**. Based on the preceding rules, here are some legal identifiers:

- String myBall
- float speed
- int ballCount
- float theBallSpeed
- boolean YouCanActuallyMakeYourVariableNamesAsLongAsYouLike
- String BALL_MANUFACTURER

Here are some illegal ones. Can you tell why?

- String Ball 1
- int 100bjs
- float -weight
- int myBall#

The reasons are as follows: Ball 1 is illegal because of the space in the identifier; 100bjs is illegal because you can't begin an identifier with a number; and -weight and myBall# are illegal because both use illegal characters: - and #, respectively.

Literals

As you will learn in the next section, a variable is something that can mean different things in different parts of the program. However, a **literal** is simply an explicit number or string constant (words or characters) used in programs. Here are some examples:

- "Sophie"
- 25
- 10346
- "abc"

Note that string literals are enclosed in quotes (usually double quotes) and numeric literals are not. In some cases, if you need a string within a string, you surround the inner string with single quotes. Here's an example:

```
"One of Shakespeare's most famous lines 'to be or not to be'
is in Hamlet"
```

Here's a sketch that outputs some literal values:

```
String announceDate = "I'm writing this on: ";
String currentMonth = "March ";
int currentDay = 5;
String currentDayName = "Sunday";
int currentYear = 2006;
String comma = ", ";

print(announceDate);
println(currentDayName);
print(currentMonth);
print(currentDay);
print(comma);
println(currentYear);
```

This sketch will output the following:

```
I'm writing this on: Sunday
March 5, 2006
```

Notice how I used the print() and println() statements to help me format the outputted lines combining the literals.

Variables

Variables are essential to programming, and it is hard to imagine coding anything without them. In Processing and Java, there are two types of variables: **primitive** variables and **object reference** variables. The major differences between these two categories of variables are the kind of data they can be associated with and how this data is stored and referenced in memory. I'm only going to cover primitive variables here; I'll discuss object reference variables when I cover OOP in Chapter 8.

A primitive variable is a simply a name assigned a specific value in memory that you can recall and change. Here are a couple of examples of primitive variables:

```
int age = 6;
String name = "Ian";
boolean isABoy = true;
```

The first part of each of the statements (int, String, and boolean) declares what type of primitive data the variable can hold: int holds integers, String holds words, and boolean holds true or false. The next part (age, name, and isABoy) is the identifier of the variable, and the last part is the actual value (6, "Ian", and true) assigned to the variable.

Variable names in Processing and Java are case sensitive, meaning that xSpeed is a different variable than xspeed. A variable's name is created by the coder and needs to be a legal identifier, which was described previously. Regardless of whether you are naming a primitive variable, object reference variable, function, method, class, or object, the same legal identifier–naming rules apply. There are also some reserved keywords that you should avoid using when naming things. The reserved keywords can be found here: http://java.sun.com/docs/books/tutorial/java/nutsandbolts/_keywords.html. In addition, I would also strongly recommend not naming your custom variables, functions, objects, and so forth with any of the built-in function names in Processing; it will lead to, at best, unexpected results.

When I initially create a variable by writing int ballCount, I am not yet specifying a specific value to be assigned to the variable, but only letting the computer know what type of data is allowed to be assigned to the variable (in this case, an integer). Every variable must be associated with a data type. Some common primitive data types in Processing are int, float, char, and boolean. Data types tell the variables what they can or can't do, and also how much memory should be allocated for them. For example, a boolean type variable can only hold the values true or false, requiring only 1 bit of memory to store either a single 0 (false) or a 1 (true). It would be a waste of memory to store it any other way. A byte can hold a number between −128 to 127 (that's 256 different possible values), which requires 8 bits, or 1 byte, of memory.

3

You might be curious as to why you can get 256 unique values from a single byte (8 bits) of memory. If you get scared by this explanation, don't worry. It's not essential to know! It's because in base 2 (as opposed to the base 10 system our minds are accustomed to), a byte is an 8-digit binary number, made up only of a combination of zeros and ones. The number of distinct values of a binary number can be calculated by taking 2—only two possible values for each digit, 0 or 1—and raising it to the power of the number of places or digits in the number. So 2 to the 8th power equals 256. ints can hold up to 4 bytes (or 2 to the 32nd power), and thus can hold numbers between −2,147,483,648 and 2,147,483,647. If you've been involved in digital design for some time, you've probably converted images from 24-bit color to 8-bit color, going from 2 to the 24th power, or 16,777,216 possible colors, to 2 to the 8th power, or 256 possible colors. The old web-safe palette of 216 colors was just a subset of the 8-bit palette that looked somewhat consistent on different platforms/browsers.

When you write the variable data type and identifier (name)—for example, int ballCount—you refer to this as **declaring the variable**. When you give a variable a specific value—for example, ballCount = 3—then you say you are **initializing the variable**. These two activities can be done together in one step (e.g., int ballCount = 3), or separately, depending upon your program needs. Because variables are by default mutable, once you initialize a variable you can still change its value whenever you need to (as long as you assign it a value consistent with its originally declared data type). For example, try running the following code:

```
int ballCount = 15;
println(ballCount);
ballCount = 10;
println(ballCount);
ballCount = 100;
println(ballCount);
```

When you run this sketch, you'll get the following output:

```
15
10
100
```

Strict typing

I remember first learning Java and being confused that I had to keep writing the data types as I declared my variables, not to mention the whole case-sensitivity issue. I was used to old-school ActionScript, where variables could hold anything at any time. However, I've come to understand and appreciate the benefits of what's referred to as "strict typing" of variables. Interestingly, ActionScript, which some of you may know, now uses explicit typing of variables as well—so much for the good old days. So int ballCount can only hold integer values and float ballSpeed can only hold float values. But why is this helpful?

It's because strict typing helps create more precise and ultimately faster-running code. If you try to assign a float value—for example, 3.2—to int ballCount, Processing will spit back a compiler error that says

> **The type of the right sub-expression, "float", is not assignable to the variable, of type "int".**

This may seem obnoxious and a royal pain, especially if you are used to a loosely typed language, but it really is a useful (or at least justifiable) language feature. Save for the strange worlds of quantum physics, we would expect distinct whole balls to be held in ballCount—not parts of balls. If the compiler let you assign 3.2 (maybe entered due to a typo) to ballCount, your program would probably crash later on. To debug your program, you would then have to track down a tiny but fatal type conversion error (definitely not a happy coding accident). Additionally, in languages that do permit on-the-fly data type assignment, it takes more work for the computer to figure out what type of data is held in a variable.

Because you set the data type of variables when they are declared in Processing and Java, and that information gets put in the compiled bytecode, the virtual machine (the language interpreter) needs to do less work. Languages like Processing and Java that work this way are called **statically typed languages**. Languages like Python, on the other hand, are **dynamically typed**, and, due in part to dynamic typing, run slower than Java and Processing. Now, at the risk of really getting you rankled, what do you think would happen if you tried to assign 3 (an integer) to ballSpeed (declared as type float)? Surprisingly, you wouldn't get a compiler error. Huh! That seems to go against what I just wrote about how static typing works. The reason the compiler allows it is because the compiler converts the 3 to 3.0 automatically. Let's test this out. If I try running the following code:

```
float ballSpeed;
ballSpeed = 3;
println(ballSpeed);
```

I get the following output:

3.0

The reason the compiler lets me get away with this is because there is no danger, nor any real change, to the value. 3, 3.0, and even 3.0000000000000 are all equal. Not to get too geeky, but this type of implicit conversion is called a "widening conversion," where an int is automatically converted into a float. The rule is that any primitive type will be converted implicitly (without any help from you) into any other type only if that type supports a larger value; a float supports a larger value than an int. In regard to Processing, that would include byte to int and int to float. Bytes can become integers and integers can become floats. Converting the other way, from a float to an int to a byte (a "narrowing conversion") can actually also happen, but you have to do it explicitly (which involves a little work on your part), with something called **type casting**, which I'll cover later in the book. For now, let's put this theory stuff to bed and play with variables a little.

Here's a little program to create a stepped radial gradient (see Figure 3-2). Later on when I cover loops, I'll simplify this program, and also show you how to generate a more elegant continuous gradient. You'll create the program in three stages. The first stage will fill the

3

display window background with black. The second stage will add a white ellipse, and the third stage will create the gradient. In stages 2 and 3, you just need to add the new code shown in bold. Also, try running the sketch at each stage to see the effect of adding the new code.

Stage 1 just generates a black 200-by-200-pixel display window:

```
/*
 title: fun with variables
 description: stepped radial gradient
 created: August 7, 2005
 by: Ira Greenberg
*/

// set the sketch window size and background
size(200,200);
background(0);
```

Stage 2 utilizes some variables and draws a white ellipse in the middle of the display window:

```
/*
 title: fun with variables
 description: stepped radial gradient
 created: August 7, 2005
 by: Ira Greenberg
*/

// declare some global variables
int xpos;
int ypos;
int gradientWidth, gradientHeight;

// set the sketch window size and background
size(200,200);
background(0);

// radial width/height
gradientWidth = gradientHeight = width;

//radial center pt
xpos = width/2;
ypos = height/2;

//turn off stroke rendering
noStroke();

//create ellipses
ellipse(xpos, ypos, gradientWidth,  gradientHeight);
```

Stage 3 adds the gradient:

```
/*
 title: fun with variables
 description: stepped radial gradient
 created: August 7, 2005
 by: Ira Greenberg
*/

// declare some global variables
int xpos;
int ypos;
int interval;
int gradientWidth, gradientHeight;

// set the sketch window size and background
size(200,200);
background(0);

// define variable values
// controls banding of gradient
interval = 255/5;

// radial width/height
gradientWidth = gradientHeight = width;

//radial center pt
xpos = width/2;
ypos = height/2;

//turn off stroke rendering
noStroke();

//create ellipses
//set fill color and render ellipse
fill(interval);
ellipse(xpos, ypos, gradientWidth,  gradientHeight);
fill(interval*2);
ellipse(xpos, ypos, gradientWidth-interval, gradientHeight-interval);
fill(interval*3);
ellipse(xpos, ypos, gradientWidth-interval*2,➡
  gradientHeight-interval*2);
fill(interval*4);
ellipse(xpos, ypos, gradientWidth-interval*3,➡
  gradientHeight-interval*3);
fill(interval*5);
ellipse(xpos, ypos, gradientWidth-interval*4,➡
  gradientHeight-interval*4);
```

3

69

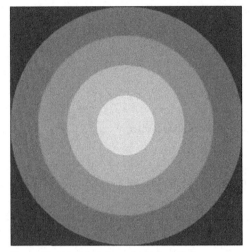

Figure 3-2. Completed stepped radial gradient

I begin the program with my standard "about the program" comments. Then I declare some global variables at the top of the program. **Global**, as opposed to **local**, means that the variables will be available from any place within the program. Later, when I cover functions, I'll discuss this concept, called **scope**, further. You'll notice I declared all the variables as type int. The line int gradientWidth, gradientHeight; declares both gradientWidth and gradientHeight variables as type int in one line. When declaring and initializing variables, you can put them on individual lines or bunch them together. For example, the following line is perfectly legal:

```
int var1 = 3, var2 = 5, var3 = 6, var4 = 0;
```

I declare four variables of type int, while also initializing them with initial values.

After declaring variables, I set the size properties and background color of the sketch window:

```
size(200,200);
background(0);
```

You might recognize these as function calls, in which dimensions (width and height) and color arguments are passed to the respective Processing functions. These functions are built into the Processing language, which is why you don't see the functions defined in the program anywhere. After you set the sketch window dimensions using the size(200, 200) command, you can then retrieve the sketch window size using Processing's built-in global properties: width and height. You'll notice these words turn a reddish color in the editor when you type them in, letting you know they are built-in properties in Processing.

Next, I assign values to some primitive variables:

```
// controls banding of gradient
interval = 255/5;
```

Because the gradient will go from black to white, I made the interval variable a factor of 255 (255 equals white). This way, I can step from black to white an equal number of steps—in this case, five. The next line may look a little strange:

```
// radial width and height
gradientWidth = gradientHeight = width;
```

If I write it out in English, its meaning will be clearer: the value of width is assigned to the variable gradientHeight, which is then assigned to the variable gradientWidth. When you use the single-equal sign (=), it means assignment, *not* equals. Assignment statements are evaluated right to left, which is why this compound assignment statement works. Also, remember that width is a built-in Processing property that holds the width I made the sketch window with the function call size(200, 200). gradientWidth and gradientHeight are variables I declared that will hold the width and height of the gradient. I could have written the statement in two lines, as well:

```
gradientHeight = width;
gradientWidth = gradientHeight;
```

Setting the center of the gradient, I defined the variables xpos and ypos with the expressions width/2 and height/2, respectively. If you've never coded before, it may look odd to use a mathematical expression as something to be assigned, but it's perfectly legal and common in programming. Remember, computers are really just super-powerful (and expensive) calculators.

```
xpos = width/2;
ypos = height/2;
```

The line noStroke(); turns off any stroke rendering, which is on by default in Processing when you render an ellipse or rectangle. noStroke() is another built-in Processing function. The rest of the program paints the gradient:

```
fill(interval);
ellipse(xpos, ypos, gradientWidth,  gradientHeight);
fill(interval*2);
ellipse(xpos, ypos, gradientWidth-interval, gradientHeight-interval);
fill(interval*3);
ellipse(xpos, ypos, gradientWidth-interval*2, ➡
  gradientHeight-interval*2);
fill(interval*4);
ellipse(xpos, ypos, gradientWidth-interval*3, ➡
  gradientHeight-interval*3);
fill(interval*5);
ellipse(xpos, ypos, gradientWidth-interval*4, ➡
  gradientHeight-interval*4);
```

The fill(interval) lines are calls to Processing's built-in fill() function. The calls pass an argument to the function that controls the fill color of the shapes. In this case, I'm working with grayscale values between 0 and 255. The ellipse(x, y, w, h) function call has four arguments for the x and y position and width and height of the ellipse. You'll also notice that the arguments I pass to the ellipse functions are both other variables and expressions that include variables. Try running the program, if you haven't already done so, and changing some of the values and/or expressions to see what happens. See also if you can increase the number of steps in the gradient, making it a little smoother. When we get to loops, I'll recode this for you, and you'll really see the power of code for doing repetitive tasks or iteration.

Operators

Some of you may remember the word *operator* from math class. Operators are the symbols you use when you write mathematical expressions. Technically speaking, operators perform a function on operands. In the expression x + 3, x and 3 are the operands and + is the operator. In terms of coding, you'll primarily use the same four operators you learned about in grade school: +, −, *, and /. Just using these operators, you're able to perform almost all the math you need to create amazing visuals. Processing and Java have additional operators besides these four, some of which I'll go over as well. Beginning to use operators is pretty simple. Coding can get complex, however, when you're figuring out the right combinations of operators needed in forming more complex expressions. You've already seen a bunch of operators in action in the last section on variables. For example, in the function call ellipse(xpos, ypos, gradientWidth-interval*4, gradientHeight-interval*4), the third and fourth arguments passed to the ellipse function, gradientWidth-interval*4 and gradientHeight-interval*4, each used two operators (− and *). Because operators return a value, you are able to use them as arguments, as shown previously.

Here are some assignment operations utilizing the four basic operators. I'll also go over some basic rules that control the order in which operators do their thing, which is referred to as **operator precedence**.

```
int x = 4+3-6;
float y = 14*3/5-2.34;
float z = 14*3/(5-2.34);
```

The order of calculation is as follows:

- Parentheses
- Multiplication and division
- Addition and subtraction

When operators have the same precedence level, the expression is evaluated from left to right.

In the first preceding example, addition and subtraction have the same precedence level, so the right side of the assignment statement is evaluated from left to right. (The assignment itself still occurs from right to left.)

The second example combines multiplication, division, and subtraction. Multiplication and division operations occur before subtraction. Since multiplication and division are at the same precedence level, this expression is evaluated left to right.

The last example uses the same operands and operators as the second example, but uses parentheses to group. Since parentheses have the highest precedence, the subtraction in the parentheses happens first, and then the multiplication/division occurs from left to right.

I've covered all the arithmetic operators but one: %, called the modulus operator. When I first learned about this operator, I found it confusing and a little scary looking and sounding. It's actually not such a big deal. The modulus operator doesn't mean percent, but rather returns the remainder of the division between two operands. The remainder is the part left over after the division.

For example, 7 % 2 would evaluate to 1, since 2 goes into 7 three times, leaving a remainder of 1. Here are some more examples:

- 17 % 9 evaluates to 8.
- 6 % 3 evaluates to 0.
- 23.4567 % 5 evaluates to 3.4567.

In addition to the five arithmetic operators you just looked at, there are quite a few others. However, you only need to concern yourself with the most common ones for now. These operators can be broken down into three categories: the equality and relational operators, the conditional (also sometimes referred to as logical) operators, and the assignment operators.

Relational operators

The **relational operators** are very important, and you will use them often. Most of these operators should look familiar to you from grade school (although probably not the last two):

- > (greater than)
- >= (greater than or equal to)
- < (less than)
- <= (less than or equal to)
- == (equal to)
- != (not equal to)

The greater than and less than arrows work the same way you remember them from school. They can also be used in conjunction with the = sign, which simply tests if one operand is greater/less than or equal to another operand. When you test with any of these operators, you're testing whether the condition is true. For example, if(4<=5) or if(3>6)—the first test is true, since 4 is less than 5, and the second test is obviously false.

With regard to the last two operators (== and !=), the double-equal sign (==) tests for equality, and the symbols != test for inequality; therefore, in the following (non-code) lines:

- if(3==3) would be true.
- if(3!=3) would be false.
- if(3!=5) would be true.

Conditional operators

The relational operators are often used in conjunction with two conditional operators for creating somewhat more complex conditions to evaluate. The two operators are

- && (logical and)
- || (logical or)

One minor warning: The operator terms *relational* and *conditional* (and also *logical*) are used inconsistently, especially around the Web. I'm classifying the operators as specified on Sun's site. See http://java.sun.com/docs/books/tutorial/java/nutsandbolts/opsummary.html for more info.

Following are some examples. To check if x is greater than 3 and less than 10:

```
if (x > 3 && x < 10) {
  //code in here would only
  //execute when condition is true
}
```

To check if x is less than 20 or greater than 50:

```
if (x <  20 || x > 50) {
  //code in here would only execute
  //when condition is true
}
```

To check if the boolean variable myLecturesAreBoring is not true:

```
if (!myLecturesAreBoring) {
  //code in here would only execute when
  //condition is true-which is always!!
}
```

By putting the exclamation symbol in front of myLecturesAreBoring, you are actually checking for the value to be false.

The relational and conditional operators are used to control the logical flow of your program. In addition to using the keyword if, you can combine it with the keyword else. These types of statements, which control the branching logic in your programs, are called conditional statements. I'll discuss them in more detail a bit later in this chapter.

Assignment operators

The only other operators you need to look at for now are used for **assignment operations**.

The simplest assignment operation just uses the = operator. For example, to assign the value 55 to the int variable speed, you'd simply write the following:

```
int speed = 55;
```

Again, the = sign is used for assignment, not equality. When you test for equality in Processing and Java, instead of writing if(speed=55), you need to write if(speed==55). The first way actually assigns the value 55 to speed; the second way tests if speed is actually equal to 55. Using the single-equal sign when testing for equality is a very common mistake new coders make. We've been conditioned to think of equality as =, not ==, so it makes sense that new coders find it confusing.

When I write an assignment statement, for example

```
x = 4;
```

I am assigning 4 to x. So now the value of x evaluates to 4. Let's say I want to add 3 to x—I could write x + 3, right? Let's try it.

Write the following two lines of code in Processing and click run.

```
int x = 4;
x + 3;
```

Surprised you got an assignment error? It's because you're adding 3 to x, but not assigning the solution anywhere. Remember that computers are really dumb. If they can't put the value anywhere, they don't know what to do. Fortunately, the Processing compiler sends out a compiler error letting you know this.

You can fix the preceding assignment in a couple of ways—but the easiest way to add 3 to x, and then assign the value back to x, is as follows:

```
x = x + 3;
```

Now this may look a little odd, having something assigned to itself. But reading the expression in English helps: add the value of x and 3 and then assign that value to x. Assignment operations happen from right to left. It may take a little time playing with this to get it clear in your brain. These operations work the same way for the other mathematical operators as well. Here's a division example:

```
float y = 10.4;
// divide by 1.25
y = y / 1.25;
```

These operations are so common in programming that there is a shortcut syntax more commonly used. The shortcut simply joins the mathematical and assignment operators. For example, the last expression (y = y / 1.25;) could be shortened to the following:

```
y /= 1.25;
```

The other mathematical operations follow the same structure. Here are some examples:

```
float temp = 98.6;
temp += 5;        // temp now equals: 103.6
temp -= .6;       // temp now equals: 103
temp *= 2;        // temp now equals: 206
temp %= 23;       // temp now equals: 22
```

The last expression may look odd; it's using the modulus operator. Remember, modulus returns the remainder of division; 23 goes into 206 eight times, leaving a remainder of 22, which then gets assigned back to the temp variable.

In the assignment operations you've been looking at thus far, the operator(s) have been surrounded by two operands. The geeky way to refer to these types of operators is as **binary operators**. Processing also uses some operators that only require one operand, which are referred to as **unary operators**. Two of these very useful operators are actually shortcuts for two other shortcuts.

If I want to add 1 to the int variable x using the shortcuts just shown, I could write the following:

```
x += 1;
```

Using a unary operator, the expression can be shortened to the following:

```
x++;
```

You'll also see this expression written as ++x;. It does matter, in some contexts, on which side you put the two operators, which I'll discuss the subtlety of later on. Besides incrementing by one, you can also decrement by one, using x-- (also --x). I recommend learning to use the shortcuts as soon as you can—they will save you keystrokes (possibly staving off carpal tunnel) and make you look like you've been coding for years.

Conditionals

Next, I want to cover conditional statements, which you got a sneak peak of when you looked at the relational and conditional operators. A conditional statement is sometimes referred to as a decision statement. Essentially, is says that if a certain condition is true, then do something; but if it is not true, do something else.

I think by now you're probably in need of some visual digression, so we'll cover the conditionals by creating a little sketch (see Figure 3-3), which creates a bouncing ball:

```
/*
 title: Bouncing Ball
 description: ball deflects off sketch window edges
 created: August 9, 2005
 by: Ira Greenberg
 */

// declare global variables
int xspeed, yspeed;
int xpos, ypos, wdth, ht;

//initialize sketch
void setup(){

  //set sketch window size and background color
  size(400, 400);
  background(0);

  //ball speed
  xspeed = 3;
  yspeed = 6;

  //ball size
  wdth = 10;
  ht = 10;

  // turn off shape stroke rendering
  noStroke();

 //initial ball placement
  xpos = width/2;
  ypos = height/2;

  frameRate(30);
}

// begin animation loop
void draw(){

  //update background
  background(0);

  //draw ball
  ellipse(xpos, ypos, wdth, ht);

  //upgrade position values
  xpos+=xspeed;
  ypos+=yspeed;
```

```
/*conditionals
  detects ball collission with sketch window edges
  also accounts for thickness of ball
 */
if (xpos>=width-wdth/2 || xpos<=wdth/2){
  xspeed*=-1;
}
if (ypos>=height-ht/2 || ypos<=ht/2){
  yspeed*=-1;
}
}
```

Figure 3-3. Screen capture of the Bouncing Ball program

When you run the Bouncing Ball program, you should see a little white ball moving in the sketch window and deflecting off the window edges. The code may look a little scary at first glance, but most of it has been covered (at least in theory). I suggest taking a little time and messing around with some of the values and seeing what happens. The worst thing you'll do is break the program. When you're done getting a little well-deserved play out of your system, you can read the brief discussion of the program that follows. Don't worry if this sketch seems over your head. I don't expect most readers to be able to fully grasp it yet. I'll be going over sketches like this many times in future chapters. My main goal here is just to give you something interesting to look at and play with.

As usual, I start the program with some comments and then declare global variables. The setup(){ ... } function is built into Processing and is used to initialize the program and define variables that may be needed later on; it runs just once. The draw() { ... } function is also built into Processing and is used for animation. When you have a single CPU in your computer, it can only really do one thing at a time. However, it can execute processes so fast that, to our slow brains, it seems like many things are happening simultaneously.

Animation is a perfect example of this effect. If at least 12 images per second move in front of your eyes, you begin to see continuous movement. But of course, you are really only looking at a series of static images.

The frameRate(30) function call at the bottom of the setup() function controls the rate at which the animation runs. You can pass different values to the frameRate() call as a single argument between the parentheses to change the speed of the animation. If you don't include the frameRate() call, the default speed is 60 frames per second. I suggest trying some different values in the call to see how it affects the speed and smoothness of your animation. The draw() function below setup() controls animation in Processing. Simply by including it, an animation loop is created in your sketch, which I'll cover in a lot more detail later.

In the draw() function, I update the background color, which helps create the illusion of the bouncing ball. Try commenting out the background(0) line by putting two forward slashes (//) in front of the command, and watch what happens. The effect is actually pretty cool, and what you would do if you wanted the background to be incrementally painted, rather than entirely updated each loop iteration.

Next I call the ellipse function, ellipse(xpos, ypos, wdth, ht);, passing in the four variables for the ball's x position, y position, width, and height. Then I increment the xpos and ypos variables using the assignment shortcut operators. This gets the ball moving. However, the ball will never stop, so I need to do some thinking for the computer and set up some conditions for when the ball should deflect or bounce off the frame.

The two conditional statements are essentially identical, except of course one controls the x movement and the other the y movement. So what I describe following for x also applies to y.

I begin the conditional with if. if is a reserved word in Java and Processing that expects a condition to follow it surrounded by parentheses. Conditional statements rely on Boolean logic (true or false) to decide how to respond. The default test is for truth. So when I write if(someStatement == true), I could also just write if (someStatement), which automatically checks for truth. If the conditional statement is true, program execution occurs on the next line following the test statement. For example:

```
if (5>4)
  print("hello");
```

The program should output hello. Although you can write your statement the way I did previously without curly braces, when there is only one line of code after the if statement, I don't recommend it. Instead, I recommend always writing it like this:

```
if (5>4) {
  print("hello");
}
```

The curly braces make it easier to read your conditional statements, and as you begin to write more complex statements, you'll need the curly braces anyway. If you do not use the curly braces, then only the next line of code will be executed if the condition is true.

Again, I always use the curly braces and will throughout the book. Getting back to the conditional statement in the bouncing ball sketch, I am actually checking for either of two conditions at the same time:

```
if (xpos>=width-wdth/2 || xpos<=wdth/2){
  xspeed*=-1;
}
```

This may look a little scary. Sorry, I had to choose between four separate conditional statements or two scary looking ones. In actuality, it's not too bad. The two vertical lines in the middle of the parentheses (||) are used to write "or" in Processing/Java. The way "and" is written is &&. So the test statement is checking to see if either statement is true. If either is true, then the ball is hitting the right edge or the left edge of the frame window, and the code between the curly braces executes.

What's important to remember in this sketch is that the event loop is continuously running; that means all the code within the draw() block is running around 30 times per second, so the test is running continuously as the ball moves. If the conditional test were up in the setup() function, it would only run once, and the window edge detection wouldn't occur. When the ball's position (really the xpos value) is greater than or equal to the width of the frame minus half the width of the ball (or xpos is less than or equal to half the width of the ball), the xspeed variable is turned positive or negative, depending on what its current state is. Remember from grade school math that when you multiply a positive and a negative number you get a negative, but two negatives multiplied equals a positive. Since xpos keeps adding the value of xspeed to itself, if the speed is positive, the ball moves to the right, and if it is negative, it moves to the left—creating the illusion of it being deflected off either of the frame wall edges. Everything I just described works the same way for the conditional statement to check the ball's y position.

I realize that this still may be confusing. I suggest playing with the code a little, setting some more extreme values to see what happens. I will be covering animation in a lot more detail later in the book, so this information will be revisited. For now, I want you to grasp how and why to use conditional statements.

Sometimes when you are checking for a condition, you want to offer one execution path if you find a condition to be true, and another one if you don't. For example:

```
if (hunger>=starving){
  eatAnything();
} else {
  eatWhatIsHealthy();
}
```

The if statement will execute the lines between the first pair of curly braces ({ eatAnthing(); }) if the condition between the parentheses (hunger>=starving) is true. If the condition is false, the code following the else statement will execute ({ eatWhatIsHealthy(); }). The conditional statement has two paths. You'll soon realize that there are a number of ways in coding to do the same thing. Some uptight computer scientists might tell you that there is a most efficient way to write code, but I don't totally buy that. Efficiency is a good thing, but you also need to find a style that suits your personality. For example, I could rewrite the preceding statements as follows:

```
if (hunger<starving){
  eatWhatIsHealthy();
} else {
  eatAnything();
}
```

The code works the same way—although it could maybe execute a little faster if most people are not starving. However, it is also more difficult to think about something not being equal vs. something being equal. Do what feels right to you, and don't obsess about efficiency or writing perfect code; it doesn't exist.

The last conditional example sent you down two possible pathways, depending on whether something was true or not. However, there are ways of checking among multiple possibilities by using a series of if...else if statements. For example:

```
if (hunger >= starving) {
  eatAnything();
} else if (hunger <= starving && belly < full) {
  eatWhatIsHealthy();
} else if (hunger <= starving && belly==full) {
  eatDessert();
} else {
  stopEating();
}
```

When the code is run, each conditional statement will be checked until a condition is true, at which time the code between the curly braces following the true conditional statement will execute. For example, if my hunger is less than starving and my belly is full, the code eatDessert() will execute. If none of the of the conditional tests are true, the code following else ({ stopEating(); }) will execute. The final else statement, which is not required, will always execute when none of the proceeding if...else if statements evaluate to true.

One word of caution: When you begin getting your coding legs and cranking out all kinds of conditional tests, pay close attention to the logic in your statements. If you make a logic error, your sketch may run without any compiler error, but you may not get the results you wanted. Logic errors are sometimes tricky to track down, because the compiler doesn't help you. Using println() statements and checking the values of your variables is normally the way to track down a logic bug.

switch statement

When you find yourself writing long if...else if statements, you may want to think about using a switch (sometimes also referred to as a case) statement. switch statements are just like if...else if statements, except that each conditional test usually has a built-in exit strategy. Here's an example switch statement:

```
switch (numberOfBurritosEaten){
  case 0:
    orderSuperBurrito(2);
    break;
  case 1:
    orderSuperBurrito(1);
    break;
  case 2:
    orderGrandeBurrito(1);
    break;
  case 3:
    orderRegularBurrito(1);
    break;
  case 4:
    orderTacos(2);
    break;
  case 5:
    orderTacos(1);
    break;
  case 6:
    orderDessert();
    break;
  default:
    seekHelp();
    break;
}
```

switch statements, unlike if...else if statements, can't check a range, but rather check for a specific value match. The condition inside the parentheses after the word switch needs to be of type int, char, or byte. The int type is for integers (e.g., –5, 0, or 2300), the char type is for individual characters on the keyboard (e.g., i, a, or /), and the byte type is a subset of integers—values between 127 and –128. I tend to use int values between the parentheses of my switch statements to keep things simple. In the newest version of Java (1.5), as of this writing, you can also use what's called an enumerated type within the parentheses of switch statements (not currently in Processing). However, enumerated types are an advanced concept that I'm not going to cover here.

When the switch statement runs, the value in the top parentheses is compared to each case, from top to bottom. If there is a match, the code after the colon is executed until it comes across a break. When it finds a break statement, the program exits the switch statement and goes to the next line below the entire switch block. The break command is optional, but if you don't use it, the program will fall through and execute the code of the next case, and continue checking all the remaining cases until it reaches the bottom of the statement. In most instances, this would be a waste of processing power. The default statement (also optional) at the end of the switch executes if no case matches were found. The last break statement is unnecessary and harmless, but possibly helpful if you happen to add more statements below and convert it to a case, so you don't eventually forget to add the break statement (a common error). I leave the choice to you.

Ternary operator

The last conditional structure I want to show you is Java's **ternary** operator—meaning that it uses three operands. The ternary operator takes some time getting used to, and some people never get used to it. I tend to hardly ever use it, but other people use it a lot, so it's worth learning. It's logic is similar to an if...else statement. Here's an example:

```
//some variables
int karma;
boolean isStillReadingThisBook;

// Here's the if/else version:
if (isStillReadingThisBook){
  karma = 100;
else {
  karma = 50;
}
// Here's the ternary operator version:
karma = isStillReadingThisBook ? 100 : 50;
```

The ternary version looks pretty terse and cryptic. Its form is really a throwback to an older style of programming. However, as you can see, it is efficient. The condition is tested, in this case the boolean variable isStillReadingThisBook; if the condition is true, then the first value after the ? is returned and assigned to the karma variable; if it is false, then the value after the : is returned. It's really up to you whether you want to use this structure. You can always use the more verbose if...else to accomplish the same thing.

Arrays and loops

The next section looks at arrays and loops. I've grouped these somewhat large topics together because of their interconnectedness. Arrays and loops aren't that complicated as concepts, but they can get a little hairy for newbie coders to implement. I'll be using them to expand on two previous sketches: the stepped radial gradient and the bouncing ball. These examples will illustrate the power of arrays and loops and also begin to show you the potential of code as a creative medium.

Arrays

There are times in coding when you'll want to assign many values to a single variable. For example, maybe you have 100 balls and you want to keep track of each of their x positions. The problem with using a primitive variable is that it can only hold one value at a time. Thus, you would need 100 separate variables to account for each ball's x position. Arrays were developed to solve this problem; they are single data structures that hold multiple values. If I wanted to animate all 100 balls, there are very easy ways to change the 100 x positions stored within the array. You can think of an array as a desk with multiple drawers. On the one hand, an array is a single entity, referred to by a single name; on the other hand, the array can hold many separate values, each accessible through an indexing system, which I'll discuss shortly. Arrays are a little difficult to get your head around at first, but they are absolutely critical to coding, and you'll be using them lots throughout the book. So if some of this explanation feels a bit abstract, don't worry—you'll be revisiting these concepts again and again.

Arrays don't have a default data type, but rather are declared with a data type just like variables are. Following is an example of an array declaration:

```
int[] xpos;
```

The declaration is done the way you'd declare a regular int variable, with the addition of the two brackets. Here are two more array declarations:

```
float[] xspeed;
String[] names;
```

You see the pattern—the type comes first, then the brackets and then the identifier or name of the array. You'll notice in the two declaration lines that I wrote "float" in all low-ercase, but "String" with an initial cap. This was not an arbitrary decision on my part; float is a primitive data type and needs to be all lowercase. String is the name of a class, and the convention is to name a class with an initial cap. I'll be covering classes later in the book, but for now you can think of a class as representing a unique data type—which you can use when you declare a variable, or in this case an array.

Arrays can be any size (actually as large as the int data type, which is big enough) and hold any legal type. However, once they are declared, their type cannot change, and once they are initialized, their size cannot change. Therefore, if I declare

```
float[] xspeed;
```

then the xspeed array can now only hold values of type float (real numbers). Here's how to initialize the xspeed array:

```
xspeed = new float[100];
```

The keyword new reserves space in memory for the array. You'll be using the keyword new a lot more when we get to OOP.

Now the xspeed array has 100 places in memory reserved for float values. Its size, like its data type, is now immutable, meaning that it can't be changed. The array now has space in the computer's memory reserved for it, although it still doesn't have any specific values assigned to those 100 places. The two lines can be put together into one declaration and initialization statement:

```
float[] xspeed = new float[100];
```

Here are a few more examples of declaring and initializing arrays:

```
int[] items = new int[50];
String[] itemNames = new String[10000];
Object[] obs = new Object[0];
```

The items array has 50 places reserved in memory for ints. The itemNames array has 10,000 places reserved in memory for Strings, and the obs array has 0 spaces in memory for Objects. In general, you wouldn't initialize an array with 0 items, but you could. Finally, there is one additional way to initialize an array, when you know ahead of time what will be in it:

```
int[] speeds = {2, 4, 445, -120, 3, 90, 54};
```

This array will have a length of 7, and, like all arrays, its size can't be changed. Here's another example with a String array:

```
String[] names = {"Lulu", "Ivan", "Myrna", "Pookie"};
```

So, once you declare and initialize arrays, how do you use them? An index system is used to access the values (called elements) stored at the different positions in the array. It's a very simple system with one caveat: arrays are zero-indexed, which means the first position in the array is at position 0, not 1. There are some benefits to this, which you'll see shortly when we get to for loops, but in the beginning it can be confusing.

Going back to the previous array, int[]speeds = {2, 4, 445, -120, 3, 90, 54}, to access the first item—the value 2—I use speeds[0]; to access the third item, 445, I use speeds[2]; and for the last item, 54, I use speeds[6]. Make sure you understand this before you move on; it's important. Arrays also have a built-in length property that you'll use often. You access the property with dot syntax. To find the length of the speeds array, you write speeds.length.

The length of the array is the actual number of items in the array, so speeds.length is equal to 7, even though speeds[6] gives you the last item in the array. You should see how working with arrays is both simple and a little complicated.

Finally, if you try to access an index that is out of range—for example, if you try to access speeds[7], which doesn't exist—you'll get a compiler error. This may seem like a pain, but again it's there to help you.

Loops

One of the best uses for computers is handling repetitive, redundant tasks that are too tedious for most people. This is accomplished in programming by using structures called loops. **Loops** are structures that continue to run, or execute, until some condition is met that causes them to stop. The two types of loops listed in the Processing language reference are while loops and for loops. In addition, we'll look at one other variation on the while loop called a do...while loop.

while

Here's an example of a while loop, (which I don't recommend you run):

```
while (true) {
  println ("help I'm in an infinite loop");
}
```

85

while is a reserved keyword in Processing, like the keywords if and else, which you've already looked at. A while loop will execute the code between its open and closed curly braces as long as the condition between the parentheses is true. In the example, the condition will always be true. true is actually another reserved keyword in Processing and Java that always means, well . . . true. Can you see why I didn't want you to run this loop example? It will never stop running, as there is no exit condition (i.e., a condition that when reached will cause the code to continue past the loop). Nasty loops like this are called **infinite loops**, and they are to be avoided. Of course, you can force the Processing application to quit, so don't panic if you did try running it (against my sage advice). Here's an improved and safe version of that last demonic loop:

```
int x = 0;
while (x<100) {
  println (x);
  x += 1;
}
```

If you run this, you should see the numbers 0 through 99 printed in the text output area at the bottom of the Processing application. The while loop runs as long as x is less than 100. With each cycle of the loop, the value of x is incremented by 1. Here's one more example:

```
int x = 1000;
while (x>=0) {
  println (x);
  x -= 100;
}
```

This loop outputs the values 1000 through 0, decrementing by 100 each cycle, or iteration, of the loop. Also, I set the condition using >=, so 0 was output as well.

do . . . while

A while loop will only execute if the condition is true. However, there are times when you'll want a loop to execute at least once no matter what. The do . . . while loop is sort of a backward while loop that always executes at least once, regardless of whether the condition is true. After the first iteration of the loop, though, it behaves just like a regular while loop. Here are two examples:

```
//example 1.
int x = 50;
do {
  println(x);
  x += 1;
}
while(x<50);

//example 2.
int x = 40;
do {
```

```
    println(x);
    x += 1;
}
while(x<50);
```

In the first example, the condition is false. Yet if you run this code, you'll get a single output of 50, because the loop will always execute at least once. In the second example, the condition begins true, and you get an output from 40 to 49, just as you'd expect using a standard while loop.

for

The for loop is my favorite loop (if that doesn't sound too pathetic). It does basically the same thing as a while loop, but I find the process of using it more elegant, especially in regard to dealing with arrays, which is where this whole discussion is going. Here's a for loop example:

```
for (int i=0; i<50; i++){
    println(i);
}
```

The for loop looks a little odd at first. There are three individual areas within the parentheses, in the head of the for loop:

- int i=0; (initialization)
- i<50; (condition)
- i++ (counter)

In the example, I created the variable i of type int and initialized it to 0. The next part of the loop checks to see if i is less than 50, and the third section increments i by one. The semicolons terminate each of these distinct sections in the for loop head, just like a normal end of line. Notice, however, that there is no semicolon after the counter. If you haven't yet, try running the example.

You should see output from 0 to 49. Even though the loop incrementation is at the head of the for loop, the variable i is not incremented until after the code in the block is executed. That's why the first value is 0, not 1.

One of the real benefits of the for loop is that the variable (i), which is declared in the initialization part of the loop, is sort of a secret variable that can only be seen between the curly braces of the for loop. This secret status is referred to as **local scope**. Local scope means that the variable is only known within the structure it is defined within. Local scope allows you to use another variable named i somewhere else in the same program or even in another separate for loop, without having the two names conflict or create ambiguity in the program. It is very common practice, and a coding convention, to use the letters *i, j*, and *k* as the names of local variables used as counters in loops. Normally, when I write a program that includes a number of simple for loops, I'll name each of the counter variables i. Besides local scope, you can also declare variables with **global scope**. When you declare variables outside of any structures (normally at the top of your program), these variables have global scope, meaning that they can be seen from anywhere within your program, including within loops. In the earlier while loop example, the variable x has global scope and can be seen anywhere in the program:

```
int x = 1000;
while (x>=0) {
  println (x);
  x -= 100;
}
```

Thus, you would not want to use x again as a counter in another loop later in the same program, as it could cause unpredictable results. Because the for loop solves this problem by keeping the counter variable local in scope, I tend to use for loops far more often than while loops.

In the next section, "Functions," I'll go more into detail on local vs. global scope. Here are a couple of other examples of for loops:

```
for (int i=1000; i>50; i-=2)
  println(i);
}

for (int i=1000, j=200; i>50; i-=2, j++)
  print("i = ");
  println(i);
  print("j = ");
  println(j);
}
```

The top example is just a variation on the for loop discussed previously. It just counts down by two instead of counting up by one. The second loop example uses multiple variables and incrementors in the head—which is legal. You just separate the different variables with commas. Try running this last loop example to view the output; it will help you understand how the for loop runs.

for loops can add tons of efficiency to your code, and used cleverly can really cut down on the number of code lines. As an example, I've recoded the stepped radial gradient (see Figure 3-4) using a for loop, converting it into a smoother continuous gradient.

```
//Continuous radial gradient
size(200,200);
background(0);

for (int i=255; i>0; i--){
  noStroke();
  fill(255-i);
  ellipse(width/2, height/2, i, i);
}
```

Figure 3-4. Continuous radial gradient

If you don't remember, the original stepped gradient example was about four times as long and not nearly as pretty.

Finally, in the latest version of Java (1.5), as of this writing, there is a new variation on the for loop, called a for-each loop, or enhanced for loop. I am not going to cover it, as it is not currently supported in Processing. Information about it can be found on Sun's site at http://java.sun.com/j2se/1.5.0/docs/guide/language/foreach.html.

Processing efficiency

You already saw that arrays hold multiple values and loops allow you to repeatedly execute code. You can use these two structures together to form a powerful and highly efficient data processing system. As an example, here's a simple mail merge program that outputs mailing addresses in the text area of the Processing application. The data is stored in six separate arrays, for first names, last names, street, city, state, and country.

```
// mail merge program
//create some arrays with address data
String[]firstName = {"Ira ", "Sophie ", "Ian ", "Robin "};
String[]lastName = {"Jed", "Rose", "Isaac", "McLennan"};
String[]street = {"4 Happy Ln, ", "19 Hunan Pl, ", ➥
  "104 Hevi Hevi St, ", "1000 Donkey Dr, "};
String[]city = {"Oxford", "Changsha", "Easton", "Edinboro"};
String[]state = {"Ohio, ", "Hunan, ", "Pennsylvania, ", "Scotland, "};
String[]country = {"USA", "China", "USA", "UK"};

// use a for loop to generate merge
for (int i=0; i<firstName.length; i++){
  print(firstName[i]);
  println(lastName[i]);
```

```
      print(street[i]);
      println(city[i]);
      print(state[i]);
      println(country[i]);
      println();
}
```

The sketch outputs the following:

```
Ira Jed
4 Happy Ln, Oxford
Ohio, USA

Sophie Rose
19 Hunan Pl, Changsha
Hunan, China

Ian Isaac
104 Hevi Hevi St, Easton
Pennsylvania, USA

Robin McLennan
1000 Donkey Dr, Edinboro
Scotland, UK
```

The for loop does all the heavy lifting by moving through the arrays, using the counter as the index to the position in the arrays. Also notice in this example that I alternated between print() and println() to format the address and line spacing correctly. Using a for loop to process four elements in each array may not seem too impressive. But imagine if each of the arrays included 10,000 elements. This simple sketch would have just as easily processed and output all that address data as well (of course, it would have taken a few more seconds). To better illustrate this, let's look at a more visually interesting example. I'm going to take the previous bouncing ball animation and beef it up some, using arrays and a loop or two. I'll also be incorporating one of Processing's handiest functions: random(value), which generates a random value between 0 and the value argument.

This example is a little long—try not to panic. You'll be looking at a lot of code like this throughout the book. I recommend running the sketch before reading through the code. You may even want to mess around with some of the values to see how it changes the output.

Here's the Many Bouncing Balls program (see Figure 3-5):

```
/*
title: Many Bouncing Balls
description: balls deflect off sketch window edges
created: August 9, 2005
by: Ira Greenberg
*/
// global variables
```

```
int ballCount = 500;
int ballSize = 8;
int ballSpeed = 3;
float[]xspeed = new float[ballCount];
float[]yspeed= new float[ballCount];
float[]xpos = new float[ballCount];
float[]ypos = new float[ballCount];
float[]wdth = new float[ballCount];
float[]ht = new float[ballCount];

//initialize sketch
void setup(){
  //set sketch window size and background color
  size(400, 400);
  background(0);

  //initialize values for all balls
  for (int i=0; i<ballCount; i++)

    // set varied ball speed
    xspeed[i] = random(1, ballSpeed);
    yspeed[i] = random(-ballSpeed, ballSpeed);

    // ball varied ball sizes
    wdth[i]= random(1, ballSize);
    ht[i]= wdth[i];

    // set initial ball placement
    xpos[i] = width/2+random(-width/3,  width/3);
    ypos[i] = height/2+random(-height/3,  height/3);
  }

  // turn off shape stroke rendering
  noStroke();
  //set the animation loop speed
  frameRate(30);
}

// begin animation loop
void draw(){

  /*updates background
   comment out to use alternate
   fill option below*/
  background(0);

  for (int i=0; i<ballCount; i++){
```

```
/*To use this fill option:
 1. uncomment fill call below
 2. comment out the background
 function call above*/
// fill(i*255/ballCount);

//draw balls
ellipse(xpos[i], ypos[i], wdth[i], ht[i]);

//upgrade position values
xpos[i]+=xspeed[i];
ypos[i]+=yspeed[i];

/*conditionals:
 detects ball collision with sketch window edges
 accounting for ball thickness.
 */
if (xpos[i]+wdth[i]/2>=width || xpos[i]<=wdth[i]/2){
  xspeed[i]*=-1;
}
if (ypos[i]+ht[i]/2>=height || ypos[i]<=ht[i]/2){
  yspeed[i]*=-1;
  }
 }
}
```

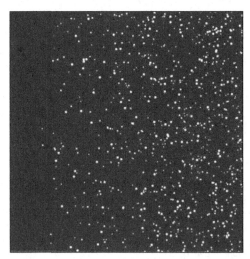

Figure 3-5. Screen capture of the Many Bouncing Balls program

Hopefully, you were able to successfully run this sketch. I created an alternative rendering option as well, which you can mess with in a bit. When you run the sketch, you should see many (actually 500) white balls moving randomly around, bouncing off the edges of the window. This code is not simple, so don't feel bad if it is a struggle to understand it. You're going to be doing a lot more of this type of coding beginning in Chapter 6—so this is really more like a teaser than something you need to fully grasp at this point. I just thought it was good to show you something a little more interesting after all the hard work you've been putting in. The main concept I want to reinforce at this point is the power of arrays and loops. Let's look at the program in sections:

```
// global variables
int ballCount = 500;
int ballSize = 8;
int ballSpeed = 3;
float[]xspeed = new float[ballCount];
float[]yspeed= new float[ballCount];
float[]xpos = new float[ballCount];
float[]ypos = new float[ballCount];
float[]wdth = new float[ballCount];
float[]ht = new float[ballCount];
```

After my comments, I declare and initialize some global variables; these variables will be accessible throughout the entire program. I chose the specific data type, in this case int or float, based on the type of value that would need to be stored in the respective variables/arrays. Obviously, ballCount could be an integer value, but a speed value would need to be a float value. The arrays are initialized with enough memory to hold the total number of balls. Remember, I can't change the arrays' sizes once they're initialized (in truth, you'll see later that there are indeed functions to do such a thing), so it's important to make them big enough at the beginning. Although the arrays are initialized to each hold 500 values (based on ballCount), there is still nothing in them.

```
//initialize sketch
void setup(){
  //set sketch window size and background color
  size(400, 400);
  background(0);

  //initialize values for all balls
  for (int i=0; i<ballCount; i++)

    // set varied ball speed
    xspeed[i] = random(1, ballSpeed);
    yspeed[i] = random(-ballSpeed, ballSpeed);

    // ball varied ball sizes
    wdth[i]= random(1, ballSize);
    ht[i]= wdth[i];
```

```
            // set initial ball placement
            xpos[i] = width/2+random(-width/3,  width/3);
            ypos[i] = height/2+random(-height/3,  height/3);
        }


        // turn off shape stroke rendering
        noStroke();
        //set the animation loop speed
        frameRate(30);
    }
```

After declaring the global variables, I do some program initialization in the setup() function. I set the window size and background color, and then I use a somewhat hairy-looking
for loop. In reality, it's not that different from the single-ball setup() function, but arrays
can look intimidating until you get used to them. The for loop

```
        for (int i=0; i<ballCount; i++)
```

uses the counter i, which is conveniently used as the first index slot in the arrays. I use the
global ballCount variable as the loop limit (in this case 500), and I increment the loop by
one each cycle. Thus, each iteration of the for loop will allow me to assign a value to each
position in the arrays; it's a very efficient system that works similarly to the mail merge
example.

In the speed arrays, I'm getting a little fancy and adding some random numbers. As I mentioned previously, I used Processing's random() function, which can take either one or two
arguments. In the book's appendix, I go through the Processing API and cover this function
in more detail. Basically, one argument generates a random number from 0 to the argument value. Two arguments give you a random value between the range of the two arguments. Processing's random() function returns a float value (a real number).

I initialized the arrays for the balls' sizes and original positions in a similar fashion to the
speed arrays, utilizing some more random values. Last, I turned off the pesky stroke rendering (noStroke();) and set the frame rate to 30 for smooth animation. Whew . . . almost
done.

```
        // begin animation loop
        void draw(){

          /*updates background
           comment out to use alternate
           fill option below*/
          background(0);

          for (int i=0; i<ballCount; i++){

            /*To use this fill option:
            1. uncomment fill call below
            2. comment out the background
```

```
    function call above*/
    // fill(i*255/ballCount);

    //draw balls
    ellipse(xpos[i], ypos[i], wdth[i], ht[i]);

    //upgrade position values
    xpos[i]+=xspeed[i];
    ypos[i]+=yspeed[i];

    /*conditionals:
    detects ball collision with sketch window edges
    accounting for ball thickness.
    */
    if (xpos[i]+wdth[i]/2>=width || xpos[i]<=wdth[i]/2){
      xspeed[i]*=-1;
    }
    if (ypos[i]+ht[i]/2>=height || ypos[i]<=ht[i]/2){
      yspeed[i]*=-1;
    }
  }
}
```

The draw() function is where all the magic happens. Once the draw() function is added to the sketch, an event loop begins refreshing the screen approximately the number of times per second specified with the frameRate(30) argument. The first thing I did was refresh the background so that the balls don't leave a trail through the window. I set an alternative rendering approach that utilizes this effect. If you read through the draw structure, I've put instructions on how to get the trails to occur. But don't do it yet—let's finish the analysis first.

Next is the second for loop. This loop draws the ellipses, increments their respective x and y position values by the speed values, and performs collision detection—which in this case means that it checks if the ball's x and y positions go beyond the window boundaries; if they do, that specific speed value's sign within the array is reversed (positive to negative or negative to positive). If xspeed is positive, then the ball moves to the right; if it's negative, then it moves to the left. If yspeed is positive, then the ball moves down; if it's negative, then it moves up.

Since all the data is housed in parallel arrays with the same number of indices, I am able to incrementally deal will all this stuff on each iteration of the for loop; this is the real power of using arrays in conjunction with loops. Now I recommend you go back and try the alternative rendering style (see Figure 3-6) and also mess with some of the values in the program. If you get something really cool, please e-mail me a screenshot. Finally, let me stress that this stuff is complicated—especially to new coders. I don't necessarily expect you to get all this yet. But hopefully some of it is beginning to stick. Many of the examples and tutorials throughout the rest of the book deal with similar patterns of coding, so I have no doubt that if you stay the course, this stuff will gel.

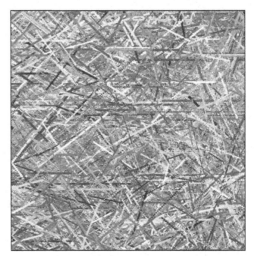

Figure 3-6. Screen capture of an alternative rendering of the Many Bouncing Balls program

Functions

I mentioned functions briefly in Chapter 2, so let's look at them again in a little more detail. Functions add structure and flexibility to your sketches, but also a little complexity. Try not to worry if some of the material seems too abstract—you'll be using functions throughout the rest of the book. My main goal here is to give you an overview of basic programming structures and a glimpse into the potential of creative coding.

In the simplest sense, functions just organize code into reusable blocks. They also have the ability to receive arguments and return a value. Here are some examples.

This first sketch draws a rectangle based on the x, y, width, and height properties passed to the drawRectangle( ) function:

```
void setup(){
  size(400, 400);
  background(255);
  drawRectangle(150, 150, 100, 100);
}
void drawRectangle(float x, float y, float w, float h){
  rect(x, y, w, h);
}
```

If you run this, you should see a 100-by-100-pixel square in the middle of the display window.

When you write your own function, you need to include Processing's setup() function, or you'll get a compile error when you try to run the sketch. A function begins with a return type (either void or a legal data type); an identifier (the name of the function); open and closed parentheses, with any optional declared parameters; and open and closed curly braces.

Here's the structure of a function:

```
return type (void or legal datatype) function name(optional ⇥
  parameters){
  code to execute when function is called;
}
```

The drawRectangle(float x, float y, float w, float h) function in the preceding sketch expects four arguments to be passed to it when it's called, as I specified four parameters between its parentheses. You'll notice that I use both the terms *parameter* and *argument*. This can be confusing to new coders (and even some experienced coders); I prefer to call the values between the parentheses in the function definition *parameters*, and the values passed to the function *arguments*. I know this may sound like an issue of semantics (or worse), but I find it easier to discuss and teach this stuff by using the two different terms.

This last example didn't do much more than Processing's plain old rect() call. The next example (see Figure 3-7) makes better use of the drawRectangle() function and also revisits for loops—yippee!

```
void setup(){
  size(400, 400);
  background(255);
  for (int i=0; i<100; i++)
    drawRectangle(random(width), random(height), random(200), ⇥
      random(200));
  }
}

void drawRectangle(float x, float y, float w, float h){
  rect(x, y, w, h);
}
```

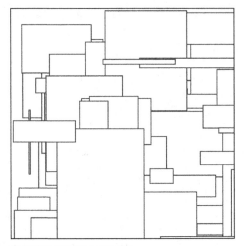

Figure 3-7. Random rectangles

This example begins to reveal the power of functions. By passing, or inputting, different values to the function, you can generate very different results. Functions create efficiencies by helping you avoid writing redundant code. They also free you from having to write all your code linearly, from top bottom, in your sketch. Once you define a function, you can call it when you need it, as well as multiple times, as I did in the last example. The next sketch uses Processing's built-in draw() function to move a box across the screen. Processing's draw() function is called automatically when you include it in your sketch. The draw() function increments the value of two speed variables I created (xspeed and yspeed), which are assigned to two position variables I created (xpos and ypos). xpos and ypos control the x and y positions of the box.

```
// simple ball
int xpos, ypos;
int xspeed=3;
int yspeed=5;

void setup(){
  size(400, 400);
}

void draw(){
  background(0);
  rect(xpos, ypos, 10, 10);
  xpos+=xspeed;
  ypos+=yspeed;
  if (xpos>=width-10 || xpos<=0){
    xspeed*=-1;
  }
  if (ypos>=width-10 || ypos<=0){
```

```
      yspeed*=-1;
    }
  }
}
```

Within the draw() function of this last sketch, I include very simple collision detection, used to reverse the direction of the box if it collides with any of the edges of the display window. Imagine if there were a lot more detection code—it could get pretty confusing looking. A better way to organize this would be to write a separate block of code (a function) to check the collisions. Not only will this code be cleaner looking, but the detection will be in a sense encapsulated (a word I'll discuss more when I get to OOP). Modularizing the code like this in a function gives the ability to potentially plug the function into other programs. Also, once I develop a template for this collision detection, I can develop variations on it, building a cool detection library—but I'm getting a bit carried way. Here's the sketch with the collision detection function added:

```
int xpos, ypos;
int xspeed=3;
int yspeed=5;
void setup(){
  size(400, 400);
}
void draw(){
  background(0);
  rect(xpos, ypos, 10, 10);
  xpos+=xspeed;
  ypos+=yspeed;
  checkCollisions(xpos, ypos);
}

void checkCollisions(int xp, int yp){
  if (xp>=width-10 || xp<=0){
    xspeed*=-1;
  }
  if (yp>=width-10 || yp<=0){
    yspeed*=-1;
  }
}
```

This new, improved code should execute exactly the same as the first version. Let's go through the function line by line.

checkCollisions(xpos, ypos); probably looks familiar to you by now. It's a function call—similar in form to size(400, 400). I pass two arguments (xpos and ypos) to the function. Also, since the function is not being assigned to some other variable, nor being used in the place of a variable, you can assume a value is not being returned by the function. If the function does not return any value, you use the reserved keyword void when you declare it; void takes the place of a data type that would need to be declared if the function did return a value. The function itself is almost exactly the same as the code that was inside the draw structure in the original version:

```
void checkCollisions(int xp, int yp){
  if (xp>=width-10 || xp<=0){
    xspeed*=-1;
  }
  if (yp>=width-10 || yp<=0){
    yspeed*=-1;
  }
}
```

You'll remember that a function head needs to have a data type or void; a legal identifier (name); and balanced (open/closed) parentheses, with any required parameters, including their data types, between the parentheses. The parameters, declared between the parentheses, in a sense catch the arguments passed to the function, and they need to match up. If the argument count or the data type doesn't match what's in the function head, the compiler will let you know. You can also use multiple versions or variations on the same named function in your program, as long as the parameter lists are different—meaning a different number of parameters or different data types. For example, the following three functions could all be included in the same program without any ambiguity:

```
void myFunction(int x, int y){
}
void myFunction(int x, int y,  int z){
}
void myFunction(float x, float y,  float z){
}
```

Since the first function uses only two parameters and the second and third functions use different data types for the parameters (int and float, respectively), the compiler will see these as unique functions. To call the functions, I could the use the following lines:

```
myFunction(2, 5);
myFunction(2, 5, 7);
myFunction(2.0, 4.2, 1.23);
```

If this looks strange to some of you who have experience with another language, this works in Processing because of an object-oriented feature built into Java called method overloading, which I'll discuss when I get to OOP in Chapter 8. Next, let's look at another function that returns a value to our current sketch. Here's the new sketch code:

```
int xpos, ypos;
int xspeed=3;
int yspeed=5;
void setup(){
  size(400, 400);
}
void draw(){
  background(0);
  rect(getXMotion(), ypos, 10, 10);
  ypos+=yspeed;
  checkCollisions(xpos, ypos);
}
```

100

```
void checkCollisions(int xp, int yp){
  if (xp>=width-10 || xp<=0){
    xspeed*=-1;
  }
  if (yp>=width-10 || yp<=0){
    yspeed*=-1;
  }
}

int getXMotion(){
  xpos+=xspeed;
  return xpos;
 }

void checkCollisions(float yp, float yp2){
  if (yp<=0){
    xspeed*=-1;
  }
  if (yp<=0){
    yspeed*=-1;
  }
}
```

I changed the first argument in the rect() function call, rect(getXMotion(), ypos, 10, 10), from a variable to another function call—which is legal, as long as the function returns a value. If you try to pass a function call as an argument that doesn't return a value, the compiler will give an error. The new function is declared with a return type of int, instead of void, and the last line is a return statement.

```
int getXMotion(){
  xpos+=xspeed;
  return xpos;
}
```

You must have a return statement as the last line in any function with a return type other than void. If you don't, you guessed it, the compiler will spit at you. There are times when you will use additional return statements in a function—for instance, when you have if...else statements—but you still must have a return statement as your last line.

I want to make one more improvement to the sketch. The getXMotion() function handles the x position only, but what about the y position? Well, I'm sure you can see that I could just easily copy the getXMotion() function and convert it to a getYMotion() function. However, that seems like too much work, and the behavior of the two functions is identical. When you find yourself repeating things or making fine adjustments to similar structures, you should be thinking that there's got to be a better way. In this case, there is. I can return an array of ints instead of a single int and convert the getXMotion() function to a getXYMotion() function. Here's the new function:

```
int[] getXYMotion(){
  xpos+=xspeed;
  ypos+=yspeed;
  int[]xypos = new int[]{xpos, ypos};
  return xypos;
}
```

The function return type is now an int[] array, not a primitive int. The function creates an xypos array each time it's called, and then returns the array. The other important aspect to this approach is knowing how to receive the array that's passed back. When I was originally just returning an int back, it was simple, because it was the only value returned. But to really benefit from this approach, the rect() call needs to be changed from:

```
rect(getXMotion(), ypos, 10, 10);
```

to

```
rect(getXYMotion()[0], getXYMotion()[1], 10, 10);
```

Does this make sense? I know it looks pretty strange. Remember, arrays are indexed, beginning at [0]. When the array is passed back, it's being received as a multivalue structure, with xpos at the 0 index and ypos at the 1 index. These values are retrieved using getXYMotion()[0] and getXYMotion()[1], respectively. If this is still not making sense, imagine replacing getXYMotion() with the array. To get the value in the first position of the array, you'd use arrayname[0]. To get the value in the second position, you'd use arrayname[1]. I hope that helps. You'll be doing stuff like this in future chapters, so try not to freak out if this stuff is hurting your head—it's supposed to in the beginning.

The last thing I want to say about functions relates to a nasty habit many coders get into. Now don't get any wrong ideas here. I'm talking about the use of magic numbers—what were you thinking of? Magic numbers are values we hard-code into a program that make the program difficult to change or customize. Using magic numbers is generally not the way to develop a modular system, but it can be a fast way of hacking out a solution without thinking of the big picture. In general, you'll want to avoid them. Following are two simple examples—the first using magic numbers:

```
//sketch using magic numbers:
size(200, 200);
background(255);
strokeWeight(5);
stroke(20);
fill(100);
rect (50, 50, 100, 100);
```

The second example improves upon this sketch, using a parameterized function instead of the hard-coded values:

```
// sketch using a nice parameterized function
void setup(){
  size(200, 200);
  background(255);
```

```
    createRect(50, 50, 100, 100, 20, 5, 100);
}

// parameterized function
void createRect(int xpos, int ypos, int wdth,
    int ht, int strokeCol,
    int strokeWt, int fillCol) {
    stroke(strokeCol);
    strokeWeight(strokeWt);
    fill(fillCol);
    rect (xpos, ypos, wdth, ht);
}
```

Both sketches should output the same centered rectangle, as shown in Figure 3-8.

Figure 3-8. Rectangle generated initially using magic numbers and then with a function

Do you see how the second approach will allow you to create any rectangle, while the first only creates one? The more modular and general you can make your code, the greater the chance you can reuse it or easily expand it. However, this type of approach takes more planning and analysis, and sometimes you just want to get coding. Because this book is about creative coding, I think it is perfectly acceptable to sometimes hack out poorly structured, "ugly" code, especially if it allows you to express yourself and find new solutions more effectively. I suspect if you're like me, you'll eventually discover things that you want to build out into larger projects, and that's where the rules and best practices stuff becomes important. So basically you have permission from me to write nasty code when necessary (to remain creatively engaged), but don't rat me out to your teacher or boss when they give you a hard time about it.

Summary

That ends the procedural programming boot camp part of the book. I hope you're not too bleary-eyed or despondent. This information takes time to assimilate, and again I suggest you treat this chapter as a reference or cheat sheet to return to as you need it. Everything covered in this chapter will resurface in examples to come throughout the book, so you'll have lots of opportunities for practice. Later, in Chapter 8, I'll cover OOP, which will be your "code boot camp part 2" experience. But of course by then, you'll be a grizzled and seasoned codehead. The next chapter will look at some of the fundamental issues involved in graphics programming.

4 COMPUTER GRAPHICS, THE FUN, EASY WAY

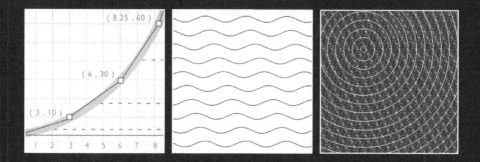

This chapter gives a simplified and highly abridged overview of computer graphics. Graphics and visualization is one of the major research areas in computer science and has a reputation for being highly complex and mathematically demanding. However, there is a wide range of research being conducted under the heading "graphics and visualization"—with varying degrees of complexity. Dr. Edward Angel, in his widely read textbook *Interactive Computer Graphics*, lists four major application areas within computer graphics:

- Display of information
- Design
- Simulation and animation
- User interfaces

Display of information involves data visualization, which can range in complexity from basic charting or plotting of simple data sets (e.g., business graphics), to visualizing molecular interactions or biological processes, to real-time mapping of complex dynamic systems (e.g., modeling of the weather).

Design (really, computer-aided design) is applied in manufacturing, engineering, and architecture. It integrates the visual (form) requirements with the analytical or structural (function) requirements. For example, an architect can design a part of a structure visually, through the manipulation of planes and cubes and other simple geometry, while the system calculates underlying structural issues.

Simulation and animation is similar to display of information, but involves time—often real time—and verisimilitude, or the appearance of reality. For example, a pilot can practice emergency landings more safely in a flight simulator than in a real plane. Haptics, another related research area in computer science, involves tactility, or touch, that complements visual and aural (sound) data used in simulation to create an immersive, real-feeling virtual experience.

User interfaces, sometimes referred to as GUIs (graphical user interfaces), make up the area of computer graphics research that people are most familiar with. We are surrounded by interfaces—not just on our PCs, but on our watches, phones, cameras, appliances, automobiles, and so forth. Yet, for all its ubiquity and apparent simplicity, user interface research is complex, because it deals with human interaction. An entire area of computer science research is devoted to this important and challenging area, called HCI (human-computer interaction).

Processing is being used, to varying degrees, in all four of these areas, and as additional code libraries are developed by readers like you, Processing's application in graphics and visualization research and development will continue to expand. Unlike proprietary languages like ActionScript and Lingo, built primarily around a specific market-driven application area (e.g., web development, CD-ROM/Kiosk development), Processing's Java core and open source status give it a vast breadth of application possibilities.

Some of the reasons coding graphics gets a reputation for being difficult is the math involved in dealing with 3D space and the low-level algorithms needed to manipulate millions of pixels in real time. 3D math is somewhat complicated, especially if you don't have a basic grounding in linear algebra and trigonometry, neither of which are really that complicated, but are usually purged from most artist's brains by the time they leave high school (if it ever got in there in the first place). Because computer monitors are 2D surfaces, there is a need in 3D to always convert 3D geometry back to a 2D projection, so we can see it on the screen.

Computationally, graphics requires a fair amount of low-level processing and lots of memory storage. For example, on a monitor with 1920 × 1200 resolution, over 2,300,000 pixels are redrawn about 70 times per second. Each pixel is made up of three color components (RGB), giving each of the 2 million–plus pixels a range of 16.7 million different colors. Once you add the actual calculations needed to generate 2D or 3D geometry, virtual light sources, textures, special effects, animation, virtual cameras, and event processing (user interaction)—well, you develop a lot of respect for engineers! As computers have gotten faster and memory has gotten cheaper, graphics programming has benefited greatly and things have gotten a little simpler, but less is definitely not more when it comes to graphics, and in spite of the technological advances, users continuously demand more from their games, films, software, and personal devices. In this chapter, I am only going to deal with 2D graphics and some basic math. In spite of all the complexity I just mentioned, Processing makes it pretty easy to get started with graphics (and of course I'll continue to take things slowly). Although this chapter only deals with 2D, everything I cover is applicable to 3D, which I'll cover near the end of the book.

Coordinate systems

A coordinate system is simply a numbered grid that allows you to locate a point in space. Two French mathematicians, René Descartes (1596–1650) and Pierre de Fermat (1601–1665) get credited with developing the Cartesian coordinate system; although Descartes gets most, if not all, of the credit. The Cartesian coordinate system is really just an extension of a number line. The number line has a 0 position; values to the right of 0 are positive and values to the left of 0 are negative—pretty basic stuff. In the coordinate system most of us remember from math class, there is a horizontal axis, usually referred to as **x** and a vertical axis, referred to as **y**. The vertical axis has its own number line, and where these two perpendicular number lines intersect (0, 0) is the origin. In the coordinate system we use in math, above the y-origin is positive and below the y-origin is negative. In computer graphics, this is often flipped, as it is in Processing—above the y-origin is negative and below the y-origin is positive. Figure 4-1 illustrates the coordinate system in Processing, in relation to the monitor. You'll notice that the origin is at the top-left corner of the coordinate system.

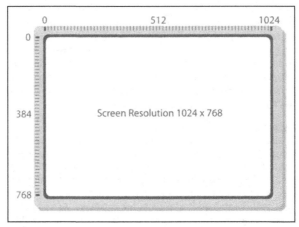

Figure 4-1. In Processing, the x-axis increases from left to right and the y-axis increases from top to bottom. The origin is in the top-left corner, at (0, 0).

If you draw a 40 pixel by 40 pixel rectangle on the monitor at (100, 100), it will be 100 pixels to the right of the left edge of the monitor and 100 pixels down from the top edge of the monitor. Since you can only plot a point to a specific pixel location on the screen, you also need to consider which point on the rectangle gets placed at (100, 100). This point is sometimes referred to as the **registration point**. In most instances, the registration point is either the top-left corner of the image or the center of the image. In Processing, there is a function named rectMode() that allows you to specify from what point a rectangle is drawn by passing different arguments to the function. For example, rectMode(CENTER) orients the rectangle at its center point, while rectMode(CORNER) uses the rectangle's top-left corner; there is also a third argument, rectMode(CORNERS), which draws the rectangle by specifying two points: the top-left and bottom-right corners of the rectangle. In Figure 4-2, the rectangle on the left is drawn from its top-left corner at (100, 100), and the one to the right is drawn from its center point.

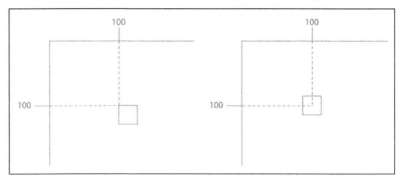

Figure 4-2. The square on the left uses its top-left corner for registration, while the one on the right uses its center point. You can explicitly set the registration point using Processing's rectMode(*MODE*) command.

When working in a 3D coordinate system, you just add another axis, called z, which follows the same rules I've been discussing for 2D. The z-axis goes into the screen and is perpendicular to both the x- and y-axes—but rest assured, for now you only need to deal with the x- and y-axes.

One other issue to consider when dealing with coordinate systems is local vs. world coordinates. For example, when you draw a rectangle on the screen at (100, 100), you can think of the rectangle living on the screen world at pixel address (100, 100). However, let's imagine you then want to put a small circle on the rectangle 3 pixels to the right of the rectangle's left edge and 3 pixels down from its top edge. What is the circle's screen pixel address? You can consider the circle's world address as (103, 103), and the circle's local address, in relation to the rectangle, as (3, 3). Now this may sound a little confusing and like an obscure point, but it is something that comes up fairly often. For example, it is often easier to work with a local coordinate system when you are assembling components on a larger structure. If you are drawing windows on a house, isn't it easier to just worry about where the windows fit in relation to the rectangle of the of building, rather than keeping track of where the windows are in relation to the edges of the screen? This way, if you ever move the building, the windows will stay in the right place in relationship to the building.

Anatomy of an image

A computer screen is (very simply put) a matrix, or grid, made up of rows and columns of pixels that can each glow a certain color, giving the illusion, when enough pixels are glowing the right color, of a continuous tone image (e.g., a photograph). Fortunately, the resolution of most of our monitors is high enough and the refresh rate fast enough to allow this matrix of pixels and constant screen redrawing to remain hidden, giving the illusion of image persistence—you see what looks like a still, smooth image. When you zoom way into an image in a program like Photoshop, you can see the pixel matrix, made up of little blocks of color. If you look under a magnifying glass at printed materials, you can also see a matrix of dots of color that, when zoomed back out, creates the same illusion of a continuous image as on a monitor. Some well-known artists, such as Roy Lichtenstein and Chuck Close, both exploited this phenomenon in their paintings, albeit in very different ways. Lichtenstein painted the dot pattern as an explicit visual element in his pop art work, directly referencing the commercial printing process. Close utilized a matrix structure originally as a production tool, dividing his images up, similar to a monitor, into small rectangular cells. Eventually his work began incorporating the grid as an explicit element as well.

Refresh rate is the rate at which the monitor redraws the screen image. Although images on a screen look constant, they're not. If you've ever shot video of your television, you've probably seen the screen flickering or jumping. The frequency of the video camera's refresh rate and the frequency of the monitor's refresh rate are not synchronized, allowing you to catch the screen refreshing. Properties like screen resolution and refresh rates are hardware-dependent and determined by the monitor and video card in your computer. You can usually select from numerous monitor display configurations through system control panels to change these properties, but actually communicating directly with the video card or monitor through the code you write in Processing is lower level than you go. Java does have a DisplayMode class, allowing you the ability to mess with this stuff (if you really want to). Above the hardware level is where you'll do most of your graphics coding in Processing.

No matter how high level the process of drawing to the screen is made for you, either through a programming language like Processing, or even more simply, a pencil tool in a graphics application, the same underlying stuff still needs to happen. These underlying processes can be quite complex in a language like Java, and involve low-level processing, pretty close to the hardware. For example, there's a class in Java called BufferedImage that provides access to much of the procedural and structural anatomy of an image. Happily, you don't need to understand the BufferedImage class to work with images in Processing; but it can be helpful, or at least interesting, to see a little of what goes into creating an image behind the scenes. I really want to stress that you don't need to understand anything about the BufferedImage class to work in Processing, but learning a little about it will give you more insight into how images work in Java and in computer graphics in general. The BufferedImage class is composed of a bunch of other classes. Figure 4-3 shows a simplified diagram of its structure.

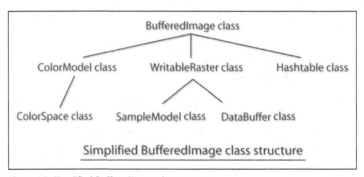

Figure 4-3. Simplified BufferedImage class structure

The BufferedImage class diagram looks pretty scary. I've had advanced computer science students brought to their knees trying to unravel it. What makes it so complicated is the abstraction involved in its design and ultimately the processing required to generate and manipulate images on a computer screen. If you begin to feel sick to your stomach reading about this stuff, just skip ahead to the "Graphic formats" section.

```
fill(0, 0, 255);
rect(0, 0, 10, 10);
```

These two lines of processing code draw a blue rectangle with a black stroke (border) to the screen. Let's look a little below the surface at what's happening. The rect() function in Processing, which relates to the Rectangle() method call in Java, is a drawing method built into the Processing language. You simply pass four arguments to the rect() function: x, y, width, and height, and the function draws a rectangle to those specifications. Drawing methods usually work by plotting points, called vertices (singular is vertex), and then connecting the vertices with some type of line. In Processing, as in numerous other programming languages with graphics capabilities, there are drawing methods to draw points, lines, and basic shapes (simple polygons). In the preceding rectangle example, four vertices are plotted, the vertices are connected with straight lines, and the space between the lines is filled in with the RGB color (R = 0, G = 0, and B = 255)—which makes blue. So far this is pretty simple, right?

If the rectangle is 10 pixels by 10 pixels, then you have 100 pixels altogether (10 X 10). You can also think about the rectangle as a table of 10 rows of pixels by 10 columns of pixels. The BufferedImage class handles these types of storage issues internally, which can get complex, as each pixel is made up of other components. In addition, the BufferedImage class maintains an internal model of an image, rather than generating an actual screen image—which is the work of a Graphics object or graphics context, which I'll discuss later on. The word "Buffer" within BufferedImage refers to a pixel buffer, which simply means an internal storage structure for the pixel data. Computer graphics relies on these types of buffers to efficiently manage the vast amounts of data involved in graphics and animation. There are numerous ways to store pixel data, based on different sample and color models. For example, pixel data can be stored in an internal table structure, with rows and columns that are essentially equivalent to the image's pixel structure on the screen; while another internal buffer can hold the pixel data organized by color. Some of the composite helper classes connected to the BufferedImage class organize pixel data into other structural units such as samples, bands, banks, and rasters, which add flexibility and power to the class, but also contribute to its complexity—it's a good thing Processing internally handles most of this stuff for us. Next, let's go in a little deeper and explore the pixel.

The pixel

Pixel, short for **picture element**, is the term used to describe the smallest unit of a digital image. Essentially, pixels are just little blocks of colors that, when grouped together en masse, form images. Each pixel on the screen has a range of possible colors dependent upon the color depth of the monitor, which is a function of both the monitor and the available memory on the computer's video card. Modern monitors and video cards are all generally capable of displaying 24-bit color depth—meaning that each pixel on the screen can utilize 24 bits of information. Remember, a bit is a unit of measure, representing the smallest unit of memory on a computer (either 0 or 1), and there are 8 bits in 1 byte. Each pixel on a color display is composed of three components, representing the colors red, green, and blue (RGB). Thus, a 24-bit pixel has 8 bits devoted to each of its three component colors. Since 8 bits is kind of meaningless to most of us as a unit of measure, let's convert 8 bits, which lives in base 2 (binary system) to our familiar base 10 (decimal system). To convert base 2 to base 10, you take the base (also called the radix), which in this case is 2 (only 2 choices for bits—0 or 1), and raise it to the power of the number of places (number of bits) in your number, in this case 8. Raising 2 to the 8th power (2^8) gives you 256. So each of the color components in the pixel then has a range of 256 different values, representing the total number of combinations of zeros and ones in an 8-digit number.

In the preceding Processing function call fill(0, 0, 255);, for each of the arguments (*R, G, B*) you can set a number between 0 and 255 (the 0 counts as a value—that's why it only goes up to 255, not 256—but the range of values, or the domain of each component, is 256). If you take the three different components (R, G, and B) and multiply each of their domains together (256 X 256 X 256), you get 16,777,216 possible colors. Another way of thinking about this (and actually closer to how the computer thinks about it) is that a

24-bit color value is literally just a 24-digit number, made up of zeros and ones, where the first 8 bits are used for blue, the next 8 bits are used for green, and the last 8 bits are used for red. If you raise 2 to the 24th power, you get the same answer as before: 16,777,216 possible colors. If you've ever used a control panel device to change your screen resolution, you've probably seen 16.7 million colors—or just "millions of colors"—as a choice. When I first got involved in computer graphics in 1992, it was common to have systems that couldn't handle 24-bit color, and you were forced to use either 16-bit or even 8-bit color depths, which only permitted a range of 65,536 colors or 256 colors, respectively. 8-bit displays required fixed palettes composed of only 256 colors. 8-bit color is referred to as **indexed color**, while 24-bit color is referred to as **true color**. Working in 8-bit color space, we were forced to choose the 256 colors we wanted to use for a project, and it was not easy to change the palette on the fly; it also didn't help that Windows and Mac had separate palettes. The web safe palette, which some of you might be familiar with, was one such made-up palette. It only included 216 of the 256 colors common to both Mac and PC platforms. These limited palettes led to pretty dithered images. **Dithering** occurs when colors outside of the range of the palette need to be approximated, which is done through the grouping of adjacent colors—optically mixing the necessary color. Dithering helps create the illusion of a wider color gamut on an 8-bit system, but usually leads to pretty grainy looking images.

Although contemporary monitors display 24 bits of information for each pixel, internally it is possible to pack even more information into a pixel data structure. Photoshop, as an example, supports 48-bit color, as do some scanners and digital cameras, allowing each pixel to utilize 16 bits for each color component—that's 65,536 unique values for each red, green, and blue component, or a total of over 281 trillion (not a typo) different colors. I know 281 trillion colors sounds bizarre, and nobody uses (or needs) all those colors, but the additional color space supports an increased range of visual detail in areas like shadows. Digital photographers especially benefit from the increased bit depth, as they can combine numerous exposures into a single image, creating images with a higher dynamic range than possible with traditional methods. 48-bit images are also utilized in 3D as radiance maps for rendering composited images, in which a 3D, computer-generated model is seamlessly blended into a photographic environment. The radiance maps work as powerful sources of illumination in the rendering process.

Java's BufferedImage class can handle 32 bits per pixel, and adds an additional 8-bit alpha component to the RGB 24-bit structure. Alpha controls the translucency of the pixel, ranging from 100 percent, which is opaque, to 0 percent, which is transparent. The integer data type in Java and Processing is 32 bits in length, making it very convenient to store pixel values as individual integers—holding red, blue, green, and alpha, commonly abbreviated as RGBA. If your head isn't spinning yet, you can see that, in spite of its complexity, the BufferedImage class really handles a lot. And in spite of the complexity involved in using it, coding graphics in Java would still be a lot scarier if you had to deal with all the mathematical calculations and color transformations the BufferedImage class handles internally. In contrast to using the BufferedImage class in Java, in Processing you can simply call two or three functions to get some similar low-level access. Of course, you have less access and flexibility than working in pure Java—but most of the stuff you really need or want to use is available in Processing, so you really can have your cake and eat it too. As I mentioned in earlier chapters, as you get deeper into graphics programming, Processing's genius really shines. And remember, as you progress in Processing, you have the freedom and flexibility to utilize Java classes such as BufferedImage, or even work in pure Java in the Processing environment.

Graphic formats

Those of you with lots of computer graphics application experience can probably skim this section. I do cover a little of the inner workings of both raster and vector graphics, which might be new or of interest, however. In computer graphics, graphic image types are generally broken down into two basic categories: raster graphics and vector graphics. **Raster graphics** are usually continuous tone images, like photographs, that are not delineated into precise shapes with smooth edges, but are built up as a series of pixels, like a painting. The pixels blend together to form the illusion of a single image. The BufferedImage class is a structure designed to handle raster graphics. **Vector graphics** are usually simpler images, in terms of number of colors and detail. They have distinct parts, each delineated with a concise edge. While raster graphics are a matrix of the actual pixels displayed on the screen (or an approximation), vector graphics are mathematically described shapes, with color fills, strokes, and other rendering attributes. Vector graphics can require much less memory compared to raster graphics, as they represent the plots of mathematical expressions. Since the computer is really a glorified calculator, it grooves on equations, but having to keep track of millions of pixels in real time is more demanding. Ultimately though, in the rendering process to the screen, eventually everything must be converted to screen pixels. However, before the screen rendering, vector graphics are able to be stored as simple expressions, rather than large arrays of RGBA color values, as with raster graphics. Raster and vector graphics each have their strengths and weaknesses, and are generally utilized for different purposes.

Raster graphics

Raster graphics are typically utilized for photographic or other highly detailed continuous tone images, where edges are not distinct and there is a large variation in color or value. Common raster graphic image file formats include TIF, BMP, and JPG. Raster formats also generally utilize some compression algorithms to ease their memory storage requirements. Compression can be **lossy**, in which the image quality is actually degraded with compression, like in JPG; or **lossless**, with no image loss, as in LZW compression, used commonly with the TIF file format. Raster images have variable resolution, meaning that you can specify how many dots of image information you want to pack into each inch. The more dots per inch (dpi), the finer the image detail or resolution, but also the higher the memory requirements. Monitor screen resolution is 72 dpi (Mac) and 96 dpi (Windows). That means that it is only possible to see 72 dpi on the screen on a Mac; any higher will not improve the quality of the screen image. So why would you want more resolution if you can't see it? Well, if you are only working on the Web, then you don't need any additional resolution—you're done (assuming the image is the size you want it). However, if you ever need to print your images, then you need more resolution; how much more is dependent upon how you're going to print. Offset printers that print magazines, posters, this book, and so forth typically utilize a line screen, composed of dots that lay a dot pattern down when they print. The frequency of the line screen is measured in lines per inch, or LPI. As long as the line screen is fine enough, the dot pattern is not noticeable. However, tighter line screens also require papers that bleed less and can hold the distinct dot pattern. There is a formula you can use to calculate required dpi, based on the line screen frequency and image size. A simpler rule, however, is to just double the frequency of the line screen to determine image dpi. So for grainy newspaper printing, a line screen frequency might be 85 LPI, but for a coffee table art book, the frequency might be 200 LPI; thus the image would need to be around 170 dpi and 400 dpi, respectively. You would also need to make sure that your image was at the actual printing size at that resolution. That being said, I recommend that when you land that huge print job, you discuss the image and printing resolution issues with the printer.

Vector graphics

Vector graphics are typically used for simple illustrations, logos, and images that require distinct and precise contours. Computer text is vector-based, normally just wrapped in a text-based object that includes certain methods for editing the text. In vector-based graphics applications like Illustrator, FreeHand, and Flash, you can create outlines from text objects, or break them apart and get down to the vector information. Vector graphics are made up of vertices (points) and strokes. The lines can be straight or curved, and are generated mathematically. Straight lines are simple linear equations, like $y = 4x + 3$. In Processing, you don't need to worry about the math; you can simply use the line function to generate a line:

```
line(x1, y1, x2, y2)
```

The first two coordinates in the function are the starting point and the last two coordinates are the line's endpoint. Processing and Java utilize internal drawing methods that handle the algebra and draw the line. Curves are a little more complex and require higher-degree polynomials (don't scream). The preceding linear equation is a first-degree polynomial, so a second-degree would just have x to the 2nd power. For example, $y = 2x^2 + 3x - 4$ is a simple second-degree polynomial, also called a quadratic equation. (Is this ringing some dusty old bells?) So I'm bugging you with all this math because second-degree (quadratic) and third-degree (cubic) polynomials are used to generate the smooth curves that are made with the common Bézier pen tools found in all major graphics applications. But again, all you have to do is put in the points and Processing will crank out the math and curves; it is actually a little more complicated than that, but not much. I'll discuss the actual implementation in the next few chapters.

The pixels contained within the bounds of the vector shapes do not need to be stored in memory as they would for raster graphics, because the shapes, including color fills and strokes, are calculated during runtime (when the program runs). Because vector graphics are just plots of a set of vertices, they can be moved or transformed very easily. It is no sweat for the computer to take in the list of coordinates and perform some calculations on the data and redraw the shapes with the updated vertices. However, since the vertices need to be stored in memory, and the computer needs to sequentially plot each of the vertices, too may vertices can become a performance drain on the computer and even potentially yield worse performance than with raster graphics.

Vector graphics are also resolution independent—one of their best attributes. You are able to scale vector shapes up or down without any loss in quality. It is just as easy for the computer to calculate 1000 as 9999, so size is essentially irrelevant with regard to vector graphics. Additionally, you can edit vector graphics by manipulating their vertices individually—so they may be deformed in real time, leading to possibilities such as character animation or shape morphing. One of the reasons a program like Flash became so popular was because of its strength as a vector-based animation program, which allowed it to effectively overcome the bandwidth issues associated with the Web, especially back in the days when we all had slow dial-up modems.

4

Animation

Animation is really just an extension of static imaging, and everything covered thus far in this chapter applies to animation. In the simplest sense, animation is a series of still images displayed sequentially. If the rate of change between images, commonly called the **frame rate**, is fast enough, our brains can't detect the transitions, and you see fluid motion. This effect is referred to as persistence of vision. In actuality, we perceive the physical world in much the same way. Light enters our cornea, moves through the pupil and lens, and eventually reaches the retina. The retina is the light-sensing part of the eye, containing photosensitive structures called rods and cones. The rods detect low light, while the cones detect color and detail. The received light is transformed, through a chemical process, into electrical impulses, which then pass through the optic nerve into the brain to form vision. Thus, our vision is not static, but—similar to animation—a perpetual sequence of dynamic 2D data. When I taught painting, I tried to encourage my students to see two-dimensionally, to record the actual visual data the eye was seeing, not the interpreted image the brain was forming. I argued that if you wanted other viewers to read 3D space in the painting, you needed to record the actual perceptual 2D cues that the eyes were seeing, which would then naturally lead to the perception of 3D space in the viewer's brain. Our binocular vision (two eyes) and our brain provide the illusion that we see three-dimensionally and that the visual field is constant. One simple way to prove the brain's giant cover-up of the true visual chaos surrounding us is to detect the eye's blind spot. At the back of each of our eyes, where the optic nerve exits the retina, is a structure called the optic disc. The optic disc has no rods or cones on it to receive light and thus causes a literal blind spot in our field of vision—actually a blind spot in each eye. However, each of our clever eyes compensates for the other eye's blind spot—blinding us to our own blind spots (ignorance is bliss). Figure 4-4 provides a little example of how to fool the brain and reveal the holes in your vision. Close your left eye and stare at the dot on the left in the figure. Don't look at the star, but you should be able to see it in your peripheral vision. Slowly move toward the page and keep looking at the dot. When you get to about a foot away or so, the star on the right should disappear—that's your blind spot. For a good article on how vision works, check out http://science.howstuffworks.com/eye1.htm.

Figure 4-4. Blind spot example

Some persistence of vision begins at a fairly low frame rate. Flip books are a good example of this; it doesn't take too much speed to get some sense of animated motion. Film has a frame rate of 24 fps (frames per second). NTSC video is about 30 fps (actually, 29.97, with two interlaced fields each refreshing at that rate to avoid flicker). Web animation/ video ranges from 12 fps to over 30 fps, depending upon connection speed, file size, the processor, and so on. At 12 fps, you notice a flicker in animation, but 12 fps was about as good as it got in the early days of the Web. Faster modems and the proliferation of broadband now allow web animation to approach comparable frame rates to film and video. In addition, web streaming technologies and improved codecs (compression algorithms) were developed to allow motion data to begin playing in the browser while content was still downloading, increasing image quality and eliminating long download delays. Outside of the Web, it is also possible to shoot film or generate computer animation with much higher frame rates than 30 fps, allowing you to do things like slow down the film and still get smooth motion. This is precisely what artist Bill Viola did in his video art piece *The Quintet of Remembrance*, installed at The Metropolitan Museum of Art in New York. Viola shot 60 seconds of footage for the piece with very high-speed film. He then slowed the piece down to over 16 minutes. In the piece, five actors, standing in a tight grouping, are each expressing intense emotion, referencing three important historical paintings. The silent piece unfolds incredibly slowly, yet with absolute clarity and free of any flicker, creating a very unique and memorable viewing experience. The high-speed film obviously captured enough frames to allow it to be played back 16 times slower, while still maintaining at least a 24 fps frame rate. Here's a link to the piece: www.metmuseum.org/toah/ ho/11/na/ho_2001.395a-I.htm.

Popular computer animation software applications such as Flash, After Effects, and LightWave borrow concepts from traditional animation, film, and video. These applications are timeline-based, in which users specify **keyframes**—the beginning and ending points of animated sequences—and the software generates the frames between the keyframes, or the **in-betweens**, in animation speak. In the golden days of traditional cell animation, the master animator created the keyframes, while the apprentice animators (the human in-betweeners) handled the rest of the frames. In digital animation, it doesn't matter if the animated object or effect is an imaging filter, 3D character, ball, light, camera, texture map, or particle generator; every object has a set of properties (x and y coordinates, width, height, etc.) that can be changed over time by setting keyframes on the timeline. Some of the higher-end animation tools even have their own proprietary programming languages built into the application, allowing code to control these timeline envelopes as well.

Animation software applications can be divided up by their core functionality. For example, the three popular animation packages I referenced—Flash, After Effects, and LightWave— are each used for different primary purposes. Flash is used for 2D web-based animation and web design/development; After Effects is used for motion design, compositing, and imaging effects for film and video; and LightWave is used for 3D modeling and animation.

Within each of these application areas are numerous other competitive packages as well. In addition, there are nonlinear digital editing tools for film and video—Apple's Final Cut Pro is one such tool. These tools, often timeline-based as well, are used to edit and output finished animations, films, and videos. Compared to all these powerful time-based applications, Processing and Java, or any programming language for that matter, seems pretty sparse. Processing doesn't have a timeline, keyframes, or the gazillion other dialog boxes commonly found in these commercial applications. Theoretically, you could build all these constructs within Processing and generate your own animation application, but wouldn't it be way more productive to just use one of the existing applications? Why use Processing for animation? (I'll assume you all have unlimited budgets for new software acquisition, so the fact that Processing is open source and completely free wouldn't figure into your decision).

Earlier in the book, I discussed the difference between using Photoshop filters for cool effects and finding less common and more personally expressive possibilities using code. Again, let me stress that I am not being critical of Photoshop or the other amazing animation tools I mentioned earlier; I love these tools. However, in the creative process it is often helpful to get down to basics and make more fundamental inquiries. Traditionally, artists have grabbed a pencil and paper or a lump of clay, and scribbled and poked away in the process of conceptualizing and finding new possibilities. The simplicity of the process and the directness of the materials lent themselves to the process of discovery. It is often in the process of playing with the materials, without explicit application, that new approaches and forms are uncovered. I assert, and know from personal experience, that it is possible to do this with code. Processing was designed primarily around this approach to coding and is the reason Processing programs are referred to as sketches. In addition, quality in art has never been a function of quantity or effect. One can use the most powerful software tools imaginable and still make overly simple and uninteresting work. At the other extreme, artists such as da Vinci, Ingres, and Constable have used simple drawing tools to produce some of the most complex and beautiful images ever created. Processing fits somewhere between the software bells and whistles and a pencil in its complexity, and is a great tool to explore/create time-based art.

The joy of math

The title of this section may seem like an oxymoron. Rather than joy, you may have other associations with math (dread, boredom, pain, unpleasant memories from high school, etc.). I can identify with the dread response, as I spent many hours staring out of public school windows during math class. It wasn't the subject matter that put me in a zombie state, it was the way it was presented. Being a creative and process-oriented kid, I wanted to feel a connection to the stuff I was learning and also wanted to see its relevancy in the world around me. In an art class, there is a direct response between one's action and some tangible result. Even in a science class, there is the possibility of a lab result or some process making a relevant connection. But in math, back when I was in school, we seemed to primarily concentrate on drilling, rote memorization, and things being right or wrong.

However, turning 40 (yikes!), I don't totally trust my memory of those days, so if you happen to be one of the inspired math teachers I had and selectively forgot, my deepest apologies. Recently, I decided to sit in a calculus class where I was teaching. I'd retrained myself in math (just the math I actually needed), and was really looking forward to the experience, which I know might sound odd to some of you. I did enjoy the class, and the professor tried to find some relevant connections, but that old dread came back in spite of the fact that I wasn't even enrolled in the class, not to mention that I already had my degrees and a job. I especially found the tests disagreeable, where rigid constraints of time and a very limited solution set took most of the joy away. Ironically, I love trying to solve complex technical and analytical problems, as one finds continuously in programming. However, in programming, as opposed to a math class, technical problems are directly linked to the process of creating. Rather than having to plot some nondescript curve I could care less about (with little or no aesthetic payoff), I'd prefer to create an aesthetically based organic form, generated through a series of curve expressions. In addition, coding allows you to chart your own procedural course when solving a problem. For example, five different coders can each solve the same problem five different ways. I believe this type of flexibility is essential to the creative process—whether you're painting a tree or creating a series of mathematical expressions to plot a tree.

For your purposes, you only need a small part of math, and mostly pretty basic stuff. However, programming is really a form of applied math—a very creative form! If you want to move something on the screen, change the color of a pixel, or have the user interact with one of your Processing sketches, you need to deal with coordinates and usually simple addition, subtraction, multiplication, or division. For example, if you create a virtual ant and want it to wander around the sketch window, avoiding some obstacles and searching for food, you need to continuously add values to the mouse's x and y coordinates and keep checking if the ant's coordinates are interfering with either the obstacle or food coordinates. If you want the food to slowly disappear as the ant eats it, you can slowly shift the value of the pixels making up the food to the background color of the screen. This section is going to take a quick look at basic math utilized in graphics programming. The material should be viewed more as a math primer than a proper elucidation of this material. If you don't fully get it here, don't panic—it will be revisited later on. Some of these concepts are also expanded upon in Appendix B.

Elementary algebra

Algebra is old. It has been used continuously and developed for over 3,000 years, with early contributions made by cultures worldwide including the ancient Egyptians, Babylonians, Greeks, and Chinese. Algebra was first introduced into Europe in the beginning of the 13th century by Leonardo Fibonacci of Pisa. Fibonacci got famous for trying to figure out the breeding capacity of rabbits. What he realized was that there is a predictable sequence of numbers, based on a simple rule, connected to the rabbits' breeding rates. In fact, this numeric progression is not only tied to rabbit breeding, but tree growth, numbers of petals on a flower, the spiral in the golden section, and many other natural phenomena. To learn more about Fibonacci and his rabbits, check out www.mcs.surrey.ac.uk/Personal/ R.Knott/Fibonacci/fibnat.html#rabeecow.

The actual word *algebra* comes from a ninth century Persian treatise, written by al-Khwarizmi (mentioned in Chapter 2 in the discussion about algorithms). Al-Khwarizmi is widely hailed as the father of algebra (as well as one of the greatest math geniuses of all time). Al-Khwarizmi, or *algoritmi*, as his name translates into Latin, is where the word algorithm comes from. Elementary algebra is absolutely fundamental to programming. In many ways, programming is algebra. However, programming is the kind of algebra you do but don't realize you're doing it—sort of like the cardiovascular heath benefits you receive from certain bedroom activities. Algebra relies on variables, numbers, and operators to form expressions—which is identical to programming. In programming, though, you need to use slightly different syntax based on the language you are using. For example, Table 4-1 shows some algebraic expressions and the corresponding Processing implementations.

Table 4-1. Algebraic expressions and their corresponding Processing implementations

Algebraic expression	Processing implementation
2x + 2	2 * x + 2
x^2 – 3x + 4	x * x – 3 * x + 4
$\dfrac{5x^3}{4}$	(5 * pow(x, 3)) / 4

Elementary algebra also has some very basic rules or laws that help us solve equations. Some of these laws are also central to programming. For your purposes, though, you just need to apply them—you don't have to worry about formal definitions or proofs. Following is a list—sort of a cheat sheet—of the elementary algebraic laws that most apply to beginning graphics programming.

Operation order (a.k.a. operator precedence)

Operations happen in a certain order, which can have a direct effect on results. For most operations, simply remember that what's inside the parentheses is evaluated first, then multiplication and division, and then addition and subtraction. If the operators have the same precedence in a compound expression, and there are no parentheses (e.g., **4 + 20 + 5**), then the expression is evaluated from left to right. The following list provides some examples:

- **6 * 3 – 4 = 14**: The multiplication is done first, and then the subtraction.
- **7 – 9 / 3 = 4**: The division is done first, and then the subtraction.
- **(7 – 9) / 3 = –2/3**: The operation inside the parentheses is done first, and then the division.
- **4 * 5 / 2 * 3 = 30**: The precedence of each operation is equal, so the equation is solved from left to right.
- **4 * 15 / 2 – 13 * 9 + 5 = –82**: The multiplication and division are done first, and then the subtraction and addition, from left to right.

For a complete list of operator precedence in Java and Processing, check out http://java.sun.com/docs/books/tutorial/java/nutsandbolts/expressions.html.

Associative property

When performing addition, grouping doesn't matter, so you don't need parentheses, but if you include them, it won't do any damage:

(a + b) + c = a + (b + c) = a + b + c

121

In multiplication, grouping doesn't matter, so you don't need parentheses in this case either:

(a * b) * c = a * (b * c) = a * b * c

Non-associative property

Most of your expressions will be non-associative, and will therefore require grouping. In the examples in the following list, notice how the placement of the parentheses changes the value of the expression. (Remember, what's between the parentheses is evaluated first.) Please also note that the operator != means "does not equal."

(a * b) + c != a * (b + c)

(4 * 5) + 6 = 26

4 * (5 + 6) = 44

4 * 5 + 6 = 26 (Multiply first, and then add)

(a – b) – c != a – (b – c)

(8 – 5) – 4 = –1

8 – (5 – 4) = 7

8 – 5 – 4 = –1 (Solved from left to right)

When in doubt, use parentheses to group; it can never hurt.

Distributive property

When multiplying an expression involving addition or subtraction (which is just addition of a negative number) by another value, you need to multiply all the different elements in the expression by the value, as the following three examples show:

4 * (a + b) = 4a + 4b

–(a + b) = –1(a + b) = –1a + –1b

6 * (a + b – c + d) = 6a + 6b – 6c + 6d

You can use the distributive property to multiply two binomials, as shown following:

(2x + 3) * (3x – 2)

= (2x * 3x) + (2x * –2) + (3 * 3x) + (3 * –2)

= 6x^2 + 5x – 6

This is a second-degree polynomial, or a quadratic equation.

Geometry

Like algebra, geometry dates way back to ancient Egypt and Babylonia (2000 to 500 BC), where knowledge of geometry was demonstrated through building and development projects. However, it was Greek influence, beginning with Thales and Pythagoras in around 600 BC, through to Archimedes in around 200 BC, that gave us what we think of as Euclidian geometry today. Of all the Greeks, it was Euclid of Alexandria, in around 300 BC, who would leave the most lasting mark on Greek geometry with his famous 13-book treatise, *The Elements of Geometry*. This treatise formalized Greek thought on geometry up to that point, and is even considered by some to be the first textbook ever written. It is certainly one of the most important and influential books ever written on mathematics, with versions of it still in print—over 2,500 years after it was written—that would be a lot of royalties for Euclid!

The word *geometry* comes from the Greek words for *earth* and *measure*, and suggests its original use in building, surveying, astronomy, and other real-world applications. Geometry was introduced to Europe during the early Renaissance, and its influence is obvious and ubiquitous, especially in Renaissance architecture and the visual arts. However, with regard to computer graphics, the major development in geometry didn't occur until the 17th century, with the advent of analytical or coordinate geometry, developed by René Descartes and Pierre de Fermat. Analytical geometry utilizes the Cartesian coordinate system (also developed by Descartes) as a system to study geometric curves and shapes plotted utilizing algebraic equations, which is precisely what is done in computer graphics. (Thankfully, most of the math is actually done behind the scenes for us.)

Points

The point is the most basic geometric element we deal with. A point has 0 dimensions; although in Processing, you do see a 1 pixel by 1 pixel output to the screen when you write the following command (making this technically a 1-pixel-long line—but we'll let it pass).

```
point(x, y);
```

Points, as data structures, are primarily used to store coordinate locations for plotting curves and shapes. Java has some convenient data structures, or classes, for this very purpose, such as the aptly named Point class. Remember, in Processing, you have the option of using Java classes as you see fit.

Lines

Lines occupy one dimension, as they have length, but no width. Lines can be expressed algebraically with the expression **y = mx + b**.

This equation for a line is referred to as the **slope-intercept** form, where **m** is the slope of the line and **b** is the y-intercept (the place where the line intercepts the y-axis). **x** and **y** are the two components of any point on the line. Slope is an important property of a line or curve in math and computer graphics, and often relates graphically to motion and acceleration. For example, the graph of the line in Figure 4-5 shows an object moving at a constant rate. The vertical axis of the graph is distance, and the horizontal axis is time. The slope of the line can be found by looking at the change in y (Δ **y**) over the change in x (Δ **x**) at any two points on the graph. People commonly refer to the slope as **rise** over **run**.

Since the graph is of a line, the slope will be constant for any two points, and thus the speed will be continuous, without any acceleration. This issue will become more relevant later on, when you begin to animate objects. If you want to create more natural motion, you need acceleration and deceleration; thus, lines and linear equations are not typically used to generate organic motion. However, you can animate any property; and for some of these properties, linear equations are the perfect solution (e.g., an object floating in space or a mechanical device operating at a steady speed). Figure 4-5 graphs speed as a linear equation, with distance and time as the y- and x-axes.

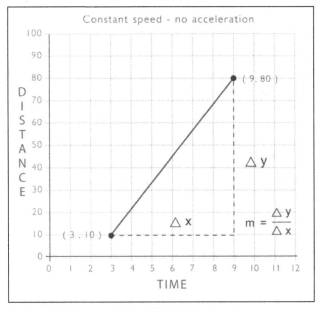

Figure 4-5. Plotting constant speed (distance/time) as a line

Curves

Curves are much more complex than lines, and there are many varieties. Here's a link with a collection of over 850 different curves: www.2dcurves.com/. For your purposes, you just need to understand some basic aspects of curves and how to generate a few. As a simple rule, you can generate a smooth, continuous curve with any second-degree (or higher) polynomial. In addition, you can predict the type of curve you'll get for some of these, especially second-degree (quadratic curve) and third-degree (cubic curve) polynomials. By predicting curves, I mean knowing how many changes in direction (or turning points) the curve can have. For example, an arc or parabola would have one change of direction, while an s-shaped curve would have two. The rule is that an even-degree curve—like a second-degree polynomial—can have an odd number of turning points one less than its degree, and an odd-degree curve—like a third-degree polynomial—can have an even number of turning points one less than its degree. I know this sounds a little confusing, but if you read it again, you'll see it's pretty simple. What this rule means is that a quadratic (second-degree) curve has one turning point and a cubic (third-degree) curve can have either zero or two turning points. This info will become more relevant when you get to Chapter 7 and see how curves are actually generated in Processing. Here are two little Processing sketches that generate the quadratic and cubic curves shown in Figures 4-6 and 4-7, respectively:

```
/*
 Simple Quadratic Curve
 equation: f(x) = x*x - 20x + 200
 Ira Greenberg, October 10, 2005
 */

float x, y;
// adjusts y to fit in sketch window coordinate space
float curveFittingFactor = .03;

void setup(){
  size(400, 400);
  background(255);
  fill(0);
  for (int i=-102; i<124; i++){
    x = i;
    y = pow(i, 2)-20*x+200;
    ellipse(x+200, y*curveFittingFactor, 4, 4);
  }
}
```

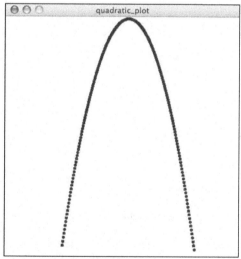

Figure 4-6. Quadratic curve

```
/*
Simple Cubic Curve
equation: f(x) = .2*x*x*x - 50*x*x - 50*x + x-100
Ira Greenberg, October 10, 2005
*/

float x, y;
// adjusts y to fit in sketch window coordinate space
float curveFittingFactor = .0001;

void setup(){
  size(400, 400);
  background(255);
  fill(0);
  for (int i=-102; i<300; i+=2){
    x = i;
    y = pow(i, 3)*.2+x*x*-50+x-100;
    ellipse(x+100, y*curveFittingFactor+200, 2, 2);
  }
}
```

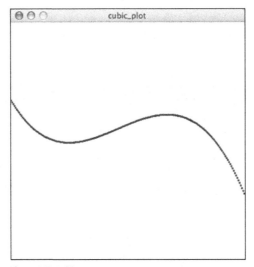

Figure 4-7. Cubic curve

Smoothness and continuity are two other important characteristics of curves. **Smoothness** means there are no cusps, or sharp kinks, in the curve, and **continuity** means that the curve doesn't stop and start again, which happens with a tangent function, for example. These properties are significant in things like calculus, but that's obviously not your concern. When a curve has a cusp or stops abruptly, and you are using it to animate or control some aspect of a program, there will be, at best, an abrupt jolt to otherwise smooth movement or possibly even a complete crash of your program. You'll experiment with these properties in later chapters. For now, there are two simple curves worth looking at that will help you code organic motion—one describes acceleration and the other deceleration.

Figures 4-8 and 4-9 show an acceleration curve and a deceleration curve, with time on the x-axis and distance on the y, as in the previous linear example.

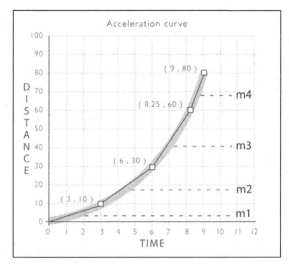

Figure 4-8. Acceleration curve

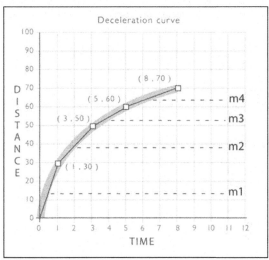

Figure 4-9. Deceleration curve

Notice that the acceleration curve is concave, like the front of a spoon, while the shape of the deceleration curve is convex. As you look at the figures, think about how much distance is being covered over what time period. Is distance increasing more rapidly than time or vice versa, and is the rate of change constant, increasing, or decreasing at different parts of the curve? Is the curve smooth and continuous? The graph shows smooth acceleration and deceleration beginning at point (0, 0), meaning that no time or distance have elapsed.

In Figures 4-8 and 4-9, I divided each of the curves into four straight segments, between the white points. These straight segments, approximating the curve, are called **secant lines**. By looking at the slope of these lines, labeled m1 through m4, you can predict how the rate of speed is changing in the graphs. It is also possible to more precisely calculate the slope of each of these secant lines by using the x and y components of the points at the ends of each of the secant lines and dividing the change in the two y components (Δ y) by the change in the two x components (Δ x). For example, to calculate the slope of the first secant line (m1) in the deceleration curve, you can do the following:

m1 = Δ y / Δ x

m1 = 30 − 0 / 1 − 0

m1 = 30

If you take the time to calculate the remaining slopes of m2, m3, and m4, you'll get 10, 5, and 3.33, respectively. Since this is a deceleration curve, it makes sense that the slopes of the secant lines decrease over time. (Of course, it's a lot less work to simply guess how the rate of change is affected based on how vertical the secant lines are.)

It is a little confusing thinking about rate of change vs. speed. **Speed** is the rate of motion, which is simpler to think about. Speed is simply distance divided by time. If I move a rectangle 30 pixels in 3 seconds, the rectangle is moving 10 pixel per second (pps); that's its speed. For example, the following simple Processing sketch moves a rectangle across the screen at approximately 30 pps:

```
//linear motion
int w = 20;
int h = 10;
int x = 0;
int y;

void setup(){
  size(400, 400);
  y = height/2;
  frameRate(30);
}

void draw(){
  background(255);
  rect(x++, y, w, h);
}
```

This linear motion would plot as a straight line, as its rate of change is constant. If, however, I initially move a ball 30 pps, and then I keep doubling the rate at which I move the ball (1 second equals 30 pps, 2 seconds equals 30 pps, 3 seconds equals 120 pps, 4 seconds equals 240 pps, etc.) based on a geometric progression, I end up with acceleration. Here's the same sketch converted from linear motion to accelerated motion. However, to keep the speed down, rather than continuously doubling the rate, I continuously increase it by 10 percent—which still gets the rectangle cruising. Don't worry if you can't follow the code yet—I'll be going over this again later in the book, in painstaking detail.

```
//Example 1: accelerated motion using multiplication
int w = 20;
int h = 10;
int x = 0;
int y;
float speed = 1;

void setup(){
  size(400, 400);
  y = height/2;
  frameRate(30);
}

void draw(){
  background(255);
  speed*=1.1;
  rect(speed, y, w, h);
}
```

There is another simple way to code acceleration, which uses addition and double implementation. I've included it here for your viewing pleasure:

```
// Example 2:
// accelerated motion using addition
int w = 10;
int h = 10;
int x = 0;
int y;
float speed;
float acceleration = .1;

void setup(){
  size(400, 400);
  y = height/2;
}

void draw(){
  background(255);
  speed += acceleration;
  rect(x+=speed, y, w, h);
}
```

When you run the sketches, notice how the box actually accelerates. If you plotted the equations that generated this motion, you'd get approximations of the acceleration curve. Later in the book you'll experiment with both constant and accelerated motion more, as well as add cool features like gravity, collisions, and springs. One final point about working with these types of equations is the potential of generating extremely large or small numbers very quickly—approaching positive or negative infinity. Actually, you don't have to worry about reaching infinity, forgetting about the obvious paradoxical aspect, as Processing will give you an error way before that. As an exercise in futility, but perhaps also some small interest, try running the following sketch, which simply begins with the value 1 and continues doubling it for 100 steps (if smoke begins pouring out of your computer, I'm sure it's just a sad coincidence):

```
double n = 1.0;
for (int i=1; i<=100; i++){
  println("step " + i + " = " + (n*=2));
}
```

If you were scared to run the sketch, don't worry—I pasted steps 70 through 80 of the output following:

```
step 70 = 1.1805916207174113E21
step 71 = 2.3611832414348226E21
step 72 = 4.722366482869645E21
step 73 = 9.44473296573929E21
step 74 = 1.888946593147858E22
step 75 = 3.777893186295716E22
step 76 = 7.555786372591432E22
step 77 = 1.5111572745182865E23
step 78 = 3.022314549036573E23
step 79 = 6.044629098073146E23
step 80 = 1.2089258196146292E24
```

The **E** in the numbers means exponential notation. The number at step 80 is 1.2089258196146292 to the 24th power. If you want to get rid of the exponential notation, just move the decimal point to the right 24 places.

In 2003, our known universe got much bigger. Prior to 2003, reports of the known universe's diameter were estimated to be between as little as 10 billion light years to nearly 40 billion light years. Now, don't get me wrong, that's pretty far. However, in 2003, Neil Cornish of Montana State University estimated the known universe's diameter to be 156 billion light years—now that's big! (I should also note that prior to his current position at Montana, Dr. Cornish worked in Stephen Hawking's research group at Cambridge—so his credentials are decent.) Well, how long is a light year? Light travels at 186,000 miles per second. There are 60 seconds in a minute, 60 minutes in an hour, 24 hours in a day, and 365 days in a year. If you multiply these together, you can determine that light travels 5,865,696,000,000 miles in a year. Multiplying that by 156 billion gives you 1.091019456E24 miles. This makes the diameter of the known universe a little less than step 80 in the preceding code output. Remember how the output was generated—I simply started with 1 and began doubling. By step 80, the output had surpassed the diameter of the known universe—but it goes way beyond that. In fact, each step from 80 to 100 is another doubling in size—my head's beginning to hurt, and I think you get the point.

Trigonometry

The Latin word *trigonometry*, coined in the 16th century, was formed from three Greek words that translate to "three-angle measure," and simply means the study of triangles. This is precisely what trig was used for in the second century BC, when the astronomer Hipparchus of Rhodes created one of the first tables of trigonometry values (it was called a table of chords back then). Unfortunately, most of Hipparchus's work has been lost, and we mostly know of him through the writings of others, especially Ptolemy, who based much of his work on Hipparchus's earlier work. Ptolemy, you may remember, is the guy who said that Earth was at the center of the universe, which was eventually refuted by Copernicus 1,400 years later. Hipparchus apparently used his chord tables to help him predict things like eclipses, star positions, distance to the moon, and the length of a year, which he predicted to within 6.5 minutes. I think it's time we give Hipparchus his due.

Hipparchus's reputation aside, solving for angles and sides of triangles is not terribly inspiring, and precisely what contributed to my dazed stare out the classroom window when I first studied it. Since ancient times (even before I was in junior high school), trig has emerged as a fundamental tool in many fields, from astronomy to architecture to engineering to 3D gaming, and yes, also to code art. Trig is much more than the study of triangles; it figures significantly in the study of waves, impacting our understanding of sound, radio, and light, among other physical phenomena.

Trigonometry is also really simple. I know this may sound odd, but aside from having to learn a couple scary Greek symbols and basic theory, trig is really just an extension of the Pythagorean theorem (at least the part of trig you'll need). Although some basic theory is helpful to begin to grasp the full power of trigonometry, it is possible to begin playing with the trig functions almost immediately, learning experientially as you experiment with them. The trig functions that you'll mostly use are sine, cosine, and tangent. There are a few others you'll look at later on in the book, but an amazing amount of stuff can be done with just these three.

I like to think of the trig functions almost as dabs of paint on my palette. I begin playing with the trig dabs, inserting different values here and there, and watching what happens. Sometimes I end up with really long and convoluted expressions, completely outside of my understanding, that make engaging, beautiful images or animations; other times I get a garbled mess. Part of the fun is in not exactly knowing what you're going to get. Fortunately, as an artist, I can get away with this aesthetically driven, semi-clueless approach to trig. I also can't help wondering, had math been taught this way when I was in school, perhaps I would have enjoyed math class more and done less window gazing. Interestingly, as I've gotten older, I've found the more I play with stuff like trig, the more interested I get in understanding the underlying theory. I also think this aesthetic approach to learning math increases retention, especially for artists.

The best way to get a sense of what trig can do is to see it in action. The three code examples that follow are not intended as a lesson on trig in Processing—that begins in Chapter 6. These examples are intended just to, hopefully, spark your latent zeal for trig (or at least make you hate it less). I don't intend newbie coders to be able to follow the code in these examples (yet).

The first trig example is of a simple repeating sine curve that creates a wave pattern, as shown in Figure 4-10.

Figure 4-10. Repeating sine curve

```
/*Simple Repeating Wave Pattern
 Ira Greenberg, October 13, 2005
 */

float y = 0;
float angle = 0;
float amplitude = 5;
float waveGap = 24;
float frequency = 5;

void setup(){
  size(400, 400);
  background(255);
  noFill();
  frameRate(30);
}

void draw(){
  // stop drawing at the bottom of the sketch window
  if (y<height){
    float py = 0;
    for (int i=0; i<width; i++){
      py = y+sin(radians(angle))*amplitude;
      point(i, py);
      angle+=frequency;
    }
    y+=waveGap;   //step waves down
  }
}
```

This sketch creates a simple sine curve across the x-axis and then repeats it down the window. I've created variables for some of the settings, which you can experiment with. One of the cool things about wave patterns is what happens when they get close together or even cross. Try changing the amplitude in the example code as well as the waveGap and frequency. Figure 4-11 was created with these altered settings:

- amplitude = 72;
- waveGap = 14;
- frequency = 6;

133

Figure 4-11. Repeating distorted sine curve

When patterns overlap and interfere with each other, interesting things happen, such as moiré patterns. In printing, moiré patterns are usually an unwanted phenomenon, occurring from interfering line screen frequencies. However, these patterns can also be quite beautiful, causing interesting visual distortions and secondary patterns to emerge. In the following example sketch (shown in Figure 4-12), the wave pattern continuously redraws itself, with some of the waveform properties controlled by the position of the mouse during runtime. In addition, a second concentric ring pattern moves around with the cursor, causing some interesting distortions to occur. You can also press the mouse and hold it, and the ring pattern will grow; when you let go, it will shrink back to its original size.

```
/* Interference and moiré pattern
 Ira Greenberg, October 18, 2005 */

float interval;
float spacer;

// Experiment with these values
float angle = 0;
float amplitude = .05;
```

```
float waveGap = 10;
float frequency = .1;
float ringGrowthRate = .5;
boolean isInactive = true;

void setup(){
  size(400, 400);
  interval = width*.03;
  spacer = interval;
  noFill();
  frameRate(30);
}

void draw(){
  background(0);
  stroke(255);
  float py = 0;
  /* This nested for loop fills the frame
      with a wave pattern. Some of its properties
      are controlled, in part, by the mouse position*/
  for (int i=0; i<height; i+=waveGap){
    for (int j=0; j<width; j++){
      py = i+sin(radians(angle))*mouseY*amplitude;
      point(j, py);
      angle+=mouseX*frequency;
    }
  }

  // draw concentric ring pattern
  for (int i=0; i<width/2*spacer/interval; i+=spacer){
    ellipse(mouseX, mouseY, 10+i, 10+i);
  }

  // describe mouse press behavior
  if (mousePressed){
    angle = 0;
    isInactive = false;
    // grow rings
    if (spacer < interval*2){
      spacer += ringGrowthRate;
    }
  }
  // shrink rings
  if (isInactive){
    if (spacer> interval){
      spacer -= ringGrowthRate;
    }
  }
}
```

4

```
// allows ring to shrink
void mouseReleased(){
  isInactive = true;
}
```

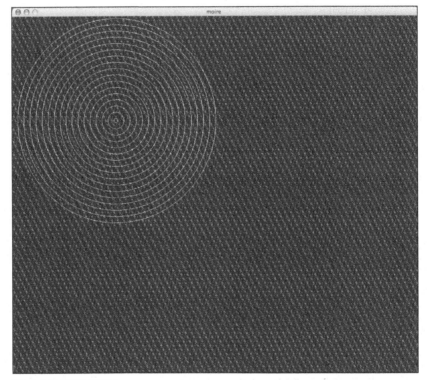

Figure 4-12. Moiré pattern

The final example simulates organic motion. The development of this example is also worth describing, as it's a good illustration of the power of "happy coding mistakes," as I described in Chapter 2.

I originally set out to create an example entitled Springy Serpent. I imagined a series of nodes, connected by tethers, moving around the screen in a snake-like manner, with springs controlling some of the motion of the serpent's body. I'd solved similar problems to this in the past, but I tend to not look at old code when I begin creating, and I couldn't quite visualize (or remember) how to pull this off. I don't necessarily recommend this "start from scratch" approach, and I'd say most coders take the exact opposite approach—using snippets of their older code and not repeating the same mistakes over and over again. One benefit of my illogical approach is the interesting stuff I find along the way. In the process of developing the springy serpent, I made some initial logic errors in my algorithm. I got some of the behavior, but not all of it. I also realized that I really needed to get a piece of paper and do a little more involved math to properly solve the problem. Being impetuous, manic, and very sleep-deprived, I just kept furiously hacking at the code—hoping for some quick (magical) fix; It wasn't going too well, and I actually went so far as to find a pencil. Eventually something emerged, but it didn't look very much like a serpent. Instead, I found a strange, smoky, self-organizing blob (see Figure 4-13). In the end, I think I got something more interesting than I originally planned for, and I learned something in the process—so embrace the chaos! The code to this sketch, entitled Puff, follows. This is not simple code, but it is an excellent demonstration of the expressive power of trig.

```
/* puff
 Ira Greenberg, October 22, 2005 */

// for puff head
float headX;
float headY;
float speedX = .7;
float speedY = .9;

// for puff body
int cells = 2000;
float[]px= new float[cells];
float[]py= new float[cells];
float[]radiiX = new float[cells];
float[]radiiY = new float[cells];
float[]angle = new float[cells];
float[]frequency = new float[cells];
float[]cellRadius = new float[cells];

void setup(){
  size(400, 400);
  // begin in the center
  headX = width/2;
  headY = height/2;

  //fill body arrays
  for (int i=0; i< cells; i++){
    radiiX[i] = random(-7, 7);
    radiiY[i] = random(-4, 4);
    frequency[i]= random(-9, 9);
    cellRadius[i] = random(16, 40);
  }
  frameRate(30);
}

void draw(){
  background(0);
  noStroke();
  fill(255, 255, 255, 5);
```

```
//follow the leader
for (int i =0; i< cells; i++){
  if (i==0){
    px[i] = headX+sin(radians(angle[i]))*radiiX[i];
    py[i] = headY+cos(radians(angle[i]))*radiiY[i];
  }
  else{
    px[i] = px[i-1]+cos(radians(angle[i]))*radiiX[i];
    py[i] = py[i-1]+sin(radians(angle[i]))*radiiY[i];

    //check collision of body
    if (px[i] >= width-cellRadius[i]/2 || px[i] <= cellRadius[i]/2){
      radiiX[i]*=-1;
      cellRadius[i] = random(1, 40);
      frequency[i]= random(-13, 13);
    }
    if (py[i] >= height-cellRadius[i]/2 || py[i] <= cellRadius[i]/2){
      radiiY[i]*=-1;
      cellRadius[i] = random(1, 40);
      frequency[i]= random(-9, 9);
    }
  }
  // draw puff
  ellipse(px[i], py[i], cellRadius[i], cellRadius[i]);
  // set speed of body
  angle[i]+=frequency[i];
}

// set velocity of head
headX+=speedX;
headY+=speedY;

//check boundary collision of head
if (headX >= width-cellRadius[0]/2 || headX <=cellRadius[0]/2){
  speedX*=-1;
}
if (headY >= height-cellRadius[0]/2 || headY <= cellRadius[0]/2){
  speedY*=-1;
}
}
```

As always, there are interesting ways to mess with some of the settings in this sketch to get dramatically different results. I utilized Processing's random() function a lot throughout the example. You might remember that the function has two forms and can take either one or two arguments. The single-argument function generates a random float value between 0 and the value of the argument. The double-argument version of the function generates a random number between the two argument values. Try messing with these numbers to see what happens. Throughout the book, you'll also look at a bunch of other interesting trig experiments, but much more slowly and in detail. There is also a section on trigonometry in Appendix B of the book.

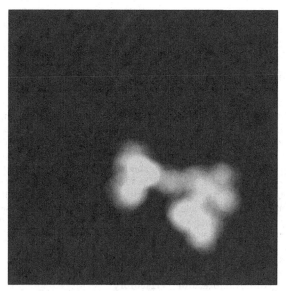

Figure 4-13. Puff

Interactivity

People take for granted that when a mouse or other pointing device is connected to their computer, the computer will respond to all their wants and desires—or at least clicks. Obviously, the computer needs a little more motivation than that. Mouse presses, releases, hovers, enters, exits, moves, and drags are all loosely classified as **mouse events**, which can be further classified more generally as simply events. Event handling is the basis of interactivity. Events can be mouse behavior, but they can also be window events (resizing a window), keyboard events (pressing a key), menu events (selecting from a pull-down menu), or focus events (selecting a dialog window, palette, or text field as the active area, which usually then accepts additional input such as filling in a text field with a word). Essentially, any input or state change that the computer can detect can be processed as an event. There are two main aspects to interactivity or working with events: event detection and the event handling.

Event detection

Processing and Java have a built-in low-level event detection mechanism, which is a good thing. If they didn't, we would be forced to create an endless event loop, constantly checking to see if events were occurring. This approach, called **polling**, is complicated and eats up CPU cycles (CPU processing time). Part of the reason it is potentially confusing deals with the very nature of how the computer works. A single-processor machine (with one CPU) ultimately needs to handle one operation or process at a time. The CPU might be able to handle billions of operations per second, but each process is still distinct. The illusion that a single computer processor is handling simultaneous events is a function of our relatively slow eyes and their inability to see the tiny delays.

Event handling

Returning to Processing and Java's event mechanism, if we don't need to create our own loop to detect events, how is it done? Java's runtime environment, the Java Virtual Machine (JVM), takes care of it for us. In addition, there is an Event class that encapsulates event properties and methods. When an event occurs, the Event class detects it and in a sense broadcasts it throughout the program. How we receive the broadcast and what we do with it is mostly what we have to worry about. This efficient system makes event handling relatively easy in Java and, as you might suspect, even easier in Processing. Here's a simple interactive example in which you can click the screen to randomize the sketch. The event detection code in the example happens within the if statement in the draw() function, checking the mousePressed condition. When the mouse is pressed, the condition evaluates to true and the setRandomStyle() function is called.

```
// click to randomize
float x, y, squareSize;
color bgColor, strokeColor, fillColor;
float strokeWt;
void setup(){
  size(400, 400);
  rectMode(CENTER);
  x = width/2;
  y = height/2;
  setRandomStyle();
  frameRate(30);
}
void draw(){
  background(bgColor);
  strokeWeight(strokeWt);
  stroke(strokeColor);
  fill(fillColor);
  rect(x, y, squareSize, squareSize);
  if (mousePressed){
    setRandomStyle();
  }
}
void setRandomStyle(){
  bgColor = color(random(255), random(255), random(255));
  strokeColor = color(random(255), random(255), random(255));
  fillColor = color(random(255), random(255), random(255));
  strokeWt = random(5, 100);
  squareSize = random(10, 300);
}
```

Events will be covered and implemented much more in future chapters. If you'd like to play with another more elaborate interactive example now, download the Tetherball sketch from the code download area on the friends of ED website (`www.friendsofed.com/`). The sketch includes a fun springing effect, allowing you to drag a bouncy tetherball-like object around the screen.

Summary

If Chapter 3 was a crash course in coding, this chapter has been a crash course in graphics programming. I discussed some general theory as well as a few application areas in the dynamic field of computer graphics. Taking an image apart and looking under the hood at some low-level graphics processing, you examined the anatomy of computer images down to the pixel level, as well as some of the underlying mathematical and procedural models utilized in their creation. You tackled some of the math theory and equations commonly used in graphics programming, and hopefully you got a sense of the expressive power and creative potential of some of these relatively simple equations. Finally, you learned a little about how interactivity works in Java and Processing. Most of the things covered in this chapter will be revisited throughout the book and expanded upon, so please don't stress out if you found this chapter overwhelming. I designed it as a general primer, and I realize that it contains a lot of technical information—not to mention some scary math. I suspect that some readers will want to periodically come back to this chapter, especially those totally new to computer graphics; others might want to review some of the equations or code examples in Appendix B. In the next chapter, you'll explore the Processing language and environment in detail.

4

5 THE PROCESSING ENVIRONMENT

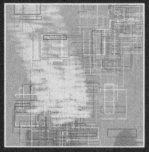

Processing, besides being a language of sorts, is an integrated development environment (IDE)—an IDE created by artists for artists. The Processing development environment is simple to learn and use, and doesn't add to the complexity of learning to program, as with many other IDEs. In fact, the Processing IDE really does substantially simplify the process of coding, even for absolute beginners. Even Flash, which is another very popular IDE of sorts, also geared toward artists, has a steep learning curve, and its complexity can get in the way on pure coding projects. In contrast, the Processing IDE has a well-designed interface and core functionality that allows you to work efficiently; it's a huge improvement over working in your old text editor.

Processing is also a language-specific IDE—a Java IDE—but as you'll soon see, a pretty unique one. Processing's seeming simplicity is deceptive, and in one very significant way, Processing goes further than most other IDEs. Processing has its own built-in procedural programming language that enables coders to write Java graphics programs (**sketches** in Processing speak) without the complexity or rigid object-oriented structure normally required to write Java. In addition, Processing has three modes of working, allowing coders, as they increase their programming literacy, to move from Processing's simplified procedural approach, to a hybrid approach that uses some more-advanced programming constructs, to ultimately working in pure Java—all in the same IDE. This multimode capability makes Processing a great environment in which to learn graphics programming, and it's one of the reasons that it's being included in more and more digital arts curricula at schools around the world.

In this chapter, I'll show you how the IDE works, walk you through the features of the environment, and introduce you to various concepts that are useful to know before you get started.

How it works

When you double-click the Processing icon, the Processing environment opens up, which as mentioned is a Java program—technically a Java application. Java applications run through a Java interpreter, or Java Virtual Machine (JVM), installed on your computer. The JVM was either installed with your operating system, as with OS X, or when you installed Processing (or Java separately), on other platforms. The virtual machine is part of Java's runtime environment, commonly referred to as the JRE. Java also has a software development kit, or JDK. The JRE includes the JVM, Java's core classes, and some supporting files. The JDK includes everything in the JRE, plus a compiler and some additional tools and files. The JVM installed on your system was built for your specific operating system and translates or interprets between your compiled Java programs and your specific operating system (OS). What's cool, or at least efficient, about this approach is that, theoretically, the same code you write on a Mac will run on a Linux or Windows system, with each of the virtual machines on the different platforms doing the translation at runtime. I wrote "theoretically" because there are some cross-platform display issues, but it essentially works. This cross-platform functionality is one of Java's strengths, allowing Java to be used across different operating systems, as well as on the Web and in other devices—all that is required is a JVM.

Returning to Processing—your launched Processing program is being run by the built-in JVM on your computer as a regular Java application. Processing sketches, however, are written within the Processing environment, or from within the running Java application. How can the sketches you write be compiled and then launched by Java if Java is already being used to run the Processing application? This is a good question (if I do say so myself). If you look within the Processing application folder, you'll notice something called jikes (see Figure 5-1).

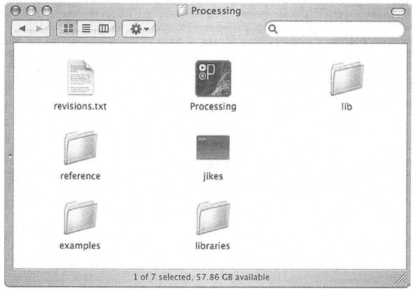

Figure 5-1. Screen capture of the Processing application folder

This is not an exclamation, as in "Holy jikes!" but rather an open source, free Java compiler from IBM. Compilers take the higher-level code we humans write and convert it to a lower-level language that machines like. In some languages, like C and C++, compiling converts your program code to a very low-level machine code that is specific to your operating system. So compiling C code on a Mac yields different machine code than compiling the same code on Windows. However, in Java and Processing, the compiled Java code, called bytecode, will be the same on any platform; and it is the interpreter, or JVM, that is responsible for translating the bytecode for your specific operating system. If you want to learn a little more about jikes, check out http://jikes.sourceforge.net/. In the standard JDK from Sun is another complier, javac, which is also free to use, but not open source.

When you launch the Processing application, which already comes compiled, it's executed, as I stated before, by the JVM installed on your computer. Your Processing sketches, which you write from within the Processing environment, are compiled into Java bytecode (the class files that the JVM can read) by jikes when you run your sketch. Running your sketches causes the Processing application to open a new display window, which is a relatively

5

simple thing to do, and executes your compiled sketch code within the new display window, all by the same virtual machine. From the virtual machine's perspective, your sketch is just another process in the larger running program.

Tour de Processing

Figure 5-2 shows most of the Processing application interface. I didn't include/expand the top menu bar, which I'll cover shortly. You'll notice, at first glance, that the interface is pretty simple, without extra dialogs, panels, inspectors, and the like cluttering up the environment. However, the information you need is visible and accessible. Additionally, the environment has an intuitive, non-techie look and feel, and doesn't seem to have a steep learning curve. As you roll over buttons, you get instant feedback about what they do, in plain simple language (Run, Stop, New, etc.).

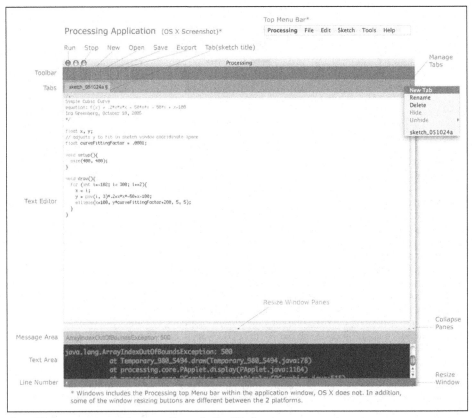

Figure 5-2. Screen capture of the Processing application interface

The Processing window is divided into horizontal bands of varying height. I'll deal with each, from the bottom up.

The **line number**, at the very bottom of the window, shows you what line of code you are currently working on, based on your cursor position.

The **text area** gives you verbose feedback about bugs in your code. It can be scary and frustrating to new coders to see all these errors come up in the text area when they first begin coding; rest assured, it happens to all of us. New coders often struggle to even find the errors in their code, and it can seem impossible that a typo or logic error could still possibly exist in code you've painstakingly gone through numerous times. The errors will likely also seem annoyingly cryptic, but over time you'll learn to understand the messages and more quickly track down your bugs. However, there are times when even experienced coders struggle to eradicate bugs. I usually find taking a break helps (as well as screaming obscenities at the top of my lungs). Eventually, you'll appreciate these verbose error messages and see how valuable they are in the debugging process. Processing also includes two commands, print() and println(), that allow you to output information about your sketch to the text area.

The **message area** gives you quick feedback during saving and exporting, and tells you in plain, simple language about errors in your code.

The **text editor** is where you write your sketch code; it's essentially your old text editor. If you play with it, you'll notice that there are clear feedback color cues, showing you what line your cursor is on, what text is selected, and if a word you typed is a legal keyword in the language.

The **tabs** show you what files you are working with. Tabs are really handy when your sketch requires multiple files. At the right side of the tabs area is a right-facing arrow button. Pressing this button opens a pop-up menu that allows you to create and manage your tabs. When you open an existing sketch in Processing, any Java or PDE files in your sketch directory will be automatically put into the tabs layout. The benefit of this will become clearer when you begin to work with external functions and classes. By default, there will always be at least one tab open, with its name at the bottom of the tab pop-up menu. This tab will be your current main sketch PDE file (it's called a PDE file because .pde is just the suffix that Processing sketches use—it stands for "Processing development environment"). As more tabs are created, you'll see the new tab names at the bottom of the tabs pop-up menu as well. You can select one of these names by clicking on it to give the tab focus (make it the active window) in the Processing project window. When you click on the tabs arrow button, the pop-up menu allows you to do the following:

- Create a new tab
- Rename a tab
- Delete a tab
- Hide/unhide a tab
- Move focus to the previous/next tab

When you create a new tab, you'll be prompted to give it a name. Processing requires PDE and Java file names to begin with a letter or underscore and contain no spaces. You may use numbers in the name after the initial character, and names should be no more than 64 characters in length. If you try to name a PDE or Java file using an illegal character, Processing will rename your file automatically, converting the illegal character to an underscore. For example, the name function 1 will be renamed function_1. In addition, you have the option of adding a .pde or .java suffix. If no suffix is added, Processing assumes the new file is of type PDE. You won't see the .pde suffix displayed in the tabs, but if you look in your project directory, you'll see it there. If you specify .java as a suffix, then the file should be a standard Java file, and you should see the .java suffix in the tab; although the suffix doesn't come up at the bottom of the tabs pop-up menu.

Any other suffix you add will be removed and appended to the root of the name, and the file will be of type PDE. For example, if you accidentally try to save your sketch with the name newfilename.ppe, the full file name will be converted to newfilename_ppe.pde. Again, in the tab, you'll only see the newfilename_ppe part. Finally, if you hide a tab, it does more than just temporarily change the tab's visibility. When you run or export your project, if a tab is hidden, then the file associated with the tab will not be compiled or included in the applet subdirectory. The Hide function is a convenient way to ensure that classes and functions not being used in your final sketch do not unnecessarily bloat your program when you compile. If you accidentally hide a tab, but still reference it in your code, the compiler will give you an error—either "No accessible method," for a missing function; or "Type . . . was not found," for a missing class. If you look in your sketch directory (see Figure 5-3), you'll notice that hidden files get appended with .x after the .pde or .java suffix.

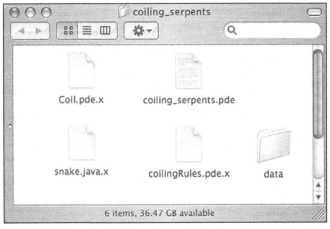

Figure 5-3. Screen capture of a Processing sketch directory

The **toolbar** conveniently contains Processing's six main control buttons. These buttons also have equivalent commands in the menu bar, which I'll cover a bit later. These are not the only commands in the Processing application, but they are probably the most often used ones. From left to right, these buttons are Run, Stop, New, Open, Save, and Export. The following list describes the functions of each (when applicable, I've included the Mac and Windows keyboard shortcuts for each in parentheses after the button name):

- Run **(Cmd+R on OS X; Ctrl+R on Windows)**: Compiles your code, launches a display window, and executes your sketch within this window.

- Stop: Terminates your running program, but leaves the display window open.

- New **(Cmd+N on OS X; Ctrl+N on Windows)**: Creates a new sketch within a new project directory. Both the directory and the PDE file (Processing's own file format) will share this name. By default, new sketches are saved with the root sketch_, the date (in the form yy/mm/dd), and a secondary character beginning with the next alphabetically available character. For example, my current sketch is named sketch_051024a. If I save this sketch using this name, and then create a new sketch, that sketch will be named sketch_051024b; the next one will be sketch_051024c. Be aware that the default preference state in Processing is to delete empty sketches upon quit. Therefore, if you do not enter any code into the text editor window, you will not be able to actually save the project to disk—which I guess makes sense since there's nothing to save in the file. If you want to change this setting, you can do so in the preferences, found under the Processing menu in OS X and the File menu in Windows.

- Open **(Cmd+O on OS X; Ctrl+O on Windows)**: Displays a menu that lets you choose between opening a sketch residing on your local hard drive or across a network, through a standard file navigator; selecting from a list of available sketches, residing within your sketchbook location directory; or loading an example sketch that came bundled with the Processing software, from the examples directory residing within the main Processing directory. You can set the location of your sketchbook, where the sketches you create will reside, through the preferences—again found under the Processing menu in OS X and the File menu in Windows.

- Save **(Cmd+S on OS X; Ctrl+S on Windows)**: Writes the current sketch to disk. You will not be prompted to confirm that you are writing over the previous state. If you want to keep your original sketch and also save the current one, you should use Save As, found under File menu. Again, please note that Processing requires sketch names to begin with a letter or underscore and contain no spaces. You may use numbers in the sketch name after the initial character, and sketch names should be no more than 64 characters in length. If you try to name a Processing sketch using an illegal character, Processing will bark at you and rename your file, converting the illegal character to an underscore.

5

- Export **(Cmd+E on OS X; Ctrl+E on Windows)**: Creates a Java applet of your sketch and places it within an "applet" subdirectory, inside your current sketch directory. Once this subdirectory is created, Processing opens it up for you, displaying five files, which I'll discuss in a moment. Applets are Java programs that can be viewed in any Java-enabled browser, which includes most modern browsers. These browsers have a built-in Java interpreter, more commonly known as the JVM. Java programs can run as applets or as stand-alone applications on the desktop. However, the source code is not identical for applets and applications, so it does take a little work to convert an applet to an application and visa versa—that is, if you're not using Processing. Processing includes the ability to export both Java applets and stand-alone Java applications.

The applet subdirectory contains these five files:

- `index.html`: The HTML page you load into the browser, with the embedded applet.

- `yourfilename.pde`: Your original processing file.

- `yourfilename.jar`: A JAR (Java Archive) file, which is downloaded and run by the browser's virtual machine. It contains the Processing core classes, other custom classes, and any media files (images, fonts, etc.) residing within the "data" subdirectory of your sketch directory. Since everything within the subdirectory is packed into the JAR file when you export, you should remove unneeded data from the subdirectory before exporting. If your sketch doesn't use any external media, you don't need a data subdirectory.

- `yourfilename.java`: A Java file created by Processing from the main sketch (PDE) file. Java files are compiled by the JVM into bytecode (class files). These class files get packed into the JAR file.

- `loading.gif`: The artwork initially shown as your page loads; it's replaced by the applet when it's loaded.

Finally, if you're running Processing in OS X, there are three places in which you can alter the Processing window structure (as shown in Figure 5-2). Some of these adjustments can be made in Windows as well. You can drag the bar between the text editor and message area up and down to resize the window panes. You can resize the entire Processing application window by dragging the lower-right corner of the window. The "collapse panes" buttons (OS X) work as follows: if the window is in its default state, showing both the text editor and the message area, clicking the up arrow expands the message area while collapsing the text editor, and the down arrow does the opposite.

File menu

This menu is pretty straightforward, and most of it should be self-explanatory. In Figure 5-4, the Sketchbook submenus are exploded. Please note that in Windows, the Processing menu is contained within the Processing application window, while in OS X, the menu system is separate from the Processing application. Aside from appearances, the two menus on the different platforms have identical functionality and command sets.

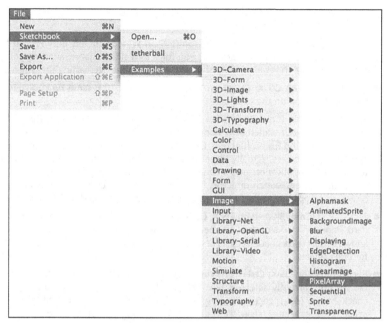

Figure 5-4. Screen capture of Processing's File ➤ Sketchbook submenus

The File menu contains the following eight commands:

- New **(Cmd+N on OS X; Ctrl+N on Windows)**: This has the same functionality as the New button on the toolbar.

- Sketchbook: The top of the Sketchbook submenu includes the Open command, which has the same functionality as the Open button on the toolbar, discussed previously. Additional content within the Sketchbook submenu includes sketches you've created, residing at your sketchbook location, specified in the Processing preferences; and an Examples directory. The Sketchbook submenu checks for PDE files, each enclosed within their own directory, within the specified Sketchbook directory. The PDE file and its directory must have the same name. You can also create additional outer directories (for organizational purposes) around your related sketches. Processing's Examples directory, which I'll discuss in a moment, is organized this way. PDE files not enclosed within a same-named directory will not be visible from the Sketchbook submenu. You can still explicitly open them with the Open command, but Processing will alert you that a directory is required and will actually create one and move your file into it when you click OK—which is pretty cool. By default, Processing generates this required directory and naming structure whenever you create a new sketch, so you only need to mess with this stuff if you really want to. The Examples directory, at the bottom of the Sketchbook submenu, is installed with Processing, in the same directory as the Processing application. It is possible to expand the Examples directory simply by placing your own sketch examples within it.

- Save **(Cmd+S on OS X; Ctrl+S on Windows)**: This has the same functionality as the Save button on the toolbar.

- Save As **(Cmd+Shift+S on OS X; Ctrl+Shift+S on Windows)**: This is similar to the Save function, except that it prompts you for a new sketch name, allowing you to save the current changed version of your sketch without overwriting the original.

- Export **(Cmd+E on OS X; Ctrl+E on Windows)**: This has the same functionality as the Export button on the toolbar.

- Export Application **(Cmd+Shift+E on OS X; Ctrl+Shift+E on Windows)**: This allows you to export your sketch as a stand-alone, platform-specific executable application. Similar to the Export function, Export Application generates an entire directory structure (in this case, actually three separate directories) with all the required files to launch an application under Linux, OS X, and Windows. This command also opens the current sketch directory, revealing the three newly created application directories (application.linux, application.macosx, and application.windows).

- Page Setup **(Cmd+Shift+P on OS X; Ctrl+Shift+P on Windows)**: This opens the standard Page Setup dialog box to specify printing options. This function has some known bugs. Please check http://dev.processing.org/bugs/show_bug.cgi?id=435 for bug updates.

- Print **(Cmd+P on OS X; Ctrl+P on Windows)**: This prints all the code within the main tab or the currently selected tab. This function has some known bugs. Please check http://dev.processing.org/bugs/show_bug.cgi?id=27 and http://dev.processing.org/bugs/show_bug.cgi?id=28 for bug updates, as well as the Processing discourse board, at http://processing.org/discourse/yabb_beta/YaBB.cgi, for the most current information about Processing's printing capabilities.

Edit menu

Figure 5-5 shows a screenshot of Processing's Edit menu.

Figure 5-5. Screen capture of Processing's Edit menu

The Edit menu contains the following eight commands:

- Undo **(Cmd+Z on OS X; Ctrl+Z on Windows)**: Cancels the previous action, including any addition or deletion of code within the text editor. To reverse Undo, select Redo.

- Redo **(Cmd+Y on OS X; Ctrl+Y on Windows)**: Reverses the last Undo command, restoring your sketch to the state immediately prior to selecting Undo.

- Cut **(Cmd+X on OS X; Ctrl+X on Windows)**: Copies the selected text into clipboard memory and removes the selected text from the text editor.

- Copy **(Cmd+C on OS X; Ctrl+C on Windows)**: Copies the selected text into clipboard memory and leaves the copied text as is within the text editor.

- Paste **(Cmd+V on OS X; Ctrl+V on Windows)**: Adds the contents of the clipboard memory to the text editor window at the cursor's position, replacing any selected text.

- Select All **(Cmd+A on OS X; Ctrl+A on Windows)**: Highlights all the text within the text editor window.

- Find **(Cmd+F on OS X; Ctrl+F on Windows)**: Allows you to find and replace keywords within the text editor window. You can replace individual words or all instances of words, and optionally specify whether searches should be case sensitive or not.

- Find Next **(Cmd+G on OS X; Ctrl+G on Windows)**: Allows quick and persistent searches of the last keyword you entered into the Find field. For example, if I attempt to find the keyword "ball" with the Find command, later on I can simply select Find Next, and the next occurrence of the word "ball" will be highlighted in the text editor. The keyword used by Find Next does not persist between Processing sessions—so if you quit and restart Processing, you'll lose your keyword in the Find command field.

Sketch menu

Figure 5-6 shows a screenshot of Processing's Sketch menu.

Figure 5-6. Screen capture of Processing's Sketch menu

The Sketch menu contains the following six commands:

- Run **(Cmd+R on OS X; Ctrl+R on Windows)**: Has the same functionality as the Run button on the toolbar.

- Present **(Cmd+Shift+R on OS X; Ctrl+Shift+R on Windows)**: Creates a full-screen display of your executing sketch. The sketch window is centered against a neutral background. You can stop the display by selecting the Stop command in the lower-left corner of the screen, or by pressing the Esc key.

- Stop: Stops a running sketch.

- Import Library: Adds a required import statement to the top of your sketch, allowing you to use the classes in the imported code library. The current core Processing libraries (which can be selected from the Import Library drop-down menu) include the following:

  - candy
  - dxf
  - javascript
  - net
  - opengl
  - pdf
  - serial
  - videos
  - xml

  If you select Sketch ➤ Import Library ➤ opengl, then the following line of code is added to the top of your sketch: import processing.opengl.*;. Using import statements is standard practice in Java, for which related classes of code are grouped in directories called packages. Packages allow you to organize code libraries for reuse and distribution. They also provide a way of helping to ensure that class names don't collide or interfere with one another. For example, if I create a class called Ball, and you create a class called Ball, and both of our classes are within a common code library, Java won't know which one to use. We can solve this problem by putting each of our classes in a uniquely named package (directory) and then importing the package with the version of the Ball class we need. Then, even if we use both Ball classes, as long as the class files reside in their own distinctive packages, there will be no naming conflict.

- Show Sketch Folder **(Cmd+K on OS X; Ctrl+K on Windows)**: Opens up the directory of your current sketch. Normally, your current sketch directory will reside within your main sketchbook directory. If you remember, your main sketchbook location is specified in the preferences.

- Add File: Opens a file navigator, allowing you to load an image, font, or other media into a data subdirectory within your sketch directory. If no data directory exists, Processing will automatically create one for you.

Tools menu

Figure 5-7 shows a screenshot of Processing's Tools menu.

Figure 5-7. Screen capture of Processing's Tools menu

The Tools menu contains the following five commands:

- Auto Format **(Cmd+T on OS X; Ctrl+T on Windows)**: This command attempts to format the code layout for optimal readability. Skipped lines, also referred to as whitespace, are retained. Syntax errors, such as missing semicolons, are not corrected. Auto Format was originally called "beautify," which is the name of a similar function in Processing's forebear, Design By Numbers (DBN). Here is an example of how Auto Format works. If I type the following code into the text editor and select Auto Format:

```
void setup(){}void draw(){}
```

then the code will be reformatted to the following:

```
void setup(){
}
void draw(){
}
```

- Create Font: One of the challenges of designing for the Web is the incompatibility of system resources such as installed fonts, which will often be different from machine to machine and across platforms. One solution is to use only a very limited set of fonts that can be assumed to be installed on most systems—such as Arial, Times, and Sans. However, from a design perspective, this is pretty limiting. Another solution is to bundle bitmap **glyphs** (actual raster graphics of each character in a font family) with a project to allow the use of fonts that aren't likely to be installed on a user's machine. The Create Font command does just this. The command opens the Create Font dialog box, which allows you to select any font installed within your system (see Figure 5-8). This dialog includes the options Size, Filename, Smooth (for anti-aliasing), and All Characters. The font generated is a copy of an existing font in your system, created in the VLW font format and installed within a data subdirectory in the current sketch directory. Similar to loading other media into Processing, a data directory is automatically created, if one doesn't already exist. There are some memory concerns involved in creating fonts this way. The larger the font size you specify, the more memory the font will use, as each font includes the actual raster information needed to draw the individual characters; normally, fonts are created using vector data. In addition, the Smooth option also requires a little more memory, as does the All Character option, which includes

155

non-English characters, such as ü and Å. As an example, I generated a series of fonts, based on the font AbadiMT-CondensedExtraBold, under OS X. At 48 points, with no options selected, the font was 144 KB; with only the Smooth option selected, it went up to 164 KB; and with the Smooth and All Character options selected, it went up to 212 KB. At 12 points, with no options selected, it went down to 24 KB.

Figure 5-8. Screen capture of Processing's Create Font dialog box

- Color Picker: This is a simple color picker, showing you the HSB (hue, saturation, brightness), RGB, and hexadecimal color values of the color selected (see Figure 5-9).

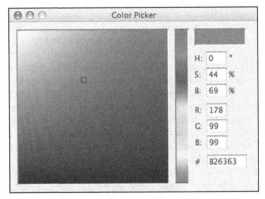

Figure 5-9. Screen capture of Processing's Color Picker dialog

156

- Copy for Discourse: It is very common for Processing users, especially those currently stuck and/or confused (which happens to all of us), to paste code snippets on the Processing discourse board. Unfortunately, the pasted results don't always look very good, as some of the formatting gets lost. Some of us with HTML backgrounds simply try inserting HTML tags directly in our code, to fix the formatting—to no avail. The Processing discourse board uses YaBB, a free, open source bulletin board system. For security reasons, YaBB doesn't allow the use of HTML tags in posts. Thus, you're forced to learn yet another proprietary tag system, called YaBB Code (YaBBC) to fix your formatting. *Or*, you can simply select Copy for Discourse, and Processing will write the YaBBC for you—cool indeed!

  Here's how it works: when you select Copy for Discourse, your sketch code is copied to your computer's clipboard and converted into YaBBC for the discourse board; simply paste to the board to recreate your Processing sketch code. In reality, YaBBC is pretty darn close to HTML, so it doesn't take an experienced coder much time to learn it—but why waste the brain cells? To learn more about YaBB/YaBBC, visit www.yabbforum.com/community/YaBB.pl?action=help.

- Archive Sketch: This command creates a ZIP archive of the current sketch, prompting you with a Save dialog to choose a location to save the archive.

Help menu

Figure 5-10 shows a screenshot of Processing's Help menu.

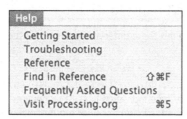

Figure 5-10. Screen capture of Processing's Help menu

The Help menu contains the following:

- Getting Started: This launches your default web browser, loading information on the Processing environment. This functionality does not require an Internet connection, as the information is stored locally within the Processing application directory. The information is divided into three sections. The first, Overview, covers the Processing development environment, Processing's three programming modes, and the different rendering modes. The second section, Platforms, lists the supported platforms and some platform-specific information (both the good news and the less-than-good news). One of the nicest aspects of the Processing community is the transparency and lack of marketing hype when it comes to what Processing can (currently) do and not do. The last section, Export, provides information about exporting your sketches as both applets and applications. For the very latest information, refer to http://processing.org/reference/environment/index.html.

- Troubleshooting: This page covers many of the common "Help me, something's not right with the Processing universe!" concerns voiced on the discourse board; you can think of this page as the triage FAQ.

- Reference: This provides you with reference to the entire Processing language API, which is stored locally on your hard drive. This is the place to go to learn about specific commands in the Processing language. Please note that this page opens to an abridged language reference. You'll need to select the Extended option to see the entire language. For the very latest information, refer to http://processing. org/reference/index.html.

- Find in Reference (Cmd+Shift+F on OS X; Ctrl+Shift+F on Windows): Select a word in your sketch and then select Find in Reference. If the word exists in the Processing API, the relevant reference information will be opened in your default web browser.

- Frequently Asked Questions: This command opens a list of questions and answers to some common Processing issues. The online version is at http://processing.org/ faq.html.

- Visit Processing.org (Cmd+5 on OS X; Ctrl+5 on Windows): This command launches your default web browser and loads http://processing.org/.

Programming modes

Processing supports three different modes of coding, allowing users with different skill and experience levels to work most efficiently and comfortably, all within the same environment. It is even possible to mix these different modes within the same project.

Basic mode

In basic mode, users simply type individual lines of commands sequentially into the text editor window, without the added complexity of more complex structures, such as functions or classes. This is an excellent mode for brand new coders to learn about programming fundamentals—such as basic syntax, coordinates, variables, and loops—and also to get more familiar with the Processing language and environment. The following code is structured in basic mode and generates a simple tan circle, with a black stroke on a lavender background:

```
size(200, 200);
background(130, 130, 240);
stroke(0);
fill(200, 150, 101);
int x = 100;
int y = 100;
int w = 140;
int h = 140;
ellipse(x, y, w, h);
```

Continuous mode

In continuous mode, users build upon what they've learned in basic mode, with the edition of code structures called functions and classes. As you recall, functions are the main building blocks used in procedural programming, and are simply groupings of lines of code that execute only when they are explicitly called. Classes are much more complicated structures than functions, and are utilized in OOP. I'll cover classes in detail in Chapter 8. In basic mode, code is executed linearly (line by line). Functions and classes, on the other hand, allow code to be executed nonlinearly. These structures are only executed when they are explicitly called, not when they are initially read into memory.

In continuous mode, two basic Processing functions are provided, which allow you to add your own custom structures (functions or classes). The two functions are as follows:

```
void setup(){
}

void draw(){
}
```

The setup() function is called only once, at the start of the program. This is the place where you normally initialize variables that will be used later in the program. Adding the setup() function to your sketch allows you to add your own additional custom functions and classes. The draw() function adds animation capabilities to your sketch and has a built-in loop, more accurately called a thread or timer. By default, adding the draw() function to your sketch causes any code between the curly braces of this structure to continuously execute. There are a number of ways of controlling this behavior, which I'll cover in Chapter 11. You can also read more about Processing's draw() function in Appendix A.

The following sketch example is built in continuous mode and uses two custom functions, fadeScreen() and paintOutlines(). The sketch is a little drawing program. I've added comments throughout the sketch to explain the program flow, although I don't necessarily expect you to fully grasp the code. The sketch allows you to draw by moving and also dragging the mouse (holding down the mouse button as you move the mouse). A screenshot of the output of the sketch is shown in Figure 5-11.

```
/*
Drawing Shapes
Ira Greenberg, November 2, 2005
*/

//declare global variables
float  radiusX, radiusY;

//controls rate of screen fade
int screenFadeValue = 20;

//controls maximum size of shape
int sizeMax = 30;
```

5

159

```
//setup structure runs once
void setup(){
  size(400, 400);
  background(130, 130, 240);
  noFill();
}

/*draw function begins loop
 required by mouseMoved and mouseDragged
 functions later in the code*/
void draw(){
}

/*custom function incrementally
 paints the screen-called when
 the mouse is pressed*/
void fadeScreen(){
  fill(130, 130, 240, screenFadeValue);
  noStroke();
  rect(0, 0, width, height);
}

/*custom function paints shapes,
 boolean argument 'isDragged' controls
 shape style*/
void paintShapes(boolean isDragged){
  if (isDragged){
    noStroke();
    ellipse(mouseX, mouseY, radiusX, radiusY);
  }
  else {
    noFill();
    stroke(random(255));
    rect(mouseX, mouseY, random(sizeMax), random(sizeMax));
  }
}

/* set shape size and
 fill color on press*/
void mousePressed(){
  // call custom function to clear screen
  fadeScreen();
  radiusX = random(sizeMax);
  radiusY = random(sizeMax);
  // set fill color for drawing
  fill(random(255), random(255), random(255), 100);
}
```

```
// paint stroked rectangles
void mouseMoved(){
  // call custom function
  paintShapes(false);
}

// paint filled ellipses
void mouseDragged(){
  // call custom function
  paintShapes(true);
}
```

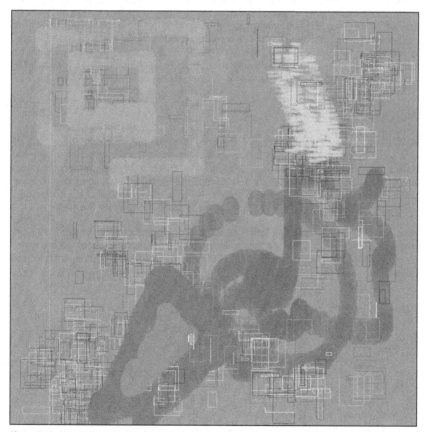

Figure 5-11. Screen capture of the Drawing Shapes sketch

Java mode

This mode allows you to work in pure Java, from directly within the Processing text editor. Java mode is extremely flexible, giving you access to the entire Java API. However, this mode is for advanced users who already have a working knowledge of Java. I'll discuss Java mode in more detail in Chapter 14.

Rendering modes

Processing, as of this writing, has three rendering modes: JAVA2D, P3D, and OPENGL. The mode can be explicitly set as an optional argument within Processing's size() method. For example, to use the P3D rendering mode, you would write: size(200, 200, P3D);. The rendering modes control how visual data is rendered, or converted to pixels on the screen. In addition to these three modes, there is a fourth mode, called P2D, that will likely be functional in the near future (it very well may be active by the time you're reading this). P2D is an alternative renderer (obviously for 2D rendering) to JAVA2D.

JAVA2D mode

JAVA2D uses Java's 2D graphics library for creating 2D rendering. According to Sun, Java 2D is "a set of classes for advanced 2D graphics and imaging." The library contains over 100 classes organized into packages according to related functionality (e.g., imaging, drawing, and color). JAVA2D is the default rendering mode in Processing. Thus, when no rendering argument is explicitly specified within the size() function, JAVA2D is used. Coders normally don't bother adding the JAVA2D argument to the size() call for this reason.

Here is a JAVA2D example that generates a polygon, in this case an octagon. You can change the value of the sides variable to generate other types of polygons. All the examples in the book thus far have been in JAVA2D mode. Figure 5-12 shows the output of the example.

```
/*
Polygon
Ira Greenberg, November 3, 2005
*/

// declare variables
int sides = 8; // change to create other polys
float angle;
float radius = 100;
float px, py, cx, cy;
float[]ptsX= new float[sides];
float[]ptsY= new float[sides];

//initialize sketch
void setup(){
  size(200, 200, JAVA2D);
```

```
  cx = width/2;
  cy = height/2;
  background(255);

 // collect points to plot shape
  for (int i = 0; i< sides; i++){
    px = cx+cos(radians(angle))*radius;
    py = cy+sin(radians(angle))*radius;
    ptsX[i] = px;
    ptsY[i] = py;
    angle+=360/sides;
  }
  // call custom function
  drawShape();
}

//custom function plots a polygon
void drawShape(){
  noFill();
  for (int i = 0; i< sides; i++){
    // if last point, connect to initial point to close shape
    if (i == sides-1){
      line(ptsX[i], ptsY[i], ptsX[0], ptsY[0]);
    }
    else {
      line(ptsX[i], ptsY[i], ptsX[i+1], ptsY[i+1]);
    }
  }
}
```

5

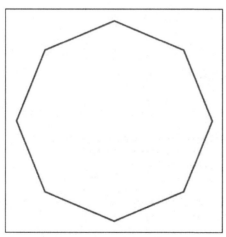

Figure 5-12. Screen capture of the Polygon sketch

P3D mode

P3D mode gives you access to a custom 3D engine in Processing. A 3D engine is just software (no oil or gears) that allows you to deal with a z-axis, in addition to the standard x- and y-axes. In 3D, geometry is calculated in three dimensions, which is just a simple math problem for a computer. However, the darn computer screen is only 2D, so the engine has to translate the 3D data back to a 2D screen projection. In the real world, we perceive images decreasing in size as they move farther away from us. We can simulate this virtually (both with traditional materials and through software) by using a system of perspective. I'm sure some of you remember doing simple two and three-point perspective exercises in an intro art class. Perspective works similarly in P3D mode, but without the need to grab a ruler or get your hands dirty. 3D-to-2D projections on the computer are generally tied to the concept of a virtual camera, which is capable of very wide-angle views (in which things are large, close, and often distorted—think fish-eye lens) as well as very distant views.

Besides virtual camera capabilities, P3D has virtual lights and simple texture mapping (image mapping), allowing an image to be attached to the points (vertices) of 3D geometry. This capability, called u-v mapping, allows image maps on the geometry to move with the form. P3D mode is built for speed, a little at the expense of rendering quality. However, P3D mode is a great and relatively easy way to begin experimenting with coding 3D with a minimal amount of code and complexity. The following short example rotates three concentric polyhedra (polyhedra are basically 3D polygons) and also responds to both the x and y mouse positions. Figure 5-13 shows the output of the sketch.

```
/*
Rotating Polyhedra
Ira Greenberg, November 3, 2005
*/

//declare variables
float rotY;
float rotX;

void setup(){
  size (400, 400, P3D);
  frameRate(30);
}
void draw(){
  background(255);
  /* ensures shapes are drawn at the
  center of the display window. In addition,
  mouse y postion controls the distance
  the shapes are drawn along the z-axis.
  As the shapes moves further into space,
  they will diminish in size*/
  translate(width/2, height/2, mouseY-100);
```

```
// rotate around Y and X axes
rotateY(rotY+=.05);
rotateX(rotX+=.1);
// mouse x position controls level
// of detail of sphere geometry
sphereDetail(mouseX/32);
fill(0);
stroke(255);
//draw sphere
sphere(30);
fill(50, 50, 50, 175);
noStroke();
//draw box
box(80);
noFill();
sphereDetail(8);
stroke(0);
// draw larger outer sphere
sphere(80);
}
```

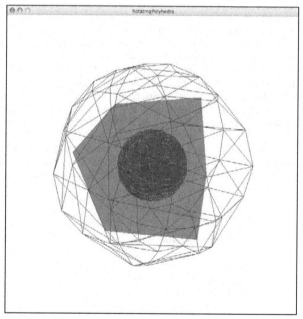

Figure 5-13. Screen capture of the Rotating Polyhedra sketch

OPENGL mode

P3D mode utilizes a software-based 3D engine, meaning that all the 3D calculations are handled by Java, just as normal 2D calculations are; the 3D math is crunched and converted to 2D data before being sent to the graphics hardware to draw the image to the screen. The hardware isn't even aware the data began life as 3D geometry. However, your graphics hardware has the capability to crunch numbers, and in fact can do it much faster than Java. The trick, though, is in communicating directly with the graphics hardware to speed things up.

OpenGL is a platform-independent library that functions as an interface between your code and the graphics hardware. OpenGL was developed in 1992 by Silicon Graphics, but is now overseen by a large group of organizations, under the heading OpenGL Architecture Review Board. Designed as a set of specifications, OpenGL is platform agnostic and can be utilized by practically all systems that have OpenGL-accelerated hardware. Processing and Java interface with OpenGL through JOGL. JOGL, developed by the Game Technology Group at Sun, is technically considered a Java binding (as in "the ties that bind") to OpenGL, and gives Processing sketches that use the OPENGL rendering mode the ability to render more stuff faster and at larger sizes. However, to benefit from this mode, you need an OpenGL-accelerated graphics card. Fortunately, most modern machines have one. To learn more about OpenGL, see www.opengl.org/; and to learn more about JOGL, see https://jogl.dev.java.net/.

Utilizing the OpenGL library couldn't be simpler in Processing. Simply select Sketch ➤ Import Library ➤ opengl, which adds an import line to your sketch, and then add the OPENGL string as a third argument to the size function call: size (800, 600, OPENGL);. The following 3D example (shown in Figure 5-14) can be run in either P3D or OPENGL rendering mode; simply change the third size argument from OPENGL to P3D. It is worth trying both 3D modes to get a sense of how hardware acceleration dramatically impacts performance. One word of caution to beginners though: 3D programming is difficult—even Processing's greatly simplified version. If you're feeling overwhelmed from information overload, don't worry about the 3D renderers. I won't cover them until the last two chapters in the book, at which time you'll be ready. I do recommend running the example to see what it does. It's a little complicated, though, so unless you have prior coding experience, I wouldn't spend too much time dwelling on it. 3D can be tough, but also pretty cool.

```
/*
Space Junk
Ira Greenberg, November 4, 2005
*/

/*need to import opengl library to use OPENGL
 rendering mode for hardware acceleration*/
import processing.opengl.*;

//used for oveall rotation
float ang;
```

```
//cube count-lower/raise to test P3D/OPENGL performance
int limit = 600;

//array for all cubes
Cube[]cubes = new Cube[limit];

void setup(){
  //try substituting P3D for OPENGL
  //argument to test performance
  size(800, 550, OPENGL);

  //instantiate cubes, passing in random vals for size and postion
  for (int i = 0; i< cubes.length; i++){
    cubes[i] = new Cube(int(random(-20, 20)), int(random(-20, 20)), ➡
      int(random(-20, 20)), int(random(-340, 340)), ➡
      int(random(-340, 340)), int(random(-340, 340)));
  }
  frameRate(30);
}

void draw(){
  background(0);
  fill(200);

  //set up some different colored lights
  pointLight(51, 102, 255, 65, 60, 100);
  pointLight(200, 40, 60, -65, -60, -150);

  //raise overall light in scene
  ambientLight(70, 70, 10);

  /*center geometry in display window.
   you can change 3rd argument ('0')
   to move block group closer(+)/further(-)*/
  translate(width/2, height/2, 150);

  //rotate around y and x axes
  rotateY(radians(ang));
  rotateX(radians(ang));

  //draw cubes
  for (int i = 0; i< cubes.length; i++){
    cubes[i].drawCube();
  }
  //used in rotate function calls above
  ang++;
}
```

5

```
//simple Cube class, based on Quads
class Cube {

  //properties
  int w, h, d;
  int shiftX, shiftY, shiftZ;

  //constructor
  Cube(int w, int h, int d, int shiftX, int shiftY, int shiftZ){
    this.w = w;
    this.h = h;
    this.d = d;
    this.shiftX = shiftX;
    this.shiftY = shiftY;
    this.shiftZ = shiftZ;
  }

  /*main cube drawing method, which looks
   more confusing than it really is. It's
   just a bunch of rectangles drawn for
   each cube face*/
  void drawCube(){
    beginShape(QUADS);
    //front face
    vertex(-w/2 + shiftX, -h/2 + shiftY, -d/2 + shiftZ);
    vertex(w + shiftX, -h/2 + shiftY, -d/2 + shiftZ);
    vertex(w + shiftX, h + shiftY, -d/2 + shiftZ);
    vertex(-w/2 + shiftX, h + shiftY, -d/2 + shiftZ);

    //back face
    vertex(-w/2 + shiftX, -h/2 + shiftY, d + shiftZ);
    vertex(w + shiftX, -h/2 + shiftY, d + shiftZ);
    vertex(w + shiftX, h + shiftY, d + shiftZ);
    vertex(-w/2 + shiftX, h + shiftY, d + shiftZ);

    //left face
    vertex(-w/2 + shiftX, -h/2 + shiftY, -d/2 + shiftZ);
    vertex(-w/2 + shiftX, -h/2 + shiftY, d + shiftZ);
    vertex(-w/2 + shiftX, h + shiftY, d + shiftZ);
    vertex(-w/2 + shiftX, h + shiftY, -d/2 + shiftZ);

    //right face
    vertex(w + shiftX, -h/2 + shiftY, -d/2 + shiftZ);
    vertex(w + shiftX, -h/2 + shiftY, d + shiftZ);
    vertex(w + shiftX, h + shiftY, d + shiftZ);
    vertex(w + shiftX, h + shiftY, -d/2 + shiftZ);
```

```
//top face
vertex(-w/2 + shiftX, -h/2 + shiftY, -d/2 + shiftZ);
vertex(w + shiftX, -h/2 + shiftY, -d/2 + shiftZ);
vertex(w + shiftX, -h/2 + shiftY, d + shiftZ);
vertex(-w/2 + shiftX, -h/2 + shiftY, d + shiftZ);

//bottom face
vertex(-w/2 + shiftX, h + shiftY, -d/2 + shiftZ);
vertex(w + shiftX, h + shiftY, -d/2 + shiftZ);
vertex(w + shiftX, h + shiftY, d + shiftZ);
vertex(-w/2 + shiftX, h + shiftY, d + shiftZ);

endShape();

//add some rotation to each box for pizazz.
rotateY(radians(1));
rotateX(radians(1));
rotateZ(radians(1));
    }
}
```

Figure 5-14. Screen capture of the Space Junk sketch

Summary

This chapter has looked at the Processing environment in depth, and how its simple, clean, highly functional interface provides an intuitive and friendly environment for new coders and an efficient workspace for seasoned developers. Built on top of Java, Processing utilizes a Java interpreter or virtual machine installed within your operating system as well as within the browser. Offering three working paths, or programming modes (basic, continuous, and Java), Processing supports multiple skill levels and learning styles, all within the same environment; you can even combine these different approaches in the same sketch. Finally, I covered Processing's exciting 3D rendering options, including a look at a fast 3D software engine and the OpenGL library. The next chapter will begin Part 2 of the book, the tutorial-based section that will help you put the theory into practice.

PART TWO **PUTTING THEORY INTO PRACTICE**

I've been looking forward to writing this part of the book—this is the part where you can focus less on programming theory and language details, and begin playing with this fascinating medium—which is really what this book is all about. Please try not to worry—if you haven't quite mastered all the theory and memorized the entire Processing API, I'll be revisiting all this in the context of exploring fundamental aesthetic principles. In the next few chapters, you'll be using Processing and code as an experimental, creative medium, not unlike how you would use more traditional materials. In addition, you'll see how the code medium is distinctive, vis-à-vis other materials, with its own underlying materiality, expressive potential, and aesthetic. This examination will naturally also include concepts of craft, process, and personal expression. I recommend that you keep the Processing environment open as you work through these hands-on chapters, and run the examples as they are covered.

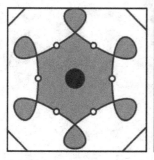  

6 LINES

This chapter will concentrate on lines and how they are represented though code. You'll also look at how lines can represent more multidimensional space, such as shapes and volume.

It's all about points

Before you can understand a line, you need to move back one dimension and take a look at points. Here is arguably the simplest graphic program you can write in any language (see Figure 6-1):

```
point(50, 50);
```

Figure 6-1. Single-point sketch

I mentioned before in the book that a point really has no dimension. Wikipedia says of points: "A point in Euclidean geometry has no size, orientation, or any other feature except position." Thus, your point, as output in Processing, is arguably a tiny square, with a width and height of a 1 pixel. However, what fun would it be to plot a point that didn't appear? In fact, your point is really a Processing line, with the same starting and ending points. The following line function call will yield the same result as the previous point function call:

```
line(50, 50, 50, 50);
```

However, this second approach is more complicated than necessary—it's certainly better to only have to pass two arguments instead of four—so stick with the point() function. Because point(x, y) is implemented internally with line(x, y, x, y), if you want to change the color of a point, you need to use the stroke() function, not fill().

There aren't many things you can do staring at a single static point, other than perhaps sitting lotus style and meditating on its oneness—which does have some value. However, enlightenment-seeking aside, let's add another point (see Figure 6-2):

```
point(33, 50);
point(66, 50);
```

Figure 6-2. Two-point sketch

Adding another point really changes things; it brings up issues of symmetry, balance, and the gestalt (seeing a face), and begins to suggest a line.

Now add a third point (see Figure 6-3):

```
point(25, 50);
point(50, 50);
point(75, 50);
```

Figure 6-3. Three-point sketch

The line gestalt is certainly getting pretty strong now. The three dots divide top and bottom and have a certain horizontal velocity as your eye sweeps across them.

Now add some code to format the display window, and also add a couple more points (see Figure 6-4):

```
size(300, 300);
background(0);
stroke(255);
point(30, 150);
point(60, 150);
point(90, 150);
point(120, 150);
point(150, 150);
point(180, 150);
point(210, 150);
point(240, 150);
point(270, 150);
```

Figure 6-4. Emerging line sketch

This is beginning to look like a real program, and it also has an insistent line. There is something simple and beautiful about the sharpness and delicateness of the white points against the black. You'll notice that I called stroke(255), which sets the stroke state of the sketch to white. I use the term "stroke state" because any drawing executed after the stroke(255) call that involves rendering a stroke will be white, until I explicitly make another call to change the rendering state of the stroke color—for example, stroke(127);. I discuss the idea of a rendering state in the color section of the language reference, found in Appendix A. The sketch is now 12 lines (of code) long and beginning to get a little unwieldy, especially for making global changes to the program. For example, if you want to now add a tenth point and still keep the line centered in the display window, it's time-consuming (and annoying) to have to go and change the value for each point. There are two ways to simplify this process. The first is to base your point positions on the size and shape of the display window, and the second is to add a looping structure that will handle the iteration for you.

Here's a solution for using ten points, implementing the first improvement:

```
size(300, 300);
background(0);
stroke(255);
point((width/11)*1, height/2);
point((width/11)*2, height/2);
point((width/11)*3, height/2);
point((width/11)*4, height/2);
point((width/11)*5, height/2);
point((width/11)*6, height/2);
point((width/11)*7, height/2);
point((width/11)*8, height/2);
point((width/11)*9, height/2);
point((width/11)*10, height/2);
```

This solution is procedurally an improvement—it uses the computer to handle the calculation of the division by 11. Next, I'll show you how to implement a while loop.

Streamlining the sketch with a while loop

```
size(300, 300);
background(0);
stroke(255);
int i = 1;
while (i<11){
  point((width/11)*i, height/2);
  i++;
}
```

This has gotten the sketch down to eight lines. If you really want to, you can shave it further by a line or two, which I'll show you shortly. Although the while loop solution is denser, the reduction in lines of code, I think, makes it more worthwhile than the previous solution. For example, if you had 100 points, the complexity vs. the convenience clearly would become an even more palatable trade-off. Before you squeeze the code down yet further, I want to go over each line of the sketch to make sure you are following along. If this stuff looks completely unfamiliar, I suspect you began the book after Chapter 3—which is OK. However, I do cover the fundamentals of programming, including loops, in detail in Chapter 3, so you'll want to review some of this stuff. If you are a seasoned coder, you can probably skip or skim the following description.

Line 1 sets the display size with the function call size(300, 300);. This is a standard Processing function call, passing two arguments (display window width and display window height). The next two function calls work very similarly, each taking an argument and setting the background color and the stroke color. You may remember that it is possible to set a background or stroke color with more arguments. For example, background(255, 255, 0) creates a yellow background. Next in the sketch I declare and initialize a variable i of type int. Declaring i of the int primitive type means that i can only be assigned integer values. For example, if I try to assign 2.3 to i (i = 2.3;), I'll get the following compiler error:

> The type of the right sub-expression, "float", is not assignable to the variable, of type "int".

Errors like this can be annoying to new coders, but this type checking mechanism is really there to help you, so you don't make a hard-to-find mistake that gets buried in code—which can lead to a much more annoying bug (as well as uncontrolled cussing). The while loop runs over and over, until some explicit limit is reached. In this case, the while loop will run as long as i is less than 11. Since i keeps increasing in value, it is also convenient to use i in your programs, as is done in setting the point position calculation point(width/11*i, height/2);. The last line in the while loop increments the value of i by 1. If I don't do this, my loop will never end. Hopefully this seems pretty straightforward.

I mentioned a paragraph or so back that you could still trim a line or two off the sketch; the first way is to increment the counter i within another expression. Here's the program, one line thinner:

```
size(300, 300);
background(0);
stroke(255);
int i = 1;
while (i<11){
  point(width/11*i++, height/2);
}
```

One of the trade-offs of condensing code like this is that the code becomes slightly harder to read. Finally, if you replace with while loop with a for loop, you can also remove the line int i = 1;. Make sure that you also remove the ++ after the i in the point() function call.

Streamlining the sketch further with a for loop

```
size(300, 300);
background(0);
stroke(255);
for  (int i=1; i<11; i++){
  point(width/11*i, height/2);
}
```

This is pretty lean now. However, what would make this structure even better and more usable as a multipurpose code block would be the removal of the number 11, which we call a "magic number" in programming. **Magic numbers** are constant values stuck in the code—usually hastily put in to quickly solve a specific problem. Although they can be effective hacks or quick fixes, they tend to also be poorly thought-out solutions that don't lend themselves to code reuse. For example, if you want to now use 100 points, you would have to change the value 11 to 101 in both places in the code. In many programs, there could be a lot more instances of this value throughout the code. Finally, here's the sketch that I might really write (depending on how I was feeling at the moment) to solve this problem:

```
size(300, 300);
background(0);
int totalPts = 100;
float steps = totalPts+1;
stroke(255);
for  (int i=1; i<steps; i++){
  point((width/steps)*i, height/2);
}
```

You'll notice that I actually added two lines of code, but now my sketch can handle any number of points. If you raise the totalPts number to over 200, you'll begin to see a pure line formed from the closely packed points. The line float steps = totalPts+1; seems to use the magic number 1, and it may seem odd to all of a sudden introduce the float type into the sketch. Although the 1 is a constant, it also expresses a state that is a constant. There will always be one more column than the number of points when the points are spaced out evenly using outer columns, and one less column than points if outer columns aren't used (see Figure 6-5).

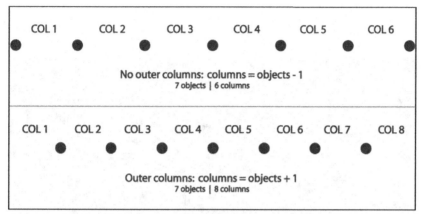

Figure 6-5. Calculating columns based on number of objects

The float type keeps rounding errors from shifting the points during division in the for loop. This is a subtle but very important point. For example, the simple expression 5 / 2 will not give the answer you might suspect; the answer, in Processing, is is 2. This is because two *integers* are divided together, which returns another integer. To get the right mathematical answer (**5.0 / 2 = 2.5**), one of the operands needs to be a float.

In the sketch, change the float type to int, set totalPts to 30 or 60 points, and run the sketch. Then, set totalPts to 29 or 59 points and run it again; the problem will go away, as 29 + 1 and 59 + 1 yields an even multiple of 300. You can use other values to demonstrate this as well. When steps is declared as type int, and you use it in the for loop (i.e., (width/steps)*i,), the answer gets rounded to an int. If you want to see the calculations, try putting the statement println((width/steps)*i), within the for loop. You'll see that all the values are integers. Now switch steps type from int back to float, and the output should be real numbers (numbers with fractional parts after the decimal point).

Creating organic form through randomization

OK, so you can draw a line with some points—no big deal, right? Well, there are some interesting things you can do now that you have your line being described procedurally. For example, to create a more organic or fuzzy line, you can use Processing's random() function within the loop (see Figure 6-6):

```
size(300, 300);
background(0);
int totalPts = 300;
float steps = totalPts+1;
stroke(255);
for  (int i=1; i< steps; i++){
  point((width/steps)*i, (height/2)+random(-2, 2));
}
```

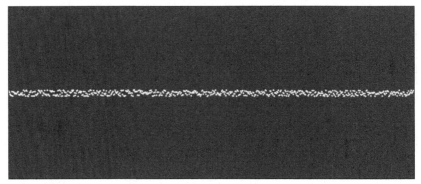

Figure 6-6. Randomized point line

The function random(-2, 2) generates a random number between the range specified by the min and max arguments passed to the function. Try passing larger and smaller and also asymmetrical arguments to the function to see what happens. Also try changing the number of points. This flexibility and ease with which you can experiment and iterate through different possibilities is what creative coding is all about. It's also the reason it's worth taking the time to code your projects efficiently, using well-structured loops and a minimal amount of magic numbers. Perhaps you'd like the random effect to change over time as well so that the line is not so consistent. Since the random() function is just looking for two float arguments, you can pass those as variables. For example, the following generates a particle spray (shown in Figure 6-7). Notice I added another variable called rand.

```
size(300, 300);
background(0);
int totalPts = 300;
float steps = totalPts+1;
stroke(255);
float rand = 0;
for  (int i=1; i< steps; i++){
  point((width/steps)*i, (height/2)+random(-rand, rand));
  rand+=.2;
}
```

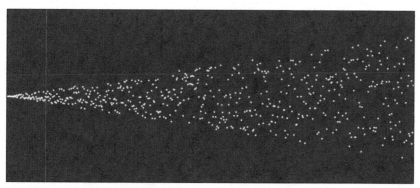

Figure 6-7. Randomized particle spray

You can even use a random() function to generate values for another random() function. Run the next example a couple of times to see the range of output (one example of which is shown in Figure 6-8); it's pretty interesting and getting fairly organic. As always, play with the numbers to see the expressive potential of the algorithm.

```
size(300, 300);
background(0);
int totalPts = 300;
float steps = totalPts+1;
stroke(255);
float rand = 0;
for  (int i=1; i< steps; i++){
  point((width/steps)*i, (height/2)+random(-rand, rand));
  rand+=random(-5, 5);
}
```

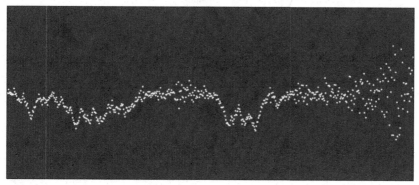

Figure 6-8. Doubly randomized particle line

Once you have a single line doing some interesting stuff, you can try to extend the concept with multiple lines. One way of thinking of this is as looping a loop. You can pretty easily put your existing for loop within another for loop and move your line down the display window, repeating the structure over and over again. It is often through these types of overlapping iterative processes that really unexpected and interesting stuff starts emerging out of the code. One caution, though: if you've been reading this stuff pretty quickly and not thoroughly experimenting with these structures along the way, you're missing many interesting possibilities, and more importantly, the feature creep in the sketches is going to quickly overwhelm you. I really recommend reading this chapter in small bites and then thoroughly chewing through the code possibilities. It's the best way to begin to remember all the weird syntax and keywords. The next example runs the previous code through another outer loop and adds some other modifications, drawing a series of lines down the display window (see Figure 6-9).

```
/*
Razor Tooth Pattern
Ira Greenberg, November 20, 2005
*/
size(300, 300);
background(0);
int totalPts = 1000;
float steps = totalPts+1;
int totalRows = 50;     // needs to be < = 300
int rowShift = height/totalRows;
float rowNudge = -.4;
float rowHop = 0;
int randNudge = 5;
stroke(255);
for (int i=rowShift; i<height; i+=rowShift ){
  for  (int j=1; j<steps; j++){
    rowHop-=rowNudge;
    if (j % (1 + (int)(random(randNudge))) == 0){
      rowNudge*=-1;
    }
    point((width/steps)*j, i+rowHop);
  }
}
```

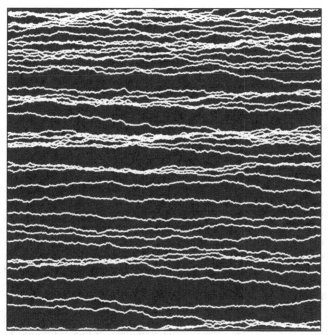

Figure 6-9. Multiple randomized particle lines

I imagine some of you might need a little clarification on parts of this last example. Although this is a simple program in number of code lines, parts of it are a bit dense. When you nest a for loop, as in the example, it is important to understand how the loop executes. The outer for loop initializes i to height/totalRows. This loop will run as long as i is less than the height of the display window. i will be incremented by the same amount i is originally initialized to, height/totalRows. On the first iteration of the outer for loop, the inner for loop runs through an entire loop cycle. In this case, j is initialized to 1 and also incremented by 1 as long as it remains less than the value of steps. After the inner loops runs through all its iterations, control goes back to the outer loop, which is incremented by height/totalRows; and then the process repeats itself, with the inner loop again going through its entire iterative loop cycle. This process will continue until the condition in the outer loop no longer evaluates to true (i is no longer less than the height of the display window). As you might imagine, if you're not careful, you can pretty easily create nested loops that take a lot of time to finish.

One other significant point regards how you name your variables in the loops. Within a code structure bounded by curly braces (for loops, if statements, functions, etc.), variables declared in the head or body of the structure (or passed in, as in the case of parameters in the head of a function) have local scope. This is in contrast to variables declared at the top of a program, which have global scope. Because of local scope, the variable i, declared in the head of the for loop, only exists between the curly braces of the for loop; it has no existence outside the loop. That's why it's possible to use the same-named variable i in all your non-nested for loops. However, when you nest a loop, the inner loop sees all of the variables you created in the outer loop; that's why you're forced to use a new name for the loop variable j in the inner loop. If you've been following this scope logic, do you think the outer loop can see the variable declared in the inner loop? The answer is no because the rules of local scope still apply.

Getting back to the code example, within the inner loop are a few lines that might be confusing:

```
rowHop-=rowNudge;
if (j % (1+ (int)(random(randNudge))) == 0){
  rowNudge*=-1;
}
```

The first line is a standard shortcut assignment operation. The variable rowHop moves the points up and down on the y-axis, and rowNudge is the value that it's either incremented or decremented by. I use the term "shortcut" because this operation does both an arithmetic operation (subtraction) and an assignment operation. The next line uses the modulus operator, which is usually foreign to non-coders. Modulus returns the remainder of division between two operands. The reason I used it was to generate a somewhat random result in the loop. I tested for the modulus expression to evaluate to 0, meaning that the division would yield no remainder. As i increases, there is a greater possibility that division will have no remainder. For example, 4 has three factors (1, 2, and 4) that go into it evenly, but 12 has six (1, 2, 3, 4, 6, and 12). In addition, I used a random number generator for the right operand to make the process more chaotic. The reason I added 1 to the value of the random() function before doing the modulus operation was to avoid division by 0, which is illegal and will cause a compiler error. Since the random() function will generate a random value between 0 and the argument value, periodically 0 will come up. In addition, I am converting the float value, evaluated by the random() function, to an integer, so the modulus expression has a chance of evaluating to 0. When you convert a float to an int by using the int() function, values are rounded down, so .999 still evaluates to 0. Thus, the statement (int)(random(randNudge)) can generate a lot of zeros. I used parentheses around the entire expression (1 + (int)(random(randNudge))) to make sure that the addition happens before the division. Normally multiplication and division, including modulus, are evaluated before addition and subtraction, but you can use parentheses to change the order of precedence, which is discussed at more length in Chapter 3. Finally, the shortcut assignment operation rowNudge*=-1; switches the direction in which the statement rowHop-=rowNudge; is pushing the points on the y-axis, giving a razor-tooth pattern to the line output. Hopefully this description wasn't too rough on the head. Make sure you play, tweak, experiment, and bust apart the code to get a better sense of what's going on.

There are two more modifications I'll make to the current sketch, and then I'll (finally) move on to using Processing's "real" line functions. The first modification involves laying a more regular grid pattern on top of the razor-tooth pattern, and the second modification involves shifting value.

Coding a grid

To begin, I'll show you how to generate a simple grid. First, you'll generate some columns of equally spaced parallel points (see Figure 6-10). This code should look similar to what you've been doing thus far.

```
size(300, 300);
background(0);
int cellWidth = width/30;
stroke(255);
//vertical lines
for (int i=cellWidth; i<width; i+=cellWidth){
  for  (int j=0; j<height; j++){
    point(i, j);
  }
}
```

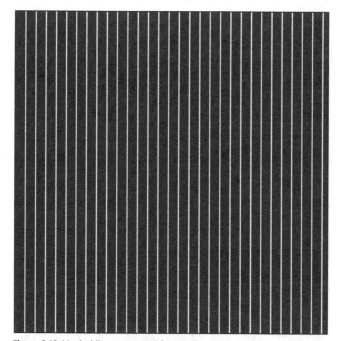

Figure 6-10. Vertical lines generated from points

If you mess with the cellWidth variable, you can change the spacing frequency. Now let's add the horizontal lines (see Figure 6-11):

```
size(300, 300);
background(0);
int cellWidth = width/20;
int cellHeight = height/30;
stroke(255);
//vertical lines
for (int i=cellWidth; i<width; i+=cellWidth){
  for  (int j=0; j<height; j++){
    point(i, j);
  }
}
//horizontal lines
for (int i=cellHeight; i<height; i+=cellHeight){
  for  (int j=0; j<width; j++){
    point(j, i);
  }
}
```

Figure 6-11. Horizontal and vertical lines, forming a symmetrical grid, generated from points

Notice that you can make the value of cellWidth different than the value of cellHeight, creating an alternative grid (see Figure 6-12). Finally, let's add some random() functions throughout the program.

Figure 6-12. Alternative grid made from points

One of the advantages of generating a line this way, using adjacent points, is the ability to alter the spacing of the points, as in the next example (see Figure 6-13):

```
/*
Point Grid
Ira Greenberg, November 20, 2005
*/
size(300, 300);
background(0);
// grid variables
int cellWidth = width/20;
int cellHeight = height/20;
int ptGap = 3;
int randHt = 4;
int randWdth = 10;
stroke(255);
//vertical lines
for (int i=cellWidth; i<width; i+=cellWidth+int(random(randWdth))){
```

```
    for  (int j=0; j<height; j+=ptGap){
      point(i, j);
    }
  }
}
//horizontal lines
for (int i=cellHeight; i<height; i+=cellHeight+int(random(randHt)) ){
  for  (int j=0; j<width; j+=ptGap){
    point(j, i);
  }
}
```

Figure 6-13. Alternative grid with spaced-out points

Now that you have your grid, let's bring the razor-tooth code back and put the two patterns together, as shown in Figures 6-14 and 6-15:

```
/*
 Yin Yang
 Ira Greenberg, November 20, 2005
 */
size(300, 300);
background(0);
//razor tooth variables
int totalPts = 1000;
```

```
float steps = totalPts+1;
int totalRows = 50;      // needs to be < = 300
int rowShift = height/totalRows;
float rowNudge = -.8;
float rowHop = 0;
int randNudge = 8;
stroke(255);
// razor tooth pattern
for (int i=rowShift; i<height; i+=rowShift ){
  for  (int j=1; j< steps; j++){
    rowHop-=rowNudge;
    if (j % (1 + (int)(random(randNudge))) == 0){
      rowNudge*=-1;
    }
    point(width/steps*j, i+rowHop);
  }
}

// grid variables
int cellWidth = width/60;
int cellHeight = height/60;
int ptGap = 1;
int randHt = 5;
int randWdth = 5;
//grid overlay
//vertical lines
stroke(40);
for (int i=cellWidth; i<width; i+=cellWidth+int(random(randWdth))){
  for  (int j=0; j<height; j+=ptGap){
    point(i, j);
  }
}

//horizontal lines
stroke(10);
for (int i=cellHeight; i<height; i+=cellHeight+int(random(randHt)) ){
  for  (int j=0; j<width; j+=ptGap){
    point(j, i);
  }
}
```

This is not such a simple program anymore. Besides the two different patterns coming together, there are now three places to change the value of the stroke. Really mess around with this sketch for a while before you move on to the next example. There is a lot of stuff to learn and many cool visual possibilities to be discovered. If you think you've found some especially cool output, please send it to me via e-mail. If I ever use/reproduce it, I'll be sure to give you proper credit.

6

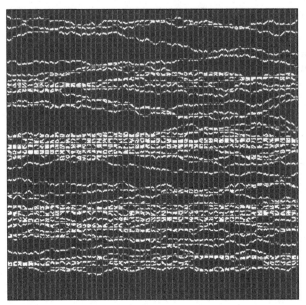

Figure 6-14. Yin Yang sketch, variation 1

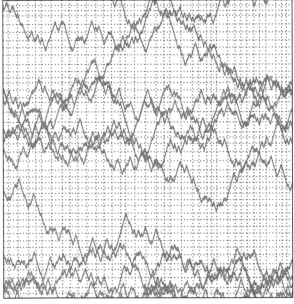

Figure 6-15. Yin Yang sketch, variation 2

Creating space through fades

Your last modification will be shifting the value of the stroke. Since color is represented numerically, you can easily shift the color's value/chroma just by applying some calculations to the color's numeric value. Going back to the vertical lines example, here's the output fading to black. Notice how it feels like the form goes back into space (see Figure 6-16).

```
size(300, 300);
background(0);
float cellWidth = width/30.0;
// find ratio of value range(255) to width
float val = cellWidth*(255.0/width);
//vertical lines
for (float i=cellWidth, v=255; i<width; i+=cellWidth, v-=val){
  stroke(v);
  for  (int j=0; j<height; j++){
    point(i, j);
  }
}
```

6

Figure 6-16. Horizontal fade to black

There is one new concept in this example and a little mathematical expression that may need some clarification. The expression that might be problematic is the following:

```
float val = cellWidth*(255.0/width);
```

I need the decrementation of the color value to coincide with the number of steps in the for loop. To ensure that this happens, I need to find the ratio between the width of the display window and the maximum value of the color (255). I simply multiply this ratio by the cellWidth interval to calculate how much to decrement the color value each step of the loop. This gives me a smooth transition from 255 to 0 (or white to black). The new concept I mentioned refers to using multiple statements within the head of the for loop, separated by commas. This is a convenient thing to do. I could also have initialized a variable outside of the loop and explicitly incremented/decremented it within the loop block, but that's more work. In truth, all three parts in the head of the for loop are optional (you do need the semicolons, though). For example, this for loop will compile and run fine. I used the break; command so that the loop doesn't run infinitely.

```
for(;;){
  print("i'm in this weird for loop");
  break;
}
```

In the next modification, I applied the value shifting to both the vertical and horizontal lines (see Figure 6-17). I also broke out of the square format to illustrate how the grid can automatically size itself to the display window size/format. This is a good example of why you want to try to base program measurements (if it's at all practical) on the dimensions of the display window, which allows your program to scale and adapt to different environments.

```
size(500, 200);
background(0);
float cellWidth = width/50.0;
// find ratio of value range(255) to width
float valw = cellWidth*(255.0/width);
//vertical lines
for (float i=cellWidth, v=255; i<width; i+=cellWidth, v-=valw){
  stroke(v);
  for  (int j= 0; j<height; j++){
    point(i, j);
  }
}

float cellHeight = height/50.0;
// find ratio of value range(255) to height
float valh = cellHeight*(255.0/height);
//horizontal lines
for (float i=cellHeight, v=255; i<height; i+=cellHeight, v-=valh){
  stroke(v);
```

```
    for  (int j=0; j<width; j++){
      point(j, i);
    }
  }
```

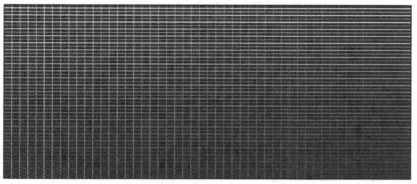

Figure 6-17. Horizontal and vertical fade to black

The last thing I'll do with the beleaguered point method is combine the gradient stroke grid with the razor-tooth pattern. Two examples of the sketch's output can be seen in Figures 6-18 and 6-19.

```
/*
 Yin Yang Fade
 Ira Greenberg, November 20, 2005
 */
size(700, 200);
background(0);

// grid variables
float cellWidth = width*.01;
float cellHeight = height*.01;
int ptGap = 1;
int randHt = 0;
int randWdth = 0;
// find ratio of value range(255) to height and width
float valh = cellHeight*(255.0/height);
float valw = cellWidth*(255.0/width);

//grid overlay
//vertical lines
for (float i=cellWidth, v=255.0; i<width; i+=cellWidth + ➥
        int(random(randWdth)), v-=valw ){
  stroke(v);
  for  (int j=0; j<height; j+=ptGap){
```

```
      point(i, j);
    }
  }
//horizontal lines
for (float i=cellHeight, v=255.0; i<height; i+=cellHeight + ➥
        int(random(randHt)), v-=valh ){
  stroke(v);
  for  (int j=0; j<width; j+=ptGap){
    point(j, i);
  }
}

//razor tooth variables
float totalPts = 1000.0;
float steps = totalPts+1.0;
int totalRows = 50;     // needs to be < = 300
int rowShift = height/totalRows;
float valr = 255.0/steps;  // used for value shift
float rowNudge = -.7;
float rowHop = 0;
int randNudge = 8;
// razor tooth pattern
for (int i=rowShift; i<height; i+=rowShift ){
  for  (float j=1,  v=255; j< steps; j++, v-=valr){
    stroke(v);
    rowHop-=rowNudge;
    if (j % (1 + (int)(random(randNudge))) == 0){
      rowNudge*=-1;
    }
    point(width/steps*j, i+rowHop);
  }
}
```

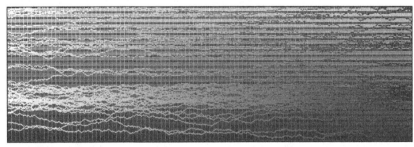

Figure 6-18. Yin Yang Fade sketch, variation 1

Figure 6-19. Yin Yang Fade sketch, variation 2

Try running this code a couple times to see how it changes. The shift from black to white, in both the grid and razor-tooth pattern, creates an interesting example of sfumato (or smoke), giving the image a sense of atmosphere. You'll notice in the code that I reversed the order of the grid and the razor-tooth pattern code blocks. Putting the grid down first created more clarity in the final image. Try reversing the blocks of code to see the difference. In the next examples, you'll explore some other ways of generating lines in Processing.

Creating lines with pixels

Besides using Processing's point() function to generate lines, you can also directly set the value of a line of pixels. In the next example, a PImage object is created, and the pixels along the horizontal, vertical, and diagonal center axes are set to black (see Figure 6-20). Please note that the PImage object is not automatically rendered to the screen; to do so, you need to explicitly call the image() function (see the last line of code in the example).

```
size(500, 300);
background(255);
// used by diagonal lines
float slope = float(height)/float(width);
PImage img = createImage(width, height, RGB);
color c = color(0, 0, 0);
//horizontal line
for (int i=0; i<width; i++){
  img.set(i, height/2, c);
}
//vertical line
for (int i=0; i<height; i++){
  img.set(width/2, i, c);
}
//diagonal line (TL-BR)
for (float i=0; i<width; i++){
  img.set(int(i), int(i*slope), c);
```

```
}
//diagonal line (BL-TR)
for (float i=0; i<width; i++){
  img.set(int(i), int(height-i*slope), c);
}
image(img, 0, 0);
```

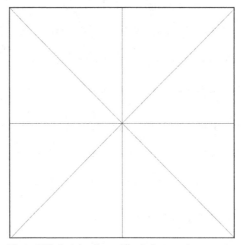

Figure 6-20. Drawing lines with pixels example

This approach is pretty low level for simply drawing some lines, and isn't much of an improvement (if any) over using the point() method. I'll return to PImage later in the book. However, one detail worth noting in the last example is the simple equation used to generate the diagonal lines. Since the lines were set by incrementing pixels across the image, I needed to the know the slope of the lines I wanted to draw, which is really how the line changes on the y-axis in regard to how it changes on the x-axis. The stroke equation is just the change in y divided by the change in x (the rise over the run). Normally for a line, you just take the beginning and ending points, do the subtraction between the two y and x components, and then perform the division. Since in the example the diagonal lines span the entire display window (from corner to corner), I could just use the display window height divided by the width to get my slope.

Processing's line functions

Fortunately, Processing has two other far more simplified approaches to generating lines that also give you more rendering capabilities, such as setting the weight or thickness of the line. The first approach you'll look at uses Processing's line() function. This function comes in two varieties, 2D and 3D. The 3D version works just like the 2D function, but requires six arguments instead of four. These arguments are the x and y (and for 3D, also z) coordinates of the line. For example, to draw a 2D line across the screen, you pass the initial point's coordinate, (x1, y1), and the endpoint's coordinate, (x2, y2), to the line(x1, y1, x2, y2) function. Figure 6-21 shows the output.

```
size(500, 300);
background(255);
line(0, height/2, width, height/2);
```

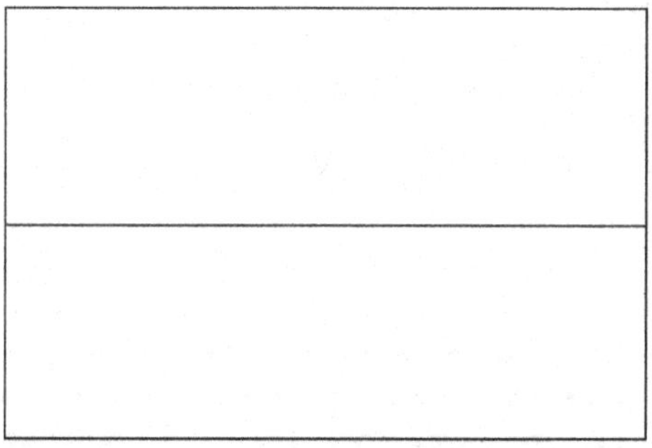

Figure 6-21. Drawing a 2D line with Processing's line() function

If you were using one of the 3D rendering options (P3D or OPENGL), you could pass in a third coordinate, referencing the z-axis. If you run the next example, you'll notice that the line doesn't appear to reach the end of the display, as it did in the last example. This is because the line is stretching back 300 pixels into virtual space, and the P3D renderer is simulating perspective, which causes things to converge and decrease in scale (visually of course) as they recede into space (see Figure 6-22).

```
size(500, 300, P3D);
background(255);
// line(x1, y1, z1, x2, y2, z2);
line(0, height/2, 0, width, height/2, -300);
```

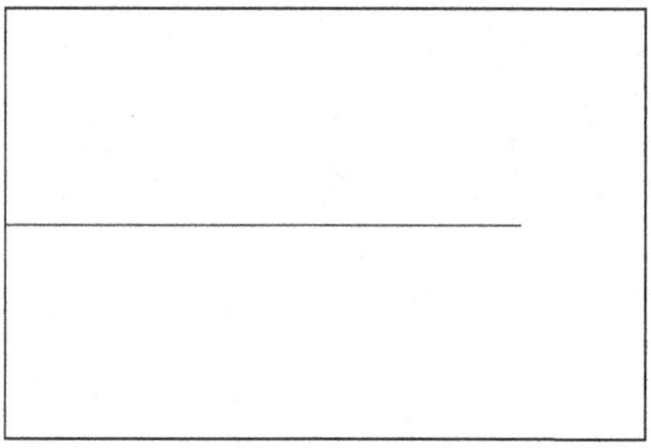

Figure 6-22. Drawing a 3D line with Processing's line() function

The rest of the examples in this chapter will be 2D. (Drawing in 3D will be discussed later in the book.) Utilizing the line() function, you can more easily create complex linear structures than using either the point() or PImage approaches. Aside from specifying the position and length of a line, you can use some of Processing's rendering style functions to affect the rendering state of the line. Next is a very simple example demonstrating the use of the strokeWeight() function (see Figure 6-23).

```
size(500, 300);
background(255);
int step = height/10;
for (int i=step; i< height; i+=step ){
  strokeWeight(i*.1);
  line(20, i, width-20, i);
}
```

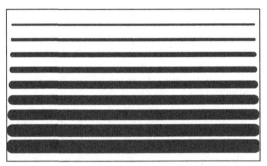

Figure 6-23. Stroke weight variation example

As the line or stroke increases in weight, the end caps of the line become very prominent. The default style is ROUND. However, end caps can be set using the strokeCap() function by passing one of three constants, ROUND, PROJECT, or SQUARE, to the function. I recoded the last example, changing some of the end caps (see Figure 6-24). Please also note the strokeCap() function only works with the default JAVA2D rendering mode. If you specify any of the other modes (P3D, OPENGL, or P2D), this feature will not work.

```
size(500, 300);
background(255);
int step = height/10;
int[]caps = {ROUND, PROJECT, SQUARE};
int j = 0;
for (int i=step; i<height; i+=step ){
  strokeWeight(i*.1);
  strokeCap(caps[j++]);
  if (j>2){
    j=0;
  }
  line(20, i, width-20, i);
}
```

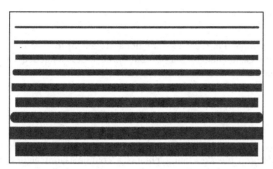

Figure 6-24. End cap variation example

Running this code should give you a clear sense of the differences between the end cap styles. These caps become a more significant concern as you begin to join lines into more complex structures. However, before you do that, let's review some of the code in the last example.

The line int[]caps = {ROUND, PROJECT, SQUARE}; declares and initializes an array of type int, and fills the index positions [0], [1], and [2] with the three constants ROUND, PROJECT, and SQUARE. I discussed arrays in detail in Chapter 3. As a review, arrays are data structures that hold multiple variables of any type. All the elements in an array need to be of the same data type. To access an item stored in an array, you use an index number placed between brackets, directly to the right of the array name, as in caps[0]. Arrays are zero-indexed, meaning that the first position in the array is 0, not 1. The three end cap styles, ROUND, PROJECT, and SQUARE, which look like strings, are actually immutable (unchangeable) integer constants. Specifying an unchanging value as a constant and using all uppercase letters in naming it are common programming approaches. In Java, the keyword final is used to specify that a variable's value is immutable. To find the corresponding int values for the constants, run the following example:

```
println("ROUND = " + ROUND);
println("SQUARE = " + SQUARE);
println("PROJECT = " + PROJECT);
// uncomment the next line to generate a semantic error.
//ROUND = 27;
```

Now, to prove that you can't change a constant's value, uncomment the last line of the code and run the sketch again, which should generate a compiler error telling you can't assign another value to ROUND.

Processing has a ton of constants defined in the language that work the same way. Each constant is usually assigned an integer value (but not always). Mostly, constants add meaning to the coding process. Isn't it easier to remember the cap style ROUND than the number 2? You can see Processing's constants at http://dev.processing.org/source/index.cgi/trunk/processing/core/src/processing/core/PConstants.java?view=markup.

Joining lines

In the previous example, I also used a conditional statement to keep looping through the caps arrays. Since each end cap was output three times, I needed to keep resetting the array counter back to 0, which is exactly what the conditional statement does:

```
if (j>2){
    j=0;
}
```

The next sketch, shown in Figure 6-25, illustrates the joining implications of the different end caps. In addition, the sketch implements a column layout algorithm, with simple padding between the corresponding cells. Try changing the value of the strokeWeight() argument as well as the shapes and padding variables to see what happens.

```
/*
 Auto Layout
 Ira Greenberg, November 21, 2005
 */
size(500, 300);
background(255);
int[]caps = {ROUND, PROJECT, SQUARE};
strokeWeight(20);
int shapes = 3;
int padding = 200;

float w = (width-padding)/shapes;
float h = w;
float colSpan = (width-shapes*w)/(shapes+1);
float x = colSpan;
float y = height/2-h/2;
for (int i=0, j=0; i<shapes; i++){
  strokeCap(caps[j++]);
  if (j>2) j=0;
  line(x, y, x+w, y);
  line(x+w, y, x+w, y+h);
  line(x, y+h, x+w, y+h);
  line(x, y+h, x, y);
  x+=w+colSpan;
}
```

Figure 6-25. Auto Layout sketch

This sketch utilizes a fair amount of variables, so it might look a bit confusing. Definitely take your time going through it. I think the auto-layout feature is worth taking the time to understand, as this type of process is quite valuable when you're doing visual stuff. You'll also notice that I initialized a second local variable (j) in the for loop head, which I use to cycle through the caps[] array. There is also a conditional statement that keeps resetting j to 0, ensuring that the index of the array stays within bounds. Remember, arrays are zero-indexed—so if you have three items in an array, the last index number will be 2, or array.length-1. If you make a request to access an index position in an array that doesn't exist, you'll get an error. This is a very common mistake, and usually pretty easily (and happily) resolved.

I also snuck in some formatting that hopefully will look quite suspect: if (j>2) j=0;. This is actually a normal conditional statement that I put on one line, leaving off the curly braces. Yes, this is legal code, as long as you only use one statement in the block of the code (between where the curly braces would have been). You can even use an else statement after the if block—but again, only one line of code will be recognized by the structure if you don't include curly braces. You'll also get a compiler error if you include the else and have more than one line in the if block. Regardless of how you format your if statement, it makes no difference whether you put it on one line or skip a line between each part (at least to the compiler). Whitespace is ignored by the compiler, except if it's between quotation marks, which it then sees as character spaces. In the next examples, the first two snippets works fine, but the last two don't work.

Here's Example 1, which works:

```
for (int i =0; i<5; i++){
// no braces, but only one line in both the if and else blocks
  if (i==3)
    println("i = " + i + " hello");
  else
    println("i = " + i + " goodbye");
}
```

Example 2 also works, but looks pretty ridiculous.

```
for(int i=0;i<5;i++){if (i==3)println(" hello");else
println("goodbye");}
```

Example 3 doesn't work properly (although it will compile and run fine). If you run the code, you'll notice that the second line in the if block (below the comment) outputs each iteration of the loop, regardless of whether the conditional statement is true—this a great way to create a hard-to-track-down and really annoying bug.

```
for (int i=0; i<5; i++){
  if (i==3)
    print("i = " + i + " hello");
    /* Without using curly braces, the next line will always execute,
        regardless of the outcome of the conditional (true or false)*/
    println(" there");
}
```

Example 4 won't even compile, which is a good thing:

```
for (int i=0; i<5; i++){
  if (i==3)
    print("i = " + i + " hello");
    println(" there");
  else
    print("i = " + i + " goodbye");
}
```

In spite of this flexibility in form, I almost always use curly braces and format my statements on multiple lines. However, there are many coders who use these other forms, so it's good to be able to recognize them and, most importantly, recognize when they'll work properly or not.

Creating a table structure

Since you've got the auto-format code working for columns, let's set it up for rows as well, and then let's try to do something visually interesting with it (see Figure 6-26).

```
/*
Table Layout I
Ira Greenberg, November 21, 2005
*/
size(500, 300);
background(255);
int[]caps = {ROUND, PROJECT, SQUARE};
strokeWeight(1);
int cols = 30;
int rows= 40;
```

```
int xPadding = 150;
int yPadding = 100;
float w = (width-xPadding)/cols;
float h = (height-yPadding)/rows;
float colSpan = (width-cols*w)/(cols+1);
float rowSpan = (height-rows*h)/(rows+1);
float x;
float y = rowSpan;
for (int i=0; i<rows; i++){
 x = colSpan;
   for (int j=0, k=0; j<cols; j++){
     strokeCap(caps[k++]);
     if (k>2){
        k=0;
     }
     line(x, y, x+w, y);
     line(x+w, y, x+w, y+h);
     line(x, y+h, x+w, y+h);
     line(x, y+h, x, y);
     x += w+colSpan;
   }
   y+=h+rowSpan;
}
```

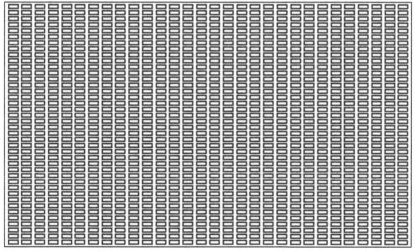

Figure 6-26. Table Layout I sketch

You've got a nice, flexible table structure now. Running the sketch, you should see a tightly packed pattern of small rectangles. Try decreasing the padding and increasing/decreasing the stroke weight. Since your table doesn't need to hold well-formatted tabular data, you can do "stupid" but fun things to it (the theme of my life). For example, what does negative padding do to the table structure? You can also make things more interesting by adding randomization directly into the plotting algorithm. Your table will then go from an array of cells or windows to (potentially) many little individual works of art (see Figure 6-27).

```
/*
Table Layout II
Ira Greenberg, November 21, 2005
*/
void setup(){
  size(700, 500);
  background(0);
  drawTable();
}

void drawTable(){
  stroke(255);
  int[]caps = { ROUND, PROJECT, SQUARE };
  strokeWeight(.1);
  int cols = 20;
  int rows= 20;
  int xPadding = 100;
  int yPadding = 100;
  float w = (width-xPadding)/cols;
  float h = (height-yPadding)/rows;
  float colSpan = (width-cols*w)/(cols+1);
  float rowSpan = (height-rows*h)/(rows+1);
  float x;
  float y = rowSpan;
  for (int i=0; i<rows; i++){
    x = colSpan;
    for (int j=0, k=0; j<cols; j++){
      strokeCap(caps[k++]);
      if (k>2){
        k=0;
      }
      line(x+random(-4, 4), y+random(-4, 4), x+w+random(-4, 4), ➥
        y+random(-4, 4));
      line(x+w+random(-4, 4), y+random(-4, 4), x+w+random(-4, 4), ➥
        y+h+random(-4, 4));
      line(x+random(-4, 4), y+h+random(-4, 4), x+w+random(-4, 4), ➥
        y+h+random(-4, 4));
      line(x+random(-4, 4), y+h+random(-4, 4), x+random(-4, 4), ➥
        y+random(-4, 4));
      x += w+colSpan;
    }
    y+=h+rowSpan;
  }
}
```

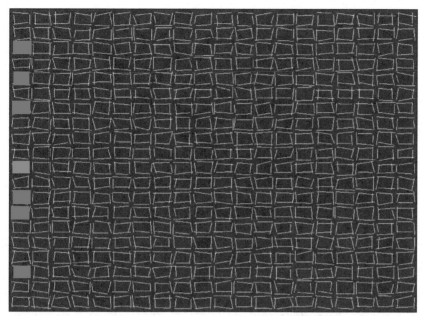

Figure 6-27. Table Layout II sketch

This was a pretty brute-force and inefficient way to add randomization to the algorithm, and you should notice all the magic numbers lurking in the line() function calls (yuck). But running the sketch, you'll see that things are beginning to get more interesting. Wouldn't it be cool if you could do this to HTML table structures (on purpose)? I also added some more formatting to the code to make it more modular, such as the drawTable() function.

When you add your own custom functions to Processing, you also need to include Processing's setup() function. setup() is executed only once when a sketch launches, and is a good place to initialize program variables. Since setup(), like all functions, is structured with external curly braces surrounding a main block, it follows the same rules of scope as I discussed with for loops—variables declared within the block are only visible from within the block (they have local scope). If you want variables to be accessible throughout the entire program, you need to declare them outside of the setup() function, at the top of the program.

Although functions add another layer of abstraction to your code, they provide tremendous processing power, as they modularize a process, allowing it to be used like an independent machine or engine. By utilizing user-defined inputs (parameters) with a function, the same function can generate a wide range of output possibilities. In the next example, I added a number of parameters to the drawTable() function, greatly increasing the sketch's expressive potential. Three examples of the sketch's output are shown in Figures 6-28, 6-29, and 6-30.

```
/*
Table Explode
Ira Greenberg, November 21, 2005
*/

void setup(){
  size(700, 500);
  background(0);
  int cols = 24;
  int rows = 24;
  color[]clrs = new color[cols*rows];
  float[]strokeWts = new float[cols*rows];
  int xPadding = -20;
  int yPadding = -50;
  float[]r1 = new float[16];
  float[]r2 = new float[16];
  float randomFactor = 6;
  int colorMin = 0;   // 0 = black
  float strokeWtMax = 2;
  int overDraw = 10;

  for (int i=0; i<r1.length; i++){
    r1[i] = random(-randomFactor);
    r2[i] = random(randomFactor);
  }

  for  (int i=0; i<clrs.length; i++){
    clrs[i] =  colorMin + int(random(255-colorMin));
    strokeWts[i] = random(strokeWtMax);
  }
  // calls main drawing function
  for (int i=0; i<overDraw; i++){
    drawTable(r1, r2, clrs, cols, rows, strokeWts, ➥
        xPadding, yPadding);
  }
}

void drawTable(float[]r1, float[]r2, color[]clrs, int cols, ➥
        int rows, float[]strokeWts, int xPadding, int yPadding){
  int[]caps = {ROUND, PROJECT, SQUARE};
  float w = (width-xPadding)/cols;
  float h = (height-yPadding)/rows;
  float colSpan = (width-cols*w)/(cols+1);
  float rowSpan = (height-rows*h)/(rows+1);
  float x;
  float y = rowSpan;
  int ttlCounter = 0;
```

```
for (int i=0; i<rows; i++){
  x = colSpan;
  for (int j=0, k=0; j<cols; j++){
    strokeCap(caps[k++]);
    if (k>2){
      k=0;
    }
    // stroke colors
    stroke(clrs[ttlCounter]);
    // stroke weight
    strokeWeight(strokeWts[ttlCounter++]);
    line(x+random(r1[0], r2[0]), y+random(r1[1], r2[1]), ➥
        x+w+random(r1[2], r2[2]), y+random(r2[3], r2[3]));
    line(x+w+random(r1[4], r2[4]), y+random(r1[5], r2[5]), ➥
        x+w+random(r1[6], r2[6]), y+h+random(r1[7], r2[7]));
    line(x+random(r1[8], r2[8]), y+h+random(r1[9], r2[9]), ➥
        x+w+random(r1[10], r2[10]), y+h+random(r1[11], r2[11]));
    line(x+random(r1[12], r2[12]), y+h+random(r1[13], r2[13]), ➥
        x+random(r1[14], r2[14]), y+random(r1[15], r2[15]));
    x += w+colSpan;
  }
  y+=h+rowSpan;
}
}
```

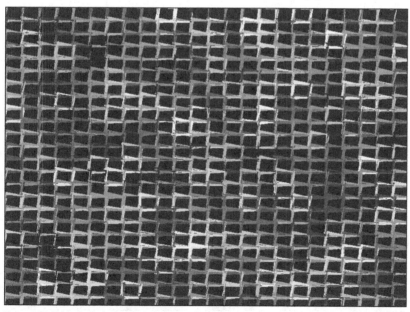

Figure 6-28. Table Explode sketch, variation 1

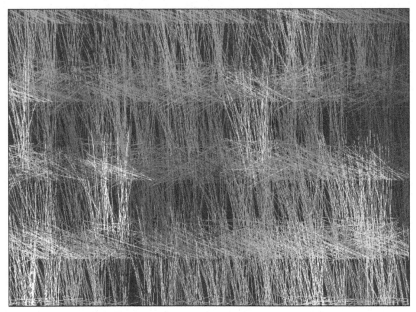

Figure 6-29. Table Explode sketch, variation 2

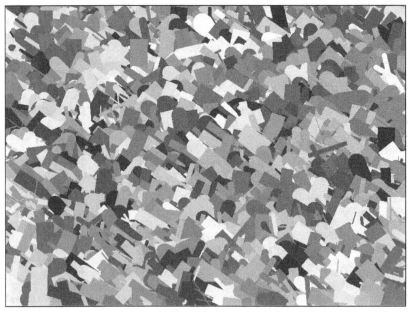

Figure 6-30. Table Explode sketch, variation 3

This is the same drawTable() function as in the last example, only many of the values in the main algorithm have been converted into parameters. Parameters are the variables, including their type declaration, that are placed between the parentheses of a function head when a function is defined. When you call or invoke the function, the values you pass to the function parameters are referred to as **arguments**. This can be confusing to new coders. The parameters define the number and type of arguments the function requires to be called. Another term you may come across is the function **signature**, which is just the name of the function, its parameters, and the return type. The return type relates to what, if any, value the function returns. A function that doesn't return any value has a void return type. You always need to specify either a return type or void when you define a function. That's why both the setup() and drawTable() functions are prefaced by the void keyword. Functions that return a specific value need to be prefaced by the data type of that value. For example, to return an int, a function should be prefaced with int. The same rule holds true for any data type that a function returns. Functions may return any legal data type.

The parameters in the new, improved drawTable() function open up a ton of cool possibilities, a few of which you can see in the included figures. Try changing any of the following argument values to see what happens: cols, rows, xPadding, yPadding, randomFactor, colorMin, strokeWtMax, and overDraw. You can change these values at the top of the setup() function, before the drawTable() function call is made. Really take the time to experiment with this sketch. It covers a lot of stuff you'll see again and again. I also think you'll be surprised at the range of output you can get with relatively few lines of code (although I realize that this might look like a lot of code to some of you).

In the next section, you'll look at the vertex() function, along with the companion beginShape() and endShape() functions. Using the vertex() function opens up even more exciting possibilities.

Vertex functions

A vertex is just another word for a point. However, what separates the vertex() function from the point() function is that the vertex() function utilizes the companion beginShape() and endShape() functions, allowing the vertices to be connected into lines, curves, 2D shapes, and even 3D forms. Since coordinate locations in a Cartesian system require a coordinate component for each axis, it makes sense that any form plotted on the computer would be reducible to a series of point locations, or vertices. The beginShape() function takes a mode argument that controls how the vertices are joined. The seven mode arguments are POINTS, LINES, TRIANGLES, TRIANGLE_STRIP, TRIANGLE_FAN, QUADS, and QUAD_STRIP. (Please note that POINTS mode is no longer documented in the official language API, but continues to work as of this writing.) If no option is specified, the line strip mode is used, which can be closed to form a polygon. This chapter will only look at how to use these modes to generate points, lines, open line strips, and closed line strips (polygons).

The vertex() function takes either two or three arguments (of type int or float), for coordinates in 2D or 3D, respectively:

```
vertex(x, y)
vertex(x, y, z)
```

This chapter will only look at vertices in two dimensions; in later chapters, you'll plot forms in 3D. Here's a really simple example of the vertex() function in action, using the POINTS mode (see Figure 6-31):

```
size(300, 300);
background(0);
stroke(255);
strokeWeight(5);
beginShape(POINTS);
vertex(50, 50);
vertex(width-50, 50);
vertex(width-50, height-50);
vertex(50, height-50);
vertex(width/2, height/2);
endShape();
```

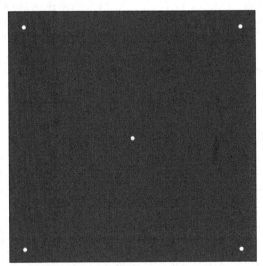

Figure 6-31. POINTS mode sketch example

This is not a very impressive example, and I believe it shows that using the vertex() function to generate points doesn't offer much advantage over using the good old point() function covered earlier. You'll notice that the vertex() calls occur between the beginShape() and endShape() function calls. In a sense, the beginShape() function begins recording drawing instructions, and the endShape() function stops recording and then renders the drawing data to the screen. As usual, Processing makes this stuff look incredibly easy. The benefit of internally recording the coordinate data is that the data can be plotted based on different drawing algorithms. Using different mode arguments within the beginShape() and endShape() functions, Processing can use the same vertex() data to draw different types of geometry.

As a little example of how this internal recording process works, the following sketch (shown in Figure 6-32) re-creates some of the functionality of vertex(), using the point() and line() functions already covered. Although this may seem like an exercise in futility, I think it is helpful to have a sense of what's happening internally, before you rely on these higher-level commands. In addition, you'll see that by going a little lower level, other interesting creative possibilities arise. Afterward, we'll look at similar functionality, the *easy way*.

```
/*
Point Recorder/Plotter
Ira Greenberg, November 23, 2005
*/

void setup(){
  size(300, 300);
  background(0);

  // create arrays to hold x, y coords
  float[]x = new float[4];
  float[]y  = new float[4];
  // create a convenient 2 dimensional
  // array to hold x, y arrays
  float[][]xy = {x, y};

  //record points
  //x positions
  xy[0][0] = 50;
  xy[0][1] = 250;
  xy[0][2] = 250;
  xy[0][3] = 50;

  //y positions
  xy[1][0] = 50;
  xy[1][1] = 50;
  xy[1][2] = 250;
  xy[1][3] = 250;

  // call plotting function
  makeRect(xy);
}

void makeRect(float[][]pts){
  stroke(255);
  smooth();
```

```
for (int i=0; i<pts[0].length; i++){
//plots vertices
strokeWeight(5);
point(pts[0][i], pts[1][i]);

//plot connecting lines
strokeWeight(.5);
if (i>0){
  line(pts[0][i], pts[1][i], pts[0][i-1], pts[1][i-1]);
}
if (i== pts[0].length-1){
  line(pts[0][i], pts[1][i], pts[0][0], pts[1][0]);
}
}
}
```

Figure 6-32. Point Recorder/Plotter sketch

Hopefully some of this looks familiar. You've already used for loops to run through the indices of an array, as well as created your own custom functions to modularize a process. This example also introduces a new variation on an older theme—2D arrays—and also utilizes another simple rendering option, the smooth() function. However, before I discuss either of these new structures, let's look at what's happening in this sketch.

Within setup(), I created a couple of arrays and populated them with coordinate data describing the vertices of a square. Obviously, if you were going to use a vertex coordinate recording process like this for real, you would not hard-code in the coordinate values, which if you remember are called magic numbers and are generally to be avoided. However, to keep things simple I broke my own rule. After I fill the array with these values,

I call my custom function makeRect(), passing the arrays to the function. makeRect() plots points based on the coordinate data in the arrays, and then draws lines between the points. I needed to use the two conditional if statements to ensure that the connecting lines were drawn to the right points, based on the value of i in the for loop. Remember that arrays are zero-indexed, meaning that the first position is at [0], not [1]. If you request an index position in an array that doesn't exist, you'll get an error. The first conditional statement ensures that this doesn't happen. The second conditional statement checks when the loop is in its last cycle, and then simply connects the last point back to the initial point, closing the path. Another way to have done this would be to have eliminated the last conditional statement and just put a line after the for loop, connecting the last point back to the first, such as line(pts[0][pts[0].length-1], pts[1][pts[0].length-1], pts[0][0], pts[1][0]);.

This last code line may look pretty confusing, mostly because of the 2D arrays. These structures are really not that confusing to conceptually grasp, but they are visually and procedurally complex to work with. If you really don't like them, you don't need to use them, as you can always substitute two regular one-dimensional arrays in their place. However, many people use them, so it's good to be able to recognize and understand how they work. In truth, there is really no such thing as a multidimensional array structure in Processing or Java. Since arrays can hold any data type in Processing and Java, they can also hold other arrays. Multidimensional arrays are just arrays of arrays. In the code example, I created two coordinate arrays, float[]x and float[]y, and then to be a pest, stuck these into another 2D array, float[][]xy. I covered arrays in detail in Chapter 3, but a little review on how to declare/initialize them might be helpful. There are two ways to declare/initialize arrays in Processing. The first way is as follows:

```
float[]x = new float[array length];
```

This creates a new array object and reserves a number of indices in memory. After you declare and instantiate an array this way, each index will have a default value assigned to it, based on the data type you're using; for float arrays, that would be 0.0. You still need to assign specific values to each index position in the array. For example:

```
x[0] = .2;
x[1] = .3;
x[2] = .7;
x[3] = .1;
```

The second way to declare and initialize an array is somewhat of a shortcut:

```
float[]x = {val 1, val 2, val 3, ...};
```

This approach works great when you already know the values to put in the array.

Both of these approaches can also be broken into two steps, which you might use if you needed your array variable to be declared at the top of your program (giving it global scope), but also wanted to instantiate the array in setup().

```
float[]x;
x = new float[array length];
```

This other way is less common:

```
float[]x;
x = new float []{val-1, val-2, val-3...};
```

Getting back to the 2D array float[][]xy, this array just holds two other arrays. In this case, both of the internal arrays x[] and y[] are the same size, or length, but they don't actually need to be. For example, the following is perfectly legal:

```
int[]months = new int[12];
int[]weeks = new int[52];
int[]days = new int[365];
int[][]year = {months, weeks, days};
```

year is still a 2D array, even though it contains three arrays, each with a different length. A 3D array, which I don't recommend using, would be an array containing 2D arrays (yuck).

To access the first value in the first array in xy[][], you use xy[0][0];. To access the second value in the first array, you use xy[0][1];. To access the first value in the second array, you use xy[1][0]; to access the second value in the second array, you use xy[1][1]. Do you see the pattern? Here's one more: if you wanted to access the 17th value in the 26th array, you'd write *arrayname*[25][16]. One other metaphor that might help you visualize a 2D array is a multi-drawer filing cabinet. The first set of brackets of a 2D array can be thought of as the drawers of the filing cabinet, and the second set of brackets represent the files in each drawer. You'll be using arrays a whole lot throughout the book, so rest assured—if it didn't stick this time, it will eventually.

Anti-aliasing using the smooth function

The other new function I used in the plotter example was smooth(), which anti-aliases the screen output. Anti-aliasing is essentially a blending trick, providing a smooth edge to screen output. Since the screen is composed of discrete rectangular pixels in a rigid grid, diagonal and curved edges won't coincide precisely with the pixel grid, and will thus appear jagged. Anti-aliasing compensates for this by filling in edge pixels with varying colors/values, based on an anti-aliasing algorithm. For example, a relatively simple anti-aliasing algorithm could be to evaluate the percent a pixel is overlapped by a shape's ideal edge (the edge if it weren't converted to jagged pixels), and then fill those overlapped pixels with a color value based on the edge color multiplied by the percent of overlap. A popular, but far more processor-intensive anti-aliasing technique is called **supersampling**, in which an image in internally rendered to a pixel buffer (not to the screen) multiple times larger than it actually is. Thus, numerous pixels now represent each original image pixel. Color values can then be evaluated at different points on the original pixel (where each of the extra pixels now represent a part of the original pixel) and averaged. After the averaging is completed, the image is reduced to its normal size and rendered to the screen.

As you might suspect, anti-aliasing techniques can dramatically impact performance, as the anti-aliasing calculations take time. Processing therefore has two functions: smooth() and noSmooth(). The first turns anti-aliasing on and the second turns it off. Anti-aliasing is off by default in Processing. This simple example illustrates the visual difference between aliasing and anti-aliasing in Processing; the ellipse on the left of Figure 6-33, using the default rendering state, is aliased, and the ellipse on the right is anti-aliased using Processing's smooth() function.

```
size(430, 220);
strokeWeight(2);
ellipseMode(CORNER);
//aliased
ellipse(10, 10, 200, 200);
smooth();
//anti-aliased
ellipse(220, 10, 200, 200);
```

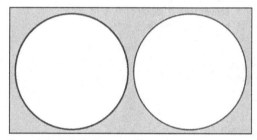

Figure 6-33. Anti-aliasing example

Please note that calling smooth() can slightly reduce the stroke weight of fine lines. This can become a factor when you specify small stroke weights. Type in Processing utilizes its own anti-aliasing procedure, so calling smooth() will have no impact on the type's edges. To specify anti-aliasing with type, you need to either specify the smooth parameter when calling the createFont() function, or go to Tools ➤ Create Font and select the Smooth option. Type is always anti-aliased in OS X.

Returning to the Point Recorder/Plotter sketch, I want to give one further example illustrating another cool feature of using this record/plot approach. Since the point data is recorded in the xy[][] array and then plotted to the screen, I can manipulate or utilize the point information in the middle of the plotting. The best way to handle this is to create another simple function that I can pass the point data to for further processing. You can think of this process like an assembly line, where, for example, a mechanical arm moves a component down the line, while other machines paint, weld, and bend it. In the next example, as the points are processed in the makeRect() function, they get sent to the scribble() function, which creates scribbly lines between the points. See Figure 6-34 for the screen output of this example.

```
/*
 Scribble Plotter
 Ira Greenberg, November 24, 2005
 */

//some scribble style constants that control
//how the scribble plotting works
int SCRIBBLE = 0;
int HATCHING = 1;

void setup(){
  size(300, 300);
  background(0);

  // create arrays to hold x, y coords
  float[]x = new float[4];
  float[]y  = new float[4];
  // create a convenient 2 dimensional
  // array to hold x, y arrays
  float[][]xy = {x, y};

  //record points
  //x positions
  xy[0][0] = 50;
  xy[0][1] = 250;
  xy[0][2] = 250;
  xy[0][3] = 50;

  //y positions
  xy[1][0] = 50;
  xy[1][1] = 50;
  xy[1][2] = 250;
  xy[1][3] = 250;

  // call plotting function
  makeRect(xy);
}

void makeRect(float[][]pts){
  stroke(255);
  smooth();

  // scribble variables, that get passed as arguments
  // to the scribble function
  int steps = 100;
  float scribVal = 3.0;
  for (int i=0; i<pts[0].length; i++){
    //plots vertices
    strokeWeight(5);
    point(pts[0][i], pts[1][i]);
```

```
    //call scribble function
    strokeWeight(.5);
    if (i>0){
      scribble(pts[0][i], pts[1][i], pts[0][i-1], pts[1][i-1], ➥
          steps, scribVal, SCRIBBLE);
    }
    if (i== pts[0].length-1){
    // show some hatching between last 2 points
      scribble(pts[0][i], pts[1][i], pts[0][0], pts[1][0], steps, ➥
          scribVal*2, HATCHING);
    }
  }
}


/*
scribble function plots lines between end points,
determined by steps and scribVal arguments.
2 styles are available: SCRIBBLE and HATCHING, which
are interestingly only dependent on parentheses
placement in the line() function calls.
*/
void scribble(float x1, float y1, float x2, float y2, int steps, ➥
        float scribVal, int style){

  float xStep = (x2-x1)/steps;
  float yStep = (y2-y1)/steps;
  for (int i=0; i<steps; i++){
    if(style == SCRIBBLE){
      if (i<steps-1){
        line(x1, y1, x1+=xStep+random(-scribVal, scribVal), y1+= ➥
            yStep+random(-scribVal, scribVal));
      }
      else {
        // extra line needed to attach line back to point-
        // not necessary in HATCHING style
        line(x1, y1, x2, y2);
      }
    }
    else if (style == HATCHING){
      line(x1, y1, (x1+=xStep)+random(-scribVal, scribVal), ➥
          (y1+=yStep)+random(-scribVal, scribVal));
    }
  }
}
```

6

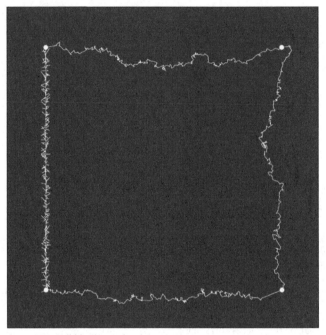

Figure 6-34. Scribble Plotter sketch

There's nothing new in this sketch. However, there are a few details that might need a little clarification. The two constant variables SCRIBBLE and HATCHING have global scope since I declared them at the top of the program.

```
int SCRIBBLE = 0;
int HATCHING = 1;
```

I passed them in as arguments from the makeRect() function to the scribble() function. They are capitalized, denoting that they are constants and should not be assigned a new value. If I really wanted to enforce that they shouldn't be changed, I could have prefaced the declaration statements with the word final, as in final int HATCHING = 1. final is technically a Java keyword—it's not within the Processing API—but it can be used within Processing. If you expand upon this sketch (which I hope you do), and want to add another scribble-style algorithm, then create a new constant, pass it as an argument, and detect for it in the scribble() function.

Hopefully you can make some sense of the scribble() function. I'm dividing up the x and y distances between the starting and ending points (passed into the function), and then plotting lines to those intermediate positions. The random() function just jitters the placement of the line vertices. The SCRIBBLE style requires an extra line of code to ensure that the final line connects back to the original point. Try commenting out the line() function call within the else block inside the scribble function() conditional block.

```
else {
        // extra line needed to attach line back to point- ➡
            not necessary in HATCHING style
        line(x1, y1, x2, y2);  //try commenting this line out
}
```

The HATCHING style doesn't require this fix. Finally, you'll notice that I use the same variable name, steps, for the local variable in the makeRect() function and the parameter in the scribble() function. I can do this because the steps variable is declared within the makeRect() function, not at the top of the sketch. Therefore, it is local in scope to the makeRect() function and not visible anywhere else. Thus, I can use the same-named variable in both functions without any conflict. Of course, you can use unique names if that seems simpler to you. Personally, I find it hard to keep coming up with new related names, so I tend to reuse local variable names.

Well, enough of this low-level point recording business—let's luxuriate through the rest of this chapter using Processing's user-friendly vertex() function.

Applying the vertex function

The vertex() function is called between the beginShape() and endShape() functions, which internally take care of the point recording and rendering just discussed. You've looked at the POINTS mode already. The LINES mode works similarly, except instead of rendering points, vertices are connected by lines in groups of two. For example, the following code generates a horizontal line:

```
size(300, 300);
background(255);
beginShape(LINES);
vertex(20, height/2);
vertex(width-20, height/2);
endShape();
```

Since the lines are laid down in groups of two vertices, adding a third vertex() function call will have no effect on the output:

```
size(300, 300);
background(255);
beginShape(LINES);
vertex(20, height/2);
vertex(width-20, height/2);
vertex(width/2, height-20);  //will have no effect
endShape();
```

I need a fourth vertex() call to generate another line:

```
size(300, 300);
background(255);
beginShape(LINES);
vertex(20, height/2);
vertex(width-20, height/2);
vertex(width/2, height-20);
vertex(width/2, 20);
endShape();
```

This mode isn't much of an improvement over just calling two line() functions. The following code, for example, gives the exact same output as the last, but in four lines rather than eight:

```
size(300, 300);
background(255);
line(20, height/2, width-20, height/2);
line(width/2, height-20, width/2, 20);
```

Creating line strips

The situation, however, changes once you try to generate a line strip, which uses a no-argument version of beginShape(). By default, beginShape() creates an open and filled path. You need to call noFill() if you want to generate an unfilled line strip. For example, the next sketch, shown in Figure 6-35, fills the display window with random vertices all connected by a continuous path. If you used the line() function, you would need to keep feeding previous second point positions into the next line call. I implemented this approach as a comparison, which I think you'll agree is a much less elegant solution.

```
// elegant vertex() appraoch
size(300, 300);
background(255);
strokeWeight(3);
noFill();
smooth();
beginShape();
for (int i=0; i<100; i++){
  vertex(random(width), random(height));
}
endShape();

// kludgy line() approach
size(300, 300);
background(255);
strokeWeight(3);
```

```
smooth();
float x = random(width);
float y = random(height);
for (int i=0; i<100; i++){
  float x2 = random(width);
  float y2 = random(height);
  line(x, y, x2, y2);
  x = x2;
  y = y2;
}
```

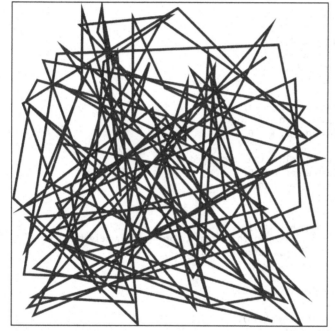

Figure 6-35. Line Strip sketch

Generating line strips opens up some interesting possibilities. One of these is maze creation. Rather than considering maze structures as purely logic puzzles, which are also very interesting, I'm going to focus on the aesthetics of the geometric patterning of mazes. One fairly simple pattern is a concentric path, which begins at either an outer or inner boundary and proceeds to the opposite boundary with some predetermined rule pattern. For example, the rule might be to turn 90 degrees when you get within a certain distance of an existing boundary.

The following sketch creates a concentric maze, but instead of using a more elegant rule-based algorithm, my cruder solution simply alters a vertical and horizontal stepping variable each iteration of the loop, beginning at the outer boundary. My implementation does allow you to have asymmetry with regard to the x- and y-axes, as well as use any display window size. I also utilize a few new functions in the loop that will require some clarification. Figure 6-36 shows the output of the code.

```
/*
Concentric Maze
Ira Greenberg, November 25, 2005
revised October 18, 2006
*/

size(400, 400);
background(0);
strokeWeight(1);
stroke(255);
smooth();
float x = width-1;
float y = height-1;
float y2 = 0, x2 = 0;
float h = 0, w = 0;

//these values can be changed
float wStep = 10.0;
float hStep = 10.0;
noFill();
beginShape();
vertex(x-w, y2+h);
for (int i=min(width, height); i>min(width, height)/2; ➥
        i-=max(wStep, hStep)){
  vertex(x-w, y-h);
  vertex(x2+w, y-h);
  vertex(x2+w, y2+h);
  w+=wStep;
  vertex(x-w, y2+h);
  h+=hStep;
}
endShape();
```

Figure 6-36. Concentric Maze sketch

Before I describe the new min() and max() functions I used in the sketch, I just want to make sure you fully understand the following statements:

```
float x = width-1;
float y = height-1;
float y2 = 0, x2 = 0;
float h = 0, w = 0;
```

In the first two lines, I subtract 1 from the width and height properties. I do this so that I can see the maze output on the right and bottom edges of the display window. Try removing the subtraction to see the difference. In the next two lines, I declare both the y2 and x2 variables as floats, and do the assignment on a single line. This is just a shortcut. I could have done the assignment on two lines as well. I do the same thing on the next line with the w and h variables. All four of these lines could also have been put on one line.

```
float y2 = 0, x2 = 0, h = 0, w = 0;
```

However, the benefit of only having to write "float" once is offset by the visual complexity of so many assignments. Ultimately, these type of issues are a matter of personal style.

The new function calls I used, min() and max(), are stuck in the head of the for loop:

```
for (int i=min(width, height); i>min(width, height)/2; i-=max(wStep,
hStep)){...
```

The min() and max() functions each take two arguments and spit back the lower or higher value, respectively. I used them to ensure that the maze was drawn correctly, regardless of what the display window or wStep and hStep values were set to. The problem they solve is correcting for potential asymmetrical values assigned to the aforementioned variables. For example, if the width and height arguments in the size() function were set to 600 and 400, my loop wouldn't be able to adjust itself if I were using width to control the loop limit. I would always need the smaller dimension to be the loop limit for the auto-adjustment to work. Since (theoretically) users may sometimes make the width argument bigger than height, or vice versa, there is no way to hard-code a value as the loop limit. By using the min() and max() functions, the loop automatically figures out the limiting variable (either the minimum value of either width or height, or the maximum value of wStep or hStep) and adjusts itself appropriately. This is a hard concept to explain in words, so I suggest playing with the values for width, height, wStep, and hStep. You can also try substituting the following for loop head into the sketch:

```
for (int i=width; i>width/2; i-=wStep)
```

while continuing to change all four values. You may notice that the substitute loop head creates less ordered but more interesting output.

Next I created a tiled version of the maze (see Figure 6-37). The sketch puts together a bunch of concepts discussed thus far in this chapter. There's a lot more that could be done with this sketch—for example, adding the scribble() function or additional random() functions. You could also add another maze pattern algorithm in the createMaze() function. I've included comments that show you what variables you can safely change. (Of course, safety aside, it's also helpful to sometimes break the code to get a better sense of how it works.)

```
/*
Maze Tile 1
Ira Greenberg, November 25, 2005
revised October 18, 2006
*/

// declare some vars
float x, y, y2, x2, h, w, xShift, yShift;

//these values can be changed
int xSclFactor = 3;
int ySclFactor = 3;
float wStep = 4;
float hStep = 4;
```

```
void setup(){
  //these values can be changed
  size(400, 400);
  background(0);
  strokeWeight(1);
  stroke(255);
  noFill();
  smooth();
 //end changeable stuff

  x = width/xSclFactor;
  y = height/ySclFactor;
  y2 = x2 = 0;
  for (int i=0; i<width; i+=x){
    for (int j=0; j<height; j+=y){
      h = w = 0;
      yShift = j;
      xShift = i;
      createMaze();
    }
  }
}

void createMaze(){
  beginShape();
  vertex((x-w)+xShift, (y2+h)+yShift);
  for (float i=min(width/xSclFactor, height/ySclFactor); ➥
      i>min(width/xSclFactor, height/ySclFactor)/2; ➥
      i-=max(wStep, hStep)){
    vertex((x-w)+xShift, (y-h)+yShift);
    vertex((x2+w)+xShift, (y-h)+yShift);
    vertex((x2+w)+xShift, (y2+h)+yShift);
    w+=wStep;
    vertex((x-w)+xShift, (y2+h)+yShift);
    h+=hStep;
  }
  endShape();
}
```

6

Figure 6-37. Maze Tile 1 sketch

Line loops

It's also possible to close a line strip, turning it into a line loop. The endShape() function has an optional CLOSE argument that closes the strip. Since the CLOSE mode generates complete shapes, I thought it would be fun to generate some polygonal geometry; and the best (and easiest) way to do that is to use a little trigonometry. Here's a very simple sketch that generates a triangle (see Figure 6-38). (Yes, I know Processing comes with a triangle() function; but it's actually a lot easier to use a little trig to calculate the vertices of a triangle rather than having to explicitly set the vertices. Also, once you have the triangle code, you can easily modify it to generate any regular polygon—which I'll show you how to do shortly.)

```
//Create a Triangle
size(400, 400);
background(0);
stroke(255);
strokeWeight(5);
smooth();
noFill();
float x = 0, y = 0;
// sets initial shape rotation
float angle = 30;

beginShape();
for (int i=0; i<3; i++){
  x = width/2+cos(radians(angle))*width/2.5;
  y = height/2+sin(radians(angle))*width/2.5;
  vertex(x, y);
  // create an equilateral tirangle
  angle+=120;
}
endShape(CLOSE);
```

Figure 6-38. Create a Triangle sketch

Save for the two trig functions, the rest of this sketch should look pretty familiar. I think you'll also soon agree that implementing trig is relatively easy in Processing. The triangle code relies on trig relationships, based on the unit circle, to do its thing. I discuss trigonometry briefly in Chapter 4, but also provide a more detailed explanation, including an illustration of the unit circle, in Appendix B. Essentially, the unit circle tells you that the location of any point on a circle can be found by using an angle of rotation, commonly called **theta**, and the radius of the circle. However, the unit circle lives in a polar coordinate system, not the happy Cartesian system we use on a computer screen. Thus, you also need to convert from the polar to the Cartesian coordinate system to get your x and y coordinates. The two general statements to do all of this are as follows:

x coordinate = x position of the center of circle + cos(angle of rotation in radians) * radius

y coordinate = y position of the center of circle + sin(angle of rotation in radians) * radius

Returning to the two trig expressions in the triangle sketch, I used the center of the display window as the center point of the unit circle, which will also be the center point of the triangle. The function radians(angle) converts from degrees to radians; the actual conversion expression is **(angle in radians) = (angle in degrees) * pi / 180**, which is what the radians() function encapsulates. Lastly, I used width/2.5 as the radius.

Processing includes a function that lets you control how lines join together. Earlier, you looked at the function strokeCap(), which controls the end caps of lines. The function strokeJoin() controls the way the end caps come together to form joints. There are three different join options, in the form of integer arguments (constants): MITER, which is the default; BEVEL; and ROUND. This next example uses the triangle code to show the difference in the respective join options (see Figure 6-39 for the output).

```
//create 3 triangles
size(600, 200);
background(0);
stroke(255);
noFill();
strokeWeight(10);
smooth();
float x = 0, y = 0;
// sets initial shape rotation
float angle = 30;
// join types
int[]joins = {MITER, BEVEL, ROUND};
for (int j=1; j<4; j++){
  beginShape();
  strokeJoin(joins[j-1]);
  for (int i=0; i<3; i++){
    x = (width/4)*j+cos(radians(angle))*width/8;
    y = height/2+sin(radians(angle))*width/8;
    vertex(x, y);
    // create an equilateral tirangle
    angle+=120;
  }
  endShape(CLOSE);
}
```

Figure 6-39. Create 3 Triangles sketch

Polygons and patterns

Now that you have a basic understanding about how the trig functions can be used to identify a point on a circle, you can exploit that knowledge to generate any regular polygon. (Even if you don't yet fully grasp—or even care—how the trig functions work, you can still use them. In fact, through using them, you'll get a better understanding of how they work than through reading about them). The following example incorporates the beginShape() and endShape(CLOSE) functions in a basic polygon-creation algorithm (the output is shown in Figure 6-40):

```
/*
Poly Maker
Ira Greenberg, November 26, 2005
revised October 18, 2006
*/

void setup(){
  size(400, 400);
  background(0);
  smooth();
  noFill();
  makePoly(width/2, height/2, 9, 150, 255, 8, MITER);
}

void makePoly(int x, int y, int points, float radius, ➡
  int strokeCol, float strokeWt, int strokeJn){
  float px=0, py=0;
  float angle = 0;
  stroke(strokeCol);
  strokeJoin(strokeJn);
  strokeWeight(strokeWt);
  beginShape();
```

6

```
  for (int i=0; i<points; i++){
    px = x+cos(radians(angle))*radius;
    py = y+sin(radians(angle))*radius;
    vertex(px, py);
    angle+=360/points;
  }
  endShape(CLOSE);
}
```

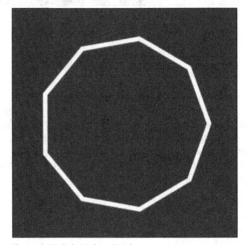

Figure 6-40. Poly Maker sketch

Try changing some of the argument values in the function call makePoly(width/2, height/2, 9, 150, 255, 8, MITER);. You can now use the makePoly() function to do some interesting things. Overlapping geometry can lead to fascinating patterns. This was one of the first experiments I did when I was learning to program that got me really excited about the aesthetic potential of code.

The last three sketches in the chapter generate geometric patterns. I've included two screen shots for each sketch. The first sketch, shown in Figures 6-41 and 6-42, is a polygonal table structure, with a bunch of random() functions thrown in. The second, shown in Figures 6-43 and 6-44, is a spiral built of polygons; and the third, shown in Figures 6-45 and 6-46, is a polystar constructed of overlapping radial geometry. This last example utilizes a modified polygon function that creates both regular polygons and poly-stars. A "polystar," which is my own made-up name, is just a polygon with a second radius, like a star. These two radii can also have both negative and positive values. As always, there are numerous values to change in all three of these sketches, with a wide range of poten-tial output. These examples incorporate much of the stuff covered in this chapter, so I'd take some time with them before heading to Chapter 7. Also try not to worry if some/most of the code still looks like gobbledygook. You'll be revisiting all the coding concepts in this chapter throughout the rest of the book.

Poly Pattern I (table structure)

```
/*
Poly Pattern I
Ira Greenberg, November 26, 2005
revised October 18, 2006
pattern: table structure
*/
void setup(){
  size(400, 400);
  background(0);
  smooth();

  //you can change these values
  int hGap = 12;
  int wGap = 12;
  int[]rads = { 3, 4, 5, 6, 7, 8 };
  int randSize = 3;
  int randPos = 3;

  for (int j=0; j<=width; j+=wGap){
    for (int i=0, radCntr=0; i<=height; i+=hGap, radCntr++){
      makePoly(j+random(-randPos, randPos), i+randPos, rads[radCntr],➡
        wGap/2+random(-randSize, randSize), 255, radCntr*.4, MITER);

      // reset counter to avoid ArrayIndexOutOfBounds error
      if (radCntr>rads.length-2){
        radCntr = 0;
      }
    }
  }
}

void makePoly(float x, float y, int points, float radius, ➡
      int strokeCol, float strokeWt, int strokeJn){
  float px=0, py=0;
  float angle = 0;
  stroke(strokeCol);
  noFill();
  strokeJoin(strokeJn);
  strokeWeight(strokeWt);
  beginShape();
  for (int i=0; i<points; i++){
    px = x+cos(radians(angle))*radius;
    py = y+sin(radians(angle))*radius;
    vertex(px, py);
    angle+=360/points;
  }
  endShape(CLOSE);
}
```

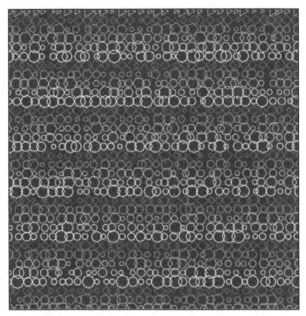

Figure 6-41. Poly Pattern I (table structure) sketch, variation 1

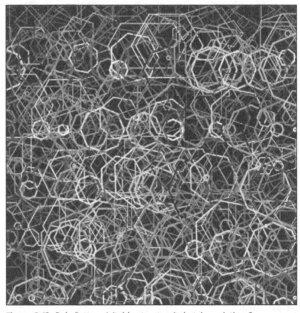

Figure 6-42. Poly Pattern I (table structure) sketch, variation 2

Poly Pattern II (spiral)

```
/*
Poly Pattern II
Ira Greenberg, November 26, 2005
revised October 18, 2006
pattern: spiral
*/

void setup(){
  size(400, 400);
  background(0);
  smooth();
  float radius = 0, radius2 = 0;
  float x = 0, y = 0;
  float ang = 0;
  while(x<width*1.5){
    y = height/2+sin(radians(ang))*radius;
    x = width/2+cos(radians(ang))*radius;
    makePoly(x, y, 8,  radius2, int(radius2*30), 6, BEVEL);

    // you can change these values
    ang+=1.1;
    radius+=.059;
    radius2+=.0016;
  }
}

void makePoly(float x, float y, int points, float radius, ➡
              int strokeCol, float strokeWt, int strokeJn){
  float px=0, py=0;
  float angle = 0;
  stroke(strokeCol);
  noFill();
  strokeJoin(strokeJn);
  strokeWeight(strokeWt);
  beginShape();
  for (int i=0; i<points; i++){
    px = x+cos(radians(angle))*radius;
    py = y+sin(radians(angle))*radius;
    vertex(px, py);
    angle+=360/points;
  }
  endShape(CLOSE);
}
```

6

Figure 6-43. Poly Pattern II (spiral) sketch, variation 1

Figure 6-44. Poly Pattern II (spiral) sketch, variation 2

Poly Pattern III (polystar)

```
/*
Poly Pattern III
Ira Greenberg, November 26, 2005
revised October 18, 2006
Pattern: PolyStar
*/

void setup(){
  size(400, 400);
  background(random(255));
  smooth();
  float ang = 0;
  int steps = int(random(30, 200));
  for (int i=0; i<steps; i++){
    makePolyStar(width/2, height/2, int(random(3, 10)), ➡
                 ang+=360/steps, random(-width/2, width/2), ➡
                 random(-width/2, width/2), int(random(255)), ➡
                 random(.25, 5), MITER);
  }
}

void makePolyStar(float x, float y, int points, float initAngle, ➡
    float radius, float radius2, int strokeCol, float strokeWt, ➡
    int strokeJn){
  float px=0, py=0;
  float angle = initAngle;
  float initRadius = radius;
  float halfRadius = radius2;
  stroke(strokeCol);
  noFill();
  strokeJoin(strokeJn);
  strokeWeight(strokeWt);
  beginShape();
  // if 2nd radius create polystar
  // else create regular poly
  if (radius2 !=0){
    points*=2;
  }
  for (int i=0; i<points; i++){
    //alternates radius length if polystar
    if (radius2 != 0 && i%2 == 0){
      radius = halfRadius;
    }
    else {
      radius = initRadius;
    }
    px = x+cos(radians(angle))*radius;
```

6

```
    py = y+sin(radians(angle))*radius;
    vertex(px, py);
    angle+=360/points;
  }
  endShape(CLOSE);
}
```

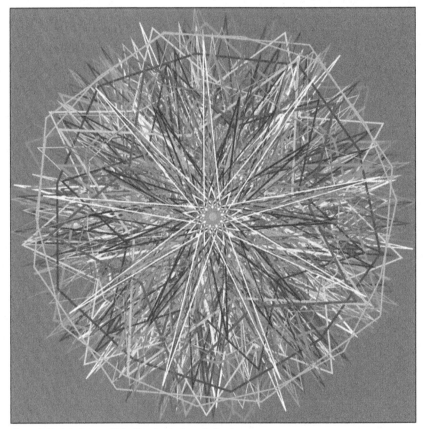

Figure 6-45. Poly Pattern III (polystar) sketch, variation 1

Figure 6-46. Poly Pattern III (polystar) sketch, variation 2

Summary

The beginning of this chapter let you look a little under Processing's hood, and it discussed how Processing functions are internally implemented. Once you got past this section, you dove into Processing's point() and line() functions, and generated a couple of interesting linear outputs. This chapter utilized lots of randomization in the sketches, demonstrating the power of controlled chaos as a creative coding force. You began with some simple, unstructured sketches that executed one line at a time, and continued on to more complex sketches that utilized modular structures, such as Processing's setup() function, as well as some custom functions and nested loops.

You worked with a number of Processing's functions in this chapter, including point(), line(), vertex(), beginShape(), and endShape(). You also looked briefly at PImage, which you'll return to again in later chapters. Using the vertex() function, you created some fairly complex table structures and maze patterns, and even tackled a little trigonometry with the polygonal sketches.

A lot has been covered in this chapter, and I'd say you have earned a little brain downtime. The next chapter will look at curves, which will include a review of a lot of the concepts covered in this chapter. Of course, there will also be a fair amount of new (and I think cool) stuff. I recommend, after your earned downtime, reviewing some of the sketches covered in this chapter before moving on. I also think it might be a good time to refer to the reference material in the earlier chapters (as well as the language reference in Appendix A) on some of the more irksome concepts you might still be fuzzy on. Of course, moderation aside, if you're feeling up to it, just turn the page and dive into the joy of curves.

7 CURVES

Curvy stuff is difficult for people to understand. Had I taken a calculus class earlier in my life, this fact would have been blatantly obvious. When drawing directly from a model, edges are indistinct and there are all sorts of subtle foreshortening. In time, you learn how to, in a sense, "not draw" what's not there, which is often the secret to allowing the curve structures to emerge in the drawing. When it comes to coding, curves again prove especially challenging, and often require a more "mathy" approach than when working with lines. Processing does make it relatively easy to generate simple curves, but being able to precisely control a combination of curves to create a form such as a human figure is very difficult.

That being said, the additional effort and added complexity of dealing with curves is well worth it, as there is something exciting about seeing organic forms and animation emerge; it's what really got me hooked on coding to begin with. In my classes, at the beginning of a semester I'll often show organic code-based animation examples to my students; this always gets them oohing and ahhing. (Of course, they make other sounds when they begin wrestling with the actual curve implementation and math.)

This chapter will explore curves in detail, beginning with how to make the transition between straight lines and curves. After that, I'll discuss creating curves using trig and polynomials, and then I'll explain Processing's curve functions in depth.

Making the transition from lines to curves

I began the last chapter with a discussion about points, and showed how a line is really just a continuous path of points. I eventually showed you how to utilize a more efficient system of terminal vertices to describe the beginning and ending points of lines. Processing's line() function takes four arguments (the x and y components of two points) and joins the points with a straight line. In beginning to think about curves, you need to consider how Processing connects the two points with a line, which you can then modify into a curve. As a review, here is a simple script to generate a vertical line utilizing a series of points, as shown in Figure 7-1:

```
size(200, 200);
background(255);
int margin = height/15;
strokeWeight(5);
for (int i=margin; i<height-margin; i++){
  point(width/2, i);
}
```

Figure 7-1.
Combining points
into a line

Hopefully this looks very familiar. The for loop generates a vertical line in the middle of the display window from a series of points, beginning at margin and ending at height (of the display window) minus margin. You'll remember that point() is really a call to the line() function, using the same two points as arguments; that's why I was able to change the thickness of the points, and thus the line, with strokeWeight(5). As an example, here's the same sketch using line():

```
size(200, 200);
background(255);
int margin = height/15;
strokeWeight(5);
for (int i=margin; i<height-margin; i++){
  line(width/2, i, width/2, i);  // notice both points are the same
}
```

In this simple sketch, it can be said in describing the line that the x position of the line remains constant while the y position changes. You may remember that the slope of a line is the change in y divided by the change in x. If you tried to figure out the slope of the vertical line, you would use the following expression:

```
y²-y¹/x²-x¹
= ((height-margin)-margin)/(width/2-width/2)
= 174/0 // oops, can't divide by 0
slope = undefined
```

You see the problem with this expression—you can't divide by 0. Therefore, a vertical line has no slope, or the slope is undefined. How about a horizontal line? Following is the sketch modified to make a horizontal line:

```
size(200, 200);
background(255);
int margin = width/15;
strokeWeight(5);
for (int i=margin; i<width-margin; i++){
  line(i, height/2, i, height/2);  // both points are the same
}
```

Calculating the slope of this line results in the following:

```
= (height/2-height/2)/((width-margin)-margin)
= 0/174
slope = 0
```

Confusingly, a horizontal line has a slope of 0. This is the kind of annoying detail that contributes to many cases of "math coma." We're not going to focus on vertical and horizontal lines (which aren't terribly exciting). Instead, I'll start with diagonals, which will lead to curves—which are actually very interesting (honestly).

The equation for the vertical line was **x = height/2**, and the equation for the horizontal line was **y = width/2**. You don't need to really worry so much about equations, but it's helpful to understand a little about what's happening to the x and y values when plotting different types of lines and curves. You'll notice in both the vertical and horizontal line equations that only one value (x or y) is needed to describe the line. That's because only one of the values is changing; the other remains constant as the line is plotted. To describe a diagonal line, both of the x and y values need to change as the line is plotted. There are a couple ways to express a line, but I think the simplest is using the slope-intercept form:

$y = mx + b$. **y** and **x** are just the coordinate values, **m** is the slope, and **b** is the place on the y-axis that the line intercepts. Again, you don't need to explicitly use the classical equations, but knowing them can help you better understand what's happening in your sketch.

Here's a diagonal line example (shown in Figure 7-2):

```
/*
Diagonal Line I
Ira Greenberg, December 3, 2005
*/
size(200, 200);
background(255);
int margin = width/15;
strokeWeight(5);
smooth();
float x = margin, y = margin;
float deltaX = 1.2;
float deltaY = 1.2;

if (deltaX>deltaY){
  while(x<width-margin){
    point(x, y);
    x += deltaX;
    y += deltaY;
  }
} else{
  while(y<height-margin){
    point(x, y);
    x += deltaX;
    y += deltaY;
  }
}
```

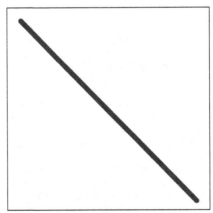

Figure 7-2. Combining points into a diagonal

You should notice some familiar structures in this example. I called the smooth() function to turn on anti-aliasing, and I used two while loops nested within a conditional if...else structure to ensure that the line stays in the display window. Try changing the values of the deltaX and deltaY variables to see how the diagonal changes (see Figures 7-3 and 7-4 for a couple of examples).

```
deltaX = .7;
deltaY = 1.2;
```

Figure 7-3. A more vertical diagonal

```
deltaX = 1.4;
deltaY = .2;
```

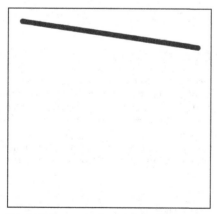

Figure 7-4. A more horizontal diagonal

As the deltaX and deltaY values become farther apart, the line visually approaches either a vertical or horizontal line. The most diagonal line (if there is such a thing) is when deltaX and deltaY are equal, or the change in x and the change in y are equal. As you might have guessed, this is also when the slope is 1. Slope is a very important property in describing motion, which I'll cover in Chapter 11. Speed is the rate at which position is changing. When you plot a diagonal line as a function of distance and time, as shown in Figure 7-5, the slope of the plotted line is speed.

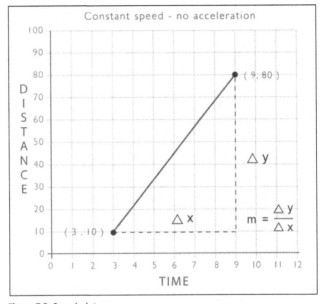

Figure 7-5. Speed plot

Creating your first curve

Without acceleration, speed is a constant and will always generate a straight line, as the rate of change will be constant. Starting with different constant values of speed, you can change the steepness, or slope, of the line, as the previous example showed, but you can never get a curve if you keep the speed (or slope) constant. Thus, it would seem logical, if you wanted to generate a curve, to use a changing speed value—which is precisely what you'll do next. This is also the reason why curves, with regard to motion, describe acceleration, or the change in speed. This next sketch (shown in Figure 7-6) is a curve plot:

```
/*
Curve I
Ira Greenberg, December 3, 2005
*/
size(200, 200);
background(255);
```

```
int margin = height/15;
strokeWeight(5);
smooth();
float x = margin, y = margin;
float xSpeed = 1.1, ySpeed = 1.02;
while(y<height-margin){
  point(x, y);
  x+=xSpeed; // arithmetic progression
  y*=ySpeed; // geometric progression
}
```

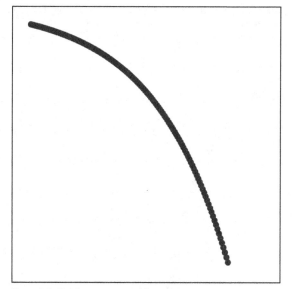

Figure 7-6. Simple curve created from points

Congratulations, you just plotted your first curve! There are many ways to implement a curve plot. I used a simple approach that increments x by xSpeed (using addition):

```
x+=xSpeed; // arithmetic progression
```

and y by ySpeed (using multiplication).

```
y*=ySpeed; // geometric progression
```

Notice that the initial values I assigned to the two speed variables are very different. In the while loop, x is incremented by xSpeed in a similar fashion to how x was incremented by deltaX in the diagonal example. x increases by 1.1 each iteration of the loop. This type of progression, generated by adding a constant value (in this case 1.1) is called an **arithmetical progression**. Here are the first and last three values of the progression, where the initial values of x and y are both 13 (margin value):

7

247

- **First three values**: 14.1, 15.2, 16.3
- **Last three values**: 159.3, 160.4, 161.5

As you can see, the change between any two consecutive values will always be xSpeed (1.1). In contrast, y is incremented by the constant 1.02 using multiplication. This is called a **geometric progression**. Here are the first and last three values in this progression:

- **First three values**: 13.26, 13.53, 13.80
- **Last three values**: 181.04, 184.66, 188.35

The difference between any consecutive values will no longer be a constant value throughout the entire progression. This change in speed generates a curve. Let's alter some values in the curve plot to see how it effects the curve (see Figures 7-7 and 7-8):

```
float xSpeed = .5, ySpeed = 1.02;
```

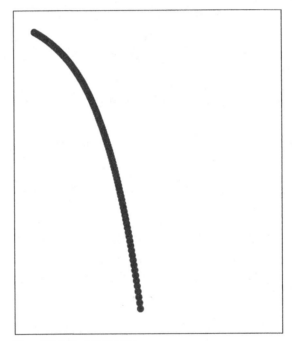

Figure 7-7. Faster falling curve

```
float xSpeed = 6.6, ySpeed = 1.11;
```

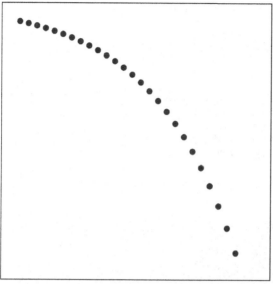

Figure 7-8. Revealing the points making up the curve

In Figure 7-7, I just decreased xSpeed, making the curve fall faster, since the x progression is slower. In the second example, I increased both variables considerably, maintaining a similarly shaped curve, but with a much faster overall progression, revealing the points making up the curve.

I want to look at some other relatively simple ways to generate curves; but before I do, here are some more interesting examples building upon what you just learned (see Figure 7-9). (If you don't see any output in the examples, try raising the strokeWeight(1.5) argument from 1.5 to 2 or above).

```
/*
Curves I
Ira Greenberg, December 4, 2005
*/
int steps = 300;
float[]x = new float[steps];
float[]y = new float[steps];
float[]xSpeed = new float[steps];
float[]ySpeed = new float[steps];

void setup(){
  size(400, 400);
  background(255);
  float margin = height*.1;
  smooth();
  strokeWeight(1.5);
```

```
for (int i=0; i<steps; i++){
  x[i] = 0;
  y[i] = random(margin);
  xSpeed[i] = random(.75, 1.2);
  ySpeed[i] = random(1.0075, 1.04);
}

for (int i=0; i<steps; i++){
  while(y[i]<height){
    point(x[i], y[i]);
    x[i]+=xSpeed[i];
    y[i]*=ySpeed[i];
  }
}
}
```

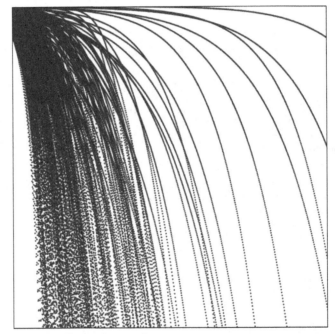

Figure 7-9. Falling random strands

This example uses arrays to generate 300 curves, with some random values. The overlapping curves generate interesting forms, suggestive of flowing strands of hair or water. As the points begin spacing out, a system of particles begins emerging. You can exploit this phenomenon further by adding a minimal amount of collision detection, allowing the particles to deflect off the display window edges. The next example, shown in Figure 7-10, is implemented a little differently and includes window edge detection.

```
/*
Curves II
Ira Greenberg, December 4, 2005
*/
int particles = 25;
float[]x = new float[particles];
float[]y = new float[particles];
float[]xSpeed = new float[particles];
float[]ySpeed = new float[particles];
float[]accel = new float[particles];
float gravity = .75;

void setup(){
  size(800, 400);
  background(0);
  smooth();
  strokeWeight(1.5);
  stroke(255);

  //fill speed arrays with initial values
  for (int i=0; i<particles; i++){
    xSpeed[i] = random(.75, 1.2);
    accel[i] = random(.005, .2);
  }

  for (int i=0; i<particles; i++){
    //stop particle on collision with right edge of display window
    while(x[i]<width){
      x[i]+=xSpeed[i];

      // double assignment creates y acceleration
      ySpeed[i] += accel[i];
      y[i]+=ySpeed[i];
      point(x[i], y[i]);

      // check ground detection only
      if ( y[i]>=height){
        // reverse particle direction
        ySpeed[i]*=-1;
        // lower particle speed
        ySpeed [i]*=gravity;
        // keep particle from sliding out of window
        y[i]=height;
      }
    }
  }
}
```

7

Figure 7-10. Falling random bouncing strands

This example is similar to the last, but I achieved the curved motion using a slightly different algorithm. Instead of multiplying y by a ratio, I used a double arithmetic incrementation. The lines

```
ySpeed[i] += accel[i];
y[i] += ySpeed[i];
```

create the acceleration. It may not be immediately apparent how this works. However, if you look at a few values during the loop iterations, it becomes clear what's happening. To keep things simple, let's assume the value assigned to accel, for one of the particles, is .1. Following are the ySpeed and y values after five iterations:

```
iteration1: ySpeed= .1,   y = .1
iteration2: ySpeed = .2,  y = .3   (y change: .2)
iteration3: ySpeed = .3,  y = .6   (y change: .3)
iteration4: ySpeed = .4,  y = 1.0  (y change: .4)
iteration4: ySpeed = .5,  y = 1.5  (y change: .5)
```

Notice how the y value is changing by an increasing interval: .2, .3, .4, .5; this is what generates the acceleration.

The display window collision detection allows the particles to remain active longer and thus graphically add to the image. The detection is pretty straightforward: if a particle's y position is greater than or equal to the height of the display window, then reverse the direction of the particle and also multiply ySpeed by the gravity variable. Here's the code snippet:

```
// check ground detection only
    if ( y[i]>=height){
      // reverse particle direction
      ySpeed[i]*=-1;
```

```
        // lower particle speed
        ySpeed[i]*=gravity;
        // keep particle from sliding out of window
        y[i]=height;
    }
```

This expression slowly reduces the particle's velocity (ySpeed) until it is very near zero. However, because ySpeed will actually never reach zero, I am forced to add the final assignment, y[i]=height, which keeps the particles from slowly creeping off the bottom of the screen. I'll revisit this issue again in more detail in Chapter 11. As always, play with the code. If you comment out this last assignment, you should notice the output is a little lower in relation to the display window.

In the next example (shown in Figure 7-11), I pushed this particle effect a little further, utilizing a new material property, more randomization, and additional display edge detection. There's nothing really new in the example, but it should reveal some more of the interesting effects you can get coding curved motion. This example can take a long time to render—up to 30 seconds. Decreasing the strokeWtMin and strokeWtMax argument values will speed things up. However, on some systems, too small a value may make the curves undetectable.

```
/*
Curves III
Ira Greenberg, December 4, 2005
// this takes some time to render
*/

// changeable variables
int particles = 125;
int timeLimit = 2000;
float particleSpan = 2;
float accelMin = .005;
float accelMax = .2;
float strokeWtMin = 1.25;
float strokeWtMax = 1.6;
float materialMin = .25;
float materialMax = .99;
float gravity = .9;

// not meant to be changed
int timer;
float[]x = new float[particles];
float[]y = new float[particles];
float[]xSpeed = new float[particles];
float[]ySpeed = new float[particles];
float[]accel = new float[particles];
float[]material = new float[particles];
float[]strokeWts = new float[particles];
```

```
void setup(){
  size(800, 400);
  background(0);
  smooth();
  stroke(255);

  //fill speed arrays with initial values
  for (int i=0; i<particles; i++){
    x[i] = random(width/2-10, width/2+10);
    xSpeed[i] = random(-particleSpan, particleSpan);
    accel[i] = random(accelMin, accelMax);
    material[i] = random(materialMin, materialMax);
    strokeWts[i] = random(strokeWtMin, strokeWtMax);
  }

  for (int i=0; i<particles; i++){
    //timer controls while loop
    timer = 0;
    strokeWeight(strokeWts[i]);

    while(timer++ < timeLimit){
      x[i]+=xSpeed[i];
      // double assignment creates y acceleration
      ySpeed[i]+=accel[i];
      y[i]+=ySpeed[i];
      point(x[i], y[i]);

      // check ground detection
      if ( y[i]>=height){
        // reverse particle direction
        ySpeed[i]*=-1*material[i];
        // lower particle speed
        ySpeed[i]*=gravity;
        // keep particle from sliding out of window
        y[i]=height;
      }
      // check wall detection
      if ( x[i]>=width || x[i]<0){
        // reverse particle horizontal direction
        xSpeed[i]*=-1;
      }
    }
  }
}
```

Figure 7-11. Curves simulating a fountain

Creating curves using trig

Another relatively easy way to generate a curve is to utilize a trig function. Sine and cosine functions both generate a repeating periodic wave. Here's a simple example (shown in Figure 7-12):

```
//trig wave
size(400, 200);
background(0);
stroke(255);
float angle = 0;
float amplitude = 10;
float x = 0, y = 0;
float xSpeed = 1;
float frequency = 3.0;
smooth();

for (int i=0; i<width; i+=xSpeed){
  strokeWeight(30);
  x+= xSpeed;
  //sin
  y = height/3 + sin(radians(angle))*amplitude;
  point(x, y);
  //cosine
  y = 2*(height/3) + cos(radians(angle))*amplitude;
  point(x, y);
  angle+=frequency;
}
```

7

Figure 7-12. Creating simple curves with trigonometry

The sin() and cos() functions are controlled by the incrementation of the angle (frequency) and the value of the amplitude. Try changing these variables to see how the plots are affected. You can also use a damping variable (which acts like gravity in the particle example) to decrease the amplitude of the trig functions over time. Here's an example of this (see Figure 7-13):

```
//waves with damping
size(400, 200);
background(0);
stroke(255);
float angle = 0;
float amplitude = 30;
float x = 0, y = 0;
float xSpeed = 1;
float frequency = 6.0;
float damping = .994;
strokeWeight(3);
smooth();

for (int i=0; i<width; i+=xSpeed){
  x+=xSpeed;
  //sin
  y = height/3 + sin(radians(angle))*amplitude;
  point(x, y);
  //cosine
  y = 2*(height/3) + cos(radians(angle))*amplitude;
  point(x, y);
  amplitude*=damping;
  angle+=frequency;
}
```

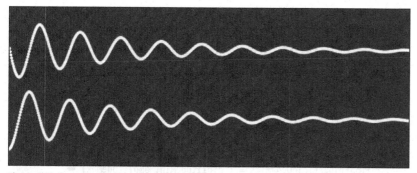

Figure 7-13. Damping effect on curves

In the last chapter, I demonstrated a scribble function, where endpoints of a line were sent to a function that randomly jittered points between the terminal points, creating a more organic-looking line. You can use trig functions in a similar capacity. I thought it might be interesting to put the particle effect together with the trig function to create particle waves (see Figure 7-14); it will also be a good review of using custom functions.

This is a fairly complex sketch. Each part of it is encapsulated in a function, and there are no global variables. Thus, the individual functions speak to each other through function calls. I recommend playing with the sketch for a while before reviewing the code. I completely parameterized the main particle function, so it's easy to mess with the variables in the setup() structure—seeing how the changes affect the output, as illustrated in Figure 7-15—before diving into the code guts.

```
/*
Particle Wave
Ira Greenberg, December 5, 2005
revised January 26, 2007
*/

void setup(){
  size(800, 400);
  background(0);
  smooth();

  /*lots of stuff to manipulate. I packed
   the arguments into arrays just to make the
   setParticles function argument/parameter
   lists less unwieldy*/
  //particle style
  /* increase strokeWt if
  you don't see any output*/
  float strokeWt = 1.5;
  float strokeCol= 255;
  float[]strokeStyle = { strokeWt, strokeCol   };
```

257

```
//particle limits
int timeLimit = 1000;
int particleCount = 100;
int[]particleLimits = {  timeLimit, particleCount    };

//particle dynamics
float amplitudeMin = .5;
float amplitudeMax = 4.0;
float frequencyMin = 4.0;
float frequencyMax = 40.0;
float materialMin = .25; // lead
float materialMax = .99; // rubber
float[]particleDynamics = { amplitudeMin, amplitudeMax, ➡
  frequencyMin, frequencyMax, materialMin, materialMax};

// speed limits
float accelMin = .005;
float accelMax = .2;
float xSpeedMin = -2.0;
float xSpeedMax = 2.0;
float[]speedLimits = { xSpeedMin, xSpeedMax, ➡
  accelMin, accelMax    };

float gravity = .85;
//position of particle emitter
float emitterX = width/2;
float emitterY = 0;
float[]world = {  gravity, emitterX, emitterY    };

//start particle engine
setParticles(strokeStyle, particleLimits, ➡
  particleDynamics, speedLimits, world);
}

// main particle engine - fully parameterized
void setParticles(float[]strokeStyle, int[]particleLimits,
  float[]particleDynamics, float[]speedLimits,  float[]world){
  //create arrays
  float[]xSpeed = new float[particleLimits[1]];
  float[]ySpeed = new float[particleLimits[1]];
  float[]accel = new float[particleLimits[1]];
  float[]x = new float[particleLimits[1]];
  float[]y = new float[particleLimits[1]];
  float[]amplitude = new float[particleLimits[1]];
  float[]frequency = new float[particleLimits[1]];
  float[]material = new float[particleLimits[1]];
```

```
    // particle style
    strokeWeight(strokeStyle[0]);
    stroke(strokeStyle[1]);

    //angle used as argument for makeWaves function call
    float angle = 0;

    //fill arrays
    for (int i=0; i<particleLimits[1]; i++){
      xSpeed[i] = random(speedLimits[0], speedLimits[1]);
      accel[i] = random(speedLimits[2], speedLimits[3]);
      amplitude[i] = random(particleDynamics[0], particleDynamics[1]);
      frequency[i] = random(particleDynamics[2], particleDynamics[3]);
      material[i] = random(particleDynamics[4], particleDynamics[5]);
      //emitter initial position
      x[i] = world[1];
      y[i] = world[2];
    }

    // dynamics engine
    for (int i=0; i<particleLimits[1]; i++){
      for (int j=0; j<particleLimits[0]; j++){
        x[i]+=xSpeed[i];
        // add waviness to call to makeWaves function
        x[i]=makeWaves(x[i], angle+=frequency[i], amplitude[i]);
        ySpeed[i]+=accel[i];
        y[i]+=ySpeed[i];
        // plot function just calls point() method
        plot(new float[]{
          x[i], y[i]          }
        );

        //ground detection
        if (y[i]>=height){
          ySpeed[i]*=-1*material[i];
          ySpeed[i]*=world[0];
          y[i] = height;
        }
        //wall detection
        if (x[i]>=width || x[i]<=0){
          xSpeed[i] *=-1;
        }
      }
    }
}
```

7

```
//generate wave
float makeWaves(float x, float angle, float amplitude){
  x+=sin(radians(angle))*amplitude;
  return x;
}

// draw points
void plot(float[]pt){
  point(pt[0], pt[1]);
}
```

Figure 7-14. Curves as particle waves, example 1

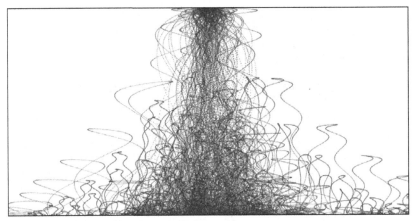

Figure 7-15. Curves as particle waves, example 2

By using functions to organize a program, you get the benefit of modularity, but also the burden of added abstraction. It doesn't help that so many of the parameters are index positions in arrays. However, with a sketch this complex, you need ways of cutting down on the variable clutter. Another, and better, way to code this sketch would be using an object-oriented approach. This would allow for even greater modularity and potential code reuse. For example, I could create a class for each of the main elements in the sketch: Particle, Emitter, Dynamics, Wave, World, and so forth. This would allow me to really encapsulate the functionality of each of these constructs. I would also design the relationships between these different classes. Of course, this approach also brings lots of added abstraction to the process, so it's not the best approach for new coders. Later in the book, when you're an old, salty hackster, I'll approach some problems using object-oriented programming (OOP). Before moving on, though, I want go over a few elements in the last particle wave example.

I avoided global variables and declared local variables within the functions. This encourages code reuse, as each function is a self-contained processing unit. To use the function, you just need to know the parameter list, or the interface to the function. The parameter list shows the input that the function requires to do its thing. The return type of the function shows what value, if any, the function returns when it is called. For example, the float makeWaves() function returns a float value every time it's called. Returning a value should not be confused with outputting something to the display window. The plot() function, for example, outputs points to the screen, but the function doesn't return any value when it is called. Another benefit of using all local variables defined within functions is that there is no danger of name collisions. I can use the same named variables in each function without any ambiguity because each variable has local scope. If I need the value of a variable outside the function, I need to pass it as an argument, as I do throughout the program.

I used a bunch of convenience arrays in the setup() function. I use the term "convenience" because I could have just passed the variables individually as arguments to the setParticles() function. However, the parameter list, defined in the head of the setParticles() function, would have needed to account for all these variables, including their type. This list would have included 17 parameters. Instead, by packaging the variables into logical arrays, I only needed to pass five arguments to the setParticles() function (which of course needed five parameters of the same type declared in the head of the function). The burden of this organizational abstraction is that once in the setParticles() function, I needed to, as the function designer, carefully decode what value each array index contained. However, since all the values required by the function are passed in as arguments, once completed, I theoretically never have to mess with the insides of this function again. If I want to change the output of the function, I simply change the values I pass to it—it's a black box construction.

One issue in this example that may be confusing to new coders is my use of function calls within other functions, especially with regard to using a returned value in an assignment. For example, from within the setParticles() function, I call the makeWaves() function:

```
// called from within the setParticles() function
x[i]=makeWaves(x[i], angle+=frequency[i], amplitude[i]);
```

Try not to get confused by all the array notation (all the [i]s) in the function. Everything is efficiently getting processed in a for loop, and each of the variables is a primitive array;

7

the loop incrementally moves through each index of the array, processing all the data. However, in any single iteration of the loop, only one value in each of the arrays is being processed/used at a time. So, for example, the second iteration of the for loop i is equal to 1, and therefore the second value in each of the arrays is the one being processed/used. You should also notice that I am using x[i] as both the variable receiving the assignment and the first argument in the makeWaves() function call. I remember being really confused when I first came across this sort of thing—it didn't seem to make sense. To understand what's happening, you need to consider the order in which things take place. Assignment operations happen from right to left. Thus, the function will do its thing before the assignment takes place. Since the makeWaves() function returns a float value, the returned value is assigned to x[i] after the function finishes. I am just using the makeWaves() function to increment the x[i] value by the trig function. The second argument, angle+= frequency[i], increments the angle variable each iteration of the loop by the current value of frequency[i]. The increasing angle value is needed by the makeWaves() function to keep its internal trig function moving. The last minor syntax issue that might be confusing to some readers is the following line:

```
plot(new float[]{ x[i], y[i] });
```

The plot() function requires a float array argument. The argument new float[]{ x[i], y[i] } is an anonymous float array that I'm passing to the plot() function. It's anonymous because I didn't assign the array to any variable; thus, its scope is limited to that moment in the function, which is all I needed. I could also have put the statement on two lines, like this:

```
float[] myPts = { x[i], y[i] };
plot(myPts);
```

Creating curves using polynomials

The last curve creation approach I'll look at briefly before diving into the Processing API is the use of polynomial equations. Polynomials sound scarier than they really are. In fact, you've already used polynomials in this chapter. Even the simple equation **x = 3** is a polynomial—albeit not a very inspiring one. **y = 3** will generate a horizontal line at 3 on the y-axis. **x = 3** will generate a vertical line at 3 on the x-axis. Equations that only use a constant (a number) are considered zero-degree polynomials. In contrast, the statement **y = 3x** is a first-degree polynomial, and will no longer only give a plain horizontal or vertical line. As x increases or decreases in value, the value of y will change. For example, the following sketch (shown in Figure 7-16) creates 100 points based on this equation, yielding a diagonal line:

```
// First-degree polynomial
// y = 3x
size(200, 200);
background(255);
strokeWeight(3);
float x = 0, y = 0;
```

```
for (int i=0; i<100; i++){
  x = i;
  y = 3*x;
  point(x, y);
}
```

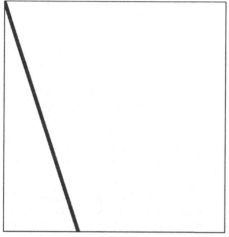

Figure 7-16. Generating a diagonal line with a first-degree polynomial

You can also add or subtract a constant to or from the equation without changing its degree, as in y = 3x + 50;. To modify the last sketch with this new polynomial, just change y = 3*x; to y = 3*x + 50;. When you run it, you'll notice that the diagonal line is moved 50 pixels down from the top of the display window.

So, none of this is terribly exciting or too complicated. Besides, this chapter is really about curves. As you might suspect, or more likely already know, if you increase the polynomial equation by one more degree, you'll arrive in curve land. The following sketch (shown in Figure 7-17) plots the second-degree polynomial $y = 2x^2 - 3x + 19$.

```
// Second-degree polynomial
// y = 2x² -3x + 19;
size(200, 200);
background(255);
strokeWeight(3);
float x = 0, y = 0;
for (int i=0; i<100; i++){
  x = i;
  y = 2* pow(x, 2)-3*x + 19;
  point(x, y);
}
```

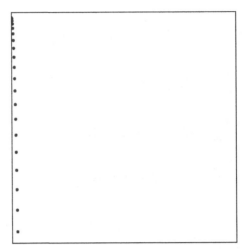

Figure 7-17. Generating a curve with a second-degree polynomial

You can see a bit of a curve, but the problem is that the value of y grows so fast that most of the curve is out of the window. In fact, after 100 iterations, y is equal to 19324.0 (pixels)—but the display window is only 200 pixels tall. To better see the curve, you can calculate the percentage of the display window to the y maximum value and multiply y by this ratio: y*(height/19324.0). This will, in a sense, remap the curve to the viewing space. Here's the modified sketch (shown in Figure 7-18):

```
/* Second-degree polynomial
y = 2x² -3x + 19;
 curve fits within display window*/
size(200, 200);
background(255);
strokeWeight(3);
float x = 0, y = 0;
int loopLimit = 100;
/*Instead of using the magic number 19324.0 in the ratio, I used the
polynomial and plugged in the loop limit to get the maximum. This
way if the window size changes, the program should still work.*/
float ratio = height/(2*pow(loopLimit-1, 2)-3*loopLimit-1 + 19);
for (int i=0; i<loopLimit; i++){
  x = i;
  y = 2* pow(x, 2)-3*x + 19;
  point(x, y*ratio);
}
```

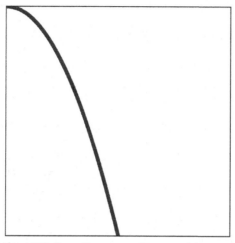

Figure 7-18. Generating a curve with a second-degree polynomial, mapped to the display window

The scary-looking line `float ratio = height/(2*pow(loopLimit-1, 2)-3*loopLimit-1 + 19);` is your quadratic equation converted into code. The `pow(loopLimit-1, 2)` part uses Processing's built-in `pow()` function. The function takes two arguments: the first is the value to act upon (the base), and the second is the power to raise the value to (the exponent), so `pow(loopLimit-1, 2)` is equal to **(loopLimit − 1)²**. In this case, the base is the expression **loopLimit − 1**.

There is another important property of second-degree polynomials, also known as quadratic curves, that you're not seeing in the plot. Quadratics don't just form any old curves—they form parabolas, or bell-shaped symmetrical curves. However, to see the bell shape, you need to shift the curve to the right by `width/2`, and also begin your `for` loop at `-width/2`. Here's the modified sketch code (shown in Figure 7-19):

```
/* parabola
 y = 2x² -3x + 19;
parabola fits within display window*/
size(400, 400);
background(255);
strokeWeight(3);
float x = 0, y = 0;
int loopLimit = 200;
//shifts curve to the right
int xShift = width/2;
/*Instead of using the magic number 19324.0 in the ratio, I used the
polynomial and plugged in the loop limit to get the maximum. This
way if the window size changes, the program should still work.*/
float ratio = height/(2*pow(loopLimit-1, 2)-3*loopLimit-1 + 19);
```

7

```
for (int i=-xShift; i<loopLimit; i++){
  x = i;
  y = 2* pow(x, 2)-3*x + 19;
  point(x+xShift, y*ratio);
}
```

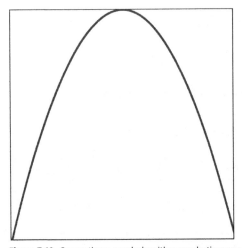

Figure 7-19. Generating a parabola with a quadratic curve

If all this math is making your eyes glaze over (sorry), we're almost done. Curves are not so simple, even using Processing's built-in functions, as you'll see shortly. But it's helpful to have some sense of what's happening under the hood. The last curve equation I'll look at briefly is a third-degree polynomial, or cubic curve. These curves, like quadratics, are fundamental to computer graphics. Cubic curves give you one additional feature that quadratic curves don't, and that is a **point of inflection**. Inflection means the curve changes direction. Think of the difference between the letters *C* (quadratic curve) and *S* (cubic curve); the *S* contains an inflection point. What's really significant about this change of direction, with regard to polynomials, is that it's always a smooth transition.

Higher-degree polynomials (above third-degree) will also include inflection points, but they require more processing power to calculate, and are ultimately harder to control. Thus, most curved lines and surfaces in computer graphics rely in some way on quadratic and cubic curves. This last polynomial example generates a cubic curve from the equation $y = 4x^3 - 6x^2 + 3x - 20$. I've taken the liberty of shifting and scaling the output so that it fits happily within the display window, as shown in Figure 7-20.

```
/* Third-degree polynomial
  y = 4x³-6x²+3x-20*/
size(400, 400);
background(255);
strokeWeight(3);
smooth();
```

266

```
float x = 0, y = 0;
int loopLimit = 200;
//shifts curve to the right
int xShift = width/2;
//shifts curve down
int yShift = height/2;
//fits curve to window
float ratio = height/(4* pow(loopLimit-1, 3)-6*pow(loopLimit-1, 2) ➡
  + 3*loopLimit-1 - 20);
for (int i=-xShift; i<loopLimit; i++){
  x = i;
  y = 4* pow(x, 3)-6*pow(x, 2) + 3*x - 20;
  point(x+xShift, y*ratio+yShift);
}
```

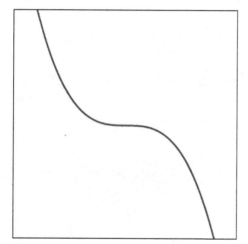

Figure 7-20. Plot of a cubic curve (third-degree polynomial)

Using Processing's curve functions

Congratulations! You just made it through the scary math section of the chapter. It only gets easier from here. It's time to look at Processing's built-in curve functions. The Processing language reference includes numerous functions dealing with curves, all housed under the Shape subheading. These functions simplify curve generation, handling most of the scary math internally. Within the Shape section is a section called Curves, which includes eight curve functions. In addition, in the Vertex section are two more vertex curve functions. Finally, there's one other lonely curve function hanging out in the 2D Primitives section, called arc(), which I'll begin with.

arc()

An arc is a curve segment of the circumference of a circle. The arc() function allows you to draw a curve segment by specifying the x and y position of the center of the circle, the width and height of the circle, and the beginning and ending angles (in radians) describing the arc rotation. It is helpful to remember that 2 * pi equals a full rotation around a circle. In the next sketch (shown in Figure 7-21) I create two arcs, each rotating halfway around the circle. The first arc begins at 0 and goes to pi, and the second begins at pi and ends at 2 * pi (please note that pi is written as PI in Processing):

```
//concave/convex curve
size(200, 200);
background(255);
int x = width/2, y = height/2;
int w = 100, h = 100;
strokeWeight(4);
smooth();
fill(0);
arc(x, y-h/2, w, h, 0, PI);
noFill();
arc(x, y+h/2, w, h, PI, PI*2);
```

Figure 7-21. Using Processing's arc() function

The arc() function is easier to use than it looks. Because it requires six arguments, two of which are angles, it can seem overly complicated—but it really isn't. It helps to think of the arc() function as a partial ellipse() function. In fact, if you really want to, you can use arc() in place of ellipse(). arc() also has both a fill and a stroke option, just like ellipse(). Here's a simple modification to the program that creates two concentric circles using arc(), as shown in Figure 7-22:

```
//concentric circles
size(200, 200);
background(255);
int x = width/2, y = height/2;
int w = 100, h = 100;
strokeWeight(4);
smooth();
fill(0);
arc(x, y, w-50, h-50, 0, PI*2);
noFill();
arc(x, y, w, h, 0, TWO_PI);
```

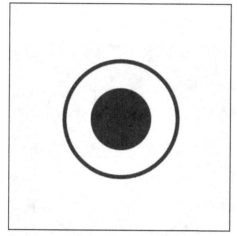

Figure 7-22. Creating circles with arc()

The arc() function's first four arguments are identical to ellipse()'s arguments: x, y, width, and height. You can also specify an ellipseMode() when using arc() to control from what point the arc is drawn; the default mode is CENTER. The arc() function's last two arguments are the start and end angles of the arc's rotation, specified in radians. If you prefer to work in degrees, just convert the degrees to radians, using the radians(angle) function. You'll notice in my examples that I used PI as my value of rotation. PI, in radians, specifies 180 degree rotation around an ellipse. PI*2, in radians, gives one complete rotation (360 degrees). Processing actually has a constant for this as well: TWO_PI, which I used in the second arc() statement.

Although arc() is easy to use, it is somewhat lacking as a general-purpose curve tool. For example, to create a continuous curve path, it's a little annoying trying to get a series of arcs to line up. I'll look at other Processing curve functions that do a better job with that. One cool thing you can do with arc() is make wedge shapes. A not-so-exciting application of this would be your standard pie chart. Here's a simple example (shown in Figure 7-23):

```
//pie chart
size(400, 400);
background(0);
smooth();
stroke(127);
fill(0);
int radius = 150;
int[]angs = {40, 10, 20, 35, 55, 30, 60, 110};
float lastAng = 0;
for (int i=0; i<angs.length; i++){
  fill(random(255));
  arc(width/2, height/2, radius*2, radius*2, lastAng, ➥
    lastAng+=radians(angs[i]));
}
```

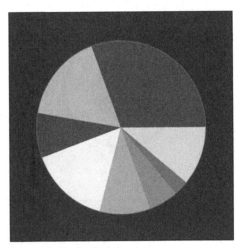

Figure 7-23. Simple pie chart

There's nothing too earth shattering about this last example. One subtle issue, though, which can really mess things up if not handled properly, is the correct use of data types in calculations. After running the pie chart sketch a few times, switch the data type of the lastAng variable from float to int and run the program again. You won't get any compiler errors, but you'll notice that only a partial pie forms. To better understand how a subtle change like this can wreck your pretty pie chart, add println(lastAng) below the arc() call, and try both data types again. When lastAng is declared as an int, println() outputs 0, 0, 0, 0, 0, 0, 1, 2; when declared as a float instead, the output is 0.698..., 0.873..., 1.222..., 1.833..., 2.793..., 3.316..., 4.363..., 6.283.... The reason for the discrepancy is that when lastAng is declared as an int, the line lastAng+=radians(angs[i]) rounds down the value of radians(angs[i]) from a float value to an int—so anything under 1.0 becomes 0, anything between 1.0 and 2.0 becomes 1.0, and so on.

Pie charts, although valuable as visualization tools, don't do much for me. The next sketch, shown in Figure 7-24, is a progression of a pie wedge from a thin fragment to a full pie. I also incremented the value of the wedge fill color.

```
//Progressive Arcs
size(400, 400);
background(50);
smooth();
noStroke();
float diameter = 40;
float ang = 0;
float col = 0;
float xCount = width/diameter;
float yCount = height/diameter;
float cellTotal = xCount*yCount;
float angIncrement = radians(360.0/cellTotal);
float colIncrement = 255.0/cellTotal;
for (float i=diameter/2; i<=height; i+=diameter){
  for (float j=diameter/2; j<=width; j+=diameter){
    ang+=angIncrement;
    col += colIncrement;
    fill(col);
    arc(j, i, diameter, diameter, 0, ang);
  }
}
```

Figure 7-24. Progression of pie wedge shapes within a table structure

271

The sketch relies on a basic table structure made up of pie wedge shapes. There's nothing new here, as you've looked at similar code in earlier examples. The sketch is a little more visually interesting than the pie chart, but can obviously be pushed further. By simply decreasing the value of the diameter variable and adding some randomization, you can improve the output quite a bit, as shown in Figure 7-25.

```
//Pie Fragments
size(400, 400);
background(255);
smooth();
noStroke();
float radius = 10;
for (int i=0; i<=width; i+=radius/2){
  for (int j=0; j<=height; j+=radius/2){
    float size = (random(radius*2));
    fill(255);
    arc(random(i), random(j), size, size, random(PI*2), random(PI*2));
    fill(0);
    arc(random(i), random(j), size, size, random(PI*2), random(PI*2));
  }
}
```

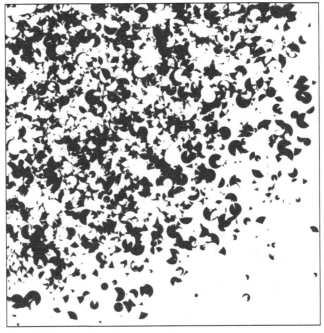

Figure 7-25. Randomized pie wedge texture

curve() and bezier()

The next two Processing curve functions I'll look at are curve() and bezier(). I'll consider these functions together, as they share some common implementation issues. As you've probably gathered by now, the implementation of curves is a little complex. Fortunately, Processing's curve() and bezier() functions simplify curve generation quite a bit. These functions encapsulate pretty sophisticated mathematical ideas, including cubic polynomials—which you looked at a little—as well as some calculus. I'm not going to deal with the calculus here, nor mess directly with polynomials. The functions each require eight arguments, representing the x and y components of four points. The bezier() function uses two points (the first two parameters and the last two parameters) to describe the ends of the curves (anchor points), and two additional points (the middle four parameters) to control how the curve moves between the endpoints (referred to as control points). Here's an example (shown in Figure 7-26). Please note that I took the liberty of connecting the control and anchor points with lines to help illustrate how the structure works.

```
//Bézier sketch
size(400, 400);
background(255);
smooth();
/*I used Java's Point class, a convenient
 data type for holding x,y coords, with public
 access to x and y properties (pt.x or pt.y)*/
Point pt1 = new Point(150, 300);
Point pt2 = new Point(100, 100);
Point pt3 = new Point(300, 100);
Point pt4 = new Point(250, 300);
//plot curve
stroke(0);
bezier(pt1.x, pt1.y, pt2.x, pt2.y, pt3.x, pt3.y, pt4.x, pt4.y);
//draw control points connected to anchor points
stroke(150);
line(pt1.x, pt1.y, pt2.x, pt2.y);
line(pt3.x, pt3.y, pt4.x, pt4.y);
//control points
ellipse(pt2.x, pt2.y, 10, 10);
ellipse(pt3.x, pt3.y, 10, 10);
//anchor points
rectMode(CENTER);
rect(pt1.x, pt1.y, 10, 10);
rect(pt4.x, pt4.y, 10, 10);
```

7

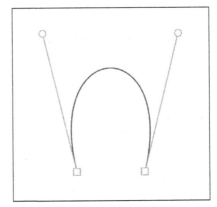

Figure 7-26. Bézier curve plot showing anchor and control points

I utilized Java's Point class in the example as a simple data structure. The Point class is not part of the Processing API, but I find it handy to use because it provides direct access to an x and a y property, which I used to help keep track of the different anchor and control points. You can create a new Point object by simply writing Point pt1 = new Point(150, 300);. The two arguments you pass, 150 and 300, will be the values of the x and y properties, respectively. So, to access the x and y values, I just write pt1.x and pt1.y. The rest of the code in the sketch is stuff you've seen numerous times before in earlier examples (and will see a lot more of).

If you've ever used a pen tool in a graphics application like Illustrator, Photoshop, or FreeHand (and I assume most of you have), then you've experienced Bézier curves, and maybe you've even messed directly with their control points. Bézier curves are named after Pierre Bézier, a French mathematician and engineer who worked for the car manufacturer Renault. To learn more about Bézier and his curve, check out http://cg.scs.carleton.ca/~luc/bezier.html.

There is a dynamic tension in a Bézier curve, determined by the placement of the control points (the small ellipse handles in the example) and their relative position to the anchor points (the small squares at ends of curve). You'll notice in the example that the curve seems to bend toward the control points. The situation is actually a little more complicated than that. The extra lines I rendered between the control points and the anchor points represent the slopes of the curves at the anchor points (also known as tangent lines). Slope is the change in y over the change in x (the rise over the run). Finding slopes of curves is a little tricky, since the curves are constantly changing, unlike straight lines, in which the slope is constant. On curves, you can take slope readings at distinct points. For a more generalized approach to solving for the slope of a curve, you need basic calculus—so I'll stop there. In a sense, the Bézier curve between the two anchor points is calculated by blending, or interpolating, the two slopes of the curve at the anchor points, as well as factoring in the distance between the anchor and control points.

Next is an interactive example that illustrates this interpolation process as a simple geometric progression. The sketch (shown in Figure 7-27) plots a quadratic curve using two anchor points and a single control point, and interpolates between these three points. Technically, the area defined by the control and anchor points is called a convex hull. Each time you click within the example, another iteration occurs, dividing the previous segments in half and plotting the path, slowly approximating the curve.

```
/* Interpolating a Bézier
curve within a convex hull
*************************
Click the screen a couple of
times to iteratively generate
the curve*/

int startingPoints = 3;
// Uses Java's Point class
Point[] bezier = new Point[startingPoints];

void setup(){
  size(600, 400);
  background(255);
  smooth();
  // create external bezier
  bezier[0] = new Point(10, 390);
  bezier[1] = new Point(300, 10);
  bezier[2] = new Point(590, 390);
  // plot initial convex hull
  plot(bezier);
}

Point[] plotBezier(Point[] pts){
  Point[] path = new Point[pts.length+1];
  path[0] = pts[0];
  for (int i=1; i<path.length-1; i++){
    path[i] = new Point((pts[i-1].x+pts[i].x)/2, ➥
      (pts[i-1].y+pts[i].y)/2);
  }
  path[path.length-1] = pts[pts.length-1];
  plot(path);
  return path;
}

void plot(Point[] pts){
  /*** render hull ***/
  if (pts.length==startingPoints){
    noFill();
    stroke(0);
    strokeWeight(2);
    //path
```

275

```
beginShape();
for (int i=0; i<pts.length; i++){
  vertex(pts[i].x, pts[i].y);
}
endShape();

//points
fill(255);
for (int i=0; i<pts.length; i++){
  if (i>0 && i<pts.length-1){
    rectMode(CENTER);
    // control point
    rect(pts[i].x, pts[i].y, 12, 12);
  }
  else {
    // anchor points
    ellipse(pts[i].x, pts[i].y, 12, 12);
  }
}
}
/*** render interpolated path ***/
else {
  // path
  noFill();
  stroke(100);
  strokeWeight(1);
  beginShape();
  for (int i=1; i<pts.length-1; i++){
    vertex(pts[i].x, pts[i].y);
  }
  endShape();
  // points
  fill(0);
  for (int i=1; i<pts.length-1; i++){
    ellipse(pts[i].x, pts[i].y, 4, 4);
  }
}
}

/* draw function required when
 including mousePressed function*/
void draw(){}
void mousePressed(){
  bezier = plotBezier(bezier);
}
```

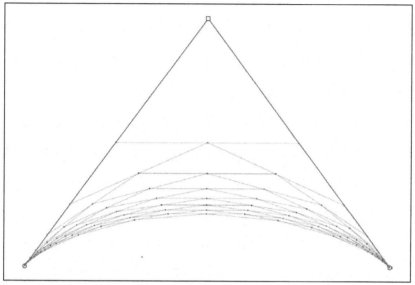

Figure 7-27. Interpolating a Bézier curve within a convex hull

There's nothing new in the last sketch, but I hope it illustrates how the convex hull (the shape defined by the three initial points) dictates the placement and shape of the curve. You can use this same sketch to approximate a cubic Bézier curve as well, with four initial points instead of three. You'll remember that cubic curves can contain an inflection point in the curve, or a change in direction, as shown in Figure 7-28. To generate this image, simply make the following changes to the values in the last sketch, and rerun it:

```
int startingPoints = 4;

bezier[0] = new Point(200, 700);
bezier[1] = new Point(100, 50);
bezier[2] = new Point(1100, 750);
bezier[3] = new Point(1000, 100);
```

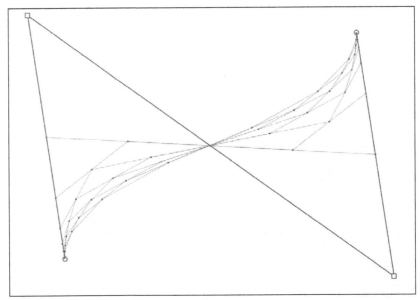

Figure 7-28. Cubic Bézier curve

Figure 7-28 shows an approximation of a Bézier curve based on a third-degree (cubic) polynomial, which I discussed earlier in the chapter. These are the most commonly used equations for calculating curves in computer graphics; although lower- and higher-degree polynomials can also be used. Wikipedia provides some excellent animations illustrating how polynomials generate Bézier curves. I was really tempted to recode these in Processing, but I think I'll leave that for you. You can find the animations at http://en.wikipedia.org/wiki/Bezier_curve.

Bézier curves can also be strung together to form longer continuous curves. The following example (shown in Figure 7-29) does just that:

```
// Bézier path
size(500, 500);
background(255);
rectMode(CENTER);

bezier(150, 100, 200, 50, 300, 50, 350, 100);
line(150, 100, 200, 50);
rect(150, 100, 10, 10);
ellipse(200, 50, 10, 10);
line(350, 100, 300, 50);
rect(350, 100, 10, 10);
ellipse(300, 50, 10, 10);
```

```
bezier(350, 100, 400, 150, 350, 250, 350, 300);
line(350, 100, 400, 150);
rect(350, 100, 10, 10);
ellipse(400, 150, 10, 10);
line(350, 300, 350, 250);
rect(350, 300, 10, 10);
ellipse(350, 250, 10, 10);

bezier(350, 300, 300, 350, 100, 250, 100, 400);
line(350, 300, 300, 350);
rect(350, 300, 10, 10);
ellipse(300, 350, 10, 10);
line(100, 400, 100, 250);
rect(100, 400, 10, 10);
ellipse(100, 250, 10, 10);
```

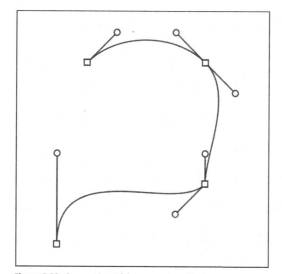

Figure 7-29. Connecting Bézier curves together

In this last example, notice how the control handles change the curve. The control handles that are aligned, forming a straight line at the second anchor point, generate a really smooth curve segment. However, the next anchor point forms a cusp, or kink, in the curve, as the handles don't align. This independence of the two control handles is both a benefit and liability of using Bézier curves. Cusps in the curve can translate to jerky motion in object or camera animations in 3D animation programs, or create an unwanted detail in a vector illustration or typeface design. However, in spite of these challenges, Bézier curves are very efficient, with a lot of descriptive capabilities, and are used widely in computer graphics.

Another way you can generate more complex curves, without depending solely on stringing so many Bézier segments together, is to use higher-degree polynomials. Higher-degree curves provide more inflection points (the places where curves change direction), and also require more control points. The number of control points is determined by the polynomial degree minus 1—that's why the standard Bézier, third-degree curve has two control handles. The ability for a curve to change direction a number of times should make it useful as a design or animation tool. However, the complexity and computational cost of using these higher-degree curves offsets most of the benefits. Thus, you're pretty much stuck with the cubic (third-degree) and quadratic (second-degree) curves you've already looked at.

However, there is one other important approach to creating smooth, continuous curves that simplifies some of the challenges of simply stringing together Bézier curves. This approach is encapsulated (within Processing) in the curve() function. I'll show you how the curve() function actually works in a minute, but first I'll jump in with a curve() example (see Figure 7-30) that plots the same curve generated in the preceding Bézier example to help highlight the difference between the two functions:

```
// Catmull-Rom spline curve
size(500, 500);
background(255);

Point p0 = new Point(150, 100);
Point p1 = new Point(350, 100);
Point p2 = new Point(350, 300);
Point p3 = new Point(150, 300);
Point p4 = new Point(100, 400);

//curve segments
curve(p4.x, p4.y, p0.x, p0.y, p1.x, p1.y, p2.x, p2.y);
curve(p0.x, p0.y, p1.x, p1.y, p2.x, p2.y, p3.x, p3.y);
curve(p1.x, p1.y, p2.x, p2.y, p3.x, p3.y, p4.x, p4.y);
curve(p2.x, p2.y, p3.x, p3.y, p4.x, p4.y, p0.x, p0.y );

//control points
ellipse(p0.x, p0.y, 10, 10);
ellipse(p1.x, p1.y, 10, 10);
ellipse(p2.x, p2.y, 10, 10);
ellipse(p3.x, p3.y, 10, 10);
ellipse(p4.x, p4.y, 10, 10);
```

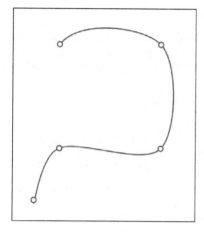

Figure 7-30.
Spline curve using Processing's curve() function

The curve() function is a spline curve implementation, or more precisely a **Catmull-Rom** spline implementation. The name "Catmull-Rom" comes from computer scientists Edwin Catmull and Raphael Rom. Catmull later went on to establish a small independent animation studio in 1986, called Pixar. Thus, you might assume that Catmull-Rom splines are relevant to 3D animation—and you'd be right. They're important for efficiently generating complex, smooth geometry—creating motion paths, among other things. In addition to curve(), Processing has a related function, called vertexCurve(), that implements the same Catmull-Rom spline. I think vertexCurve() is a little simpler to use than curve() (I'll look at this function after I slog through the curve() function a bit).

In the last example, I created five initial points to hold the curves' control points. Hopefully you noticed that there were no control points off the path, as in the earlier bezier() example. This is one of the main differences between a Bézier curve and a Catmull-Rom spline curve. After creating the five points, I call my curve() functions. Like the bezier() function, curve() uses eight parameters—the x and y components of four points. However, unlike bezier(), curve() doesn't use a system of anchor and control points. Instead, all four of the points, in a sense, function as control points. The curve then follows the path of the control points. Look closely at the curve() calls in my last example. Here they are again:

```
curve(p4.x, p4.y, p0.x, p0.y, p1.x, p1.y, p2.x, p2.y);
curve(p0.x, p0.y, p1.x, p1.y, p2.x, p2.y, p3.x, p3.y);
curve(p1.x, p1.y, p2.x, p2.y, p3.x, p3.y, p4.x, p4.y);
curve(p2.x, p2.y, p3.x, p3.y, p4.x, p4.y, p0.x, p0.y);
```

In the first curve() call, points p0 and p1 are at the left and right edges of the first segment of the curve. p4 and p2 are the extra control points on either side. In the next curve() call, I copy p1 to the left point position of the second curve. This will allow the first curve's right point and the second curve's left point to align. I then use p2 for the right point of the second curve. Since each point also needs a control point on the left and right, I put p0 to the left of p1, and p3 to the right of p2. This same pattern repeats itself in the next two calls. The only thing that may look odd is the last p0 in the final curve. Since

7

I used p4 to its left, I chose to go back to the beginning of my curve, ensuring that p4 had a control point to its right. (I know this is confusing and not intuitive at all.) One other little trick that may make this more comprehensible is that if you copy the third through the eighth parameters of a curve() function call and paste them in another curve() call, then the curves will connect. You'll still need to add a seventh and eighth parameter to this new curve. Look at these two lines:

```
curve(p0.x, p0.y, p1.x, p1.y, p2.x, p2.y, p3.x, p3.y);
curve(p1.x, p1.y, p2.x, p2.y, p3.x, p3.y);
```

Notice how the third through eighth parameters in the first curve() call repeat as the first through the sixth parameters in the next curve() call. I still need to add the last two parameters to the second curve, which I do by continuing the cycle from p3 to p4 for the seventh and eighth parameters:

```
curve(p0.x, p0.y, p1.x, p1.y, p2.x, p2.y, p3.x, p3.y);
curve(p1.x, p1.y, p2.x, p2.y, p3.x, p3.y, p4.x, p4.y);
```

Finally, there is one other cool function available to control the tension of the spline curve; it works similarly to how control points on a Bézier curve exaggerate or flatten a curve, depending upon where the handles are located. Using curve(), you don't literally drag any handles or set extra control points off the curve. Instead, you simply pass a value to the curveTightness(value) function. The value can be negative or positive. In this next example (shown in Figure 7-31), I create a series of identical spline curves, with varying degrees of curve tightness, using the values -2, -1, 0, 1, and 2 as arguments in the curveTightness(value) function (please note that you need to use Processing's noFill() function if you don't want your curves filling in):

```
// Catmull-Rom spline curve
// Curve Tightness
size(600, 400);
background(0);
stroke(255);
strokeWeight(2);
smooth();
int curveWdth = 50;
int cols = 5;
int xPadding = (width-curveWdth*cols)/(cols+1);
int x = xPadding;

for (int i=-2; i<3; i++){
  curveTightness(i);
  Point p0 = new Point(x, 100);
  Point p1 = new Point(x+curveWdth, 100);
  Point p2 = new Point(x+curveWdth, 300);
  Point p3 = new Point(x, 300);
  Point p4 = new Point(x, 200);
  x+=curveWdth+xPadding;
```

```
//curve segments
noFill(); // comment this line out  to see how the curve fills
curve(p4.x, p4.y, p0.x, p0.y, p1.x, p1.y, p2.x, p2.y);
curve(p0.x, p0.y, p1.x, p1.y, p2.x, p2.y, p3.x, p3.y);
curve(p1.x, p1.y, p2.x, p2.y, p3.x, p3.y, p4.x, p4.y);
curve(p2.x, p2.y, p3.x, p3.y, p4.x, p4.y, p0.x, p0.y );

//control points
fill(255);
ellipse(p0.x, p0.y, 5, 5);
ellipse(p1.x, p1.y, 5, 5);
ellipse(p2.x, p2.y, 5, 5);
ellipse(p3.x, p3.y, 5, 5);
ellipse(p4.x, p4.y, 5, 5);
}
```

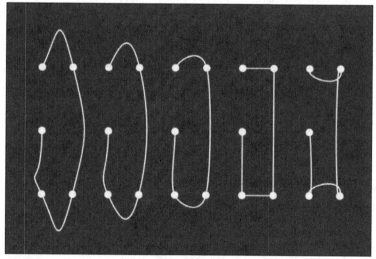

Figure 7-31. Controlling curvature using Processing's curveTightness() function

All right, so that covers most of the theory part of curves. I realize it may have been a bit rough to get through. One of my goals in this book is to try to provide detailed and clear explanations of important concepts that are often not well articulated in existing sources (that I can find). For example, in doing research on splines, I was amazed at how inscrutable most of the explanations were. This was mostly due to the dense mathematical explanations. The concepts themselves aren't that complicated, but when they're explained as a page of Greek symbols, matrices, and complex graphs, well—you're not going to entice many artists. I also expect you to move through this material pretty quickly (on the first read through), mostly just remembering that it's covered in the book. As you progress in your work and develop more coding chops, there will be times you'll need/want to deal with some of these more complex issues.

Next, I want to put this material to better use and cover just a few more curve functions. But don't worry, most of the really difficult stuff is over (at least in this chapter). I won't formally be covering interactivity until Chapter 12. However, it can be helpful in trying to understand curve concepts to be able to play around with the curves, including yanking on their control points. I'm not going to go into all the interactive theory here, so some of the code in the upcoming interactive examples may look odd (and possibly scary). You can peek ahead to Chapter 12 if you want to, but I'd suggest just playing with the stuff for now, and get to the learning part a little later. You're entitled to fool around a bit, in blissful ignorance.

More curve and Bézier variations

The next two examples, shown in Figures 7-32 and 7-33, are just variations on a theme. You'll eventually use the bezier() function to plot a more ambitious sketch consisting of a very interactive ellipse, which you'll be able to mess around with in real time. Hopefully this example will reveal some of the creative potential of having to deal with curve complexity. First, however, I'll look at two more functions: bezierVertex() and curveVertex(). These functions are really just alternative forms of the bezier() and curve() functions. The following example plots three spirals using the bezier() and bezierVertex() functions. Again, I've added extra code to render the control handles to show how their placement affects the spiral. I didn't bother to render the anchor points in this example, and I also doubled up the line() and ellipse() calls to save a few trees.

```
// bezier() vs. bezierVertex()
size(650, 225);
background(255);
rectMode(CENTER);
strokeWeight(2);

//bezier() - no fill
noFill();
bezier(50, 50, 92, 15, 134, 15, 175, 50);
bezier(175, 50, 215, 92, 215, 134, 175, 175);
bezier(175, 175, 135, 205, 105, 205, 75, 175);
bezier(75, 175, 50, 145, 50, 105, 75, 75);
bezier(75, 75, 100, 54, 125, 54, 150, 75);
bezier(150, 75, 175, 100, 175, 125, 150, 150);
bezier(150, 150, 134, 160, 118, 160, 100, 150);
bezier(100, 150, 92, 140, 92, 130, 100, 115);

//lines connecting anchor points to control handles
strokeWeight(1);
line(50, 50, 92, 15);   line(134, 15, 175, 50);
line(175, 50, 215, 92);  line(215, 134, 175, 175);
line(175, 175, 135, 205);  line(105, 205, 75, 175);
line(75, 175, 50, 145);  line(50, 105, 75, 75);
line(75, 75, 100, 54);  line(125, 54, 150, 75);
line(150, 75, 175, 100);  line(175, 125, 150, 150);
line(150, 150, 134, 160);  line(118, 160, 100, 150);
line(100, 150, 92, 140);  line(92, 130, 100, 115);
```

```
//control handles
fill(255);
ellipse(92, 15, 8, 8);  ellipse(134, 15, 8, 8);
ellipse(215, 92, 8, 8);  ellipse(215, 134, 8, 8);
ellipse(135, 205, 8, 8);  ellipse(105, 205, 8, 8);
ellipse(50, 145, 8, 8);  ellipse(50, 105, 8, 8);
ellipse(100, 54, 8, 8);  ellipse(125, 54, 8, 8);
ellipse(175, 100, 8, 8);  ellipse(175, 125, 8, 8);
ellipse(134, 160, 8, 8);  ellipse(118, 160, 8, 8);
ellipse(92, 140, 8, 8);  ellipse(92, 130, 8, 8);

//bezierVertex() - closed and no fill
strokeWeight(2);
int x = 200;
noFill();
beginShape();
vertex(50+x, 50);
bezierVertex(92+x, 15, 134+x, 15, 175+x, 50);
bezierVertex(215+x, 92, 215+x, 134, 175+x, 175);
bezierVertex(135+x, 205, 105+x, 205, 75+x, 175);
bezierVertex(50+x, 145, 50+x, 105, 75+x, 75);
bezierVertex(100+x, 54, 125+x, 54, 150+x, 75);
bezierVertex(175+x, 100, 175+x, 125, 150+x, 150);
bezierVertex(134+x, 160, 118+x, 160, 100+x, 150);
bezierVertex(92+x, 140, 92+x, 130, 100+x, 115);
endShape(CLOSE);

//lines connecting anchor points to control handles
strokeWeight(1);
stroke(0);
line(50+x, 50, 92+x, 15);  line(134+x, 15, 175+x, 50);
line(175+x, 50, 215+x, 92);  line(215+x, 134, 175+x, 175);
line(175+x, 175, 135+x, 205);  line(105+x, 205, 75+x, 175);
line(75+x, 175, 50+x, 145);  line(50+x, 105, 75+x, 75);
line(75+x, 75, 100+x, 54);  line(125+x, 54, 150+x, 75);
line(150+x, 75, 175+x, 100);  line(175+x, 125, 150+x, 150);
line(150+x, 150, 134+x, 160);  line(118+x, 160, 100+x, 150);
line(100+x, 150, 92+x, 140);  line(92+x, 130, 100+x, 115);

//control handles
fill(255);
ellipse(92+x, 15, 8, 8);  ellipse(134+x, 15, 8, 8);
ellipse(215+x, 92, 8, 8);  ellipse(215+x, 134, 8, 8);
ellipse(135+x, 205, 8, 8);  ellipse(105+x, 205, 8, 8);
ellipse(50+x, 145, 8, 8);  ellipse(50+x, 105, 8, 8);
ellipse(100+x, 54, 8, 8);  ellipse(125+x, 54, 8, 8);
ellipse(175+x, 100, 8, 8);  ellipse(175+x, 125, 8, 8);
ellipse(134+x, 160, 8, 8);  ellipse(118+x, 160, 8, 8);
ellipse(92+x, 140, 8, 8);  ellipse(92+x, 130, 8, 8);
```

7

```
//bezierVertex() - open and filled
strokeWeight(2);
x = 400;
fill(127);
beginShape();
vertex(50+x, 50);
bezierVertex(92+x, 15, 134+x, 15, 175+x, 50);
bezierVertex(215+x, 92, 215+x, 134, 175+x, 175);
bezierVertex(135+x, 205, 105+x, 205, 75+x, 175);
bezierVertex(50+x, 145, 50+x, 105, 75+x, 75);
bezierVertex(100+x, 54, 125+x, 54, 150+x, 75);
bezierVertex(175+x, 100, 175+x, 125, 150+x, 150);
bezierVertex(134+x, 160, 118+x, 160, 100+x, 150);
bezierVertex(92+x, 140, 92+x, 130, 100+x, 115);
endShape();

//lines connecting anchor points to control handles
strokeWeight(1);
stroke(0);
line(50+x, 50, 92+x, 15);  line(134+x, 15, 175+x, 50);
line(175+x, 50, 215+x, 92);  line(215+x, 134, 175+x, 175);
line(175+x, 175, 135+x, 205);  line(105+x, 205, 75+x, 175);
line(75+x, 175, 50+x, 145);  line(50+x, 105, 75+x, 75);
line(75+x, 75, 100+x, 54);  line(125+x, 54, 150+x, 75);
line(150+x, 75, 175+x, 100);  line(175+x, 125, 150+x, 150);
line(150+x, 150, 134+x, 160);  line(118+x, 160, 100+x, 150);
line(100+x, 150, 92+x, 140);  line(92+x, 130, 100+x, 115);

//control handles
fill(255);
ellipse(92+x, 15, 8, 8);  ellipse(134+x, 15, 8, 8);
ellipse(215+x, 92, 8, 8);  ellipse(215+x, 134, 8, 8);
ellipse(135+x, 205, 8, 8);  ellipse(105+x, 205, 8, 8);
ellipse(50+x, 145, 8, 8);  ellipse(50+x, 105, 8, 8);
ellipse(100+x, 54, 8, 8);  ellipse(125+x, 54, 8, 8);
ellipse(175+x, 100, 8, 8);  ellipse(175+x, 125, 8, 8);
ellipse(134+x, 160, 8, 8);  ellipse(118+x, 160, 8, 8);
ellipse(92+x, 140, 8, 8);  ellipse(92+x, 130, 8, 8);
```

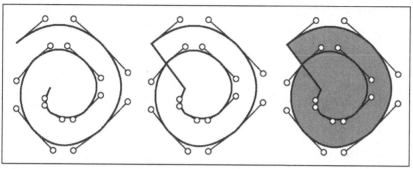

Figure 7-32. bezier() vs. bezierVertex() sketch

The bezierVertex() function needs to be called between beginShape() and endShape(), with the initial call being a single vertex() call. Remember that beginShape() begins recording coordinate data until endShape() is called, at which time the data is rendered to the screen and filled by default. Although the shape will be filled, the path defining the shape will not be closed unless the CLOSE argument is included in the endShape(CLOSE) call. Of course, visually, you can make the path appear closed by making sure that the anchor point in the last bezierVertex(controPt1, controlPt2, anchorPt) call is placed at the same coordinate location as the initial vertex(x, y) call. If the starting and ending points are not in the same location, using the CLOSE argument will connect the two points with a straight line, which is what occurs in the second spiral in the last example. By default, the shape will be filled following the same rule, as illustrated in the third spiral, even though this spiral is technically not closed. This same pattern of rules holds true for the curve() and curveVertex() functions. For the sake of thoroughness, here's a curve()/curveVertex() version of the last example:

```
//curve() vs. curveVertex()
size(650, 225);
background(255);
rectMode(CENTER);
strokeWeight(2);

//curve()
noFill();
curve(92, 15, 92, 15, 134, 15, 175, 50);
curve(92, 15, 134, 15, 175, 50, 175, 175);
curve(134, 15, 175, 50, 175, 175, 75, 175);
curve(175, 50, 175, 175, 75, 175, 75, 75);
curve(175, 175, 75, 175, 75, 75, 150, 75);
curve(75, 175, 75, 75, 150, 75, 150, 150);
curve(75, 75, 150, 75, 150, 150, 100, 150);
curve(150, 75, 150, 150, 100, 150, 100, 150);
```

287

```
//control points
strokeWeight(1);
fill(255);
ellipse(92, 15, 8, 8);
ellipse(134, 15, 8, 8);
ellipse(175, 50, 8, 8);
ellipse(175, 175, 8, 8);
ellipse(75, 175, 8, 8);
ellipse(75, 75, 8, 8);
ellipse(150, 75, 8, 8);
ellipse(150, 150, 8, 8);
ellipse(100, 150, 8, 8);

//curveVertex - closed and unfilled
strokeWeight(2);
int x = 200;
beginShape();
curveVertex(92+x, 15);
curveVertex(92+x, 15);
curveVertex(134+x, 15);
curveVertex(175+x, 50);
curveVertex(175+x, 175);
curveVertex(75+x, 175);
curveVertex(75+x, 75);
curveVertex(150+x, 75);
curveVertex(150+x, 150);
curveVertex(100+x, 150);
curveVertex(100+x, 150);
endShape(CLOSE);

//control handles
strokeWeight(1);
fill(255);
ellipse(92+x, 15, 8, 8);
ellipse(134+x, 15, 8, 8);
ellipse(175+x, 50, 8, 8);
ellipse(175+x, 175, 8, 8);
ellipse(75+x, 175, 8, 8);
ellipse(75+x, 75, 8, 8);
ellipse(150+x, 75, 8, 8);
ellipse(150+x, 150, 8, 8);
ellipse(100+x, 150, 8, 8);

//curveVertex() - open and filled
x = 400;
strokeWeight(2);
fill(127);
beginShape();
```

```
curveVertex(92+x, 15);
curveVertex(92+x, 15);
curveVertex(134+x, 15);
curveVertex(175+x, 50);
curveVertex(175+x, 175);
curveVertex(75+x, 175);
curveVertex(75+x, 75);
curveVertex(150+x, 75);
curveVertex(150+x, 150);
curveVertex(100+x, 150);
curveVertex(100+x, 150);
endShape();

//control handles
strokeWeight(1);
fill(255);
ellipse(92+x, 15, 8, 8);
ellipse(134+x, 15, 8, 8);
ellipse(175+x, 50, 8, 8);
ellipse(175+x, 175, 8, 8);
ellipse(75+x, 175, 8, 8);
ellipse(75+x, 75, 8, 8);
ellipse(150+x, 75, 8, 8);
ellipse(150+x, 150, 8, 8);
ellipse(100+x, 150, 8, 8);
```

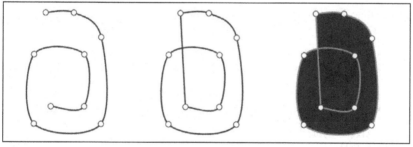

Figure 7-33. curve() vs. curveVertex() sketch

I think the curveVertex() function is less work to use than curve(). Obviously, having to deal with two arguments is definitely better than eight. From bezier() to bezierVertex(), you go from eight to six arguments, so I'm not so sure for normal open paths if there is much advantage. For closed or fill paths, you'll want to use bezierVertex() or curveVertex(). Although you can fill individual bezier() and curve() curves, the fill won't span multiple connected curve segments. To see an example of this, replace the noFill() call with fill(127) before the first spiral code in either of the last two examples.

One interesting thing to do with both the bezier() and curve() functions is to create elliptical plots, where the control points can be manipulated to create various interconnected curve patterns. The following example (shown in Figure 7-34) allows you to click the screen to generate a random ellipse pattern. I've also a coded a more advanced, highly interactive version of the example (shown in Figure 7-35), entitled Interactive Bézier Ellipse, which you can download from the Download section on the friends of ED site (www.friendsofed.com).

```
/*
Bézier Ellipse
Ira Greenberg, December 19, 2005
Revised: November 15, 2006
*/

// arrays to hold ellipse coordinate data
float[] px, py, cx, cy, cx2, cy2;

// global variable - points in ellipse
int pts = 4;

color controlPtCol = #222222;
color anchorPtCol = #BBBBBB;

void setup(){
  size(600, 600);
  setEllipse(pts, 130, 130);
}

void draw(){
  background(145);
  drawEllipse();
}

// draw ellipse with anchor/control points
void drawEllipse(){
  strokeWeight(1.125);
  stroke(255);
  noFill();
  // create ellipse
  for (int i=0; i<pts; i++){
    if (i==pts-1) {
      bezier(px[i], py[i], cx[i], cy[i], cx2[i], cy2[i], ➡
        px[0], py[0]);
    }
    else{
      bezier(px[i], py[i], cx[i], cy[i], cx2[i], cy2[i], ➡
        px[i+1], py[i+1]);
    }
  }
```

```
    strokeWeight(.75);
    stroke(0);
    rectMode(CENTER);

    // control handles and tangent lines
    for (int i=0; i<pts; i++){
      if (i==pts-1){  // last loop iteration - close path
        line(px[0], py[0], cx2[i], cy2[i]);
      }
      if (i>0){
        line(px[i], py[i], cx2[i-1], cy2[i-1]);
      }
      line(px[i], py[i], cx[i], cy[i]);
    }

    for (int i=0; i<pts; i++){
      fill(controlPtCol);
      noStroke();
      //control handles
      ellipse(cx[i], cy[i], 4, 4);
      ellipse(cx2[i], cy2[i], 4, 4);

      fill(anchorPtCol);
      stroke(0);
      //anchor points
      rect(px[i], py[i], 5, 5);
    }
}

// fill up arrays with ellipse coordinate data
void setEllipse(int points, float radius, float controlRadius){
  pts = points;
  px = new float[points];
  py = new float[points];
  cx = new float[points];
  cy = new float[points];
  cx2 = new float[points];
  cy2 = new float[points];
  float angle = 360.0/points;
  float controlAngle1 = angle/3.0;
  float controlAngle2 = controlAngle1*2.0;
  for (int i=0; i<points; i++){
    px[i] = width/2+cos(radians(angle))*radius;
    py[i] = height/2+sin(radians(angle))*radius;
    cx[i] = width/2+cos(radians(angle+controlAngle1))* ➥
      controlRadius/cos(radians(controlAngle1));
    cy[i] = height/2+sin(radians(angle+controlAngle1))* ➥
      controlRadius/cos(radians(controlAngle1));
    cx2[i] = width/2+cos(radians(angle+controlAngle2))* ➥
```

```
      controlRadius/cos(radians(controlAngle1)));
    cy2[i] = height/2+sin(radians(angle+controlAngle2))* ➥
      controlRadius/cos(radians(controlAngle1)));

    //increment angle so trig functions keep chugging along
    angle+=360.0/points;
  }
}

void mousePressed(){
  setEllipse(int(random(3, 36)), random(-200, 300), random(-200, 300));
}
```

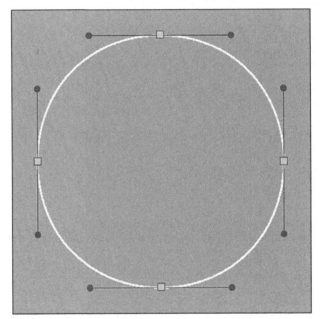

Figure 7-34. Bézier Ellipse sketch, example 1

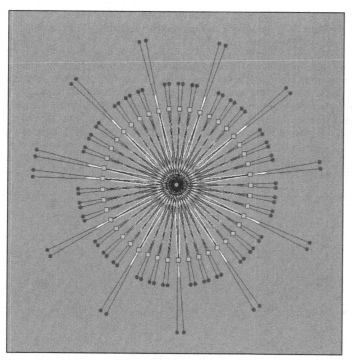

Figure 7-35. Bézier Ellipse sketch, example 2

The program plots a closed ellipse using the bezier() function with a little help from sin() and cos(). When plotting a circle using a Bézier curve, which you might remember is a cubic curve (third-degree polynomial), the two control points get placed between the two anchor points, dividing the curve into equal thirds, from anchor 1 to control 1 to control 2 to anchor 2. If you were using a quadratic curve (second-degree polynomial), as is used by ActionScript's curveTo() method, for example, you'd put your single control point halfway between the two adjacent anchor points. When using cubic Bézier curves, you can approximate a circle using only four anchor points; a quadratic Bézier requires eight—however, neither of these generates a perfect circle. In the example, I used two different radius variables (radius and controlRadius), one for the anchor points and one for the control points. I did this so that you can eventually morph the ellipse into more interesting forms by changing the spatial relationships between the control and anchor points. However, I also wanted to maintain some of the original symmetry, so the variations aren't purely random.

The two functions that do most of the work are drawEllipse() and setEllipse(). setEllipse() fills the anchor and control point arrays (px, py, cx, cy, cx2, and cy2) based on the trig equations. Notice that I instantiated the arrays and initialized their sizes at the top of the setEllipse() function, based on the number of points passed into the function. Since this needs to happen at both the start of the sketch and whenever anyone clicks the screen, it seemed most efficient to create a function, rather than include the same basic code in two different places in the sketch. When a user clicks, setEllipse() is called, passing in a bunch of random values: setEllipse(int(random(3, 36)), random(-200, 300), random(-200, 300));.

The drawEllipse() function is called each frame from the draw() function. You'll be using draw() extensively a little later in the book. draw() is used for animation, and by including it, Processing continually redraws the screen (by default) around 60 frames per second. You can update values within draw(), as I'm doing by repeatedly calling drawEllipse(). Also notice that the first line in the draw() structure is a background(145) call. If I don't include this, the screen will not be cleared between draw loops, and changes to the curve plot will build up on the screen. This could be used to very good effect, so you might want to try commenting out the background(145) call. Then run the sketch and click the screen repeatedly. Figure 7-36 shows a screenshot of my attempt.

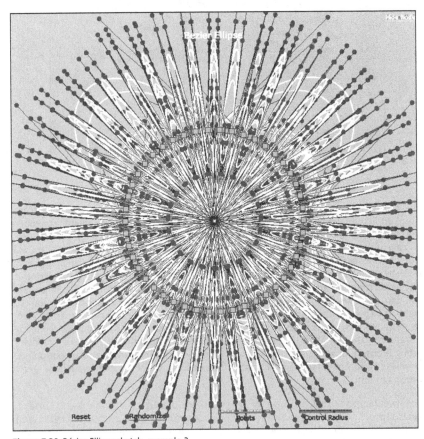

Figure 7-36. Bézier Ellipse sketch, example 3

I included one last example (shown in Figure 7-37) on how to create an elliptical spline plot using shape() and shapeVertex(). I also included a more generalized spline ellipse–creation function. Notice how the curveTightness settings affect the different curves, creating interesting path details. Similarly to the bezier() example, I initially populate the coordinate arrays with ellipse point data, using some trig expressions. However, unlike bezier(), I'm not burdened with anchor and control points. When drawing the closed curves, I followed the control point order I covered earlier in the chapter. This is not terribly intuitive, so it might help to mess with the node order in the curve() functions a little to see how it affects the curve. I implemented the first ellipse using curve(), and the second using curveVertex(). I'm not sure which is easier—probably curveVertex(), since it uses a shorter parameter list. The problem with the initial ellipse plots is that they are hard-coded for four points and can't easily be customized. Thus, I created a more general spline ellipse function as well, allowing you to control the number of points, as well as the x and y position, radius, and curve tightness, among other properties. The function is used to generate the two inner curves. This modular approach will be looked at in more depth in the next chapter, as you begin to apply some object-oriented approaches to the examples.

```
/*
Curve Ellipse
Ira Greenberg, December 20, 2005
revised November 15, 2006
*/

float radius = 165;
float angle = 0;

//outer circle
float[]cx = new float[4];
float[]cy = new float[4];

//middle circle
float[]cx2 = new float[4];
float[]cy2 = new float[4];

void setup(){
  size(400, 400);
  background(255);
  strokeWeight(1.5);
  smooth();

  for (int i =0; i<4; i++){
    //outer ellipse
    cx[i] = width/2+cos(radians(angle))*radius;
    cy[i] = height/2+sin(radians(angle))*radius;

    //middle ellispe
    cx2[i] = width/2+cos(radians(angle))*(radius*.85);
    cy2[i] = height/2+sin(radians(angle))*(radius*.85);
```

7

```
    angle+=360.0/4.0;
  }

  //outer curve
  curveTightness(-3);
  curve(cx[3], cy[3], cx[0], cy[0], cx[1], cy[1], cx[2], cy[2]);
  curve(cx[0], cy[0], cx[1], cy[1], cx[2], cy[2], cx[3], cy[3]);
  curve(cx[1], cy[1], cx[2], cy[2], cx[3], cy[3], cx[0], cy[0]);
  curve(cx[2], cy[2], cx[3], cy[3], cx[0], cy[0], cx[1], cy[1]);

  //middle curve
  curveTightness(2);
  noFill();
  beginShape();
  curveVertex(cx2[3], cy2[3]);
  curveVertex(cx2[0], cy2[0]);
  curveVertex(cx2[1], cy2[1]);
  curveVertex(cx2[2], cy2[2]);
  curveVertex(cx2[3], cy2[3]);
  curveVertex(cx2[0], cy2[0]);
  curveVertex(cx2[1], cy2[1]);
  endShape();

  for (int i=0; i<4; i++){
    fill(255);
    ellipse(cx[i], cy[i], 10, 10);
    ellipse(cx2[i], cy2[i], 10, 10);
  }

  //inner curve
  curveEllipse(6, width/2, height/2, radius*.2, -8, 127, true);
  //inner, inner curve
  curveEllipse(8, width/2, height/2, radius*.05, 0, 0, false);
}

// general spline ellipse plotting function
void curveEllipse(int pts, int x, int y, float radius, ➥
  float tightness, int fillCol, boolean isNodeVisible){
  float[]cx = new float[pts];
  float[]cy = new float[pts];
  float angle = 0;

  for (int i=0; i<pts; i++){
    cx[i] = x+cos(radians(angle))*(radius);
    cy[i] = y+sin(radians(angle))*(radius);
    angle+=360.0/pts;
  }
```

```
curveTightness(tightness);
beginShape();
fill(fillCol);
for (int i=0; i<pts; i++){
  if (i==0){
    curveVertex(cx[pts-1], cy[pts-1]);
  }
  curveVertex(cx[i], cy[i]);
  if (i==pts-1){
    curveVertex(cx[0], cy[0]);
    curveVertex(cx[1], cy[1]);
  }
}
endShape(CLOSE);
// render control points
if (isNodeVisible){
  fill(255);
  for (int i=0; i<pts; i++){
    ellipse(cx[i], cy[i], 10, 10);
  }
}
}
```

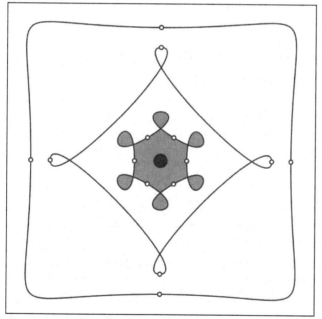

Figure 7-37. Curve Ellipse sketch

297

The nastiness with the spline curves is in figuring out the order of the control points. It's important to remember that each point needs a control point on either side of itself. In the block of code for the outer curve:

```
curve(cx[3], cy[3], cx[0], cy[0], cx[1], cy[1], cx[2], cy[2]);
curve(cx[0], cy[0], cx[1], cy[1], cx[2], cy[2], cx[3], cy[3]);
curve(cx[1], cy[1], cx[2], cy[2], cx[3], cy[3], cx[0], cy[0]);
curve(cx[2], cy[2], cx[3], cy[3], cx[0], cy[0], cx[1], cy[1]);
```

notice the order of the indices in the array brackets:

```
3, 0, 1, 2
0, 1, 2, 3
1, 2, 3, 0
2, 3, 0, 1
```

Each succeeding row begins with the second through the fourth values, and then the next logical value is added. Once you get to the highest value (in this case, 3), you go back to 0. I recommend messing with this order to see how it affects the curve.

The curveEllipse() function adds flexibility to the curve-creation process. You generally want to structure your code to build in as much flexibility as possible. Functions and eventually objects offer this possibility. Notice that the curveVertex() calls in the curveEllipse() function require some conditional statements within the for loop, ensuring that the correct ordering of indices is followed, as discussed earlier:

```
for (int i=0; i<pts; i++){
  if (i==0){
      curveVertex(cx[pts-1], cy[pts-1]);
    }
    curveVertex(cx[i], cy[i]);
    if (i==pts-1){
      curveVertex(cx[0], cy[0]);
      curveVertex(cx[1], cy[1]);
    }
  }
}
```

Before concluding this chapter, I just want to briefly mention a few more curve-related Processing functions. bezierDetail() and curveDetail() allow you to control the detail of the curve rendering, anywhere from a straight line to a stepped curve to a smooth, flowing curve. However, these functions do not work with the JAVA2D renderer, the current default rendering mode. You can use them with the P3D and OPENGL renderers, which are covered in Chapters 13 and 14. As of this writing, the P2D renderer is not functional. However, if/when that renderer is resurrected, these functions should work with it as well. In addition, there are three other functions—curvePoint(), bezierPoint, and bezierTangent()—that allow points and tangent lines to be plotted along curve paths. These are interesting, but also a little complex, and I think you've had enough of that sort of thing in this chapter. More information about these functions can be found in Processing's language reference.

Summary

Curves, and the math behind them, offer all sorts of expressive possibilities for creative coding. They are the basis for generating organic forms and, as you'll see in Chapter 11, natural motion. Of course, all this power does come with some added complexity. As I illustrated in this chapter, Processing allows you to generate curves using standard polynomial and trigonometric equations. Of course, if the math doesn't do it for you, you can also use Processing's built-in curve functions. As you progress as a coder, though, I think you'll find the math stuff really helpful—allowing you to more fully exploit the built-in functions. In Chapter 8, I'll depart from the math (for a while) and introduce object-oriented programming.

7

8 OBJECT-ORIENTED PROGRAMMING

Mammal

Quadruped

Canine

anShepherd

Object-oriented programming (OOP) is a deep and complex subject, and a detailed discussion of it is beyond the scope of this book. However, in this chapter I will give you a solid grounding in OOP to get you started. While OOP is challenging to start with, it is fundamental to Java and therefore Processing, and it is very rewarding once you get the hang of it, so don't despair if you find this chapter difficult to follow. As you work through the rest of the book, it will help you to keep returning to this chapter to look up OOP concepts as you meet them in all the applied examples you come across. It will get easier as you practice, I promise.

A new way of programming?

The answer to this question is both yes and no. While very different from procedural programming, OOP can at the same time be thought of as a natural extension of it. In procedural programming, you use functions to modularize code, adding efficiency, organization, and some portability. Classes, the main building blocks of OOP, work similarly. However, OOP takes the modularization of code a couple of magnitudes further. Functions are like data processing machines. They input data, perform some computation with/on the data, and spit the data back out to be used somewhere else. Users who utilize a function only need to know what the function does (not how it does it) and what type of data the function is expecting as input. This type of approach is often referred to as "black-box" design. Electrical components work this way (thankfully). Imagine if you had to understand all the details of how your DVD player works just to watch a film. Instead, you just need to know how to plug it in and hit play. Functions and classes both provide their own variations on black-box design; they encapsulate their internal implementation while providing a public interface to utilize the structure.

Classes, like functions, are modular, can process data, and allow code to be organized into logical structures, adding more organization to the coding process. However, classes go much further than functions in their ability to be independent, modular, reusable entities. In addition, classes have built-in variables, called **properties**, and their own functions, called **methods**—these properties and methods can be used beyond anything a function could provide. In OOP, we say that we interact with a class through its public interface, which can be thought of as the portal to communicate with the class's black box. Also, unlike functions—which are singular, static processing units—classes provide customized copies of themselves called **instances**, allowing a single class to have a wide range of unique states or instances. Instances of a class are also referred to as **objects**, which, if it isn't obvious, is where the term object-oriented programming comes from.

For example, if I create a Box class, I can then use the class to create Box instances of varying size, shape, color, and so on. Each of the Box instances would share certain core attributes (properties), but these attributes could each be expressed uniquely. Classes can also extend other classes. For example, I can create a class called Shape, which I can then extend to create Rectangle, Circle, and Triangle classes. Each of these three more-specific classes would share certain common attributes, such as position, size, and color, defined within the common Shape class. Aside from the common attributes, instances of these classes will also have their own unique characteristics, such as a specific plotting algorithm, a radius (for a circle), width/height (for a rectangle), an orientation (for a triangle), and so on. These unique attributes would be defined within the specific Rectangle, Circle, and Triangle classes.

The ability for classes to extend other classes is a powerful feature of OOP, allowing libraries of classes to be developed for reuse. For example, if I create a simple drawing program, I could incorporate the existing Rectangle, Circle, and Triangle classes just discussed, rather than rebuilding from scratch. Most programming languages come with extensive libraries of classes, greatly simplifying the development process. Processing takes this concept one step further by creating a procedural front-end (allowing you to simply call functions) on top of the classes it relies on. The Java language, which you'll work with toward the end of the book, is a great example of a mature object-oriented language with thousands of prewritten classes at your disposal.

Now these are a lot of new concepts to absorb without any pictures (or at least code snippets), so let's get to work with some code. Following is an OOP example, based on the creation (and hopefully consumption) of a Burrito class.

BurritoRecipe class

Classes are often used to model specific objects or processes in the real world. I like burritos quite a bit—so let's make a BurritoRecipe class. Since a class is composed of properties and methods, you need to think about what properties or characteristics a burrito recipe has and what methods or actions would be associated with a burrito recipe. I know this sounds very simplistic, but this really is classic object-oriented thinking.

In OOP, you create an abstraction (the class), internally grouping the class's properties with methods that act upon these properties, raising program design issues to a higher level where you can think like a person (albeit a hungry person), rather than like a machine. For example, once you create your BurritoRecipe class, you could use it by writing something like burritoRecipe1 = new BurritoRecipe(). If you wanted to select pinto beans for your recipe, you could then write something like burritoRecipe1.setBeans("pinto"). Classes are often also thought of as blueprints. You use the blueprints to make objects (also known as instances) of the class. For example, the aforementioned burritoRecipe1 is an object of the BurritoRecipe class. Each object created from a class has access to the same structure (the class's internal properties and methods), but each object can also choose to express itself differently from other objects derived from the same class. Thus, I can use the BurritoRecipe class to make a bean burrito recipe, and you can use it to make a chicken burrito recipe (or better yet, a chicken and bean burrito recipe).

Here are some BurritoRecipe properties: size, tortillaFlavor, meatType, beanType, toppings, salsaTemperature.

Here are some Burrito methods: getSize(), setSize(), getTortillaFlavor(), setTortillaFlavor(), setMeatType(), getMeatType(), setBeanType(), getBeanType(), getToppings(), setToppings(), setSalsaTemperature(), getSalsaTemperature(), and printRecipe(). It is the convention, where applicable, to create **get** and **set** methods for the class's properties. In the preceding list of methods, all of the methods except printRecipe() either get or set properties of the class.

Of course, within the BurritoRecipe class, there could be additional methods and properties relating, for example, to side dishes, calories, costs, and so on. In OOP, your class design decisions are not unlike decisions you would make in the real world if you really were to make, serve, sell, or eat a burrito.

Before you actually create your BurritoRecipe class, have a look at the basic framework of a simple generic class:

```
class ClassName {

  // properties
  int property1;
  float property2;

  // constructors
  ClassName(){
  }

  ClassName(int prop1, float prop2){
    property1 = prop1;
    property2 = prop2;
  }

  // methods
  void setProperty1(int prop1){
    property1 = prop1;
  }
  int getProperty1(){
    return property1;
  }

  void setProperty2(float prop2){
    property2 = prop2;
  }
  float getProperty2(){
    return property2;
  }

}
```

A class begins with the keyword class, followed by a legal identifier (the name) of the class. The naming of classes follows the same naming rules described in Chapter 3. The convention is to begin class names with a capital letter. When using a compound name (a name made up of multiple words), such as ClassName, you also capitalize the initial letter of any nested words. Following the class identifier is an open curly brace. The class is closed with a final terminating curly brace, at the very bottom of the class. Between the open and closed curly braces are the class's properties, constructors, and methods.

The properties are variables declared within the class with a data type, an identifier, and an optional initial value. (If you don't assign an initial value, the properties are assigned default values based on their specific data type). The properties defined at the top of the class have global scope within the class, just like variables declared at the top of a sketch in Processing. Variables declared within the head of a constructor or method (parameters), or within the constructor/method blocks, are local to that respective structure. This all works the same way as functions work in Processing.

The **constructors** are simply methods (functions declared within a class) with the same exact name as the class and no specified return type. These special methods are invoked automatically when an object of the class is created. You can have multiple constructors (each with the same name as the class) as long as the number and type of parameters in the constructor head (also known as the signature) is different. This also works the same way as functions work in Processing. Here's an example of multiple constructors for a Shape class. Notice that each constructor has the same name as the class, but a unique parameter list. (This code is not intended to be run.)

```
class Shape{
  // 1st constructor
  Shape(){
  }
  // 2nd constructor
  Shape(float x, float y){
  }
  // 3rd constructor
  Shape(float x, float y, float w, float h){
  }
}
```

As I mentioned previously, methods are just functions declared within a class. Like functions, they can return a value or not, and they can also accept arguments passed into them. If a method doesn't return a value, you declare the method using the void keyword. If the method returns a value, you need to declare it with the specific data type it returns.

Now you're ready to look at a complete class. Please note that the class definition is just one part of the process of using a class. Following my description of the BurritoRecipe class, I'll show you how to actually incorporate it into a sketch. The class code is a little lengthy, but I'll spend some time going over it.

```
class BurritoRecipe {

  // properties
  int size;
  String tortillaFlavor;
  String meatType;
  String beanType;
  String[]toppings;
  int salsaTemperature;

  //3 constructors--default, basic, monster
  //default burrito recipe constructor
  BurritoRecipe (){
  }
```

8

305

```
//regular burrito recipe constructor
BurritoRecipe (String tortillaFlavor, String beanType, ➡
        String meatType){
  //initialize properties
  this.tortillaFlavor = tortillaFlavor;
  this.beanType = beanType;
  this.meatType = meatType;
}

//monster burrito recipe constructor(uuummmm)
BurritoRecipe (String tortillaFlavor, String beanType, ➡
        String meatType, String[]toppings, int salsaTemperature){
  //initialize properties
  this.tortillaFlavor = tortillaFlavor;
  this.beanType = beanType;
  this.meatType = meatType;
  this.toppings = toppings;
  this.salsaTemperature = salsaTemperature;
}

//get/set methods
int getSize() {
  return this.size;
}

void setSize(int size) {
  this.size = size;
}

String getTortillaFlavor(){
  return this.tortillaFlavor;
}

void setTortillaFlavor(String tortillaFlavor){
  this.tortillaFlavor = tortillaFlavor;
}

String getMeatType(){
  return this.meatType;
}

void setMeatType(String meatType){
  this.meatType = meatType;
}

String getBeanType(){
  return this.beanType;
}
```

```
    void setBeanType(String beanType){
      this.beanType = beanType;
    }

    String[] getToppings(){
      return this.toppings;
    }

    void setToppings(String[] toppings){
      this.toppings = toppings;
    }

    int getSalsa(int salsaTemperature){
      return this.salsaTemperature;
    }

    void setSalsa(int salsaTemperature){
      this.salsaTemperature = salsaTemperature;
    }

    void printRecipe(){
      println("Burrito Recipe:");
      println("---------------");
      if (this.tortillaFlavor!=null){
        println("Steam or lightly pan heat a " + this.tortillaFlavor + ➡
            " tortilla.");
        if (this.beanType!=null){
          println("Sauté fresh onions, garlic, cilantro, slowly ➡
              mixing in " + this.beanType + " beans and white wine.");
        }
        if (this.meatType!=null){
          println("Grill " + this.meatType + " along with fresh green ➡
                  pepper, jalapeno pepper, chile pepper, ➡
                  onions and garlic.");
        }
        if (this.toppings!=null){
          for (int i =0; i< toppings.length; i++){
            println("Add " + toppings[i]+".");
          }
        }
        if (this.salsaTemperature>0){
          println("Finish off with a generous spritz of "+ ➡
            this.salsaTemperature+" alarm salsa.");
        }
      }
      else {
        println("Uh, you'll need to give me some ingredients\n" + ➡
              "if you actually want me to produce a recipe.");
      }
```

```
            // go to next line after printing
            // cooking instructions to the screen
            println();
        }
    }
```

Class declaration

```
    class BurritoRecipe {
```

As I discussed, to declare a class, you use the `class` keyword followed by the identifier (BurritoRecipe) of the class. Following the class identifier, there needs to be an open curly brace.

Properties declaration

```
        // properties
        int size;
        String tortillaFlavor;
        String meatType;
        String beanType;
        String[]toppings;
        int salsaTemperature;
```

Properties are declared at the top part of the class. As in previous examples with variables, properties need a data type and a legal identifier to be declared; they can also be assigned initial values. In this example, I just declare the properties. Notice that of the six properties, two are of type `int`, three are of type `String`, and one is of type `String[]` (array of Strings). The six declared properties are technically known as **instance properties**, and each object created (or instantiated) from the BurritoRecipe class will have access to its own unique copies of these properties. This is an important point and illustrates the blue-print nature of classes. The properties and methods defined in the class are the core structural elements (commonly referred to as members) of each object instantiated from the class, and each object can express itself uniquely via its own copies of the class's properties and methods.

In addition to instance properties, classes can also have static properties and static methods. These are declared with the keyword `static`. Static properties are also known as class properties. I will provide an example of some static variables when I cover composition shortly. The main difference between instance properties and static properties is that each object or instance created from a class can assign different values to its instance properties, but all objects of a class share the same values assigned to the class's static properties. In Java and Processing, static variables are used mostly to create constants (with the additional keyword `final` added in the declaration). Constants are variables that are immutable (can't be changed). For example, in Processing and Java, PI is a constant, and its declaration in Java's Math package could be something like the following:

```
    static final double PI 3.141592653589793;
```

Obviously, PI is never going to change, and the complier will enforce this if you use the static and final keywords in declaring it. If someone eventually tries to assign some other value to PI, the compiler would generate an error and prevent them from doing it. For the curious among you, the keyword double is the Java data type associated with PI. The double data type is similar to the float type, except a double requires twice as much storage as a float (8 bytes vs. 4 bytes), and also has greater precision (accuracy to 15 digits). However, double precision is not really necessary for the types of things most people do with Processing, so float was made the default primitive data type for any decimal values in Processing.

Constructors

As mentioned before, constructors are methods with the same name as the class, automatically invoked when an object is instantiated (created with the new keyword, as in new BurritoRecipe()). In addition, the constructor returns a reference to the object created. Thus, in the complete instantiation statement

```
BurritoRecipe myRecipe = new Burrito Recipe();
```

the variable myRecipe, declared of type BurritioRecipe, is assigned a reference to the newly created BurritoRecipe object.

```
//3 constructors--default, basic, monster
 //default burrito recipe constructor
 BurritoRecipe (){
 }

 //regular burrito recipe constructor
 BurritoRecipe (String tortillaFlavor, String beanType, ➡
      String meatType){
   //initialize properties
   this.tortillaFlavor = tortillaFlavor;
   this.beanType = beanType;
   this.meatType = meatType;
 }

 //monster burrito recipe constructor(uuummmm)
 BurritoRecipe (String tortillaFlavor, String beanType, ➡
      String meatType,  String[]toppings, ➡
   int salsaTemperature){
   //initialize properties
   this.tortillaFlavor = tortillaFlavor;
   this.beanType = beanType;
   this.meatType = meatType;
   this.toppings = toppings;
   this.salsaTemperature = salsaTemperature;
 }
```

8

In the BurritoRecipe class, I included three constructors, which allows the class to be initialized three different ways, depending on what arguments are passed to the constructor when the object is instantiated. Within the constructors' parentheses are any optional parameters. When you create a new object, passing arguments to a constructor, there must be a constructor with the same number and type of parameters or the compiler will spit out an error, which if you remember is similar to how functions work as well. The following object instantiations are valid, based on the available constructors in the BurritoRecipe class:

```
// uses default BurritoRecipe constructor
BurritoRecipe recipe1 = new BurritoRecipe();

//uses regular BurritoRecipe constructor
BurritoRecipe recipe2 = ➡
        new BurritoRecipe ("spinach", "pinto", "chicken");
```

However, the following instantiation will generate a compiler error, as there is no constructor with an appropriate parameter list:

```
// generates a compiler error.
BurritoRecipe recipe3 = new BurritoRecipe ("spinach", "chicken");
```

Within the code blocks (the code between the curly braces) of the bottom two constructors are a number of assignment lines that initialize the class's instance properties with the values passed in via the arguments:

```
this.tortillaFlavor = tortillaFlavor;
this.beanType = beanType;
this.meatType = meatType;
```

These lines may look a little odd at first. I remember being pretty confused when I first saw code like this. In naming the parameters, I used the same names as the properties declared at the top of the class. This was technically not necessary, and I could have made the names different. However, I actually find it easier to remember what parameter value initializes what property when they have the same names. Perhaps some of you may be thinking, "When two different things have the same name, couldn't that create a problem, especially if the properties declared up top have global scope and can be seen anywhere within the class?" This is a good question. The answer is yes and no. Following, I illustrate a good way and a bad way of performing the constructor initialization when both the parameters and the properties have the same names.

Here's the good code:

```
this.tortillaFlavor = tortillaFlavor;
this.beanType = beanType;
this.meatType = meatType;
```

And here's the bad code:

```
tortillaFlavor = tortillaFlavor;
beanType = beanType;
meatType = meatType;
```

Hopefully you noticed that the only difference between the good and bad code is the absence of the this keyword at the beginning of the bad code assignments. If you don't use the this keyword, the compiler uses the local parameters on both sides of the assignment operator.

The special keyword this refers to the class itself. Thus, this.meatType is the property, not the parameter of the same name. As I mentioned, if you don't use the keyword this, the compiler will only use the local parameter within the constructor block—so an assignment like meatType = meatType doesn't pass a value to the property, but just uselessly assigns the parameter value back to the parameter—meaning nothing really happens. I realize that if this is totally new to you, it may seem like an obscure point, but it really isn't. Is there any way to avoid using the this keyword? Well, there is, actually. If I had used distinct property and parameter names, I could have avoided using the this keyword. For example, the following constructor could be safely substituted for the second constructor in the BurritoRecipe class example:

```
//basic burrito recipe--add toppings later
BurritoRecipe(String tortFlavor, String bType, String mType){
  //initialize properties
  tortillaFlavor = tortFlavor;
  beanType = bType;
  meatType = mType;
}
```

I still could use the this keyword in front of the properties on the left of the assignments if I wanted to, but it is not required any longer. Ultimately, you can do your constructor initializations either way: using the same named properties and parameters and the this keyword in front of the properties, or keeping the property and parameter names distinct. In my humble opinion, using the same names for the properties and parameters ultimately makes things simpler, and also helps you to see what parameter to assign to what property. But not everyone would agree with me. When you start looking at other people's code, you'll see this handled both ways—even though I think I'm right.

Methods

After the constructors, there is a long list of methods, in the following style:

```
int getSize() {
  return this.size;
}
void setSize(int size) {
  this.size = size;
}
```

In OOP, there is a convention to structure methods utilizing the get/set prefix appended to the property names (commonly referred to as get/set methods, or "getters" and "setters"), as illustrated in the preceding code. Not all your methods will be getters and setters, but generally it is desirable to have a get and set method for each property. In pure OOP (which you're not totally burdened with here), the idea is that a class's properties

311

should not be targeted directly and the properties should actually be made private, using the optional private keyword (called an access modifier) in front of the property declaration. For example

```
private String meatType
```

If you make the property private, you will not be allowed to directly target it from outside the class. Instead, you are forced to use its respective public get/set methods.

So, instead of myBurritoRecipe.meatType = "chicken" or String meat = myBurritoRecipe. meatType;, classic OOP says you must use myBurritoRecipe.setMeatType("chicken"); or String meat = myBurritoRecipe.getMeatType();—I suspect this might be confusing, so for now, you can go ahead and be naughty and just target your properties directly, which is actually encouraged in Processing.

In addition to the getter and setter methods, most classes also have additional methods that do more interesting things (thank goodness). For example, the printRecipe() method in this program outputs burrito cooking instructions.

```
void printRecipe(){
    println("Burrito Recipe:");
    println("---------------");
    if (this.tortillaFlavor!=null){
      println("Steam or lightly pan heat a " + this.tortillaFlavor + ➥
              " tortilla.");
      if (this.beanType!=null){
        println("Sauté fresh onions, garlic, cilantro, slowly ➥
                mixing in " + this.beanType + " beans and white wine.");
      }
      if (this.meatType!=null){
        println("Grill " + this.meatType+" along with fresh green ➥
            pepper, jalapeno pepper, chile pepper, onions and garlic.");
      }
      if (this.toppings!=null){
        for (int i =0; i< toppings.length; i++){
          println("Add " + toppings[i]+".");
        }
      }
      if (this.salsaTemperature>0){
        println("Finish off with a generous spritz of " + ➥
          this.salsaTemperature+" alarm salsa.");
      }
    }
    else {
      println("Uh, you'll need to give me some ingredients\n" + ➥
              "if you actually want me to produce a recipe.");
    }
    // go to next line after printing
    // cooking instructions to the screen
```

```
        println();
    }
}
```

This method may look complex at first glance, but it is really just a bunch of `if` statements sending output to the text window. One thing that is new in the method is the use of the keyword `null` in some of the `if` statements. For example

```
    if (this.tortillaFlavor!=null){
```

The conditional expression `!=` means "is not equal to." So the `if` statement is then true when `this.tortillaFlavor` is not equal to `null`. This type of logic can seem tricky when you first start using it. Just try to remember that `if` statements are checking if the condition between the parentheses is true, not for a universal truth. So, if I say `ira = tall` (I'm not really), then the conditional `if (ira==tall)` would evaluate to true, as would `if (ira!=short)`. To explain why I used the `null` keyword in the first place, I need to go back to the discussion about declaring variables/properties.

Notice that in the class, when I declare a property using the `String` data type, that `String` has an initial cap. (Remember that Java and Processing are case sensitive, so the capital `S` matters.) Also, throughout the book, when variables of a primitive type have been declared—such as `int` or `float`—all lowercase letters were used. The capital `S` in `String` should inform you that the `String` data type is a class. Variables or properties declared of type `String`, or of any class for that matter, are not primitive types like `int`, `float`, or `boolean` that actually evaluate to specific values, but instead are object reference variables that evaluate to the memory address where the objects are stored. Now you don't need to worry about memory addresses. But what you do need to know is that the default value of an object reference, once it has been declared and before it has been defined, is `null`.

In the `printRecipe()` method, I needed to find a way to keep the program from crashing when it couldn't a find a value it expected. By writing the `if` statements the way I did, I ensured that if the property was initialized, and therefore wasn't equal to `null`, the block of code would run. However, if it was still equal to `null`, then the relevant print statement would be skipped, keeping the program from crashing. This is actually a pretty common thing to do in coding, and you will see more of it later on in the book.

Throughout the method, I also used the concatenation operator, `+`, to join the string literals in quotes with the properties. Remember, literals are just actual words or numbers that you write—for example, "art" (a string literal) or 10 (a number literal, which is referred to as a constant). A literal's meaning or value is explicitly what is written. To join a literal with a property or variable, you need to use the concatenation operator, as follows:

```
    this.beanType + " beans and white wine."
```

Also notice within the method that most of the `if` statements are nested within an outer `if` statement, which determines if there is a tortilla. If there isn't a tortilla, then the program skips the remaining statements and outputs the following:

```
    "Uh, you'll need to give me some ingredients if you actually want me
    to produce a recipe."
```

Alas, if there is no tortilla, there is no way to make a burrito. Lastly, notice how the for loop is used to run through the list of toppings. Using an array for the toppings and the array's length property as the limit on the for loop, any number of toppings can be added to the recipe, and the for loop will automatically loop through the entire array, using the value of the array's length property to determine when to stop. Throughout the rest of the book, you'll see many similar examples using for loops and arrays.

Finally, here's a complete Processing implementation that actually uses the class. Enter all the following code into Processing and run the sketch—or better yet, download the complete code (BurritoRecipe.pde) from the Download section of the friends of ED site (www.friendsofed.com/).

```
/*
title: BurritoRecipe class example
description: create some tasty burritos
created: August 9, 2005
revised: March 10, 2006
        October 23, 2006
by: Ira Greenberg
note: Enjoy and use plenty of guac.
*/

void setup(){
  // create some burrito recipes
  //use constructor 1
  BurritoRecipe b1 = new BurritoRecipe();
  b1.printRecipe();

  //use constructor 2
  BurritoRecipe b2 = new BurritoRecipe("spinach", "black", "chicken");
  b2.printRecipe();

  //use constructor 3
  String[]tpgs = {"tomato", "lettuce", "corn"};
  BurritoRecipe b3 = new BurritoRecipe("whole wheat", "pinto", ➥
          "beef", tpgs , 8);
  b3.printRecipe();
}


class BurritoRecipe {

  // properties
  int size;
  String tortillaFlavor;
  String meatType;
  String beanType;
```

```
    String[]toppings;
    int salsaTemperature;

    //3 constructors--default, basic, monster
    //default burrito recipe constructor
BurritoRecipe (){
    }

    //regular burrito recipe constructor
BurritoRecipe (String tortillaFlavor, String beanType, ➥
         String meatType){
      //initialize properties
      this.tortillaFlavor = tortillaFlavor;
      this.beanType = beanType;
      this.meatType = meatType;
    }

    //monster burrito recipe constructor(uuummmm)
BurritoRecipe (String tortillaFlavor, String beanType, ➥
         String meatType, String[]toppings, int salsaTemperature){
      //initialize properties
      this.tortillaFlavor = tortillaFlavor;
      this.beanType = beanType;
      this.meatType = meatType;
      this.toppings = toppings;
      this.salsaTemperature = salsaTemperature;
    }

  //get/set methods
  int getSize() {
    return this.size;
  }

  void setSize(int size) {
    this.size = size;
  }

  String getTortillaFlavor(){
    return this.tortillaFlavor;
  }

  void setTortillaFlavor(String tortillaFlavor){
    this.tortillaFlavor = tortillaFlavor;
  }

  String getMeatType(){
    return this.meatType;
  }
```

8

```
void setMeatType(String meatType){
  this.meatType = meatType;
}

String getBeanType(){
  return this.beanType;
}

void setBeanType(String beanType){
  this.beanType = beanType;
}

String[] getToppings(){
  return this.toppings;
}

void setToppings(String[] toppings){
  this.toppings = toppings;
}

int getSalsa(int salsaTemperature){
  return this.salsaTemperature;
}

void setSalsa(int salsaTemperature){
  this.salsaTemperature = salsaTemperature;
}

void printRecipe(){
  println("Burrito Recipe:");
  println("---------------");
  if (this.tortillaFlavor!=null){
    println("Steam or lightly pan heat a " + this.tortillaFlavor + ➥
        " tortilla.");
    if (this.beanType!=null){
      println("Sauté fresh onions, garlic, cilantro, slowly ➥
          mixing in " + this.beanType + " beans and white wine.");
    }
    if (this.meatType!=null){
      println("Grill " + this.meatType+" along with fresh green ➥
        pepper, jalapeno pepper, chile pepper, onions and garlic.");
    }
    if (this.toppings!=null){
      for (int i =0; i< toppings.length; i++){
        println("Add " + toppings[i]+".");
      }
    }
    if (this.salsaTemperature>0){
      println("Finish off with a generous spritz of " + ➥
```

```
          this.salsaTemperature+" alarm salsa.");
      }
    }
    else {
      println("Uh, you'll need to give me some ingredients\n" + ➡
            "if you actually want me to produce a recipe.");
    }
    // go to next line after printing
    // cooking instructions to the screen
    println();
  }
}
```

There are a couple of ways of using a class in Processing. For one, you can simply add it in your main tab with the rest of your sketch code, just as you've been doing with functions. (To use a custom class or function, you must also include Processing's setup() function.) You can also enter a class (or function) in a separate tab. The sketch will still see it/treat it as if it exists in the main tab. Finally, you can also work in Java mode, which I'll cover in Chapter 14. For the BurritoRecipe example, I used the simplest solution, and just entered the class code directly below the setup() function. At the top of the sketch, within the setup() function, I instantiated three BurritoRecipe objects, and called the printRecipe() method for each of them. When the sketch runs, it outputs burrito cooking directions, based on the arguments I passed when I instantiated the three BurritoRecipe objects.

In the first instantiation statement, I didn't pass any arguments:

```
BurritoRecipe b1 = new BurritoRecipe();
```

The printRecipe() method outputs the following:

```
Burrito Recipe:
----------------
Uh, you'll need to give me some ingredients
if you actually want me to produce a recipe.
```

In the second instantiation statement, I passed three arguments:

```
BurritoRecipe b2 = new BurritoRecipe ("spinach", "black", "chicken");
```

The printRecipe() method outputs the following:

```
Burrito Recipe:
----------------
Steam or lightly pan heat a spinach tortilla.
Sauté fresh onions, garlic, cilantro, slowly mixing in black beans ➡
      and white wine.
Grill chicken along with fresh green pepper, jalapeno pepper, ➡
      chile pepper, onions and garlic.
```

8

Finally, when I created the third `BurritoRecipe` object, I passed in a bunch of stuff:

```
String[]tpgs = {"tomato", "lettuce", "corn"};
BurritoRecipe b3 = new BurritoRecipe("whole wheat", "pinto", ➥
        "beef", tpgs , 8);
```

The `printRecipe()` method outputs the following:

```
Burrito Recipe:
---------------
Steam or lightly pan heat a whole wheat tortilla.
Sauté fresh onions, garlic, cilantro, slowly mixing in pinto beans ➥
        and white wine.
Grill beef along with fresh green pepper, jalapeno pepper, ➥
        chile pepper, onions and garlic.
Add tomato.
Add lettuce.
Add corn.
Finish off with a generous spritz of 8 alarm salsa.
```

Hopefully, this example has given you a clear sense of how OOP is implemented in Processing. However, I don't think my (albeit very tasty) example properly illustrated the potential power of OOP. One simple way OOP is useful is in sheer efficiency. It may not seem worth it to generate a whole `BurritoRecipe` class just to generate a few burritos, but what if you needed to generate thousands of different burrito recipes. Clearly, the time spent creating the class begins to pay off big-time. Another way OOP is useful is in organizing the coding process. Let's say I decide to construct an interactive recipe book of 100 favorite dishes from around the world, and of course I want to include my burrito recipe. My little `BurritoRecipe` class included 5 properties and 13 methods, and the other 99 world recipes would each contain around the same level of detail. If I don't use classes, I might try to code all the hundreds of properties as global and local variables. I'd then need to use lots and lots of functions to sort all this stuff out—pretty much a nightmare scenario.

Besides this being a royal pain, I would also lose the connection of each property to its respective recipe. Instead, if I use classes, each recipe will enclose, or encapsulate, its respective properties and methods, shielding users of the class from much of the internal procedural complexity and organizing all the hundreds of properties into logical conceptual structures (classes). Remember, OOP was developed based on the real world and our brains' predilections for thinking of things as discrete units. Going one step further, it would even be possible to create a `RecipeBook` class that could encapsulate the individual recipe objects within the larger organizing class. The bottom line is, as coding problems get more complex, the benefits gained from OOP begin to far outweigh the costs of implementing it.

Advanced OOP concepts

Next, I'll introduce some advanced OOP concepts, including encapsulation/information hiding, inheritance, composition, interfaces, and polymorphism. These concepts are fundamental to OOP, but they're somewhat difficult to grasp and even harder to effectively apply. Understanding these concepts becomes increasingly important as your projects increase in size and complexity, especially when you want to create reusable code. If you're a new coder (and are still recovering from the basic OOP whirlwind tour), you might want to skip this next section (for now). Just be sure to return to it, as you'll definitely want to know about this stuff to fully leverage the power of Processing and Java. Fortunately, you can learn these concepts incrementally as you progress as a coder. It's also possible, if you're anything like me, that you may end up finding this stuff fascinating.

Encapsulation and data hiding

Encapsulation is one of the more "slippery" terms you'll stumble across when you begin to learn programming. On the one hand, its meaning in programming is similar to its meaning in English—the encasing or enclosing of something. You can think about the way a function encases lines of code into an invokable unit as a form of encapsulation. One of the benefits of this arrangement is that the interface to a function and the implementation within the function are separated; this allows the implementation to change over time while still maintaining a consistent interface. For example, if I have a function called createPortrait() that initially draws a lousy stick-figure head, over time I can improve the algorithm to generate a more photorealistic head. The user, then, can just keep calling createPortrait() as the interface to the function remains constant, in spite of the improvements made to the guts of the function.

In OOP, encapsulation refers to the encasing and grouping of an object's data fields (properties) with its methods. As mentioned earlier, objects are created from classes, each with its own copies of the properties and methods defined in the class. In classic OOP, you don't generally interact with an object's properties directly. Instead, you use the object's methods to get or set its property values. This principle is referred to as data or information hiding. In Java, for example, you normally use the keyword private when declaring properties to make them inaccessible. You declare methods (which are the structures that users of the class must use to interact with the properties) as public to get and set their values. For example, if I have class that has a name property, I would declare the property as private like this:

```
private String name;
```

And I would create public get and set methods to provide indirect access to the private name property, as follows:

```
public String getName (){
  return name;
}
public void setName (String n){
  name = n;
}
```

8

One of the benefits of data hiding is that dependencies between properties can be better managed. For example, if an object uses the values of a number of properties to calculate something, and users are allowed to go in willy-nilly and change any property values directly, calculations could be adversely affected. However, if you use a method, property values can be both set and checked prior to performing any calculation, improving upon both program efficiency and reliability.

All that being said, in Processing, everything is public by default, meaning that to a user of the Processing API, everything is directly accessible. This design decision was made to keep Processing as simple as possible. However, it is possible, especially when working in Java mode, to make your properties private and enforce data hiding. In Chapter 14, you'll work in Java mode, making your object properties private and using public get and set methods to interact with them. To learn more about this concept, check out http://java.sun.com/docs/books/tutorial/java/concepts/object.html.

Inheritance

Inheritance in OOP is the ability of a class A to inherit or extend another class, B, enabling class A to have access to the properties and methods within the extended class B. In this constructed relationship, class B is referred to as the **superclass** that class A extends, and class A becomes the **subclass** that extends class B. In addition, class A can add its own additional properties and methods, and even overwrite specific properties and methods of class B (its extended superclass). Inheritance proceeds in a general-to-specific direction. For example, if I have a class called GermanShepherd, I could start with a very general base class, called Mammal, a subclass of Mammal called Quadruped, a subclass of Quadruped called Canine, and a subclass of Canine called GermanShepherd. A Feline class could also inherit from Quadruped, while a Human class might come from a Biped class that inherited from Mammal. Figure 8-1 shows a diagram of this.

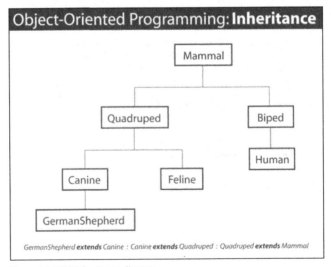

Figure 8-1. OOP inheritance diagram

Inheritance in Java is absolutely fundamental to the language's design. In fact, every class in Java except the Object class has at a minimum one superclass, and every class except the Object class has a lineage that goes back to Object. For example, when you export a Processing sketch, a Java applet is created. Here is the Applet class's lineage:

```
java.lang.Object
  java.awt.Component
      java.awt.Container
          java.awt.Panel
              java.applet.Applet
```

The classes are the words that start with an initial cap (Object, Component, Container, Panel, and Applet). The words connected to them by a dot are the packages the classes live in. Packages are just directories or folders that hold class files. In this lineage, Applet inherits from Panel, which inherits from Container, which inherits from Component, which inherits from Object. Therefore, the Applet class has access to all the accessible properties and methods declared within its own class and from all the classes above it—giving the Applet class access to over 200 methods. However, the inheritance chain doesn't go the other way. Object doesn't have access to any properties or methods besides those declared within its own class description, as it is at the top of the inheritance chain for all classes. On the other hand, the Panel class has access to methods/properties in Container, Component, and Object—but not Applet.

Applying inheritance

Using inheritance is pretty straightforward. In the following example, I have a very simple Shape class and Polygon class. The Polygon class inherits from (or extends) the Shape class.

```
class Shape {
  //class properties
  int x;
  int y;
  int w;
  int h;

  //constructors
  Shape (){
  }

  Shape (int x, int y, int w, int h){
    this.x = x;
    this.y = y;
    this.w = w;
    this.h = h;
  }
}

class Polygon extends Shape{
  int pts;
  //constructor
```

```
Polygon (int x, int y, int w, int h, int pts){
  //Optional call to superclass constructor must come first
  super(x, y, w, h);
  // add any remaining initializations
  this.pts = pts;
}

//method to draw poly
void create(){
  float px = 0, py = 0;
  float angle = 0;
  beginShape();
  for (int i=0; i<pts; i++){
    px = cos(radians(angle))*w;
    py = sin(radians(angle))*h;
    vertex(px, py);
    angle+=360.0/pts;
  }
  endShape(CLOSE);
}
}
```

The Shape class is very simple and hopefully makes some sense to you. The Polygon class has some new syntax. The class declaration uses the extends keyword to create the inheritance relationship between the superclass (Shape) and the subclass (Polygon). A superclass-subclass relationship is purely contextual. Therefore, if I create a new ComplexPolygon class that extends the Polygon class, then in that context, Polygon is the superclass and ComplexPolygon is the subclass. Polygon would still be a subclass in regard to the Shape class. Simply using the extends keyword is all it takes to create an inheritance relationship.

Within the Polygon constructor is the other new keyword, **super**. The super keyword, as you might have guessed, refers to the superclass. If you call super from within a constructor, it needs to be the first line in the subclass's constructor, or else the complier will give an error. The call to super in this context is a call to the superclass constructor. So all I'm doing here is initializing the properties in the Shape class by passing through the arguments sent to the subclass's constructor when the object was instantiated. You don't need to explicitly call the superclass constructor from the subclass; it's generally only done when you want to initialize properties within the superclass, as I did in the example. In Processing, a subclass like Polygon has access to its superclass's properties and methods, meaning that it can use those properties and methods as if they were declared within itself. That's why in the Polygon create() method I'm able to use the w and h properties that were only declared within the Shape superclass. (Don't get confused with the use of the same named w and h parameters in the Polygon constructor. Those are local variables to the constructor and not visible down in the create() method.) To try out the Polygon class (and its Shape superclass) from within Processing, add the following setup function along with the two classes:

```
void setup(){
  size(400, 400);
  background(50);
  smooth();
  Polygon p = new Polygon(0, 0, 175, 175, 8);
  translate(width/2, height/2);
  p.create();
}
```

One final point: Processing and Java allow a superclass to be assigned an object reference to any class that has extended it or is below it in the inheritance lineage. Thus, an object of the Object class can be assigned an object reference to any class, because the Object class sits alone at the very top of the entire class lineage. So it is perfectly legal and common to write a statement like this:

```
Shape myShape = new Polygon(10, 19, 233, 100, 8);
```

Inheritance gives Processing and Java a lot of power, efficiency, and flexibility. Applying it judiciously, however, is not always so simple. One of the potential problems with inheritance is that classes get locked into dependencies. So, if I eventually decide to change a class for reuse, I may inadvertently mess up another program that depends, through inheritance, on a certain implementation within a superclass. This scenario and how to deal with it is a pretty advanced and subtle concern that won't apply to most new coders, but it is something to keep in the back of your mind as you begin to develop larger and more complex projects.

Composition

One alternative (and also complimentary) approach to inheritance is called **composition**. Composition is another technique for developing relationships between classes. Composition is pretty straightforward to implement, and I think easier to get your head around than inheritance. Let's imagine I'm trying to develop a virtual house. My house will be really simple; it will only contain windows. The windows, however, are pretty fancy. In OOP, it is virtuous to be able to modularize a construct into a class, encapsulating its properties and behavior. Thus, it would be a good idea to create a Window class and have the class internally take care of creating and customizing the windows. Then, in my House class, I could just worry about where the windows are going to go and maybe how big to scale them; the Window class would take care of everything else. This is good OOP design. However, this approach also involves having multiple classes interacting with one other. The challenge of this inter-class communication is that unless there is an inheritance relationship, an object from one class can't effectively communicate with an object of an unrelated class. In my previous inheritance example, the Polygon class extended the Shape class. This made sense because a polygon *is a* type of shape. Can I do the same thing with the House and Window? Not really, as a window is not a type of house. Thus inheritance doesn't conceptually seem like the right choice.

8

Composition can solve this problem elegantly. Although I can't say that a window is a type of house, I can say that a house *has a* window. This is the difference between inheritance and composition. Inheritance involves an **is-a** relationship and composition involves a **has-a** relationship. Which approach would work with the following class groupings?

- Mammal, Cat
- Artist, CreativeCoder
- Monkey, Tail
- Foot, Finger
- EatingTool, Spoon, Fork

Well, a cat *is* a mammal, and a creative coder *is* an artist—these are both examples of inheritance. A monkey *has* a tail, which is an example of composition. A foot, however, doesn't have a finger; nor is a finger a type of foot—so neither relationship makes sense—this is an annoying tricky one. Lastly, a spoon and a fork *are both* eating tools, which is another example of inheritance.

Following is some class code illustrating how to apply the composition relationship.

```
class Window {
  /* declare static properties: the final keyword ensures
     that these constant values can't be changed. */
  static final int RECTANGLUAR = 1;
  static final int ELLIPTICAL = 2;
  static final int OCTAGONAL = 3;

  // instance properties
  int panes;
  boolean isDoublePaned;
  int configuration;

  // constructor
  Window (int panes, boolean isDoublePaned, int configuration){
    this.panes = panes;
    this.isDoublePaned = isDoublePaned;
    this.configuration = configuration;
  }
  // other Window methods would go here
}

class House {
  // instance properties
/* The House class contains a property
   of type Window */
  Window win;

  // constructor
  /* The House constructor expects
```

```
    a Window object argument */
  House(Window win){
    this.win = win;
  }
  // other House methods would go here
}
```

From within Processing, I could use these classes like this (assuming, of course, that the two classes were pasted below the setup() function, or each in their own separate tab):

```
void setup(){
  Window myWin = new Window(4, true, Window.ELLIPTICAL);
  House myHouse = new House(myWin);
}
```

Notice that I included three constants in the Window class. It is a coding convention to use all caps for constant names. One of the most common uses for constants is for preset values. In my example, I am giving a user of the Window class a choice of three different window configurations. I could have just forced the user to type in a number, but it is easier for most people to remember a name. In my Window class, I would eventually want to add a method that figures out what constant the user selected (which is just an int value), and then have that type of window created. You'll notice in the Processing setup() function that I use the static ELLIPTICAL property by attaching it to the class name with a dot (Window.ELLIPTICAL). Static properties are class properties that are accessible from any class. There is no need to instantiate an object of the class to use them. Remember also that Processing and Java are case sensitive, so when using the class name, you need the initial capital.

After the static properties, I declare three instance properties, which should hopefully look familiar by now. Next, in the Window constructor, I do my normal parameter-to-property assignments. I didn't include any other methods in the class for the sake of brevity (as if that were still possible).

The House class is very short, but gives a clear example of class composition. I only declared one instance variable, and you'll notice it is of type Window. Now this may look pretty odd, as you normally declare a property or variable as a valid data type, built into the Processing and Java core languages. Well, it so happens that any class you create is a valid data type. The subtlety of this concept took me some time to fully grasp. Just remember that a class is a data type. So it is perfectly valid to declare a property of a class type.

In the House constructor, there is a parameter of type Window that requires that an argument of type Window be passed in when a House object is instantiated. Within the House constructor, I do a standard assignment, using the parameter and property—both of type Window. The really cool thing is that now I can communicate directly with the Window object from within the House class, through its internal reference passed into the House constructor. Of course, if I were to finish the class, I would want to include additional properties and methods, allowing the Window object to be placed and sized within the house.

8

There are many advantages for House and Window to have this special compositional relationship. By letting the house control when and where to draw the windows, it can ensure that the windows always fit, regardless of whether the house is resized or moved. By letting the windows take care of actually drawing themselves, the house only has to worry about the number of windows, their scale, and where they go. This is good, clean OOP in action.

I realize that this is not easy stuff to grasp in its entirety, but I hope you are getting a sense of what OOP is and why it might be useful. The best way to learn OOP is to practice and experiment writing classes/programs. You can read this stuff over and over, but until you apply it, it's hard to get it to stick. The final concepts we'll look at in this long chapter are not easy, so read at your own risk. If you choose to jump ahead, which is fine, do try to come back at some point.

Interfaces

In the example on inheritance a couple of pages back, a Polygon class extended a Shape class. This allowed the Polygon class to access the class members of the Shape class. This made sense because of the is-a relationship. A polygon *is a* shape. In the composition example, the House class contained a reference to the Window class through an instance variable of type Window. This was the right solution because a house *has a* window, but a window is not a house. I could have also used the Shape class as a base class for both the House and Window classes, as both a window and a house are shapes (of a sort). It is possible and actually very common to combine inheritance and composition when designing classes.

However, there are times when you'll have a class that has an is-a relationship to two or more classes. For example, a Bicycle class could have an is-a relationship to a Vehicle class and also a SportsGear class. Since the SportsGear class and the Vehicle class don't have much in common, you can't logically create an inheritance chain, where the Bicycle class extends the SportsGear class that extends the Vehicle class. The most logical solution is one of multiple inheritance, where the Bicycle class extends both the Vehicle class and the SportsGear class. In a language like C++, this could be done. However, in Java and Processing, this is illegal, as the languages don't support multiple class inheritance, which many people think is a good thing. If you want to learn more about this issue, check out www.javaworld.com/jw-12-1998/jw-12-techniques.html. However, Java/Processing does support another approach to multiple inheritance, often referred to as multiple inheritance of interface.

Interfaces are class-like constructs that can only include method definitions and constants. Interfaces can't include method implementations, the stuff between the curly braces. Method definitions include a return type (or the keyword void), the identifier (name) of the method, and the number and type of parameters. For example, method definitions in a SportsGear interface might include the following:

```
String getBrandName();
float getUnitCost();
void setUnitCost(float unitCost);
void printWarranty();
```

The entire SportsGear interface in Processing would be:

```
interface SportsGear{
  String getBrandName();
  float getUnitCost();
  void setUnitCost(float unitCost);
  void printWarranty();
}
```

It's pretty simple to create interfaces. However, using them is a bit trickier, and using them polymorphically is trickier still. We'll take it one step at a time. Here's a Bicycle class that extends a Vehicle class and implements the SportsGear interface (this code is not meant to be run):

```
class Bicycle extends Vehicle implements SportsGear{
  //instance variables
  String brandName;
  float unitCost;

  // constructor
  Bicycle(String brandName, float unitCost){
    this.brandName = brandName;
    this.unitCost = unitCost;
  }

  /* We're required to implement all methods
      from the SportsGear interface*/

  String getBrandName(){
    return brandName;
  }
  float getUnitCost(){
    return unitCost;
  }
  void setUnitCost(float unitCost){
    this.unitCost = unitCost;
  }
    void printWarranty(){
      println("Bicycle:  full replacement value for 1 year");
  }
}
```

To keep things simple in the example, I didn't bother adding any properties or methods to the Vehicle class, or extra properties/methods to the Bicycle class. Instead, the Bicycle class gets all of its members just by implementing the SportsGear interface. Whenever a class implements an interface—through the use of the implements keyword—the class must implement all the methods in the interface, which means that it needs to include all the method definitions contained within the interface, as well as fill in the method blocks. This is enforced by the compiler, which will generate an error if it's not done.

8

When I first learned about interfaces, by about this point in the discussion I got kind of annoyed. I was able to follow how to code interfaces, but I didn't get the benefit. I mean, if you are forced to implement all the methods in the interface, why not just add the methods directly to the class to begin with? Wouldn't this be less work and less confusing? What is the interface really giving you for this added effort? I think in retrospect that this was a good question. At this point, there is not much apparent benefit.

Let's now create another class that also implements the SportsGear interface, to see if you can begin to see the power of interfaces. (This code is not intended to be run either—I'll get to that shortly.)

```
class Skis implements SportsGear{
  //instance variables
  String brandName;
  float unitCost;

  // constructor
  Skis(String brandName, float unitCost){
    this.brandName = brandName;
    this.unitCost = unitCost;
  }
  // required implemented interface methods
  String getBrandName(){
    return brandName;
  }
  float getUnitCost(){
    return unitCost;
  }
  void setUnitCost(float unitCost){
    this.unitCost = unitCost;
  }
  void printWarranty(){
      println("Skis: full replacement value for 5 years");
  }
}
```

In the Skis class, you can see that I included the same method definitions as in the Bicycle class. Notice also that I implemented the printWarranty() method a little differently in each of the two classes. I have the freedom to do this because the interface methods are empty. This is one of the benefits of using interfaces. They provide a shared interface for communicating with a group of related classes, but still allow a customized implementation of each of the common methods. As you get more experienced with coding, you'll begin to recognize some recurring patterns in how related classes are designed, and even eventually be able to guess at some of the classes' methods

The customized implementation benefit I just mentioned is helpful, but still for my money, not quite enough to add so much complexity or extra work to my process. However, before you write off interfaces, there is another much more powerful benefit to using them that justifies the extra effort—polymorphism.

Polymorphism

Polymorphism sounds a lot worse than it really it is; it just means assuming multiple forms or shapes. Whether you realize it or not, you're already very familiar with how polymorphism works. For example, imagine you and a friend decide to spend one Sunday building a birdhouse. You'd probably want some tools—say, a screwdriver and a saw. These tools don't have much in common with one another except their general classification as tools. In OOP speak, we could say that each tool has two types: the type Tool and also its more specific type (Screwdriver or Saw). As you're building the birdhouse, your friend is holding a screw and asks you to pass him a tool. Unless you're a prankster, you pass him the screwdriver. Even though your friend didn't specify which tool; the context determined which was appropriate. Also, since both the screwdriver and the saw are tools, there was no risk (when he asked for a tool) of you passing him a ham sandwich or whatever. This dynamic binding between a more general classification (tool) and a specific object (screwdriver), based on context, is precisely how polymorphism works in OOP.

In technical terms, polymorphism in Processing/Java is based on the JVM's ability to be able to link a method to a specific class's implementation on the fly, making it possible for a well-designed program to actually expand and grow over time, without necessarily going back into the source code. For example, let's say you created a video game that included creatures who could each cast different magical spells. Using polymorphism, it would be possible to code a system that could handle any number of creatures, including new ones you added after the main game engine was complete—without ever having to go back into the engine's source code. Here's a very simple code example of this scenario that you can run in Processing:

```
// polymorphism example using inheritance
void setup(){
  Creature c = new Creature();
  Ogre o = new Ogre();
  Elf  e = new Elf();
  Engine eng = new Engine();
  eng.addCreature(c);
  eng.addCreature(o);
  eng.addCreature(e);
}

//superclass
class Creature{
  void castSpell(){
    println("nothing to say");
  }
}

//subclass 1
class Ogre extends Creature{
  void castSpell(){
    println("I miss ya donkey");
  }
}
```

8

329

```
//subclass 2
class Elf extends Creature{
  void castSpell(){
    println("Gotta make the cookies");
  }
}

/* game engine--with embedded superclass
 reference in the addCreature() method */
class Engine{
  void addCreature(Creature c){
    c.castSpell();
  }
}
```

In the example, the Ogre and Elf classes each extend the Creature class. Through this inheritance relationship, any Ogre and Elf objects instantiated will now also be of the secondary type Creature. Thus, it would be perfectly legal to assign new Ogre and Elf objects to variables declared of type Creature.

```
Creature o = new Ogre();
Creature e = new Elf();
```

However, as you continue to expand this example, you'll want the Ogre and Elf objects to be assigned to variables of type Ogre and Elf, respectively—so if you tried using the preceding superclass assignment lines (which would work for now), make sure you put them back to what they were:

```
Ogre o = new Ogre();
Elf  e = new Elf();
```

This capability of unrelated objects (created from different classes) to have a relationship through a common parent class (which each class extends) allows you to create more-flexible programs. For example, if you create a game that includes the Ogre and Elf creatures, inside the game engine you'd either have to hard-code reference variables for each of the creatures, or use a common extended class. For only two creatures, either option might be fine. However, what if your game included 20 creatures, or even the capability for players to create their own creatures? The last thing you'd want to do is to keep going into your game engine code and adding new reference variables every time a player created a new creature. Rather, by including a common superclass reference variable in your engine, you could simply require players creating a new creature class to extend your base Creature superclass. This would allow your game to scale up, without you're ever having to touch the game engine source code.

Besides including a reference to the superclass in your game engine, you'd also need common methods within the Creature superclass and all the individual subclasses. In my last example, notice the common castSpell() method within the Creature superclass and both the Ogre and Elf subclasses. These methods have identical signatures (same name and parameter list). However, their implementations (the code between the curly braces of the methods) are different. As I mentioned earlier, one of the benefits of inheritance is that a subclass has access to the superclass's methods (and properties). It's also possible for a subclass to override methods within the superclass. This is accomplished by creating methods in the subclass with identical signatures to methods in its superclass.

In the last example, the following three instantiation lines

```
Creature c = new Creature();
Ogre o = new Ogre();
Elf e = new Elf();
```

create Creature, Ogre, and Elf objects (the Ogre and Elf objects are also of type Creature, through inheritance). The addCreature(Creature c) method in the Engine class includes a parameter of type Creature, allowing not only objects of type Creature to be passed to the method as arguments, but also any subclasses of Creature. Inside this method is a call, using the passed-in object reference, to the common castSpell() method. Here's where the magic happens. In setup(), when I call the Engine addCreature() method three times:

```
eng.addCreature(c);
eng.addCreature(o);
eng.addCreature(e);
```

passing in Creature, Ogre, and Elf objects, respectively, the JVM automatically figures out which implementation of the castSpell() method to call, based on the passed-in argument. In the first call, I'm passing in an object of type Creature, so the castSpell() implementation in the superclass is used. But in the next two calls, the castSpell() implementations within the Ogre and Elf subclasses, respectively, are used. This is polymorphism in action and a powerful feature of Processing and Java.

Polymorphism with interfaces

> At the risk of scaring readers away from the last few pages of this chapter, I feel it's only fair to warn you that you're about to head down a double black diamond trail (of the mind). This material is very advanced and presented in a condensed format. Read it at your own risk.

Another variation on polymorphism in Java/Processing involves the use of interfaces. As I mentioned earlier, classes are data types, and a class that extends another class becomes of that secondary type as well. Interfaces are also legal data types—you can declare an object reference variable as an interface type, just like a class type. In the SportsGear interface discussion a few pages back, the Bicycle and Skis classes each implemented the SportsGear interface. Thus, instantiated Bicycle and/or Skis objects would also both be of the secondary type SportsGear. The Bicycle class also extended a Vehicle class, so it would actually be of three types: Bicycle, Vehicle, and SportsGear. In Processing and Java, a class is only allowed to extend a single class, but it can implement as many interfaces as you'd like. This is why it is said that multiple inheritance of interface is permitted in Processing/Java.

Returning to the creature engine example, let's say some of the creatures have archery capabilities. It would be possible to add archery capabilities directly within the Creature class (which each class extends), but of course not all creatures would be archers, so it really doesn't belong in the Creature superclass. Another possible option might be to create a new Archer class, but the problem there is that you're not allowed to have a class in Processing/Java extend more than one class. Since each creature needs to extend the Creature class, it wouldn't be possible to also extend the Archer class. Using an interface can help solve this problem. As discussed, an interface can only include constants and unimplemented methods (method signatures). Here's a very simple Archer interface:

```
interface Archer{
  void shoot();
}
```

This interface only includes a shoot() method; notice the absence of curly braces following the shoot() method signature. To use the interface, you need to add the implements keyword along with the interface name to the end of another class declaration. I'll add the interface to the Elf class and also to a new Knight class. Here's what the class declaration statements look like:

```
class Elf extends Creature implements Archer
class Knight extends Creature implements Archer
```

And here are the completed Elf and Knight classes:

```
// Elf class
class Elf extends Creature implements Archer{
  void castSpell(){
    println("Gotta make the cookies");
  }

  // required method from interface
  void shoot(){
    println("Elf shoots");
  }
}

//Knight class
class Knight extends Creature implements Archer{
  void castSpell(){
    println("Mirror, mirror on thw wall...");
  }
   // required method from interface
  void shoot(){
    println("Knight shoots");
  }
}
```

Notice that both classes contain the shoot() method, including their own unique implementations. It's important to remember that any class that implements an interface is forced to literally implement the interface—meaning add curly braces and fill in the body of the method. Next, I'll add a launchArrow(Archer a) method to the Engine class, which includes a parameter of the Archer interface type. Here's the completed Engine class:

```
class Engine{
  void addCreature(Creature c){
    c.castSpell();
  }
  void launchArrow(Archer a){
    a.shoot();
  }
}
```

The launchArrow() method works the same way as the addCreature() method. When the launchArrow() method is called, the respective shoot() method implementation (in a class implementing the Archer interface) will be selected based on what specific type the more general Archer types evaluate to. Finally, here's the updated setup() function, including the new Knight instantiation and launchArrow() method calls:

```
void setup(){
  Creature c = new Creature();
  Ogre o = new Ogre();
  Elf e = new Elf();
  Knight k = new Knight();
  Engine eng = new Engine();

  eng.addCreature(c);
  eng.addCreature(o);
  eng.addCreature(e);

  eng.launchArrow(e);
  eng.launchArrow(k);
}
```

I want to make one final modification to this example. In the setup() function, I originally instantiated the Creature object only to help illustrate how method implementations can be dynamically selected, based on the type of the passed argument. When I passed in a subclass object, its castSpell() implementation was used, but when I passed in the super-class object, the castSpell() implementation within the superclass was actually used. In reality, you generally wouldn't want to instantiate a Creature object. Instead, you're only interested in using the Creature class as a base for more specific creatures.

Java includes the reserved keyword abstract, which can be used to enforce this behavior. You simply preface the class declaration with the abstract keyword, turning the class into an abstract class. Here's the Creature class as an abstract class:

```
abstract class Creature{
  void castSpell(){
    println("nothing to say");
  }
}
```

333

Once a class is declared abstract, the complier will not allow it to be instantiated. So, in the last example, if I add the abstract keyword in front of the Creature class, I'll get an error when I try to run the sketch. However, if I remove the Creature instantiation line as well as the line below it, where the engine adds the Creature object c, the sketch will run fine. Besides enforcing this behavior, abstract classes also allow you to add abstract methods to the class. Abstract methods are simply method declarations (like in interfaces) that also require the abstract keyword. Here's an example:

```
abstract String getCreatureName();
```

Also similar to interfaces, any class that extends an abstract class must implement all abstract methods within the superclass. However, unlike interfaces, abstract classes also allow you to include concrete methods (regular implemented methods) within the class. It is not necessary for a subclass to reimplement the abstract superclass's concrete methods, but of course, as in the example, it can override them. Here's the completed polymorphism example, including the Archer interface and abstract Creature superclass. I also added an abstract getCreatureName() method to the Creature superclass, which I then implemented in each of the (concrete) subclasses.

```
/* polymorphism example using
   inheritance, interface and
   an abstract class */
void setup(){
  Ogre o = new Ogre();
  Elf e = new Elf();
  Knight k = new Knight();
  Engine eng = new Engine();

  eng.addCreature(o);
  eng.addCreature(e);

  eng.launchArrow(e);
  eng.launchArrow(k);

  println(o.getCreatureName());
  println(e.getCreatureName());
  println(k.getCreatureName());
}

// abstract Creature superclass
abstract class Creature{
  /* this method will be overriden by
   Creature subclasses */
  void castSpell(){
    println("nothing to say");
  }

  //abstract getCreatureName method
  abstract String getCreatureName();
}
```

```
// Ogre subclass
class Ogre extends Creature{
  // overriden method within Creature superclass
  void castSpell(){
    println("I miss ya donkey");
  }

  /* required method implementation
   from abstract Creature superclass */
  String getCreatureName(){
    return "I am an an Ogre";
  }
}

// Elf subclass
class Elf extends Creature implements Archer{
  // overriden method within Creature superclass
  void castSpell(){
    println("Gotta make the cookies");
  }

  /* required method implementation
   from interface Archer */
  void shoot(){
    println("Elf shoots");
  }

  /* required method implementation
   from abstract Creature superclass */
  String getCreatureName(){
    return "I am an an Elf";
  }
}

// Knight subclass
class Knight extends Creature implements Archer{
  // overriden method within Creature superclass
  void castSpell(){
    println("Mirror, mirror on thw wall...");
  }

  /* required method implementation
   from interface Archer */
  void shoot(){
    println("Knight shoots");
  }
```

8

```
        /* required method implementation
         from abstract Creature superclass */
        String getCreatureName(){
          return "I am a Knight";
        }
      }

      interface Archer{
        void shoot();
      }

      /* game engine-with embedded superclass
       reference in the addCreature() method
       and embedded interface reference in
       launchArrow method */
      class Engine{
        void addCreature(Creature c){
          c.castSpell();
        }
        void launchArrow(Archer a){
          a.shoot();
        }
      }
```

Sorry if the text output is anticlimactic. Later on in the book, you'll use OOP and polymorphism to generate some interesting visuals. In this chapter, we needed to get some theory out of the way—which we've now done.

Summary

This was not an easy chapter. OOP introduces many abstract concepts to an already abstract activity—programming. However, as you begin to create more complex sketches, the organizational and reusability benefits of OOP make it well worth the added complexity. Also, like any craft-based pursuit, the process gets easier through practice. The first part of the chapter dealt with the basics of OOP—classes and objects. I think you'll find working with simple classes in Processing straightforward and helpful. For example, when creating an animation, it's helpful to encapsulate the animated object's properties (e.g., x, y, width, and height) inside a class, allowing you to target the properties using dot syntax (e.g., animatedObject.x). In the advanced OOP section, you looked at some pretty complex concepts, including inheritance, interfaces, abstract classes, and polymorphism. Understanding and implementing these concepts takes time. Fortunately, you can do a lot without them. However, as you build ever more complex sketches, these advanced features can provide much greater flexibility and efficiency to your sketch design. You'll be using most of the features discussed in this chapter throughout the book (to accomplish more interesting things than getting some text output).

9 SHAPES

Shapes are a natural extension of lines and curves. In the simplest sense, a shape is just the enclosed space formed between three or more lines. Of course, a single continuous curve can enclose space as well (e.g., an ellipse). Shapes can be generally categorized. For example, an enclosed three-sided shape is referred to as a triangle, even if its size or configuration can't be determined. Fundamental 2D shapes (e.g., rectangles, circles, and triangles) are commonly referred to as **primitives**. Primitives are essential building-block shapes, which when combined allow you to (efficiently) construct most other shapes. Processing includes both 2D and 3D primitive functions. In this chapter, you'll just be dealing with 2D shape functions.

I'll begin by creating some simple sketches based on Processing's primitive 2D shape functions. These sketches will also provide a quick review of some of the core concepts covered in earlier chapters. Using Processing's drawing commands, I'll then show you how to create your own custom shapes, and eventually you'll work your way to implementing an OOP approach for shape creation—putting to good use some of the concepts you looked at in the last chapter. Before you dive in, first a word of encouragement.

Patterns and principles (some encouragement)

Hopefully by this point in the book you're beginning to recognize some common coding and implementation patterns, duplicated in many of the examples. From my experiences in the classroom, I find most students are able to grasp these coding patterns and principles much more quickly than they can remember the specific language commands/syntax. You can always look up a command—that's what the language reference (API) is for. Conceptualization and design are far more important factors than language retention. Thus, if you're beginning to get the bigger picture, but are still struggling with implementation details, you're doing well. If on the other hand, fundamental coding concepts such as variables, loops, conditional statements, and arrays still seem unclear, you might want to review Chapter 3 again.

Processing's shape functions

Processing comes with pre-made shape creation commands, some you've looked at already. However, I'll discuss each again with some simple examples. As you review these functions, I recommend trying to deduce the underlying algorithms operating within the functions, rather than simply trying to memorize how to apply them. For example, if you were to create your own rectangle-drawing function, how would you do it? This algorithm-centered approach will lead you to a deeper understanding of coding and Processing, and ultimately allow you to code any shape, rather than make you helplessly reliant on the few functions included in the API.

The first shape I'll cover is the rectangle. Using Processing, creating a rectangle couldn't be easier (and something you're probably very familiar with by now). The following code creates the rectangle shown in Figure 9-1:

```
void setup(){
  size(400, 400);
  background(255);
  strokeWeight(10);
  fill(127);
  rect(100, 50, 200, 300);
}
```

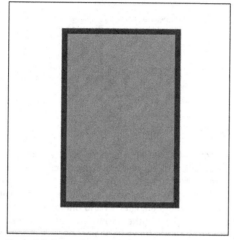

Figure 9-1. Processing's rect() function

The shape functions in Processing rely on a drawing mode variable for defining their origin—the point from which the shapes are drawn. The default origin point for a rectangle is the top-left corner, while for an ellipse it's the center. However, you can easily change these by calling rectMode() or ellipseMode() before calling the rect() or ellipse() function, respectively. This next example (shown in Figure 9-2) draws three rectangles utilizing three different drawing modes: rectMode(CORNER), rectMode(CENTER), and rectMode(CORNERS).

```
void setup(){
  size(400, 400);
  background(255);
  strokeWeight(10);
  fill(127);
  rect(103, 120, 130, 100);
  rectMode(CENTER);
  rect(103, 120, 130, 100);
  rectMode(CORNERS);
  rect(233, 220, 363, 320);
}
```

9

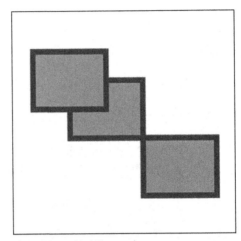

Figure 9-2. rectMode() example

The default mode is rectMode(CORNER), which draws the rectangle from the top-left corner. Since this is the default, I didn't need to explicitly call it in the sketch. The CENTER and CORNER modes treat the four rect() arguments as x, y, width, and height. However, the CORNERS mode treats the four arguments as x1, y1, x2, y2, specifying the top-left and bottom-right corner points of the rectangle. If I add one more rect() call to the bottom of the program, without specifying another drawing mode call, what mode do you think will be used? This question is a little tricky, as many people will assume the default state (CORNER) will be used, but the answer is actually (CORNERS). Every time you issue one of these drawing mode commands in a program, you change the current state of the drawing mode. This type of programming change is referred to as a **state change**, as you are changing the drawing state of the program, at least in terms of drawing rectangles.

Processing's ellipse() function, which has the same four parameters as rect(int x, int y, int w, int h), works similarly. However, as mentioned earlier, the default drawing mode for ellipse() is ellipseMode(CENTER). ellipse() also has access to one additional mode, ellipseMode(CENTER_RADIUS). This mode does the same thing as CENTER, only it treats the width and height arguments as radii rather than diameters. One somewhat useful thing to do with these two modes together is to quickly generate an ellipse within an ellipse (see Figure 9-3):

```
size(400, 400);
background(255);
strokeWeight(10);
fill(127);
ellipseMode(CENTER_RADIUS);
ellipse(200, 200, 170, 170);
fill(255);
ellipseMode(CENTER);
ellipse(200, 200, 170, 170);
```

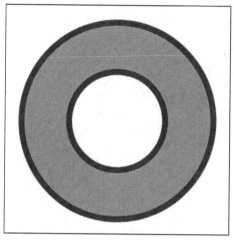

Figure 9-3. ellipseMode() example

This next example is the earlier rectMode example converted to draw ellipses (see Figure 9-4). I left in the rect() calls, treating them as bounding boxes around the ellipses.

```
//Ellipses with Bounding Boxes
void setup(){
  size(400, 400);
  background(255);
  strokeWeight(10);
  fill(127);
  ellipse(103, 120, 130, 100);
  ellipseMode(CORNER);
  ellipse(103, 120, 130, 100);
  ellipseMode(CORNERS);
  ellipse(233, 220, 363, 320);

  // bounding boxes
  strokeWeight(1);
  noFill();
  rect(103, 120, 130, 100);
  rectMode(CENTER);
  rect(103, 120, 130, 100);
  rectMode(CORNERS);
  rect(233, 220, 363, 320);
}
```

9

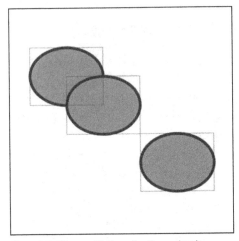

Figure 9-4. Ellipses with Bounding Boxes sketch

A bounding box is the smallest rectangular region that encloses a shape. Bounding boxes are important in computer graphics, as it's simpler and less computationally demanding for the computer to calculate the area of a rectangle than an ellipse or some other irregular shape. Thus, in a game, for example, collision detection can be calculated with regard to the bounding box of a shape, instead of the shape's actual perimeter. This will allow the game to perform better (but there may be some loss of accuracy with regard to how the actual detection looks on the screen).

In addition to the rect() and ellipse() shape functions, Processing includes point(), arc(), triangle(), and quad() functions. I discussed point() exhaustively in Chapters 6 and 7, and technically a point is not a shape (mathematically speaking), so I'll skip it. I also covered arc() in the context of curves—but here's one more example, illustrating the arc() function's pie shape feature (see Figure 9-5):

```
//Arcs with Bounding Boxes
void setup(){
  size(400, 400);
  background(255);
  strokeWeight(10);
  fill(127);
  arc(103, 120, 130, 100, 0, PI);
  ellipseMode(CORNER);
  arc(103, 120, 130, 100, 0, HALF_PI);
  ellipseMode(CORNERS);
  arc(233, 220, 363, 320, 0, TWO_PI-HALF_PI);

  // bounding boxes
  strokeWeight(1);
  noFill();
```

```
  rect(103, 120, 130, 100);
  rectMode(CENTER);
  rect(103, 120, 130, 100);
  rectMode(CORNERS);
  rect(233, 220, 363, 320);
}
```

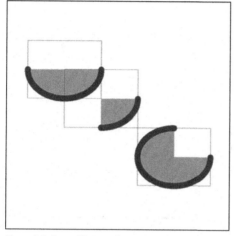

Figure 9-5. Arcs with Bounding Boxes sketch

In this last sketch, I used the ellipse() example code and simply switched the ellipse keyword with arc, adding the two additional required start and end angle arguments. (The angle arguments need to be specified in radians, and the value of PI in radians is equivalent to 180 degrees, or 1/2 rotation around an ellipse.) I was able to use the ellipse() example source code, as arc() shares the same four initial arguments as ellipse() and also uses the ellipseMode() function to specify its drawing mode. Really, an arc and an ellipse are related, as both are internally implemented the same way using cosine and sine functions. Later in the chapter, I'll show you how to create an ellipse in Processing using some trig functions. As I demonstrated in Chapter 7, if you use 0 and TWO_PI as your two angle arguments when calling arc(), you'll get an ellipse. I leave that for you to try on your own, if you missed it earlier. Next is an example that uses Processing's triangle() function (see Figure 9-6):

```
//Triangle
Point[]p = new Point[3];
void setup(){
  size(400, 400);
  background(190);
  p[0] = new Point(2, height-2);
  p[1] = new Point(width-2, height-2);
  p[2] = new Point(width/2, 2);
```

9

```
    stroke(0);
    strokeWeight(2);
    fill(225);
    triangle(p[0].x, p[0].y, p[1].x, p[1].y, p[2].x, p[2].y);
}
```

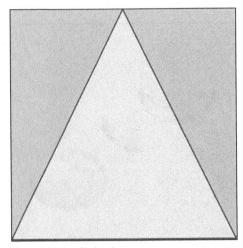

Figure 9-6. Triangle sketch

The examples thus far in the chapter have been pretty dull, so we'll do something a little more interesting with the triangle() function. Also note that I used Java's Point class again, as I find it very convenient when plotting stuff. This class is not included in Processing, so you won't find it in the Processing reference. However, it's in the Java API (see http://java.sun.com/j2se/1.4.2/docs/api/java/awt/Point.html). Arrays in Processing and Java can be declared of any data type. (Remember from Chapter 8 that a class is also a data type.) Point is a class in Java and thus a valid data type. This allowed me to create a Point array and to refer to each Point object in the array by a single index value (e.g., p[0] or p[1]). Since each Point object has an x and y property, this is a convenient data type for keeping track of both components (x and y) at the same time. If I had just used arrays of type float instead of the Point class, I'd need to use either two separate parallel arrays—one for x and one for y—or I'd need to use a multidimensional array (p[][]). I think using an array of Points is the simplest solution. Here's a little variation on the Triangle sketch (see Figure 9-7):

```
    //Triangle Zoom
    Point[]p = new Point[3];
    float shift = 10;
    void setup(){
      size(400, 400);
      background(190);
      smooth();
      p[0] = new Point(1, height-1);
```

```
        p[1] = new Point(width-1, height-1);
        p[2] = new Point(width/2, 1);
        stroke(0);
        strokeWeight(1);
        fill(225);
        triangle(p[0].x, p[0].y, p[1].x, p[1].y, p[2].x, p[2].y);
        triBlur();
    }
    void triBlur(){
      triangle(p[0].x+=shift, p[0].y-=shift/2, p[1].x-=shift, ↩
            p[1].y-=shift/2, p[2].x, p[2].y+=shift);
      if(p[0].x<width/2){
        // recursive call
        triBlur();
      }
    }
```

Figure 9-7. Triangle Zoom sketch

This sketch introduces a new advanced concept called recursion. **Recursion** is a process in which a function calls itself, as happened in triBlur() in the last example. I didn't need to use recursion in this last example—I could have also handled the multiple calls to triangle() iteratively using a while or for loop, but it was a good excuse to demonstrate how recursion works. One danger in using recursion is the increased possibility of generating an infinite loop, which is a lot easier to do than you might assume. The notion of something calling itself can be a little confusing, and therefore it's not that hard to make a simple logic mistake. I avoided an endless loop by wrapping the recursive call in a conditional statement. Since I increased the value of p[0].x each time the function executed, I used the conditional to ensure that p[0].x would never exceed the midpoint of the display window. Next, I'll add a gradient blur effect to the sketch (see Figure 9-8):

```
//Triangle Blur
Point[]p = new Point[3];
float shift = 2;
float fade = 0;
float fillCol = 0;
void setup(){
  size(400, 400);
  background(0);
  smooth();
  fade = 255.0/(width/2.0/shift);
  p[0] = new Point(1, height-1);
  p[1] = new Point(width-1, height-1);
  p[2] = new Point(width/2, 1);
  noStroke();
  triBlur();
}
void triBlur(){
  fill(fillCol);
  fillCol+=fade;
  triangle(p[0].x+=shift, p[0].y-=shift/2, p[1].x-=shift, ➥
           p[1].y-=shift/2, p[2].x, p[2].y+=shift);
  if(p[0].x<width/2){
    // recursive call
    triBlur();
  }
}
```

Figure 9-8. Triangle Blur sketch

The blur was generated by incrementing the fill color from black to white each loop iteration, based on the fade factor. I also turned off the stroke and decreased the value of the shift variable to make the transition seamless. Hopefully you've been able to follow all this. With the exception of the recursion, there's nothing new here. In the next modification, I'll introduce a new concept. I'll add some rotation to the triangles, which in itself isn't very complicated. However, the first attempt won't pan out as you might expect. I'll then discuss some new concepts to get the sketch working. Here's the flawed initial attempt (see Figure 9-9):

```
//Triangle Spin
Point[]p = new Point[3];
float shift = 2;
float fade = 0;
float fillCol = 0;
float spin = 0;

void setup(){
  size(400, 400);
  background(0);
  smooth();
  fade = 255.0/(width/2.0/shift);
  spin = 360.0/(width/2.0/shift);
  p[0] = new Point(1, height-1);
  p[1] = new Point(width-1, height-1);
  p[2] = new Point(width/2, 1);
  noStroke();
  triBlur();
}
void triBlur(){
  fill(fillCol);
  fillCol+=fade;
  rotate(spin);
  triangle(p[0].x+=shift, p[0].y-=shift/2, p[1].x-=shift, ➥
           p[1].y-=shift/2, p[2].x, p[2].y+=shift);
  if(p[0].x<width/2){
    // recursive call
    triBlur();
  }
}
```

9

Figure 9-9. Triangle Spin sketch

Transforming shapes

In the last example, I wanted to create a nice, even rotation around the center point of the triangles. Instead, what I got was the triangles spinning out of the display window. What happened? The computer didn't actually do anything wrong (although I suspect you realized that). I asked it to rotate 3.6 degrees each iteration of the loop, and it did just that. When you call the rotate() function, Processing rotates around the origin, which is (0, 0), or the top-left corner of the display window. The triangles, however, are centered in the middle of window. So Processing did exactly what I asked of it—it rotated around the origin, not the center point of the triangles or the display window.

To fix this issue, I either need to write my own custom triangle and rotate functions using some trig functions, or (the much simpler way) I can draw my triangles centered around the origin (0,0), and then use Processing's translate() function to move them to the center of the display window. In reality, this shifts the graphics context of the entire display window, not just the triangles. The graphic context is the virtual drawing space of the display window. Here's the last example corrected using Processing's translate() function (see Figures 9-10 and 9-11):

```
//Triangle Flower
Point[]p = new Point[3];
float shift = 1.0;
float fade = 0;
float fillCol = 0;
float rot = 0;
```

```
float spin = 0;
void setup(){
  size(400, 400);
  background(0);
  smooth();
  fade = 255.0/(width/2.0/shift);
  spin = 360.0/(width/2.0/shift);
  p[0] = new Point(-width/2, height/2);
  p[1] = new Point(width/2, height/2);
  p[2] = new Point(0, -height/2);
  noStroke();
  translate(width/2, height/2);
  triBlur();
}
void triBlur(){
  fill(fillCol);
  fillCol+=fade;
  rotate(spin);
  // another interesting variation: uncomment the line below
  // rotate(rot+=radians(spin));
  triangle(p[0].x+=shift, p[0].y-=shift/2, p[1].x-=shift, ➥
          p[1].y-=shift/2, p[2].x, p[2].y+=shift);
  if(p[0].x<0){
    // recursive call
    triBlur();
  }
}
```

Figure 9-10. Triangle Flower sketch, variation 1

Figure 9-11. Triangle Flower variation sketch, variation 2

Look at this sketch carefully, as the concepts are important. Also notice that I included a second rotate() option. Simply uncomment the // rotate(rot+=radians(spin)); statement to see the effect.

If you want to create any multi-shape object, you usually need to deal with translation. In Java, the class that encapsulates this sort of thing is called AffineTransform. **Affine transform** is a term used to describe a special type of transformation involving matrices. You can simply think of a matrix (singular of matrices) as a table structure composed of rows and columns. In computer graphics, the use of matrices is an efficient way to represent coordinate geometry. It is possible to use a matrix to store the position, scale, and rotation of point coordinates. It is also possible to transform the data in the matrix, and ultimately the coordinate geometry, using simple operations (e.g., addition and multiplication). Matrices are too complex an issue to cover in depth here, but here's a good link with information about them: http://en.wikipedia.org/wiki/Matrix_%28mathematics%29.

An affine transformation allows shapes to be moved, scaled, rotated, and even sheared without distortion by ensuring that lines that are parallel and/or straight prior to the transformation remain so afterwards. Affine transformations in Processing affect the graphics context and are cumulative. In other words, If I rotate with the function call rotate(PI), and then again with rotate(HALF_PI), the graphics context will be rotated 1 1/2 pi, or 270 degrees. What has already been drawn on the screen won't be effected, but any new data added to the screen will now be initially rotated 1 1/2 pi. This same cumulative effect occurs when using the rotate(), translate(), and scale() functions. Transformations can be confusing when you first start using them. Here's a simple example that uses a series of transformations to construct a little truck (see Figure 9-12):

```
//Toy Truck
int truckW = 300;
int truckH = 100;
int truckX = -truckW/2;
int truckY = -truckH/2;

void setup(){
  size(500, 200);
  background(0);
  smooth();

  //body1
  translate(width-truckW/2-50, height/2);
  rect(truckX, truckY, truckW, truckH);

  //body2
  translate(-width+316, 17);
  scale(.2, .65);
  rect(truckX, truckY, truckW, truckH);

  //body3
  translate(-width+250, 20);
  scale(.7, .59);
  noStroke();
  rect(truckX, truckY, truckW, truckH);

  //tires
  stroke(255);
  strokeWeight(7);
  scale(.70, .75);
  translate(160, 172);
  ellipse(truckX, truckY, truckW, truckH);
  translate(1300, 0);
  ellipse(truckX, truckY, truckW, truckH);
  translate(1800, 0);
  ellipse(truckX, truckY, truckW, truckH);
  translate(400, 0);
  ellipse(truckX, truckY, truckW, truckH);

  //window mask
  translate(-3355, -284);
  scale(.7, .9);
  noStroke();
  fill(0);
  triangle(truckX, truckY + truckH, truckX+truckW, ➡
           truckY, truckX, truckY);
}
```

9

353

Figure 9-12. Toy Truck sketch

When looking at the code in the last example, I hope some of you protested, exclaiming "Hey, you can't use all those magic numbers!" It's true, it isn't good practice to use magic numbers. And this really is a pretty lousy implementation of a truck (although it's kind of cute, don't you think?). The problem I faced was dealing with all the accumulating matrix transformations and having to manually plug in and try different values until I got my truck. Because of the scaling effect, some of the translation values got pretty wacky, with a few values far exceeding the display window dimensions. Fortunately, there is a much better way to handle resetting the matrix values, which I'll discuss shortly.

The last basic shape function I'll cover is quad(). This function works just like the triangle() function, but uses four vertices instead of three. The function requires eight arguments, defining the x and y components of each of the four vertices. Unlike the rect() function, in which each corner is 90 degrees, quad() can create a four-point polygon with different angles for each corner. In the following simple quad() example, I illustrate this using the random() function for each vertex (see Figure 9-13):

```
// Simple Quad
size(300, 300);
background(0);
noStroke();
smooth();
// quad(p1.x, p1.y, p2.x, p2.y, p3.x, p3.y, p4.x, p4.y)
quad(50+random(-25, 25), 50+random(-25, 25), ➥
    250+random(-25, 25), 50+random(-25, 25), ➥
    250+random(-25, 25), 250+random(-25, 25), ➥
    50+random(-25, 25), 250+random(-25, 25));
```

Figure 9-13. Simple Quad sketch

Next is a more interesting quad() example that also includes Processing's resetMatrix()
function, used to reset the affine transformation matrix discussed earlier (see Figure 9-14):

```
// Disintegrating Quad Wall

float randShift = .2;
int quadW = 15;
int quadH = quadW;
float[]q = { -quadW/2, -quadH/2, quadW, quadH };

void setup() {
  size(600, 600);
  background(255);
  smooth();
  noStroke();
  /* generate a table structure of
   quads progressivley adding more
   randomization to each quad */
  for (int i=0, k=1; i<height-quadH; i+=quadH, k++){
    /* resetting the transformation matrix
     keeps the translations from continually
     accumulating. Try commenting out the
     resetMatrix() call to see the effect. */
    resetMatrix();
    translate(0, quadH*k);
    for (int j=0; j<width-quadW; j+=quadW){
      translate(quadW, 0);
      fill(random(0, 255));
      // r(k) is a function call
      quad(q[0]+r(k), q[1]+r(k), ➡
```

```
        q[0]+q[2]+r(k), q[1]+r(k), ➡
        q[0]+q[2]+r(k), q[1]+q[3]+r(k), ➡
        q[0]+r(k), q[1]+q[3]+r(k));
    }
  }
}

float r(int i){
  return random(-i*randShift, i*randShift);
}
```

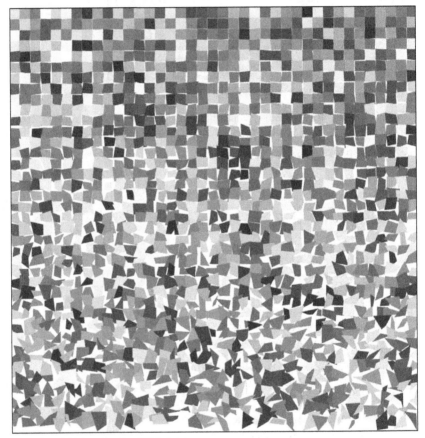

Figure 9-14. Disintegrating Quad Wall sketch

This is a dense little sketch, so it may not be apparent at first glance what's happening. The nested for loop generates a table structure of quadrilaterals. In the outer for loop head, I initialized two variables (i and k) since I needed one variable to be incremented by quadH (i) and one to be incremented by 1 (k). The first line in the loop, after the comment, is the function call resetMatrix(). This simple step clears the transformation matrix at the beginning of each iteration of the loop. Since the matrix was getting reset each time, I couldn't use it to step down the rows of the table. I solved this by multiplying the second argument (which controls the y position) in the outer loop translate() call with k, as in translate(0, quadH*k). However, by resetting the matrix, I was able to repeatedly call translate(quadW, 0) within the inner loop, which took care of stepping the quadrangles across the display window. Finally, I set up a convenient little function, r(val), to add a random offset to the quadrangle points. Since I used the outer loop variable k to specify the random range, randomization increased as the loop ran. Try changing the randShift variable at the top of the sketch to see how it affects the output.

Before moving on to some other drawing functions, I want to provide one more example that will hopefully help clarify the matrix transformations. The next sketch uses a convenient Processing function, printMatrix(), which actually prints to the screen the current contents of the transformation matrix. As I mentioned earlier, transformations affect the virtual drawing, or graphics context, so in this next example, all I include are the actual matrix transformations—which is all I need to see how the individual transformation function calls affect the overall matrix. You don't need to spend too much time on this, but just look at which part of the matrix is affected by each call (see Figure 9-15):

```
// printMatrix()
//initial state
println(" before transformations");
printMatrix();

//translate
translate(150, 225);
println(" after translate()");
printMatrix();

//scale
scale(.75, .95);
println(" after translate() and scale()");
printMatrix();

//rotate
rotate(PI*.3);
println(" after translate(), scale() and rotate()");
printMatrix();

//reset
resetMatrix();
println(" after resetMatrix()");
printMatrix();
```

9

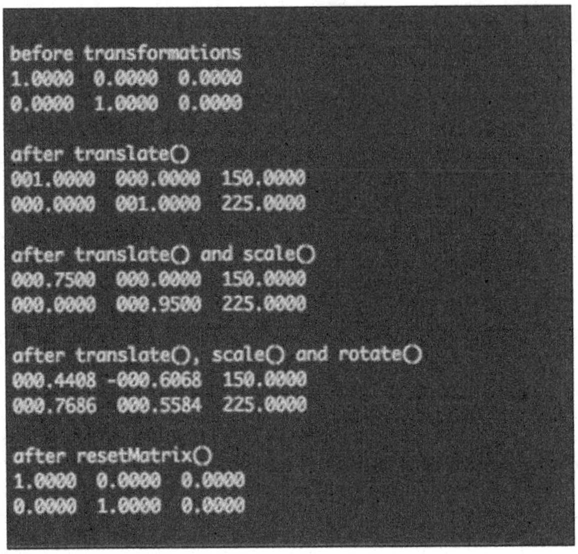

```
before transformations
1.0000  0.0000  0.0000
0.0000  1.0000  0.0000

after translate()
001.0000  000.0000  150.0000
000.0000  001.0000  225.0000

after translate() and scale()
000.7500  000.0000  150.0000
000.0000  000.9500  225.0000

after translate(), scale() and rotate()
000.4408 -000.6068  150.0000
000.7686  000.5584  225.0000

after resetMatrix()
1.0000  0.0000  0.0000
0.0000  1.0000  0.0000
```

Figure 9-15. printMatrix() sketch

Plotting shapes

Although the basic shape functions rect(), ellipse(), triangle(), and quad() offer some convenience, they are also pretty limited. Processing has a more general and versatile approach to shape creation that you've looked at before. Utilizing beginShape(), endShape(), and a series of vertex() commands, any shape can be created using Processing. These shapes can include combinations of both straight and curved sections. beginShape() also offers some advanced modes, allowing more complex polygonal structures to be created. You've used these functions before, so some of this will likely be review. I'll begin by examining the default closed mode, which will generate a polygon (see Figure 9-16):

```
//Octagon
size(400, 400);
background(255);
smooth();
int margin = 50;
fill(0);
stroke(127);
strokeWeight(6);
beginShape();
vertex(3, height/2);
vertex(margin, margin);
```

```
vertex(width/2, 3);
vertex(width-margin, margin);
vertex(width-3, height/2);
vertex(width-margin, height-margin);
vertex(width/2, height-3);
vertex(margin, height-margin);
endShape(CLOSE);
```

Figure 9-16. Octagon sketch

The default beginShape() mode is a filled but open shape. By adding the CLOSE argument to the endShape() call, the shape is closed (by connecting the last vertex to the initial vertex), as illustrated in the Octagon example. Plotting the octagon wasn't too difficult because an 8-sided regular shape on a 4-sided window boils down to plotting vertices at the corners and midpoints of the display window—but what about switching to a pentagon or heptagon (7 sides), or even an enneakaidecagon (a 19-sided polygon)? Using a little trig, you can very easily create a general-purpose polygon creator. In the following example, I've parameterized lots of details to make the makePoly() function useful. I've also called this function a bunch of times in the sketch to showcase the range of images it can create (see Figure 9-17).

```
/*
Polygon Creator
Ira Greenberg, December 26, 2005
*/
void setup(){
  size(600, 600);
  background(127);
  smooth();
  /*
```

```
        //complete parameter list
        makePoly(x, y, pts, radius 1, radius 2, initial rotation, ➡
        stroke Color, stroke Weight, fill Color, endcap, stroke join)
        */
        // makePoly function calls
        makePoly(width/2, height/2, 72, 420, 270, 45, color(0, 0, 0), ➡
            16, color(255, 255, 255));
        makePoly(width/2, height/2, 16, 300, 250, 45, color(200, 200, 200),➡
            10, color(20, 20, 20));
        makePoly(width/2, height/2, 60, 210, 210, 45, color(255,255,255), ➡
            8, color(0,0,0), PROJECT, ROUND);
        makePoly(width/2, height/2, 60, 200, 155, 45, color(120, 120, 120),➡
            6, color(255, 255, 255), PROJECT, ROUND);
        makePoly(width/2, height/2, 50, 280, -200, 45, ➡
            color(200, 200, 200), 6, color(50, 50, 50), PROJECT, ROUND);
        makePoly(width/2, height/2, 8, 139, 139, 68, color(255, 255, 255), ➡
            5, color(0,0,0));
        makePoly(width/2, height/2, 24, 125, 60, 90, color(50, 50, 50), 12,➡
            color(200, 200, 200), ROUND, BEVEL);
        makePoly(width/2, height/2, 4, 60, 60, 90, color(0,0,0), 5, ➡
            color(200,200,200), ROUND, BEVEL);
        makePoly(width/2, height/2, 4, 60, 60, 45, color(255, 255, 255), 5,➡
            color(20, 20, 20), ROUND, BEVEL);
        makePoly(width/2, height/2, 30, 30, 30, 90, color(75, 75, 75), 10, ➡
            color(60,60,60), ROUND, BEVEL);
        makePoly(width/2, height/2, 30, 28, 28, 90, color(255, 255,255), 2,➡
            color(60,60,60), ROUND, BEVEL);
        makePoly(width/2, height/2, 24, 10, -25, 45, #000000, .75, ➡
            color(255, 255, 255), SQUARE, MITER);
    }

    //default - if no args passed
    void makePoly(){
      // call main makePoly function
      makePoly(width/2, height/2,  4, width/4, width/4, ➡
        45, #777777, 4, #AAAAAA, SQUARE, MITER);
    }

    // x, y, pts args
    void makePoly(float x, float y, int pts){
     // call main makePoly function
      makePoly(x, y, pts, width/4, width/4, ➡
        45, #777777, 4, #AAAAAA, SQUARE, MITER);
    }
```

```
// x, y, pts, rad1, rad2 args
void makePoly(float x, float y, int pts, float rad1, float rad2){
 // call main makePoly function
  makePoly(x, y, pts, rad1, rad2, 45, #777777, 4, #AAAAAA, ➥
    SQUARE, MITER);
 }


// x, y, pts, rad1, rad2,, initRot, strokeCol, strokeWt, fillCol args
void makePoly(float x, float y, int pts, float rad1, float rad2, ➥
  float initRot, color strokeCol, float strokeWt, color fillCol){
// call main makePoly function
  makePoly(x, y, pts, rad1, rad2, initRot, strokeCol, strokeWt, ➥
    fillCol, SQUARE, MITER);
}


// main function - called by other overloaded functions/methods
void makePoly(float x, float y, int pts, float rad1, float rad2, ➥
    float initRot, color strokeCol, float strokeWt, ➥
    color fillCol, int endCap, int endJoin){

  float px = 0, py = 0, angle = initRot;
  stroke(strokeCol);
  strokeWeight(strokeWt);
  strokeCap(endCap);
  strokeJoin(endJoin);
  fill(fillCol);

  beginShape();
  for (int i = 0; i< pts; i++){
   if (i%2 == 0){
     px = x+cos(radians(angle))*rad1;
     py = y+sin(radians(angle))*rad1;
   }
   else {
     px = x+cos(radians(angle))*rad2;
     py = y+sin(radians(angle))*rad2;
   }
   vertex(px, py);
   angle+=360/pts;
  }
  endShape(CLOSE);
}
```

9

Figure 9-17. Polygon Creator sketch

The trig functions, based on unit circle relationships, do most of the real work in this sketch. I've included `sin()` and `cos()` expressions in numerous examples earlier in the book, and a general discussion about trig and the unit circle can be found in Chapter 4 and also in Appendix B. In addition, I owe some debt to Ric Ewing, who a couple years ago published a series of wonderful drawing methods for ActionScript that have informed my own approach (see `www.macromedia.com/devnet/flash/articles/adv_draw_methods.html`).

I nested the trig functions in a conditional `if...else` structure as a simple way to generate two radii. I've used this technique in other places in the book as well. The modulus operator, `%`, returns the remainder of the division between the two operands (e.g., **9 % 5 = 4**, as 5 goes into 9 once, leaving a remainder of 4). I used (`i%2 == 0`) in the head of the conditional so that points would alternate between radius 1 and radius 2. If you don't see it yet, this works because only even numbers will return 0, but odds won't.

The other possibly surprising aspect of this sketch is the use of five `makePoly()` function definitions, in which—in all but one of them—another `makePoly()` function is called. This approach of creating multiple functions (or methods) with the same name is a common technique in OOP, and is referred to as **method overloading**. As long as the method signatures are different, the compiler sees them as unique structures. The signature, in Java and Processing, is a combination of the method name and parameter list (including the number and type of parameters). If the number and/or type of parameters is different in the signatures, then the compiler sees the methods as unique, regardless of whether the methods share the same name. This is a convenient implementation, as it gives users a choice of how to call/use the method.

I created five versions of the makePoly() function. It is possible to create a lot more, although it's probably not necessary. Only one of the makePoly() functions includes the full parameter list; the others use a partial list, and one of them includes no parameter. Each of the four makePoly() functions (without the full parameter list) internally calls the makePoly() function with the full list. I did this so that the actual plotting algorithm could be put in one place—inside the makePoly() function with the full parameter list.

When one of the functions without the full parameter list is called, it internally passes the arguments it received—adding default values for the remaining ones—to the makePoly() function with the full parameter list and plotting implementation. I recommend trying to add your own version of a makePoly() function to the sketch to get a better sense of how this all works.

Regular and star polygons are fine, but there are some other useful shapes that you can build by modifying the last algorithm a bit. Here's a sprocket creator sketch, in which I call the makeSprocket()function a bunch of times to demonstrate the range of shapes the function is capable of generating (see Figure 9-18).

```
/*
Sprocket Creator
Ira Greenberg, December 27, 2005
*/

void setup(){
  size(600, 600);
  background(65);
  smooth();

  makeSprocket(width/2, height/2, 20, 280, 440, 45, color(0, 0, 0), ↪
      20, color(255, 255, 255), SQUARE, MITER);
  makeSprocket(width/2, height/2, 120.0, 275, -230, 45, ↪
      color(200, 200, 200), 2, color(20, 20, 20), SQUARE, ROUND);
  makeSprocket(width/2, height/2, 20.0, 250, 120, 45, color(0, 0, 0),↪
      12, color(255, 255, 255), PROJECT, MITER);
  makeSprocket(width/2, height/2, 8.0, 120, 190, 45, ↪
      color(20, 20, 20), 14, color(200, 200, 200), PROJECT, MITER);
  makeSprocket(width/2, height/2, 8.0, 120, 170, 22.5, ↪
      color(245, 245, 245), 20, color(10, 10, 10), PROJECT, MITER);
  makeSprocket(width/2, height/2, 25.0, 90, 35, 45, ↪
      color(255, 255, 255), 2, color(0, 0, 0), PROJECT, MITER);
  makeSprocket(width/2, height/2, 8.0, 25, 10, 45, ↪
      color(127, 127, 127), 4, color(255, 255, 255), PROJECT, MITER);
}

void makeSprocket(float x, float y, float spokes, float rad1, ↪
    float rad2, float initRot, color strokeCol, float strokeWt, ↪
    color fillCol, int endCap, int endJoin){
```

```
float px = 0, py = 0, angle = initRot;
float ang = (360.0/spokes)/2.0;
float ang2 = (360.0/spokes)/4.0;
stroke(strokeCol);
strokeWeight(strokeWt);
strokeCap(endCap);
strokeJoin(endJoin);
fill(fillCol);

beginShape();
for (int i = 0; i<spokes; i++){
  px = x+cos(radians(angle))*rad1;
  py = y+sin(radians(angle))*rad1;
  vertex(px, py);
  angle+=ang;
  px = x+cos(radians(angle))*rad1;
  py = y+sin(radians(angle))*rad1;
  vertex(px, py);
  angle+=ang2;
  px = x+cos(radians(angle))*rad2;
  py = y+sin(radians(angle))*rad2;
  vertex(px, py);
  angle+=ang2;
}
endShape(CLOSE);
}
```

Figure 9-18. Sprocket Creator sketch

The Sprocket Creator sketch is similar to the Polygon Creator sketch. The main difference is the few extra trig expressions in the makeSprocket() function. Instead of plotting vertices at equal angle rotations, each spoke of the sprocket is composed of three vertices. The first and second share the same radius and are the outer edge of the spoke. The third vertex is an inner radius, and is at the base between each spoke. Notice also that I used two different angle values. I somewhat arbitrarily defined the angle between the two spoke vertices (within the spoke) as twice as large as the angle between the spokes. The final angle incrementation (angle+=ang2) ensures that there is symmetry between each spoke.

As reading descriptions like this can be confusing, I suggest playing with the sketch and creating some of your own sprockets. You might also want to try to spin your own shape by modifying the existing drawSprocket() method.

Creating hybrid shapes

The beginShape() and endShape() functions allow you to combine straight and curved lines to form hybrid shapes. Once you introduce curves into your shapes, calculating coordinates can get a little tricky. It often helps to break the problem down into more manageable sections—in the next two example sketches, I do just that. In the first sketch, I hack out a list of coordinates (using magic numbers) and individual drawing function calls that create a hybrid shape. In the second sketch, I develop a more general plotting algorithm, removing all the magic numbers. Here's the initial code in all its magic number glory (see Figure 9-19):

```
// Hybrid Shape
size(600, 600);
curveTightness(-.4);
smooth();

beginShape();
curveVertex(200, -300);
curveVertex(200, 100);
curveVertex(400, 100);
curveVertex(400, -300);

vertex(500, 100);
vertex(500, 200);

curveVertex(800, 200);
curveVertex(500, 200);
curveVertex(500, 400);
curveVertex(800, 400);

vertex(500, 500);
vertex(400, 500);
```

```
curveVertex(400, 800);
curveVertex(400, 500);
curveVertex(200, 500);
curveVertex(200, 800);

vertex(100, 500);
vertex(100, 400);

curveVertex(-200, 400);
curveVertex(100, 400);
curveVertex(100, 200);
curveVertex(-200, 200);

vertex(100, 100);
endShape(CLOSE);
```

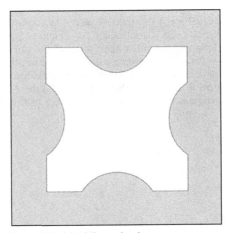

Figure 9-19. Hybrid Shape sketch

The next step was looking at the ugly code I had written and seeing if I could figure out an algorithm to generalize the form. This backward approach—making before thinking—seems to be a general pattern I use when I get stuck. I guess if you're better at math than me, you might be able to lay down clean algorithms by just thinking about problems, but I usually have to get my hands dirty first. Because the shape created in the sketch is symmetrical, and there is a recurring pattern of function calls in the code, I knew it would be possible, without too much hair pulling, to figure out the algorithm. I also knew, because of the radial symmetry, that using trig functions would somehow be the easiest solution. Here's what I got (see Figure 9-20):

```
// Hybrid Shape 2
size(600, 600);
curveTightness(-.4);
smooth();
strokeWeight(10);
float sides = 8;
float angle = 360.0/sides/2;
float px = 0, py = 0;
float cx = 0, cy = 0;
float ang = 360.0/(sides+sides/2.0);
float ang2 = ang/2.0;
float rad1 = 250.0;
float rad2 = rad1*2.0;
int x = width/2;
int y = height/2;

beginShape();
for (int i=0; i<sides; i++){
  cx = x+cos(radians(angle))*rad2;
  cy = y+sin(radians(angle))*rad2;
  curveVertex(cx, cy);
  px = x+cos(radians(angle))*rad1;
  py = y+sin(radians(angle))*rad1;
  curveVertex(px, py);
  angle+=ang;
  px = x+cos(radians(angle))*rad1;
  py = y+sin(radians(angle))*rad1;
  curveVertex(px, py);
  cx = x+cos(radians(angle))*rad2;
  cy = y+sin(radians(angle))*rad2;
  curveVertex(cx, cy);
  px = x+cos(radians(angle))*rad1;
  py = y+sin(radians(angle))*rad1;
  vertex(px, py);
  angle+=ang2;
  px = x+cos(radians(angle))*rad1;
  py = y+sin(radians(angle))*rad1;
  vertex(px, py);
}
endShape(CLOSE);
```

9

Figure 9-20. Hybrid Shape 2 sketch

This sketch makes a good gear shape. If you change the value of the sides variable in the example, the shape scales nicely. I think it would be a good exercise to try to "functionalize" this last example. In other words, try sticking the main drawing routine in a function with a bunch of parameters, as I did with the polygon and sprocket examples. Besides curveVertex(), you can also use bezierVertex() in conjunction with regular vertex() calls, but I'll also leave that for you to try on your own.

The other shape modes

There are a number of additional shape modes. Many of these are more applicable to 3D than 2D, for creating a skin or polygonal mesh around a 3D form. In the 3D chapters, you'll learn how to plot some 3D forms. For now, I'm just going to give a brief overview of what the other modes do. The first two you'll look at, TRIANGLES and QUADS, don't form a contiguous mesh, but rather simply create individual triangles and quadrangles from lists of coordinates. In the next example, I'll generate 90 triangles using a for loop and the TRIANGLES mode (see Figure 9-21):

```
//Random Triangles
size (500, 500);
background(255);
smooth();
beginShape(TRIANGLES);
for (int i=0; i<90; i++){
  stroke(random(0, 200));
  fill(random(225, 255), 150);
  strokeWeight(random(.5, 5));
  vertex(random(width), random(height));
}
endShape();
```

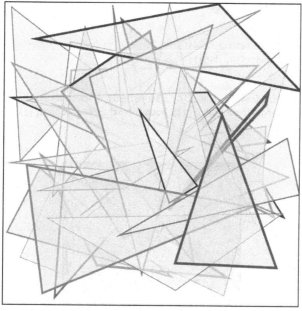

Figure 9-21. Random Triangles sketch (TRIANGLES mode)

Although you could relatively easily write your own function to pull this sort of thing off, it is still convenient having this option. It would be a good exercise to try to re-create the functionality of the beginShape(TRIANGLES) mode using the triangle() function or the no-argument version of beginShape().

Notice the extra argument in the command fill(random(225, 255), 150);, after the closed parentheses of the random call. This optional second argument allows you to control the alpha, or transparency, of the grayscale fill. The value range is from 0 to 255 (0 being transparent and 255 being completely opaque). If you don't specify an argument, the default value is 255. The stroke() and fill() commands each allow you to specify one, two, three, or four arguments. In the next chapter, I'll discuss color and imaging, and concepts like alpha in greater detail.

beginShape(QUADS) mode works similarly to TRIANGLE mode, except that shapes are closed in groups of four vertex() calls instead of three. In this next example, I generate random quads, bounded within a rectangular region, forming a sort of shape texture (see Figure 9-22).

```
//Random Bounded Quads
size (250, 250);
background(255);
smooth();
int[]boundinBox = {50, 50, 150, 150};
fill(0);
```

```
rect(boundinBox[0], boundinBox[1], boundinBox[2], boundinBox[3]);
strokeJoin(BEVEL);
beginShape(QUADS);
for (int i=0; i<1000; i++){
  stroke(random(50, 255));
  fill(0, 0);
  strokeWeight(random(.5, 2));
  vertex(random(boundinBox[0], boundinBox[0]+boundinBox[2]), ➥
       random(boundinBox[1], boundinBox[1]+boundinBox[3]));
}
endShape();
```

Figure 9-22. Random Bounded Quads sketch
(QUADS mode)

You'll notice in the output that the shapes don't form a pattern of little rectangles, even though they were generated by using QUADS mode. This is because a quadrilateral is not necessarily a rectangular structure. It is possible to create a quadrilateral in which no two sides are parallel; this shape is sometimes referred to as a trapezium. If any two of the sides are parallel, it's usually called a trapezoid, which I assume you remember from some math class. There is a simple and complex classification for polygons, which affects quadrilaterals as well. Simple polygons don't intersect with themselves, while complex ones do. Here's an example of each, using QUADS mode (see Figure 9-23):

```
//Simple/Complex Quads
size (300, 150);
smooth();
beginShape(QUADS);
//simple quad
vertex(25, 40);
vertex(125, 30);
```

```
vertex(120, 120);
vertex(20, 118);
//complex quad
vertex(175, 40);
vertex(275, 30);
vertex(170, 118);
vertex(270, 120);
endShape();
```

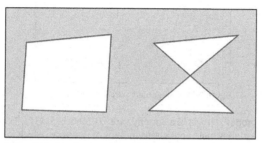

Figure 9-23. Simple/Complex Quads sketch

Simple vs. complex polygons is a big issue in 3D, where quadrilateral surfaces can become non-planar and cause anomalies when rendering. Triangles, on the other hand, are always planar. For our current purposes, in 2D, complex quads just form an interesting pattern. If you want to learn more about quads in general, check out http://en.wikipedia.org/wiki/Quadrilateral (I especially like the taxonomic classification chart). One other minor but significant point about using either TRIANGLE or QUADS mode is that you'll want to make sure that you use the right number of vertex() commands. The number of commands should be divisible by 3 for TRIANGLES and 4 for QUADS. Additional vertex() lines that aren't grouped in three or four lines, respectively, will be disregarded. For example, as shown in Figure 9-24, the fourth and fifth lines in the following sequence will be disregarded:

```
size (120, 120);
beginShape(TRIANGLES);
vertex(20, 20);
vertex(100, 100);
vertex(40, 100);
vertex(30, 60);
vertex(20, 50);
endShape();
```

Figure 9-24. Disregarded extra vertex() calls

The last three modes I'll discuss briefly are TRIANGLE_STRIP, TRIANGLE_FAN, and QUAD_STRIP. These modes build contiguous meshes of polygons, which is very useful in 3D. They work sort of similarly to the last two modes discussed, except that the multiple forms created are attached. Also, extra vertex() lines are not disregarded. However, a minimum number of vertex() commands need to be issued—three for TRIANGLE_STRIP and TRIANGLE_FAN, and four for QUAD_STRIP—before any shapes are rendered. Here's an example using TRIANGLE_STRIP mode (see Figure 9-25):

```
// TRIANGLE_STRIP Mode
size(400, 400);
smooth();
int x = width/2;
int y = height/2;
int outerRad = 150;
int innerRad = 200;
float px = 0, py = 0, angle = 0;
float pts = 36;
float rot = 360.0/pts;

beginShape(TRIANGLE_STRIP);
for (int i=0; i<pts; i++) {
  px = x+cos(radians(angle))*outerRad;
  py = y+sin(radians(angle))*outerRad;
  angle+=rot;
  vertex(px, py);
  px = x+cos(radians(angle))*innerRad;
  py = y+sin(radians(angle))*innerRad;
  vertex(px, py);
  angle+=rot;
}
endShape();
```

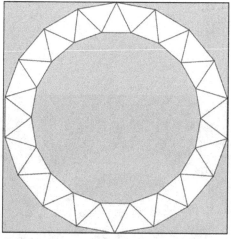

Figure 9-25. TRIANGLE_STRIP Mode sketch

I reused the basic trig functions I've been using throughout the book for generating an ellipse. By setting an outer and inner radius, this shape could be useful as an end cap for a hollow 3D cylinder. Next, I simply decreased the radii and fill color value (from white to black) each loop iteration, creating a spiral (see Figure 9-26):

```
// TRIANGLE_STRIP Spiral
size(400, 400);
background(0);
smooth();
int x = width/2;
int y = height/2;
int outerRad = 160;
int innerRad = 200;
float px = 0, py = 0, angle = 0;
int pts = 36;
float rot = 360.0/pts;
int fillCol = 255;
int fillfade = fillCol/pts;

beginShape(TRIANGLE_STRIP);
for (int i=0; i<pts; i++) {
  px = x+cos(radians(angle))*outerRad;
  py = y+sin(radians(angle))*outerRad;
  angle+=rot;
  vertex(px, py);
  px = x+cos(radians(angle))*innerRad;
  py = y+sin(radians(angle))*innerRad;
  vertex(px, py);
  outerRad-=4;
```

9

373

```
      innerRad-=4.25;
      fill(fillCol);
      fillCol-=fillfade;
      angle+=rot;
    }
  endShape();
```

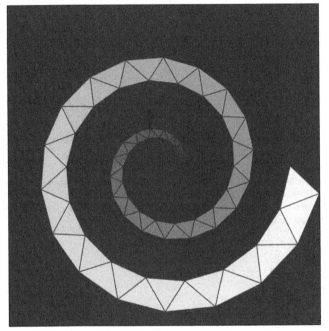

Figure 9-26. TRIANGLE_STRIP Spiral sketch

Tessellation

Another interesting thing you can do with these functions is create a tessellation. A **tessellation** is a pattern of shapes that fit together, without any gaps, covering a surface. For more of a definition, have a look at what Wikipedia has to say about tessellations, at http://en.wikipedia.org/wiki/Tessellation. TRIANGLE_FAN mode is a little tricky, as it needs to rotate clockwise, and the initial point should define the center part of the fan. In 3D, forms are commonly converted to and/or rendered as triangle meshes. TRIANGLE_FAN mode is a somewhat convenient function for triangulating planar geometry. Triangulating means converting a larger polygon into triangles, which is a form of tessellation. Since triangles are always planar and simple (with regard to polygons—not a commentary on their intelligence), they are easier for the computer to render than quadrilaterals. This mode works by defining the center point of the fan and then selecting the vertices in a clockwise fashion along the perimeter of the shape you want to triangulate. Once again, the trig functions come in handy. Here's an example sketch that triangulates any regular polygon, using TRIANGLE_FAN mode (see Figure 9-27):

```
//TRIANGLE_FAN
size(400, 400);
smooth();
strokeWeight(1.5);
float px = 0, py = 0;
float angle = 0;
float radius = 150;
int pts = 8;
int x = width/2;
int y = height/2;

// needs to rotate clockwise
beginShape(TRIANGLE_FAN);
vertex(x, y);
for (int i=0; i<=pts; i++){
  px = x+cos(radians(angle))*radius;
  py = y+sin(radians(angle))*radius;
  vertex(px, py);
  angle+=360/pts;
}
```

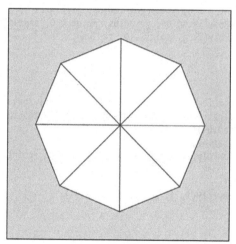

Figure 9-27. TRIANGLE_FAN sketch

Next, I'll use the last solution as part of a sketch for a tessellated plane (see Figure 9-28):

```
/*
 Tessellated Plane
 Ira Greenberg, December 30, 2005
 */
void setup(){
  size(400, 400);
  smooth();
  tesselate(6, 20);
}

void tesselate(int points, int radius){
  /* catch and handle out of
   range point count */
  if (points<=5){
    points = 4;
  }
  else {
    points  = 6;
  }

  // eventually add some more patterns
  switch(points){
  case 4:
    for (int i = 0, k = 0; i<=width+radius; i+=radius*2, k++){
      for (int j = 0; j<=height+radius; j+=radius*2){
        drawPoly(i-radius, j-radius, points, 0, radius);
        drawPoly(i, j, points, 0, radius);
      }
    }
    break;
  case 6:
    for (float i = 0, k = 0; i<=width+radius; i+=radius*1.5, k++){
      for (float j = 0; j<=height+radius*2; j+=(cos(radians(30))* ➥
            radius)*2){
        if (k%2==0){
          drawPoly(i, j-cos(radians(30))*radius, points, 0, radius);
        }
        else{
          drawPoly(i, j, points, 0, radius);
        }
      }
    }
    break;
  }
}
```

```
// draw triangle fan
void drawPoly(float x, float y, int pts, float initAngle, float rad){
  strokeWeight(1.5);
  float px = 0, py = 0;
  float angle = initAngle;
  // needs to rotate clockwise
  beginShape(TRIANGLE_FAN);
  vertex(x, y);
  for (int i=0; i<=pts; i++){
    fill(255/pts*i);
    px = x+cos(radians(angle))*rad;
    py = y+sin(radians(angle))*rad;
    vertex(px, py);
    angle+= 360/pts;
  }
}
```

Figure 9-28. Tesselated Plane sketch

This last example is fairly complex; though not much is new. It took some finessing to get the geometry to tile properly and a bit of trig for the hexagon tiling. There are two things that I think are significant about this sketch. The first involves encapsulation and the latter involves exception handling. Both custom functions tessellate() and drawPoly() involve somewhat complicated implementations. However, to use both functions in the last example, all that needed to be called was `tessellate(6, 20);`. When you encapsulate procedural complexity into self-contained modular units such as functions, it becomes relatively simple to use even the most complexly implemented procedures. This illustrates a general notion of the concept of encapsulation. There is also the more specific but related definition of encapsulation (discussed in Chapter 8) that applies specifically to OOP.

The second point, exception handling, is illustrated by the conditional statement at the top of the `tessellate()` function. The conditional syntax you've seen before, but the concept is new. I only wrote tessellation routines for four- and six-sided polygons. However, someone could conceivably use the function at some point and put in a value other than 4 or 6. Rather than generate an unexpected error, I wrote code to catch the out-of-range value and correct it. Eventually, additional tessellation routines could be added to the program, at which time you would simply update the conditional. The concept of building in code structures to catch and deal with input errors is generally referred to as **exception handling**. In a language like Java, exception handling is formalized, with numerous class structures. Processing doesn't have its own native exception handling structures (but you're free to use Java's structures). Generally speaking, though, a formalized exception handling process is beyond what most people will want to do with Processing. In addition, the places where exception handling is required in Processing (e.g., input/output) are already encapsulated and invisible to the user. Remember that this is kind of the whole point of Processing—to minimize the annoying lower-level stuff, allowing people to more freely express themselves. So there may be times, as in my last example, that you might want to build in some simple safety checks. If, however, you do end up building something that you feel requires a more elaborate and formal error-checking system, you'll want to look into Java's exception handling capabilities. Here's some info from Sun: http://java.sun.com/docs/books/tutorial/essential/exceptions/.

Applying OOP to shape creation

The last section of this chapter utilizes an OOP approach. Chapter 8 dealt exclusively with OOP, but I'll review some of the fundamental concepts here as well. OOP is not easy for new coders to get their heads around, so try not to be too hard on yourself if you find some of the material difficult—it really is.

The "object-oriented" part of OOP is an approach to programming that treats concepts (both things and processes) as self-contained modular units. These units, called classes, are like blueprints describing a concept, which includes attributes (properties) and functions (methods) contained within the class definition. For example, if you create a class called Rectangle, the properties of this class might include its x and y position, its width and height, its stroke and fill color, and so on. Its methods might include getting and setting its width or height, and drawing itself. To use the Rectangle class, you create (instantiate) objects from it. Since the class is like a blueprint, when you make an object, you get a copy of all the properties and methods defined in the class; and each object remains independent from all the other objects made from the same class. This allows you to have ten rectangle objects, each with different postion, size, color, and so on. Since I've gone this far with the rectangle metaphor, let's actually construct a simple rectangle class and implement it in Processing.

```
void setup(){
  // create new rectangle object
  new Rectangle();
}

// class description
class Rectangle {
}
```

This is all it takes to create a class in Processing. Of course, this class won't do anything, but it's a start. To create a class, you use the class keyword followed by the name of the class. You capitalize the name of your classes. To create an object from the Rectangle class, you use the new keyword. Typically, you also assign the new object to a variable so that you can refer to it later in your program. In the last example, even though I created a Rectangle object, I can't communincate with it, as there is no variable assigned a reference to the object. Figure 9-29 shows an improved (and more useful) version of the last sketch:

```
// object (reference) variable
Rectangle r1;

void setup(){
  // create new rectangle object
  r1 = new Rectangle(100, 200, 150, 150);
}

// class description
class Rectangle {

  //class constructor
  Rectangle(int x, int y, int w, int h) {
    println("x pos = "+ x+"\ny pos = " + y);
    println("width = "+ w+"\nheight = " + h);
  }
}
```

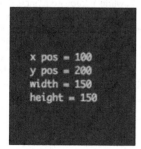

Figure 9-29. OOP println() output example

This wasn't much of an improvement, but I got some output at least. However, there are a bunch of new concepts to discuss in this sketch. At the top of the program, I declared a variable of type Rectangle. Remember that variables in Processing and Java need to be declared of a data type. The data type controls things like how much memory is allocated to the variable and what type of data the variable can be assigned. As I discussed earlier in the book, there are two types of variables in Processing: primitive and reference.

Primitive variables, which were discussed extensively in Chapter 3, are assigned actual values. int, float, and char are examples of primitive variable types. Primitive variables are relativley simple for the computer to handle, as each evaluates to a single value.

Reference variables are more complex, as they each often need to refer to multiple values. To solve this problem, reference variables, rather than directly being assigned a value, hold a reference or link to the data in memory. Thus, the Rectangle r1 variable will ultimately hold a reference to the Rectangle object data, not the data directly. There are some important issues due to this arrangement, but nothing you need to worry about right now. The important point to remember is that the data type of the variable dictates what type of data can be assigned to it; and each class you create is a unique data type. Rectangle r1 can be assigned object references of the Rectangle type (or a subclass of the Rectangle type), but it can't be assigned an int or a String value or reference of another data type.

Looking at the class definition, you'll notice that I added a constructor. Remember that the constructor begins with the same name as the class and also utilizes parentheses for a parameter list. When an object is created from a class, a constructor inside the class is always run. You can think of a constructor as an object initializer function. If you don't explicitly include a constructor, a default (internal) class constructor is called that has no parameters. By creating my own constructor, new Rectangle objects will now use my constructor, instead of the default one. Therefore, if a Rectangle object is now created without four int arguments, an errror will occur. Try replacing r1 = new Rectangle(100, 200, 150, 150); with r1 = new Rectangle(); to see what happens. When the constructor is called successfully, the code within its block (between the curly braces) is executed.

In this revised version of the sketch, the constructor outputs some sensational information about the Rectangle object's properties. (Don't worry, you'll make some images eventually.) Also notice the syntax I used in the println() commands. I generated four lines of output with just two println() calls by using the newline escape sequence, \n. Escape sequences are little character shortcuts you can include in strings to do things like add a new line or include special characters. For example, if you need to include a quote character in output, you'd do it like this: println("\"Help! I'm surrounded by quotes\"");. For a list of escape character sequences, check out http://java.sun.com/docs/books/jls/second_edition/html/lexical.doc.html. Finally, the following code gets the Rectangle class to actually draw something (see Figure 9-30):

```
// Drawing with OOP
// object (reference) variable
Rectangle r1;

void setup(){
  size(400, 400);
  background(255);
```

```
  // create new rectangle object
  r1 = new Rectangle(100, 200, 150, 150);
}

// class description
class Rectangle {

  //class constructor
  Rectangle(int x, int y, int w, int h) {
   rect(x, y, w, h);
  }
}
```

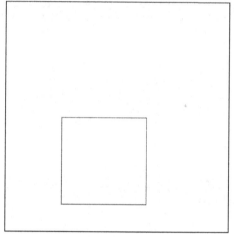

Figure 9-30. Drawing with OOP sketch

Creating a neighborhood

Hopefully, this last sketch makes some sense. Don't worry if it doesn't yet. Also, you'd be correct in thinking that it doesn't really make much sense to go through the bother of creating a class just to call rect(), which you could call from within setup(). This is certainly true. So let's add some stuff to make all this class business worth it. Let's build a simple house, with a door, some windows, and a roof, and then let's put a couple houses together to form a little neighborhood. I'm going to make a class for each of the following elements: door, window, roof, and house. In this example, I'll keep things simple by not adding decorative features like paint, shingles, cornices, and so on. And I'll keep all the classes within the same PDE file (which isn't really necessary). Later in the book, I'll show you how to begin working with multiple files in separate Processing tabs.

Door class

In designing these really simple classes, it helps to think a little bit about how the house will fit together. I'll begin with the door—what properties will the door have? I want to keep everything really simple for now. The door will have an x position, a y position, width and height, and a doorknob. What methods will the door have? Working in pure Java, I would set up a set and get method for each of the properties. For example, for the x property, I'd have a setX() and a getX() method. In addition, in pure Java, I'd make the properties private, meaning that users couldn't call the properties directly (e.g., d1.x), but would be forced to use the respective set and get methods for each property (e.g., d1.getX()). Although this is the classic OOP approach, it is not really the Processing approach. So I won't make the properties private, nor will I create set and get methods for all the properties, which will actually save me a ton of work. The only methods I will add to the Door class are setknob() and drawDoor(). The setknob() method will control the side of the door on which the doorknob is drawn, and the drawDoor() method will draw the door. Here's the Door class:

```
class Door{
  // instance properties
  int x;
  int y;
  int w;
  int h;

  // for knob
  int knobLoc = 1;

  // constants - class properties
  final static int RT = 0;
  final static int LFT = 1;

  // constructor
  Door(int w, int h){
    this.w = w;
    this.h = h;
  }

  // draw the door
  void drawDoor(int x, int y) {
    rect(x, y, w, h);
    int knobsize = w/10;
    if (knobLoc == 0){
      //right side
      ellipse(x+w-knobsize, y+h/2, knobsize, knobsize);
    }
    else {
      //left side
      ellipse(x+knobsize, y+h/2, knobsize, knobsize);
    }
  }
```

```
    // set knob position
    void setKnob(int knobLoc){
      this. knobLoc = knobLoc;
    }
  }
```

At the top of the class, I declared some variables. The first five variables are properties that each Door object will have access to; these are called, in OOP terminology, instance variables or object properties. Each Door object will have its own unique set of these variables, so an object can assign its own values to the variables without affecting any other Door objects. For the doorknob, I needed some variables to specify which side of the door the knob should be on. I created two variables, LFT and RT, which I declared as constants. I used the Java keyword final to specify that the value of the two constants can't be changed—which is precisely what a constant is. Secondly, I used the Java keyword static to specify that these constants are static variables, also sometimes referred to as class variables.

Static variables, unlike instance variables, are not unique to each object created from the class. Instead they each hold a single value, accessible from any class, using the syntax *class name.property*. For example, if I wanted to use the Door class's LFT property, I would simply write Door.LFT. I don't need to create an object to do this, and I can do it from any class. So theoretically, if you ever needed the value 1, you could use Door.LFT. However, I don't recommend doing that unless using the constant name makes sense in the context of the program, as in setKnob(Door.LFT);. You'll see more how these constants are used shortly, when an actual door is created.

The next code block is the constructor, in which I included two parameters for the door's width and height (which is perhaps the measurements you'd think about if you were to actually purchase a door). OOP is modeled after the physical world, so it's not a bad idea when designing classes to think about how you would accomplish the same task in the real world. Within the constructor block are two possibly odd looking assignments (although they're discussed in Chapter 8):

```
this.w = w;
this.h = h;
```

Since the instance variables declared at the top of the class and the parameters specified between the parentheses of the constructor have the same identifiers (names), I need a way to identify which is which. I could have simply given the parameters different names from the instance variables. However, it is pretty common practice to use the same names for instance variables and parameters in the constructor, and I tend to like doing it.

The parameters represent the values that will be passed into the constructor when an object is created. These values will need to be seen throughout the class. However, parameters only have local scope (meaning they can only be "seen" within the method or function they're declared in). This is a problem if another method in the class wants to be able to access these values. By assigning the value of the parameters to the instance variables declared at the top of the class—giving them global scope—the values can now be seen throughout the class. Since the parameters have this special relationship to their partner instance variables, I find it convenient to give them the same name.

383

Outside of the constructor, w and h always refer to the values of the instance variables by those names. But in the constructor, w and h refer to the values of the parameters. That's because local scope takes precedence over global scope. By using the special keyword this preceding the instance variable names (connected with a dot), this.w and this.h are now seen as the instance variables, not the parameters. The w and the h, when not preceded with this, are still the parameters.

Let's skip the drawDoor() method for a moment and look at the setKnob() method. This method contains another assignment, similar to the ones in the constructor. In the drawDoor() method, which I'll discuss next, you'll need to know which side to draw the doorknob on. By assigning a value to the knobLoc instance variable in the setKnob() method, the drawDoor() method will now be able to assess the side on which to attach the knob. Notice also that at the top of the class I gave the knobLoc variable an initial value when I declared it. I did this just in case a position wasn't eventually specified using the setKnob() method.

Finally, in the drawDoor() method, I simply draw the door, using Processing's rect() function. Using a conditional statement and the knobLoc property, the method also figures out which side to draw the knob on, which it then does using Processing's ellipse() function. The next sketch uses the Door class to actually draw a door (see Figure 9-31):

```
// Drawing a Door
// object (reference) variable
Door door1;

void setup(){
  size(200, 350);
  background(200);
  smooth();

  // create new Door object
  door1 = new Door(100, 250);
  door1.setKnob(Door.LFT);
  door1.drawDoor(50, 50);
}

class Door{
  //door properties
  int x;
  int y;
  int w;
  int h;

  // for knob
  int knobLoc = 1;
  //constants
  final static int RT = 0;
  final static int LFT = 1;
```

```
// constructor
Door(int w, int h){
  this.w = w;
  this.h = h;
}

// draw the door
void drawDoor(int x, int y) {
  rect(x, y, w, h);
  int knobsize = w/10;
  if (knobLoc == 0){
    //right side
    ellipse(x+w-knobsize, y+h/2, knobsize, knobsize);
  }
  else {
    //left side
    ellipse(x+knobsize, y+h/2, knobsize, knobsize);
  }
}

// set knob position
void setKnob(int knobLoc){
  this. knobLoc = knobLoc;
}
}
```

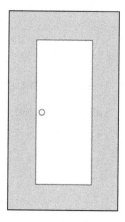

Figure 9-31. Drawing a Door sketch

The three lines at the top of the sketch create the door.

```
door1 = new Door(100, 250);
door1.setKnob(Door.LFT);
door1.drawDoor(50, 50);
```

9

First, I need to create the Door object; in OOP this is called **instantiation**. Then I optionally set its knob position. Notice how I used the static variable LFT, preceded by the class name and a dot. Finally, the door is drawn. Look carefully at the syntax—the door object door1 is attached directly to its method with a dot. If you eventually wanted to change the value of one of the properties, you'd target it the same way. For example, to change the x property to 194, you'd write: door1.x = 194. Of course, this command would have to come after the Door object has been instantiated: door1 = new Door(100, 250);. Before you move on to the Window class, I strongly recommend you review the Door class a few times, as well as my description. I also suggest trying to make some more doors on your own. This little sketch covers a lot of important issues that will be built upon.

Window class

A window shares certain characteristics with a door. Both have an x and y position, as well as width and height. If this example were more detailed, both objects might also have color, material, price, and inventory number characteristics. There is a way of minimizing this redundancy between classes in OOP, called inheritance (covered extensively in Chapter 8), in which classes can inherit properties and methods from other classes. However, inheritance adds another level of abstraction and complexity, so for this example I'll redundantly create the same properties in the different classes. Later on in the book, when you're an advanced object-oriented programmer, you'll apply inheritance. Here's a sketch that draws three windows using the new Window class (see Figure 9-32):

```
// Drawing Some Windows
void setup(){
  size(450, 250);
  background(200);
  smooth();

  Window window1 = new Window(100, 150);
  window1.drawWindow(50, 50);
  Window window2 = new Window(100, 150, true, Window.DOUBLE);
  window2.drawWindow(175, 50);
  Window window3 = new Window(100, 150, true, Window.QUAD);
  window3.drawWindow(300, 50);
}

class Window{
  //window properties
  int x;
  int y;
  int w;
  int h;

  // customized features
  boolean hasSash = false;
```

```
// single, double, quad pane
int style = 0;
//constants
final static int SINGLE = 0;
final static int DOUBLE = 1;
final static int QUAD = 2;


// constructor 1
Window(int w, int h){
  this.w = w;
  this.h = h;
}
// constructor 2
Window(int w, int h, int style){
  this.w = w;
  this.h = h;
  this.style = style;
}
 // constructor 3
Window(int w, int h, boolean hasSash, int style){
  this.w = w;
  this.h = h;
  this.hasSash = hasSash;
  this.style = style;
}

// draw the window
void drawWindow(int x, int y) {
  //local variables
  int margin = 0;
  int winHt = 0;
  int winWdth = 0;

  if (hasSash){
    margin = w/15;
  }

  switch(style){
  case 0:
    //outer window (sash)
    rect(x, y, w, h);
    //inner window
    rect(x+margin, y+margin, w-margin*2, h-margin*2);
    break;
  case 1:
    winHt = (h-margin*3)/2;
    //outer window (sash)
    rect(x, y, w, h);
```

9

```
          //inner window (top)
          rect(x+margin, y+margin, w-margin*2, winHt);
          //inner windows (bottom)
          rect(x+margin, y+winHt+margin*2, w-margin*2, winHt);
          break;
        case 2:
          winWdth = (w-margin*3)/2;
          winHt = (h-margin*3)/2;
          //outer window (sash)
          rect(x, y, w, h);
          //inner window (top-left)
          rect(x+margin, y+margin, winWdth, winHt);
          //inner window (top-right)
          rect(x+winWdth+margin*2, y+margin, winWdth, winHt);
          //inner windows (bottom-left)
          rect(x+margin, y+winHt+margin*2, winWdth, winHt);
           //inner windows (bottom-right)
          rect(x+winWdth+margin*2, y+winHt+margin*2, winWdth, winHt);
          break;
      }
    }

    // set window style (number of panes)
    void setStyle(int style){
      this.style = style;
    }
  }
```

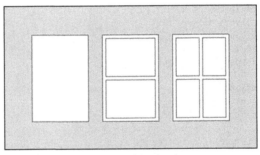

Figure 9-32. Drawing Some Windows sketch

Although the Window class is longer than the Door class, it works very similarly. In the sketch, I created three windows, each with different features. The major difference between the Door and Window classes is the use of multiple constructors in the Window class. Remember that in Processing, you're allowed to name multiple methods and functions with the same identifier, as long as their signatures are different. In OOP speak, this is called method overloading. It is quite common practice to do this with constructors, as it provides an easy way for users to instantiate objects with various initial configurations and values, as I did in this last example. One other minor point is that I created a couple local variables in the drawWindow() method:

```
//local variables
int margin = 0;
int winHt = 0;
int winWdth = 0;
```

Like parameters, these variables are only scoped within the method that they are defined within. In general, it's a good rule to only give variables the scope they require. These variables are only used within the drawWindow() method, so it made sense to make them local. Take a few minutes to look at the switch statement in the drawWindow() method, as well as the procedure I used to draw the different windows. Again, I relied on Processing's rect() function to take care of all the drawing.

Roof class

The last piece of our house I need is the roof. Next is a sketch that draws a roof using the new Roof class (see Figure 9-33):

```
// Drawing Some Roofs
void setup(){
  size(400, 150);
  background(200);
  smooth();
  Roof roof1 = new Roof();
  roof1.drawRoof(25, 100, 100, 150);
  Roof roof2 = new Roof(Roof.GAMBREL);
  roof2.drawRoof(150, 100, 100, 150);
  Roof roof3 = new Roof(Roof.DOME);
  roof3.drawRoof(275, 100, 100, 100);
}

class Roof{
  //roof properties
  int x;
  int y;
  int w;
  int h;

  // roof style
  int style = 0;
  //constants
  final static int CATHEDRAL = 0;
  final static int GAMBREL = 1;
  final static int DOME = 2;
```

9

```
// default constructor
Roof(){
}

 // constructor 2
 Roof(int style){
  this.style = style;
}

// draw the roof
void drawRoof(int x, int y, int w, int h) {
  switch(style){
  case 0:
    beginShape();
    vertex(x, y);
    vertex(x+w/2, y-h/3);
    vertex(x+w, y);
    endShape(CLOSE);
    break;
  case 1:
   beginShape();
    vertex(x, y);
    vertex(x+w/7, y-h/5);
    vertex(x+w/2, y-h/2.75);
    vertex(x+(w-w/7), y-h/5);
    vertex(x+w, y);
    endShape(CLOSE);
    break;
  case 2:
    ellipseMode(CORNER);
    arc(x, y-h/2, w, h, PI, TWO_PI);
    line(x, y, x+w, y);
    break;
  }

 }

 // set roof style
 void setStyle(int style){
   this.style = style;
 }
}
```

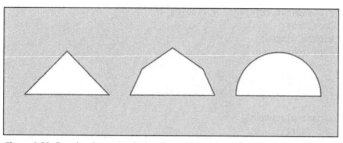

Figure 9-33. Drawing Some Roofs sketch

There is nothing new in this sketch, and I now have all the House component classes built. The next thing to do is put them all together. Again, it is worthwhile considering this problem in the context of the real world. If you were really building a house, you would be at the stage at which you have identified your door, window, and roof suppliers, and have established an agreed upon set of properties and methods. In a sense, you have developed a contractual agreement with your suppliers. This is precisely how OOP works.

House class

The public properties and methods of a class are referred to as the **public interface** to the class. If you know the public interface to a class, you don't even need to know what happens within the class. The interface, in a sense, enforces the contract. Classes should be as modular and self-contained as possible. Thus, each of the classes takes care of calculating and drawing itself. The House class is no exception. The House class, besides drawing some type of external structure, will need to orchestrate how the Door, Window, and Roof component classes are used in its own creation. To make this happen, you need to somehow include these classes within the House class. You also want to be able to customize these component classes. There is a classic OOP way to solve this problem, which is called **composition**. I'll actually include variables of the respective component types within the House class. In other words, I'll include reference variables of the Door, Window, and Roof data types within the House class definition. When I instantiate the House class, I'll actually pass in Door, Window, and Roof object references as arguments, which, you'll remember, will need to be received by parameters of the same data type within a House constructor.

Here's the House class. Please note that the following code is not a finished sketch yet, but only the House class. Shortly, I'll put all the classes (Window, Door, Roof, and House) together into a sketch to draw a little neighborhood.

```
class House{
  //house properties
  int x;
  int y;
  int w;
  int h;
```

```
//component reference variables
Door door;
Window window;
Roof roof;

//optional autosize variable
boolean AutoSizeComponents = false;

//door placement
int doorLoc = 0;
//constants
final static int MIDDLE_DOOR = 0;
final static int LEFT_DOOR = 1;
final static int RIGHT_DOOR = 2;

//constructor
House(int w, int h, Door door, Window window, Roof roof, ➡
      int doorLoc) {
  this.w = w;
  this.h = h;
  this.door = door;
  this.window = window;
  this.roof = roof;
  this.doorLoc = doorLoc;
}

void drawHouse(int x, int y, boolean AutoSizeComponents) {
  this.x = x;
  this.y =y;
  this.AutoSizeComponents = AutoSizeComponents;

  //automatically sizes doors and windows
  if(AutoSizeComponents){
    //autosize door
    door.h = h/4;
    door.w = door.h/2;

    //autosize windows
    window.h = h/3;
    window.w = window.h/2;

  }
  // draw bldg block
  rect(x, y, w, h);

  // draw door
  switch(doorLoc){
  case 0:
```

```
            door.drawDoor(x+w/2-door.w/2, y+h-door.h);
            break;
        case 1:
            door.drawDoor(x+w/8, y+h-door.h);
            break;
        case 2:
            door.drawDoor(x+w-w/8-door.w,  y+h-door.h);
            break;
        }

        // draw windows
        int windowMargin = (w-window.w*2)/3;
        window.drawWindow(x+windowMargin, y+h/6);
        window.drawWindow(x+windowMargin*2+window.w, y+h/6);

        // draw roof
        roof.drawRoof(x, y, w, h);
    }

    // catch drawHouse method without boolean argument
    void drawHouse(int x, int y){
        // recall with required 3rd argument
        drawHouse(x, y, false);
    }
}
```

The House class is implemented similarly to the Door, Window, and Roof classes. It contains a constructor; it has x, y, w, and h instance variables; and it has some constants and a drawHouse() method. Again, the redundant elements and structures in these classes could be handled more efficiently using inheritance, which I covered in Chapter 8 and will also use in later chapters. What's markedly different between these classes, however, is the compositional relationship between the House class and its component classes. The House class contains reference variables of the Door, Window, and Roof classes. When I instantiate the House class, I'll include Door, Window, and Roof objects as arguments that will be sent to the House constructor.

Within the House constructor, the Door, Window, and Roof instance properties declared at the top of the House class will each be assigned the values (object references) of their matching parameters. Remember, the parameters declared within the constructor head (between the parentheses) are local to the constructor, so it's necessary to do these assignments in the constructor to create global visibility for these passed-in values so that they may be seen throughout the class. Because the House class will now contain object references to these component classes (Door, Window, and Roof), the properties and methods of each of these classes can be utilized from within the House class with the normal syntax *object.property* (e.g., roof1.x) or *object.method* (e.g., window1.drawWindow()). Without the object references being passed into the House constructor, the House class would have no way of communicating with its Door, Window, or Roof components.

9

The abstraction of OOP takes some time to get your head around. So if your head is spinning, you're definitely not alone. It's helpful to remember that each class in OOP should be a self-contained modular unit. Someone using the class shouldn't need to look inside the class to see how it's implemented. Instead, they just need to know the class's pubic interface (its public properties and methods, including any constructors). When you use a class, the class should, in a sense, take care of itself. So when you create a window and then ask the window to draw itself, you don't need to be privy to how it actually implements the drawing; you just need to make sure you ask properly—using the correct method and any required arguments.

When the House class creates itself through its drawHouse() method, it will need to compose its components—position and size its door, window, and roof. For the House class to be able to do this, it needs the object references to these components, and when requested to do so, each of the components will be responsible for drawing itself. Since the position of each of the house's components is ultimately dependent on the size and position of the house, it makes sense for the house to make these calls after its own position and size have been determined.

One last point is that it's also possible (albeit not very desirable) to totally encapsulate the creative (customization) process from the user. In the upcoming neighborhood sketch, I'll provide the user the capability to customize the individual House components (Door, Window, and Roof) as each component object is instantiated. The user will then simply pass these customized component objects as arguments when instantiating a House object. Instead of giving the user this customization ability—to select a roof style, for example—you could just let the House class set all the style properties for the individual components. The House class could even take care of instantiating the component Door, Window, and Roof objects from within its own class, hiding this process entirely from the user and avoiding the need to pass in any object reference arguments. This greatly simplifies the process of using the House class for the user, but also removes any customization options. Thus, balance needs to be considered carefully when you design a class—on one hand, you should think about ease of use, but on the other, you should think about providing users with enough creative freedom to make the class ultimately worth using.

I'm going to end this chapter with a completed Neighborhood sketch (see Figure 9-34), including the Door, Window, Roof, and House classes. However, the following example code only includes the final sketch's setup() function, since the four finished classes are printed in their entirety earlier in the chapter. To run the sketch, of course, you'll need to add the Door, Window, Roof, and House classes to the sketch. (Note that when adding the class code, you should not include the setup() functions from the earlier individual class sketch examples—just the code beginning with class, down to the final closing curly brace at the bottom of the entire class.) You can either type/paste the class code directly into Processing, below the setup() function at the top of the Neighborhood sketch, or better yet, download the completed Neighborhood sketch code from the book's Download section on the friends of ED site (www.friendsofed.com/).

The Neighborhood sketch's setup() function primarily includes instantiation statements. Each of the three houses in the Neighborhood sketch has its own Door, Window, and Roof objects passed into its constructor when instantiated. Notice how I instantiate the component classes first and then pass the reference variables for each of the component objects as arguments when I instantiate the House.

394

In laying out the neighborhood, I used the previous house's x and w positions to ensure that the houses lined up properly, but also didn't overlap.

In spite of the sketch's length (when the four classes are added), the object-oriented structure adds organization and (reusable) modularity to the code, as compared to a long series of function calls. In addition, the OOP structure provides a logical framework in which to add new features to the entire neighborhood, the House class, or any of the component classes. Really take your time going through (and playing) with this example. I also suggest trying to reimplement some of the internal drawing methods. For example, the cathedral roof could be drawn with Processing's triangle() function, and the dome roof could be created with the bezier() or curve() function. Changing the internal implementation of a class, if done properly, should have no effect on how you use the class. In addition (if you're feeling ambitious), you could even try to apply a tessellated texture as a skin to some of the houses.

```
/*
 Neighborhood
 Ira Greenberg, January 1, 2006
 Happy New Year!
 */
void setup(){
  size(600, 400);
  background(190);
  smooth();
  //ground plane
  int groundHeight = 10;
  fill(0);
  rect(0, height-groundHeight, width, groundHeight);
  fill(255);

  // Houses
  Door door1 = new Door(40, 80);
  Window window1 = new Window(100, 125, false, Window.DOUBLE);
  Roof roof1 = new Roof(Roof.DOME);
  House house1 = new House(150, 150, door1, window1, roof1, ➡
        House.MIDDLE_DOOR);
  house1.drawHouse(50, height-groundHeight-house1.h, true);

  Door door2 = new Door(40, 80);
  Window window2 = new Window(100, 125, true, Window.QUAD);
  Roof roof2 = new Roof(Roof.GAMBREL);
  House house2 = new House(200, 120, door2, window2, roof2, ➡
        House.LEFT_DOOR);
  house2.drawHouse(50+house1.w, height-groundHeight-house2.h, true);

  Door door3 = new Door(40, 80);
  door3.setKnob(Door.RT);
  Window window3 = new Window(125, 125, true, Window.SINGLE);
```

```
    Roof roof3 = new Roof(Roof.CATHEDRAL);
    House house3 = new House(150, 200, door3, window3, roof3, ➥
        House.RIGHT_DOOR);
    house3.drawHouse(house2.x+house2.w, height-groundHeight-house3.h, ➥
        true);
}
// add Door class
// add Window class
// add Roof class
// add House class
```

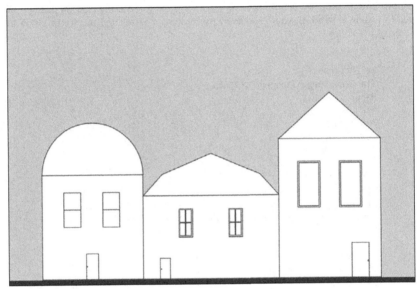

Figure 9-34. Neighborhood sketch

Summary

Beginning with Processing's simple shape commands, rect(), ellipse(), triangle(), arc(), and quad(), this chapter introduced some of the underlying computer graphics principals involved in generating and working with shapes, including the definition of an origin point, the use of bounding boxes, and the concept of state changes. Moving beyond simple shape functions, you learned about a more general and powerful approach for shape creation, using Processing's vertex() function and companion beginShape() and endShape() record functions. Utilizing a powerful programming technique called recursion, you learned about an alternative approach to iterating, including the risk of generating infinite loops with recursion. You looked under the hood at Processing's matrix functions and how drawing in Processing happens internally in a graphics context, which has its own local coordinate system. Finally, you looked at applying an object-oriented approach to generating shapes, developed a simple neighborhood example, and used an advanced OOP concept called composition. Next chapter, I'll introduce color/imaging techniques using Processing, and also expand the discussion of OOP to incorporate some more advanced concepts.

9

10 COLOR AND IMAGING

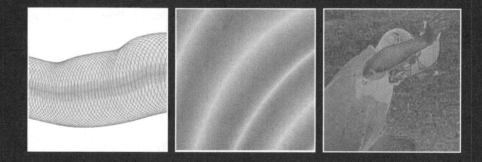

Thus far in the book I've focused on the structural aspects of creative coding—an armature upon which to build. However, I've barely scraped the surface of Processing's expressive potential. Nowhere is this potential more evident than in Processing's extensive color and imaging capabilities. I'll begin this chapter by exploring Processing's high-level color and imaging functions, which conceal the internal mathematics while still providing lots of creative range. Working at the pixel level, you'll learn how to generate custom gradients and even spin some of your own cool imaging filters. Finally, you'll apply an object-oriented approach to imaging and color, building upon the OOP concepts introduced in Chapters 8 and 9.

The importance of color

One of the major contributing factors in creating expressive work is color. This is not in any way to imply that powerfully expressive work can't be done in grayscale—artists such as Francisco de Goya, Franz Kline, and William Kentridge immediately come to mind. However, I've found that I have a different relationship with my work and process when I work in color. As a painter, I found I could express a wider range of thoughts and feelings when my palette included a full range of color, as opposed to just grayscale. I think this holds true for creative coding as well.

In the beginning, when you are first learning the basics of coding, the whole process might seem purely analytical, but like any discipline, once you develop some fluency, certain processes go on autopilot, freeing you to access other cognitive states. Coding grayscale normally uses 8 bits of information per pixel, providing 256 different values from black to white—black being 0 and white being 255. Color generally uses 24 bits of information per pixel (or 256 × 256 × 256, giving you 16,777,216 different colors). In addition, an extra 8 bits of data is often used for alpha, or transparency. At the risk of sounding overly new-agey, color seems to provide us with a wider range of responses to map to a wider range of emotions than grayscale does. Once we begin to explore color at the pixel level we are only a few steps away from digital imaging, or using code and procedural processing to affect all or a range of the pixels making up a continuous tone image—like a photograph. Processing comes with a bunch of cool functions for doing just this. In addition, this chapter will explore how to spin some of your own imaging filters. To begin, though, let's look at some simple color examples (see Figure 10-1):

```
// Color Shift
size(800, 450);
background(50);
noStroke();
int spacing = 50;
int w = (width-spacing*2)/2;
int h = w;
color swatch = color(100, 100, 120);
```

```
//left squares
fill(255, 120, 0);
rect(spacing, spacing, w, h);
fill(swatch);
rect(spacing+w/3, spacing+h/3, w/3, h/3);

//right squares
fill(45, 140, 255);
rect(w+spacing, spacing, w, h);
fill(swatch);
rect(w+spacing+w/3, spacing+h/3, w/3, h/3);
```

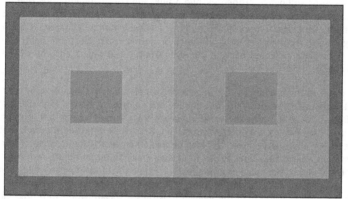

Figure 10-1. Color Shift sketch

Color theory

For those of you with degrees in art, the preceding example will look familiar. To those of you who escaped the torture of cutting out hundreds of little pieces of colored paper while squinting and gluing your fingers together, this sketch illustrates an exercise for studying the relativity of color, specifically color interaction. Two important artists and teachers, Josef Albers and Johannes Itten, formalized the modern study of color for artists. Their artwork and writings led to the creation of color theory foundation courses in Western art curricula throughout the world. The sketch illustrates a classic exercise in which two identical small swatches of color are placed on two larger sheets of differing colors. The problem involves trying to make the smaller swatches appear to be two different colors, by substituting different colors behind the swatches. This and similar studies developed by Albers, Itten, and others reveal interesting and unexpected color phenomena, including color and value shifts, afterimages, scale distortions, and even 3D spatial movements—sometimes referred to as "push-pull," a term coined by another major artist/colorist/educator, Hans Hofmann.

Not everyone seems to be able to see these often subtle color relationships. Squinting or crossing your eyes, turning an image upside down, or changing your viewing distance to an image are techniques that can sometimes help you to better see these phenomena. I've had very bright, talented students really struggle when it came to seeing and mixing color, while other students seem to take to it very naturally. It's led me to believe that, just as some people can more naturally distinguish subtle modulations in pitch (I'm not one of them), there is a similar mechanism for perceiving and differentiating color. However, I feel it's also important to point out that great art has been created by both strong and weak colorists. Some artists/art professors even believe that innate gifts, such as color sensitivity or drawing facility, can even at times impede a person's development as an artist. So if you can't see the color shift in the example, try not to freak out.

Color has three distinctive properties: hue, value, and chromatic intensity. **Hue** relates to the actual names we associate colors with (red, green, blue, etc.). Hue is controlled by the wavelength of the light. For example, the hue of a ripe lemon is yellow, while the hue of a stop sign is red. An object absorbs all the colors in the visual spectrum (light) except the color we perceive reflected back to our eyes. Thus, a red object absorbs all the colors except red.

Value relates to the brightness vs. darkness of the color. Value is also strongly determined by light. Although it is possible to shift the hue of a color, as in the last example, it can only be shifted so far in the physical world. However, the value of a color has less constancy. The value of the color on an orange's surface is drastically different in a dark room than outside in the sun. Value often confuses people when first learning about color. When looking at an object, they tend to see what they know about an object—which is usually primarily defined by the hue. For example, if I create a still life and place an egg in shadow next to an eggplant under a light source, most beginning art students will assume the egg surface has greater value than the eggplant, as they associate white with brightness and the eggplant's dark purple as darkness. Under the same exact lighting conditions, an eggplant would be darker than an egg, so the gestalt function in our mind codes a predictable pattern, which usually holds true, until some sneaky art professor sticks an eggplant under a bright lamp.

The last component of color is **chromatic intensity**. Two colors can have similar hue and value, but very different chromatic intensities. Consider the difference in color between a brick and an orange. The hue in both is orangish, and the value could be very similar, but there is still a difference in the color, which is controlled by chromatic intensity. When a color loses some of its chromatic intensity, we speak of it getting neutralized or moving toward gray. In the artist's color wheel, which we'll look at next, certain colors have a complimentary relationship. When two complimentary colors mix, they neutralize each other, reducing the chromatic intensity of each. Before you look at the color wheel, I want to make sure you understand the syntax in these two lines of code:

```
color swatch = color(100, 100, 120);
fill(swatch);
```

color is a Processing data type. The function call color(100, 100, 120) returns a color value, which I assigned to the variable swatch, declared of the type color. The three arguments I passed to the color function represent the red, green, and blue components of the color. Up to this point in the book, I've been passing single integer arguments to the fill() and stroke() functions, generating grayscale values. However, to generate color, you can pass three (or four) arguments to the fill()/stroke() calls, representing red, green, and blue (and alpha); or combine the three values into a color variable, as I did in the example. Thus, the following two fill() calls are equivalent:

```
color swatch = color(100, 100, 120);
fill(swatch);

fill(100, 100, 120);
```

Here's a simple example using random stroke colors, shown in Figure 10-2:

```
//Rotated Triangle
size(350, 350);
background(255);
smooth();
strokeWeight(3);
noFill();
translate(width/2, height/2);
for (int i=0; i<20; i++){
  stroke(random(255), random(255), random(255));
  triangle(-120, 120, 120, 120, 0, -120);
  rotate(TWO_PI/20);
}
```

Figure 10-2. Rotated Triangle sketch

In the next example, I use the color data type to create some arrays in conjunction with the fill() command. Hopefully, the output in Figure 10-3 looks familiar.

```
/*
Subtractive Color Wheel
Ira Greenberg, January 4, 2005
primaries (r, y, b)
secondaries(g, p, o)
tertiaries(y-o, r-o, r-p, b-p, b-g, y-g)
*/
int segs = 12;
float rotAdjust = radians(360/segs/2);
float radius = 175.0;
float ratio = .65;
float interval = TWO_PI/segs;
int SHADE = 0;
int TINT = 1;

void setup(){
  size(800, 400);
  background(0);
  smooth();
  ellipseMode(CENTER_RADIUS);
  noStroke();
  createWheel(width/4, height/2, SHADE);
  createWheel(width - width/4, height/2, TINT);
}

void createWheel(int x, int y, int valueShift){
  radius = 175;
  ratio = .65;
  if (valueShift == SHADE){
    // left wheel
    for (int j=1; j<5; j+=1){
      color[]cols = {
        color(255/j, 255/j, 0), color(255/j, (255/1.5)/j, 0), ➥
          color(255/j, (255/2)/j, 0), color(255/j, (255/2.5)/j, 0), ➥
          color(255/j, 0, 0), color(255/j, 0, (255/2)/j), ➥
          color(255/j, 0, 255/j), color((255/2)/j, 0, 255/j), ➥
          color(0, 0, 255/j), color(0, 255/j, (255/2)/j), ➥
          color(0, 255/j, 0), color((255/2)/j, 255/j, 0)
      };
      for (int i=0; i<segs; i++){
        fill(cols[i]);
        arc(x, y, radius, radius, interval*i+rotAdjust, ➥
            interval*(i+1)+rotAdjust);
```

```
      }
      radius*=ratio;
      ratio-=.1;
    }
  }
  else if (valueShift == TINT){
    //right wheel
    for (float j=0; j<1.5; j+=.3){
      color[]cols = {
        color(255, 255, 255*j), color(255, (255/1.5)+255*j, 255*j),
        color(255, (255/2)+255*j, 255*j),
        color(255, (255/2.5)+255*j, 255*j), color(255, 255*j, 255*j),
        color(255, 255*j, (255/2)+255*j),
        color(255, 255*j, 255), color((255/2)+255*j, 255*j, 255),
        color(255*j, 255*j, 255),
        color(255*j, 255, (255/2)+255*j), color(255*j, 255, 255*j),
        color((255/2)+255*j, 255, 255*j) };
      for (int i=0; i<segs; i++){
        fill(cols[i]);
        arc(x, y, radius, radius, interval*i+rotAdjust, ➥
            interval*(i+1)+rotAdjust);
      }
      radius*=ratio;
      ratio-=.1;
    }
  }
}
```

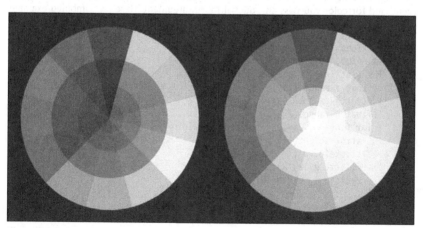

Figure 10-3. Subtractive ColorWheel sketch

405

I'm sure most of you recognized the output as the classic color wheel, composed of the three primaries (red, yellow, and blue), the three secondaries (green, purple, and orange) and the six tertiaries (yellow-orange, red-orange, red-purple, blue-purple, blue-green, and yellow-green). The two wheels (one showing shades of the colors and the other showing tints) represent color relationships as perceived off a reflective colored surface, such as a painting. This color model is referred to as **subtractive**. When the full spectrum of colors is mixed together in the subtractive model, we get a dark, neutral color that approaches black. In contrast, the colors we perceive on a computer monitor, through projected light, are considered **additive**. These colors, when mixed together, create white light. In addition, the primaries in the additive model are red, green, and blue, as opposed to red, yellow, and blue, as in the subtractive model.

The preceding sketch uses the arc() function to create a series of circles (composed of pie wedges) that overlap one another. The overlapping circles get progressively smaller, while the value of the color darkens and lightens on the left and right circles, respectively. Since the colors are fully opaque, there is no mixing of the overlapping pie wedges—rather, the shift in value is determined solely by the calculations within the cols[] array. The array uses Processing's color data type. I create and fill the arrays from scratch each iteration of the loop, using anonymous color objects; they're anonymous only in the sense that I'm not assigning each color object to a variable. As a fun problem to try on your own, try modifying the previous sketch to generate two similar wheels based on the additive model.

Controlling alpha transparency

Besides the color component properties, you can also specify an alpha component, which controls the transparency of the color. For grayscale, you pass an optional second argument, and for color you pass an optional fourth argument. Here's a combined example that shows both (see Figure 10-4):

```
// Alpha
size(400, 315);
for (int i=0; i< height; i+=width/15){
  float r=random(255);
  float g=random(255);
  float b=random(255);
  for (int j=0, a=255; j<width; j+=width/10, a*=.8){
    strokeWeight(5);
    stroke(0, a);
    fill(r, g, b, a);
    rect(j, i, width/10, width/10);
  }
}
```

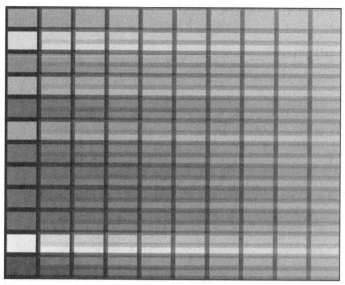

Figure 10-4. Alpha sketch

In this example, each row of cells overlaps the preceding row, illustrating some of the beautiful translucent effects you can get by procedurally altering the alpha. By incorporating color and alpha modulations with some of the other techniques you've looked at earlier—such as generating a series of simple shapes iteratively through translations—you can create aesthetically interesting images of layered geometry that begin to approximate other media, such as painting. Here's an example, shown in Figure 10-5:

```
/*
Fade-Spin
Ira Greenberg, January 7, 2006
*/

int w = 20, h = 20;
float ang = 0;
float amp = 60;
void setup(){
  size(500, 300);
  background(170, 120, 150);
  noStroke();
  smooth();

  for (int i=0, x=0; i<width; i++, x++){
    fill(200-255/width*i, 200-255/width*i, 165/width*i, 140);
    resetMatrix();
    translate(x, height/4);
    rotate(radians(x*.45));
```

10

```
        rect(-w, -h, w*.2, h*random(-.1, .4));
  }

  resetMatrix();
  for (int i=0, x=0; i<width; i++, x++){
    fill(255.0/width*i, 255.0-255.0/width*i, 127.0/width*i, 95);
    pushMatrix();
    translate(x,  height-height/5);
    rotate(radians(x*1.75));
    rect(-w, -h, w,  h);
    popMatrix();
  }

  for (float i=0, x=0, y=0; i<width; i++, x++){
    fill(160-50/width*i, 255.0/width*i, 200-190/width*i, 20);
    pushMatrix();
    translate(x, height/2+y);
    rotate(radians(x*1.75));
    rect(-w*.55, -h*.55, w*.55+y*.125,  h*.55+y*.125);
    popMatrix();
    y = sin(radians(ang+=2))*amp+random(15);
  }

  for (float i=0, x=0, y=0; i<width; i++, x+=1.5, y++){
    fill(50.0-255.0/width*i, 127.0-255.0/width*i, 200.0/width*i, 10);
    pushMatrix();
    translate(-50+x, y);
    rotate(radians(x*1.75));
    rect(-w*3.55, -h*3.55, w*3.55,  h*3.55);
    popMatrix();
  }
}
```

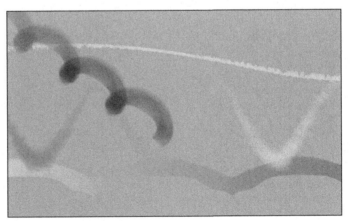

Figure 10-5. Fade-Spin sketch

A quick review of creating transformations

I think the preceding sketch illustrates nicely how numbers, code, and even rigid geometry can begin to approximate organic forms. You may have also noticed that I snuck in two new commands, pushMatrix() and popMatrix(), and also used resetMatrix(), which you looked at a little in Chapter 9. In that chapter, I also discussed Processing's translate() function and talked a little bit about the underlying affine transformation matrix that controls how the coordinate geometry you create is ultimately mapped to the display window. This is important (albeit a little confusing) information, so I want to review some of it again. Processing's display window is technically a Java component. Components include such things as buttons, panels, frames, and labels. Components utilize a graphics object to actually paint stuff in the component. The graphics object is just a Java class that encapsulates lower-level rendering stuff, which you don't have to worry about. If, however, you would like to learn some more about these under-the-hood issues, check out http://java.sun.com/products/jfc/tsc/articles/painting/.

When the display window's graphics object does its thing, coordinate data is mapped from a kind of a virtual object coordinate space to the actual display window coordinate space. By default, these two spaces start out in sync. However, when I call a function like translate(), I can shift the virtual object space in reference to the display window—making the two coordinate spaces no longer in sync. For example, prior to calling translate(), the call rect(50, 50, 100, 100) draws a rectangle 50 pixels down and to the right from the top-left corner of the display window. However, if I call translate(25, 25) prior to the rect(50, 50, 100, 100) call, the rectangle will be drawn 75 pixels down and to the right of the top-left corner of the display window. In addition, the transformed virtual coordinate space will remain in this changed state. So, with any additional drawing calls I make, the new geometry will be shifted 25 pixels down and to the right. If I call translate(25, 25) again, all new drawing calls will now be shifted 50 pixels down and to the right from the literal values passed to the respective drawing calls.

When resetMatrix() is called, Processing in a sense resets the transformation state—putting the object coordinate space back in sync with the display window space. However, there are times when you don't want to reset the entire transformation, and that's when the functions pushMatrix() and popMatrix() come in.

10

Pushing and popping the matrix

When you surround a transform operation (such as translate(), rotate(), or scale()) with the function calls pushMatrix() and popMatrix(), the original state of the matrix before the pushMatrix() call is restored after the popMatrix() call, regardless of what happens between the pushMatrix() and popMatrix() calls. Here's an example that prints the matrix values before, during, and after to illustrate this point (see Figure 10-6):

```
// Transformation Matrix
printMatrix();

pushMatrix();
translate(50, 50);
rotate(PI);
scale(.5);
printMatrix();
popMatrix();

printMatrix();
```

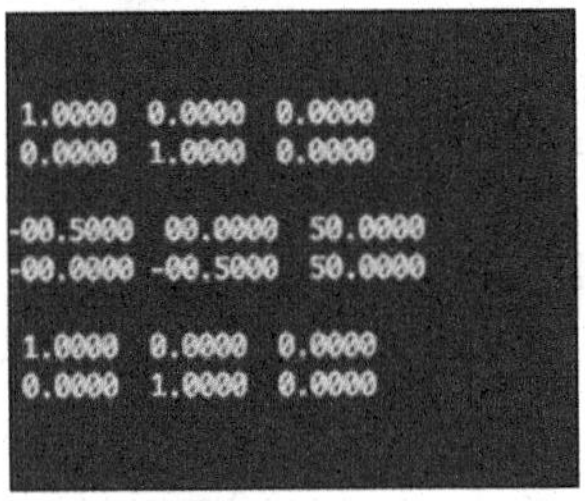

Figure 10-6. Transformation Matrix sketch

If you look at the output, you'll see that the transformation matrix output is the same before and after the pushMatrix()/popMatrix() calls. Using pushMatrix() and popMatrix(), I was able to localize the transformation so that the transformation state isn't changed for all future calls. Returning to the earlier Fade-Spin example, I used the push and pop calls to do precisely the same thing. Try commenting out the pushMatrix()/popMatrix() calls to see what happens. To learn some more about transformations, check out www.developer.com/net/vb/article.php/626051#_Introduction.

Finally, the Fade-Spin example was procedurally a little dense, as I used for loops to initialize and increment a bunch of values. Also, you'll notice that sometimes I initialized the loop values as type int and other times as type float. If you specify a variable as type int and then try to increment it with a non-integer value, you'll get unexpected results due to rounding, which can drastically change a sketch. Look at the values in this example:

```
for (int i=0; i<10; i+=1.5){
  println(i);
}
```

Even though I'm asking the loop to increment by 1.5, the values get rounded down to the nearest integer value because i is of type int. Before moving on, I want to look at one more example that uses overlapping geometry. A few years ago, I started a series of images generated with code that I called Protobytes. The Protobytes are formed from overlapping geometry. I was interested in generating organic forms that had some loose connections to natural organisms. I built the forms up incrementally, as I'll try to do here in a few separate steps. Since trig functions generate smooth repeating curves, I find them especially handy for this type of experimentation. This next example, shown in Figure 10-7, is entitled Nematode.

410

```
/*
 Nematode - stage 1
 Ira Greenberg, January 7, 2006
 stage 1
*/
size(500, 300);
background(255);
strokeWeight(.2);
smooth();
noFill();
float radius = 0;
float thickness = .35;
float x = 0;
float y = height/2;
float amp = .5;
float angle = 0;
for (int i=0; i<width; i++){
  stroke(65, 10, 5);
  translate(2, y);
  ellipse(-radius/2, -radius/2, radius*.75, radius);
  y = sin(radians(angle+=5))*amp;
  radius+=thickness;
    if (i==width/4){
      thickness*=-1;
    }
}
```

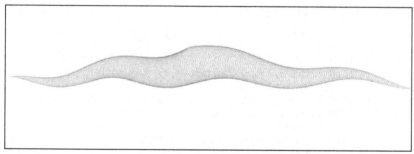

Figure 10-7. Nematode sketch (stage 1)

In the first stage of the sketch, I created the basic outer structure of the nematode. By overlapping a series of ellipses and altering their position and scale slightly, I was able to generate the body. I used a sin() function to control the y position, and by altering the thickness of the radius I was able to define the end sections of the organism. Let's add a little internal structure and some more detail (see Figure 10-8):

```
/*
 Nematode - stage 2
 Ira Greenberg, January 7, 2006
 */
size(500, 300);
background(255);
strokeWeight(.2);
smooth();
noFill();
float radius = 0;
float thickness = .35;
float x = 0;
float y = height/2;
float amp = .5;
float angle = 0;
float angle2 = 0;
for (int i=0; i<width/2-15; i++){
  stroke(65, 10, 5);
  noFill();
  translate(2, y);
  if (i >= width/2-40) {
    fill(195, 110, 105, 70);
  }
  else if (i >= width/4-40 && i <= width/2-100){
    fill(195, 110, 105, 8);
  }
  else {
    fill(195, 110, 105, 2);
  }
  ellipse(-radius/2, -radius/2, radius*.75, radius);
  noStroke();
  fill(205, 110, 105, 40);
  ellipse(-radius/2, -radius/2, radius*.25, radius*.25);
  fill(205, 110, 105, 200);
  ellipse(-radius/2, -radius/2, radius*.05, radius*.05);
  y = sin(radians(angle+=5))*amp;
  radius+=thickness;
  radius+=sin(radians(angle2+=random(30)))*.4;
  if (i==width/4){
    thickness*=-.9;
  }
}
```

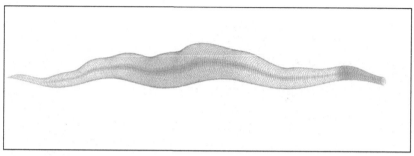

Figure 10-8. Nematode sketch (stage 2)

In this stage, I mostly just added some more ellipses, controlling their radii and color/alpha. I also added a sin() function, with random amplitude to add some jitter to the nematode's body. I think nematodes are actually pretty smooth, but I'll invoke artistic license here. Here's a finished nematode (see Figure 10-9):

```
/*
 Finished Nematode
 Ira Greenberg, January 7, 2006
 */
void setup(){
  size(500, 300);
  background(255);
  smooth();
  strokeWeight(.2);
  noFill();
  float radius = 0;
  float thickness = .35;
  float x = 0;
  float y = height/2;
  float amp = .5;
  float angle = 0;
  float angle2 = 0;

  //ground plane
  stroke(150, 100, 20);
  line(0,50, width, 50);

  for (int i=0; i<width/2-15; i++){
    noFill();
    translate(2, y);
    // add some surface shading
    if (i >= width/2-40) {
      fill(195, 110, 105, 50);
    }
    else if (i >= width/4-40 && i <= width/2-100){
      fill(195, 110, 105, 10);
```

```
    }
    else {
      fill(195, 110, 105, 2);
    }
    //outer shell 1
    stroke(145, 10, 5, 175);
    ellipse(-radius/2, -radius/2, radius*.75, radius);

    //outer shell 2
    stroke(65, 10, 100, 150);
    ellipse(-radius/2, -radius/2, radius*.71, radius*.71);

    // organs 1
    stroke(200, 200, 30, i*.8);
    ellipse(-radius/2, -radius/2, segment(radius, angle), ➥
          segment(radius, angle));

    // organs 2
    noStroke();
    fill(150, 75, 100, 28);
    ellipse(-radius/2, -radius/2, segment(radius*.7, angle), ➥
          segment(radius*.7, angle));

    // inner tube
    fill(205, 110, 105, 40);
    ellipse(-radius/2, -radius/2, radius*.25, radius*.25);

    // inner vein
    fill(205, 110, 105, 200);
    ellipse(-radius/2, -radius/2, radius*.05, radius*.05);
    y = sin(radians(angle+=5))*amp;
    radius+=thickness;
    radius+=sin(radians(angle2+=random(30)))*.4;
    if (i==width/4){
      thickness*=-.9;
    }
  }
}

float segment(float rad, float angle){
  if(rad>25){
    rad*=1.5+random(.15);
  }
  else{
    rad*=random(.2);
  }
  float r = cos(radians(angle*=1.3))*rad*.5;
  return r;
}
```

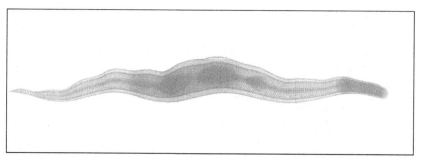

Figure 10-9. Finished Nematode sketch

There's so much more that could be done with the nematode, but I'll leave that to you. However, I'll include one more nematode image, shown in Figure 10-10, on a dark background with some minor changes to a few of the stroke values. Since the nematode image is translucent, when you add a dark background, the image takes on an interesting look and feel, resembling a film negative or X-ray.

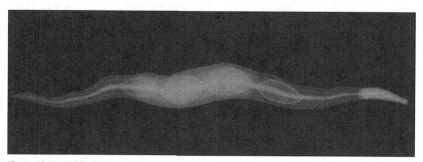

Figure 10-10. Finished Inverted Nematode sketch

10

Setting the color mode

So far, this chapter has been using the fill() and stroke() functions with the default RGB color mode. Using this mode, each of the R, G, and B color components can be assigned an int or float value from 0 to 255. However, Processing has an alternative HSB color mode, which can be set by calling colorMode(HSB). HSB stands for hue, saturation, and brightness. These components correlate to the three color properties of hue, chromatic intensity, and value, which I discussed earlier in the "Color theory" section of the chapter. By default, RGB and HSB modes use a value range of 0 to 255 for each of the three components. In the next example, I create the six primary and secondary colors and cyan using both modes (see Figure 10-11):

```
// Color Modes RGB/HSB
size(400, 114);
smooth();
color red1 = color(255, 0, 0);
color orange1 = color(255, 127, 0);
color yellow1 = color(255, 255, 0);
color green1 = color(0, 255, 0);
color cyan1 = color(0, 255, 255);
color blue1 = color(0, 0, 255);
color purple1 = color(255, 0, 255);

colorMode(HSB);
color red2 = color(0, 255, 255);
color orange2 = color(21.25, 255, 255);
color yellow2 = color(42.5, 255, 255);
color green2 = color(85, 255, 255);
color cyan2 = color(127.5, 255, 255);
color blue2 = color(170.0, 255, 255);
color purple2 = color(212.5, 255, 255);

color[][]cols = { ➥
  { red1, orange1, yellow1, green1, cyan1, blue1, purple1 },
  { red2, orange2, yellow2, green2, cyan2, blue2, purple2 }
};

int w = width/cols[0].length;
int h = w;
for (int i=0; i<2; i++){
  for (int j=0; j<cols[i].length; j++){
    fill(cols[i][j]);
    rect(w*j, h*i, w, h);
  }
}
```

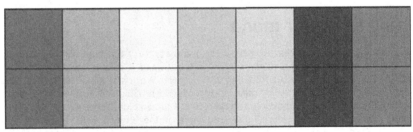

Figure 10-11. Color Modes RGB/HSB sketch

If you look carefully at the HSB section in the last example, you'll notice that, with the exception of orange2, all the colors represent an increase of 42.5. 42.5 is equal to 255 divided by 6. This progression in color from red to purple follows the same color order as

416

the decreasing wavelengths of the individual colors forming the visible light spectrum—the small fraction of the total electromagnetic spectrum our eyes can see. Red's wavelength is approximately 700 nanometers (nm), and violet's is around 400 nm. Perhaps you remember roy g biv (red, orange, yellow, green, blue, indigo, violet), a mnemonic many of us learned to remember the colors in the rainbow. Following is a simple sketch that creates a smooth color gradient across the visual spectrum (see Figure 10-12):

```
// ROY G BIV
size(400, 120);
noStroke();
colorMode(HSB);
float w = width/(255-42.5);
for (int i=0; i<width; i+=w){
  fill(i, 255, 255);
  rect(w*i, 0, w, height);
}
```

Figure 10-12. ROY G BIV sketch

There are times when it would be more convenient to use a different range than 0 to 255 to control the color components. In the last example, I was forced to do a little math to figure out the ratio of the width of the display window to the range of color values, in the line float w = width/(255-42.5);. I don't mean to be lazy, but it would have been easier to simply specify the range of color from 0 to the display window width and let the calculation-loving computer deal with the crunching. Happily, Processing includes a simple way to do just that. The colorMode() function has some optional arguments for setting a range of color values. For example, here's a math-lite version of the last sketch.

```
// ROY G BIV
// math-lite version
size(400, 120);
noStroke();
colorMode(HSB, width);
for (int i=0; i<width; i++){
  fill(i, width, width);
  rect(i, 0, i, height);
}
```

10

This sketch is not a pure copy, as there is some extra red at the end of the spectrum. To remove this, I'd still need to deal with the extra one-sixth of color range—which means I'm back to doing a little math—so I'll tolerate the extra pretty red on the right. Not only can you specify the overall range, you can do it per component, and the ranges you assign to each component can be bizarrely different. Here's a rather silly example illustrating this (see Figure 10-13):

```
// Multi Modes
size(720, 100);
noStroke();
// standard values
colorMode(HSB, 360, 100, 100);
for (int i=0; i<360; i++){
  for (int j=0; j<100; j++){
    fill(i, j, j);
    rect(i, j, 1, 1);
  }
}

// ridiculous, but possible
colorMode(HSB, 1.0, .01, 3000);
for (float i=0, ii=0; i<1.0; i+=1.0/360.0, ii++){
  for (float j=0, jj=0, k=0; j<.01; j+=.01/100.0, ➥
              jj++, k+=3000.0/100.0){
    fill(i, j, k);
    rect(360+ii, jj, 1, 1);
  }
}
strokeWeight(2);
stroke(0);
noFill();
rect(0, 0, 360, 100);
rect(360, 0, 360, 100);
```

Figure 10-13. Multi Modes sketch

The first gradient was generated using 360, 100, and 100 as the ranges for the H, S, and B components, respectively. This is actually a standard way for representing HSB, where 360 represents the degrees around the color circle and the two 100s represent 100 percent saturation and 100 percent brightness. I then created an identical gradient using bizarre values, just to illustrate the possibility. This second nested for loop is pretty frightening looking, so don't give yourself a hard time if you don't feel like unraveling it. You can also specify individual component color ranges for RGB mode, again specifying one or three optional arguments when calling the colorMode(RGB) function; I'll leave that for you to try on your own.

More convenient color functions

Before moving on to imaging, I want to look at some more convenient color functions included in Processing. For creating quick, easy color blends, Processing includes two functions: blendColor() and lerpColor(). Here's a blendColor() example, shown in Figure 10-14:

```
//blendColor
size(400, 400);
smooth();
noStroke();
color c1 = color(255, 127, 0);
color c2 = color(0, 75, 150);

color[] blends = {
  blendColor(c1, c2, ADD), /*tan*/
  blendColor(c1, c2, SUBTRACT), /*red*/
  blendColor(c1, c2, DARKEST), /*green*/
  blendColor(c1, c2, LIGHTEST)  /*pink*/
};

// background
fill(c1);
rect(0, 0, width, height);

for (int i=0; i<4; i++){
  fill(blends[i]);
  arc(width/2, height/2, width/1.25, height/1.25, ➡
      PI/2*i, PI/2*i+PI/2);
}

// front circle
fill(c2);
arc(width/2, height/2, width/4, height/4, 0, TWO_PI);
```

10

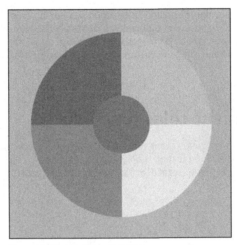

Figure 10-14. blendColor() sketch

blendColor() takes two colors as arguments and a third mode argument that controls how the two colors are blended. The different modes are BLEND, ADD, SUBTRACT, DARKEST, and LIGHTEST. The underlying math behind each of these modes is a little complicated—I'll look at that a bit later in the chapter when I discuss imaging, which includes a similar blending function. (Please note that as of this writing, BLEND mode, which I did not include in the example, requires the second color argument in the blendColor() call to have an alpha setting below 255, or no apparent blend will be detectable.)

An alternative to blendColor() is lerpColor(). The lerp part of the function name refers to linear interpolation. **Interpolation** just means finding values between other discrete values. Processing actually includes a math function called lerp() that does just this. Here's a lerp() example:

```
// lerp()
int a = 1;
int b = 2;
int steps = 5;
float interpolationValue = 1.0/steps;
for (int i=1; i<steps; i++){
  println(lerp(a, b, interpolationValue*i));
}
```

This example outputs the values 1.2, 1.4, 1.6, and 1.8. lerp() requires three arguments: the two discrete values to interpolate between and an interpolation value (a percentage expressed as a value between 0 and 1.0). For example, to find a value midway between two numbers, you'd use an interpolation value of .5. A more useful and common application of interpolation in computer graphics is for finding points along a path.

lerpColor() uses the same approach as lerp(), but applies it to blending colors. It also requires three arguments: two colors and an interpolation value. Here's a lerpColor() example (see Figure 10-15):

```
// lerpColor()
size(400, 400);
noStroke();
color c1 = color(255, 255, 0);
color c2 = color(150, 0, 150);

// change these values to alter gradient
float stepsH = 16;
float stepsW = 16;

/* ratio to remap any number of
 cells into 0 - 1.0 range for
 lerpColor interpolation argument */
float remapFactor = 100.0/(stepsH*stepsW);

float cellW = width/stepsW;
float cellH = height/stepsH;
int cellCounter = 0;

for (int i=0; i<stepsH; i++){
  for (int j=0; j<stepsW; j++){
    fill(lerpColor(c1, c2, (remapFactor*cellCounter)*.01));
    rect(j*cellW, i*cellH, cellW, cellH);
    cellCounter++;
  }
}
```

10

Figure 10-15. lerpColor() sketch

I used a changing interpolation value in the last example to create a gradient blend between the two color arguments through the display window. Try changing the starting color values as well as the variables stepsH and stepsW (which can be different from one another) to alter the color gradient.

In addition to blendColor() and lerpColor(), Processing includes seven other handy functions for accessing individual color component values. I've included six of these functions within the next example, which outputs the individual color components (R, G, and B) as well as hue, saturation, and brightness values; I didn't include alpha(), but it works similarly to the other six (the sketch output can be seen in Figure 10-16):

```
// Color Component Functions
color c1 = color(123, 200, 52);
println("Default RGB, 255");
println("red = "+ red(c1));
println("green = "+ green(c1));
println("blue = "+ blue(c1));
println("hue = "+ hue(c1));
println("saturation = "+ saturation(c1));
println("brightness = "+ brightness(c1));

println("\nStandard HSB 360, 100, 100");
colorMode(HSB, 360, 100, 100);
println("red = "+ red(c1));
println("green = "+ green(c1));
println("blue = "+ blue(c1));
println("hue = "+ hue(c1));
println("saturation = "+ saturation(c1));
println("brightness = "+ brightness(c1));

println("\nAlternative RGB 1.0");
colorMode(RGB, 1.0);
println("red = "+ red(c1));
println("green = "+ green(c1));
println("blue = "+ blue(c1));
println("hue = "+ hue(c1));
println("saturation = "+ saturation(c1));
println("brightness = "+ brightness(c1));
```

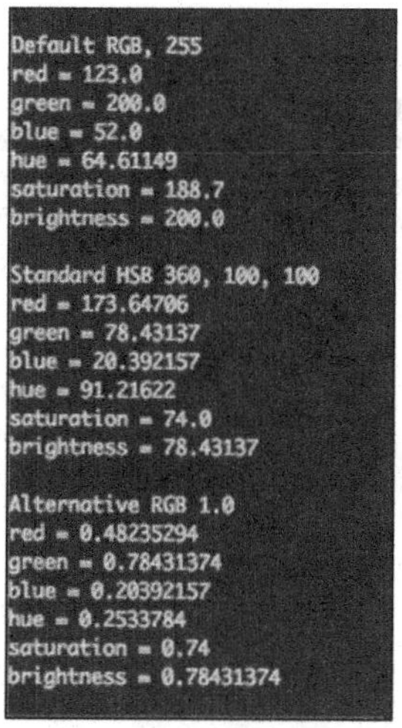

```
Default RGB, 255
red = 123.0
green = 200.0
blue = 52.0
hue = 64.61149
saturation = 188.7
brightness = 200.0

Standard HSB 360, 100, 100
red = 173.64706
green = 78.43137
blue = 20.392157
hue = 91.21622
saturation = 74.0
brightness = 78.43137

Alternative RGB 1.0
red = 0.48235294
green = 0.78431374
blue = 0.20392157
hue = 0.2533784
saturation = 0.74
brightness = 0.78431374
```

Figure 10-16. Color Component Functions sketch

I want to mention two final points about using these functions. First, according to the Processing API reference, these functions are somewhat slow—say, for extracting component data from many colors at a time. The reference suggests using bitwise operations if speed is an issue. I cover bitwise operations in detail in Appendix B, and I also look at some examples that utilize them a little later in this chapter. Second, these seven functions return a float value, regardless of whether you originally specified int values when you created the color. So, for example, if you created a color using the default RGB mode (e.g., color c = color(200, 150, 74)) and you then called red(c), the value returned would be 200.0, not 200. I know it's just a 0 after the dot, but this could cause problems if you tried to assign the returned value to a variable declared as type int. Try running the following three lines; you should get a compiler error:

```
//generates a compiler error
color c = color(200, 134, 119);
int r = red(c);
```

10

Imaging

Thus far in the book, I've been utilizing a vector graphics approach, in which images are created and manipulated using mathematical expressions that plot a shape and apply rendering attributes, such as stroke weight, fill color, corner joins, and so on. Processing has the ability to work deeper, down at the pixel or raster level. In a sense, you've been getting near the pixel level when you used 1 × 1 pixel rectangles to create some gradients. However, using rectangles to represent pixels is a very inefficient way to approach imaging. In addition, most people connect photo manipulation with imaging, which you'd be hardpressed to do with a series of rect() calls.

Gradients

I'll begin with some simple pixel gradients and then play with some images. This first sketch, shown in Figure 10-17, creates a linear gradient and utilizes Processing's set() function. This function allows me to change the color of a pixel, as well as load an image into the display window. For now, I'll just show you how to change some pixels. The function expects three arguments: set(x, y, color).

```
// Simple Linear Gradient
// January 12, 2006
// x and y axis

// constants
int Y_AXIS = 1;
int X_AXIS = 2;

void setup(){
  size(400, 400);

  // create some gradients
  // background
  color b1 = color(190, 190, 190);
  color b2 = color(20, 20, 20);
  setGradient(0, 0, width, height, b1, b2, Y_AXIS);
  //center squares
  color c1 = color(255, 120, 0);
  color c2 = color(10, 45, 255);
  color c3 = color(10, 255, 15);
  color c4 = color(125, 2, 140);
  color c5 = color(255, 255, 0);
  color c6 = color(25, 255, 200);
  setGradient(50, 50, 150, 150, c1, c2, Y_AXIS);
  setGradient(200, 50, 150, 150, c3, c4, X_AXIS);
  setGradient(50, 200, 150, 150, c2, c5, X_AXIS);
  setGradient(200, 200, 150, 150, c4, c6, Y_AXIS);
}

void setGradient(int x, int y, float w, float h, ➡
        color c1, color c2, int axis ){
  // calculate differences between color components
  float deltaR = red(c2)-red(c1);
  float deltaG = green(c2)-green(c1);
  float deltaB = blue(c2)-blue(c1);

  // choose axis
  if(axis == Y_AXIS){
    /*nested for loops set pixels
      in a basic table structure */
```

```
    // column
    for (int i=x; i<=(x+w); i++){
      // row
      for (int j=y; j<=(y+h); j++){
        color c = color( ➡
            (red(c1)+(j-y)*(deltaR/h)), ➡
            (green(c1)+(j-y)*(deltaG/h)), ➡
            (blue(c1)+(j-y)*(deltaB/h)) );
        set(i, j, c);
      }
    }
  }
  else if(axis == X_AXIS){
    // column
    for (int i=y; i<=(y+h); i++){
      // row
      for (int j=x; j<=(x+w); j++){
        color c = color( ➡
            (red(c1)+(j-x)*(deltaR/h)), ➡
            (green(c1)+(j-x)*(deltaG/h)), ➡
            (blue(c1)+(j-x)*(deltaB/h)) );
        set(j, i, c);
      }
    }
  }
}
```

Figure 10-17. Simple Linear Gradient sketch

The Simple Linear Gradient example uses a custom setGradient() function that allows you to specify the size, position, colors, and axis of the gradient within the display window. The nested for loops in the function may look a little confusing. The math stuff is simpler than it looks. Initially in the function, the three local variables deltaR, deltaG, and deltaB are assigned the differences between the R, G, and B components, respectively, within the two colors. The rest of the problem involves iterating each component from color c1 to color c2 evenly in the for loops. By dividing the delta values by the axis dimension, I get the ratio of the delta to the height, which I then multiply by the counter j. This way, even though j is incremented by 1 in the loop, the ratio will translate to the appropriate value for the color component, creating a smooth, continuous gradient. Also, the reason I subtract the y and x from j in both loop options is to ensure that the beginning of the gradient begins with c1, not c1 plus the value of x or y. As always, play with this sketch and change things. I also recommend calling some println() commands and checking on the values of variables during the for loops. When I debug my programs (which takes up too much of my time), I am constantly calling println() with a variable name as an argument to see how the program is working.

Next, I'll create the radial gradient shown in Figure 10-18. (Please be patient—this sketch can take some time to render.)

```
// Simple Radial Gradient
// January 12, 2006
void setup(){
  size(400, 400);
  background(0);
  smooth();

  // create a simple table of gradients
  int columns = 4;
  int radius = (width/columns)/2;
  // create some gradients
  for (int i=radius; i<width; i+=radius*2){
    for (int j=radius; j<height; j+=radius*2){
      createGradient(i, j, radius, ➥
        color(int(random(255)), int(random(255)), int(random(255))), ➥
        color(int(random(255)), int(random(255)), int(random(255))));
    }
  }
}

void createGradient (float x, float y, float radius, ➥
          color c1, color c2){
  float px = 0, py = 0, angle = 0;

  // calculate differences between color components
  float deltaR = red(c2)-red(c1);
  float deltaG = green(c2)-green(c1);
  float deltaB = blue(c2)-blue(c1);
  // hack to ensure there are no holes in gradient
```

```
   // needs to be increased, as radius increases
   float gapFiller = 8.0;

   for (int i=0; i<radius; i++){
     for (float j=0; j<360; j+=1.0/gapFiller){
       px = x+cos(radians(angle))*i;
       py = y+sin(radians(angle))*i;
       angle+=1.0/gapFiller;
       color c = color( ➡
           (red(c1)+(i)*(deltaR/radius)), ➡
           (green(c1)+(i)*(deltaG/radius)), ➡
           (blue(c1)+(i)*(deltaB/radius)) );
       set(int(px), int(py), c);
     }
   }
   // adds smooth edge
   // hack anti-aliasing
   noFill();
   strokeWeight(3);
   ellipse(x, y, radius*2, radius*2);
 }
```

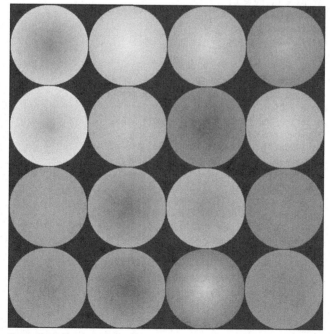

Figure 10-18. Simple Radial Gradient sketch

10

427

The radial gradient functions similarly to the linear one, except I used some trig functions. The way it works is that the radius keeps increasing each iteration of the outer for loop. The nested loop creates a circle of colored pixels at each radius length. A blend occurs between color 1 and color 2, as it did in the linear example. I had to add some minor "hacks," however. Since the set() function only takes ints, not floats, I needed to explicitly convert the px and py variables to ints with the calls int(px) and int(py). In addition, as the pixels were drawn around each circle at the respective radii lengths, I noticed some small (and annoying) gaps in the gradient. To compensate, I created the gapFiller variable, which ensures that extra pixels are drawn to fill in the gaps. I look forward to hearing from one of you on how to more elegantly solve this problem—full bragging rights extended.

Before moving on to another approach to writing pixels, let's look at one more less "regular" example. This example, shown in Figure 10-19, also takes some time to render.

```
/*
Wave Gradient
January 13, 2006
*/
size(600, 400);
background(200,200,200);
float angle = 0;
float px = 0, py = 0;
float amplitude = 30;
float frequency = 0;
float fillGap = 2.5;
color c;

for (int i=-50; i<height+50; i++){
  // reset angle to 0, so waves stack properly
  angle = 0;
  // increasing frequency causes more gaps
  frequency+=.003;
  for (float j=0; j<width+50; j++){
    py = i+sin(radians(angle))*amplitude;
    angle+=frequency;
    c = color( ➡
            abs(py-i)*255/amplitude, ➡
            255-abs(py-i)*255/amplitude, ➡
            j*(255.0/(width+50)) );
    // hack to fill gaps. Raise value of fillGap
    // if you increase frequency
    for (int filler=0; filler<fillGap; filler++){
      set(int(j-filler), int(py)-filler, c);
      set(int(j), int(py), c);
      set(int(j+filler), int(py)+filler, c);
    }
  }
}
```

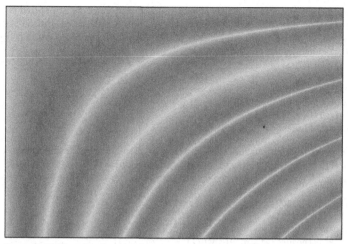

Figure 10-19. Wave Gradient sketch

Hopefully this last sketch didn't cook your computer. Between the two nested loops, there's a fair amount of processing. The gradient is determined by a simple sine wave with increasing frequency; this is what gives the gradient its asymmetry. The color is determined, somewhat arbitrarily, by some simple expressions. The red component is generated by the sine function, the green component is based on 255 (minus the value of the sine function), and the blue component is determined by the counter j. In all three cases, the component color values calculated by the expressions are remapped to a range of 0 to 255. Definitely mess around with some of the values, especially the color expressions and the frequency. At the bottom of the function, the third for loop fills gaps in the gradient, similarly to what was done in the radial gradient sketch. You can also try changing the fillGap variable to see what happens. Using the set() function is relatively straightforward, but not the fastest way to change pixel data in Processing.

Faster pixel functions

There are three other language structures (two functions and an array) that can speed things up. The three structures are loadPixels(), updatePixels(), and pixels[]. The first structure, loadPixels(), creates an array of pixels (assigned to the built-in global variable pixels[]) of the entire display window. The number of pixels in the display window can be calculated by width * height. So, for example, a 400 × 400 display would equal 160,000 pixels. Here's some evidence:

```
size(400, 400);
loadPixels();
print(pixels.length);
```

10

The pixels[] array stores each pixel as Processing's color data type, structured in consecutive rows. For example, if the sketch size is 100 × 100, then the 5,050th pixel (pixels[5049]) will be close to the center point in the display window. Here's an example that directly changes the color of that pixel:

```
size(100, 100);
background(0);
loadPixels();
pixels[5050] = color(255);
updatePixels();
```

The Processing reference includes a very simple mathematical expression to help you target a pixel in the pixels[] array of the display window: pixels[y*width+x]. Based on this expression, the last little sketch (shown in Figure 10-20) could be rewritten as follows:

```
size(100, 100);
background(0);
loadPixels();
pixels[height/2*width+width/2] = color(255);
updatePixels();
```

Figure 10-20. Pixels array (single white pixel) sketch

To change more than 1 pixel, a loop will help. The next example divides the display window in horizontal bands, assigning a different color to each band (see Figure 10-21):

```
// Color Banding with pixels[]
size(400, 400);
loadPixels();
int px = pixels.length;
int bands = 20; // should be a factor of px
color c;
```

```
for (int i=0; i<bands; i++){
  c = color(random(255), random(255), random(255));
  for (int j=(px/bands)*i; j<px/bands*(i+1); j++){
    pixels[j] = c;
  }
}
updatePixels();
```

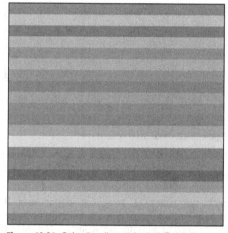

Figure 10-21. Color Banding with pixels[] sketch

You need to call loadPixels() prior to utilizing the pixels[] array. If you neglect to call loadPixels(), you'll get a null pointer error, which essentially means that you're trying to access something that hasn't been created yet. After you make any changes to pixels[], you'll need to call updatePixels() to see your changes updated in the display window. If you don't call the function, you'll neither get an error message nor see your updates. These types of (annoying) errors are categorized as "failing silently," which can be a royal pain when debugging.

In the last sketch, I created the variable px to hold the length value of pixels[]. I did this just for convenience, as px was shorter to write than pixels.length. Every array has a public length property that is especially useful when setting the limit of a loop. For example, to randomly assign a color to every pixel on the screen, I could do this (see Figure 10-22):

```
// Color Static
size(400, 400);
loadPixels();
int px = pixels.length;
color c;
for (int i=0; i<px; i++){
  c = color(random(255), random(255), random(255));
  pixels[i] = c;
}
updatePixels();
```

10

431

Figure 10-22. Color Static sketch

Image manipulation

As you might suspect, the pixels[] array has better uses than creating static. loadPixels() collects all the pixels in the window, regardless of whether the pixels make up a single color background fill or a photographic image. The more interesting latter case opens the door to all kinds of imaging possibilities. However, before looking at the next sketch, let's review how to load an image.

To work with images in Processing, you need to load them into a data directory that resides within the current sketch directory. It's a very simple process. Under Sketch in the top menu bar, select the Add File command. This command opens a file browser, allowing you to select an image to copy into the data directory. If there isn't a data directory, Processing will automatically create one for you. If you eventually make additional changes to the image using a program like Photoshop, you'll need to remember to add the altered image to your data directory again (it's not updated automatically). One cautionary note: when you add an image into the data directory with the same name as an existing image, the original image will be replaced by the image you add, without any warning. Processing can work with GIF, JPG, TGA, and PNG images.

The following sketch (shown in Figure 10-23) loads an image (my dog Heidi) into the display window (obviously, you'll need to change the name heidi.jpg to the image you're using):

```
// Load an Image
size(600, 400);
PImage img1;
img1 = loadImage("heidi.jpg");
image(img1, 0, 0);
```

Figure 10-23. Load an Image sketch

Pretty painless, don't you think? If you did run into a problem, remember that Processing is case sensitive, so .JPG is different than .jpg. In addition, Processing can't (easily) handle huge files the way a program like Photoshop can, which can utilize virtual memory (memory borrowed from the hard drive). Also remember that image size and resolution are interconnected, so just changing the size of the image's dimensions won't reduce its memory requirements; it will just increase the resolution of the smaller image.

If you're working with a very large image and run into the java.lang.OutOfMemoryError, you can try allocating more memory to Processing by selecting Preferences from the top Processing menu. Make sure that the Set Maximum Available Memory box is selected, and then try incrementally (and cautiously) raising the value. Processing's default value is 512KB. To learn more about memory issues/errors in Processing, check out http:// processing.org/faq/bugs.html#memory.

Notice in the last example that I declared the variable img1 of type PImage. Similarly to Processing's color data type, PImage is a unique Processing data type, used to store image data. The line img1 = loadImage("heidi.jpg"); in the example creates a PImage object. This line didn't actually draw the image to the screen, but constructed a PImage object containing the relevant image data.

One of the challenges of loading images or other forms of external data is the latency, or delay, between the input request and the data actually being loaded into the program. As you can imagine, this delay can be substantial for large image files. Using pure Java, loading images can be a bit involved, requiring structures for tracking the image data as it's loading—much lower-level than most of us would want to go. PImage, along with the loadImage() function, encapsulates this entire loading process (thankfully).

10

In addition to loadImage(), you can use the image() function to actually draw the image to the screen, as in the line image(img1, 0, 0);. The second and third arguments in the call (0, 0) are for the x and y position of the image. Images are positioned from the top-left corner of the image. In the last example, if I had wanted to center the image in the display window (assuming, of course, that the image was smaller than the window), I could have used the following:

```
//load and center an image
size(700, 500);
PImage img1;
img1 = loadImage("heidi.jpg");
translate(width/2, height/2);
image(img1, -img1.width/2, -img1.height/2);
```

Since PImage is a data type (think class), it includes properties (also referred to as fields) and methods. PImage objects have width and height properties, which I conveniently used in calculating the image position (centered). More information about the PImage data type, including its other fields/methods, can be found at http://processing.org/reference/PImage.html.

In the last example, I called the image() function to display my image. set() can also be called to load images—in this case, two copies of the same image—the same function called earlier to change the color of a pixel (see Figure 10-24):

```
//Loading Images with set()
size(600, 400);
background(245);
PImage img2 = loadImage("kids.jpg");
set(50, 50, img2);
set(img2.width+100, 50, img2);
```

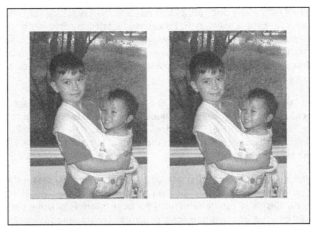

Figure 10-24. Loading Images with set() sketch

The image() function has an extra feature that I think makes it more useful than set() for loading images: the ability to resize the image as you load it. The next example, shown in Figure 10-25, tiles images in the display window using image(img, x, y, w, h). I recommend using an image approximately 400 (width) × 300 pixels to try the example.

```
//Image Tiling
size(650, 450);
PImage img2 = loadImage("heidi.jpg");
int cols = 8;
int rows = 8;
int w = width/cols;
int h = height/rows;
for (int i=0; i<height; i+=h){
  for (int j=0; j<width; j+=w){
    image(img2, j, i, w, h);
  }
}
```

Figure 10-25. Image Tiling sketch

Besides the set() function, it's probably no surprise that there's also a get() function. get() can return the color of a single pixel, an entire PImage, or a section of a PImage. This last case can be useful for creating a collage of image fragments (if that's the sort of thing you enjoy doing). Here's an example, shown in Figure 10-26, that copies four pieces of the image and pastes them in a stack on the right side of the display window. Please note that your image needs to be 650 (width) × 450 pixels for this example to render properly.

```
//Compositing
size(650, 450);
PImage img = loadImage("hong_kong.jpg");
image(img, 0, 0);
int w = width/5;
int h = height/5;
PImage[]frags = {
  get(130, 140, w, h),
  get(475, 220, w, h),
  get(220, 300, w, h),
  get(300, 205, w, h),
  get(100, 250, w, h)
    };

for (int i=0; i<5; i++){
  image(frags[i], width-w, h*i);
}
```

Figure 10-26. Compositing sketch

In the last example, I created an array of anonymous PImages using the get() command. This syntax may look odd, as I'm relying on the returned values of the get() calls (which are PImages) to populate the arrays. You'll remember that arrays can be instantiated a few different ways; one such way is to declare and populate the array at the same time, with the values specified between curly braces, as illustrated in the example.

A more ambitious but interesting thing to do with get() could be to write your own image-encrypting sketch. The simple encryption procedure will collect the image as sequential fragments and then re-create the image, reordering the image. I'll keep it really simple and just reverse the order of the fragments. You need to use an image of 600 (width) × 400 pixels to run the example (see Figure 10-27):

```
//Simple Image Encryption
int ENCRYPTION_LOW = 0;
int ENCRYPTION_MEDIUM = 1;
int ENCRYPTION_HIGH = 2;
int ENCRYPTION_VERY_HIGH = 3;

void setup(){
  size(600, 400);
  PImage img = loadImage("changsha.jpg");
  image(img, 0, 0);

 // call the fragment function
  fragment(ENCRYPTION_HIGH);
}

void fragment(int encryptionLevel){
  int fragW = 0;
  int fragH = 0;
  int frags = 0;
  // set size of blocks
  switch(encryptionLevel){
      case 0:
        fragW = width/2;
        fragH = height/2;
        frags = 4;
       break;
      case 1:
        fragW = width/4;
        fragH = height/4;
        frags = 16;
      break;
      case 2:
        fragW = width/8;
        fragH = height/8;
        frags = 64;
      break;
      case 3:
```

10

```
          fragW = width/10;
          fragH = height/10;
          frags = 100;
        break;
  }

  // fill array with image blocks
  PImage[]imgs = new PImage[frags];
  int fragCounter = 0;
  for (int i=0, ii=0; i<width; i+=fragW, ii++){
    for (int j=0, jj=0; j<height; j+=fragH, jj++){
      imgs[fragCounter++] = get(i, j, fragW, fragH);
    }
  }
  // call encryption function
  encrypt(imgs);
}

//encrypt
void encrypt(PImage[]imgs){
  PImage[]imgs2 = new PImage[imgs.length];
  for (int i=imgs.length-1; i>=0; i--){
    // reverse  fragment order
    imgs2[abs(i-(imgs.length-1))] = imgs[i];
  }
  update(imgs2);
}

// repaint Display window
void update(PImage[]imgs){
  //reset counter
  int counter = 0;
  //reassemble image
  for (int i=0; i<width; i+=imgs[0].width){
    for (int j=0; j<height; j+=imgs[0].height){
      image(imgs[counter], i, j);
      counter++;
    }
  }
}
```

Figure 10-27. Simple Image Encryption sketch

This is actually a pretty dopey encryption, but hopefully it sparks some ideas. Also, the encryption fragmentation is based on the 600 × 400 format. If you change that, you'll likely get an "array out of bounds" error. The basic encryption works by cutting the image into fragments that are used to create an array of PImages of all the fragments. At that point, you could write any sorting algorithm you'd like to encrypt (reorder) the fragments. I simply reversed the order with the following expression:

```
imgs2[abs(i-(imgs.length-1))] = imgs[i];
```

The function abs() always returns a positive value, allowing me to load the image fragments in imgs[] in reverse order into imgs2[]. Upon reviewing the code, If you have trouble seeing why this works, run the following line in the for loop within the encrypt function:

```
println("i = "+i+", abs(i-(imgs.length-1)) = " + ➥
    abs(i-(imgs.length-1)));
```

One minor caution—if you're on an older computer (sorry), be careful running the VERY_HIGH option, it might take a while.

If you've been looking through the imaging section of the Processing reference, you may have found some commands with duplicate names. For example, if you click on the PImage link, you'll see that a number of the method names are the same as function names grouped under the Pixels heading in the language reference. The commands are actually different, although functionally they do some similar things. Here's how to keep this stuff all straight.

10

Display window functions

The commands grouped under the Pixels heading of the language reference are functions that affect the pixels in the display window, regardless of whether those pixels make up a background color or an image. The pixels[] array specified under this heading is the array that holds all the pixels making up the display window (again, regardless of what's in it).

PImage methods

The PImage data type also has a pixels[] array property that is assigned the pixels making up the created PImage object. When invoking a method of the PImage class, you use a PImage object reference attached to the property or method with dot syntax. For example, to set a pixel of a PImage named img, you would write img.set(). In contrast, to set a pixel in the display window, you would just use set(). The situation can seem even more confusing once img (the PImage object) is drawn to the screen. At that point, the image data becomes part of the display window, which gets collected in the window's pixels[] array. However, img still retains its original pixel data in memory (in its own img.pixels[] array).

The next sketch, shown in Figure 10-28, uses the PImage method get() to create a pixilated image. The variable detail allows you to change the level of pixilation. The original PImage is never drawn to the screen, but rather the internal image is used for picking color values with the PImage get() method. The picked color values are then used to create a matrix of colored rectangles approximating the image. If you bring the level of detail down to (or near) 1, the colored rectangles will approximate a continuous tone image; you'll also want to uncomment the line //noStroke();. I recommend using an image the same size as the display window.

```
//Pixilate
size(600, 400);
PImage img = loadImage("changsha.jpg");
//noStroke();
int detail = 10;
for ( int i=0; i<width; i+=detail){
  for ( int j=0; j<height; j+=detail){
    color c = img.get(i, j);
    fill(c);
    rect(i, j, detail, detail);
  }
}
```

Figure 10-28. Pixilate sketch

The next sketch loads two copies of an image into the display window and increases the right image's red saturation. Remember, the loadPixels() function call collects the display window pixel data, assigning it to the display window pixels[] array (not the img.pixels[] array). After making some changes to the pixels[] array, I need to call updatePixels() to have the changes actually updated within the display window. In the example, I'm using a 400 × 400 pixel image and an 800 × 400 pixel display window (see Figure 10-29):

```
//Red Saturation
size(800, 400);
PImage img = loadImage("hong_kong.jpg");
image(img, 0, 0);
image(img, width/2, 0);
int threshold = 125;
loadPixels();
for(int j=0; j<height; j++){
  for(int i=(width/2+j*width); i<width+j*width; i++){
    if (red(pixels[i])>threshold){
      pixels[i] = color(255, green(pixels[i]), blue(pixels[i]));
    }
  }
}
updatePixels();
```

10

Figure 10-29. Red Saturation sketch

An easier way to add a tint or color overlay to an image is to use Processing's tint() function. The function requires a color argument, which can be specified five different ways:
gray, with or without alpha; RGB or RGBA color; or a single color value, using Processing's
color data type. In the next example, shown in Figure 10-30, I used an image the same size
as the display window (600 × 400 pixels):

```
// Tint()
size(600, 400);
PImage img = loadImage("highway.jpg");
image(img, 0, 0);
int tintAlpha = 255;

int[][]cols = {
  {255, 0, 0, tintAlpha}, {255, 255, 0, tintAlpha},
  {0, 0, 255, tintAlpha}, {0, 255, 0, tintAlpha},
  {255, 0, 255, tintAlpha}, {255, 127, 0, tintAlpha}
};

int columns = 3;
int w = width/columns;
int h = cols.length;

for (int i=0; i<h; i++){
  tintAlpha = 255;
  for (int j=0; j<w; j++){
    tint(color(cols[i][0], cols[i][1], cols[i][2], tintAlpha));
    image(img, j*w, i*height/h, w, height/h );
    tintAlpha-=(255/columns);
  }
}
```

Figure 10-30. Tint sketch

Speeding things up with bitwise operations

You might have noticed that this last sketch took some time to render (or maybe your computer is faster than mine). There is a faster, albeit lower-level, way to manipulate the individual color components packed inside the color data type. The color data type combines the individual color components alpha, red, green, and blue into 32 bits of data. The structure of the color data type looks like this: AAAAAAAARRRRRRRRGGGGGGGG-BBBBBBBB. Of course, the letters would be replaced by zeros and ones, depending on the color specified. For example, run the following sketch to see the bit string for blue:

```
color c = color(0, 0, 255);
println(binary(c));
```

In the sketch output, the alpha and blue bits are all ones, since I specified maximum value for blue (255), and alpha is 255 by default. Likewise, the red and green bits are all zeros, per the original color value I set—color(0, 0, 255).

Bitwise operations allow you to directly manipulate the bits, shifting and even doing simple mathematical operations on them. Bitwise operations are not for everyone, so don't fret if you can't deal with this approach. However, it's good to know that the possibility exists, and they are quite speedy. I provide a detailed overview of bitwise operations in Appendix B, so you might want to read that before trying these next few sketches. If, however, you just want to use bitwise operations with a limited understanding of how they actually work, here's the highly abridged "recipe" version:

10

To access the red, green, blue, and alpha components from a color c, use the following syntax:

```
int a =  c >> 24 & 0xFF;
int r = c >> 16 & 0xFF;
int g =  c >> 8 & 0xFF;
int b =  c & 0xFF;
```

To combine the individual color components back into a color, use:

```
// combine components back into a 32-bit integer
c = (a << 24) | (r << 16) | (g << 8) | b;
```

This next sketch combines the two steps, filling the top and bottom of the sketch window with a color manipulated using bitwise operations:

```
// bitwise operations
size(200, 300);
noStroke();
color c = color(45, 120, 96);

// fill top of window
fill(c);
rect(0, 0, width, height/2);

// get color components
int r = c >> 16 & 0xFF;
int g =  c >> 8 & 0xFF;
int b =  c & 0xFF;
int a =  c >> 24 & 0xFF;

// alter component values
r += 100;
g -= 50;
b += 100;

// combine components back into a 32-bit integer
c = (a << 24) | (r << 16) | (g << 8) | b;

// fill bottom of window
fill(c);
rect(0, height/2, width, height/2);
```

Here's an example of tinting an image using bitwise operations (shown in Figure 10-31). I used an image the same size as the display window (600 × 400 pixels).

```
/* Tint (using bitwise operations)
Created January 18, 2006
updated December 4, 2006 */
size(600, 400);
PImage img = loadImage("changsha2.jpg");
PImage img2 = createImage(img.width, img.height, RGB);
// copy pixels array from img to img2
arraycopy(img.pixels, img2.pixels);
int r, g, b, a;
int row = height/6;

for(int i=0; i<width*height; i++){
  // get untinted component values
  r =  img2.pixels[i] >> 16 & 0xFF;
  g =  img2.pixels[i] >> 8 & 0xFF;
  b =  img2.pixels[i] & 0xFF;
  a =  img2.pixels[i] >> 24 & 0xFF;

  // tint based on height in display window
  if (i<width*row){
    r =255;
  } else if (i>width*row && i<width*row*2){
    r = 255;
    g = 255;
  } else if (i>width*row*2 && i<width*row*3){
    b = 255;
  } else if (i>width*row*3 && i<width*row*4){
    g = 255;
  } else if (i>width*row*4 && i<width*row*5){
    r = 255;
    b = 255;
  } else {
    r = 255;
    g = 127;
  }

  // combine components back into a 32-bit integer
  img2.pixels[i] = (a << 24) | (r << 16) | (g << 8) | b;
}
// draw images
image(img, 0, 0);
image(img2, width/2, 0);
```

10

Figure 10-31. Tint sketch (using bitwise operations)

Again, let me stress the fact that you do not need to use bitwise operations in Processing. The Processing functions red(c), green(c), blue(c), and alpha(c) also return the individual color component values. However, once you get past the strange bitwise syntax (i.e., >> 16 & 0xFF), you'll realize they are relatively easy to use, and again, fast.

The last sketch utilized two PImages; the first was created with the line

```
PImage img = loadImage("changsha2.jpg");
```

which is the syntax I looked at earlier to create a PImage based on a loaded image. The second PImage was created with the following line:

```
PImage img2 = createImage(img.width, img.height, RGB);
```

This is the syntax to use when you want to create a PImage, but initially only specify its size and color format. Notice that I specified the size of the second PImage using the width and height properties of the first PImage, ensuring that both images were the same size.

As you may remember, every PImage includes a pixels[] array that contains all the color values in the image. Once I created the second PImage, I copied the pixels[] array from the first PImage into the second using Processing's arrayCopy(src, dest) function.

This is a pretty handy function that you need to use to copy arrays. You can't simply copy an array using syntax like array1 = array2, which only works for primitive types, such as int1 = int2. Arrays and objects are reference types. You may remember from earlier in the book that a primitive type is directly assigned a specific value (e.g., int i = 1;), but a reference type is internally assigned an address in the computer's memory where the object is stored. Thus, the syntax array1 = array2 makes the two array variables point to the same place in the computer's memory (where the array is stored)—generally not what you want to do. This is a fairly advanced topic, but something you do need to be aware of. I cover variables in detail in Chapter 3.

There are a lot of other interesting things you can do using bitwise operations. Here's a sketch, shown in Figure 10-32, that changes the contrast of an image (I used a 400 × 400 pixel image for the example).

```
/* Contrast (using bitwise operations)
 created January 18, 2006
 updated December 4, 2006 */

size(800, 400);
PImage img = loadImage("harbor.jpg");
PImage img2 = createImage(img.width, img.height, RGB);
arraycopy(img.pixels, img2.pixels);

float threshold = 127.5;
float contrast = .5; // pos or neg values
loadPixels();
for(int i=0; i<img.width * img.height; i++){
  // separate out component color values
  int r =  img2.pixels[i] >> 16 & 0xFF;
  int g =  img2.pixels[i] >> 8 & 0xFF;
  int b =  img2.pixels[i] & 0xFF;
  int a =  img2.pixels[i] >> 24 & 0xFF;

  // red
  r = int(r*(1.0 + (contrast)*((r-threshold)*.01)));
  r = constrain(r, 0, 255);

  // green
  g = int(g*(1.0 + (contrast)*((g-threshold)*.01)));
  g = constrain(g, 0, 255);

  // blue
  b = int(b*(1.0 + (contrast)*((b-threshold))*.01));
  b = constrain(b, 0, 255);

  // combine components back into a 32-bit integer
  img2.pixels[i] = (a << 24) | (r << 16) | (g << 8) | b;
}
//draw images
image(img, 0, 0);
image(img2, width/2, 0);
```

10

Figure 10-32. Contrast sketch (using bitwise operations)

This is a fairly simple contrast implementation that calculates the difference between the color component value and some threshold—in this case, the midpoint of the 255-value color range (127.5). This value is multiplied by a contrast value and then added to 1; the color component is then multiplied by this number. So, for example, if the threshold/contrast expression value evaluates to 1.2, and the color component value is 150, it will become 180. The reason I subtract the threshold from the component is to generate a nice gradient of values so that the contrast shift will be smooth. For example, a color in the mid-range (e.g., 129) would be affected very little (multiplied by 1.00225). However, colors approaching 0 or 255 would be more intensely affected (e.g., an initial component value of 240, using .15 as the value of the contrast variable, would become 280.5). The difference in values between the most minimal changes and the most severe would be across a gradient proportional to the difference between the component's original value and the threshold.

In the example, I was also forced to convert the calculated contrast values from type `float` to type `int` so that I could assign them back to the color component variables, declared as type `int`. Finally, I used Processing's `constrain()` function, which sets a minimum and maximum for a value. Since my component values needed to stay within the range of 0 to 255, I clipped them if they exceeded these limits. With a starting value of 240 and a contrast value of .15, the calculated value 280.5 would get constrained to 255. You can try commenting out the `constrain()` function calls to see what happens when the values do go out of range; it can be visually interesting. I'll finish up this section by looking some more at Processing's built-in imaging and filtering capabilities.

Imaging filters

Processing's PImage class has a method called `mask()` that allows you to use either an image or a pixel array to mask out part of an image. The mask image should be grayscale. (You can use an RGB image, but only the blue channel of the image will be used as the mask.) My suggestion is to convert your mask image to grayscale before using it.

The mask works like an alpha channel. A value of 0 (black) will conceal the image pixel, while a value of 255 (white) will fully reveal the image pixel. Values between 0 and 255 will display the masked pixels in the image with varying degrees of translucency. In the next sketch, I used one image to mask out the sky area of another image, allowing the display window background color to show through (where the 0 values of the mask pixels are). I made the sky-shaped mask image from the original image, which I was able to select and convert using Photoshop. In the two example images, the first image uses a 100 percent black sky mask, while the second uses a linear gradient from black (top of the sky) to white (bottom of the sky). The two images I used were both 600 × 480 pixels (see Figures 10-33 and 10-34):

```
// Mask the Sky
size(600, 480);
background(185, 185, 250);
PImage img = loadImage("harbor2.jpg");
PImage mask = loadImage("harbor2_mask.jpg");
img.mask(mask);
image(img, 0, 0, 600, 480);
```

Figure 10-33. Mask the Sky sketch

10

Figure 10-34. Mask the Sky with Gradient sketch

When using a pixel array mask instead of an image, the pixel array size should be the same length (number of pixels) as the image you're masking, which means that if your image is 600 × 400, your pixel array should have a length of 240,000 (image width × image height). Pixel array masks are a very cool feature in Processing that are a little hard to understand at first. Besides providing the ability to create interesting collaged effects, they can also be used to generate a dynamic mask at runtime. In the next example, shown in Figure 10-35, I'll create a pixel array mask composed of 2,000 random rectangles. The image you use needs to be the same dimensions as the display window.

```
// Pixel Array Mask
size(600, 400);
// set background--the blue channel
// contributes to pixel mask
background(180, 90, 50);

//load but don't display image
PImage img = loadImage("changsha.jpg");

// create a mask composed of rectangles
fill(255);
for (int i=0; i<2000; i++){
```

```
        rect(random(width), random(height), 5+random(15), 5+random(15));
    }
    // build pixel array of the screen
    loadPixels();

    // set mask
    img.mask(pixels);

    //draw image
    image(img, 0, 0, 600, 400);
```

Figure 10-35. Pixel Array Mask sketch

Since you can collect the pixels in the display window using loadPixels(), you can generate a mask with any of Processing's drawing functions, which is exactly what I did in this
example. Using the rect() command, I created 600 rectangles with a fill of 255, and then
I called loadPixels(), which created a pixel array of the image. If you specify an RGB fill
value, the mask utilizes the value of the blue color component of the pixels. You can also
specify a grayscale value with a single argument when calling the fill or background function. 0 (black) will be opaque, while 255 (white) will be totally transparent. Values between
0 and 255 will have varying translucency. In the example, I set the blue component in the
background color to 50, giving the pixel mask some overall slight translucency, allowing
the image to show through the background color a little. I gave the rectangles a fill of 255,
fully revealing parts of the image through the little rectangle windows. If you're still not
getting this, try changing some of the values and playing with the code—it's the best way
to really understand what's happening.

10

blend() and filter()

There are two other powerful Photoshop-esque imaging functions in Processing's toolbox: blend() and filter(). These functions each do so much that they could easily have been divided into a bunch of separate functions. They're built upon some very low-level coding—mostly using bitwise operations—and were developed as a group effort, with considerable contributions by Karsten Schmidt (a.k.a. toxi) (www.toxi.co.uk/) and Mario Klingemann (www.quasimondo.com/). If you'd like to take a look at the actual source code implementation (to better appreciate toxi and Klingemann's efforts), check out Processing's PImage class at http://dev.processing.org/source/index.cgi/trunk/processing/core/src/processing/core/PImage.java?view=markup.

I do, however, have some (small) misgivings about these functions being included in Processing, as they so deeply encapsulate very low-level processing, and—not unlike Photoshop—can become easy targets for fast, uninformed effects. In this sense, I feel their ease of use and power actually have the potential to limit creativity. For example, here's a sketch that uses the filter function to invert an image (see Figure 10-36). Please remember to add an image into your data directory for all the examples prior to using loadImage(), as in the previous examples.

```
// INVERT Filter
// image should be 600 x 400 pixels
size(600, 400);
background(255);
PImage img = loadImage("view.jpg");
image(img,0,0);
filter(INVERT);
```

Figure 10-36. INVERT Filter sketch

This last sketch couldn't be simpler. The INVERT argument inverts the pixel color component values. However, that's all you can do with it. Now, let's implement our own custom invert filter. Inverting the color component value is as simple as subtracting 255 from each component. However, doing that will also generate a negative value or 0. I want positive color component values in the range of 0 to 255, so I need to remove the negative sign. Two simple ways to do that would be to multiply each value by −1, or use Processing's abs() function, which returns the absolute value of the argument.

```
//custom invert--version 1
// image should be 600 x 400 pixels
size(600, 400);
background(255);
PImage img = loadImage("view.jpg");
image(img, 0, 0);
loadPixels();

for (int i=0; i<pixels.length; i++){
  // separate out and invert component color values
  int r = abs((pixels[i] >> 16 & 0xFF)-255);
  int g = abs((pixels[i] >> 8 & 0xFF)-255);
  int b = abs((pixels[i] & 0xFF)-255);
  int a = pixels[i] >> 24 & 0xFF;

  pixels[i] = (a << 24) | (r << 16) | (g << 8) | b;
}
updatePixels();
```

This sketch should mimic, in output, the earlier sketch that used Processing's filter(INVERT) function. I should also mention that the preceding sketch could be condensed by using a different bitwise operator, ^, which I believe is how it's actually internally implemented in Processing. Here's the condensed, albeit denser, version. I won't spend more time explaining the bitwise stuff here—but remember that I cover it in detail in Appendix B if you want more info.

```
//custom invert--version 2
// condensed verison
// image should be 600 x 400 pixels
size(600, 400);
background(255);
PImage img = loadImage("view.jpg");
image(img, 0, 0);
loadPixels();
for (int i=0; i<pixels.length; i++){
  pixels[i] ^= 0xFFFFFF;
}
updatePixels();
```

10

And if you really can't stand the bitwise stuff, you can also use the color component functions, which although not as efficient, get the job done:

```
//custom invert--version 3
// image should be 600 x 400 pixels
size(600, 400);
background(255);
PImage img = loadImage("view.jpg");
image(img, 0, 0);
loadPixels();

for (int i=0; i<(width*height); i++){
  // separate out and invert component color values
  int r = abs(int(red(pixels[i]))-255);
  int g = abs(int(green(pixels[i]))-255);
  int b = abs(int(blue(pixels[i]))-255);
  int a = int(alpha(pixels[i]));

  pixels[i] = color(r, g, b, a);
}
updatePixels();
```

So you might ask at this point, "Why would anyone (in their right mind) want to do all this customizing, when you can get the same bang for a whole lot less buck using the prebuilt function?" Using Processing's filter(INVERT) function, you will always get the same consistent result. This is not necessarily a bad thing, as it's convenient to be able to quickly and reliably invert pixels. However, what if, in inverting the pixels, you begin to digressively wonder (as artists tend to do), "What would happen if, rather than inverting the pixels, I did something else to them?" A Photoshop user might then go back to the pull-down menu and look for other cool pre-made effects. However, as a creative coder, I'm not really looking for a quick answer. Rather, I'm engaged in a search process that hopefully will to lead to discovering a yet untraveled aesthetic path. When you have a toolbox of canned effects, no matter how good, it can be pretty hard to find untrodden territory. This is not to imply you should avoid filters. I'm just suggesting taking the time to learn how some of these effects work programmatically, under the hood. Starting with the custom invert sketch, here's a variation that creates a smooth gradient between a negative and positive image. I used a 300 × 400 pixel photo (of yours truly engaged in rocket science) for this sketch (see Figure 10-37):

```
// From Neg to Pos
size(300, 400);
background(255);
PImage img = loadImage("research.jpg");
image(img, 0, 0);
loadPixels();

float invertFactor = 255.0;
for (int i=0; i<pixels.length; i++){
```

```
// separate out and invert component color values
float r = abs(red(pixels[i])-invertFactor);
float g = abs(green(pixels[i])-invertFactor);
float b = abs(blue(pixels[i])-invertFactor);
// put pixel back together
pixels[i] = color(r, g, b);

    // each row interval decrements invertFactor
    if (i>0 && i% width==0){
      invertFactor-=(255.0/height);
    }
}
updatePixels();
```

Figure 10-37. From Neg to Pos sketch

Besides showcasing a custom invert filter, this last sketch demonstrated another example of the usefulness of the modulus operator:

```
if (i>0 && i% width==0){
```

By dividing i by the display window width and checking for a 0 remainder, I ensured that the variable invertFactor would only be decremented per each row of pixels, giving me a smooth gradation down the image.

10

PROCESSING: CREATIVE CODING AND COMPUTATIONAL ART

I guess you've done enough under-the-hood gazing. Without further interruption, here are the rest of Processing's filters and blends, shown in Figures 10-38 through 10-42:

```
// THRESHOLD Filter
// filter(THRESHOLD, float threshold level)
// image should be 200 x 200 pixels

size(800, 200);
PImage img = loadImage("moonshadow.jpg");
float thresholdLevel = 1.0;
for (int i=0; i<4; i++){
  image(img, 200*i, 0, 200, 200);
  filter(THRESHOLD, thresholdLevel);
  thresholdLevel-=.25;
}
```

Figure 10-38. THRESHOLD Filter sketch

The THRESHOLD argument converts the image pixels to black or white depending on whether their value is below or above a threshold level. The threshold level is between 0.0 and 1.0. For example, if the level is .5, then pixels whose values are above 255/2 would be turned white, and those below turned black. The second threshold level argument is optional; if omitted, Processing uses .5 as the default value. One final subtle point is that the value of the pixel is determined by the highest component value, not an average of the component values. So the value of color(200, 90, 10) would evaluate to 200, not 100.

```
// GRAY Filter
// filter(GRAY)
// image should be 600 x 450 pixels
size(600, 450);
PImage img = loadImage("changsha2.jpg");
image(img, 0, 0);
filter(GRAY);
```

Figure 10-39. GRAY Filter sketch

The GRAY filter argument should be pretty self-explanatory—colored images are converted to grayscale. There are no additional optional arguments.

```
// POSTERIZE Filter
// filter(POSTERIZE, int colorLevels);
    // image should be 200 x 200 pixels
size(1000, 200);
background(255);
PImage img = loadImage("moonshadow.jpg");
int cols = 5;
int w = width/cols;
int h = height;
int[]vals = {2, 4, 8, 16, 32};
for (int i=0; i<cols; i++){
  image(img, i*w, 0, w, h);
  filter(POSTERIZE, vals[i]);
}
```

10

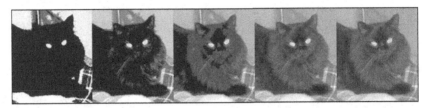

Figure 10-40. POSTERIZE Filter sketch

The POSTERIZE argument converts the number of colors per each of the RGB components to a new level based on a required second-level argument. This argument must be in the range 2 to 255. As of this writing, the POSTERIZE option is not fully stable. While testing the function, I got numerous color values out of range, especially when I utilized a level argument that didn't factor into 256. Hopefully this issue will be resolved by the time you're reading this.

```
// BLUR Filter
// filter(BLUR, int radius);
     // image should be 200 x 200 pixels
size(1000, 200);
PImage img = loadImage("moonshadow.jpg");
int cols = 5;
int w = width/cols;
int h = height;

// cumulative blur
 for (int i=0; i<cols; i++){
   image(img, i*w, 0, w, h);
   filter(BLUR);
 }
```

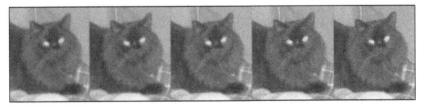

Figure 10-41. BLUR Filter sketch

The BLUR argument generates a Gaussian blur based on the value of a second radius argument passed to filter(BLUR, int radius). If no second argument is included, Processing uses a default value of 1 for the blur radius. In the sketch example, you'll notice that the image (of my cat Moonshadow) is blurred progressively more as you move from right to left. Since no blur radius argument was used, a radius value of 1 was internally set for all five calls within the loop. Since the effect happens to all the pixels in the display window cumulatively, the older images (on the left) get blurred over and over again. When the blur radius is set high, the blurring can be severe. For example, here's a very blurry image of my dog Heidi (please note that this sketch can take some time to render—and of course, no harm came to Heidi during the blurring process):

```
// Severe BLUR Filter
// image should be 600 x 400 pixels
size(600, 400);
background(255);
PImage img = loadImage("heidi.jpg");
image(img, 0, 0);
filter(BLUR, 10);
```

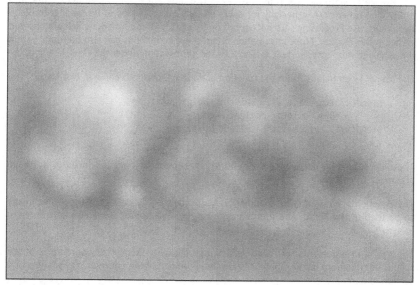

Figure 10-42. Severe BLUR Filter sketch

One final word of caution about the BLUR argument: it takes progressively more time to render as you increase the radius argument, and no exception (compiler error) is thrown for ridiculously large numbers, so be careful.

The final filter mode is OPAQUE, which I won't bother covering as it simply ensures that the alpha component of each of the pixels is at 100 percent.

blend()

Processing's blend() function, similarly to filter(), is chock-full of features. One point of potential confusion to beginning coders (as well as some more experienced folks, including myself at one point) is that there are two blend() commands within Processing. One lives as a PImage method and the other as a display window function; both also work similarly.

One way of keeping the two commands distinct is to consider the display window function blend() as a blend involving a background image. Processing's background() command can take either a color value argument or a PImage argument. If you use an image argument, the image *must* be the same size as the display window.

Here's a sketch that loads an image into the background:

```
/* image needs to be the same size as the display
   window and reside in the sketch's data directory */
size(600, 400);
background(loadImage("heidi.jpg"));
```

The PImage blend() method is used to blend two different PImages together (or one into itself). One other note, especially for users of early beta versions of Processing: to blend two colors, use Processing's blendColor() or lerpColor() commands, which are covered earlier in this chapter. More information about these commands can also be found within the language reference, in the Creating & Reading subsection under the Color heading.

The blend() commands (both the function and PImage method) come in two forms:

```
blend(srcImg, sx1, sy1, swidth, sheight, dx1, ➡
        dy1, dwidth, dheight, mode);
blend(sx1, sy1, swidth, sheight, dx1, dy1, ➡
        dwidth, dheight, mode);
```

The only difference between the two forms is that the first version includes a PImage argument.

The arguments sx1, sy1, swidth, and sheight specify the coordinates of the source image to be used in the blend. The source image can be a section of the image or the entire image.

The next four arguments, dx1, dy1, dwidth, and dheight, specify the coordinates of the final (or destination) image. These values can be the size of the entire display window or a section of it.

In the next two sketch examples, I'll create a simple blend, keeping both the source and destination coordinate values the same as the display window size. The first example uses the blend() function, and the second uses the PImage blend() method. Both sketches use the version of the blend() call that includes a PImage argument, and also include the value DARKEST as the final (mode) argument. I only include one screenshot (see Figure 10-43), as the two sketches have identical output.

```
// blend() Function Example sketch
// background image and PImage should both be 300 x 400 pixels
size(300, 400);
background(loadImage("airport.jpg"));
PImage img = loadImage("towers.jpg");
blend(img, 0, 0, 300, 400, 0, 0, 300, 400, DARKEST);
```

```
// blend() PImage Method sketch
// both PImages should be 300 x 400 pixels
size(300, 400);
PImage img1 = loadImage("airport.jpg");
PImage img2 = loadImage("towers.jpg");
img2.blend(img1, 0, 0, 300, 400, 0, 0, 300, 400, DARKEST);
image(img2, 0, 0);
```

Figure 10-43. Simple blend() sketch

Notice in the first sketch code (the function version of blend()), I didn't need to explicitly call image() to draw the blended image to the screen; while in the second example, which uses the PImage method version of blend(), I did need to call image() to see the blended image.

In the next two sketches, I'll reuse the last blend() function example, changing the source image coordinates in the first example and then the destination image coordinate values in the second (see Figures 10-44 and 10-45):

```
// blend() Function with Altered Source Image Coordinates
// background image and PImage should be 300 x 400 pixels
size(300, 400);
background(loadImage("airport.jpg"));
PImage img = loadImage("towers.jpg");
blend(img, 0, 300, 300, 10, 0, 0, 300, 400, DARKEST);
```

Figure 10-44. blend() Function with Altered Source Image Coordinates
sketch

```
// blend() Function with Altered Destination Image Coordinates
// background image and PImage should be 300 x 400 pixels
size(300, 400);
background(loadImage("airport.jpg"));
PImage img = loadImage("towers.jpg");
blend(img, 0, 0, 300, 400, 0, 200, 300, 200, DARKEST);
```

Figure 10-45. blend() Function with Altered Destination Image Coordinates sketch

In the blend() Function with Altered Source Image Coordinates example, I set the y coordinate of the source image to 300 and the height of the source image to 10. You can think of this as copying a segment (specified by these source coordinates) of the image and then stretching this segment to fit the destination coordinates, which I set to the full size of the display window.

In the second example, I made the source coordinates the size of the display window, but made the destination coordinates only include the bottom half of the display window.

Besides the source and destination coordinates, the blend() method also requires a mode argument. I specified DARKEST in the last examples, but there are a few others as well.

The blend() modes include BLEND, ADD, LIGHTEST, SUBTRACT, and DARKEST. The math behind these modes involves, as you might suspect, bitwise operations. The Processing reference lists the blending expressions as follows:

- BLEND: Linear interpolation of colors: **C = A * factor + B**
- SUBTRACT: Subtractive blending with black clip: **C = max(B − A * factor, 0)**
- ADD: Additive blending with white clip: **C = min(A * factor + B, 255)**
- DARKEST: Only the darkest color succeeds: **C = min(A * factor, B)**
- LIGHTEST: Only the lightest color succeeds: **C = max(A * factor, B)**

463

C is the blended value, and A and B represent the two colors to blend. Processing's min() and max() functions return the lowest and highest argument values, respectively. These functions are useful for clipping out-of-range values. For example, if one of the arguments passed to the SUBTRACT mode is less than 0, the max() function will return the 0 argument. All other in-range values will be returned. The "factor" specified in the preceding expressions is based on the alpha component of the source pixel, which is represented by the first 8 bits (from the left) of the 32-bit integer representing the pixel color. These leftmost bits are also referred to as the **highest byte**. Fortunately, you don't have to worry about the internal implementation to use the blend() function.

Next are examples using SUBTRACT mode (shown in Figures 10-46, 10-47, and 10-48). I'll continue to use the same airport.jpg and towers.jpg images as in the preceding DARKEST examples.

```
size(300, 400);
background(loadImage("airport.jpg"));
PImage img = loadImage("towers.jpg");
blend(img, 0, 0, 300, 400, 0, 0, 300, 400, SUBTRACT);
```

Figure 10-46. blend() Function Using SUBTRACT Argument sketch

The next sketch utilizes some for loops to dynamically change the destination coordinates, creating an interesting patterned abstraction:

```
size(300, 400);
background(loadImage("airport.jpg"));
PImage img = loadImage("towers.jpg");
int w = width/6;
int h = height/8;

for (int i=0; i<width; i+=w){
  for (int j=0; j<height; j+=h){
    blend(img, 0, 0, width, height, i, j, w, h, SUBTRACT);
  }
}
```

Figure 10-47. blend() Function Using SUBTRACT Argument in Loops sketch

The next sketch builds upon the last, adding random source coordinates:

```
/* blend() Function Using SUBTRACT
   with Random Source Coodinates */
size(300, 400);
background(loadImage("airport.jpg"));
PImage img = loadImage("towers.jpg");
int w = width/12;
int h = height/16;

for (int i=0; i<width; i+=w){
  for (int j=0; j<height; j+=h){
    // arguments need to be integers
    int srcX = int(random(width-w));
    int srcY = int(random(height-h));
    int srcW = int(random(w));
    int srcH = int(random(h));
    blend(img, srcX, srcY, srcW, srcH, i, j, w, h, SUBTRACT);
  }
}
```

Figure 10-48. blend() Function Using SUBTRACT with Random Source Coordinates sketch

In the last example, I used Processing's random() function to vary the size of the source segments. Notice that when the segments were very small they became highly pixilated when blown up in the destination image.

The other blend modes work similarly to SUBTRACT; just substitute a different mode for SUBTRACT in the blend() call in the last example to see the difference.

Saving a file

Here's one last blend() example (shown in Figure 10-49) using the LIGHTEST mode. I structured this sketch using the PImage blend() method form and reversed the order of the two images. I also threw in Processing's cool save() function.

```
/* PImage blend() Method LIGHTEST Mode
--Random Source Coodinates & save() */
size(300, 400);
PImage img1 = loadImage("towers.jpg");
PImage img2 = loadImage("airport.jpg");
int w = width/24;
int h = height/32;

for (int i=0; i<width; i+=w){
  for (int j=0; j<height; j+=h){
    // arguments need to be integers
    int srcX = int(random(width-w));
    int srcY = int(random(height-h));
    int srcW = int(random(w));
    int srcH = int(random(h));
    img1.blend(img2, srcX, srcY, srcW, srcH, i, j, w, h, LIGHTEST);
  }
}
image(img1, 0, 0);
save("tower_mosaic.tif");
```

10

The save() function saves an image of the display window to the current sketch folder. You can access the current sketch folder by selecting Show sketch folder from the Sketch menu. When naming the String argument in the save("myString.tif") call, you can specify a TIF, TGA, JPG, or PNG file. If you don't specify any extension, the image will be saved as a TIF, with .tif appended to the end of the String argument. Processing also has a variation of this function, called saveFrame(), that allows you to save multiple frames, which I'll look at next chapter. One note of caution: neither save() nor saveFrame() will work in sketches running within the browser environment.

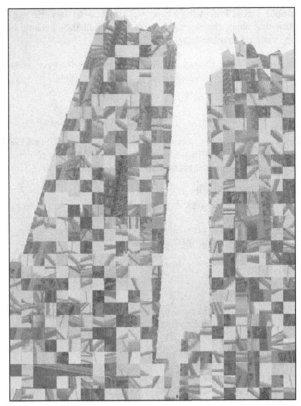

Figure 10-49. PImage blend() Method LIGHTEST Mode—Random Source Coodinates & save() sketch

An object-oriented approach

Before concluding the chapter, I'd like to apply an OOP approach to a color/imaging example (shown in Figure 10-50) that extends some of the OOP concepts looked at in the last two chapters. In Chapter 9, you used OOP to create a little neighborhood of houses composed of a number of component classes. The classes shared certain characteristics and had a number of redundant instance variables and methods. For example, the Door, Window, Roof, and House classes all had x, y, width, and height properties, as well as their own drawing methods. In programming, you usually try to avoid creating redundant elements. OOP includes some advanced concepts and language structures for minimizing redundancy and creating efficient, modular, and hopefully reusable classes. One of these key concepts is called inheritance, which I introduced in Chapter 8.

Inheritance

In OOP, **inheritance** describes the ability of one class to inherit, or extend, the attributes and capabilities of another class. For example, if I create a class called Box, I could give it attributes such as height, width, depth, x, y, color, and so forth. It might also have methods to get and set these properties, and perhaps a create() method. I could then use this Box class as the base for another class or even a set of classes. A house, a cage, and a suitcase are all radically different objects, yet they each rely on a box structure. Instead of each of these classes defining their own height, width, depth, x, y, and color properties, they could inherit these from the Box class.

In Processing and Java, when a class inherits form another class, the term *extends* is used to describe the relationship of one class inheriting from another. In addition, the term *superclass* is used to describe the class being extended from, and *subclass* is used to describe the class that extends the superclass. In the box example, Box would be the superclass and House, Cage, and Suitcase would each be subclasses of Box; it is also said that each of these subclasses extends the Box class. When a class extends a class, besides having access to the properties and methods in the superclass, the subclass can add its own additional properties and methods that would be unique to the class. For example, the House class, besides having the general properties of a box, might also have a roof property, a chimney property, and so on. There are some additional subtle and advanced concepts involved in inheritance, which I'll look at in the next few chapters. However, for now, I've created a sketch that illustrates basic inheritance. The sketch reuses the linear and radial gradient examples from earlier in the chapter, with some minor modifications.

Gradient class

The first class I designed for this example was a Gradient class. This class will be the base class for a LinearGradient class and also a RadialGradient class. In other words, the Gradient class will be the superclass, and the LinearGradient and RadialGradient subclasses will extend the Gradient class. In addition, in thinking about these class relationships, I decided that I didn't want people to be able to directly use the Gradient class (i.e., instantiate the class), but rather *only* use it as a superclass for building other types of custom gradients. Java has a keyword (abstract) that is used to enforce this condition (which Processing has access to) that I have included in the Gradient class. Here's the class (please note that this class, as well as the individual subclasses I'll look at shortly, are not intended to be run independently):

```
abstract class Gradient {

  // constants
  // these can't be changed
  final static int AXIS_VERTICAL = 0;
  final static int AXIS_HORIZONTAL = 1;

  // instance fields with default values
  // these can be changed
  color c1 = color(255);
  color c2 = color(0);
  Rectangle bounds  = new Rectangle(0, 0, width, height);
```

10

469

```
// abstract method, to be implmented by subclasses
abstract void create();

/* concrete methods*/
//getter/setters
  void setColor1(color c1){
    this.c1 = c1;
  }
  color getColor1(){
    return c1;
  }
  void setColor2(color c2){
    this.c2 = c2;
  }
  color getColor2(){
    return c2;
  }
  void setBounds(Rectangle Bounds){
    this.bounds = bounds;
  }
  Rectangle getBounds(){
    return bounds;
  }
}
```

Abstract class declaration

Notice that I began the class with the Java keyword abstract. By preceding a class declaration with abstract, you enforce the rule that the class cannot be instantiated. Therefore,
the call new Gradient() will generate a compiler error. I designed the Gradient class to be
used exclusively as a base class to extend when building custom gradients. To read what
Sun has to say about abstract classes, check out http://java.sun.com/docs/books/
tutorial/java/java00/abstract.html.

Class constants

Next, I declared two constants:

```
final static int AXIS_VERTICAL = 0;
final static int AXIS_HORIZONTAL = 1;
```

Again, I borrowed some Java modifiers (final and static) to enforce good coding practice. Constants shouldn't be changed, and the use of the final keyword ensures that the
compiler enforces this rule. Once a constant has an initial value, you'll generate a compile
error if you try to assign another value to it. Typically, constants are assigned integer
values, as I did in the Gradient class.

Declaring properties with the static keyword makes their values directly accessible using
the class name, without the use of an object. For example, to access the value of

AXIS_VERTICAL from *outside* the Gradient class (or its subclasses), you'd write Gradient.AXIS_VERTICAL; to access the value from within Gradient (or its subclass), you can just use AXIS_VERTICAL. You can use/access static properties from within any class without the need to instantiate an object of the class. Conversely, instance properties require an object to be used. Another way to think about the distinction between static and instance properties is that there is only ever a single value for any static property, but each object has its own copy of any instance properties.

Instance properties

Below the constants, I declared some instance properties. As I just discussed, these properties can only be accessed by an object of the class (or in this case, objects of the subclasses). For example, if you create a RadialGradient class and then instantiate an object using the syntax RadialGradient rg = new RadialGradient ();, you could access the object's c1 property with the syntax rg.c1 or rg.getColor1().

The instance property Rectangle r uses Java's Rectangle class. This class is really handy for holding the bounds of something. Instantiating an object of the Rectangle class takes four arguments, defining x, y, width, and height. These public properties can then be accessed directly, as in r.x, r.y, r.width, and r.height (assuming the Rectangle object is named r).

Abstract method

Below the instance properties is a strange-looking method declaration:

```
abstract void create();
```

This is an abstract method, which doesn't include any actual implementation of the method; notice that curly braces aren't even included. Abstract methods are used to enforce a rule between the abstract superclass and any subclasses: a class that extends an abstract class must implement any abstract methods within the superclass (or itself be declared an abstract class). This means that any class that extends the Gradient class must include a create() method—with the curly braces and preferably some gradient-creating code between them. You are not required to include an abstract method in an abstract class; you can just use standard implemented methods (also known as concrete methods) like the getter/setter methods included below the abstract create() method. Subclasses have no obligation to reimplement any concrete methods within the abstract superclass.

In the Gradient class, it made sense to make the create() method abstract, since the code to create each gradient (linear or radial, in this case) will be radically different. In addition, by forcing subclasses of the Gradient class to implement their own create() method, you enforce a common interface—which is a good thing. Imagine if some company took your Gradient class and extended it to create a library of 1,000 specialized Gradient subclasses (and paid you gobs of money, of course). Since your superclass requires any subclasses to implement the create() method, a user of the subclasses would have immediate insight into how to draw any of the 1,000 custom gradients. The complicated plotting algorithms for each gradient would be encapsulated inside the custom implemented create() methods in each subclass—all happily hidden from the user.

10

getters/setters

Finishing the class are getter and setter methods for the instance properties. You'll learn more about the benefit of getters and setters in Chapter 14, when I show you how to work in Java mode. For now, you can access instance properties directly, as in rg.c1 (assuming rg is the name of the gradient object), or using the method rg.getColor1().

LinearGradient class

```
class LinearGradient extends Gradient {
  int axis;

  //default constructor
  LinearGradient() {
    axis = AXIS_VERTICAL;
  }

  //constructor
  LinearGradient(color c1, color c2) {
    this.c1 = c1;
    this.c2 = c2;
    axis = AXIS_VERTICAL;
  }

  //constructor
  LinearGradient(color c1, color c2, Rectangle bounds) {
    this.c1 = c1;
    this.c2 = c2;
    this.bounds = bounds;
    axis = AXIS_VERTICAL;
  }

  //constructor
  LinearGradient(color c1, color c2, Rectangle bounds, int axis) {
    this.c1 = c1;
    this.c2 = c2;
    this.bounds = bounds;
    this.axis = axis;
  }

  // required: implemented create method
  void create(){
    // calculate differences between color components
    float deltaR = red(c2)-red(c1);
    float deltaG = green(c2)-green(c1);
    float deltaB = blue(c2)-blue(c1);
```

```
    // y axis
    if(axis == AXIS_VERTICAL){
      for (int i=bounds.x; i<=(bounds.x+bounds.width); i++){
        for (int j=bounds.y; j<=(bounds.y+bounds.height); j++){
          color c = color( ➥
              (red(c1)+(j-bounds.y)*(deltaR/bounds.height)), ➥
              (green(c1)+(j-bounds.y)*(deltaG/bounds.height)), ➥
              (blue(c1)+(j-bounds.y)*(deltaB/bounds.height)) );
          set(i, j, c);
        }
      }
    }
    // x axis
    else {
      for (int i=bounds.y; i<=(bounds.y+bounds.height); i++){
        for (int j=bounds.x; j<=(bounds.x+bounds.width); j++){
          color c = color( ➥
              (red(c1)+(j-bounds.x)*(deltaR/bounds.width)), ➥
              (green(c1)+(j-bounds.x)*(deltaG/bounds.width)), ➥
              (blue(c1)+(j-bounds.x)*(deltaB/bounds.width)) );
          set(j, i, c);
        }
      }
    }
  }

  void setAxis(int axis){
    this.axis = axis;
  }

  int getAxis(){
    return axis;
  }
}
```

Notice the extends keyword in the LinearGradient class declaration. As I've been discussing, when the Gradient class is extended, LinearGradient becomes a subclass of Gradient and has access to its properties and methods. Remember that the relationship between a superclass and a subclass is relative. If another class were to eventually extend the LinearGradient class, then that class would become a subclass to LinearGradient. LinearGradient would become its superclass, even though it's still the subclass to Gradient. Every class in Processing and Java begins life as a subclass, as there is an Object class that is the über-superclass for all other classes. Here's some info on Java's Object class: http://java.sun.com/j2se/1.4.2/docs/api/java/lang/Object.html.

I included four constructors in the LinearGradient class, giving users multiple ways to instantiate linear gradients. Notice that three of the four constructors utilize the this keyword in assigning the parameters to the instance properties of the same name. Notice that these instance properties are declared in the Gradient superclass, not directly within the

LinearGradient subclass. The subclass can utilize the (accessible) properties and methods in the superclass, and they can be referred to directly, as if they were declared directly within the subclass; any subclass of Gradient would have this capability. You can see how building a class library using inheritance can create efficiencies and ultimately speed development—not to mention create more consistency for the user.

The create() method is the abstract method inherited from Gradient that needs to be implemented. Again, *implementing* in this case means creating the method's code block (the areas between and including the curly braces). The create() method is where the custom gradients are actually created.

Finally, the LinearGradient class includes setAxis() and getAxis() methods for specifying which axis to draw the gradient across. I could have placed these two methods within the Gradient superclass, but it was more appropriate to put them in the LinearGradient subclass, as some gradients don't utilize a dominant axis (e.g., radial gradients)—which illustrates that although subclasses share certain features (inherited from their common superclass), they may (and usually do) contain their own unique properties and methods as well.

RadialGradient class

```
class RadialGradient extends Gradient {

  //default constructor
  RadialGradient() {
    super();
  }

  //constructor
  RadialGradient(color c1, color c2) {
    this.c1 = c1;
    this.c2 = c2;
  }

  //constructor
  RadialGradient(color c1, color c2, Rectangle bounds) {
    this.c1 = c1;
    this.c2 = c2;
    this.bounds = bounds;
  }

  // required: implemented create method
  void create(){
    float px = 0, py = 0, angle = 0;
    float radius1 = bounds.width/2;
    float radius2 = bounds.height/2;
    float centerX = bounds.x+radius1;
    float centerY = bounds.y+radius2;
    float radiusMax = max(radius1, radius2);
```

```
      // calculate differences between color components
      float deltaR = red(c2)-red(c1);
      float deltaG = green(c2)-green(c1);
      float deltaB = blue(c2)-blue(c1);
      // gapFiller ensures there are no holes in gradient
      float gapFiller = 8.0;

      for (int i=0; i<radiusMax; i++){
        for (float j=0; j<360; j+=1.0/gapFiller){
          if (radius1>radius2){
            px = centerX+cos(radians(angle))*i;
            py = centerY+sin(radians(angle))*(i-(radius1-radius2));
          }
          else {
            px = centerX+cos(radians(angle))*(i-(radius2-radius1));
            py = centerY+sin(radians(angle))*i;
          }
          angle+=1.0/gapFiller;
          color c = color( ➥
              (red(c1)+(i)*(deltaR/radiusMax)), ➥
              (green(c1)+(i)*(deltaG/radiusMax)), ➥
              (blue(c1)+(i)*(deltaB/radiusMax)) );
          set(int(px), int(py), c);
        }
      }
    }
  }
```

This class follows the structure of the LinearGradient class very closely. However, the RadialGradient class didn't require any additional properties/methods of its own, which made the constructor calls a bit simpler than LinearGradient's. The create() function is a bit more complex, though—but you've looked at code like this before; the gradient-creation code pretty much follows the radial gradient example from earlier in the chapter.

One extra feature I added in this version of the code is the ability to create asymmetrical elliptical gradients, with different values for width and height. I also used Processing's max(val1, val2) function, which returns the largest argument value. Since it's now possible to create a very asymmetrical ellipse, I wanted to make the largest dimension of the ellipse control the size of the gradient and for loop limits. You can try changing the max to min, which returns the smaller of the two argument values, to see what happens. Finally, here's the calling PDE main code that generates some gradients using the three classes:

```
/*
Inheritance Example
linear and radial gradients
January 25, 2006
NOTE: This sketch takes some time to render.
REQUIRED: Gradient class, LinearGradient class and
RadialGradient class.
*/
```

10

```
void setup(){
  size(400, 400);

  // fill display window with default black and white
  // linear gradient background
  LinearGradient lg = new LinearGradient();
  lg.create();

  //create 4 linear Gradients
  color c1 = color(255, 0, 0);
  color c2 = color(0, 255, 0);

  color c3 = color(255, 255, 0);
  color c4 = color(180, 0, 255);

  color c5 = color(255, 127, 0);
  color c6 = color(0, 0, 255);

  color c7 = color(0, 255, 255);
  color c8 = color(255, 180, 0);

  Rectangle r1 = new Rectangle(50, 50, 150, 150);
  Rectangle r2 = new Rectangle(200, 50, 150, 150);
  Rectangle r3 = new Rectangle(50, 200, 150, 150);
  Rectangle r4 = new Rectangle(200, 200, 150, 150);

  LinearGradient lg1 = new LinearGradient(c1, c2, r1, ➥
          Gradient.AXIS_HORIZONTAL);
  lg1.create();
  LinearGradient lg2 = new LinearGradient(c3, c4, r2);
  lg2.create();
  LinearGradient lg3 = new LinearGradient(c5, c6, r3);
  lg3.create();
  LinearGradient lg4 = new LinearGradient(c7, c8, r4, ➥
          Gradient.AXIS_HORIZONTAL);
  lg4.create();

  //create 4 radial Gradients
  c1 = color(0, 150, 200);
  c2 = color(200, 200, 100);

  c3 = color(190, 225, 290);
  c4 = color(90, 45, 20);

  c5 = color(195, 195, 90);
  c6 = color(30, 10, 70);
```

```
    c7 = color(0);
    c8 = color(255);

    r1 = new Rectangle(60, 60, 130, 130);
    r2 = new Rectangle(225, 60, 100, 130);
    r3 = new Rectangle(60, 225, 130, 100);
    r4 = new Rectangle(210, 210, 130, 130);

    RadialGradient rg1 = new RadialGradient(c1, c2, r1);
    rg1.create();
    RadialGradient rg2 = new RadialGradient(c3, c4, r2);
    rg2.create();
    RadialGradient rg3 = new RadialGradient(c5, c6, r3);
    rg3.create();
    RadialGradient rg4 = new RadialGradient(c7, c8, r4);
    rg4.create();
}
```

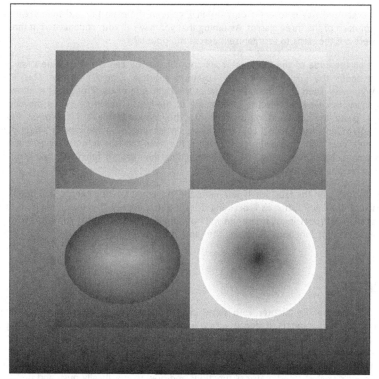

Figure 10-50. Inheritance Example (linear and radial gradients) sketch

The calling PDE code should be old hat by now. I simply created a bunch of color and Rectangle objects and passed them to the respective gradient constructors. Both the LinearGradient and RadialGradient default constructors fill the entire screen with a black-and-white linear or radial gradient, respectively. I used the former to create a background gradient. Notice the Gradient.AXIS_HORIZONTAL argument in two of the LinearGradient instantiation calls. This is a standard use of a constant. I used the class name to preface the constant name, as you'll remember that the constant was declared as a static property in the Gradient class.

In running this example, you have two options: you can type all the code (the three classes and the main PDE code just shown) into Processing, or you can download the complete code from www.friendsofed.com/downloads.

Organizing classes using multiple tabs

Once you've got all the code, there are two ways you can organize it in Processing. The first and simplest way is to add all the code (including the classes) directly into the main (leftmost) tab. This is the approach you've been using thus far in the book. A better and more organized way is to enter only the PDE code in the main tab and then create new tabs for each of the three classes. Assuming that you have all your code pasted in the main tab, here are the steps to reorganize it across multiple tabs.

Select all the code of the Gradient class and cut it—you can either use the Copy command under the Edit menu or the common shortcut Cmd+C (on the Mac)/Ctrl+C (on Windows). Then click the tabs arrow at the right side of the Processing window, and select New tab. Give the file the same name of the class (Gradient). When the new tab opens, paste the Gradient class code into the window. Repeat this process for the LinearGradient and RadialGradient classes. When you have the classes safely pasted into their own tabs, delete the class code in the main tab (the leftmost one), but make sure you keep the remaining PDE code (including the setup() function). You should be able to run the sketch now.

One final note on the tabs: when you name the individual tab documents, you don't need to include the .pde suffix, as Processing does it automatically. If you do include it, that's OK as well, as Processing is smart and will not append a second suffix. You can also create separate tabs for functions, following the same procedure I just outlined.

Summary

This has been a big chapter with some challenging—but also hopefully interesting—information and snippets. It began with a look at basic color theory, which you applied using Processing's built-in color capabilities, including selecting between color models and working with Processing's color data type. I discussed the Java graphics context and its connection to how painting occurs in Processing and Java, and I briefly discussed Processing's sophisticated matrices functions and how to specifically push and pop translations, as well as reset a matrix with the identity matrix.

In the "Imaging" section, you delved a little deeper, looking at Processing's color component functions, which I used to show how to generate a series of pixel-based gradients. I discussed speed issues when processing hundreds of thousands of pixels, and I looked at a lower-level approach to increasing performance, using bitwise operations. I also discussed the problem or challenge of managing potential rounding errors when moving between floats and ints, and how subtle changes such as these can have dramatic effects. Using Processing's loadPixels(), updatePixels(), and pixels[] functions, I discussed approaches for writing and transforming pixel data. I compared the somewhat confusing differences between using the display window functions, based on the pixesl[] array, and using Processing's PImage data type, with its own properties and methods, including another pixels[] array property.

Processing's blend and filter capabilities are extensive, and you looked in detail at each, at times going below the hood and even re-creating your own imaging effects, using both Processing functions and bitwise operations. Finally, I extended the discussion on OOP with an inheritance example, generating a simple framework for creating gradients.

In the next chapter, you'll be revisiting many of the topics covered in the book thus far, as I introduce motion into the sketches. In addition, you'll explore interesting and fun approaches to simulating organic motion and physics. And you'll also continue your exploration of OOP.

10

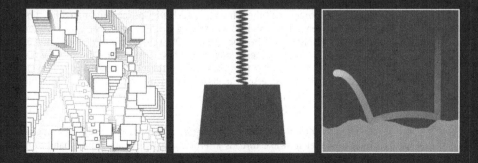

Let the fun begin! I suspect many of you have been waiting patiently (or not so patiently) for this chapter. It took a certain restraint on my part to not start flying pixels around the screen back in Chapter 1. Animation and motion design is usually what gets my students hooked on coding—and even to embrace trigonometry. This chapter, we'll explore all kinds of neat motion (including some trig), from deflecting to bouncing to easing to springing. You'll even create an asteroid shower and learn how to code all sorts of interesting collisions.

Before we dive right into the code, though, I want to discuss very briefly how computer animation works in general, and also some different strategies employed to implement it.

Animation basics

A computer monitor is an animation machine, continuously refreshing the pixels on the screen at the monitor's refresh rate. Obviously, this is not terribly engaging animation, but the fact that animation can happen in front of your eyes and be wholly undetectable is significant. Our brains are wired this way as well, as we perceive a persistent unflickering visual field, in spite of the fact that our eyes are continuously receiving new data. In animation, we exploit this phenomenon by moving data in front of the viewer's eyes at certain rates, tricking the brain into seeing smooth, continuous motion. To move this data, the computer needs to start a process that changes pixel color values over time. From a computer animator's standpoint, this could simply include dragging a shape to two different places on the screen using some timeline interface, such as found in applications like Flash, Director, Final Cut Pro, After Effects, and LightWave. Often, these high-end products employ a keyframing model, where the user sets the beginning keyframe and ending keyframe of a simple animation, and the computer generates the in-between frames. What these cool, very high-level applications don't reveal is how the actual time sequencing is handled internally by the computer—usually you just hit a play button.

Computers with a single processor execute a single instruction at a time, but very quickly (over a billion times per second). However, in a multitasking environment like we're all used to working in, we need to do more than one thing at a time. For example, I may be running five programs at the same time, each with certain automated functions occurring behind the scenes. I may also set a rendering in a 3D program and work on something else while it's completing in the background. Obviously, I wouldn't want all these different processes to be put in a line, or queue, and have to wait for each to be completed before the next task begins. Instead, the operating system splits the executing commands up so that the individual processes can be weaved together, sharing the available processing time. Since the computer can do so many things in a second, we perceive simultaneous processing.

We often refer to these individual processes as **threads**. Normally, we won't need to worry about low-level stuff like threads in Processing, as the application handles it behind the scenes. However, it's helpful to have a little understanding of how threads work, especially since threads are critical for animation.

Working in Java, creating even the simplest animation is a little complicated, as you need to explicitly create a separate thread. In contrast, animation in Processing couldn't be simpler. To illustrate this difference, I've coded a simple animation using Java, followed by the same animation using Processing's draw() function (which encapsulates the thread creation process for us). The Java version is written to be run within Processing.

```
// Animation in Java using a thread
// This code should run ok in Processing
void setup(){
  size(400, 400);
  new SimpleAnimation();
}
class SimpleAnimation implements Runnable{
  int x, xspd = 3;
  //constructor
  SimpleAnimation(){
    Thread t = new Thread(this);
    t.start();
  }
  void run() {
    while (x<width-10) {
      background(255);
      rect(x, height/2, 10, 10);
      x+=xspd;
      repaint();
      try {
        Thread.sleep(30);
      }
      catch (InterruptedException e){
      }
    }
  }
}
```

The following code shows the same animation using only Processing:

```
// Animation the Processing way
// using Processing's draw() structure
int x, xspd = 3;
void setup(){
  size(400, 400);
  frameRate(30);
}

void draw(){
  background(255);
  rect(x, height/2, 10, 10);
  x+=xspd;
}
```

11

In the previous Java example, notice that I explicitly instantiate a Thread object:

```
Thread t = new Thread(this);
```

A few lines later, in the run() method, notice the following block:

```
try {
        Thread.sleep(30);
     }
     catch (InterruptedException e){
}
```

The run() method continuously executes, which is where the drawing happens, and the Thread.sleep(30) call adds a delay between each execution (or frame); the larger the delay value, the slower the animation. Finally, I also needed to call the command repaint(), which forces the screen to be updated each frame—allowing you to see the animation. Whew! That's a lot to deal with. Fortunately, you don't need to worry about most of this stuff in Processing.

In the Processing example, notice the draw() function. This Processing function encapsulates most of the annoying stuff involved in creating animations with threads in the Java example. Simply including the draw() function in your sketch causes a thread to begin running (under the hood).

In the last two examples, the actual animation involved a rectangle moving across the screen. If it wasn't obvious, the variable x was incremented by xspd each frame, and then the rectangle was drawn with the updated x value. In a sense, I simply redrew the rectangle over and over again, at a different x position. The reason you don't see all the previous drawn rectangles is because of the call background(255); at the top of the draw() function. This call fills the screen with white between each frame, painting over the previous rectangle. This repainting of the background between draw frames is what gives the illusion that a single rectangle is moving across the screen. Try commenting out background(255); in the last sketch and rerunning it (see Figure 11-1).

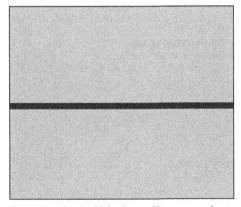

Figure 11-1. Sketch with background() commented out

You can actually use this painting effect to generate an image over time. In the next example, 100 rectangles move across the screen with varying positions, sizes, and colors (shown in Figure 11-2):

```
// Painting Stripes
int x;
float speedX = 3.0;
int shapes = 100;
float[]y = new float[shapes];
float[]w = new float[shapes];
float[]h = new float[shapes];
color[]colors = new color[shapes];
void setup(){
  size(400, 400);
  frameRate(30);
  noStroke();
  // fill arrays will random values
  for (int i=0; i<shapes; i++){
    y[i]=random(height);
    w[i]=random(15)+2;
    h[i]=w[i];
    colors[i]=color(random(255), random(255), random(255));
  }
}

void draw(){
  for (int i=0; i<shapes; i++){
    fill(colors[i]);
    rect(x, y[i], w[i], h[i]);
  }
  x+=speedX;
}
```

Figure 11-2. Painting Stripes sketch

485

One of the nice things about waiting until Chapter 11 to cover motion is that I've had time to properly introduce and reinforce basic coding principles and structures, allowing you to focus on more creative applications using these structures. Thus, I'm going to assume you understand the code in the last example. If, however, the array structures still seem confusing, I recommend a quick review of the section on arrays, in Chapter 3. I can improve this last sketch by alternating the y position of the rectangles over time and using variable speed (shown in Figure 11-3):

```
// Painting Stripes II
int shapes = 200;
float[]speedX = new float[shapes];
float[]speedY = new float[shapes];
float[]x = new float[shapes];
float[]y = new float[shapes];
float[]w = new float[shapes];
float[]h = new float[shapes];
color[]colors = new color[shapes];
void setup(){
  size(400, 400);
  frameRate(30);
  noStroke();
  // fill arrays will random values
  for (int i=0; i<shapes; i++){
    x[i]=0;
    y[i]=random(height);
    w[i]=random(2, 10);
    h[i]=w[i];
    colors[i]=color(random(255), random(255), random(255));
    speedX[i] = random(5, 10);
    speedY[i] = random(-2, 2);
  }
}

void draw(){
  for (int i=0; i<shapes; i++){
    fill(colors[i]);
    rect(x[i], y[i], w[i], h[i]);
    x[i]+=speedX[i];
    y[i]+=speedY[i];
  }
}
```

This sketch may look a little complicated because of all the arrays, but it works similarly to the previous example. One issue that often confuses my students is how and when for loops render. This is also a frequent question on the Processing discussion board. Screen redraws do not update as the for loop is churning. Rather, the screen update occurs after the for loop completes all its cycles. In the last example, the entire draw() function executes approximately 30 times per second. This rate is also commonly referred to as **frames per second**. Each frame, the entire for loop runs. When the for loop exits, the screen updates.

Figure 11-3. Painting Stripes II sketch

Simple collision detection

In the last example, when the rectangles pass the edge of the display window, they don't stop. To improve the sketch, I could add simple boundary collision detection and also a timeout function. Before I add collision detection for all the rectangles in the last example, though, let's first look at collision detection with a single moving rectangle:

```
// Single rect with boundary collision detection
float speedX, speedY;
float x, y, w, h;

void setup(){
  size(400, 400);
  x=width/2;
  y=height/2;
  w=70;
  h=w;
  speedX = 2;
  speedY = 1;
}

void draw(){
  background(255);
  rect(x, y, w, h);
```

11

```
      x+=speedX;
      y+=speedY;

      // Check display window edge collisions
      if (x > width-w){
        x = width-w;
        speedX*=-1;
      }
      else if (x < 0){
        x = 0;
        speedX*=-1;
      }
      else if (y > height-h){
        y = height-h;
        speedY*=-1;
      }
      else if (y < 0){
        y  = 0;
        speedY*=-1;
      }
    }
```

If you run the sketch, you should see a single rectangle bouncing off the four boundaries of the display window. If it isn't obvious, the key block of code that makes the rectangle bounce off the walls is the following:

```
  // Check display window edge collisions
  if (x > width-w){
    x = width-w;
    speedX*=-1;
  }
  else if (x < 0){
    x = 0;
    speedX*=-1;
  }
  else if (y > height-h){
    y = height-h;
    speedY*=-1;
  }
  else if (y < 0){
    y  = 0;
    speedY*=-1;
  }
```

Each of the four if statements controls detection on one of the display window boundaries (right, left, bottom, and top). Notice that the conditionals check if the rectangle is either greater than (>) or less than (<) the boundary, but not equal to (==) the boundary—in other words, they check whether the rectangle has actually pushed through the boundary. This is necessary because the rate at which the computer checks for the collision and the distance the rectangle moves are not perfectly synchronized; the rectangle may very well be past the boundary when the collision check occurs. By checking for collision past the boundary, we're ensured of (eventually) catching it. However, this solution is not without some problems.

Aesthetically, the rectangle may appear to go through the wall before bouncing off it. A worse problem is that if the rectangle goes too far past the edge of the window, the detection can actually catch it more than one time—causing it to get stuck (and sometimes appear to shake) on the boundary. The quick fix for these problems is to immediately place the rectangle against the display window wall after the detection, as I did in the example code. Technically, this fix is not precisely accurate, but generally good enough for "creative" coding purposes. For the more ambitious (or precise) reader, there is a more complex (and accurate) way of fixing this overlap problem, by analyzing an object's path over time and finding precisely when it makes initial contact with the boundary. Implementing such an approach is beyond this book, but most (computer science–oriented) computer graphics texts will cover this approach.

Finally, after the collision has been detected and the rectangle has been put neatly back against the display window edge, I simply reverse the sign of the speed variable by multiplying it by –1. If it's been a while since math class, remember that a negative multiplied by another negative becomes a positive (and of course a negative times a positive equals a negative).

Next, I'll just add the collision detection and a timeout feature to the previous multi-rectangle example. I'll also add a background(255) call so that we can see the discrete rectangles bouncing around (shown in Figure 11-4):

```
// Collision Detection and Timeout
int shapes = 200;
float[]speedX = new float[shapes];
float[]speedY = new float[shapes];
float[]x = new float[shapes];
float[]y = new float[shapes];
float[]w = new float[shapes];
float[]h = new float[shapes];
color[]colors = new color[shapes];
int timeLimit = 15;

void setup(){
  size(400, 400);
  frameRate(30);
  noStroke();
  // fill arrays will random values
  for (int i=0; i<shapes; i++){
    x[i]=width/2;
    y[i]=height/2;
    w[i]=random(2, 12);
    h[i]=w[i];
    colors[i]=color(random(255), random(255), random(255));
```

11

```
      speedX[i] = random(-5, 5);
      speedY[i] = random(-2, 2);
    }
  }

void draw(){
  background(255);
  for (int i=0; i<shapes; i++){
    fill(colors[i]);
    rect(x[i], y[i], w[i], h[i]);
    x[i]+=speedX[i];
    y[i]+=speedY[i];

    // check display window edge collisions
    if (x[i] > width-w[i]){
      x[i] = width-w[i];
      speedX[i]*=-1;
    }
    else if (x[i] < 0){
      x[i] = 0;
      speedX[i]*=-1;
    }
    else if (y[i] > height-h[i]){
      y[i] = height-h[i];
      speedY[i]*=-1;
    }
    else if (y[i] < 0){
      y[i] = 0;
      speedY[i]*=-1;
    }
  }

  // stop draw when timelimit reached
  if (millis() >= timeLimit*1000){
    noLoop();
  }
}
```

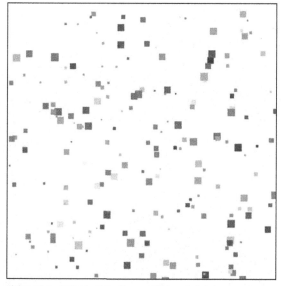

Figure 11-4. Collision Detection and Timeout sketch

Accessing time

The last sketch combined stuff you've looked at before. The collision detection block worked identically to the previous single-object example, only of course using arrays and a for loop. I did throw in two new function calls: millis() and noLoop().

millis() returns the number of milliseconds that have elapsed since the sketch began running. In addition to returning milliseconds, Processing can also communicate with your computer's internal clock, accessing the current time with the six functions second(), minute(), hour(), day(), month(), and year().

Processing's noLoop() function immediately stops the draw() structure from looping. There is also a companion loop() call that begins the draw() loop again. In the example, I compared the total elapsed milliseconds with a user-defined variable, timeLimit, allowing the draw() function to eventually stop after a certain amount of time had elapsed.

Adding some simple fading

The final modification I'll make to the multirectangle sketch is the addition of a fade to the white background, creating the illusion of some blur trails for the rectangles (shown in Figure 11-5). The code should remain the same as in the last sketch, with the exception of the replacement of the first line in the draw() function:

```
background(255);
```

491

with the following two lines:

```
fill(255, 40);
rect(0, 0, width, height);
```

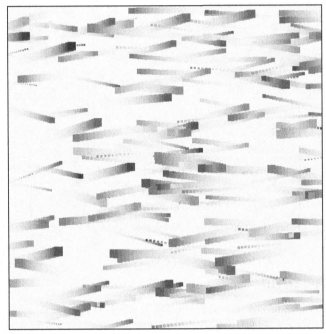

Figure 11-5. Simple Fading sketch

The new rect() call does the same thing as background() (repainting the display window), only using an alpha setting (below 255) specified for the background color. To increase the persistence of the trails, try decreasing the alpha value.

Fun with physics

Simulating physics is fun! I realize that this is a pretty nerdy thing to say. But there is something captivating about seeing a bunch of polygons moving in a naturalistic way. Think about the moving grass and flora in *Shrek*, the ocean in *The Perfect Storm*, or the fur in *Monsters, Inc.*—and of course don't forget Gollum in *The Lord of the Rings*. Regrettably, we won't begin our exploration of physics simulating reactive fur, tidal waves, or a demented self-loathing creature. Instead, we'll add some gravity to our single bouncing rectangle example (shown in Figure 11-6):

```
// Acceleration with Gravity
float speedX, speedY;
float x, y, w, h;
// acceleration force
float gravity;

void setup(){
  size(400, 400);
  x=width/2;
  w=20;
  h=w;
  fill(0);
  speedX = 4;
  // set acceleration force
  gravity = .5;
}

void draw(){
  fill(255, 60);
  rect(0, 0, width, height);

  fill(0);
  rect(x, y, w, h);
  x+=speedX;
  speedY+=gravity;
  y+=speedY;

  // Check display window edge collisions
  if (x > width-w){
    x = width-w;
    speedX*=-1;
  }
  else if (x < 0){
    x = 0;
    speedX*=-1;
  }
  else if (y > height-h){
    y = height-h;
    speedY*=-1;
  }
  else if (y < 0){
    y  = 0;
    speedY*=-1;
  }
}
```

11

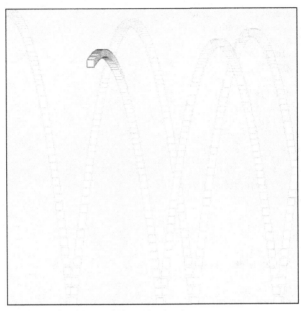

Figure 11-6. Acceleration with Gravity sketch

I reused the fade technique from the last example to help visualize the rectangle's curved motion. This sketch is structured pretty similarly to the earlier ones we looked at, with the addition of accelerated motion on the y-axis. x continues to be incremented by xSpeed (providing a constant rate of change), but I've added an extra gravity variable for the y motion. Prior to incrementing y by ySpeed, I incremented ySpeed by gravity. This extra assignment created accelerated motion, as the rate of change of y was no longer constant.

To illustrate why this double incrementation works, run the following sketch. The output, shown in Figure 11-7, shows the actual values for x and y over five iterations:

```
// Acceleration Calculations
float x = 0, x2 = 0, y = 0, y2 = 0;
float xSpeed = 3.0, ySpeed = .0;
float gravity = .5;

void setup(){
  for (int i=0; i<5; i++){
    ySpeed += gravity;
    y += ySpeed;
    println("y = " + y + "   increase = " + (y-y2));
    y2 = y;
  }
  println("");
  for (int i=0; i<5; i++){
```

```
      x+=xSpeed;
      println("x = " + x + "   increase = " + (x-x2));
      x2 = x;
    }
  }
```

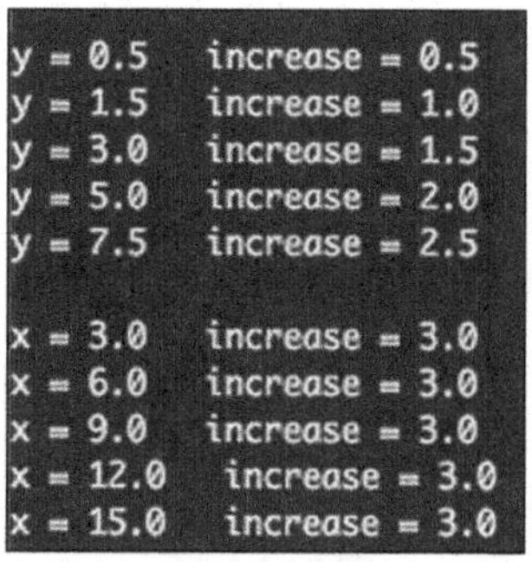

Figure 11-7.
Output of Acceleration Calculations sketch

The output shows the increase in y is changing while the increase in x remains constant at 3, which causes the curved motion in the example.

In the previous accelerated bouncing rectangle example, the rectangle collided with the ground and bounced, and then the process repeated itself while the sketch continued running. In the real world, if we dropped a bouncy box, when the box collided with the ground, there would be a transfer of some of its bouncing energy (into heat, sound, etc.), causing the box to eventually come to a rest on the ground. You may remember Newton's law of conservation of energy, which states that energy in a closed system remains constant—it can be transferred but not created or destroyed. So, in technical terms, we could say that when the rectangle collides with the ground, there is a transfer of its kinetic energy into thermal (heat) and mechanical (sound) energy. Rather than deal with the real physics of this type of energy transfer, I'll simply create a damping variable (a fractional value) and multiply ySpeed by it each time the rectangle hits the ground.

The damping variable will eventually stop the rectangle's motion along the y-axis, but I also need to stop the rectangle's movement along the x-axis—if I don't, the rectangle will continue to slide back and forth along the bottom of the display window. To fix this, I'll create a friction variable, which will gradually slow the rectangle's sideways motion using the same approach as with the damping variable. Each time the rectangle collides with the bottom of the display window, xSpeed is multiplied by the friction variable (also a fractional value). In the real world, friction would also slow the rectangle as it moved through the air and made contact with the side walls—but we'll ignore this for now (although you could easily add in these calculations as well).

```
      // Simple Motion Physics I
      float speedX, speedY;
      float x, y, w, h;
      // acceleration force
      float gravity;
```

11

```
// stops motion
float damping, friction;

void setup(){
  size(400, 400);
  x=width/2;
  w=20;
  h=w;
  fill(0);
  speedX = 4;
  // set dynamics
  gravity = .5;
  damping = .8;
  friction = .9;
}

void draw(){
  fill(255, 60);
  rect(0, 0, width, height);

  fill(0);
  rect(x, y, w, h);
  x+=speedX;
  speedY+=gravity;
  y+=speedY;

  // Check display window edge collisions
  if (x > width-w){
    x = width-w;
    speedX*=-1;
  }
  else if (x < 0){
    x = 0;
    speedX*=-1;
  }
  else if (y > height-h){
    y = height-h;
    speedY*=-1;
    speedY*=damping;
    speedX*=friction;
  }
  else if (y < 0){
    y  = 0;
    speedY*=-1;
  }
}
```

Before moving on, try experimenting with the values for xSpeed, gravity, damping, and friction. You should easily be able to simulate different gravities (as you'd encounter on different planets), as well as different materials for the rectangle and ground surface. For example, to simulate a lead block being dropped on the moon and landing on a rough surface, you could try the following settings:

```
speedX = 1;
gravity = .02;
damping = .85;
friction = .6;
```

To simulate a lacrosse ball landing on Jupiter on a super smooth, slick surface, try the following:

```
speedX = 5;
gravity = .98;
damping = .75;
friction = .99;
```

Figure 11-8 shows these two scenarios side by side, without a background() call in draw().

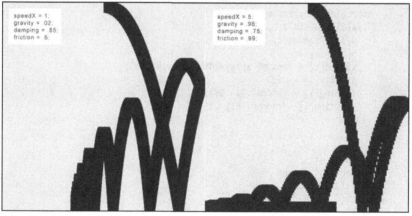

Figure 11-8. Simple Motion Physics I sketch

Converting this sketch of a single bouncing rectangle with naturalesque physics to many rectangles is as easy as creating arrays for each of the individual variables and adding for loops within the setup() and draw() functions. That being said, all the array syntax can look a little intimidating.

In addition to the arrays, I added three variables (shapeCount, birthRate, and sprayWidth) to control how the rectangles are born. Without controlling the birthrate, all the rectangles would be born at the same time, creating a much less interesting effect than the spray effect we get in the sketch. Also, by using the sprayWidth variable in setting the xSpeed[] values, I can control the width of the spray. Output from the sketch is shown in Figure 11-9.

11

497

```
// Simple Motion Physics II
int shapes = 200;
float[]w = new float[shapes];
float[]h = new float[shapes];
float[]x = new float[shapes];
float[]y = new float[shapes];
float[]xSpeed = new float[shapes];
float[]ySpeed = new float[shapes];
float[]gravity = new float[shapes];
float[]damping = new float[shapes];
float[]friction = new float[shapes];
//controls rate rects are born
float shapeCount;
float birthRate = .25;
// control width of spray when rects are born
float sprayWidth = 5;

void setup(){
  size(400, 400);
  noStroke();
  //initialize arrays with random values
  for (int i=0; i<shapes; i++){
    x[i] = width/2.0;
    w[i] = random(2, 17);
    h[i] = w[i];
    xSpeed[i] = random(-sprayWidth, sprayWidth);
    gravity[i] = .1;
    damping[i] = random(.7, .98);
    friction[i] = random(.65, .95);
  }
}

void draw(){
  //fade background
  fill(255, 100);
  rect(0, 0, width, height);
  fill(0);

  // shapeCount births rects over time
  for (int i=0; i<shapeCount; i++){
    rect(x[i], y[i], w[i], h[i]);
    x[i]+=xSpeed[i];
    ySpeed[i]+=gravity[i];
    y[i]+=ySpeed[i];

    //collision detection
    if (y[i]>=height-h[i]){
      y[i]=height-h[i];
      // bounce
```

```
        ySpeed[i]*=-1.0;
        // slow down vertical motion on ground collision
        ySpeed[i]*= damping[i];
        // slow down lateral motion on ground collision
        xSpeed[i]*=friction[i];
      }
      if (x[i]>=width-w[i]){
        x[i]=width-w[i];
        xSpeed[i]*=-1.0;
      }
      if (x[i]<=0){
        x[i]=0;
        xSpeed[i]*=-1.0;
      }
    }
    if (shapeCount<shapes){
      shapeCount+=birthRate;
    }
  }
```

Figure 11-9. Simple Motion Physics II sketch

I strongly recommend you play around with this sketch a bit before moving on. See if you can simulate some natural phenomenon, such as a spray of water, sparks, or an explosion. Don't be scared to add a few more variables to control where the rectangles are emitted from, or how the rectangles scatter when they hit the ground. You can even add other forces, such as wind, to the sketch.

11

Object interactions

The last sketch can be thought of as a very (very) simplified particle system. Particle systems are used to render organic effects and phenomena usually without a discrete and rigid form. For example, by generating a group of particles moving in certain wave patterns, we can simulate things like waving grass, a sheet blowing in the wind, or even liquid. Aside from the type of speed and acceleration variables we've been looking at, particle systems might also include more complex calculations for inter-particle attraction/repulsion, inertia, and so on.

We'll begin by considering the interaction between just two particles and build from there. One simple but interesting type of interaction is following behavior, as exhibited in a simple predator/prey dynamic. In the next two sketches, I'll make the mouse the prey and a ravenous ellipse its predator. The first example simply has the ellipse follow the mouse with a slight delay. Notice that I used Processing's pmouseX and pmouseY variables, which hold the coordinate values of the mouse one frame in the past.

```
// Ravenous ellipse I
float x, y;

void setup(){
  size(400, 400);
  x = width/2;
  y = height/2;
  smooth();
}

void draw(){
  // repaint background
  fill(255, 40);
  rect(0, 0, width, height);

  /* find distance for x and y
   between prey and predator */
  float deltaX = (pmouseX-x);
  float deltaY = (pmouseY-y);

  x += deltaX;
  y += deltaY;
  ellipse(x, y, 15, 15);
}
```

Easing

The core principle in this last (pretty dull) sketch is that we are calculating deltaX and deltaY each frame in the draw() loop, with the following lines:

```
/* find distance for x and y
   between prey and predator */
   float deltaX = (pmouseX-x);
   float deltaY = (pmouseY-y);
```

Since the ellipse and mouse are moving closer (until deltaX and deltaY eventually reach 0), we can be sure that the predator will never overshoot the prey. We can improve this sketch by varying the speed in which the predator chases the prey with an effect called **easing**. Easing simply adds some deceleration or acceleration to an object's motion.

In the next example, I'll have the predator decelerate as it nears the prey; this is also referred to as **easing out**. Easing in would be the opposite—the predator would accelerate toward the prey. To accomplish the easing out, I'll add an easing variable that will work very similarly to the damping variable used a few sketches back (shown in Figure 11-10).

```
// Ravenous Ellipse II
float x, y;
float easing = .05;

void setup(){
  size(400, 400);
  x = width/2;
  y = height/2;
  smooth();
}

void draw(){
  // repaint background
  fill(255, 40);
  rect(0, 0, width, height);

  /* find distance for x and y
   between prey and predator */
  float deltaX = (pmouseX-x);
  float deltaY = (pmouseY-y);

  // cause the predator to decelerate
  deltaX *= easing;
  deltaY *= easing;

  x += deltaX;
  y += deltaY;
  ellipse(x, y, 15, 15);
}
```

11

501

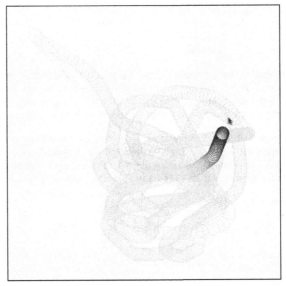

Figure 11-10. Ravenous Ellipse II sketch

Now the predatory motion is smoother and much more natural. And all I added were the two easing statements (besides of course declaring the easing variable at the top of the sketch):

```
// cause the predator to decelerate
  deltaX *= easing;
  deltaY *= easing;
```

Let's replace the ravenous ellipse with an even more ravenous triangle (shown in Figure 11-11). The triangle will not only follow the mouse, but remain oriented in a certain direction so that it can attack with its mouth (you'll have to take my word that this triangle does indeed have a mouth). I'll create the triangle and its orientation using some trig.

```
// Ravenous Triangle I
float predCntrX, predCntrY;
float predX[] = new float[3];
float predY[] = new float[3];
float predLen = 8.0;
float predAng, predRot;
float easing = .05;
```

```
void setup(){
  size(400, 400);
  predCntrX = width/2;
  predCntrY = height/2;
  smooth();
}

void draw(){
  // repaint background
  fill(255, 40);
  rect(0, 0, width, height);

  /* find distance for x and y
   between prey and predator */
  float deltaX = (pmouseX-predCntrX);
  float deltaY = (pmouseY-predCntrY);

  // cause the predator to decelerate
  deltaX *= easing;
  deltaY *= easing;

  predCntrX += deltaX;
  predCntrY += deltaY;

  // orient predator
  predRot = atan2(deltaY, deltaX);

  // draw predator
  createPredatoryTriangle();
}

void createPredatoryTriangle(){
  // draw predator with some trig
  fill(0);
  beginShape();
  for (int i=0; i<3; i++){
    predX[i] = predCntrX+cos(radians(predAng)+predRot)*predLen;
    predY[i] = predCntrY+sin(radians(predAng)+predRot)*predLen;
    vertex(predX[i], predY[i]);
    predAng += 120;
  }
  endShape(CLOSE);
}
```

11

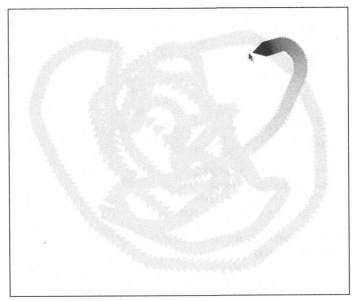

Figure 11-11. Ravenous Triangle I sketch

I used the basic unit circle relationships **cos(theta) = x** and **sin(theta) = y** to plot the triangle in the createPredatoryTriangle() function. The variables predCntrX and predCntrY give the center point of the triangle, and the variable predLen is the length of each of the triangles' three vertices from the center point. I've used these unit circle relationships to plot polygons throughout the book, so hopefully this is a review.

To get the triangle to rotate and stay oriented, I used Processing's atan2(y, x) function. The Processing documentation says this about the function: "Calculates the angle (in radians) from a specified point to the coordinate origin as measured from the positive x-axis." (See http://processing.org/reference/atan2_.html.)

Don't worry if this doesn't help much. The "atan" part of the function name refers to arctangent. Normally, using trigonometry (e.g., sine, cosine, and tangent), we begin with an angle and we can calculate the ratio of two sides of a right triangle. The arc versions of the trig functions are used when we know the ratio of two of the sides and we want to find the angle between them. In the sketch, deltaY and deltaX (representing the change in y and the change in x) provide the ratio of two sides of a right angle, which I plugged into the atan2(deltaY, deltaX) function to get the angle I need, like so:

```
predRot = atan2(deltaY, deltaX);
```

I then added predRot (which is already in radians) directly into the two trig equations that plotted the triangle:

```
predX[i] = predCntrX+cos(radians(predAng)+predRot)*predLen;
predY[i] = predCntrY+sin(radians(predAng)+predRot)*predLen;
```

A lot more can be done with this code, including creating an autonomous prey object and using it instead of the mouse. A simple tank game could be created, with a computer-controlled tank and a user-controlled one. The atan2() function will ensure that the tanks (or the tanks' gun turrets) stay oriented in the correct direction as they move.

Springing

Another fun effect to experiment with is springing. In the last few examples, the predator followed the prey, but never overshot it. There are times, though, when you might want an object to slingshot past another object and eventually come to rest. Think about a small rubber ball on an elastic string, and how it bounces around before coming to rest. Working with accurate spring equations is somewhat involved, and more than you need for most aesthetics-based creations. We can very easily simulate spring behavior just by tweaking the code used in the predator/prey scenario. In fact, the tweak we need is very similar to the tweak used to add acceleration (with gravity) to the speed example earlier in the chapter.

Here's the Ravenous Triangle I sketch converted to use a springy (yet still ravenous) triangle:

```
// Ravenous Triangle II
float predCntrX, predCntrY;
float predX[] = new float[3];
float predY[] = new float[3];
float predLen = 8.0;
float predAng, predRot;
// springing variables
float accelX, accelY;
float springing = .01, damping = .95;

void setup(){
  size(400, 400);
  predCntrX = width/2;
  predCntrY = height/2;
  smooth();
}

void draw(){
  // repaint background
  fill(255, 40);
  rect(0, 0, width, height);

  /* find distance for x and y
   between prey and predator */
  float deltaX = (pmouseX-predCntrX);
  float deltaY = (pmouseY-predCntrY);
```

11

```
                    // create springing effect
                    deltaX *= springing;
                    deltaY *= springing;

                    // conditional keeps triangle from spinning endlessly
                    if (dist( pmouseX, pmouseY, predCntrX, predCntrY)>5){
                      accelX += deltaX;
                      accelY += deltaY;
                    }

                    // move predator's center
                    predCntrX += accelX;
                    predCntrY += accelY;

                    // slow down springing
                    accelX *= damping;
                    accelY *= damping;

                    // orient predator
                    predRot = atan2(accelY, accelX);

                    createRavenousSpringyTriangle();
                  }

                  void createRavenousSpringyTriangle(){
                    // create predator with some trig
                    fill(0);
                    beginShape();
                    for (int i=0; i<3; i++){
                      predX[i] = predCntrX+cos(radians(predAng)+predRot)*predLen;
                      predY[i] = predCntrY+sin(radians(predAng)+predRot)*predLen;
                      vertex(predX[i], predY[i]);
                      predAng += 120;
                    }
                    endShape(CLOSE);
                  }
```

To create the springing effect, I need to simultaneously decrease the values of deltaX and deltaY, like so:

```
                    deltaX *= springing;
                    deltaY *= springing;
```

while incrementing accelX and accelY by deltaX and deltaY respectively, as follows:

```
                    // conditional keeps triangle from spinning endlessly
                      if (dist(pmouseX, pmouseY, predCntrX, predCntrY)>5){
                        accelX += deltaX;
                        accelY += deltaY;
                      }
```

> *Note that the if statement around the two incrementation lines just keeps the triangle from endlessly spinning when the mouse stops moving.*

The last step is damping the accelX and accelY values, which occurs in the final two lines:

```
// slow down springing
accelX *= damping;
accelY *= damping;
```

As always, I suggest playing with these values. Although it is relatively easy to implement the springing, it's not easy to fully grasp how/why it's working. Playing with the values will help you to better understand the principle.

There is so much more that can be done with both the following/easing and springing code. One really fun and interesting thing to try is to put a number of springy forms together in a series. In this next example (shown in Figure 11-12), I'll create a worm composed of 60 overlapping springy ellipses that follow an invisible moving food source. The springing for the initial ellipse will be calculated based on the position of the food source; while the springing for each of the other 59 ellipses will be based on the position of the preceding ellipse—forming a reactive chain.

```
/* Worm
 demonstrates springs in a series */

// for worm
int segments = 60;
float[] x = new float[segments];
float[] y = new float[segments];
float[] accelX = new float[segments];
float[] accelY = new float[segments];
float[] springing = new float[segments];
float[] damping = new float[segments];

// for food
float fx, fy;
float fCntrX, fCntrY;
float fAngle, fSpeedX = .25, fSpeedY = .5;

void setup(){
  size(400, 400);
  smooth();
  // initialize array values
  for (int i=0; i<segments; i++){
    /* need to decrease both springing and
      damping values as segments increase */
    springing[i] = .05*(.07*(i+1));
    damping[i] = .95-(.02*i);
  }
```

11

```
                        // food center
                        fCntrX = width/2;
                        fCntrY = height/2;
                    }

                    void draw(){
                        // repaint background
                        fill(0, 10);
                        noStroke();
                        rect(0, 0, width, height);

                        createFood();
                        createWorm();
                    }

                    void createFood(){
                        // food moves in random wave pattern
                        fx = fCntrX + cos(radians(fAngle))*random(25);
                        fy = fCntrY + sin(radians(fAngle))*random(25);

                        fCntrX+=fSpeedX;
                        fCntrY+=fSpeedY;

                        fAngle+=random(-6, 6);

                        // keep food within display window
                        if (fCntrX>width-15 || fCntrX<15 ){
                            fSpeedX*=-1;
                        }
                        if (fCntrY>height-15 || fCntrY<15 ){
                            fSpeedY*=-1;
                        }
                    }

                    void createWorm(){
                        float[] deltaX = new float[segments];
                        float[] deltaY = new float[segments];

                        for (int i=0; i<segments; i++){
                            // lead ellipse
                            if (i==0){

                                /* food position used to calculate the
                                initial ellipse of the worm */
                                deltaX[i] = (fx-x[i]);
                                deltaY[i] = (fy-y[i]);
                            }
                            else {
                            /* preceding ellipse used to calculate the
```

```
    next ellipse of the worm */
    deltaX[i] = (x[i-1]-x[i]);
    deltaY[i] = (y[i-1]-y[i]);
  }

  // create springing effect
  deltaX[i] *= springing[i];
  deltaY[i] *= springing[i];

  accelX[i] += deltaX[i];
  accelY[i] += deltaY[i];

  // move worm
  x[i] += accelX[i];
  y[i] += accelY[i];

  fill(0);
  stroke(255);
  // draw worm
  if (i<segments/2){
    ellipse(x[i], y[i], i, i);
  }
  else {
    ellipse(x[i], y[i], segments-i, segments-i);
  }
  // slow down springing
  accelX[i] *= damping[i];
  accelY[i] *= damping[i];
  }
}
```

11

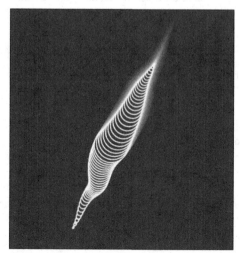

Figure 11-12.
Worm sketch

Earlier in the chapter, when we converted a single bouncing rectangle to multiple bouncing rectangles, the problem mostly boiled down to converting single variables to arrays and using for loops in setup() and draw() to process them; this is pretty much the case with this last example. The springing principle works similarly to the previous Ravenous Triangle II example. There are, however, two aspects that probably need clarification.

The first challenge with the worm was keeping the springing values within a logical range so that the worm moved properly (based on my own aesthetic sense). I actually have no idea about real worm motility—other than I suspect it involves slithering.

First, notice the for loop:

```
for (int i=0; i<segments; i++){
    /* need to decrease both springing and
     damping values as segments increase */
    springing[i] = .05*(.07*(i+1));
    damping[i] = .95-(.02*i);
}
```

This is where I initialized the springing[] and damping[] array values. I settled on the two scary-looking expressions after some trial and error. I suspect other values could yield even nicer worm movement. Since the springing of the ellipses, other than the initial one, are based on each preceding ellipse, the springing values increased rapidly, creating an interesting expanding and whipping wave pattern, but not a solid slithering worm. By reducing the values of both the springing and damping each iteration of the for loop, I was able to find a workable worm solution. Again, I urge you to mess around with these values, obliterating the worm in the process—it won't feel a thing.

For the food source, I wanted to created a simple wandering (invisible) bot that would replace mouseX and mouseY in calculating the deltaX and deltaY values. I needed the food source (fx, fy) to only control the lead ellipse, and I needed the other ellipses to each be controlled by the preceding ellipse. Here's the block of code that handles this:

```
// lead ellipse
if (i==0){
    /* food position used to calculate the
     initial ellipse of the worm */
    deltaX[i] = (fx-x[i]);
    deltaY[i] = (fy-y[i]);
}
else {
    /* preceding ellipse used to calculate the
    next ellipse of the worm */
    deltaX[i] = (x[i-1]-x[i]);
    deltaY[i] = (y[i-1]-y[i]);
}
```

The food source itself wanders around the display window based on trig functions with some random values. It also bounces off the display window boundaries, keeping the worm on the screen.

Finally, the following code, which draws the actual worm, might need a little explanation:

```
stroke(255);
// draw worm
if (i<segments/2){
  ellipse(x[i], y[i], i, i);
}
else {
  ellipse(x[i], y[i], segments-i, segments-i);
}
```

I wanted the worm to have both a narrow anterior and posterior and a wider midsection. The if...else block ensures that the ellipses would form in this basic structure. Again, try messing with these values to create some other strange organisms.

An alternative spring approach

There is another way of simulating springs that some people may find easier than the approach we just looked at. Consider the motion of a spring—does it suggest any other form? A spring undulates, usually symmetrically, in a regular wave pattern. Thus, any equation that generates a wave should be able to simulate wave behavior. We used the trig functions in Chapter 7 (on curves) to create waves, and we can use them here as well to simulate spring behavior.

The next example, shown in Figure 11-13, is of a fairly realistic weight on a spring that stretches as the weight moves. Clicking the screen resets the spring.

```
// Weight on a Spring
float x, y;
int w = 150, h = 100;
float angle, frequency = 5.0;
float amplitude, damping = .987;
int springSegments = 32, springWidth = 15;

void setup(){
  size(400, 400);
  x = width/2.0-w/2.0;
  smooth();
  strokeWeight(5);
  fill(0);
  setSpring();
}

void draw(){
  background(255);
  createSpring();
  startSpring();
}
```

11

```
void startSpring(){
  // spring behavior
  y += cos(radians(angle))*amplitude;
  amplitude*=damping;
  angle+=frequency;

  if (mousePressed){
    setSpring();
  }
}

void setSpring(){
  y = 100;
  angle = 0;
  amplitude = 26.0;
}

void createSpring(){
  // weight
  quad(x+20, y, x+w-20, y, x+w, y+h, x, y+h);
  // spring
  for (int i=0; i<springSegments; i++){
    // end segment
    if (i==springSegments-1){
      line(x+w/2+springWidth, (y/springSegments)*i, ➡
           x+w/2, (y/springSegments)*(i+1));
    }
    else {
      // alternate spring bend left/right
      if (i%2==0){
        line(x+w/2-springWidth, (y/springSegments)*i, ➡
            x+w/2+springWidth, (y/springSegments)*(i+1));
      }
      else {
        line(x+w/2+springWidth, (y/springSegments)*i, ➡
            x+w/2-springWidth, (y/springSegments)*(i+1));
      }
    }
  }
}
```

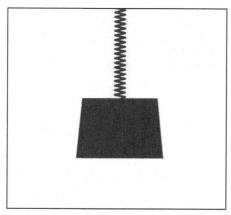

Figure 11-13. Weight on a Spring sketch

Notice the actual springing code in the setSpring() function:

```
// spring behavior
  y += cos(radians(angle))*amplitude;
  amplitude*=damping;
  angle+=frequency;
```

This code is very similar to other trig expressions used throughout the book. Again, by damping a simple sine or cosine wave over time, you can create pretty realistic spring motion. Lastly, notice within the createSpring() function that I used the modulus opera-tor (%) when drawing the spring. I needed a way of alternating the plotting of the spring coil right and left. By using the if...else block with the condition (i%2==0)—only an even number leaves a remainder of 0 when divided by 2—I was able to accomplish this easily.

We can build upon this concept by simulating some values for mass and spring strength. In the next sketch, shown in Figure 11-14, I create a series of springs that have varying sizes (representing differences in mass) and spring strengths, illustrated by varying the stroke weight when drawing the springs. Based on these variations, the sketch simulates how these different configurations might move. For example, a heavy weight attached to a spring with a small rod diameter would stretch further than the same weight on a spring with a wider diameter. The damping effect of the spring is based on the stroke weight as well. Each time you run the sketch or click the mouse in the display window, random values are generated for mass and spring strengths.

```
// Weights on Springs
int weights = 5;
float[]x = new float[weights];
float[]y = new float[weights];
float[]w = new float[weights];
float[]h = new float[weights];
float[]angle = new float[weights];
```

```
float[]frequency = new float[weights];
float[]amplitude = new float[weights];
float[]strokeWt = new float[weights];
float[]damping = new float[weights];
int springSegments = 24, springWidth = 8;

void setup(){
  size(600, 400);
  frameRate(30);
  smooth();
  fill(0);
  setSpring();
}

void draw(){
  background(255);
  for (int i=0; i<weights; i++){
    createSpring(x[i], y[i], w[i], h[i], strokeWt[i]);
    noStroke();
    fill(0);
    // draw weights
    quad(x[i], y[i], x[i]+w[i], y[i], x[i]+w[i]+w[i]*.2, ➥
         y[i]+h[i], x[i]-w[i]*.2, y[i]+h[i]);
    // spring behavior
    y[i] = y[i]+cos(radians(angle[i]))*amplitude[i];
    angle[i]+=frequency[i];
    amplitude[i]*=damping[i];
  }
  // press the mouse to reset
  if (mousePressed){
    setSpring();
  }
}

void setSpring(){
  for (int i=0; i<weights; i++){
    // size approximates mass
    w[i] = random(20, 70);
    h[i] = w[i];
    // stroke weight approximates
    // spring strength (resistance)
    strokeWt[i] = random(1, 4);
    x[i] = ((width/(weights+1))*i)+width/(weights+1)-w[i]/2.0;
    y[i] = (w[i]*3)/strokeWt[i];
    angle[i] = 0;
    // spring speed
    frequency[i] = strokeWt[i]*4;
    // amplitude based on mass/spring strength
    amplitude[i] = (w[i]*1.5)/strokeWt[i];
```

```
    // calc. damping based on strokeWeight
    // simulates resistance of spring thickness
    switch(round(strokeWt[i])){
    case 1:
      damping[i] = .99;
      break;
    case 2:
      damping[i] = .98;
      break;
    case 3:
      damping[i] = .97;
      break;
    case 4:
      damping[i] = .96;
      break;
    }
  }
}

//plot spring
void createSpring(float x, float y, float w, float h, float strokeWt){
  stroke(50);
  strokeWeight(strokeWt);
  for (int i=0; i<springSegments; i++){
    // for spring end segment
    if (i==springSegments-1){
      line(x+w/2+springWidth, (y/springSegments)*i, ➥
          x+w/2, (y/springSegments)*(i+1));
    }
    else {
      // alternate spring bend left/right
      if (i%2==0){
        line(x+w/2-springWidth, (y/springSegments)*i, ➥
            x+w/2+springWidth, (y/springSegments)*(i+1));
      }
      else {
        line(x+w/2+springWidth, (y/springSegments)*i, ➥
            x+w/2-springWidth, (y/springSegments)*(i+1));
      }
    }
  }
}
```

11

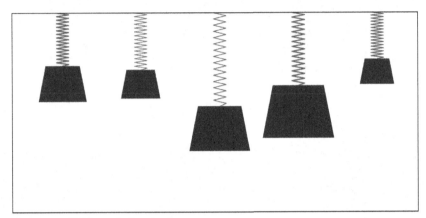

Figure 11-14. Weights on Springs sketch

Even the simplest wavy/springy behavior can be evocative and even humorous. I've created two final spring examples that illustrate this. The first sketch is of a simple undulating sine wave that moves across the display window. When I showed the initial state of this sketch to my six-year-old son, he immediately saw its connection to the way water moves, so I added an additional playful element. This example, entitled *Beach Ball*, is a bit long, so I've provided it as a download, which you can find in the Download section of the friends of ED website (www.friendsofed.com/downloads.html).

Soft-body dynamics

The second example is of a springy polygon that combines both approaches to springing we've looked at this chapter. This sketch is loosely inspired by the brilliant Java work *Sodaplay* (www.sodaplay.com/constructor/index.htm), created by Ed Burton and team at Soda Creative (http://soda.co.uk/). The example illustrates (very) simple soft-body dynamics. In rigid-body dynamics, objects collide and interact, but the objects themselves don't deform; think of a block of wood falling down the stairs. In soft-body dynamics, the objects actually deform; think of a water balloon falling down the stairs (but not exploding). People are often fascinated by these types of simulations (I know I am), and in many ways they represent the ultimate illusion. Since we are more or less squishy, soft-bodied organisms ourselves, these types of soft-body physics simulations represent a logical extension of earlier creative attempts at human depiction—from cave paintings, to terra cotta figures, to self-portraiture, to Shrek's bouncing belly. Following is the code for Hybrid Springy Dude: A Polygon with Attitude (shown in Figure 11-15):

```
/* Hybrid Springy Dude:
 A Polygon with Attitude */
// center point
float centerX = 0, centerY = 0;
float radius = 60, rotAngle = -90;
float accelX, accelY;
float springing = .0085, damping = .98;
```

516

```
//corner nodes
int nodes = 5;
float nodeStartX[] = new float[nodes];
float nodeStartY[] = new float[nodes];
float[]nodeX = new float[nodes];
float[]nodeY = new float[nodes];
float[]angle = new float[nodes];
float[]frequency = new float[nodes];
// soft-body dynamics
float organicConstant = 1;

void setup(){
  size(400, 400);
  //center shape in window
  centerX = width/2;
  centerY = height/2;
  // initialize frequencies for corner nodes
  for (int i=0; i<nodes; i++){
    frequency[i] = random(5, 12);
  }
  noStroke();
  frameRate(30);
}

void draw(){
  //fade background
  fill(255, 100);
  rect(0,0,width, height);
  drawShape();
  moveShape();
}

void drawShape(){
  // calculate node  starting locations
  for (int i=0; i<nodes; i++){
    nodeStartX[i] = centerX+cos(radians(rotAngle))*radius;
    nodeStartY[i] = centerY+sin(radians(rotAngle))*radius;
    rotAngle += 360.0/nodes;
  }

  // draw polygon
  curveTightness(organicConstant);
  fill(175);
  beginShape();
  for (int i=0; i<nodes; i++){
    curveVertex(nodeX[i], nodeY[i]);
  }
  for (int i=0; i<nodes-1; i++){
    curveVertex(nodeX[i], nodeY[i]);
```

11

```
    }
    endShape();
}

void moveShape(){
  //move center point
  float deltaX = mouseX-centerX;
  float deltaY = mouseY-centerY;

  // create springing effect
  deltaX *= springing;
  deltaY *= springing;
  accelX += deltaX;
  accelY += deltaY;

  // move polygon's center
  centerX += accelX;
  centerY += accelY;

  // slow down springing
  accelX *= damping;
  accelY *= damping;

  // change curve tightness
  organicConstant = 1-((abs(accelX)+abs(accelY))*.1);

  //move nodes
  for (int i=0; i<nodes; i++){
    nodeX[i] = nodeStartX[i]+sin(radians(angle[i]))*(accelX*2);
    nodeY[i] = nodeStartY[i]+sin(radians(angle[i]))*(accelY*2);
    angle[i]+=frequency[i];
  }
}
```

Figure 11-15. Hybrid Springy Dude sketch

Springy Dude is not an accurate physics simulation. Instead, I used some random values as an approximation for the spring and deformation. When the mouse moves, the entire polygon springs, based on the original springing code we looked at earlier in the chapter. The block of code controlling this overall movement is the following:

```
// move center point
float deltaX = mouseX-centerX;
float deltaY = mouseY-centerY;

// create springing effect
deltaX *= springing;
deltaY *= springing;
accelX += deltaX;
accelY += deltaY;

// move polygon's center
centerX += accelX;
centerY += accelY;

// slow down springing
accelX *= damping;
accelY *= damping;
```

I utilized a parenting approach with regard to the relationship between the polygon's five perimeter points (which aren't rendered) and the shape's central point. If you haven't done much computer animation before, this may not initially mean much to you. The central problem in a sketch like Hybrid Springy Dude is how to maintain the shape, while allowing both the form to move as a whole and its individual parts to move independently.

In a program like Flash, there are MovieClip data structures that can explicitly have parent and nested child clips. Most 3D animation applications employ similar constructs. In Processing, we don't have this built-in structure (though of course we could build one). Instead, in the example I used the variables centerX and centerY to represent the overall coordinating point of the entire shape, which in a sense becomes the parent (or control node).

11

I used trig functions both to calculate the nodes' starting positions (relative to the shape's center point) and to create the spring effect on the shape's vertices. To enable the shape to return to its original polygonal structure after the springing, I needed to capture the original point locations of the shape (relative to the control node). Here's the block of code that does that:

```
//  calculate node  starting locations
  for (int i=0; i<nodes; i++){
    nodeStartX[i] = centerX+cos(radians(rotAngle))*radius;
    nodeStartY[i] = centerY+sin(radians(rotAngle))*radius;
    rotAngle += 360.0/nodes;
  }
```

The nodes are then moved with two other trig expressions:

```
//move nodes
  for (int i=0; i<nodes; i++){
    nodeX[i] = nodeStartX[i]+sin(radians(angle[i]))*(accelX*2);
    nodeY[i] = nodeStartY[i]+sin(radians(angle[i]))*(accelY*2);
    angle[i]+=frequency[i];
  }
```

The two blocks of code are very similar. Again, the first block captures the nodes' original positions, which keep changing as the overall shape is moving. The second code block takes care of moving the individual points. The springing movement of both the overall form and the individual points is controlled by the variables accelX and accelY, which are calculated in the overall spring code shown earlier.

Finally, the curvy deformation—from a rigid polygonal structure to an organic blob—is based on the following line:

```
// change curve tightness
  organicConstant = 1-((abs(accelX)+abs(accelY))*.1);
```

This line calculates a curve tightness value, which is fed into Processing's curveTightness() function when the shape is plotted, using a series of curveVertex() calls:

```
// draw polygon
  curveTightness(organicConstant);
  fill(175);
  beginShape();
  for (int i=0; i<nodes; i++){
    curveVertex(nodeX[i], nodeY[i]);
  }
  for (int i=0; i<nodes-1; i++){
    curveVertex(nodeX[i], nodeY[i]);
  }
  endShape();
```

You may remember from Chapter 7 ("Curves") that the curveTightness() function controls how the curve interpolation is handled between the curve vertices. I took advantage of this really handy and simple-to-use function to create all the squishy, soft-body magic.

Advanced motion and object collisions

Earlier in the chapter we looked at a simple strategy for handling the collision of objects with the display window. The steps included placing the object flush with the edge in case the detection happened after the object had already passed through the edge, and then reversing the speed value controlling the object's motion—this was done for both axes. Here's another simple example of this basic collision approach:

```
float x, y, r = 20;
float speedX = 2, speedY = 2.5;
void setup(){
  size(400, 400);
  x = width/2;
  y = height/2;
  noStroke();
  smooth();
}
void draw(){
  background(0);
  x+=speedX;
  y+=speedY;
  ellipse(x, y, r*2, r*2);
  // check wall collisions
    if (x > width-r){
    x = width-r;
    speedX*=-1;
  }
  else if (x < r){
    x = r;
    speedX*=-1;
  }
  else if (y > height-r){
    y = height-r;
    speedY*=-1;
  }
  else if (y < r){
    y = r;
    speedY *=-1;
  }
}
```

This strategy will work fine for orthogonal collisions, when the object bounces off a horizontal or vertical surface. However, it won't work for an object hitting an angular or curved surface, including objects colliding with each other. The next section will show you how to deal with these cases.

Vectors

To begin to think about these more advanced types of collisions, you need to consider how an object's path is controlled by the speed values you increment it by. In the last example, I incremented x by 2 and y by 2.5. Obviously, since y is being increased more each frame than is x, the object moves on more of a vertical path than a horizontal one. Since neither speed value was 0, you could also predict that the object would move in some type of diagonal path. If speedX had been 0, the object would have only moved vertically. And of course the situation would have been reversed if speedY had been 0.

Returning to the original speed settings, speedX = 2, speedY = 2.5, what could you do if you wanted to double the speed of the object, but not alter its direction? You could multiply both values by 2. This would cause the object to move faster, but still along the same path. So what happened? I know this may seem pathetically simple, but the underlying concepts are very important for what we'll be doing (and not as simple as they may initially seem).

When you double the speed settings, the object's speed obviously increases, but the ratio of the two speeds remains the same, keeping the object moving in the same direction. This ratio relates to the slope of the line defining the movement of the object. You may recall that slope is calculated as the change in y (Δy) over the change in x (Δx)—or the rise over the run.

Thus, speed and direction can be thought of as two separate quantities; you can alter an object's speed while still maintaining its current direction. (It would be pretty hard to drive a car safely if we couldn't do this.) Mathematically, there is a convenient way of expressing all this, namely in a structure called a **vector**.

I've mentioned vectors earlier in the book, and we'll delve deeper into them in the final chapters (on 3D) as well. A vector, for our current purposes, is a quantity that describes both speed and direction, more commonly known as **velocity**.

In the next example, the two parts of the vector (direction and speed) are coded as separate variables, to help illustrate their relationship. The sketch moves five rectangles in the same direction, but at differing speeds.

```
float directionX = .56, directionY = .83;
float[] speeds = {.75, 1.3, 2.2, .92, 1.5};
float[] x = new float[5], y = new float[5];

void setup(){
  size(400, 400);
  noStroke();
  fill(128);
  smooth();
}
void draw(){
  background(255);
  for (int i=0; i<5; i++){
    x[i] += directionX*speeds[i];
    y[i] += directionY*speeds[i];
    rect(x[i], y[i], 6, 6);
  }
}
```

The variables directionX and directionY represent the direction the rectangles all travel. The specific values .56 and .83 can be thought of as the base ratio of change along x and y, respectively. In other words, even if we multiply both of these values by some very large common constant, we increase the overall speed value, but we don't affect the ratio between these two values (which again controls the direction the rectangles are moving).

Normalizing a vector

When working with vectors, it is common practice to find this base ratio of a vector, which is referred to as normalizing a vector. **Normalizing** simply means reducing the magnitude (length) of a vector to 1, which is done by dividing each component of a vector by its overall length. For example if you have vector *v*, you can find its length like this (expressed in code):

```
length = sqrt(v.x*v.x + v.y*v.y);
```

Then to find the base ratio, you simply divide each of the vector's components by its length:

```
normalizedVector.x = v.x / length;
normalizedVector.y = v.y / length;
```

Again, this base ratio, or normalized vector, expresses the direction of the vector. For example, if we have a line and we want to animate an ellipse at a certain speed along the line, we can treat the line as a vector. Once we have the length of the line, we can normalize it and use the normalized values as the direction for the ellipse to travel, which we can then multiply by any speed we choose. Here's a sketch that does precisely this (shown in Figure 11-16):

```
// Moving Along a Vector
float lineX1, lineY1, lineX2, lineY2;
float vectX, vectY, vectMag, directionX, directionY;
float ellipseX, ellipseY;
float ellipseSpeed = 2;

void setup(){
  size(400, 400);
  fill(128);
  smooth();
  lineX1 = 100;
  lineY1 = 75;
  lineX2 = 300;
  lineY2 = 325;

  // express line as a vector
  vectX = lineX2-lineX1;
  vectY = lineY2-lineY1;

  // find magnitude(length) of vector
  vectMag = sqrt(vectX*vectX + vectY*vectY);

  /* normalize vector to get
  base direction ratio */
  directionX = vectX/vectMag;
  directionY = vectY/vectMag;
```

11

```
      // start ellipse on line
      ellipseX = lineX1;
      ellipseY = lineY1;
    }
    void draw(){
      background(255);
      // draw line
      line(lineX1, lineY1, lineX2, lineY2);

      //draw ellipse
      ellipse(ellipseX, ellipseY, 20, 20);

      // move elipse
      ellipseX += directionX * ellipseSpeed;
      ellipseY += directionY * ellipseSpeed;

      // keeps ellipse moving along line
      if (ellipseX>lineX2 && ellipseY>lineY2 ||
        ellipseX<lineX1 && ellipseY<lineY1) {
        /* when ellipse reaches end of vector
        reverse the vector's direction */
        directionX *= -1;
        directionY *= -1;
      }
    }
```

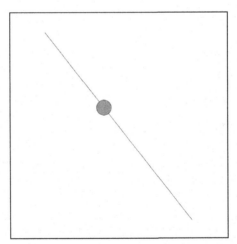

Figure 11-16. Moving Along a Vector sketch

In the sketch, I calculated the line as a vector by finding the difference between the components (x and y) of each endpoint of the line ($x_2 - x_1$, $y_2 - y_1$). Since I subtracted the leftmost point of the line from the right, I found component values independent of the placement of the vector within the larger coordinate system. This is actually a feature of vectors; it doesn't matter where you put them—their direction and magnitude will remain constant.

Once I got the vector's components, I simply calculated the vector's overall length and then divided each component by this length, giving me the base direction ratio, which I used in the calculation to move the ellipse, independent of the ellipse's speed.

Applying vectors in collisions

Let's now apply some of these vector principles to collisions. You already know how to handle collisions against orthogonal surfaces, such as the display window boundaries. However, the problem is quite a bit more complex when the collision surface is not orthogonal. The reason for this added complexity essentially boils down to a rotated coordinate system problem. For example, in Figure 11-17, the collision depicted on the left takes place against an orthogonal surface. The collision on the right, against a non-orthogonal surface, can also be thought of as an orthogonal collision in a rotated coordinate system. As you might guess, one solution to solving a non-orthogonal collision problem is to factor in this coordinate rotation. I'll discuss this solution shortly. First, however, I want to look at another approach, borrowing a principle from physics: the law of reflection.

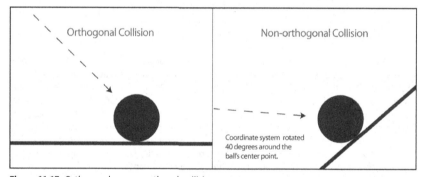

Figure 11-17. Orthogonal vs. non-orthonal collisions

The law of reflection

Figure 11-18 illustrates the **law of reflection**, which simply states that when light strikes a surface, the angle of reflection is equal to the angle of incidence, relative to the surface normal. The angle of incidence is the angle of the incoming ray striking the surface. A normal line is any line perpendicular to a surface. (It actually doesn't matter where on the surface this line is, since all perpendicular lines off a flat surface will be parallel.) Please also note that the terms *surface normal* and *normalizing a vector* are unrelated. Remember that normalizing involves dividing a vector's components by the length of the vector. In fact, in the next example, I'll actually be normalizing the surface normal. Although this law of reflection relates to how light reflects off of a surface, it works the same way for an object bouncing off a surface.

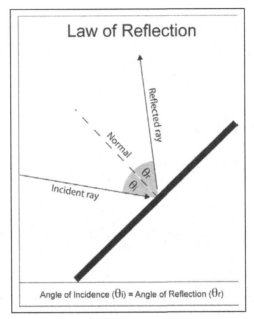

Figure 11-18. Law of reflection

There is a very handy equation you can use to apply this principle: **R = 2N(N • L) – L**, where *R* is the reflection vector, *N* is the surface normal (also a vector quantity), and *L* is the incident vector. Both the normal vector and the incident vector need to be normalized as well. The expression (N • L) represents the dot product of the surface normal and the incident vector. Since *N* and *L* are both vector quantities, you can't simply multiply them together the way you do two individual values (e.g., 5 × 4). Instead, you have two options for multiplying vectors; one approach returns a single non-vector value (the dot product) and the other approach returns another vector (the cross-product). For this example, you only need to use the dot product calculation. When you get to Chapter 14, you'll use the cross-product along with the dot product.

The beauty of using this equation is that you don't have to worry about rotating coordinates. In the next example (shown in Figure 11-19), I created a non-orthogonal base plane for the ellipse to deflect off of. To handle the actual collision detection, I treated the top of the base as an array of point coordinates and checked the distance between the ellipse and each of the individual points. Each time the ellipse hits the top of the display window, the base top is recalculated.

```
/*********************************************
 * Non-orthogonal Reflection:
 * Based on the equation R = 2N(N•L)-L
 * R = reflection vector
 * N = normal
 * L = incidence vector
```

```
  Ira Greenberg,      2/12/07
  *****************************************/
float baseX1, baseY1, baseX2, baseY2;
float baseLength;
float[] xCoords, yCoords;
float ellipseX, ellipseY, ellipseRadius = 8;
float directionX, directionY;
float ellipseSpeed = 3.5;
float velocityX, velocityY;

void setup(){
  size(400, 400);
  fill(128);
  smooth();
  baseX1 = 0;
  baseY1 = height-150;
  baseX2 = width;
  baseY2 = height;

  // start ellipse at middle top of screen
  ellipseX = width/2;

  // calculate initial random direction
  directionX = random(.1, .99);
  directionY = random(.1, .99);

  // normalize direction vector
  float directionVectLength = sqrt(directionX*directionX + ➥
          directionY*directionY);
  directionX /= directionVectLength;
  directionY /= directionVectLength;
}

void draw(){
  // draw background
  fill(0, 6);
  noStroke();
  rect(0, 0, width, height);

  // calculate length of base top
  baseLength = dist(baseX1, baseY1, baseX2, baseY2);
  xCoords = new float[ceil(baseLength)];
  yCoords = new float[ceil(baseLength)];

  // fill base top coordinate array
  for (int i=0; i<xCoords.length; i++){
    xCoords[i] = baseX1 + ((baseX2-baseX1)/baseLength)*i;
    yCoords[i] = baseY1 + ((baseY2-baseY1)/baseLength)*i;
  }
```

11

```
// draw base
fill(200);
quad(baseX1, baseY1, baseX2, baseY2, baseX2, height, 0, height);

// calculate base top normal
float baseDeltaX = (baseX2-baseX1)/baseLength;
float baseDeltaY = (baseY2-baseY1)/baseLength;
float normalX = -baseDeltaY;
float normalY = baseDeltaX;

// draw ellipse
noFill();
stroke(200);
ellipse(ellipseX, ellipseY, ellipseRadius*2, ellipseRadius*2);

// calculate ellipse velocity
velocityX = directionX * ellipseSpeed;
velocityY = directionY * ellipseSpeed;

// move elipse
ellipseX += velocityX;
ellipseY += velocityY;

// normalized incidence vector
float incidenceVectorX = -directionX;
float incidenceVectorY = -directionY;

// detect and handle collision
for (int i=0; i<xCoords.length; i++){
  // check distance between ellipse and base top coordinates
  if (dist(ellipseX, ellipseY, xCoords[i], ➥
        yCoords[i]) < ellipseRadius){

    // calculate dot product of incident vector and base top normal
    float dot = incidenceVectorX*normalX + ➥
        incidenceVectorY*normalY;

    // calculate reflection vector
    float reflectionVectorX = 2*normalX*dot - incidenceVectorX;
    float reflectionVectorY = 2*normalY*dot - incidenceVectorY;

    // assign reflection vector to direction vector
    directionX = reflectionVectorX;
    directionY = reflectionVectorY;

    // draw base top normal at collision point
    stroke(255, 128, 0);
    line(ellipseX, ellipseY, ellipseX-normalX*100, ➥
        ellipseY-normalY*100);
```

```
    }
  }

  // detect boundary collision
  // right
  if (ellipseX > width-ellipseRadius){
    ellipseX = width-ellipseRadius;
    directionX *= -1;
  }
  // left
  if (ellipseX < ellipseRadius){
    ellipseX = ellipseRadius;
    directionX *= -1;
  }
  // top
  if (ellipseY < ellipseRadius){
    ellipseY = ellipseRadius;
    directionY *= -1;
    // randomize base top
    baseY1 = random(height-300, height);
    baseY2 = random(height-300, height);
  }
}
```

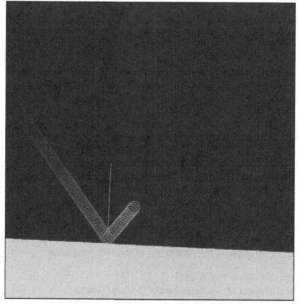

Figure 11-19. Non-orthogonal Reflection sketch

This is not a simple example, so I expect some of you may be scratching your heads a bit reviewing the code. Notice at the top of the sketch, where I declared global variables, that I created separate variables for directionX, directionY, and ellipseSpeed. Similarly, as in the last example, I conceptualized the ellipse's movement as a vector quantity, keeping direction and speed as separate quantities. I also declared initial arbitrary values for directionX and directionY. These two variables represent the direction of the incident (incoming) vector. This vector must be normalized to be useful in the larger reflection calculation ($R = 2N(N \cdot L) - L$). I normalized the vector at the bottom of the setup() function, with the following lines:

```
// normalize direction vector
  float directionVectLength = sqrt(directionX*directionX + ➥
          directionY*directionY);
  directionX /= directionVectLength;
  directionY /= directionVectLength;
```

You'll remember that to normalize a vector, you need to divide each of the vector's components by the overall length of the vector, which I did in the previous code snippet. Since the variables directionX and directionY are randomly assigned values, I couldn't assume that they formed a vector with a length of 1 (the length of a normalized vector).

Within the draw() function, I used the following lines to calculate the coordinate values of the top of the base, which were used in the collision detection:

```
// calculate length of base top
  baseLength = dist(baseX1, baseY1, baseX2, baseY2);
  xCoords = new float[ceil(baseLength)];
  yCoords = new float[ceil(baseLength)];

// fill base top coordinate array
  for (int i=0; i<xCoords.length; i++){
    xCoords[i] = baseX1 + ((baseX2-baseX1)/baseLength)*i;
    yCoords[i] = baseY1 + ((baseY2-baseY1)/baseLength)*i;
  }
```

I used the length of the base top edge to instantiate two float arrays of the same length. Since the baseLength calculation resulted in a float value, I was forced to convert the float value to an int value to be able to use this value to initialize the lengths of the two arrays. Next, using the for loop, I filled the two arrays with the coordinate values forming the base top edge. I'll assume you can make sense of the code that draws and moves the ellipse, as we've looked at code like this before, including in the last example.

To calculate the base top edge's normal, I needed to first generate the vector forming the top edge of the base. I also normalized this vector. Both of these steps were taken care of in the first two lines (following the comment) of the following code:

```
// calculate base top normal
  float baseDeltaX = (baseX2-baseX1)/baseLength;
  float baseDeltaY = (baseY2-baseY1)/baseLength;
  float normalX = -baseDeltaY;
  float normalY = baseDeltaX;
```

In two dimensions, the surface normal of a vector is really just a line perpendicular to the vector. In three dimensions, the situation is a bit more complicated and requires the use of the cross-product calculation mentioned previously. We'll look at the cross-product in the book's final chapter. Calculating the perpendicular line to a vector is very simple. To get the x component of the normal, you simply reverse the sign of the vector's y component, and to get the y component of the normal, you take the vector's x component, as illustrated in the last two lines of the previous snippet of code. Be aware, though, that every vector actually has two perpendicular lines, facing opposite directions (once you know one, just reverse its sign to find the other).

The block of code that handles most of the real heavy lifting in the draw() function is the following:

```
// normalized incidence vector
float incidenceVectorX = -directionX;
float incidenceVectorY = -directionY;

// detect and handle collision
for (int i=0; i<xCoords.length; i++){
  // check distance between ellipse and base top coordinates
  if (dist(ellipseX, ellipseY, xCoords[i], ➥
      yCoords[i]) < ellipseRadius){

    // calculate dot product of incident vector and base top normal
    float dot = incidenceVectorX*normalX + ➥
        incidenceVectorY*normalY;

    // calculate reflection vector
    float reflectionVectorX = 2*normalX*dot - incidenceVectorX;
    float reflectionVectorY = 2*normalY*dot - incidenceVectorY;

    // assign reflection vector to direction vector
    directionX = reflectionVectorX;
    directionY = reflectionVectorY;

    // draw base top normal at collision point
    stroke(255, 128, 0);
    line(ellipseX, ellipseY, ellipseX-normalX*100, ➥
        ellipseY-normalY*100);
  }
}
```

The directionX and directionY variables were normalized earlier in the sketch, so all I needed to do was reverse their signs to generate the normalized incidence vector (incidenceVectorX and incidenceVectorY). The for loop iterates though all the coordinates forming the base's top edge, and the conditional statement checks if the ellipse's distance relative to the base's top edge is less than the ellipse's radius—in which case a collision is detected. Once detected, the dot product is calculated by multiplying the incidence vector and normal vector's x and then y components, respectively, and adding these values together. This calculation works the same way for three dimensions—by simply

11

adding the z component into the mix. I'm not going to go into the theory behind the dot product here, but I will discuss it when I cover 3D in Chapter 14. If you just can't wait, though, Wikipedia has some good stuff to say about it at http://en.wikipedia.org/wiki/Dot_product.

Following the dot product calculation, I calculate the reflection vector, plugging in the values I've previously calculated. Finally, I assign the reflection vector to the original direction vector and display the normal at the point of collision. If the code is working, you should see that the angle formed between the base edge normal and the incoming incidence vector is equal to the angle between the outgoing reflection vector and the normal. The remainder of the code handles display window boundary detection and also resets the base's top edge whenever the ellipse makes contact with the top of the display window.

A better way to handle non-orthogonal collisions

Although the last example successfully handled angled collisions, there are some challenges in trying to extend this solution to handle object-object collisions as well trying to add simple physics, like gravity and drag. There is another collision solution that ActionScript guru Keith Peters writes about in his excellent book *Foundation ActionScript Animation: Making Things Move!* Although Keith's book deals with ActionScript, not Processing, I highly recommend it as a general graphics coding guide.

The solution Keith writes about deals with considering angled collisions as a rotated coordinate system problem, instead of focusing on trying to calculate the actual reflection angle. It works like this: if you take any 2D collision, you can always rotate the local coordinates so that the collision happens orthogonally (shown in Figure 11-20). For example, suppose a ball strikes a surface at a 40-degree angle. Rather than trying to calculate the angle of reflection, taking into account both the ball's incidence vector and the angle of the collision surface, you can rotate the surface and velocity vector (in this case –40 degrees) so that the collision surface is orthogonal (perfectly horizontal or vertical). Once rotated, you can handle the reflection the same way you do with collisions against the edges of the display window—simply reverse the sign of the appropriate velocity vector coordinate; finally, the last step is rotating everything back to where it was prior to the rotation.

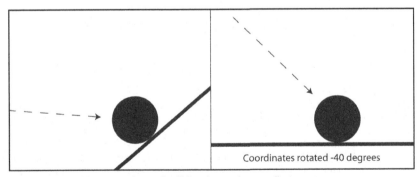

Figure 11-20. Handling non-orthogonal collisions by rotating coordinates

We'll look at this process in steps. The first step is handling the rotation of the collision surface and velocity vector. Remember your trusted rotation expressions:

```
x = cos(theta)*radius
y = sin(theta)*radius
```

These expressions hopefully look very familiar by now. They allow you to plot any point based on theta (the angle of rotation expressed in radians) and a radius. These equations are immensely handy in code art. However, there is another somewhat more complicated form of the expressions that makes them even handier (and absolutely essential for calculating 3D rotations). The two expressions just mentioned are actually derived from their more powerful trig brethren:

```
new x = cos(theta)*x - sin(theta)*y
new y = cos(theta)*y + sin(theta)*x
```

Whoa! Now don't freak out yet. The main difference between the two forms of the expressions is that the familiar shorter ones are used when the angle of rotation begins at 0. The longer forms of the expressions are used when the rotation represents a change of rotation (not necessarily beginning at 0 on the unit circle) and is also based on a specific point location (x and y). In the next example, I'll use these expressions to rotate a simple line around the center point of the display window (press the mouse to make the line rotate from its current position):

```
/* Trig Rotation Expressions
 -mouse press to rotate
Special thanks to kirupa.com*/

float[] x = new float[2];
float[] y = new float[2];
float[] newX = new float[2];
float[] newY = new float[2];
float theta;

void setup(){
  size(400, 400);
  float t = random(TWO_PI);
  /* I used the simple trig rotation form
   to generate the original line coords */
  x[0] = cos(t)*-50;
  y[0] = sin(t)*-50;
  x[1] = cos(t)*50;
  y[1] = sin(t)*50;
}

void draw(){
  background(255);
  translate(width/2, height/2);
  /* I used the longer trig rotation form to
   rotate based on the existing rotation */
```

11

```
newX[0]  = cos(theta)*x[0] - sin(theta)*y[0];
newY[0]  = cos(theta)*y[0] + sin(theta)*x[0];
newX[1]  = cos(theta)*x[1] - sin(theta)*y[1];
newY[1]  = cos(theta)*y[1] + sin(theta)*x[1];
line(newX[0], newY[0], newX[1], newY[1]);
// to rotate
if (mousePressed){
  theta += radians(1);
}
}
```

> *If you're curious how the two forms of the trig expressions relate, I'll clue you in. Starting with the long form of the expressions*
>
> ```
> new x = cos(theta)*x - sin(theta)*y
> new y = cos(theta)*y + sin(theta)*x
> ```
>
> *assume the angle of rotation starts at 0, which will make x equal to the radius (on the unit circle) and y equal to 0. Next, plug these values for x and y into the longer form, giving you the following:*
>
> ```
> new x = cos(theta)*radius - sin(theta)*0
> new y = cos(theta)*0 + sin(theta)*radius
> ```
>
> *If you then factor out the 0 values, you're left with the familiar short form:*
>
> ```
> new x = cos(theta)*radius
> new y = sin(theta)*radius
> ```
>
> *To learn more, check out Kirupa Chinnathambi's fabulous site at* www.kirupa. com/developer/actionscript/trig_multiple_axis.htm.

Notice in the last example that I used the short form of the trig expressions in the setup() function to calculate the initial coordinate values for the line, which was rotated with a random angle between 0 and 2pi. I then used the longer form of the expressions in the draw() function to further rotate the line based on the line's current coordinate locations; using the longer form allowed for a smooth transition between the rotations. One final note about these expressions: By changing the value of the signs in the expression, you can reverse the direction of the rotation. Thus, the expressions

```
new x = cos(theta)*x - sin(theta)*y
new y = cos(theta)*y + sin(theta)*x
```

rotate clockwise, but the expressions

```
new x = cos(theta)*x + sin(theta)*y
new y = cos(theta)*y - sin(theta)*x
```

rotate counterclockwise.

Asteroid shower in three stages

Now we'll apply these expressions to our non-orthogonal collision problem, for which we'll slowly develop an asteroid shower animation. In my kinder, gentler version, asteroids pummeling Earth don't cause cataclysmic destruction, but harmlessly bounce off the planet's surface.

In the first stage of the asteroid shower animation, I'll create a single orb that bounces off a non-orthogonal surface.

Stage 1: Single orb

The sketch will be developed using six tabs, including the main sketch tab. Three of the tabs you'll create will hold classes and the other two will hold functions. The first new tab I'll create is for a Ground class. Create a new tab and name it Ground. Enter the following code into the tab:

```
class Ground {
  float x1, y1, x2, y2;
  float x, y, len, rot;

  // default constructor
  Ground(){
  }

  // constructor
  Ground(float x1, float y1, float x2, float y2) {
    this.x1 = x1;
    this.y1 = y1;
    this.x2 = x2;
    this.y2 = y2;
    x = (x1+x2)/2;
    y = (y1+y2)/2;
    len = dist(x1, y1, x2, y2);
    rot = atan2((y2-y1), (x2-x1));
  }
}
```

This is a relatively simple class. Objects of the class are instantiated using four arguments, specifying the left and right coordinates of the top surface of the ground plane. In addition, within the constructor, a center point (x, y) of the surface is calculated, as is the ground surface length and the angle of rotation of the surface. Notice how I found the angle of rotation using the following expression:

```
rot = atan2((y2-y1), (x2-x1));
```

You looked at the atan2() function earlier in the chapter. Remember that you can use the standard trig functions sin(), cos(), and tan() to translate a rotation in the polar coordinate system to a specific coordinate value in the Cartesian system; and you can use the

11

inverse of these functions (referred to as the arc functions) to go in the other direction (find the angle of rotation beginning with some Cartesian coordinates).

Next I'll add an Orb class, which is very simple and self-explanatory. Add the following code to a new tab named Orb:

```
class Orb{
  float x, y, r;

  // default constructor
  Orb() {
  }

  Orb(float x, float y, float r) {
    this.x = x;
    this.y = y;
    this.r = r;
  }
}
```

I created a really simple 2D vector class for the orb's velocity. Create a tab named Vect2D and enter the following code:

```
class Vect2D{
  float vx, vy;

  // default constructor
  Vect2D() {
  }

  Vect2D(float vx, float vy) {
    this.vx = vx;
    this.vy = vy;
  }
}
```

These are all the classes you'll need. To handle the collision detection between the orb and the non-orthogonal surface, as well as the display window edges, you'll use two functions. First you'll tackle the easier, orthogonal (display window edge) collision. Create a new tab called checkWallCollision and enter the following code:

```
void checkWallCollision(){
  if (orb.x > width-orb.r){
    orb.x = width-orb.r;
    velocity.vx *= -1;
    velocity.vx *= damping;
  }
  else if (orb.x < orb.r){
    orb.x = orb.r;
    velocity.vx *= -1;
```

```
    velocity.vx *= damping;
  }
}
```

There's nothing new here. You've dealt with these types of orthogonal collisions a number of times before. The steps to handle the wall collision, as a refresher, are as follows:

1. Keep the orb from moving too far through the wall by assigning the precise value of the point of collision to the orb's x property (orb.x = width-orb.r;).

2. Reverse the orb's velocity (along the x-axis).

3. Optionally dampen the velocity along the x-axis upon collision.

Finally, the ground collision function is where you'll rotate the coordinate space to temporarily convert the challenging non-orthogonal collision problem to a much simpler orthogonal one. Create a tab named checkGroundCollision and enter the following code:

```
void checkGroundCollision() {

  // get difference between orb and ground
  float deltaX = orb.x - ground.x;
  float deltaY = orb.y - ground.y;

  // precalculate trig values
  float cosine = cos(ground.rot);
  float sine = sin(ground.rot);

  /* rotate ground and velocity to allow
   orthogonal collision calculations */
  float groundXTemp = cosine * deltaX + sine * deltaY;
  float groundYTemp = cosine * deltaY - sine * deltaX;
  float velocityXTemp = cosine * velocity.vx + sine * velocity.vy;
  float velocityYTemp = cosine * velocity.vy - sine * velocity.vx;

  // ground collision
  if (groundYTemp > -orb.r){
    // keep orb from going into ground
    groundYTemp = -orb.r;
    // bounce and slow down orb
    velocityYTemp *= -1.0;
    velocityYTemp *= damping;
  }

  // reset ground, velocity and orb
  deltaX = cosine * groundXTemp - sine * groundYTemp;
  deltaY = cosine * groundYTemp + sine * groundXTemp;
  velocity.vx = cosine * velocityXTemp - sine * velocityYTemp;
  velocity.vy = cosine * velocityYTemp + sine * velocityXTemp;
  orb.x = ground.x + deltaX;
  orb.y = ground.y + deltaY;
}
```

11

I suspect this function needs some going over. The initial lines in the function

```
// get difference between orb and ground
  float deltaX = orb.x - ground.x;
  float deltaY = orb.y - ground.y;
```

calculate the difference between the orb and the center point of the line defining the ground plane. These values, assigned to deltaX and deltaY, will be fed into the long form of the trig expressions I discussed earlier. Remember, the long form trig expressions rotate existing coordinates (represented by deltaX and deltaY) by adding to their current rotation. The current rotation we're interested in is calculated in the Ground class's constructor, which defines the amount that the ground edge is rotated from being perfectly horizontal (orthogonal).

Next in the function, the values for cosine and sine are calculated using the current rotation value (accessible through the property ground.rot):

```
float cosine = cos(ground.rot);
float sine = sin(ground.rot);
```

These two lines may look odd and even unnecessary. In truth, they are unnecessary, as you could call the individual trig functions in all the rotation expressions following in the code. However, there is a processing cost every time a trig function is called; and more importantly, each frame, all the trig-based expressions (eight in total) will use the same trig values. (Remember, by default, Processing runs your sketches at 60 frames per second.) As such, precalculated trig values make the program more efficient.

Now the fun begins. The following lines perform the rotation of the ground and the orb's velocity:

```
/* rotate ground and velocity to allow
   orthogonal collision calculations */
  float groundXTemp = cosine * deltaX + sine * deltaY;
  float groundYTemp = cosine * deltaY - sine * deltaX;
  float velocityXTemp = cosine * velocity.vx + sine * velocity.vy;
  float velocityYTemp = cosine * velocity.vy - sine * velocity.vx;
```

These expressions hopefully look familiar. The ground and orb's velocity are rotated the same amount, so that the ground surface is perfectly horizontal. This is only a temporary calculation, allowing you to perform a simpler reflection calculation (following shortly). The ground and velocity are not actually rotated. In fact, notice that the values returned from the four expressions are returned to four temporary variables: groundXTemp, groundYTemp, velocityXTemp, and velocityYTemp. Remember also that the signs in the four trig expressions relate to the direction of rotation. When I eventually rotate the ground and velocity back, I'll use the same long form trig expressions with the signs reversed.

Now that you have some values based on an orthogonal collision, you can handle the collision nearly the same way you did for the walls:

```
// ground collision
  if(groundYTemp > -orb.r){
    // keep orb from going into ground
    groundYTemp = -orb.r;
    // bounce and slow down orb
    velocityYTemp *= -1.0;
    velocityYTemp *= damping;
  }
```

Up until now, when handling orthogonal collisions, I've been checking if the object's x or y property was past its respective x or y boundary. However, in the ground collision conditional block, I'm checking if the difference (along the y-axis) between the orb and the ground is greater than the negative of the orb's radius; this reads like one of those annoying logic problems on a standardized test (sorry). You'll remember that, a few paragraphs back, the variable deltaY was assigned the difference between the orb's y position and the ground's y position; that value was then rotated and assigned to the variable groundYTemp. As the orb nears the ground, the difference between their y values will decrease, until the orb passes through the ground, at which time this value will begin increasing. Before the orb actually hits the ground, though, as the difference between the orb and ground's y value continues to decrease, there will be a point when the orb's center point is the same distance from the ground as the orb's radius—which would make the expression orb.y-ground.y equal to -orb.r. When the orb then moves one more pixel toward the ground, the difference between orb.y and ground.y, though still negative, will be greater than -orb.r, and the conditional will evaluate to true. You may have to read that a few times to get it; or just embrace the temporary confusion—I do it all the time. Once the conditional evaluates to true, the steps to reflect the orb should be old hat and self-explanatory.

Now that the ground and velocity have been rotated, allowing you to successfully detect and reflect the orb, all that's left to do is reset the ground and velocity back to their initial non-orthogonal rotations and update the position of the orb:

```
// reset ground, velocity and orb
  deltaX = cosine * groundXTemp - sine * groundYTemp;
  deltaY = cosine * groundYTemp + sine * groundXTemp;
  velocity.vx = cosine * velocityXTemp - sine * velocityYTemp;
  velocity.vy = cosine * velocityYTemp + sine * velocityXTemp;
  orb.x = ground.x + deltaX;
  orb.y = ground.y + deltaY;
```

The first four lines of code use the same long form trig functions we looked at earlier, but the signs in the expressions are reversed, and the ground and velocity temp values are now used as the current coordinates. Remember, reversing the signs in the expression will have the effect of causing the rotation to go in the opposite direction—putting the ground and velocity back in their original non-orthogonal positions. Of course, as I mentioned earlier, the ground and velocity were not actually affected, rather the four temp variables (groundXTemp, groundYTemp, velocityXTemp, and velocityYTemp) were assigned the rotated values. Now, however, the orb's velocity is updated by the trig expressions, as is the orb's position, based on the ground coordinates and the updated deltaX and deltaY variables.

11

To run the completed sketch (shown in Figure 11-21), you'll need the Orb, Ground, and Vect2D classes, the checkWallCollision() and checkGround() functions, and the following code, which should be entered in the leftmost main tab:

```
/****************************************
Non-orthogonal Collision
Based on Rotated Coordinates
****************************************
 * Based on Keith Peters's Solution in
 * Foundation ActionScript Animation:
 * Making Things Move!
 * http://www.friendsofed.com/book.html?➥
 * isbn=1590597915
 ****************************************/

Orb orb;
Vect2D velocity;
float gravity = .05, damping = 0.6;
Ground ground;

void setup(){
  size(400, 400);
  smooth();
  orb = new Orb(50, 50, 3);
  velocity = new Vect2D(.5, 0);
  // random ground slope
  ground  = new Ground(0, random(250, 390), ➥
          width, random(250, 390));
}

void draw(){
  // background
  noStroke();
  fill(0, 15);
  rect(0, 0, width, height);

  // move orb
  orb.x += velocity.vx;
  velocity.vy += gravity;
  orb.y += velocity.vy;

  // draw ground
  fill(127);
  beginShape();
  vertex(ground.x1, ground.y1);
  vertex(ground.x2, ground.y2);
  vertex(ground.x2, height);
  vertex(ground.x1, height);
  endShape(CLOSE);
```

```
// draw orb
noStroke();
fill(200);
ellipse(orb.x, orb.y, orb.r*2, orb.r*2);

// collision detection
checkWallCollision();
checkGroundCollision();
}
```

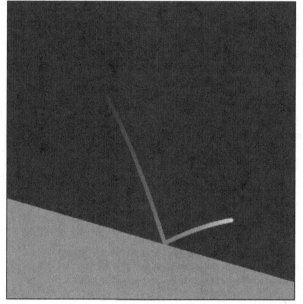

Figure 11-21. Non-orthogonal Collision Based on Rotated Coordinates
sketch

Each time you run the sketch, a randomly sloped ground plane is created. I didn't bother to actually draw the ground plane normal as I did in the earlier example, but notice how the angle of incidence of the orb and the angle of reflection are symmetrical based on where the normal would be perpendicular to the ground.

Stage 2: Segmented ground plane

In the next stage of the sketch, shown in Figure 11-22, I'll add a segmented ground plane, allowing the orb to bounce more erratically from numerous collisions on different angled surfaces. The three classes and the checkWallCollision() function will remain unchanged. Some minor modifications will need to be made to the main tab and the checkGroundCollision() function. The changes to the existing code are in bold. Here's the code for the main sketch tab:

```
/*****************************************
 * Non-orthogonal Collision with
 * Multiple Ground Segments
 *****************************************
 * Based on Keith Peters's Solution in
 * Foundation ActionScript Animation:
 * Making Things Move!
 * http://www.friendsofed.com/book.html? ⇒
 * isbn=1590597915
 *****************************************/

Orb orb;
Vect2D velocity;
float gravity = .05, damping = 0.8;
int segments = 40;
Ground[] ground = new Ground[segments];
float[] peakHeights = new float[segments+1];

void setup(){
  size(400, 400);
  smooth();
  orb = new Orb(50, 50, 3);
  velocity = new Vect2D(.5, 0);

  // calculate ground peak heights
  for (int i=0; i<peakHeights.length; i++){
    peakHeights[i] = random(height-100, height-90);
  }

  /* float value required for segment width (segs)
   calculations so the ground spans the entire
   display window, regardless of segment number. */
  float segs = segments;
  for (int i=0; i<segments; i++){
    ground[i]  = new Ground(width/segs*i, peakHeights[i], ⇒
        width/segs*(i+1), peakHeights[i+1]);
  }
}

void draw(){
  // background
  noStroke();
  fill(0, 15);
  rect(0, 0, width, height);

  // move orb
  orb.x += velocity.vx;
  velocity.vy += gravity;
  orb.y += velocity.vy;
```

```
    // draw ground
    fill(127);
    beginShape();
    for (int i=0; i<segments; i++){
      vertex(ground[i].x1, ground[i].y1);
      vertex(ground[i].x2, ground[i].y2);
    }
    vertex(ground[segments-1].x2, height);
    vertex(ground[0].x1, height);
    endShape(CLOSE);

    // draw orb
    noStroke();
    fill(200);
    ellipse(orb.x, orb.y, orb.r*2, orb.r*2);

    // collision detection
    checkWallCollision();
    for (int i=0; i<segments; i++){
      checkGroundCollision(ground[i]);
    }
  }
```

The changes to the code in the main tab all relate to dividing the ground plane into multiple segments; all the other code remains the same in this tab. The new segments variable controls how many segments the ground is divided up into. I calculated the segment coordinates in the ground[] array so that each segment would connect to the segments on either side of itself, creating one continuous undulating surface. The height of the undulation is calculated randomly, with the y-coordinates of the line stored in the peakHeights[] array. Finally, since each segment now needs to be rotated to handle a potential orb collision with its surface, I used a for loop to call checkGroundCollison(ground[i]), passing in each segment one at a time. This approach also allowed me to keep the implementation of this function almost identical to the original, by simply adding a parameter to the function signature. The following code block shows this function (changes to the original checkGroundCollison() function are displayed in bold):

```
    void checkGroundCollision(Ground groundSegment) {

    // get difference between orb and ground
    float deltaX = orb.x - groundSegment.x;
    float deltaY = orb.y - groundSegment.y;

    // precalculate trig values
    float cosine = cos(groundSegment.rot);
    float sine = sin(groundSegment.rot);

    /* rotate ground and velocity to allow
     orthogonal collision calculations */
    float groundXTemp = cosine * deltaX + sine * deltaY;
```

11

```
float groundYTemp = cosine * deltaY - sine * deltaX;
float velocityXTemp = cosine * velocity.vx + sine * velocity.vy;
float velocityYTemp = cosine * velocity.vy - sine * velocity.vx;

/* ground collision - check for surface
 collision and also that orb is within
 left/rights bounds of ground segment */
if (groundYTemp > -orb.r &&
  orb.x > groundSegment.x1 &&
  orb.x < groundSegment.x2 ){
  // keep orb from going into ground
  groundYTemp = -orb.r;
  // bounce and slow down orb
  velocityYTemp *= -1.0;
  velocityYTemp *= damping;
}

// reset ground, velocity and orb
deltaX = cosine * groundXTemp - sine * groundYTemp;
deltaY = cosine * groundYTemp + sine * groundXTemp;
velocity.vx = cosine * velocityXTemp - sine * velocityYTemp;
velocity.vy = cosine * velocityYTemp + sine * velocityXTemp;
orb.x = groundSegment.x + deltaX;
orb.y = groundSegment.y + deltaY;
}
```

The parameter groundSegment obviously needed to replace the variable ground in the original function. Other than that, the only additional change was in the conditional block that checks for the actual collision. In the original version of the function, I didn't need to check if the orb was too far left or right, since there was only one collision surface spanning the entire display window. However, once I divided the ground into segments, I needed a way to limit the collision detection to the width of each respective segment. I accomplished this by simply adding a left and right boundary check in the conditional test (shown following):

```
if (groundYTemp > -orb.r &&
    orb.x > groundSegment.x1 &&
    orb.x < groundSegment.x2 )
 ...
```

Make sure you try running this sketch and experimenting with (at least) the segments value and the peak heights random value range (displayed in bold in the following code). You can also of course mess with gravity, damping, orb, and velocity instantiation values.

```
// calculate ground peak heights
  for (int i=0; i<peakHeights.length; i++){
    peakHeights[i] = random(height-100, height-90);
  }
```

Please note that if you push the peak heights random value range really far (e.g., height-300, height-10) you might get some strange results—which I of course recommend trying.

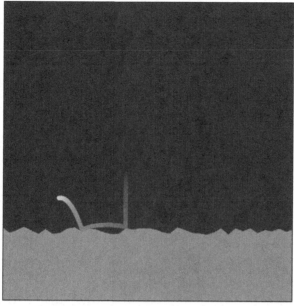

Figure 11-22. Non-orthogonal Collision with Multiple Ground Segments sketch

Stage 3: Asteroid shower

In the final stage of the sketch, shown in Figure 11-23, I'll add multiple orbs to the segmented ground plane. In addition, in the hope of creating something a little more visually interesting, I'll convert the flat, undulating ground plane to a curved, undulating planet, and I'll attach an image map to the geometry. I'll also add inspirational twinkling stars and some fiery colors to the asteroid shower.

As with stage 2, the Ground, Orb, and Vect2D classes remain unchanged. You just need to edit the code in the main tab and add some parameters to the checkGroundCollision() and checkWallCollision() functions. Following is the main tab code (note that, since the majority of the following code is different from the last sketch, I didn't put the changes in bold):

```
/******************************************
 * Asteroid Shower
 * Non-orthogonal Collision with`
 * Multiple Ground Segments and
 * Multiple Orbs
 ******************************************
 * Based on Keith Peters's Solution in
 * Foundation ActionScript Animation:
```

```
 * Making Things Move!
 * http://www.friendsofed.com/book.html? ➥
 * isbn=1590597915
 **************************************/

// orbCount minimum is 2
int orbCount = 140;
Orb[] orb = new Orb[orbCount];
Vect2D[] velocity = new Vect2D[orbCount];
color[] cols = new color[orbCount];
float[] damping = new float[orbCount];
float gravity = .03;
float sprayRadius = .3;
float birthRate = .4;
float emitter = 0;
float dampingMin = .5, dampingMax = .85;

// min of 6 segments required
int segments = 200;

Ground[] ground = new Ground[segments];
float[] peakHeights = new float[segments+1];

// controls ground undulation
float groundTexture = 3.5;

// earth image map
PImage p;

// stars
int starCount = 500;
Point[] stars = new Point[starCount];

void setup(){
  size(400, 400, P3D);

  // load image map
  p = loadImage("earth.png");

  // stars
  for (int i=0; i<starCount; i++){
    stars[i] = new Point(int(random(width)), int(random(height)));
  }

  // set array values
  for (int i=0; i<orbCount; i++){
    orb[i] = new Orb(random(5, 10), 0, random(.5, 2));
    velocity[i] = new Vect2D(1 + random(-sprayRadius, ➥
          sprayRadius), 0);
```

```
    damping[i] = random(dampingMin, dampingMax);
    cols[i] = color(random(200, 255), random(255), ➥
        random(100), random(20, 255));
  }

  // calculate ground peakHeights
  for (int i=0; i<peakHeights.length; i++){
    peakHeights[i] = random(-groundTexture, groundTexture);
  }

  // calculate points for planet surface, along arc.
  float ang = 200.0;
  float[] px = new float[segments+1];
  float[] py = new float[segments+1];
  for (int i=0; i<segments; i++){
    px[i] = width-50 + cos(radians(ang))*(width*1.3+peakHeights[i]);
    py[i] = height*1.75 + sin(radians(ang))*(height+peakHeights[i]);
    ang+=90.0/segments;
  }

  // instantiate Ground objects
  for (int i=0; i<segments; i++){
    ground[i] = new Ground(px[i], py[i], px[i+1], py[i+1]);
  }
}

void draw(){
  // background
  noStroke();
  fill(0, 15);
  rect(0, 0, width, height);

  // draw stars
  for (int i=0; i<starCount; i++){
    stroke(random(100, 255), random(255));
    point(stars[i].x, stars[i].y);
  }

  // draw earth
  noStroke();
  // bring alpha back to 100%
  fill(0, 255);
  beginShape();
  texture(p);
  float imageShiftX = 20;
  float imageShiftY = -240;
  for (int i=0; i<segments; i++){
    vertex(ground[i].x1, ground[i].y1, ground[i].x1+imageShiftX, ➥
        ground[i].y1+imageShiftY);
```

```
    }
    vertex(ground[segments-1].x1, ground[0].y1, ➡
        ground[segments-1].x1+ imageShiftX, ➡
        ground[0].y1+imageShiftY);
    vertex(ground[0].x1, ground[0].y1, ground[0].x1+imageShiftX, ➡
        ground[0].y1+imageShiftY);
    endShape(CLOSE);

    // draw and move orb
    for (int i=0; i<emitter; i++){
      orb[i].x += velocity[i].vx;
      velocity[i].vy += gravity;
      orb[i].y += velocity[i].vy;

      fill(cols[i]);
      ellipse(orb[i].x, orb[i].y, orb[i].r*2, orb[i].r*2);

      // collision detection
      checkWallCollision(orb[i], velocity[i], damping[i]);
      for (int j=0; j<segments; j++){
        checkGroundCollision(ground[j], orb[i], velocity[i], damping[i]);
      }
    }
    if (emitter < orbCount-1){
      emitter += birthRate;
    }
  }
```

Besides adding multiple orbs in this example, I added some convenient variables for changing things like birthrate of the orbs, radius of the spray of orbs, and degree of ground texture. In addition, as I mentioned earlier, I added an image of Earth, which I mapped onto the ground surface, and twinkling stars in the background. These and some other variables were declared at the top of the code (as usual), above the setup() function. Notice also that I used Java's Point class to declare the stars array. I've used this class in other places throughout the book. The Point class includes convenient public x and y properties.

I instantiated and initialized stuff in the setup() function, as you've seen me do many times before. What is new, though, is the third argument I added to the size(400, 400, P3D) function call. P3D is the name of the Processing software 3D rendering engine. When P3D is added as a third argument in size(), P3D becomes the current renderer, replacing the default JAVA2D renderer. I needed the P3D renderer to be able to map the Earth image onto the ground geometry.

I decided to use arrays for both damping and colors, allowing the orbs to bounce to different heights and also to be filled with their own colors. Since gravity should make all the objects fall at the same rate, I thought varying the damping values would create a more interesting waterfall effect once the orbs hit the planet. You can think of the damping value as controlling the elastic property of each orb.

Rather than deal with another flat, undulating surface, I used some trig functions to calculate the planet surface as an arc. The two expressions that create the arc

```
px[i] = width-50 + cos(radians(ang))*(width*1.3+peakHeights[i]);
py[i] = height*1.75 + sin(radians(ang))*(height+peakHeights[i]);
```

are pretty ugly and (dare I say) use magic numbers. I spent way too much time on this chapter, so I kind of took the easy way out (sorry). Feel free to mess with these values to change the planet's shape, or better yet, try to improve the expressions by losing the magic numbers.

In the draw() function, after drawing the fading background and stars, I created the Earth (yeah, I'm pretty powerful). Notice after the beginShape() function call, the following line:

```
texture(p);
```

This call, in a sense, turns on texture mode, allowing images to be mapped to geometry in Processing, using beginShape(), endShape(), and vertex() calls. The texture() call needs to be called between beginShape() and endShape(), and before any vertex() calls. The argument p should be the image you want to map to the geometry. This image should be loaded earlier in your sketch (after it has been added to the sketch's data directory), as I did in the setup() function.

Image mapping in Processing follows a common approach, used in other 3D environments, utilizing **uv coordinates**. *u and v r*epresent the coordinate space in which to put an image. Unlike x, y, and z, which each map to a specific axis, u and v represent a more symbolic type of space that relates to the object's vertices. For example, I can specify a point in xyz space that also has uv components. This structure allows 3D geometry to be plotted along the x-, y-, and z-axes, while also enabling an image to be attached to the geometry, with some flexibility; the image can be mapped different ways to the actual vertex geometry it's connected to. Once an image is mapped to the geometry using uv coordinates, it can be deformed along with the geometry, allowing for very realistic morphing effects. For now, I'll be focusing on simply mapping the image onto the 2D ground geometry. Later, in the 3D chapters, we'll map an image to a 3D object.

After the texture(p) call is made, the vertex calls now require two extra arguments, specifying how the image should be mapped to the vertices created between beginShape() and endShape(). By default, the mapping is based on the image's actual size. However, Processing comes with a function called textureMode(), allowing you to change the mapping from IMAGE mode (the default) to NORMALIZED mode. NORMALIZED mode allows you to specify argument values between 0 and 1.0, instead of the actual image sizes. To learn more about this option, please refer to the Processing reference at http://processing.org/reference/textureMode_.html.

The default image mapping is relatively simple to use on rectilinear geometry. For example, to map a 200 by 200 pixel image onto the same sized geometry, you would do the following (please note: the following code won't run as written—you need to specify P3D in size(), add and then load an image, and finally replace *PimageObjectNameGoesHere* with the actual name of your PImage):

```
translate(width/2, height/2);
beginShape();
texture(PimageObjectNameGoesHere)
vertex(-100, -100, 0, 0);
vertex(100, -100, 200, 0);
vertex(100, 100, 200, 200);
vertex(-100, 100, 0, 200);
endShape(CLOSE);
```

To map the image larger on the same geometry, you'd decrease the uv coordinates values (only values greater than 0 will have any effect). Increasing uv values beyond the actual size of the image will have no effect.

Returning to the Asteroid Shower sketch, it wasn't easy to map the Earth image onto the irregular ground shape. I created the two variables, as follows:

```
float imageShiftX = 20;
float imageShiftY = -240;
```

to help ensure that the image would map properly. I recommend messing with these values to see what happens.

Next in the draw() function is the drawing and moving of the orbs, which is pretty straightforward. What might be less obvious, though, is how to handle the collisions between the multiple ground segments and the multiple orbs. The crux of this problem is remembering to check the collision between each orb against every ground segment. When you come up against a programming problem with two sets of objects that need to interact like this, the solution is often a nested loop—which is precisely what I used to solve the collision problem. Thus, each orb gets born within the outer for loop and then gets passed to the checkGroundCollision() function, which is called within another nested for loop that executes the number of times there are ground segments. Each time the inner loop is called, the current orb, velocity, and damping values (controlled by the outer loop), and the ground segment (specified by the inner loop) are passed to the checkGroundCollision() function. Again, this inner loop will run the number of times there are segments and then control will return to the outer loop to begin the process over again.

The last conditional in the draw() function

```
if (emitter < orbCount-1){
   emitter += birthRate;
}
```

simply ensures that the emitter used to control the birthrate of orbs doesn't exceed the total orb count specified earlier in the sketch. We're almost done.

To keep your workload down some, I edited the checkGroundCollision() and checkWallCollision() functions in such a way that all you need to do is add some parameters to the two functions. Thus, between stage 2 and stage 3, you just need to replace

```
void checkGroundCollision(Ground groundSegment) {
```

with

```
void checkGroundCollision(Ground groundSegment, Orb orb, ➥
        Vect2D velocity, float damping) {
```

and

```
void checkWallCollision() {
```

with

```
void checkWallCollision(Orb orb, Vect2D velocity, float damping) {
```

That's really all you need to do (you can thank me later). The way I got this to work was by naming the parameters in the heads of the checkGroundCollision() and checkWallCollision() functions the same names as the global variables declared in the main tab. Remember, local variables, which include parameters, take precedence over the same named global variables. Although this was an expedient solution, it can also lead to nasty, hard-to-track-down errors. I personally often use this approach, but it's not for everybody, so enjoy and use it with caution.

Figure 11-23. Asteroid Shower sketch

There is one final thing I'd like to cover before retiring this chapter. However, before I do, I suggest playing with the Asteroid Shower sketch a bit first—doomsday scenario visualizations can be surprisingly cathartic.

Inter-object collision

In the ActionScript book I mentioned earlier, *Foundation ActionScript Animation: Making Things Move!* Keith Peters goes into glorious detail on the joys of billiard ball physics, or what happens when objects collide, taking into account not only their velocity vectors but their respective masses. This gets into a discussion on Newtonian physics, which is really good stuff (stop making faces). However, as Keith has beat me to the punch (not to mention that his elucidation on the subject rocks), and of course since we share the same publisher, in this chapter I'll include only some simple (and brief) examples dealing with the subject. However, I strongly recommend that you check out Keith's book to learn more.

Simple 1D collision

The simplest way to begin to understand these types of collisions is to move two balls along a single axis in opposite directions, not taking into account any rotation, mass, drag, wind, and so forth. In fact, we'll begin with both balls moving at the same speed as well. I've divided the sketch (shown in Figure 11-24) into five tabs: the main tab, the Ball class, the Vect2D class, the checkBoundaryCollision() function, and the checkObjectCollision() function. Of course, you can just put all the classes and functions in the main tab, below the draw() function, instead. Here's all the code, divided by tab:

```
// main sketch tab:
// 1D Collision with Swapping Velocities
Ball[] balls =  {
  new Ball(100, 200, 30), new Ball(300, 200, 30) };
Vect2D[] vels = {
  new Vect2D(1.3, 0), new Vect2D(-1.3, 0) };

void setup(){
  size(400, 400);
  smooth();
  noStroke();
}

void draw(){
  background(255);
  fill(150);
  for (int i=0; i<2; i++){
    balls[i].x += vels[i].vx;
    ellipse(balls[i].x, balls[i].y, balls[i].r*2, balls[i].r*2);
    checkBoundaryCollision(balls[i], vels[i]);
  }
  checkObjectCollision(balls, vels);
}

// Ball class:
// class Ball{
  float x, y, r;
```

```
  // default constructor
  Ball() {
  }

  Ball(float x, float y, float r) {
    this.x = x;
    this.y = y;
    this.r = r;
  }
}

// Vect2D class:
class Vect2D{
  float vx, vy;

  // default constructor
  Vect2D() {
  }

  Vect2D(float vx, float vy) {
    this.vx = vx;
    this.vy = vy;
  }
}

// checkBoundaryCollision() function:
void checkBoundaryCollision(Ball ball, Vect2D vel){
  if (ball.x > width-ball.r){
    ball.x = width-ball.r;
    vel.vx *= -1;
  }
  else if (ball.x < ball.r){
    ball.x = ball.r;
    vel.vx *= -1;
  }
  else if (ball.y > height-ball.r){
    ball.y = height-ball.r;
    vel.vy *= -1;
  }
  else if (ball.y < ball.r){
    ball.y = ball.r;
    vel.vy *= -1;
  }
}

// checkObjectCollision() function:
void checkObjectCollision(Ball[] b, Vect2D[] v){
  float d = dist(b[0].x, b[0].y, b[1].x, b[1].y);
  if (d < b[0].r + b[1].r){
```

11

```
        Vect2D vTemp = new Vect2D();
        vTemp.vx = v[0].vx;
        v[0].vx = v[1].vx;
        v[1].vx = vTemp.vx;
    }
}
```

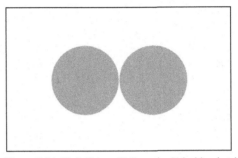

Figure 11-24. 1D Collision with Swapping Velocities sketch

Nearly all of this is straightforward. In fact, the only lines that may need some clarification are in the checkObjectcollision() function—specifically the following lines:

```
Vect2D vTemp = new Vect2D();
vTemp.vx = v[0].vx;
v[0].vx = v[1].vx;
v[1].vx = vTemp.vx;
```

I needed to create the Vect3D object (vTemp) to help me switch the velocities. Looking at the assignment operations, it should be apparent how the velocity switcheroo works. Try running the previous sketch as it's written, and then change the line

```
Vect2D[] vels = {
    new Vect2D(1.3, 0), new Vect2D(-1.3, 0) };
```

to

```
Vect2D[] vels = {
    new Vect2D(6.3, 0), new Vect2D(-1.3, 0) };
```

Try running the sketch again. Starting with different initial velocities makes it easier to see the transfer of motion.

In a moment, I'm going to present you with some pretty scary-looking equations (insert evil laugh here) to allow you to more accurately calculate the ball-ball collision. The basic principle I'll be using is as follows: a moving object carries a certain amount of momentum related to both its velocity and its mass. When two objects collide, all that combined momentum at impact has to go somewhere. In the real world, the force of this impact turns into heat, sound, cool explosions, and new motion. In a virtual world, we can control how the force is transferred. For example, when two objects collide, if we force all the momentum upon impact to go back into only new motion, then somehow the motion after the impact alone needs to be equal to the total momentum of the two objects at the point of impact. The easiest way to pull this off in code, as I did in the last example, is simply to have the two objects exchange their velocities upon impact.

Less simple 1D collision

This last example, although relatively simple, didn't take into account the mass of the objects. I used the term "transfer of motion" to describe how the balls simply switched their velocities. But what if you want to account for balls of different mass? Introducing mass requires those scary equations I mentioned earlier. Again, here's the first:

obj 1 final velocity = (obj 1 mass – obj 2 mass) * obj 1 velocity + 2 * obj 2 mass * obj 2 velocity

----

obj 1 mass + obj 2 mass

And here's the second:

obj 2 final velocity = (obj 2 mass – obj 1 mass) * obj 2 velocity + 2 * obj 1 mass * obj 1 velocity

----

obj 1 mass + obj 2 mass

I know the equations are long, but converting them to code is not a big deal, as you'll see shortly. The hard part of course would be attempting to derive the equations, which I won't bother doing. Keith Peters's book goes into some detail about where the equations come from. If you're really interested in the math, here's a link you might enjoy as well: www.euclideanspace.com/physics/dynamics/collision/oned/index.htm.

The two equations are based on the law of conservation of momentum, which I've sort of already discussed. For our purposes, the law states that in a closed system (such as the type we're coding), the total momentum of objects before a collision is equal to the total momentum after the collision. By using these equations, you'll be able to now account for mass in your ball-ball collisions.

The next example, shown in Figure 11-25, requires only some minor tweaks to the previous sketch. The sketch can be divided into five tabs like the last, with the main tab code, Vect2D class, and checkBoundaryCollision() function all remaining exactly as they were in the previous sketch, so I won't bother repeating that code. All you need to do is update the Ball class and checkObjectCollision() function. Here's the revised Ball class, with the new changes displayed in bold:

11

```
class Ball{
  float x, y, r, m;

  // default constructor
  Ball() {
  }

  Ball(float x, float y, float r) {
    this.x = x;
    this.y = y;
    this.r = r;
    m = r*.1;
  }
}
```

If it isn't obvious, all I added was a mass property to the class and based its value on the radius. Of course, the mass could also be coded as a completely separate value from the radius, as, for example, a large cork ball would certainly weigh less than a much smaller steel ball bearing. That being said, tying the mass to the radius was easiest.

The checkObjectCollision() function is where the majority of changes are, and of course it's where the scary conservation of momentum expressions are coded:

```
void checkObjectCollision(Ball[] b, Vect2D[] v){
  float d = dist(b[0].x, b[0].y, b[1].x, b[1].y);
  if (d < b[0].r + b[1].r){

    /* calculate final velocities based on
       Law of Conservation of Momentum */
    float finalVel0 = ((b[0].m - b[1].m) * v[0].vx + 2 *➡
        b[1].m * v[1].vx) / (b[0].m + b[1].m);
    float finalVel1 = ((b[1].m - b[0].m) * v[1].vx + 2 *➡
        b[0].m * v[0].vx) / (b[0].m + b[1].m);

    v[0].vx = finalVel0;
    v[1].vx = finalVel1;
  }
}
```

Hopefully, you didn't find the long expressions too frightening; they're long but pretty straightforward, and of course there's no obligation to really understand why they work (but then I'm not your Physics teacher). Following the new expressions, I simply assign the final velocities to the original velocity variables.

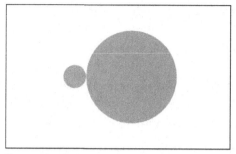

Figure 11-25. 1D Collision Using Conservation of Momentum sketch

Try running the sketch a few times and changing the radius of one of the balls. The greater the difference between the two radii, the more obvious the effect of the conservation of momentum will be.

2D collisions

Now that we got most of the easy stuff over with (I'm winking, don't worry), we'll tackle the holy grail of collisions: non-orthogonal 2D collisions. In actuality, you already know how to do this (well, sort of). I'll be using the same coordinate rotation approach I used for the Asteroid Shower sketch. The main difference is that there are now two objects colliding (shown in Figure 11-26).

The main sketch tab reuses much of the existing code from the previous example, with the changes shown in bold, as follows:

```
// Main Sketch Tab
// 2D Collision Using Conservation of Momentum
Ball[] balls = {
  new Ball(100, 400, 10), new Ball(700, 400, 40) };
Vect2D[] vels = {
  new Vect2D(4.3, -2.7), new Vect2D(-3.3, .95) };

void setup(){
  size(400, 400);
  smooth();
  noStroke();
}

void draw(){
  background(255);
  fill(150);
  for (int i=0; i<2; i++){
    balls[i].x += vels[i].vx;
    balls[i].y += vels[i].vy;
```

11

```
        ellipse(balls[i].x, balls[i].y, balls[i].r*2, balls[i].r*2);
        checkBoundaryCollision(balls[i], vels[i]);
      }
      checkObjectCollision(balls, vels);
    }
```

The checkObjectCollision() function needs a few more changes than that; here it is (brace yourself):

```
void checkObjectCollision(Ball[] b, Vect2D[] v){

    // get distances between the balls' components
    Vect2D bVect = new Vect2D();
    bVect.vx = b[1].x - b[0].x;
    bVect.vy = b[1].y - b[0].y;

    // calculate magnitude of the vector separating the balls
    float bVectMag = sqrt(bVect.vx * bVect.vx + bVect.vy * bVect.vy);
    if (bVectMag < b[0].r + b[1].r){
      // get angle of bVect
      float theta = atan2(bVect.vy, bVect.vx);
      // precalculate trig values
      float sine = sin(theta);
      float cosine = cos(theta);

      /* bTemp will hold rotated ball positions. You
         just need to worry about bTemp[1] position*/
      Ball[] bTemp = {  new Ball(), new Ball()  };
      /* b[1]'s position is relative to b[0]'s
       so you can use the vector between them (bVect) as the
       reference point in the rotation expressions.
       bTemp[0].x and bTemp[0].y will initialize
       automatically to 0.0, which is what you want
       since b[1] will rotate around b[0] */
      bTemp[1].x  = cosine * bVect.vx + sine * bVect.vy;
      bTemp[1].y  = cosine * bVect.vy - sine * bVect.vx;

      // rotate Temporary velocities
      Vect2D[] vTemp = { new Vect2D(), new Vect2D() };
      vTemp[0].vx  = cosine * v[0].vx + sine * v[0].vy;
      vTemp[0].vy  = cosine * v[0].vy - sine * v[0].vx;
      vTemp[1].vx  = cosine * v[1].vx + sine * v[1].vy;
      vTemp[1].vy  = cosine * v[1].vy - sine * v[1].vx;

      /* Now that velocities are rotated, you can use 1D
       conservation of momentum equations to calculate
       the final velocity along the x-axis. */
      Vect2D[] vFinal = {  new Vect2D(), new Vect2D()  };
      // final rotated velocity for b[0]
```

```
vFinal[0].vx = ((b[0].m - b[1].m) * vTemp[0].vx + 2 * b[1].m *
  vTemp[1].vx) / (b[0].m + b[1].m);
vFinal[0].vy = vTemp[0].vy;
// final rotated velocity for b[0]
vFinal[1].vx = ((b[1].m - b[0].m) * vTemp[1].vx + 2 * b[0].m *
  vTemp[0].vx) / (b[0].m + b[1].m);
vFinal[1].vy = vTemp[1].vy;

// hack to avoid clumping
bTemp[0].x += vFinal[0].vx;
bTemp[1].x += vFinal[1].vx;

/* Rotate ball positions and velocities back
 Reverse signs in trig expressions to rotate
 in the opposite direction */
// rotate balls
Ball[] bFinal = { new Ball(), new Ball() };
bFinal[0].x = cosine * bTemp[0].x - sine * bTemp[0].y;
bFinal[0].y = cosine * bTemp[0].y + sine * bTemp[0].x;
bFinal[1].x = cosine * bTemp[1].x - sine * bTemp[1].y;
bFinal[1].y = cosine * bTemp[1].y + sine * bTemp[1].x;

// update balls to screen position
b[1].x = b[0].x + bFinal[1].x;
b[1].y = b[0].y + bFinal[1].y;
b[0].x = b[0].x + bFinal[0].x;
b[0].y = b[0].y + bFinal[0].y;

// update velocities
v[0].vx = cosine * vFinal[0].vx - sine * vFinal[0].vy;
v[0].vy = cosine * vFinal[0].vy + sine * vFinal[0].vx;
v[1].vx = cosine * vFinal[1].vx - sine * vFinal[1].vy;
v[1].vy = cosine * vFinal[1].vy + sine * vFinal[1].vx;
  }
}
```

11

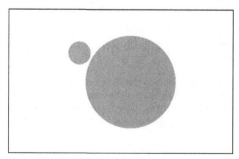

Figure 11-26. 2D Collision Using Conservation of
Momentum sketch

OK, hopefully we're still on speaking terms. Part of the reason this function is so long, with a slew of temporary object arrays, is that I wanted to make all the processes as explicit as possible. There are many ways of optimizing this code and reducing the number of lines; however, that economy comes with a cost of potential confusion. (Again, Keith Peters's book discusses a bunch of these optimizations, so I encourage you to take a look at it for a deeper discussion on this topic.)

I added a lot of comments directly within the code to help you decipher it. In addition, I'll provide a brief overview.

The code in the function combines a number of concepts we've looked at throughout this chapter, including vectors, coordinate rotation, and of course the law of conservation of momentum. I began the function by assigning the vector described by the distance between the two balls to bVect. I used this vector to determine the angle of rotation between the balls, as well as to define the reference point for rotation. Vectors, you'll remember, tell us about both direction and magnitude. I calculated the magnitude of bVect (assigned to bVectMag) and used it to determine when the balls were colliding, since the vector between the balls is also conveniently the distance between the balls.

By plugging the components of bVect into the atan2() function, I was able to find the angle (in radians) of the vector's rotation, which is precisely the value you need to rotate the ball and velocity coordinates, allowing you to treat the 2D collision between the balls as a 1D (orthogonal) collision.

When rotating the ball and velocity coordinates, you don't want to rotate in reference to the screen origin, but rather locally around the point of collision. I accomplished this by using bVect (the vector describing the distance between the balls) as the reference point of rotation. The two lines I'm referring to are the following (please note that I created a bunch of temporary Ball and Vect2D arrays (including bTemp) in the function to try to help clarify the different steps in the collision process):

```
bTemp[1].x = cosine * bVect.vx + sine * bVect.vy;
bTemp[1].y = cosine * bVect.vy - sine * bVect.vx;
```

b[1] will rotate around b[0], setting the vector between them perfectly horizontal. Thus, b[0] will act, in a sense, as the origin for the rotation, so I don't need to assign any value to bTemp[0].x and bTemp[0].y, which were both automatically assigned 0.0 when bTemp[0] was instantiated (since float values—which the x and y properties are—default to 0.0 when declared).

Next, I rotated the velocities, which should be self-explanatory, using the good old long form trig expressions.

The rotated velocities were assigned to the vTemp objects. Next, the ugly conservation of momentum expressions come into play. Notice that I only used them to find the final rotated velocities along the x-axis. The velocities along the y-axis were calculated previously, so I simply assigned vTemp.vy to vFinal.vy (for both objects).

To avoid unintentional clumping of the balls at collision, I borrowed a nice hack from Keith's example, which essentially moves the balls a little away from each other upon collision detection so that clumping is avoided. It's not a perfect fix, but it sure is nice and simple.

We're almost home now. The last steps left are to rotate the rotated ball position values and velocities back to the original rotation at collision and to update the balls' positions to the screen (remember that I treated the rotation locally with regard to the vector between the balls, rotating b[1] around b[0]). Updating the balls' screen positions just entails adding the final ball positions (bFinal) to b[0].

That's it! Definitely take some time playing with this sketch, plugging in different values for the balls' radii (which, again, control mass) and the initial velocities, both defined in the sketch's main tab.

There is so much more that could be done with this sketch, and collisions in general, including the addition of more balls. Likewise, orb-orb collisions could also be introduced to the Asteroid Shower example. That being said, I think this chapter's gone on long enough.

Summary

This chapter began with a brief overview of some of the technical issues involved in computer-based animation, including the concept of threads and the use of timeline-based keyframe models commonly found in high-end animation applications. Comparing Java and Processing animation code side by side, I showed how Processing's draw() structure encapsulates much of the low-level (and annoying) aspects of programmatic animation. Beginning with a simple moving ball and eventually adding simple physics, you explored easing, springing, and the concept of soft-body dynamics. Coding collisions, with some help from code guru Keith Peters, I introduced different approaches for handling both orthogonal and non-orthogonal 1D collisions, including ways to work with multiple surfaces and objects. Finally, I introduced an advanced 2D collision example that included conservation of momentum calculations.

In the next chapter, we'll add interactivity into the mix, allowing the user to interact with your sketches. We'll also discuss the possibilities of generating applications and graphical user interfaces (GUIs) in Processing.

11

12 INTERACTIVITY

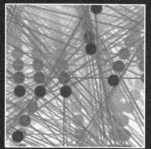

One of the most compelling aspects of digital/code art is interactivity. Interactive art is not in itself a completely new concept—for example, we've all become quite accustomed to "please touch" type children's museums. However, what is unique in code art is the fact that users can not only interact with a work of art, but in some cases they can actually redefine it, or even use the piece of art to create their own original works of art. Mark Napier's piece *net.flag* (www.guggenheim.org/internetart/welcome.html) is an excellent example of this. Viewers use Napier's web-based piece to design a flag, which (conceptually) becomes the flag of the entire Internet. Their creation remains the current flag of the Net until another viewer changes it. Each of the flags created also gets put into a permanent viewable database. Napier's piece—and others like it—represents a radical break with the established view of a work of art as contemplative object/space. Instead, in the case of *net.flag*, the work of art almost disappears, becoming a dynamic tool that others can use to express themselves.

In this chapter, you'll learn how to both detect and handle events. By **events**, I mean inputs to the system, such as mouse clicks or key presses. Of course, there are events that occur at a lower-level than the graphical user interface (GUI), as well—such as an internal timer or other system process that communicates with a running application. For example, my mail program periodically checks for incoming mail without my having to request it. It's also possible to detect other less standard high-level events, such as input from a video camera, microphone, or motion sensor. Processing has the capacity to interface with all these types of events. While in this chapter I'll only be covering mouse and key events, the principles discussed apply to most input devices.

Interactivity simplified

As you've probably come to expect by now, Processing simplifies the process of interactivity by encapsulating a bunch of the code you'd be required to include using pure Java. For an example of this, take a look at the following three sketches, each of which functions identically. The first two are written in Java and the third in Processing, but all three can be run in Processing. When run, the sketches print to the text area in the Processing application when the mouse is pressed within the Processing display window.

```
//  2 different Java approaches
// Java approach 1 implements the Java MouseListener interface:
void setup(){
  new MouseEventDemo();
}
class MouseEventDemo implements MouseListener {
  //constructor
  MouseEventDemo(){
    addMouseListener(this);
  }
  // we're required to implement all MouseListener methods
  public void mousePressed(MouseEvent e) {
    println("Java MouseListener interface example"+ ➡
            "mouse press detected");
```

```
  }
  public void mouseClicked(MouseEvent e){}
  public void mouseEntered(MouseEvent e){}
  public void mouseExited(MouseEvent e){}
  public void mouseReleased(MouseEvent e){}
}

// Java approach 2 extends the Java MouseAdapter class
void setup(){
  new MouseEventDemo();
}
class MouseEventDemo extends MouseAdapter {
  //constructor
  MouseEventDemo(){
    addMouseListener(this);
  }
  public void mousePressed(MouseEvent e) {
    println("Java MouseAdapter class example: mouse press detected");
  }
}

// Processing "easy" approach
void draw(){}  // we're required to include draw() function
void mousePressed() {
  println("Processing example: mouse press detected");
}
```

The two Java approaches are both more complex and require more code than the Processing approach. Using Java's MouseAdapter class simplifies things somewhat, as the MouseAdapter class encapsulates the necessary implementation of all the required MouseListener methods. The Processing approach takes this concept of encapsulation one step further, making it unnecessary to explicitly implement or extend another mouse event–related interface or class. In reality, the Processing approach I wrote is a little too lean, as you'd almost always want to include Processing's setup() function as well as draw(). However, all that is technically required for the mouse event detection to work in Processing is the inclusion of the draw() function.

12

Mouse events

Besides mouse press detection, Processing also includes event detection for mouse releases, clicks, moves, and drags. Mouse release detection occurs whenever the mouse button is released, regardless if the mouse position changes while the mouse is pressed. In comparison, mouse click detection occurs only if the mouse is released at the same point it was pressed. When the mouse is pressed and released at the same point, both release and then click detection occur—always in this order. Mouse move detection occurs when the mouse moves, without the mouse button being pressed, while mouse dragging detection occurs while the mouse moves with the button pressed. In addition, Processing can detect which mouse button is pressed (left, right, or center), using Processing's mouseButton system variable. With a little help from Java, it can also detect multiple button clicks, which I'll illustrate in a sketch at the end of the chapter.

Following is a better mouse event example, in which a rectangle on the screen is moved to the position of the mouse when the mouse button is pressed. The mouseX and mouseY properties are used to get the respective x and y positions of the mouse.

```
// mousePressed function
// example 1

// declare x, y
float x, y;
// declare and initialize w, h
float w = 20.0, h = 20.0;

void setup(){
  size(400, 400);
  // initialize x, y
  x = width/2.0;
  y = height/2.0;
  rectMode(CENTER);
}

void draw(){
  background(255);
  rect(x, y, w, h);
}

void mousePressed() {
  x = mouseX;
  y = mouseY;
}
```

This example utilizes a function called mousePressed(). Remember, the void in front of the function identifier just means that the function doesn't return a value. Processing also provides an alternative mousePressed Boolean variable that detects whether the mouse is pressed. The variable is equal to true if the mouse is pressed and false if it's not. As the following code shows, the previous sketch can be easily changed to use the mousePressed variable instead of the mousePressed() function:

```
// mousePressed variable
// example 2

// declare x, y
float x, y;
// declare and initialize w, h
float w = 20.0, h = 20.0;
```

```
void setup(){
  size(400, 400);
  // initialize x, y
  x = width/2.0;
  y = height/2.0;
  rectMode(CENTER);
}

void draw(){
  background(255);
  rect(x, y, w, h);

  if (mousePressed){
    x = mouseX;
    y = mouseY;
  }
}
```

This may seem confusing if you're a new coder—why have two ways of doing the same thing? Well, if you run this last example, you'll notice that the two sketches actually don't run quite the same way. This last example updates the rectangle's x and y positions continuously while the mouse is pressed, allowing the rectangle to be dragged in the display window. The earlier example only updated the rectangle when the mouse was pressed. As you look at some more complex examples, it will become clearer how these two approaches differ.

Notice also when I checked the condition (true or false) of the mousePressed Boolean variable, I just included it between the parentheses: (mousePressed). I didn't explicitly check if it was true using (mousePressed == true). This shortcut is perfectly legal, since the Boolean value will evaluate to either true or false, which is what the if statement needs to know in determining whether it should execute the code between its curly braces.

In addition to mouse press events, you can detect mouse release events. Here's an example:

```
// mouseReleased
// example 1

// declare x, y
float x, y;
// declare and initialize w, h
float w = 20.0, h = 20.0;
// rectangle fill color variable
color rectColor = color(255, 255, 255);

void setup(){
  size(400, 400);
  // initialize x, y
  x = width/2.0;
```

12

567

```
    y = height/2.0;
    rectMode(CENTER);
}

void draw(){
  background(255);
  fill(rectColor);
  rect(x, y, w, h);
}

void mousePressed() {
  x = mouseX;
  y = mouseY;
}

// randomly change fill color upon mouse release
void mouseReleased() {
  rectColor = color(random(255), random(255), random(255));
}
```

In this example, I included the original mousePressed() function and added a mouseReleased() function. When you run the sketch, you'll see that Processing can detect both parts of the mouse click (the press and release) as separate events. The mouseReleased() function creates a random color for the rectangle's fill.

> If you're a detail-oriented person (I'm really not), you may have noticed some inconsistency with Processing's automatic syntax color highlighting in the text editor. In general, Processing's built-in functions turn orange, while built-in variables turn red. However, the mousePressed() function turns red, and the mouseClicked() function remains black. The other mouse event functions, mouseReleased(), mouseMoved(), and mouseDragged(), turn orange. This is definitely confusing, and I've seen comments on the Processing discussion board saying so as well. Perhaps at some point this minor issue will be addressed; for now, just realize that it's not something you're doing wrong, and that the color of your code in the text editor has no effect on the functionality of the code. (It's also possible that by the time you read this, the issue will have been resolved.)

The mouseMoved() and mouseDragged() functions work similarly to mousePressed() and mouseReleased(). Here's a mouseDragged() example:

```
// mouseDragged Example
float x, y;
// declare and initialize radius
float r = 5.0;

void setup(){
  size(400, 400);
```

```
    // initialize x, y
    x = width/2.0;
    y = height/2.0;
    frameRate(30);
    smooth();
    noStroke();
  }

  void draw(){
    // fading background
    fill(0, 5);
    rect(0, 0, width, height);

    fill(255);
    ellipse(x, y, r*2, r*2);
  }

  void mouseDragged() {
    x = mouseX;
    y = mouseY;
  }
```

This example works similarly to the earlier mousePressed Boolean variable example. When you press the mouse in the display window and drag, the ellipse follows the mouse.

The next example adds a mouseMoved() function that controls a jitter and a scatter variable, which are set as you move the mouse around the display window (without it being pressed). The scatter variable controls the limit on a for loop, while the jitter variable controls the radius on a ring of random ellipses created in the for loop. Upon dragging the mouse (i.e., with the button pressed), the ring of ellipses will follow the cursor using the last jitter and scatter settings set. This is because mouse dragging and mouse moving, similarly to the press and release events, are processed as unique mouse event states—you can't press and release at the same time, nor can you move and drag at the same time.

```
    // mouseMoved Example
    float x, y;
    // declare and initialize radius
    float r = 1.5;
    float jitter = 5;
    float scatter = 1;

    void setup(){
      size(400, 400);
      // initialize x, y
      x = width/2.0;
      y = height/2.0;
      frameRate(30);
      smooth();
      noStroke();
```

12

```
}

void draw(){
  // fading background
  fill(0, 5);
  rect(0, 0, width, height);

  fill(255);
  for (int i=0; i<scatter; i++){
    float angle = random(TWO_PI);
    float sctterDistX = x+cos(angle)*jitter;
    float sctterDistY = y+sin(angle)*jitter;
    ellipse(sctterDistX, sctterDistY, r*2, r*2);
  }
}

void mouseDragged() {
  x = mouseX;
  y = mouseY;
}

// scatter/jitter ellipse
void mouseMoved() {
  scatter = mouseX*.05;
  jitter = mouseY*.05;
}
```

The next example, shown in Figure 12-1, combines mouse events with some of the motion principles covered in Chapter 11. I think you'll find this next sketch more aesthetically interesting than the "learning" examples you've looked at thus far in this chapter—but you've got to crawl some before you dance! This sketch allows you to plot points, or nodes, that get connected with lines. After three or more nodes are plotted, you can click back on the initial plotted node and close the shape. Once the shape is closed, some cool stuff happens. Here's the code:

```
// Shape Builder and Animator Example
float nodeRadius = 5.0;
// holds node coordinate values
float[]nodeXPos = new float[0];
float[]nodeYPos= new float[0];

color initialNode = color(0);
boolean isShapeClosed = false;

//dynamics variables (moves shape)
float gravity = .95;
float jitterRange = 5;
float elasticRangeMin = .75;
float elasticRangeMax = .95;
```

```
float friction = .85;
float[]jitter = new float[0];
float[]xSpeed = new float[0];
float[]ySpeed = new float[0];
float[]elasticity = new float[0];

void setup(){
  size(400, 600);
  frameRate(30);
  smooth();
}

void draw(){
  // create simple shape trails
  fill(255, 36);
  rect(0, 0, width, height);

  if (nodeXPos.length>1){
    // draw line between nodes
    drawEdge();
    // check if mouse is over original node
    checkOverInitialNode();
    // animate shape
    moveShape();
  }
  // draw node
  drawNode();
}

// change node fill color when mouse is over initial node
void checkOverInitialNode(){
  if (isInitialNode()){
    initialNode = color(255, 127, 0);
  }
  else {
    initialNode = color(0);
  }
}

//function to draw lines between nodes
void drawEdge(){
  stroke(100, 50, 20);
  for (int i=0; i<nodeXPos.length; i++){
    if (i>0){
      line(nodeXPos[i], nodeYPos[i], nodeXPos[i-1], nodeYPos[i-1]);
    }
    // close shape, line between last node and initial node
    if (isShapeClosed && i == nodeXPos.length-1){
      line(nodeXPos[i], nodeYPos[i], nodeXPos[0], nodeYPos[0]);
```

12

```
      }
    }
  }

  // function to draw nodes
  void drawNode(){
    // draw nodes at shape vertices
    noStroke();
    for (int i=0; i<nodeXPos.length; i++){
      // initial node has own color variable
      if (i==0){
        fill(initialNode);
      }
      else{
        fill(0);
      }
      ellipse(nodeXPos[i], nodeYPos[i], nodeRadius*2, nodeRadius*2);
    }
  }

  // function returns true/false if mouse is over initial node
  boolean isInitialNode(){
    boolean isOnNode = false;
    if (nodeXPos.length>2){
      if (dist(mouseX, mouseY, nodeXPos[0], nodeYPos[0]) < nodeRadius){
        isOnNode = true;
      }
    }
    return isOnNode;
  }

  void mousePressed(){
    if(isShapeClosed){
      // after shape is closed empty arrays
      nodeXPos = subset(nodeXPos, 0, 0);
      nodeYPos = subset(nodeYPos, 0, 0);
      xSpeed = subset(xSpeed, 0, 0);
      ySpeed = subset(ySpeed, 0, 0);
      jitter = subset(jitter, 0, 0);
      elasticity = subset(elasticity, 0, 0);

      //reset variable to false
      isShapeClosed = false;
    }

    if(!isInitialNode()){
      // if not on initial node plot at mouse position
      // increase size of node coordinate arrays
      nodeXPos = append(nodeXPos, mouseX);
```

```
      nodeYPos = append(nodeYPos, mouseY);

      // increase size of dynamics arrays
      xSpeed = append(xSpeed, 0);
      jitter = append(jitter, random(-jitterRange, jitterRange));
      elasticity = append(elasticity, random(elasticRangeMin, ➥
            elasticRangeMax));
      ySpeed = append(ySpeed, 0);
  }
  else {
    // set to true to avoid additional nodes on shape
    isShapeClosed = true;
  }
}

//function to move shape
void moveShape(){
  //animate after shape is closed
  if (isShapeClosed){
    for (int i=0; i<nodeXPos.length; i++){
      nodeXPos[i]+=xSpeed[i];
      ySpeed[i]+=gravity;
      nodeYPos[i]+=ySpeed[i];

      // set display window edge collision
      // right display window edge
      if (nodeXPos[i]>width-nodeRadius){
        nodeXPos[i] = width-nodeRadius;
        xSpeed[i]*=-1;
      }
      // left display window edge
      if (nodeXPos[i]<nodeRadius){
        nodeXPos[i] = nodeRadius;
        xSpeed[i]*=-1;
      }

      // bottom display window edge
      if (nodeYPos[i]>height-nodeRadius){
        nodeYPos[i] = height-nodeRadius;
        xSpeed[i]+=jitter[i];
        xSpeed[i]*=friction;
        jitter[i]*=friction;
        ySpeed[i]*=-1;
        ySpeed[i]*=elasticity[i];
      }
    }
  }
}
```

12

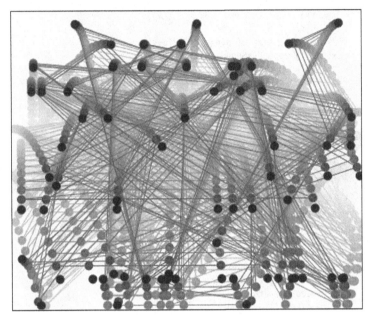

Figure 12-1. Shape Builder and Animator Example sketch

You should play with this sketch some to see what it can do. Besides running the sketch, I also recommend messing with some of the variable values declared at the top of the program.

To give you a better understanding, I'll now go over the sketch a section at a time.

```
// Shape Builder and Animator Example
float nodeRadius = 5.0;
// holds node coordinate values
float[]nodeXPos = new float[0];
float[]nodeYPos= new float[0];

color initialNode = color(0);
boolean isShapeClosed = false;

//dynamics variables (moves shape)
float gravity = .95;
float jitterRange = 5;
float elasticRangeMin = .75;
float elasticRangeMax = .95;
float friction = .85;
float[]jitter = new float[0];
float[]xSpeed = new float[0];
float[]ySpeed = new float[0];
float[]elasticity = new float[0];
```

As usual, I declare global variables at the top of the program, before the setup() function. The nodeXPos[] and nodeYPos[] arrays hold the shape coordinate data as the shapes are plotted. The initialNode color variable is used to dynamically set a color on the initial plotted node when it is moused over—this functions like a rollover effect. (Later in the chapter, I'll look at more examples of custom interactive buttons in Processing.) The Boolean variable isShapeClosed maintains the status of the closed state of the shape, which is important, as animation only occurs when this variable is true. The dynamics variables (most of which were discussed in Chapter 11) handle the animation. Many of the variables are arrays, since animation is applied to each individual node. Since it's not known how many nodes will be plotted for each shape, these arrays are initialized with zero length. Later in the sketch, as the user plots a node, values (and length) are added to the array using Processing's append() function.

```
void setup(){
  size(400, 600);
  frameRate(30);
  smooth();
}
```

The setup() function is nice and simple—hopefully, it doesn't need any explanation.

```
void draw(){
  // create simple shape trails
  fill(255, 36);
  rect(0, 0, width, height);

  if (nodeXPos.length>1){
    // draw line between nodes
    drawEdge();
    // check if mouse is over original node
    checkOverInitialNode();
    // animate shape
    moveShape();
  }
  // draw node
  drawNode();
}
```

The draw() function is relatively simple as well, considering the amount of stuff happening in this sketch. By creating some custom functions, I was able to keep the draw() function pretty lean. I wrapped the three custom function calls (drawEdge(), checkOverInitialNode(), and moveShape()) in a conditional block to ensure that at least two nodes are plotted prior to connecting the nodes with lines. drawEdge() calls a function that handles the drawing of the lines between the nodes. I called this function prior to actually drawing the nodes so that the nodes appear on top of the connecting lines. checkOverInitialNode() checks if the mouse is over the initial node, allowing the color of the node to be changed. moveShape() animates the shape after it's closed. Below the conditional block, I called drawNode(), which, as you might suspect, draws the nodes.

12

```
void checkOverInitialNode(){
  if (isInitialNode()){
    initialNode = color(255, 127, 0);
  }
  else {
    initialNode = color(0);
  }
}
```

The checkOverInitialNode() function sets the color variable initialNode to orange when the mouse hovers over the initial node, and then resets it to black when the mouse moves off the node.

```
void drawEdge(){
  stroke(100, 50, 20);
  for (int i=0; i<nodeXPos.length; i++){
    if (i>0){
      line(nodeXPos[i], nodeYPos[i], nodeXPos[i-1], nodeYPos[i-1]);
    }
    // close shape, line between last node and initial node
    if (isShapeClosed && i == nodeXPos.length-1){
      line(nodeXPos[i], nodeYPos[i], nodeXPos[0], nodeYPos[0]);
    }
  }
}
```

drawEdge() draws a line connecting the plotted nodes. The for loop is controlled by the length of the nodeXPos[] array, which increases each time a new node is plotted. The conditional blocks nested within the for loop ensure that lines are drawn only when there are at least two nodes plotted, and that the final line connects the last plotted node with the initial node, closing the shape.

```
void drawNode(){
  // draw nodes at shape vertices
  noStroke();
  for (int i=0; i<nodeXPos.length; i++){
    // initial node has own color variable
    if (i==0){
      fill(initialNode);
    }
    else{
      fill(0);
    }
    ellipse(nodeXPos[i], nodeYPos[i], nodeRadius*2, nodeRadius*2);
  }
}
```

drawNode() draws the nodes using Processing's ellipse() function and the coordinate values stored in the nodeXPos[] and nodeYPos[] arrays. The conditional if...else block fills the initial node's color using the intialNode color variable, while all the other nodes are filled with black. Using the intialNode variable allows the first plotted node's color to be changed when the mouse is over it, providing some interactive direction to the user.

```
// function returns true/false if mouse is over initial node
boolean isInitialNode(){
  boolean isOnNode = false;
  if (nodeXPos.length>2){
    if (dist(mouseX, mouseY, nodeXPos[0], nodeYPos[0]) < nodeRadius){
      isOnNode = true;
    }
  }
  return isOnNode;
}
```

The isInitialNode() function returns true if there are more than two nodes plotted and the mouse is over the initially plotted node. If neither of these conditions is true, the function returns false. Notice how I declared the function using the boolean keyword in front of the function name; this enforces that the function must return a Boolean value. Note also that the Boolean variable isOnNode, which I declared within the function, only exists locally (has local scope) within the function.

```
void mousePressed(){
  if(isShapeClosed){
    // after shape is closed empty arrays
    nodeXPos = subset(nodeXPos, 0, 0);
    nodeYPos = subset(nodeYPos, 0, 0);
    xSpeed = subset(xSpeed, 0, 0);
    ySpeed = subset(ySpeed, 0, 0);
    jitter = subset(jitter, 0, 0);
    elasticity = subset(elasticity, 0, 0);

    //reset variable to false
    isShapeClosed = false;
  }

  if(!isInitialNode()){
    // if not on initial node plot at mouse position
    // increase size of node coordinate arrays
    nodeXPos = append(nodeXPos, mouseX);
    nodeYPos = append(nodeYPos, mouseY);

    // increase size of dynamics arrays
    xSpeed = append(xSpeed, 0);
    jitter = append(jitter, random(-jitterRange, jitterRange));
    elasticity = append(elasticity, random(elasticRangeMin, ➥
          elasticRangeMax));
    ySpeed = append(ySpeed, 0);
  }
  else {
    // set to true to avoid additional nodes on shape
```

12

```
        isShapeClosed = true;
      }
   }
```

The mousePressed() function begins with a conditional block that initializes the sketch arrays when the shape is closed; this allows new shapes to be plotted when the mouse is pressed (only after the shape has been closed and has begun animating). I used Processing's subset() function to reset the primitive arrays. The function returns a subset of an array. The first argument is the array to subset, the second argument is the place in the array to begin the subset, and the third argument is the number of positions in the array to include in the subset. Since I used 0, 0 for the starting point and number of positions in the subset, an empty array was returned. Notice that I assigned the empty array back to the same array I used in the first argument; this may look odd, but it is perfectly legal. At the end of the conditional block, I reset the variable isShapeClosed to false to allow new nodes to be plotted.

The next conditional block, if(!isInitialNode()), uses the ! operator with the function call isInitialNode(). The function call returns a Boolean value (true or false). Prefacing the function call with the exclamation mark means that the conditional test will evaluate to true when the function call returns false (i.e., when the user is not pressing on the initial node). This kind of logic can hurt your head. Instead of using !isInitialNode(), you could also use isInitialNode() == false or isInitialNode() != true to handle the test.

Within the conditional block, I used Processing's append() function. This function increases the length of arrays. The function takes two arguments: the first argument is the array to append to, and the second is the value to add to the array. Like subset(), the append() function returns the changed array, which I reassigned to the same array variable. On each mouse press, all six of the arrays are appended to. Finally, if the user clicks the initial node, the arrays are not expanded, but the Boolean variable isShapeClosed is set to true.

```
void moveShape(){
  //animate after shape is closed
  if (isShapeClosed){
    for (int i=0; i<nodeXPos.length; i++) {
      nodeXPos[i]+=xSpeed[i];
      ySpeed[i]+=gravity;
      nodeYPos[i]+=ySpeed[i];

      // set display window edge collision
      // right display window edge
      if (nodeXPos[i]>width-nodeRadius){
        nodeXPos[i] = width-nodeRadius;
        xSpeed[i]*=-1;
      }
      // left display window edge
      if (nodeXPos[i]<nodeRadius){
        nodeXPos[i] = nodeRadius;
        xSpeed[i]*=-1;
```

578

```
        }

        // bottom display window edge
        if (nodeYPos[i]>height-nodeRadius){
          nodeYPos[i] = height-nodeRadius;
          xSpeed[i]+=jitter[i];
          xSpeed[i]*=friction;
          jitter[i]*=friction;
          ySpeed[i]*=-1;
          ySpeed[i]*=elasticity[i];

        }
      }
    }
  }
```

The final function in the sketch, moveShape(), controls the movement of the shape. I nested all the motion code in the conditional block (isShapeClosed), which evaluates to true only if the shape is closed. The actual motion code should look familiar, as similar code was covered in Chapter 11. The for loop ensures that speed values are added to each of the shape's nodes (the lines connecting the nodes rely on the nodes' coordinates for their placement), and the collision code makes each node bounce off the sides and bottom of the display window. The animation uses gravity and jitter, which simulate the shape falling with acceleration and deflecting off an irregular ground surface. The array variables elasticity[] and friction[] eventually bring the individual nodes to a stop at the bottom of the display window.

Adding interface elements

Next, I'll look at creating more elaborate interface elements, such as interactive buttons. Processing doesn't come with any native prebuilt buttons, but you can easily build them, as I sort of did in the last example when I tested if the mouse was pressed on the initially plotted node. The only difference between detecting a mouse event on a button and detecting a mouse event on the entire display window is in the evaluation of the size of the bounded hit area (the area that detects the event). Of course, when building a user interface, you generally want to give the user more control than they get by simply clicking the screen.

When creating a button, you can use Processing's drawing/text functions or import a graphic—I'll discuss both approaches in this chapter. This first sketch creates a single button that starts a simple animation of a rectangle moving across the screen:

```
// Start Button

// button
float btnX, btnY, btnW, btnH;

// moving rectangle
float x = 25;
```

12

```
float y = 30;
float w = 10;
float h = w;
float xSpeed = 0;

void setup(){
  size(600, 100);
  btnX = width/2;
  btnY = height-20;
  btnW = 50;
  btnH = 20;
}

void draw(){
  background(200);
  rectMode(CENTER);
  fill(250);
  stroke(150);
  rect(btnX, btnY, btnW, btnH);

  fill(0);
  noStroke();
  rect(x, y, w, h);
  x+=xSpeed;
}

void mousePressed(){
  if (mouseX>btnX-btnW/2 && mouseX< btnX+btnW/2 && ➡
      mouseY>btnY-btnH/2 && mouseY< btnY+btnH/2){
    xSpeed+=.2;
  }
}
```

In this sketch, each time the mouse is pressed on the rectangle at the bottom of the screen, the smaller square's speed increases by .02. The mouse detection is now working based on the bounds of the button. However, since no feedback is provided, the user might not understand that the sketch is working (or even that the rectangle is supposed to be a button). You could improve the sketch by giving the user some more visual cues, such as changing the cursor icon during detected mouse events, adding different rendering states to the button (up, over, and down), giving the button a label, and providing some output based on the current speed of the moving square. The following sketch is a modified version of the last that handles these improvements in two steps. The new and altered code is shown in bold.

```
// Interactive Button (step 1)

// button
float btnX, btnY, btnW, btnH;
```

```
color btnUpState = color(200, 200, 200);
color btnOverState = color(200, 200, 50);
color btnDownState = color(255, 150, 20);

color btnBackground = btnUpState;

// moving square
float x = 25;
float y = 30;
float w = 10;
float h = w;
float xSpeed = 0;

void setup(){
  size(600, 100);
  btnX = width/2;
  btnY = height-20;
  btnW = 50;
  btnH = 20;
}

void draw(){
  background(150);
  rectMode(CENTER);
  fill(btnBackground);
  stroke(100);
  rect(btnX, btnY, btnW, btnH);

  fill(0);
  noStroke();
  rect(x, y, w, h);
  x+=xSpeed;
}

void mousePressed(){
  if (mouseX>btnX-btnW/2 && mouseX< btnX+btnW/2 && ➡
      mouseY>btnY-btnH/2 && mouseY< btnY+btnH/2){
    xSpeed+=.2;
    btnBackground = btnDownState;
  }
}
void mouseReleased(){
    btnBackground = btnOverState;
}

void mouseMoved(){
  if (mouseX>btnX-btnW/2 && mouseX< btnX+btnW/2 && ➡
      mouseY>btnY-btnH/2 && mouseY< btnY+btnH/2){
    cursor(HAND);
```

12

581

```
    btnBackground = btnOverState;
  } else {
    cursor(ARROW);
    btnBackground = btnUpState;
  }
}
```

The sketch makes a little more sense visually now. Processing's cursor(cursor icon) function makes it really easy to change the cursor icon. The different built-in icons are ARROW, CROSS, HAND, MOVE, TEXT, and WAIT. Please note that once you change the cursor icon, the new icon will remain until you call the cursor(cursor icon) function again.

The final version of this sketch (shown in Figure 12-2) will make it even more user-friendly, and will also add a few more interface elements, such as buttons with labels. Unfortunately, making the sketch simpler for the user can mean more (potentially a lot more) work for the coder. Creating ergonomically friendly interfaces requires a lot of code, especially when the language (like Processing) doesn't rely on a set of prebuilt widgets (buttons, sliders, spinners, etc.).

> *Please note that the following Final Interactive Button Example sketch requires that the Processing font* Verdana-10.vlw *be installed in the sketch's data directory. You can create the font yourself by using Processing's* Create Font *command, found under the* Tools *menu, or you can download the font from the Download section on the friends of ED web site (*www.friendsofed.com/downloads.html*).*

```
// Final Interactive Button Example

// font used for button text
PFont myFont;
//buttons
float btn1X, btn1Y, btn1W, btn1H;
float btn2X, btn2Y, btn2W, btn2H;
float btn3X, btn3Y, btn3W, btn3H;

color btnUpState = color(200, 200, 200);
color btnOverState = color(200, 200, 50);
color btnDownState = color(255, 150, 20);

color btn1Background = btnUpState;
color btn2Background = btnUpState;

// moving square
float x = 25;
float w = 10;
float h = w;
// randomly place square y position on screen
float y = random(h/2, 70);
```

```
float xSpeed = 0;
color movingSquareBackground = color(random(255), ➡
        random(255), random(255));

//controls mouse trails
boolean isTrailable = false;
// mouse trails check box
boolean isTrailsSelected = false;

void setup(){
  size(600, 100);
  // load font from within the sketch's data directory
  myFont = loadFont("Verdana-10.vlw");
  textFont(myFont, 10);

  //buttons
  //speed- button
  btn1X = 250;
  btn1Y = height-20;
  btn1W = 50;
  btn1H = 20;

  //speed+ button
  btn2X = width-250;
  btn2Y = height-20;
  btn2W = 50;
  btn2H = 20;

  // check box controls mouse trails
  btn3X = width-60;
  btn3Y = height-20;
  btn3W = 10;
  btn3H = 10;
}

void draw(){
  rectMode(CENTER);

  // mouse trails
  if (isTrailable){
    fill(150, 16);
    rect(width/2, height/2, width, height);
  }
  else {
    background(150);
  }

  stroke(100);
  //btn 1 - decreases speed
```

12

```
          fill(btn1Background);
          rect(btn1X, btn1Y, btn1W, btn1H);
          fill(75);
          text("speed -", btn1X-17, btn1Y+btn1H/4);

          //btn2 - increases speed
          fill(btn2Background);
          rect(btn2X, btn2Y, btn2W, btn2H);
          fill(75);
          text("speed +", btn2X-17, btn2Y+btn2H/4);

          //btn3 - check box controls mouse trails
          fill(255);
          rect(btn3X, btn3Y, btn3W, btn3H);
          fill(75);
          text("trails", btn3X+10, btn3Y+btn3H/4);
          if (isTrailsSelected){
            // draw x in box
            line(btn3X-btn3W/2, btn3Y-btn3H/2, btn3X+btn3W/2, btn3Y+btn3H/2);
            line(btn3X-btn3W/2, btn3Y+btn3H/2, btn3X+btn3W/2, btn3Y-btn3H/2);
          }

          //moving square
          fill(movingSquareBackground);
          noStroke();
          rect(x, y, w, h);
          x+=xSpeed;
          // show speed
          rect(x, y, w, h);
          fill(75);
          text(xSpeed, 10, height-10);
          // ensure square stays on screen
          if (x>width){
            x = 0;
            y = random(h/2, 70);
            movingSquareBackground = color(random(255), ➡
                   random(255), random(255));
          }
          else if (x<0){
            x = width;
            y = random(h/2, 70);
            movingSquareBackground = color(random(255), ➡
                   random(255), random(255));
          }
        }

        void mousePressed(){
          if (mouseX>btn1X-btn1W/2 && mouseX< btn1X+btn1W/2 && ➡
            mouseY>btn1Y-btn1H/2 && mouseY< btn1Y+btn1H/2){
```

584

```
      xSpeed-=.2;
      btn1Background = btnDownState;
    }
    if (mouseX>btn2X-btn2W/2 && mouseX< btn2X+btn2W/2 && ➡
      mouseY>btn2Y-btn2H/2 && mouseY< btn2Y+btn2H/2){
      xSpeed+=.2;
      btn2Background = btnDownState;
    }
    if (mouseX>btn3X-btn3W/2 && mouseX< btn3X+btn3W/2 && ➡
      mouseY>btn3Y-btn3H/2 && mouseY< btn3Y+btn3H/2){
      if (isTrailsSelected) {
        isTrailsSelected = false;
        isTrailable = false;
      }
      else {
        isTrailsSelected = true;
        isTrailable = true;
      }
    }
  }
}
void mouseReleased(){
  if (btn1Background==btnDownState){
    btn1Background = btnOverState;
  }
  else if (btn2Background==btnDownState){
    btn2Background = btnOverState;
  }
}

void mouseMoved(){
  if (mouseX>btn1X-btn1W/2 && mouseX< btn1X+btn1W/2 && ➡
    mouseY>btn1Y-btn1H/2 && mouseY< btn1Y+btn1H/2){
    cursor(HAND);
    btn1Background = btnOverState;
  }
  else {
    cursor(ARROW);
    btn1Background = btnUpState;
  }

  if (mouseX>btn2X-btn2W/2 && mouseX< btn2X+btn2W/2 && ➡
    mouseY>btn2Y-btn2H/2 && mouseY< btn2Y+btn2H/2){
    cursor(HAND);
    btn2Background = btnOverState;
  }
  else {
    cursor(ARROW);
    btn2Background = btnUpState;
  }
```

12

```
//button 3
if (mouseX>btn3X-btn3W/2 && mouseX< btn3X+btn3W/2 && ➡
  mouseY>btn3Y-btn3H/2 && mouseY< btn3Y+btn3H/2){
  cursor(HAND);
}
else {
  cursor(ARROW);
}
}
```

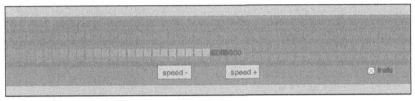

Figure 12-2. Final Interactive Button Example sketch

The finished interactive buttons example is likely a little intimidating, mostly due to its length. One of the (annoying) difficulties of coding graphical interfaces is the sheer amount of required code. Although verbose, interface code is not overly complex. Much of the code is redundant. For example, the last sketch included three buttons (one of which operated as a check box) which all shared a lot of common functionality.

```
// font used for button text
PFont myFont;
// buttons
float btn1X, btn1Y, btn1W, btn1H;
float btn2X, btn2Y, btn2W, btn2H;
float btn3X, btn3Y, btn3W, btn3H;

color btnUpState = color(200, 200, 200);
color btnOverState = color(200, 200, 50);
color btnDownState = color(255, 150, 20);

color btn1Background = btnUpState;
color btn2Background = btnUpState;
```

All three buttons are defined by btn#x, btn#y, btn#w, and btn#h properties. (The # symbol just represents the different button numbers.) I could have made this example more efficient and elegant by creating a Button or even Widget class, since all the objects have the same four properties. This would be an excellent thing to try on your own. The rest of the example should be straightforward, and stuff you've seen before. For example, notice the following conditional statement within the draw() function:

```
// mouse trails
  if (isTrailable){
    fill(150, 16);
    rect(width/2, height/2, width, height);
  }
  else {
    background(150);
  }
```

The if...else statement paints either a semi-opaque layer or an opaque layer, based on the state of the isTrailable Boolean variable. Clicking the trails check box button controls whether the variable is true or false. Within the draw() function, the drawing of each of the buttons is handled with the following code:

```
stroke(100);
//btn 1 - decreases speed
fill(btn1Background);
rect(btn1X, btn1Y, btn1W, btn1H);
fill(75);
text("speed -", btn1X-17, btn1Y+btn1H/4);

//btn2 - increases speed
fill(btn2Background);
rect(btn2X, btn2Y, btn2W, btn2H);
fill(75);
text("speed +", btn2X-17, btn2Y+btn2H/4);

//btn3 - check box controls mouse trails
fill(255);
rect(btn3X, btn3Y, btn3W, btn3H);
fill(75);
text("trails", btn3X+10, btn3Y+btn3H/4);

if (isTrailsSelected){
  // draw x in box
  line(btn3X-btn3W/2, btn3Y-btn3H/2, btn3X+btn3W/2, btn3Y+btn3H/2);
  line(btn3X-btn3W/2, btn3Y+btn3H/2, btn3X+btn3W/2, btn3Y-btn3H/2);
}
```

The last snippet in the preceding code controls whether the check box is filled or empty, based on another Boolean variable, isTrailsSelected.

Each time the square exits the screen, either right or left, it is mapped back to the opposite side so that it will keep moving. Also, just for some variety, the color and y position of the box change randomly:

```
if (x>width){
  x = 0;
  y = random(h/2, 70);
  movingSquareBackground = color(random(255),⟶
```

12

```
                    random(255), random(255));
      }
      else if (x<0){
        x = width;
        y = random(h/2, 70);
        movingSquareBackground = color(random(255), ➥
             random(255), random(255));
      }
```

The main crux of the sketch is the mouse detection code. In the discussion that follows, I'll look at each mouse event separately. Here's the first event:

```
      void mousePressed(){
        if (mouseX>btn1X-btn1W/2 && mouseX< btn1X+btn1W/2 && ➥
          mouseY>btn1Y-btn1H/2 && mouseY< btn1Y+btn1H/2){
          xSpeed-=.2;
          btn1Background = btnDownState;
        }
        if (mouseX>btn2X-btn2W/2 && mouseX< btn2X+btn2W/2 && ➥
          mouseY>btn2Y-btn2H/2 && mouseY< btn2Y+btn2H/2){
          xSpeed+=.2;
          btn2Background = btnDownState;
        }
        if (mouseX>btn3X-btn3W/2 && mouseX< btn3X+btn3W/2 && ➥
          mouseY>btn3Y-btn3H/2 && mouseY< btn3Y+btn3H/2){
          if (isTrailsSelected) {
            isTrailsSelected = false;
            isTrailable = false;
          }
          else {
            isTrailsSelected = true;
            isTrailable = true;
          }
        }
      }
```

When the mouse is pressed, the code checks if the mouse is over one of the buttons by comparing the button's coordinates to the mouse position. To keep things simple, I used a bunch of redundant code in the three conditional statements. When either of the speed buttons are pressed, I set the fill color of the buttons with the lines:

```
      btn1Background = btnDownState;
```
or
```
      btn2Background = btnDownState;
```

These buttons also obviously increment/decrement the xSpeed of the moving square. When the check box is pressed, it is toggled either on or off depending upon its current state, setting the Boolean variable isTrailsSelected. When isTrailsSelected is true, an x fills the box. I also set the Boolean variable isTrailable to the same value as isTrailsSelected, which changes the display window's background fill from 100 percent alpha to 16 percent alpha with the following conditional block in the draw() function:

```
if (isTrailable){
    fill(150, 16);
    rect(width/2, height/2, width, height);
}
else {
    background(150);
}
```

Next, I'll look at the mouse Release event:

```
void mouseReleased(){
    if (btn1Background==btnDownState){
    btn1Background = btnOverState;
    }
    else if (btn2Background==btnDownState){
    btn2Background = btnOverState;
    }
}
```

The mouse release event just returns the buttons to their over states. I used the over state instead of the up state, as the mouse will still be over the button during the mouse release.

```
void mouseMoved(){
    if (mouseX>btn1X-btn1W/2 && mouseX< btn1X+btn1W/2 && ➡
       mouseY>btn1Y-btn1H/2 && mouseY< btn1Y+btn1H/2){
    cursor(HAND);
    btn1Background = btnOverState;
    }
    else {
    cursor(ARROW);
    btn1Background = btnUpState;
    }

    if (mouseX>btn2X-btn2W/2 && mouseX< btn2X+btn2W/2 && ➡
       mouseY>btn2Y-btn2H/2 && mouseY< btn2Y+btn2H/2){
    cursor(HAND);
    btn2Background = btnOverState;
    }
    else {
    cursor(ARROW);
    btn2Background = btnUpState;
    }

    //button 3
    if (mouseX>btn3X-btn3W/2 && mouseX< btn3X+btn3W/2 && ➡
       mouseY>btn3Y-btn3H/2 && mouseY< btn3Y+btn3H/2){
    cursor(HAND);
```

12

589

```
    }
    else {
      cursor(ARROW);
    }
  }
```

The mouse move event code is functionally not very important with regard to actually moving the square. However, it is critically important with regard to the ergonomics of the sketch. By changing the cursor and adding a rollover state, when the user hovers over one of the interactive elements, the GUI feels more responsive and responds in a more expected way vis-à-vis other modern software applications. This last example could be greatly expanded, particularly through the addition of more GUI components and standardization of the elements and functionality.

Most programming languages have dedicated code libraries or GUI toolkits for handling GUI elements (widgets) such as buttons, dialog boxes, sliders, and so on. AWT and Swing are two popular Java GUI toolkits for this purpose (see `http://java.sun.com/products/jfc/` for more information on AWT and Swing).

> Please note that it is not recommended that any AWT or Swing components be incorporated in Processing sketches. For the official statement on this and other GUI-relevant information, check out `http://dev.processing.org/reference/core/index.html`.

As of this writing, Processing has five (user-contributed) GUI libraries, which you can access from within the Processing application by choosing Help ➤ Reference ➤ Libraries, or online at `http://processing.org/reference/libraries/index.html`. I will not be covering Processing's libraries within this book. The best place to learn more about them is by searching Processing's online discussion board at `http://processing.org/discourse/yabb_beta/YaBB.cgi`. As Processing continues to evolve, it's likely that other GUI libraries will be created, and eventually maybe even a visual editor that will allow you to drag and drop pre-made components right into your sketches.

Creating a simple drawing application

Before moving on from the topic of mouse events, I thought it might be fun to create a simple drawing program. Within this program, you'll create pencil, paint, and eraser tools, as well as a selectable palette. There are two basic paths you could take here: a vector-based drawing program or a raster-based program (of course, you could also combine the two).

A vector-based program would allow you to select and edit the shapes you draw, as in a program such as Adobe Illustrator. However, programming this level of interactivity comes at the cost of added complexity (lots of it). With a simpler, raster-based approach, the display window pixels are colored directly—there is no functionality allowing the selection of shapes. The following example, in spite of being raster-based, is still a bit complicated; and similar to the last example, the GUI elements require quite a bit of code—therefore, the sketch will be built in stages. Figure 12-3 shows the completed drawing application.

Figure 12-3. Simple Drawing Application sketch

With this sketch, I tried to create a user-friendly interface with reactive interactive elements that clearly alert users when they can do something. The inclusion of both button over states and event-specific cursors should make users feel more comfortable mousing around the sketch. Although the sketch is over 350 lines of code, the functionality and feature set is still very simple. You can draw with a pencil, paintbrush, or eraser. The current selected paint color is the background color surrounding the three tool buttons. I found this solution simple to code in comparison to the addition of a highlight box on the actual palette or some other more complicated alternative. The pencil tool draws a continuous line, and the brush tool draws a line composed of a series of strokes; the faster you move the brush, the straighter the strokes making up the paint mark. The eraser paints the background color over whatever it moves across. You can control the size of the marks all three tools make by using the slider in the top-right of the sketch. I gave the slider handle an over state as well, similar to the tool buttons, again to give users feedback as they mouse over it. The clear button fills the entire screen with the currently selected color. Other things that might be fun to add to the sketch could include a series of pre-made shapes that you could draw with (simple polygons, ellipses, stars, etc.). I imagined that these could be created as buttons on the top bar of the sketch (between the Processing Paint title and the slider). You could also add some imaging filters, such as blur and contrast. In addition, a save function could be added to allow users to capture a screenshot of the art they create with the sketch.

12

591

To ensure that the sketch functions properly, please enter the following code into Processing in the exact order that I present it. As usual, the sketch begins with a title and global variable declarations:

```
/* Basic Drawing Application Example
Ira Greenberg, April 17, 2006 */
// fonts
PFont titleFont, clearFont;
```

The PFont variables were used for label text. I chose to dynamically generate a font by using Processing's createFont() function. This function attempts to convert a typeface installed on your system into the format Processing needs. Later in the sketch, I specified Arial as the typeface to convert, as it's a very common face. Don't worry if you don't have Arial installed on your system—you'll be able to substitute a different face.

```
// canvas background color
color canvasBg = color(255);

// paint color
color paintColor;

// palette
color[]palette = new color[156];
```

The palette array was initialized with 156 slots in memory, based on a table 6 swatches across and 26 swatches down (6 × 26 = 156). This size was arbitrarily based on the size of the overall palette, as well as the size of each swatch.

```
// create 3 icons
PImage pencil, brush, eraser;
```

I used imported images for the three tool buttons and Processing's built-in PImage data type. These images need to live in Processing's data directory. You can download these images from the Download section of the friends of ED web site (www.friendsofed.com/downloads.html).

```
// panels coordinate arrays
float[] menu, tools, canvas;

// buttons coordinate arrays
float[] pencilBtn, brushBtn, eraserBtn;
```

Each section of the drawing interface, as well as the buttons, was broadly defined as a coordinate array (with a length of 4), holding each section/button's x, y, width, and height values.

```
//create button state colors
color buttonUp = color(175, 175, 50, 150);
color buttonOver = color(255, 130, 20, 175);
color buttonSelected = color(250, 250, 30, 175);
```

```
// set initial button background colors
color pencilBg = buttonSelected;
color brushBg = buttonUp;
color eraserBg = buttonUp;

// button booleans
boolean isPencilSelected = true;
boolean isBrushSelected = false;
boolean isEraserSelected = false;
```

As in the last example, I created up, over, and selected states for each of the buttons, as well as Boolean values to hold the specific button states. For example, I initialized the sketch by making the pencil active and the other tools inactive. Thus, I set isPencilSelected to true and isBrushSelected and isEraserSelected to false.

```
// slider
float[] sliderBar, sliderHandle;
boolean isSliderMovable = false;
color sliderHandleUp = color(255, 127, 0);
color sliderHandleOver = color(255, 200, 0);
color sliderHandleBg = sliderHandleUp;
float sliderValue = 0;

//clear button
float[]clearBtn;

color clearBtnOver = color(50, 50, 150);
color clearBtnUp = color(0, 0);
color clearBtnBg = clearBtnUp;
```

The slider and the clear button were handled very similarly to the tool buttons. I could have encapsulated this more and removed some of the redundant structures, but the code would have become denser and more inscrutable. I could have also used an object-oriented structure—building a base widget class and having each specific interactive element extend (inherit) it and then add its own specific properties/methods. This OOP approach would be an excellent exercise to try on your own.

After declaring all the global variables, I then initialized many of them in the setup() function.

```
void setup(){
    size(600, 400);
    background(canvasBg);
    frameRate(30);

    // create fonts
    titleFont = createFont("Arial", 11);
    clearFont = createFont("Arial", 10);
```

12

The createFont() function dynamically generates a font based on the typeface name argument passed to the function. Again, I used Arial as it's a very common face, and is likely installed on your computer. If you don't have Arial (or if you dislike it), you can substitute it with any face installed on your computer. If you're not sure what faces are installed, you can run the command println(PFont.list()); in Processing, which will output all your installed fonts.

```
// create icons
pencil = loadImage("pencil_cursor.png");
brush = loadImage("brush_cursor.png");
eraser = loadImage("eraser_cursor.png");
```

To load the cursor PNG images, you need to first import them into the sketch's data directory using the Add File command, found under the Sketch menu.

```
// create panel coordinate arrays
menu = new float[]{
  0, 0, width, 25     };
tools = new float[]{
  0, menu[3], 50, 165     };
canvas = new float[]{
  tools[2], menu[3], width-tools[2], height-menu[3]+1     };

// create button coordinate arrays
pencilBtn = new float[]{
  tools[0]+5, tools[1]+10, tools[2]-11, 45     };
brushBtn = new float[]{
  tools[0]+5, pencilBtn[1]+ pencilBtn[3]+5, tools[2]-11, 45     };
eraserBtn = new float[]{
  tools[0]+5, brushBtn[1]+ brushBtn[3]+5, tools[2]-11, 45     };

// create slider coordinate arrays
sliderBar = new float[]{
  width-150, menu[1]+menu[3]/2, 75, menu[1]+menu[3]/2  };
sliderHandle = new float[]{
  sliderBar[0]+sliderBar[2]/2, sliderBar[1]-3, 6, 6     };

// create clear button coordinate array
clearBtn = new float[]{
  width-45, 6, 31, 13     };
```

I initialized the coordinate arrays, using existing interface elements as references in defining the specific coordinate values. Laying out an application based on these types of relationships adds flexibility to the GUI. For example, if three buttons are sized and placed based on the width of the tool pane, it doesn't matter if the application window eventually scales up or down—the buttons will resize appropriately and remain in the correct place in the interface. In this sketch, I didn't follow this rule religiously, but rather used it when it seemed convenient. Although laying elements relative to each other adds flexibility, it also makes the code a little harder to read. I tried to find a balance in the example, using a minimal amount of hard-coded magic numbers, or specific values put directly into the code. As mentioned previously, magic numbers are generally to be avoided.

```
//temporarily set colorMode to HSB
colorMode(HSB, 6, 26, 26);

//construct palette values
int paletteCounter = 0;
for (int j=0; j<6; j++){
  for (int i=palette.length/6; i>0; i--){
    if (i>13){
      palette[paletteCounter] = color(random(6), random(26)+5, ➥
       random(26)+5);
    }
    if (i<=13){
      palette[paletteCounter] = color(j, i*2, i*4);
    }
    paletteCounter++;
  }
}

//set initial color
paintColor = palette[23];

//reset colorMode to RGB
colorMode(RGB, 256, 256, 256);
}
```

In generating the palette, I used Processing's color data type. The top of the palette is generated with random color values, while the bottom part includes color gradients. I switched color modes from RGB to HSB, as I found it simpler to code the gradients this way. The colorMode() function not only allows you to select between the RGB and HSB modes, but it also lets you define the numeric range for each color component. This is a very handy function, especially for generating something like a gradient based on specific loop counter values. After I finished generating the color values, which I stored in an array, I switched back to the default RGB mode, with a range of 256 values for each color component. Next, we'll look at the draw() function:

```
void draw(){
  strokeWeight(1.0);

  // menu bar
  fill(40, 40, 60);
  noStroke();
  rect(menu[0], menu[1], menu[2], menu[3]);

  // tool panel
  fill(paintColor);
  noStroke();
```

12

```
rect(tools[0], tools[1], tools[2], tools[3]);

// title
fill(175, 175, 220);
textFont(titleFont);
text("Processing Paint", 5, menu[1]+menu[3]-8);

// slider (controls stroke width)
stroke(255, 127, 0);
noFill();
// slider artwork
rect(sliderBar[0]-10, sliderBar[1]-1.5, 3, 3);
rect(sliderBar[0]-8.5, sliderBar[1]-.5, 3, 3);
// slider bar
rect(sliderBar[0]+sliderBar[2]+5, sliderBar[1]-3.5, 7, 7);
rect(sliderBar[0]+sliderBar[2]+7.5, sliderBar[1]-1, 7, 7);
stroke(255);
line(sliderBar[0], sliderBar[1], sliderBar[0]+ sliderBar[2], ➡
    sliderBar[3]);
// slider handle
fill(sliderHandleBg);
stroke(150);
rect(sliderHandle[0], sliderHandle[1], sliderHandle[2], ➡
    sliderHandle[3]);

// clear button
stroke(255, 200, 0);
fill(clearBtnBg);
rect(clearBtn[0],clearBtn[1], clearBtn[2], clearBtn[3]);
fill(255, 200, 0);
textFont(clearFont);
text("clear", width-40, menu[1]+menu[3]-10);

// pencil button
fill(pencilBg);
stroke(200);
rect(pencilBtn[0], pencilBtn[1], pencilBtn[2], pencilBtn[3]);
image(pencil, pencilBtn[0]+pencilBtn[2]/2-pencil.width/2, ➡
    pencilBtn[1]+pencilBtn[3]/2-pencil.height/2);

// brush button
fill(brushBg);
stroke(200);
rect(brushBtn[0], brushBtn[1], brushBtn[2], brushBtn[3]);
image(brush, brushBtn[0]+brushBtn[2]/2-brush.width/2, ➡
    brushBtn[1]+brushBtn[3]/2-brush.height/2);

// eraser button
fill(eraserBg);
```

```
stroke(200);
rect(eraserBtn[0], eraserBtn[1], eraserBtn[2], eraserBtn[3]);
image(eraser, eraserBtn[0]+eraserBtn[2]/2-eraser.width/2, ➡
    eraserBtn[1]+eraserBtn[3]/2-eraser.height/2);
```

The code to draw all the interface elements, although verbose, is very straightforward, with the elements positioned in the display window in reference to other existing elements. Notice the numerous calls to the fill() and stroke() functions. As you'll remember, these calls set the rendering state of the program; if I call fill(255, 0, 0) until I call fill() again with different values, all future shapes will be filled with red. Also notice that I did not include any interactive code (the code that makes the buttons work) directly with the GUI elements.

```
// draw palette
int paletteCounter=0;
for (float i=0; i<tools[2]-8; i+=8){
  for (float j=menu[3]+tools[3]; j<height-8; j+=8){
    fill(palette[paletteCounter++]);
    strokeWeight(.5);
    rect(i, j, 8, 8);
  }
}
```

The nested for loops in the palette code are a little scary (and ugly) looking. The color palette is really just a series of rectangles filled with the colors stored in the palette color array, which was filled back in the setup() function. Users are able to select colors out of the palette through Processing's get() function, which simply returns a color value at a specific point in the display window. The mouse position will be used to define this point, like this: get(mouseX, mouseY);.

```
if (mousePressed && mouseX>tools[0]+tools[2] && ➡
  mouseY>menu[1]+menu[3]) {
  smooth();

  //pencil
  if (isPencilSelected){
    stroke(paintColor);
    strokeWeight(sliderValue);
    line(mouseX, mouseY, pmouseX, pmouseY);
  }
  //brush
  else if (isBrushSelected){
    strokeWeight(.25);
    float nozzleRadius = sliderValue;
    float sprayFeather = sliderValue*4;
    float strokeAngle = 0;
    float px = 0, py = 0, px2 = 0, py2 = 0;
    stroke(paintColor);
    for (int i=0; i<360; i++){
      px = mouseX-nozzleRadius*2+cos(radians(strokeAngle))* ➡
```

12

```
      nozzleRadius+random(sprayFeather);
      py = mouseY-nozzleRadius*2+sin(radians(strokeAngle))* ➥
      nozzleRadius+random(sprayFeather);
      px2 = pmouseX-nozzleRadius*2+cos(radians(strokeAngle))* ➥
      nozzleRadius+random(sprayFeather);
      py2 = pmouseY-nozzleRadius*2+sin(radians(strokeAngle))* ➥
      nozzleRadius+random(sprayFeather);
      line(px, py, px2, py2);
      strokeAngle+=1;
    }
  }
  //eraser
  else if (isEraserSelected){
    stroke(canvasBg);
    strokeWeight(sliderValue*4);
    line(mouseX, mouseY, pmouseX, pmouseY);
  }
}
```

From within draw(), the value of Processing's built-in mousePressed Boolean variable can be checked. As I already discussed, Processing also has a mousePressed() function, which I use a bit later in the sketch and outside of the draw() function. In the preceding code, I used an outer if clause to check if the mouse is pressed over the drawing canvas. If this is true, the nested if clauses check which tool is currently selected. If the pencil tool is selected, then the process is pretty straightforward: a stroke color and stroke weight are set, and Processing's line() function is called. The line() function uses Processing's mouse and pmouse x and y variables: line(mouseX, mouseY, pmouseX, pmouseY);. mouseX and mouseY are the current mouse coordinates, while pmouseX and pmouseY are the mouse x and y coordinates one frame prior to the current one. These are very convenient variables that work great for allowing you to easily simulate a drawing tool. Skipping the brush tool for a moment, the eraser tool works identically to the pencil tool—only the stroke is a little wider and the stroke color is always the color of the canvas background.

The brush code is a bit more complicated: as the brush is dragged, a series of lines are drawn somewhat randomly around the mouse position, giving a brushy look to the mark. I used the trig functions to generate the points around the current mouse position. You've looked at code like this in numerous other places in the book, as well as earlier in the chapter. The cos() function is used to get the x coordinate and sin() is used to get the y coordinate. The expression nozzleRadius+random(sprayFeather); controls how far the lines are drawn around the mouse position. You'll notice that I subtracted nozzleRadius*2 at the beginning of each of the px, py, px2, and py2 lines. I did this so that the cursor would appear in the center of the paint mark, not at the top-left corner. Try removing nozzleRadius*2 from each of the lines if you want to see how the cursor shifts. When painting with the brush, if you drag it quickly, the brush marks will straighten out, which is a nice (unexpected) effect, thanks again to the pmouseX and pmouseY variables.

```
    //slider dragging
    if (isSliderMovable && mousePressed && mouseX > ➥
        sliderBar[0] && mouseX<sliderBar[0]+sliderBar[2]){
      sliderHandle[0] = mouseX-sliderHandle[2]/2;
```

```
    }
    sliderValue = (sliderHandle[0]-sliderBar[0]+10)*.25;
  }
```

The last code snippet in draw() controls the slider event behavior. If the mouse is pressed on the slider handle, it can be dragged only across the x-axis, constrained between the ends of the slider bar. In setting the sliderValue variable, I needed to add 10 and multiply the actual coordinate value by .25 so that the value of sliderHandle's x position could be used for setting the pencil, brush, and eraser tools' stroke sizes, which are controlled by the slider.

After the draw() function is the mousePressed() function:

```
void mousePressed(){
  //pencil
  if (mouseX>pencilBtn[0] && mouseX<pencilBtn[0]+pencilBtn[2] && ➥
    mouseY>pencilBtn[1] && mouseY<pencilBtn[1]+pencilBtn[3]){
    // set selected button background color
    pencilBg = buttonSelected;
    // set boolean
    isPencilSelected = true;
    //set other buttons to unselected
    deselectBtns(0);
  } else
  //brush
  if (mouseX>brushBtn[0] && mouseX<brushBtn[0]+brushBtn[2] && ➥
    mouseY>brushBtn[1] && mouseY<brushBtn[1]+brushBtn[3]){
    // set selected button background color
    brushBg = buttonSelected;
    // set boolean
    isBrushSelected = true;
    //set other buttons to unselected
    deselectBtns(1);
  } else
  //eraser
  if (mouseX>eraserBtn[0] && mouseX<eraserBtn[0]+eraserBtn[2] && ➥
    mouseY>eraserBtn[1] && mouseY<eraserBtn[1]+eraserBtn[3]){
    // set selected button background color
    eraserBg = buttonSelected;
    // set boolean
    isEraserSelected = true;
    //set other buttons to unselected
    deselectBtns(2);
  } else
  // set painting color
  if (mouseX>tools[0] && mouseX<tools[0]+tools[2] && ➥
    mouseY>tools[1]+tools[3] && mouseY<height){
    paintColor = get(mouseX, mouseY);
  }
}
```

12

The pencil, brush, and eraser snippets all work similarly. With this code, I detect if the mouse is pressed on any of the buttons. If a button is pressed, I change the background color of the pressed button to show that it has been selected. In addition, I set a Boolean variable (either isPencilSelected, isBrushSelected, or isEraserSelected) to true. In draw(), I am checking for one of these to be true to allow drawing to occur. The last statement in each of these conditional blocks is deselectBtns(number); (number is replaced with either 0, 1, or 2 (for pencil, brush, or eraser, respectively). This function ensures that only one button is selected at a time. It wouldn't make sense for two drawing tools to be selected at the same time, so this function, in a sense, treats the three buttons as a group, preventing multiple selections. Radio buttons often work this way, allowing you only to select one button in a group.

The last part of the mousePressed() function is the code to select the paint color from the palette. As I discussed earlier, you can get specific color pixel values from Processing very simply, by using Processing's get() function and the mouse's current coordinate. The conditional block ensures that the mouse is pressed on the palette, but doesn't ensure that the mouse isn't on a line; so it's possible to select the color from the lines separating the swatches as the painting color.

```
void mouseReleased(){
  // clear button repaints background
  if (mouseX>clearBtn[0] && mouseX<clearBtn[0]+clearBtn[2] && ➡
    mouseY>clearBtn[1] && mouseY<clearBtn[1]+clearBtn[3]){
    canvasBg = paintColor;
    fill(canvasBg);
    rect(canvas[0], canvas[1], canvas[2], canvas[3]);
  }
}
```

I used the mouseReleased() function for the clear button. I could have used the mousePressed() function, but I thought it might be helpful to have an example of this function as well. mouseReleased() works very similarly to mousePressed(), except that the event is triggered when the button is released. Next, we'll look at the mouseMoved() function. This function provides the visual cues to the viewer (e.g., mouse over states), making the application interaction easy to understand.

```
void mouseMoved(){
  //pencil
  if (!isPencilSelected){
    if (mouseX>pencilBtn[0] && mouseX<pencilBtn[0]+pencilBtn[2] && ➡
      mouseY>pencilBtn[1] && mouseY<pencilBtn[1]+pencilBtn[3]){
      cursor(HAND);
      // set buttonOver background color
      pencilBg = buttonOver;
    }
    else {
      pencilBg = buttonUp;
    }
  }
```

600

```
    if (!isBrushSelected){
      if (mouseX>brushBtn[0] && mouseX<brushBtn[0]+brushBtn[2] && ➥
        mouseY>brushBtn[1] && mouseY<brushBtn[1]+brushBtn[3]){
        cursor(HAND);
        // set buttonOver background color
        brushBg = buttonOver;
      }
      else {
        brushBg = buttonUp;
      }
    }

    if(!isEraserSelected){
      if (mouseX>eraserBtn[0] && mouseX<eraserBtn[0]+eraserBtn[2] && ➥
        mouseY>eraserBtn[1] && mouseY<eraserBtn[1]+eraserBtn[3]){
        cursor(HAND);
        // set buttonOver background color
        eraserBg = buttonOver;
      }
      else {
        eraserBg = buttonUp;
      }
    }
```

The three conditionals for the pencil, brush, and eraser tools ensure that the cursor hand shows when the mouse is hovering over a button (if a button tool is not currently selected), and also changes the buttons' over states. Since the over states are just changes in fill color, the color needs be to reset to the button up color once the mouse has moved off the button (e.g., eraserBg = buttonUp).

```
    // set palette cursor
    if (mouseX>tools[0] && mouseX<tools[0]+tools[2] && ➥
      mouseY>tools[1]+tools[3] && mouseY<height){
      cursor(ARROW);
    }
    // set painting cursor
    if (mouseX>tools[0]+tools[2] && mouseX<width && ➥
      mouseY>menu[1]+menu[3] && mouseY<height){
      cursor(CROSS);
    }
```

These conditionals set the cursor state when the mouse is over the palette and drawing part of the window (the canvas).

```
    // slider handle detection and cursor
    if (mouseX>sliderHandle[0] && mouseX<sliderHandle[0]+ ➥
        sliderHandle[2] &&
      mouseY>sliderHandle[1] && mouseY<sliderHandle[1]+ ➥
        sliderHandle[3]){
      cursor(HAND);
```

12

```
            isSliderMovable = true;
            sliderHandleBg = sliderHandleOver;
        } else {
            //cursor(CROSS);
            isSliderMovable = false;
            sliderHandleBg = sliderHandleUp;
        }

        // clear button detection and cursor
        if (mouseX>clearBtn[0] && mouseX<clearBtn[0]+clearBtn[2] && ➡
          mouseY>clearBtn[1] && mouseY<clearBtn[1]+clearBtn[3]){
            cursor(HAND);
            clearBtnBg = clearBtnOver;
        } else {
            clearBtnBg = clearBtnUp;
        }
    }
```

The slider handle and clear button code work very similarly to the other buttons we looked at. The slider handle button uses a isSliderMovable Boolean variable that works in conjunction with code in draw(), only allowing the slider handle to be dragged when the mouse is pressed directly on the handle.

```
    // reset unselected buttons (pencil, brush, eraser)
    void deselectBtns(int index){
        switch(index){
        case 0:
            brushBg = buttonUp;
            eraserBg = buttonUp;
            isBrushSelected = false;
            isEraserSelected = false;
            break;
        case 1:
            pencilBg = buttonUp;
            eraserBg = buttonUp;
            isPencilSelected = false;
            isEraserSelected = false;
            break;
        case 2:
            pencilBg = buttonUp;
            brushBg = buttonUp;
            isPencilSelected = false;
            isBrushSelected = false;
            break;
        }
    }
```

The deselectBtns() function is used to maintain only one active drawing tool button at a time. Again, I structured these three buttons like a radio button group, where only one selection can be active at a time. The function, by receiving the index of the current tool, resets the other unselected tools, including setting their up states.

If you've entered all the code in the order I presented it, your drawing application should now be able to be run. Please remember that if you don't have the typeface Arial installed (you probably do), you'll need to specify a different (installed) typeface on your computer, in the following two lines:

```
titleFont = createFont("Arial", 11);
clearFont = createFont("Arial", 10);
```

Remember to also add the cursor PNGs to the sketch's data directory.

Whew! I realize that was a lot of code, but hopefully you're starting to see the redundancy, especially in the GUI implementation. By restructuring a program like this using an object-oriented approach, you could eliminate some of the redundancy (but not necessarily use less code). If I were going to scale this program to a much larger application, the added organizational aspects of OOP would make it worthwhile to do so.

Keystroke events

In addition to mouse events, interactivity often includes keystroke events. As usual, Processing simplifies the process, making it really easy to add keystroke control to your sketches. Processing includes built-in functions to detect key presses and releases and to also determine what specific key was pressed. For example, this sketch changes the rectangle's color to red on the key press and blue on the key release:

```
color rectBackground = color(0, 0, 255);
void setup(){
  size(400, 400);
  background(255);
  rectMode(CENTER);
}
void draw(){
  fill(rectBackground);
  rect(width/2, height/2, 200, 200);
}
void keyPressed(){
  rectBackground = color(255, 0, 0);
}
void keyReleased(){
  rectBackground = color(0, 0, 255);
}
```

Obviously, you'll usually want to know what key was pressed when detecting a key event. The next sketch adds arrow key detection to the key press event, giving each directional arrow control over a different color fill:

12

```
color rectBackground = color(0, 0, 255);
void setup(){
  size(400, 400);
  background(255);
  rectMode(CENTER);
}
void draw(){
  fill(rectBackground);
  rect(width/2, height/2, 200, 200);
}
void keyPressed(){
  if(key == CODED){
    if (keyCode == UP) {
      rectBackground = color(255, 0, 0);
    }
    else if (keyCode == DOWN) {
      rectBackground = color(255, 255, 0);
    }
    else if (keyCode == RIGHT) {
      rectBackground = color(0, 255, 0);
    }
    else {
      rectBackground = color(255, 0, 255);
    }
  }
}
```

The keyCode property is used to check special keys on the keyboard, such as the arrow keys. Processing defines these keys with constants (that's why the arrow direction names are in all caps). Before checking the individual key codes, you need to check if the key is coded at all; this is handled by the external conditional if(key == CODED){}. For an up-to-date list of the available key codes in Processing, please refer to the online reference at http://processing.org/reference/keyCode.html.

In addition to key codes, it's also possible to detect the value of each standard key. The next sketch is based on the last example, replacing the arrow keys with the keys A, S, W, and Z, for left, right, up, and down, respectively.

```
color rectBackground = color(0, 0, 255);
void setup(){
  size(400, 400);
  background(255);
  rectMode(CENTER);
}
void draw(){
  fill(rectBackground);
  rect(width/2, height/2, 200, 200);
}
void keyPressed(){
  if(key == 'a'){
```

```
    rectBackground = color(255, 0, 0);
  }
  else if (key == 's') {
    rectBackground = color(255, 255, 0);
  }
  else if (key == 'w') {
    rectBackground = color(0, 255, 0);
  }
  else if (key == 'z') {
    rectBackground = color(255, 0, 255);
  }
}
```

Finally, instead of using the keyPressed() function, you can use a keyPressed Boolean variable directly within the draw() function. We already looked at this multiple approach to solving a problem earlier in the chapter, when I discussed the mousePressed() function vs. the mousePressed Boolean variable. Here's the code:

```
color rectBackground = color(0, 0, 255);
void setup(){
  size(400, 400);
  background(255);
  rectMode(CENTER);
}
void draw(){
  fill(rectBackground);
  rect(width/2, height/2, 200, 200);

  // keyPressed boolean variable
  if (keyPressed){
    if(key == 'a'){
      rectBackground = color(255, 0, 0);
    }
    else if (key == 's') {
      rectBackground = color(255, 255, 0);
    }
    else if (key == 'w') {
      rectBackground = color(0, 255, 0);
    }
    else if (key == 'z') {
      rectBackground = color(255, 0, 255);
    }
  }
}
```

12

I've included one more somewhat lengthy interactive example that takes advantage of Processing's easy-to-use key event detection (see Figure 12-4). The piece is a motion painting application that uses an animated brush, which is completely controlled by the keyboard. I've killed enough trees this chapter, so I've added my descriptions about the sketch directly within the code as comments. I recommend running the example first before going through the code. Happy motion painting!

```
/* Motion Painter
Ira Greenberg, April 17, 2006 */

/* Begin declaring global variables above
 the setup() function. */
int points = 5;

/*parentNode[] array holds x and y position of
 center of moving brush shape.*/
float[]parentNode = new float[2];

/*shape[][] 2-dimensional array holds x and y position
 of up to 8 points making up the vertices of each
 brush shape. Each brush shape can have a minimum
 of 2 points or a maximum of 8 points.*/
float[][]shape = new float[8][2];

float shapeRadius = 10.0;
float strokeAlpha = 255;
float speed = 2;
float rotation  = 15;
float rotationSpeed = 4;
float xSpeed = 0.0;
float ySpeed = 0.0;
byte xDirection = 1;
byte yDirection = 1;
float strokeWt = 1;

/*strokeColor[][] 2-dimensional array holds
 color values for each edge of the brush shapes.*/
float[][]strokeColor = new float[8][3];

boolean isWallSolid = true;
int canvasWidth;
int canvasHeight;
PFont font;

void setup(){
  size(600, 400);
  canvasWidth = width;
  canvasHeight = height-100;
  background(255);
  smooth();
  frameRate(30);

  /*Initialize parentNode to center of canvas, which
```

```
    is smaller (vertically) than the entire display window.*/
  parentNode[0] = canvasWidth/2;
  parentNode[1] = canvasHeight/2;

  /*Fill pallete with random colors for brush shape edges.
   Each shape can have between 2 and 8 edges*/
  setPalette();

  // Font for key commands at bottom of sketch
  font = createFont("Verdana", 12);
}

void draw(){
  /*xSpeed and ySpeed variables controlled by trig functions.
   rotation variable is controlled by user, through keystroke
   commands. x and y value of parentNode is incremented by
   xSpeed and ySpeed. The brush shape is drawn around the
   parentNode as its origin, ensuring the brush shape moves
   with the parentNode*/
  xSpeed = cos(radians(rotation))*speed*xDirection;
  ySpeed = sin(radians(rotation))*speed*yDirection;
  parentNode[0]+=xSpeed;
  parentNode[1]+=ySpeed;

  /*If isWallSolid boolean variable is true, the shape bounces off
   the canvas edges. If false, the shape exits the canvas and is
   remapped to the opposite side of the canvas. The isWallSolid
   variable is controlled by the user with the keystrokes 'b' for
   bounce or 'n' for no bounce.*/
  if (!isWallSolid){
    if (parentNode[0]>canvasWidth+shapeRadius*2){
      parentNode[0] = 0;
    }
    else if (parentNode[0]<-shapeRadius*2){
      parentNode[0] = canvasWidth;
    }
    if (parentNode[1]>canvasHeight+shapeRadius*2){
      parentNode[1] = 0;
    }
    else if (parentNode[1]<-shapeRadius*2){
      parentNode[1] = canvasHeight;
    }
  }
  else {
    if (parentNode[0]>canvasWidth-shapeRadius/2){
      xDirection*=-1;
    }
    else if (parentNode[0]<shapeRadius/2){
      xDirection*=-1;
```

12

```
  }
  if (parentNode[1]>canvasHeight-shapeRadius/2){
    yDirection*=-1;
  }
  else if (parentNode[1]<shapeRadius/2){
    yDirection*=-1;
  }
}

/*drawShape() function draws a 2-8 point polygon, which
 functions as a brush shape. The number of sides to
 the shape is determined by the user pressing keys 2-8.*/
drawShape();

/*keyPressed boolean property
 checks for specific keys*/
if (keyPressed){
  if(key == '+') {
    //Increase shape size
    shapeRadius++;
  }
  else if(key == '_') {
    //Decrease shape size
    shapeRadius--;
  }
  else if(key == 'a') {
    if (strokeAlpha>0){
      //Decrease alpha
      strokeAlpha-=5;
    }
  }
  else if(key == 's') {
    if (strokeAlpha<255){
      //Increase alpha
      strokeAlpha+=5;
    }
  }
  else if(key == 'b') {
    //Causes shape to bounce off canvas edges.
    isWallSolid = true;
  }
  else if(key == 'n') {
    //Causes shape to pass through canvas edges.
    isWallSolid = false;
  }
  else if(key == 'c') {
    //Set new random color palette for each shape edge.
    setPalette();
  }
```

```
  //keys 2-8 control number of edges for brush shape.
  else if(key == '2') {
    points = 2;
  }
  else if(key == '3') {
    points = 3;
  }
  else if(key == '4') {
    points = 4;
  }
  else if(key == '5') {
    points = 5;
  }
  else if(key == '6') {
    points = 6;
  }
  else if(key == '7') {
    points = 7;
  }
  else if(key == '8') {
    points = 8;
  }
}
//Bottom info panel
fill(130);
noStroke();
rect(0, canvasHeight, canvasWidth, height-canvasHeight);

textFont(font);
fill(255, 200, 0);
text("key commands:", 10, canvasHeight+20);
fill(0);
//left column
text("UP Arrow: speed ++", 10, canvasHeight+35);
text("DOWN Arrow: speed --", 10, canvasHeight+50);
text("RIGHT Arrow: rotate right", 10, canvasHeight+65);
text("LEFT Arrow: rotate left", 10, canvasHeight+80);

//middle column
text("',' stop", 200, canvasHeight+20);
text("'.' start", 200, canvasHeight+35);
text("'+' (requires shift key): size ++", 200, canvasHeight+50);
text("'-' (requires shift key): size --", 200, canvasHeight+65);
text("'c' randomize color: size --", 200, canvasHeight+80);

//right column
text("change shapes (keys: 2-8)", 430, canvasHeight+20);
text("'a' alpha --", 430, canvasHeight+35);
text("'s' alpha ++", 430, canvasHeight+50);
```

12

```
    text("'b' bounce", 430, canvasHeight+65);
    text("'n' no bounce", 430, canvasHeight+80);
}

//keyPressed function
//Check built-in coded keys
void keyPressed(){
  if(key == CODED) {
    if (keyCode == UP) {
      if (speed<10){
        speed+=.25;
      }
    }
    else if (keyCode == DOWN) {
      if (speed>-10){
        speed-=.25;
      }
    }
    else if(keyCode == RIGHT) {
      rotation+=rotationSpeed;
    }
    else if(keyCode == LEFT) {
      rotation-=rotationSpeed;
    }
  }
  else {
  // check for 2 more uncoded keys
    if(key == '.') {
      //start motion
      loop();
    }
    else if(key == ',') {
      //stop motion
      noLoop();
    }
  }
}

//Randomly fill palette
void setPalette(){
  for (int i=0; i<8; i++){
    for (int j=0; j<3; j++){
      strokeColor[i][j] = random(255);
    }
  }
}

//Trig functions draw 2-8 sided polygon around parentNode.
void drawShape(){
```

610

```
strokeWeight(strokeWt);
float angle = 0;
for (int i=0; i<points; i++){
  shape[i][0] = parentNode[0]+cos(radians(angle+rotation)) ⮡
      *shapeRadius;
  shape[i][1] = parentNode[1]+sin(radians(angle+rotation)) ⮡
      *shapeRadius;
  angle+=360/points;
}

// Each edge of the polygon (brush shape)
// has a different color.
for (int i=0; i<points; i++){
  stroke(strokeColor[i][0], strokeColor[i][1], ⮡
      strokeColor[i][2], strokeAlpha);
  if (i==points-1){
    //If last point, connect to initial point to close polygon.
    line(shape[i][0], shape[i][1], shape[0][0], shape[0][1]);
  }
  else {
    //If not last point, draw line from current point to next point.
    line(shape[i][0], shape[i][1], shape[i+1][0], shape[i+1][1]);
  }
}
}
```

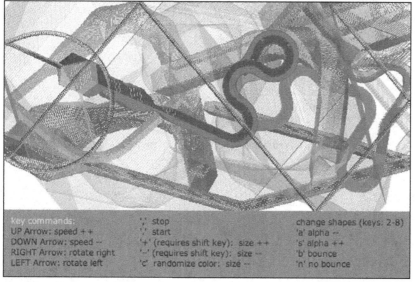

Figure 12-4. Motion Painter sketch

I mentioned at the beginning of the chapter that Processing (with a little help from Java) allows you to detect multiple mouse clicks. To close the chapter, I've included one last simple example that utilizes multiple mouse clicks on the display window to dynamically change the number of sides of a polygon. The simple piece of Java code that allows you to detect multiple mouse clicks is mouseEvent.getClickCount(), which returns an integer value of the number of clicks. The time delay between clicks determines if the series of clicks is considered a multiple click input or a series of individual clicks.

```
// Detecting Multiple Mouse Clicks
int clickCount = 0;
void setup(){
  size(400, 400);
  smooth();
}

void draw(){
  background(255);
  translate(width/2, height/2);
  rotate(frameCount*PI/180);
  drawPoly();
}

void mouseClicked(){
  clickCount = mouseEvent.getClickCount();
}

void drawPoly(){
  // draw point if single click
  if (clickCount==1){
    point(0, 0);
  }
  else {
    float ang = 0;
    int verts = clickCount;
    beginShape();
    for (int i=0; i<verts; i++){
      ang += 360.0/verts;
      vertex(cos(radians(ang))*150.0, sin(radians(ang))*150.0);
    }
    endShape(CLOSE);
  }
}
```

Summary

We began this chapter comparing Java and Processing's approach to coding interactivity. As usual, compared to pure Java, Processing simplifies interactivity. Using Processing's built-in mouse event functions, I coded some simple sketches that reacted to the user's mouse presses, as well as mouse releases. I compared functions such as mousePressed() with their companion Boolean variables of the same name (mousePressed), and looked at some examples that used both. I also discussed the difference between Processing's mouseMoved() and mouseDragged() functions. Developing some longer examples, I created a node-based shape-building and animation sketch and also a simple paint program, including a custom GUI with reactive multi-state buttons and a draggable slider. After the mouse events, we looked at Processing's keyboard events, which work similarly to the mouse events. I compared coded keys, such as the arrow keys, defined as constants in Processing, with the standard keyboard keys—letters, numbers, and so forth. Finally, I created an animated paint program that was completely controlled by keyboard events. To learn more about pushing Processing's event detection and handling capabilities beyond the mouse and keyboard, check out the Processing libraries (http://processing.org/reference/libraries/index.html).

The final two chapters of the book introduce coding 3D in Processing—one of the most exciting features of the language.

12

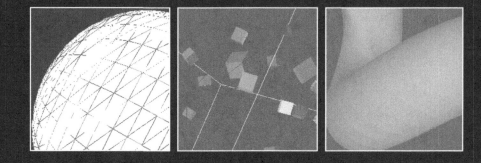

The term *approach-avoidance* describes a psychological state in which people are attracted to and also repulsed by something. This tension aptly describes the relationship many of my past art students had with 3D animation. On the one hand, they were enamored by the cool 3D effects they watched in their favorite games and films. On the other hand, they became easily frustrated trying to learn the extremely dense and unintuitive software. Popular 3D modeling and animation applications such as LightWave, Maya, and 3ds Max (which handle the coding behind the scenes) are extremely complex, specialized pieces of software, presenting steep, drawn-out learning curves. Attempting to teach these same art students 3D programming would have been unthinkable. For this reason, coding 3D has been the domain of computer science types, requiring lots of scary math and very low-level programming—that is, until Processing came along. Processing has full 3D support and even includes two separate 3D renderers, and of course it's free. Most importantly, Processing greatly simplifies the process of coding 3D for creative folks, allowing us to begin "creating" in 3D almost immediately.

In this chapter, you'll learn about Processing's built-in 3D support, based on the custom P3D rendering engine. Working with some simple 3D functions, such as box(), you'll learn how to create that sexy spinning cube in no time. I'll revisit the concept of transformations, but in 3D space using Processing's pushMatrix() and popMatrix() functions. Then I'll go a little beneath the hood and teach you how to code your own 3D rotations as well as create some custom 3D geometry. First, I'll start with the basics.

Processing 3D basics

Here's the ubiquitous spinning cube I promised, using only nine lines of code (see Figure 13-1):

```
void setup(){
  size(400, 400, P3D);
}
void draw(){
  background(0);
  translate(width/2, height/2);
  rotateY(frameCount*PI/60);
  box(150, 150, 150);
}
```

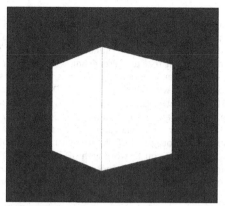

Figure 13-1. Spinning Cube 1

Man, that was even easier than using code-free 3D animation software.

In the preceding example, the cube only spun around the y-axis. The following code creates a cube that spins around the x- and y-axes (see Figure 13-2):

```
void setup(){
  size(400, 400, P3D);
}
void draw(){
  background(0);
  translate(width/2, height/2);
  rotateY(frameCount*PI/60);
  rotateX(frameCount*PI/60);
  box(150, 150, 150);
}
```

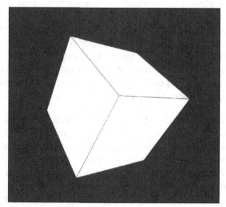

Figure 13-2. Spinning Cube 2

13

If you compare the code in the preceding two sketches carefully, you'll notice all I had to do to get the second rotation was add a single line of code: rotateX(frameCount*PI/60);. The sketch is very simple, but it does introduce a few new concepts. First, I included an extra argument in the size(400, 400, P3D) function call. In reality, the size() function always includes a third argument that tells Processing what renderer to use. If you don't specify a renderer, then the default renderer (JAVA2D) is used. P3D is a 3D renderer, also referred to as a 3D engine, built within in Processing. A **3D engine** is just software that calculates the math of 3D coordinate space (x, y, and z), and then remaps the 3D space back to a 2D projection so that you can view it on a monitor. Since our monitors still rely on a flat, illuminated 2D surface, they can't really plot 3D information. In a sense, what you see on your monitor is sort of a photograph of 3D that has been flattened to 2D coordinate space. 3D engines typically allow you to work with 3D geometry, light sources, textures, and even virtual cameras. Besides that, 3D works very similarly to 2D, allowing you to set properties like fills, strokes, position, and scale, and animate these properties as well.

3D transformation

In the last two examples, Processing's box() function took three arguments (width, height, and depth), and placed the box, centered, at (0, 0, 0). Since you're using three dimensions now, you use three values (x, y, and z) to identify a point in space. To move the box to the center of the display window, you can use Processing's translate() function. Try running the last sketch again, but commenting out the translate(width/2, height/2); call. You should see the box spinning around the top-left corner of the display window, centered at (0, 0, 0).

You can also translate along the z-axis. In the last sketch, change translate(width/2, height/2); to translate(width/2, height/2, -400); and run the sketch. You should now see a smaller cube spinning in the display window. You can also try using a larger positive value for the third argument; for example, translate(width/2, height/2, 130); will generate a cube that fills the entire display window.

I referred to the cube getting smaller and larger when translated along the z-axis. More accurately, the cube remains the same size (with regard to its internal width/height/depth properties), but its translation along the z-axis moves it within a virtual space modeled after space in the physical world, in which objects appear to decrease and increase in size as they move away from or toward a viewer, according to the rules of perspective. 3D engines attempt to simulate this phenomenon by coding perspective projection, usually through a virtual camera that can be moved, rotated, and even zoomed. I'll discuss virtual cameras in Processing in Chapter 14.

The process of translating the contents of the display window is a little confusing and takes some time to get used to. This shouldn't be a completely new concept, though, as it was covered earlier in the book in the discussion of 2D space, and the same principles apply. The benefit of translation becomes apparent when you try to rotate a shape drawn in the middle of the display window. The next sketch draws a 2D rectangle in the center of the screen and then rotates it. I used the rect() command, since it takes x- and y-coordinate and dimension arguments (as opposed to box() and sphere(), which only take dimension arguments).

```
void setup(){
  size(400, 400);
}
void draw(){
  background(0);
  rotate(frameCount*PI/60);
  rect(50, 50, 150, 150);
}
```

If you run the sketch, you may be surprised to see the rectangle rotating off the screen, around the origin, instead of around its own center point. This is a common error new coders make. Intuitively, it seems that rotate() should spin the shape around its center point. However, rotate() doesn't actually spin the shape; it spins the entire contents of the display window. If you're used to graphics applications like Illustrator, FreeHand, or Flash, which internally handle translations when you draw highly encapsulated shape objects, it can seem frustrating to have to think about the translation process in Processing. A basic rule of thumb is to draw your objects initially around the origin (0, 0, 0) and then translate them. Here's a new version of the last sketch, correctly implemented for centered rotation:

```
void setup(){
  size(400, 400);
}
void draw(){
  background(0);
  translate(width/2, height/2);
  rotate(frameCount*PI/60);
  rect(-75, -75, 150, 150);
}
```

The order of transformations also has an effect on how and where in the display window things are drawn.

The next sketch (see Figure 13-3) uses Processing's sphere() function. I call translate() after rotateY(), which doesn't get the sphere rotating around the center of the window. However, if I switch the order of the rotateY(frameCount*PI/60); and translate(width/2, height/2); commands, the rotation happens as expected, around the center of the window.

```
void setup(){
  size(400, 400, P3D);
}
void draw(){
  background(0);
  // the next 2 lines should be switched in order
  rotate(frameCount*PI/60);
  translate(width/2, height/2);
  sphere(100);
}
```

13

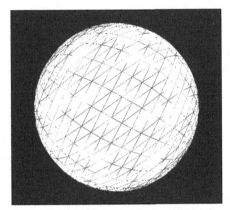

Figure 13-3. Order of Transformations example

The problem becomes a little trickier when using multiple objects. For example, the next sketch tries to rotate four cubes as one larger block. Each cube will be 100 × 100 × 100, so I need to offset each block by 50. For example, I want the top-left block to be at –50 on the x-axis and –50 on the y-axis; the top-right block at 50 on the x-axis and –50 on the y-axis; the bottom-left block at –50, 50; and the bottom-right one at 50, 50. In addition, I want the entire group of four blocks to be centered in the display window. The intuitive thing to try is to initially translate everything to the center of the display window, as I did in the previous example, and then call a series of translations for each block, using the offset values I just mentioned. Unfortunately, this won't work as expected. But don't take my word for it; give it a try (see Figure 13-4):

```
// Multiple Translations
void setup(){
  size(400, 400, P3D);
}
void draw(){
  background(0);
  translate(width/2, height/2);
  rotateY(frameCount*PI/60);

  translate(-50, -50);
  fill(255, 0, 0);
  box(100, 100, 100);

  translate(50, -50);
  fill(255, 255, 0);
  box(100, 100, 100);

  translate(-50, 50);
  fill(0, 0, 255);
  box(100, 100, 100);
```

```
    translate(50, 50);
    fill(0, 255, 0);
    box(100, 100, 100);
  }
```

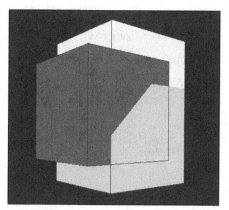

Figure 13-4. Multiple Translations example

So what happened? Translations are cumulative. Each time you call translate(), the entire drawing context of the display window is translated. For example, here's a series of translations that move a box across the screen (see Figure 13-5):

```
void setup(){
  size(400, 100, P3D);
}
void draw(){
  background(255);
  translate(10, height/2);
  for (int i=10; i<width-20; i+=10){
    translate(10, 0);
    box(10, 10, 10);
  }
}
```

Figure 13-5. Cumulative Translations example

You'll notice that I called translate() twice. The first call happens within draw(), while the second call is inside the for loop within draw(). When a transformation such as a translation happens within draw(), it is reset each time that draw() executes. Thus, not to contradict myself from the earlier paragraph, but the first call, translate(10, height/2), is actually not cumulative. However, the second call, translate(10, 0); within the for loop, executes 37 times each time draw() runs, which creates the cumulative translations as the block is offset across the stage. Returning to the rotating block wall, how would you solve this problem?

Processing comes equipped with two handy functions to solve the problem: pushMatrix() and popMatrix(). These functions work in pairs and allow you to temporarily offset the drawing context of the display window, draw something, and then put the drawing context back to where it was before you transformed it. Pretty cool, right? Here's the fixed rotating wall utilizing the two functions (see Figure 13-6):

```
// Multiple Translations with pushMatrix() and popMatrix()
void setup(){
  size(400, 400, P3D);
}
void draw(){
  background(0);
  translate(width/2, height/2);
  rotateY(frameCount*PI/60);

  pushMatrix();
  translate(-50, -50);
  fill(255, 0, 0);
  box(100, 100, 100);
  popMatrix();

  pushMatrix();
  translate(50, -50);
  fill(255, 255, 0);
  box(100, 100, 100);
  popMatrix();

  pushMatrix();
  translate(50, 50);
  fill(0, 0, 255);
  box(100, 100, 100);
  popMatrix();

  pushMatrix();
  translate(-50, 50);
  fill(0, 255, 0);
  box(100, 100, 100);
  popMatrix();
}
```

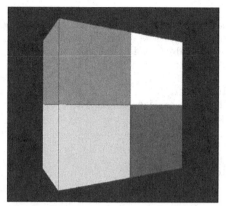

Figure 13-6. Multiple Translations with pushMatrix()
and popMatrix() example

Notice how the pushMatrix() and popMatrix() functions surround the translate() and box() calls. pushMatrix() must come before popMatrix(), and they need to work as a pair. The underlying math and theory behind these functions is not simple, but using them really is. You can even nest these function calls, as long as you have a popMatrix() for each pushMatrix(). The next example, shown in Figure 13-7, constructs a cube of cubes. The fill color is controlled by the counters in the three for loops. I also made the color translucent, in order to reveal the multicube structure.

```
// Cubic Grid
float boxSize = 40;
float margin = boxSize*2;
float depth = 400;
color boxFill;

void setup(){
  size(400, 400, P3D);
  noStroke();
}

void draw(){
  background(255);
  // center and spin grid
  translate(width/2, height/2, -depth/2);
  rotateY(frameCount*PI/60);
  rotateX(frameCount*PI/60);

  // build grid using multiple translations
  for (float i=-depth/2+margin; i<=depth/2-margin; i+=boxSize){
    pushMatrix();
    for (float j=-height/2+margin; j<=height/2-margin; j+=boxSize){
      pushMatrix();
```

13

```
      for (float k=-width/2+margin; k<=width/2-margin; k+=boxSize){
        // base fill color on counter values, abs function
        // ensures values stay within legal range
        boxFill = color(abs(i), abs(j), abs(k), 50);
        pushMatrix();
        translate(k, j, i);
        fill(boxFill);
        box(boxSize, boxSize, boxSize);
        popMatrix();
      }
      popMatrix();
    }
    popMatrix();
  }
}
```

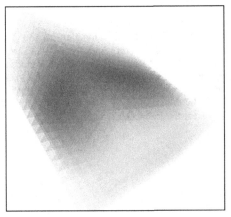

Figure 13-7. Cubic Grid sketch

So 3D seems pretty easy, right? Well, as you no doubt suspect, there is a *lot* of stuff going on beneath Processing's surface when it come to 3D—stuff that looks truly scary (even to folks who enjoy math). Not to pop your happy bubble, but I'd like to take just a little look under the hood (but well above the really nasty stuff). Since I've been using Processing's box() function, I'll show you how to create a custom version of the command, as well as some custom rotation methods. I think seeing how a cube is constructed will give you a better sense about how to think in 3D. I also think it will begin to give you insight into how to create other 3D geometry besides Processing's box and sphere. You'll continue to use Processing's translate() function to center your geometry; so you'll design your cube to be centered at the origin, which, if you'll remember, is (0, 0, 0) in 3D. You'll also build the cube using object-oriented methodology, with classes. Finally, you'll give your cube an extra feature or two beyond Processing's built-in version.

Creating a custom cube

To begin to think about a cube, you need to think about the components of a cube. A cube can be thought of in a number of ways: as a group of points defining the cube's vertices, sometimes referred to as a point cloud; as a wireframe, representing the lines connecting the cube's vertices; or as a solid, composed of polygonal sides or faces. In a more advanced example, you might also look at different shading and surface material algorithms to create a photorealistically textured cube. This section will begin with the creation of a simple class that holds the three x, y, and z coordinates for each of the cube's vertices. The class will be named Point3D.

```
/*
Extremely simple class to
 hold each 3D vertex
 */
class Point3D{
  float x, y, z;

  // constructors
  Point3D(){
  }

  Point3D(float x, float y, float z){
    this.x = x;
    this.y = y;
    this.z = z;
  }
}
```

I hope this class looks self-explanatory. I'm using the class simply to group the three component properties of each vertex. As a refresher, to create a Point3D object and then output its component properties, you'd write the following:

```
void setup(){
  Point3D p1 = new Point3D(-50, -50, -50);
  println(p1.x + ", " + p1.y + ", " + p1.z);
}

/*
Extremely simple class to
 hold each 3D vertex
 */
class Point3D{

  float x, y, z;

  // constructors
  Point3D(){
  }
```

```
Point3D(float x, float y, float z){
  this.x = x;
  this.y = y;
  this.z = z;
  }
}
```

If you run this, you should see the following output: -50.0, -50.0, -50.0.

Next, you'll create your Cube class.

I should point out that technically a cube would be composed only of equal-area square faces. However, my Cube class will allow you to specify different values for width, height, and depth; sorry if this offends any of you purists out there.

The Cube class will rely on the Point3D class in a compostional relationship, in which I'll embed variables of type Point3D directly within the Cube class. Remember, each cube will be created around the origin, so I won't account for an x, y, or z property for the entire cube; only the cube's overall width, height, and depth properties will be specified, similarly to how Processing's box() function works. (The class code that follows will not execute on its own, but you probably realize that by now.)

```
class Cube{
  Point3D[] vertices = new Point3D[24];
  float w, h, d;

  // constructors
// default constructor
  Cube(){
  }

  Cube(float w, float h, float d){
    this.w = w;
    this.h = h;
    this.d = d;

    // cube composed of 6 quads
    //front
    vertices[0] = new Point3D(-w/2,-h/2,d/2);
    vertices[1] = new Point3D(w/2,-h/2,d/2);
    vertices[2] = new Point3D(w/2,h/2,d/2);
    vertices[3] = new Point3D(-w/2,h/2,d/2);
    //left
    vertices[4] = new Point3D(-w/2,-h/2,d/2);
    vertices[5] = new Point3D(-w/2,-h/2,-d/2);
    vertices[6] = new Point3D(-w/2,h/2,-d/2);
    vertices[7] = new Point3D(-w/2,h/2,d/2);
    //right
```

```
        vertices[8] = new Point3D(w/2,-h/2,d/2);
        vertices[9] = new Point3D(w/2,-h/2,-d/2);
        vertices[10] = new Point3D(w/2,h/2,-d/2);
        vertices[11] = new Point3D(w/2,h/2,d/2);
        //back
        vertices[12] = new Point3D(-w/2,-h/2,-d/2);
        vertices[13] = new Point3D(w/2,-h/2,-d/2);
        vertices[14] = new Point3D(w/2,h/2,-d/2);
        vertices[15] = new Point3D(-w/2,h/2,-d/2);
        //top
        vertices[16] = new Point3D(-w/2,-h/2,d/2);
        vertices[17] = new Point3D(-w/2,-h/2,-d/2);
        vertices[18] = new Point3D(w/2,-h/2,-d/2);
        vertices[19] = new Point3D(w/2,-h/2,d/2);
        //bottom
        vertices[20] = new Point3D(-w/2,h/2,d/2);
        vertices[21] = new Point3D(-w/2,h/2,-d/2);
        vertices[22] = new Point3D(w/2,h/2,-d/2);
        vertices[23] = new Point3D(w/2,h/2,d/2);
    }

  void create(){
      // draw cube
      for (int i=0; i<6; i++){
        beginShape(QUADS);
        for (int j=0; j<4; j++){
          vertex(vertices[j+4*i].x, vertices[j+4*i].y, ➥
              vertices[j+4*i].z);
        }
        endShape();
      }
    }
  }
```

The Cube class is divided into two constructors and a create() method. The first constructor is just the default no-arguments constructor, in case a Cube object is instantiated without any initial values. The second constructor takes three arguments and assembles the data, while the create() method actually handles the drawing. In comparison to the Cube class, Processing's box() function, which seems to handle both instantiation and drawing, might initially seem like a better procedural model—it's certainly less work. However, suppose you wanted to pass Cube objects to another class that would then take care of positioning and drawing the cubes—you'd need to separate the object creation from the actual drawing of the object, as in the preceding example. The second constructor initializes the vertices array, which holds 24 Point3D objects. Although a cube looks like it only has eight unique points, it's simpler (for now) to think of a cube as six separate quadrangle faces composed of four points each. This will prevent you from having to use some of the points for more than one face (which you'll eventually learn how to do as well).

13

The create() method includes a nested for loop that is a bit dense to untangle. I needed an algorithm that would run through the vertices array and treat each individual face as a self-contained quadrangle (composed of four points). Notice that the beginShape() and endShape() functions are nested within the outer for loop as well, allowing each face to be drawn as a separate unit. This structure will also allow you to easily customize the color of each face, which we'll look at shortly. However, before getting into that, I'll show you how to use the two classes just created to generate a cube.

Here's some runnable code. (Please note that I didn't repeat the code from the Point3D and Cube classes shown previously. Just make sure you add the two classes beneath the following code, or put each class in its own tab.)

```
Cube c1;
void setup(){
  size(400, 400, P3D);
  c1 = new Cube(200, 200, 200);
  c1.create();
}
// Don't forget to add the Point3D and Cube classes code
```

I also want to translate the cube to the middle of the drawing space, or at least have it move around some. I'll use Processing's translate() and rotate() functions in conjunction with the classes to achieve this. In addition, I'll create an overloaded create(color[]quadBG) method for customizing the color of each quad face.

> You may remember that an overloaded method is an object-oriented concept meaning that more than one method with the same name exists in a class. What differentiates the same named methods is the number and type of parameters between the parentheses in the head of the method. You can read more about overloaded methods and other object-oriented concepts in Chapter 8.

The next example, shown in Figure 13-8, creates two cubes, using the two overloaded create() methods. Since I added an additional create() method to the Cube class, I've included the updated class code in the following example. I didn't repeat the Point3D class, which you'll need as well to run the example; simply paste it below the Cube class or put it into its own tab.

```
// Two Rotating Custom Cubes

// custom Cube reference variables
Cube c1, c2;
// array to hold different face colors
color[]quadBG = new color[6];

void setup(){
  size(400, 400, P3D);
  quadBG[0] = color(175, 30, 30, 150);
  quadBG[1] = color(30, 175, 30, 150);
```

```
    quadBG[2] = color(30, 30, 175, 150);
    quadBG[3] = color(175, 175, 30, 150);
    quadBG[4] = color(175, 30, 175, 150);
    quadBG[5] = color(175, 87, 30, 150);
    c1 =  new Cube(200, 200, 200);
    c2 =  new Cube(100, 100, 100);
}

void draw(){
  background(100);
  translate(width/2, height/2);
  rotateX(frameCount*PI/50);
  rotateY(frameCount*PI/60);
  // create larger colored cube
  noStroke();
  c1.create(quadBG);
  // create inner black cube
  fill(0, 200);
  stroke(255);
  c2.create();
}

// Updated custom Cube class
class Cube{
  Point3D[] vertices = new Point3D[24];
  float w, h, d;

  // Constructors
  // default constructor
  Cube(){
  }

  // constructor 2
  Cube(float w, float h, float d){
    this.w = w;
    this.h = h;
    this.d = d;

    // cube composed of 6 quads
    //front
    vertices[0] = new Point3D(-w/2,-h/2,d/2);
    vertices[1] = new Point3D(w/2,-h/2,d/2);
    vertices[2] = new Point3D(w/2,h/2,d/2);
    vertices[3] = new Point3D(-w/2,h/2,d/2);
    //left
    vertices[4] = new Point3D(-w/2,-h/2,d/2);
    vertices[5] = new Point3D(-w/2,-h/2,-d/2);
    vertices[6] = new Point3D(-w/2,h/2,-d/2);
    vertices[7] = new Point3D(-w/2,h/2,d/2);
```

13

```
      //right
      vertices[8] = new Point3D(w/2,-h/2,d/2);
      vertices[9] = new Point3D(w/2,-h/2,-d/2);
      vertices[10] = new Point3D(w/2,h/2,-d/2);
      vertices[11] = new Point3D(w/2,h/2,d/2);
      //back
      vertices[12] = new Point3D(-w/2,-h/2,-d/2);
      vertices[13] = new Point3D(w/2,-h/2,-d/2);
      vertices[14] = new Point3D(w/2,h/2,-d/2);
      vertices[15] = new Point3D(-w/2,h/2,-d/2);
      //top
      vertices[16] = new Point3D(-w/2,-h/2,d/2);
      vertices[17] = new Point3D(-w/2,-h/2,-d/2);
      vertices[18] = new Point3D(w/2,-h/2,-d/2);
      vertices[19] = new Point3D(w/2,-h/2,d/2);
      //bottom
      vertices[20] = new Point3D(-w/2,h/2,d/2);
      vertices[21] = new Point3D(-w/2,h/2,-d/2);
      vertices[22] = new Point3D(w/2,h/2,-d/2);
      vertices[23] = new Point3D(w/2,h/2,d/2);
    }
    void create(){
      // draw cube
      for (int i=0; i<6; i++){
        beginShape(QUADS);
        for (int j=0; j<4; j++){
          vertex(vertices[j+4*i].x, vertices[j+4*i].y, ➥
              vertices[j+4*i].z);
        }
        endShape();
      }
    }
    void create(color[]quadBG){
      // draw cube
      for (int i=0; i<6; i++){
        fill(quadBG[i]);
        beginShape(QUADS);
        for (int j=0; j<4; j++){
          vertex(vertices[j+4*i].x, vertices[j+4*i].y, ➥
              vertices[j+4*i].z);
        }
        endShape();
      }
    }
  }
  // This example requires the Point3D class.
```

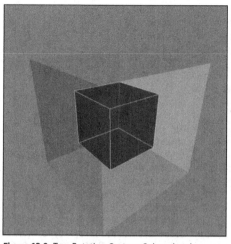

Figure 13-8. Two Rotating Custom Cubes sketch

I made the cubes translucent in this example (by lowering the fill color alpha to below 255) so that you can see the inner cube. Notice how the two create() method calls automatically invoke the correct version of the method, based on the argument passed to the method.

I created another example using the Cube class that's a little more interesting, and of course a little more complicated. The sketch includes a bunch of small rotating, moving cubes within a larger rotating cube (see Figure 3-9). When the inner cubes hit the boundaries of the outer cube, they reverse direction. In addition, the cubes are all connected by a line. There's actually nothing in this sketch that you haven't already looked at. However, thinking in 3D space is definitely more confusing than in 2D. Again, I didn't bother repeating the code from the updated Cube or Point3D classes; just remember to include both classes beneath the following code or in their own tabs.

```
// Cubes Contained Within a Cube
Cube stage; // external large cube
int cubies = 50;
Cube[]c = new Cube[cubies]; // internal little cubes
color[][]quadBG = new color[cubies][6];

// controls cubie's movement
float[]x = new float[cubies];
float[]y = new float[cubies];
float[]z = new float[cubies];
float[]xSpeed = new float[cubies];
float[]ySpeed = new float[cubies];
float[]zSpeed = new float[cubies];
```

13

```
// controls cubie's rotation
float[]xRot = new float[cubies];
float[]yRot = new float[cubies];
float[]zRot = new float[cubies];

// size of external cube
float bounds = 300;

void setup(){
  size(400, 400, P3D);
  for (int i=0; i<cubies; i++){
    // each cube face has a random color component
    float colorShift = random(-75, 75);
    quadBG[i][0] = color(175+colorShift, 30, 30);
    quadBG[i][1] = color(30, 175+colorShift, 30);
    quadBG[i][2] = color(30, 30, 175+colorShift);
    quadBG[i][3] = color(175+colorShift, 175+colorShift, 30);
    quadBG[i][4] = color(175+colorShift, 30, 175+colorShift);
    quadBG[i][5] = color(175+colorShift, 87+colorShift, 30);

    // cubies are randomly sized
    float cubieSize = random(5, 15);
    c[i] =  new Cube(cubieSize, cubieSize, cubieSize);

    //initialize cubie's position, speed and rotation
    x[i] = 0;
    y[i] = 0;
    z[i] = 0;

    xSpeed[i] = random(-2, 2);
    ySpeed[i] = random(-2, 2);
    zSpeed[i] = random(-2, 2);

    xRot[i] = random(40, 100);
    yRot[i] = random(40, 100);
    zRot[i] = random(40, 100);
  }
  // instantiate external large cube
  stage =  new Cube(300, 300, 300);
}

void draw(){
  background(50);
  // center in display window
  translate(width/2, height/2, -130);
```

```
// outer transparent cube
noFill();
// rotate everything, including external large cube
rotateX(frameCount*PI/225);
rotateY(frameCount*PI/250);
rotateZ(frameCount*PI/275);
stroke(255);
// draw external large cube
stage.create();

//move/rotate cubies
for (int i=0; i<cubies; i++){
  pushMatrix();
  translate(x[i], y[i], z[i]);
  rotateX(frameCount*PI/xRot[i]);
  rotateY(frameCount*PI/yRot[i]);
  rotateX(frameCount*PI/zRot[i]);
  noStroke();
  c[i].create(quadBG[i]);
  x[i]+=xSpeed[i];
  y[i]+=ySpeed[i];
  z[i]+=zSpeed[i];
  popMatrix();

  // draw lines connecting cubbies
  stroke(10);
  if (i<cubies-1){
    line(x[i], y[i], z[i], x[i+1], y[i+1], z[i+1]);
  }

  // check wall collisions
  if (x[i]>bounds/2 || x[i]<-bounds/2){
    xSpeed[i]*=-1;
  }
  if (y[i]>bounds/2 || y[i]<-bounds/2){
    ySpeed[i]*=-1;
  }
  if (z[i]>bounds/2 || z[i]<-bounds/2){
    zSpeed[i]*=-1;
  }
}
}
```

13

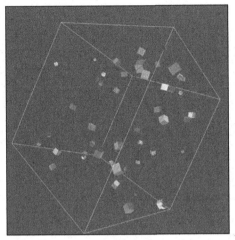

Figure 13-9. Cubes Contained Within a Cube sketch

This example is long—but again, it's stuff you've looked at before. The most complex part of the sketch is the following code snippet, within the for loop of the draw() function:

```
pushMatrix();
translate(x[i], y[i], z[i]);
rotateX(frameCount*PI/xRot[i]);
rotateY(frameCount*PI/yRot[i]);
rotateX(frameCount*PI/zRot[i]);
noStroke();
c[i].create(quadBG[i]);
x[i]+=xSpeed[i];
y[i]+=ySpeed[i];
z[i]+=zSpeed[i];
popMatrix();
```

It is sometimes confusing, when using the pushMatrix() and popMatrix() functions, to determine what commands need to be called between them. Since I'm using a loop to process an array of items, I need to make sure that each transformation only affects its respective item; otherwise, the transformations will become cumulative, so objects stored later in the array will be affected much more than the earlier ones. It is helpful to break down the last example by commenting out the pushMatrix() and popMatrix() calls and then rerunning the sketch to see the effect. In addition, I recommend playing with some of the values in the sketch, especially the variables in the following code:

```
int cubies = 50;
float bounds = 300;
float cubieSize = random(5, 15);
xSpeed[i] = random(-2, 2);
ySpeed[i] = random(-2, 2);
zSpeed[i] = random(-2, 2);
```

As complicated as this last sketch might have seemed, it only scratches the surface of what's possible. For example, a more advanced version of the sketch could include physics calculations: gravity, collisions, angular or rotational velocities, and so on. Well, don't worry, I won't torture you further with this example. However, before moving on, there is one more fundamental concept used in the last example that I'd like to discuss: 3D rotations.

3D rotations

Thus far in the chapter, I've been happily using Processing's 3D rotation functions: rotateX(), rotateY(), and rotateZ(). These are really easy to use, which is a good thing—but it's also valuable to understand how these functions operate beneath the hood. I actually already covered the basic math that controls 3D rotation when I discussed 2D rotation around the z-axis. In 2D, when you want to rotate around the origin, you use the following trig functions:

```
y = sin(theta)*radius
x = cos(theta)*radius
```

Hopefully, these expressions seem like old friends by now (if so, you're well on your way to geek certification). In 3D, the situation isn't much more complicated than applying these same rotation expressions to the x- and y-axes. To perform rotations around each of the three individual axes, you'd use the following expressions:

```
z-axis rotation
x = cos(theta)*radius
y = sin(theta)*radius

x-axis rotation
y = cos(theta)*radius
z = sin(theta)*radius

y-axis rotation
z = cos(theta)*radius
x = sin(theta)*radius
```

These expressions work fine for single-axis rotations, but if you want to put a bunch of these together, or allow a user to randomly rotate a shape around any axis in real time, you need slightly more complicated versions of these equations. Before looking at those, here's a simple implementation that rotates three rectangles around the x-, y-, and z-axes (see Figure 13-10):

```
// Single Axis 3D Rotation

// rectangle vertices
float[][]rectX = new float[3][4];
float[][]rectY = new float[3][4];
float[][]rectZ = new float[3][4];
```

13

```
// rotation variables
float[]angle = {45, 45, 45};
float[]rot = {1, 1, 1};

void setup(){
  size (400, 200, P3D);
}

void draw(){
  background(255);
  for (int i=0; i<3; i++){
    pushMatrix();
    // spread rects evenly across window
    translate(75+(125*i), height/2);
    beginShape();
    for (int j=0; j<4; j++){
      // rotation around z-axis
      if (i==0){
        rectX[i][j] = cos(radians(angle[i]))*50;
        rectY[i][j] = sin(radians(angle[i]))*50;
      }
      // rotation around x-axis
      else if (i==1){
        rectY[i][j] = cos(radians(angle[i]))*50;
        rectZ[i][j] = sin(radians(angle[i]))*50;

        // offset added just to show rotation better
        rectX[i][j] = 10;
      }
      // rotation around y-axis
      else if (i==2){
        rectZ[i][j] = cos(radians(angle[i]))*50;
        rectX[i][j] = sin(radians(angle[i]))*50;

        // offset added just to show rotation better
        rectY[i][j] = 10;
      }
      vertex(rectX[i][j], rectY[i][j], rectZ[i][j]);
      angle[i]+=360/4;
      angle[i]+=rot[i];
    }
    endShape(CLOSE);
    popMatrix();
  }
}
```

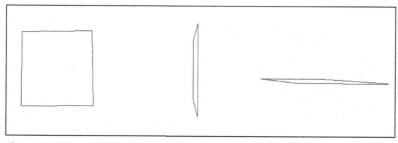

Figure 13-10. Single Axis 3D Rotation sketch

I coded this procedurally, but of course I could have created a custom rectangle class to do the same thing. The rectangles are plotted using the two trig equations by increment- ing the angle[] variable in the trig functions by 90 degrees. To make the rectangles spin, I just incremented angle[] by the rot[] variable. Again, the order of translations and placement of the pushMatrix() and popMatrix() functions are significant; try comment- ing out the functions or moving them to see what effect this has on the output. You'll notice I also added an extra offset statement (rectX[i][j] = 10; and rectY[i][j] = 10;) for the x-axis and y-axis rotations, respectively. I only did this so that you could better see the rotations. If you comment these lines out, two of the rotations will be perpendicular to the screen and thus look like two shifting lines instead of planes.

The problem with the last implementation is that you can't do much with it, unless of course you're really into single-axis rotations. It would be better to be able to rotate around all three axes. To do this, you need to, in a sense, keep track of where the vertices are as they are rotating so that you can smoothly transition them to a new rotation. Internally, Processing does this with its own 3D rotation functions, allowing you to call each of the functions in succession, without the last one overriding the previous ones. The three x, y, and z rotation calls blend into a seamless and interesting rotation. I've discussed this previously—but here's another really simple example, using Processing's box() func- tion and three built-in rotation functions:

```
void setup(){
  size(400, 400, P3D);
}
void draw(){
  background(150);
  translate(width/2, height/2, 200);
  rotateX(PI*frameCount/60);
  rotateY(PI*frameCount/80);
  rotateZ(PI*frameCount/100);
  box(50, 50, 50);
}
```

And here's an interactive version, allowing the user to perform axis rotations by moving the mouse. (Since the mouse normally only moves along the x- and y-axes, I only included rotations around these axes.)

13

```
float rotX, rotY;
void setup(){
  size(400, 400, P3D);
}
void draw(){
  background(150);
  translate(width/2, height/2, 200);
  rotateX(rotX);
  rotateY(rotY);
  box(50, 50, 50);
}
void mouseMoved(){
  rotX = radians(mouseY);
  rotY = radians(mouseX);
}
```

So that was the easy way. Of course, you by now know that I can't leave well enough alone. Next, I'll show you how to re-create the functionality of Processing's three rotation functions, which mostly just means altering the trig functions. Here they are, along with some declared variables to help illustrate how they work. (Please note that this code is not meant to be run.)

```
float originalX, originalY, originalZ;
float x2, y2, z2;
float x3, y3, z3;
float finalX, finalY, finalZ;

// rotation around x-axix
y2  = cos(angleX) * originalY - sin(angleX) * originalZ;
z2 = sin(angleX) * originalY + cos(angleX) * originalZ;

// rotation around y-axis
z3 = cos(angleY) * z2 - sin(angleY) * x2;
x3 = sin(angleY) * z2 + cos(angleY) * x2;

// rotation around z-axis
finalX = cos(angleZ) * x3 - sin(angleZ) * y3;
finalY = sin(angleZ) * x3 + cos(angleZ) * y3;
```

Although the expressions may at first seem a little confusing, if you look at them carefully, you'll see that they're pretty redundant. A key feature to using these expressions, which some books don't seem to clarify properly, is that the expressions use existing x, y, and z values as inputs. So, for example, if you wanted to do rotations around all three axes, you'd need to keep feeding the new values calculated from the previous axis rotations into the next set of expressions, as I illustrated by using the different variables. I accomplish this in the next example by using three separate vertices arrays in addition to the original array of vertices; it's mostly an organizational problem.

The first example I'll look at simply rotates a rectangle, which is coded procedurally. In the second example, I'll reuse the Cube and Point3D classes to rotate a cube. Here's the code for the first example (shown in Figure 13-11):

```
// Custom Rotation of a Rectangle Around the X-, Y-, and Z-Axes

// rectangle's vertices before rotation
float[][]originalVertices = new float[4][3];

// rectangle's vertices after rotation
float[][]transformedVertices = new float[4][3];

// control rectangle rotations
float angleX, angleY, angleZ;

void setup(){
  size(400, 400, P3D);

 /* generate initial rectangle coordinate data
     filling originalVertices array */
// creates rectangle parallel to window
  float angle = 45;
  for (int i=0; i<4; i++){
    originalVertices[i][0] = cos(radians(angle))*50;
    originalVertices[i][1] = sin(radians(angle))*50;
    originalVertices[i][2] = 0;
    angle+=360/4.0;
  }
}

void draw(){
  background(100);
 // rotate rectangle around all 3 axes
  myRotateX(2);
  myRotateY(6);
  myRotateZ(3);

  //draw rect
  createRect();
}

void myRotateX(float deg){
  angleX+=deg;
}
void myRotateY(float deg){
  angleY+=deg;
}
void myRotateZ(float deg){
  angleZ+=deg;
}
```

13

```
void createRect(){
  translate(width/2, height/2, 200);
  transformedVertices = rotateVertices();
  beginShape();
  for (int i=0; i<4; i++){
    vertex(transformedVertices[i][0], transformedVertices[i][1], ➥
        transformedVertices[i][2]);
  }
  endShape(CLOSE);
}

// called every frame
float[][]rotateVertices(){

  // arrays to temporarily store rotated vertices
  float[][]rotatedVertices_XAxis = new float[4][3];
  float[][]rotatedVertices_YAxis = new float[4][3];
  float[][]rotatedVertices_ZAxis = new float[4][3];

  for (int i=0; i<4; i++){
    // rotation around x-axis
    rotatedVertices_XAxis[i][0] = originalVertices[i][0];
    rotatedVertices_XAxis[i][1] = cos(radians(angleX))* ➥
        originalVertices[i][1] - sin(radians(angleX))* ➥
        originalVertices[i][2];
    rotatedVertices_XAxis[i][2] = sin(radians(angleX))* ➥
        originalVertices[i][1] + cos(radians(angleX))* ➥
        originalVertices[i][2];

    // rotation around y-axis
    rotatedVertices_YAxis[i][1] = rotatedVertices_XAxis[i][1];
    rotatedVertices_YAxis[i][2] = cos(radians(angleY))* ➥
        rotatedVertices_XAxis[i][2] - sin(radians(angleY))* ➥
        rotatedVertices_XAxis[i][0];
    rotatedVertices_YAxis[i][0] = sin(radians(angleY))* ➥
        rotatedVertices_XAxis[i][2] + cos(radians(angleY))* ➥
        rotatedVertices_XAxis[i][0];

    // rotation around z-axis
    rotatedVertices_ZAxis[i][0] = cos(radians(angleZ))* ➥
        rotatedVertices_YAxis[i][0] - sin(radians(angleZ))* ➥
        rotatedVertices_YAxis[i][1];
    rotatedVertices_ZAxis[i][1] = sin(radians(angleZ))* ➥
        rotatedVertices_YAxis[i][0] + cos(radians(angleZ))* ➥
        rotatedVertices_YAxis[i][1];
    rotatedVertices_ZAxis[i][2] = rotatedVertices_YAxis[i][2];
  }
  return rotatedVertices_ZAxis;
}
```

Figure 13-11. Custom Rotation of a Rectangle Around
the X-, Y-, and Z-Axes example

The 2D array float[][]originalVertices is used to store the original rectangle vertices
data, and float[][]transformedVertices is used eventually to receive the transformed
vertices data, which is then passed to Processing's vertex() function for drawing. In the
setup() function, I create the original rectangle with the standard sin() and cos() function approach described in numerous sections of the book. I don't draw the rectangle
here, but rather construct it in data and assign that data to the originalVertices[][]
array. Next, in draw(), I call some custom rotate functions that update the values of the
angleX, angleY, and angleZ variables used in the rotation calculations. Finally, I call the
createRect() function, which internally calls the rotateVertices() function and draws
the rectangle on the screen. It is in the rotateVertices() function that most of the
sketch's real heavy lifting occurs.

At the top of the rotateVertices() function I declare three 2D arrays. These arrays are
used to temporarily store the transformed vertices data. To make things simpler (honestly), I set up the sketch to call the rotateVertices() function every time draw()
executes. This isn't the most efficient approach, but it avoids things like having to check
which rotation function commands were invoked; I just assume they're all being called.
However, if you comment out any/all of the following lines:

```
myRotateX(2);
myRotateY(6);
myRotateZ(3);
```

the program will still work properly. The rotateVertices() function will still be called
from within createRect(), but some/all of the rotation angle values won't change, so
you'll get less or no rotation. Reading though the rotateVertices() function should be
straightforward, even though it's kind of dense. The important thing to notice is how the
previous array's values are input into the next set of expressions, and how these expressions are assigned to one of the temporary arrays. I chose to have the function return the
final array, which is why I used the expression transformedVertices = rotateVertices();
in the createRect() function and created the three temporary arrays (rotatedVertices_
XAxis[][], rotatedVertices_YAxis[][], and rotatedVertices_ZAxis[][]) locally within

13

the rotateVertices() function; there are certainly other ways to implement this. Before you move on to the cube example, I strongly recommend you play/experiment with this one for a while.

I'll reuse the Point3D and Cube classes to build the next example. I'll need to create another method to handle the combined 3D rotations. I could redesign the Cube class and add the new rotation method directly in there. But a much better a way to deal with adding the new method is to create a new class as a subclass of the Cube class. This approach gives me the benefit of using the original class without having to alter it, still allowing me to extend its capabilities. As discussed earlier in the book, the term *inheritance* in OOP is used to describe this extending approach. Although I could have gone into my original Cube class and added a rotation method, it's best practice to not edit existing classes, as other dependent classes could be adversely affected. The following code gives the completed example (shown in Figure 13-12). I didn't include the Point3D or Cube class code, just the new SpinnyCube class (Cube subclass); so don't forget to add the Point3D and Cube classes before running the example. (Remember, you can either create a new tab for each class, or simply paste the classes beneath your current sketch code.)

```
// Rotation of a Custom Cube Around the X-, Y-, and Z-Axes

// custom Cube reference variable
SpinnyCube c1;

// array to hold different face colors
color[]quadBG = new color[6];

void setup(){
  size(400, 400, P3D);
  quadBG[0] = color(175, 30, 30, 255);
  quadBG[1] = color(30, 175, 30, 255);
  quadBG[2] = color(30, 30, 175, 255);
  quadBG[3] = color(175, 175, 30, 255);
  quadBG[4] = color(175, 30, 175, 255);
  quadBG[5] = color(175, 87, 30, 255);

  //instantiate cube
  c1 = new SpinnyCube(200, 200, 200);
}

void draw(){
  background(100);
  translate(width/2, height/2);

  if (mousePressed){
    //interactive rotation
    c1.spinnyRotateX(mouseY);
    c1.spinnyRotateY(mouseX);
  }
  else {
```

```
    //automatic rotation
    c1.spinnyRotateX(frameCount*PI);
    c1.spinnyRotateY(frameCount*PI/4);
    c1.spinnyRotateZ(frameCount*PI/5);
  }

  //draw cube
  noStroke();
  c1.create(quadBG);
}

// SpinnyCube class
class SpinnyCube extends Cube{
  float angleX, angleY, angleZ;
  Point3D[] transformedVertices = new Point3D[24];

  // default constructor
  SpinnyCube(){
  }

  // constructor
  SpinnyCube(float w, float h, float d){
    // call superclass constructor
    super(w, h, d);
  }

  // rotation method
  void spinnyRotateXYZ(){
    // temporary vertices arrays
    Point3D[] rotatedVertices_XAxis = new Point3D[24];
    Point3D[] rotatedVertices_YAxis = new Point3D[24];
    Point3D[] rotatedVertices_ZAxis = new Point3D[24];

    for (int i=0; i<24; i++){
      // initialize temp vertices arrays
      rotatedVertices_XAxis[i] = new Point3D();
      rotatedVertices_YAxis[i] = new Point3D();
      rotatedVertices_ZAxis[i] = new Point3D();

      // rotation around x-axis
      rotatedVertices_XAxis[i].x = vertices[i].x;
      rotatedVertices_XAxis[i].y = cos(radians(angleX))* ➥
            vertices[i].y - sin(radians(angleX))*vertices[i].z;
      rotatedVertices_XAxis[i].z = sin(radians(angleX))* ➥
            vertices[i].y + cos(radians(angleX))*vertices[i].z;

      // rotation around y-axis
      rotatedVertices_YAxis[i].y = rotatedVertices_XAxis[i].y;
      rotatedVertices_YAxis[i].z = cos(radians(angleY))* ➥
```

13

```
                        rotatedVertices_XAxis[i].z - sin(radians(angleY))* ➥
                        rotatedVertices_XAxis[i].x;
            rotatedVertices_YAxis[i].x = sin(radians(angleY))* ➥
                        rotatedVertices_XAxis[i].z + cos(radians(angleY))* ➥
                        rotatedVertices_XAxis[i].x;

            // rotation around z-axis
            rotatedVertices_ZAxis[i].x = cos(radians(angleZ))* ➥
                        rotatedVertices_YAxis[i].x - sin(radians(angleZ))* ➥
                        rotatedVertices_YAxis[i].y;
            rotatedVertices_ZAxis[i].y = sin(radians(angleZ))* ➥
                        rotatedVertices_YAxis[i].x + cos(radians(angleZ))* ➥
                        rotatedVertices_YAxis[i].y;
            rotatedVertices_ZAxis[i].z = rotatedVertices_YAxis[i].z;
        }
        // update transformedVertices arrays
        transformedVertices = rotatedVertices_ZAxis;
    }

    // assign rotation angles for each axis
    void spinnyRotateX(float angle){
        angleX = angle;
    }
    void spinnyRotateY(float angle){
        angleY = angle;
    }
    void spinnyRotateZ(float angle){
        angleZ = angle;
    }

    /* SpinnyCube (subclass) create() methods will
       override Cube (superclass) create() methods. */
    void create(){
        // draw cube
        spinnyRotateXYZ();
        stroke(0);
        for (int i=0; i<6; i++){
            beginShape(QUADS);
            for (int j=0; j<4; j++){
                vertex(transformedVertices[j+4*i].x, transformedVertices[j+ ➥
                        4*i].y, transformedVertices[j+4*i].z);
            }
            endShape();
        }
    }
    void create(color[]quadBG){
        // draw cube
        spinnyRotateXYZ();
```

```
        for (int i=0; i<6; i++){
          fill(quadBG[i]);
          beginShape(QUADS);
          for (int j=0; j<4; j++){
            vertex(transformedVertices[j+4*i].x, transformedVertices[j+ ➥
                4*i].y, transformedVertices[j+4*i].z);
          }
          endShape();
        }
      }
    }
```

Figure 13-12. Rotation of a Custom Cube Around the
X-, Y-, and Z-Axes example

The example begins similarly to the earlier cube example, except that I'm using my new
SpinnyCube reference type to declare variable c1. Remember, a class is a legal data type,
just as float, int, and color are. Since the SpinnyCube class extends the Cube class, I was
able to instantiate the SpinnyCube object with the help of the constructor in the Cube
superclass. If this doesn't make sense yet, it will become clearer shortly (and you can
always refer back to Chapter 8 for a review on OOP).

Within the draw() function, I set up a simple if...else block that starts the cube spinning
and allows the user to drag and rotate the cube. The last line in draw() is the create()
method that handles drawing the cube. Below the draw() function is the SpinnyCube class.

Even though I used an OOP approach for this example, the SpinnyCube class is implemented quite similarly to the last procedural spinning rectangle example. I declared a
transformedVertices[] array to eventually handle the rotated vertices. The drawing code
uses this array. I didn't need to create the original vertices[] array, as I have access to all
the members (properties and methods) in the Cube class (through inheritance), which

13

contains this array. The SpinnyCube constructor accepts the same three arguments as the Cube class, for the width, height, and depth of the cube. The first line of the SpinnyCube constructor

```
super(w, h, d);
```

passes the arguments through to the superclass (Cube) constructor. This is a very efficient structure that allows you to build upon base and component classes. One little reminder— if there had been any other code in the SpinnyCube constructor, it would need to be put after the super() call, which (when included) must always be the first line in the subclass constructor. (However, you are not required to include a call to super() in a subclass constructor.)

> *I recommend always adding a default no-argument constructor to any class that will be extended, since the superclass constructor is always invoked, even without an explicit call to* super(). *To learn more about this and related (albeit geeky and low-level) issues, check out* www.beginner-java-tutorial.com/ *and* http://java.sun.com/docs/books/jls/second_edition/html/classes.doc.html.

Following the constructors is the spinnyRotateXYZ() method. This method works practically identically to the rotateVertices() function in the previous example. To keep things organized, I declared and initialized all the temporary vertices arrays locally within this method. As in the last example, the transformed vertices need to be plugged into the next set of expressions. Finally, at the end of the method, I assigned the updated vertices to the transformedVertices[] array used to draw the cube. Following this method are three simple utility methods (spinnyRotateX(), spinnyRotateY(), and spinnyRotateZ()) that update rotation angles, used by the expressions in the spinnyRotateXYZ() method.

The last methods in the SpinnyCube class are two overloaded create() methods, just as in the Cube class. Creating two more methods with the same name may seem confusing and unnecessary, since the subclass has access to the superclass's create() methods. I wanted to call the spinnyRotate() method internally from within the create() methods, and I didn't want to make that change to the cube's original create() methods. Since the create() methods in the SpinnyCube subclass have the same method signatures (parameter lists) as the create() methods in the Cube superclass, the methods in the subclass will override the same named ones in the superclass. In other words, when I call

```
c1.create(quadBG);
```

and c1 is of type SpinnyCube, the create() method in the SpinnyCube subclass is executed, not the one with the identical signature in the Cube class. The SpinnyCube create() methods are implemented nearly identically to the ones in the Cube class, except that they have additional lines for calling the spinnyRotateXYZ() method.

Beyond box() and sphere()

While there are many common 3D primitives (including cylinders, pyramids, cones, and toroids), Processing's built-in primitive-creation functions are limited to the measly box() and sphere(). I'll show you how to construct a few of these—which is mostly a matter of creating algorithms. What I mean by this is that you need a set of logical instructions to create these forms (unless you're a math genius, which I'm not). Sometimes forms seem complex until you see the steps to generate them. Before switching shapes, I'll develop an algorithm to construct a brick tower (shown in Figure 13-13) that includes a crenellated roof, using the existing Cube class.

The tower will be constructed of rings of bricks with a rotational offset between the brick rows, allowing the vertically adjacent brick seams to alternate, like in a regular brick wall. The first part of the algorithm generates a single ring of bricks; next, the graphics context (the object that controls the actual drawing) is translated the distance equal to the height of a brick and rotated one-half the ring rotation angle so that the vertical seams alternate. Then the first step is repeated until some specified height is reached. Finally, the last step involves creating the crenellation, which uses the same basic routine as step 1 (generating a brick ring), but with every other brick removed (actually never added).

To generate the initial brick ring, I used the following trig expressions:

```
z = cos(radians(angle))*radius;
x = sin(radians(angle))*radius;
```

These expressions, which were discussed earlier in the chapter, can be used to generate a regular polygon that is flipped to face the top and bottom of the display window. In addition to placing the bricks in a ring in the xz plane, I also need to rotate the bricks so that they are aligned with the ring path. I accomplished this by rotating each brick the same number of degrees I displaced it to form the ring. To help understand this, imagine that you have a brick floating in front of your eyes. The brick's wide side is facing you, as if you were looking straight at a building. Now displace the brick 90 degrees around your head (but don't rotate it), so that it's next to your left ear. The brick's end is now facing your ear. To make the wide side of the brick again face your head (actually, your ear), you need to rotate the brick around its center point the same number of degrees it was displaced (i.e., 90 degrees).

Following is the code for the example, which requires the Cube and Point3D classes:

```
// Brick Tower

// Point3D and Cube classes required.
float bricksPerLayer = 16.0; // value must be even
float brickLayers = 25.0;
Cube[]bricks = new Cube[int(bricksPerLayer*brickLayers)];
float brickWidth = 60, brickHeight = 25, brickDepth = 25;
float radius = 150.0;
float angle = 0;
```

13

```
void setup(){
  size(400, 400, P3D);

  //instantiate bricks
  for (int i=0; i<bricks.length; i++){
    bricks[i] = new Cube(brickWidth, brickHeight, brickDepth);
  }
}

void draw(){
  background(100, 125, 200);
  float tempX = 0, tempY = 0, tempZ = 0;
  fill(175, 87, 20);
  stroke(100, 50, 10);
  // add basic light setup
  lights();
  translate(width/2, height*1.2, -550);
  // tip tower to see the inside
  rotateX(radians(-45));
  // slowly rotate tower
  rotateY(frameCount*PI/60);
  for (int i=0; i<brickLayers; i++){
    // increment rows
    tempY-=brickHeight;
    // alternate brick seams
    angle = 360.0/bricksPerLayer*i/2;
    for (int j=0; j<bricksPerLayer; j++){
      tempZ = cos(radians(angle))*radius;
      tempX = sin(radians(angle))*radius;
      pushMatrix();
      translate(tempX, tempY, tempZ);
      rotateY(radians(angle));
      // add crenelation
      if (i==brickLayers-1){
        if (j%2 == 0){
          bricks[j].create();
        }
      }
      // create main tower
      else {
        bricks[j].create();
      }
      popMatrix();
      angle += 360.0/bricksPerLayer;
    }
  }
}
// Point3D and Cube classes required
```

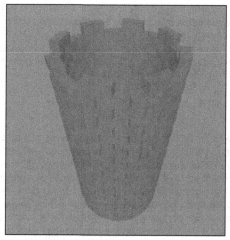

Figure 13-13. Brick Tower sketch

This is a pretty long example, but I assure you you've seen it all before. I reused the Point3D and Cube classes, which really simplified things. If you build your classes well, you can continue to reuse or extend them, which will increase your efficiency over time. This is one of the great benefits of OOP. The only somewhat complicated parts of the sketch are the code that controls the alternating brick layer rotation and the crenellation code. Since I knew what angle of rotation I needed to generate the brick ring, I wrote the expression

```
angle = 360.0/bricksPerLayer*i/2;
```

to control the alternating seams per each brick layer. Remember the order of operations (which does make a difference): when the operators are of the same precedence level, the expression is solved from left to right. This was the case with this expression, as multiplication and division have the same precedence level. The expression evaluates alternating values per loop cycle between an even multiple of the angle and one-half of an even multiple, which gives me the alternating brick seams. (The actual angle value doesn't really matter.) Try removing the /2 from the expression to see what happens when the seams don't alternate.

The crenellation code uses the modulus operator, which I've discussed in numerous chapters throughout the book; remember that it evaluates to the remainder of a division. I used the operator so that every other brick would be drawn.

```
// add crenellation
    if (i==brickLayers-1){
      if (j%2 == 0){
        bricks[j].create();
      }
    }
```

I guess with crenellation like this (one brick high), you'd need very tall bricks (or very short soldiers).

Hopefully, the rotating castle tower didn't bring your computer to a standstill. Calculating all that 3D data in real time is demanding. There are some advanced and frighteningly low-level approaches to optimizing 3D that I won't go into. However, Processing includes a really simple way to speed things up, which I'll look at in the next chapter (sorry to be a tease). For now, if the code is executing really slowly, try lowering the number of brick layers and/or increasing the speed of the rotation.

Extrusion

To begin to generate forms such as cylinders, cones, spheres, and toroids (also sometimes referred to as toruses), it helps to understand the concept of lathing. However, to understand lathing, you need to understand extrusion (lots of annoying terms, I know). **Extrusion** simply pushes 2D geometry into 3D space by adding a depth component to the 2D shape. For example, a rectangle on the xy plane is extruded into a cube that now exists in xyz space. Next is a simple interactive extrusion example beginning with a rectangle (shown in Figure 13-14). Move your mouse right and left to rotate the rectangle, and drag the mouse up and down to extrude it (remember, dragging requires the mouse button to be pressed).

```
/* Extrusion Example
move right to left to rotate
drag up and down to extrude
*/
float depth = 0, boxDepth = 0;
float mousePt_Y = 0;

void setup(){
  size(500, 300, P3D);
}

void draw(){
  background(25);
  lights();
  fill(100, 100, 175);
  stroke(200);
  translate(width/2, height/2);
  rotateY(radians(mouseX));
  box(100, 50, boxDepth);
}

void mouseDragged(){
    boxDepth = depth + (mousePt_Y-mouseY);
}
void mousePressed(){
  mousePt_Y = mouseY;
}
void mouseReleased(){
  depth = boxDepth;
}
```

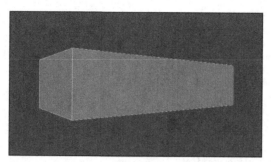

Figure 13-14. Extrusion Example sketch

In reality, my example is a pretty cheap version of extrusion, since I used Processing's box() command, which created the rectangle in 3D space, allowing me to just interactively change the value of the depth argument in the box() call. If I had started with a "real" rectangle, I would have had to deal with adding and attaching new geometry to have enough vertices (at least eight) to make a box. Notice in the example that when you drag the mouse up, the rectangle becomes a solid box, but when you drag it down, the box exterior seems to become strangely transparent. This occurrence isn't a quantum paradox, but one of the clever ways 3D is optimized for our still slow computers. Since we normally aren't interested in the inside of a form (the part we can't see), 3D engines tend not to waste processing power rendering that information. Thus, in 3D, polygons are usually single-sided. So, when the mouse is dragged down and the box collapses in on itself, the inside surfaces become the outside surfaces; however, since the inside faces are invisible, you can see through them to the original outside surfaces, which are now inside the box—oy vey!

Lest you think I got off too easy borrowing Processing's box() function in the last extrusion example, I'll follow it up with a better one. Using the keyboard, you can control the length of the extrusion and the number of segments. You can also set the rendering as wireframe, hollow shaded, or filled solid. The left and right arrows control extrusion length, the up and down arrows control the addition/deletion of segments, the S key toggles between solid shaded and hollow shaded, and the W key toggles between wireframe and shaded. All the surfaces are double-sided, allowing you to see both the inside and outside of the box when in hollow shaded mode. I included three screenshots generated by the sketch, shown in Figures 13-15 through 13-17.

```
/* Better Extrusion Example
Arrow keys control segments (up/down)
and extrusion length (left/right)
's' key controls solid rendering
'w' key controls wireframe rendering
*/

// begin as a flat cube
int segments = 1;
int pts = 8;
float rectWidth = 150, rectHeight = 100;
float extrudeLength;
```

13

```
boolean isSolid = true;
boolean isWireFrame = false;
// vertices arrays
float[]verticesX = new float[pts];
float[]verticesY = new float[pts];
float[]verticesZ = new float[pts];

void setup(){
  size(500, 300, P3D);
  float px, py, pz;
  float angle = 45;
  // initialize vertices
  // initially create 2 planes in the same position,
  for (int i=0; i<pts; i++){
    px = cos(radians(angle))*rectWidth/2;
    py = sin(radians(angle))*rectHeight/2;
    pz = 0;
    verticesX[i] = px;
    verticesY[i] = py;
    verticesZ[i] = pz;
    angle+=360/4;
  }
}

void draw(){
  background(25);
  lights();
  if(isWireFrame){
    noFill();
  } else {
    fill(100, 100, 175);
  }

  stroke(200);
  translate(width/2, height/2);
  rotateY(frameCount*PI/200);
  rotateZ(frameCount*PI/190);
  rotateX(frameCount*PI/180);
  extrude();
}

// add/subtract points to vertices arrays
// called from within Key event functions below
void setSegments(int seg){
  //increase/decrease segment count
  segments+=seg;

  /*
  Temp array used to add another segment to vertices
```

```
  arrays. The x and y values don't change between planes.
  The extruded z values are calculated in extrude function
  */
  float[][]inputArray = {
    {verticesX[0], verticesX[1], verticesX[2], verticesX[3]},
    {verticesY[0], verticesY[1], verticesY[2], verticesY[3]},
    {verticesZ[0], verticesZ[1], verticesZ[2], verticesZ[3]}
  };

  // add new segment to vertices array, using
  // Processing's splice() function
  verticesX = splice(verticesX, inputArray[0], verticesX.length);
  verticesY = splice(verticesY, inputArray[1], verticesY.length);
  verticesZ = splice(verticesZ, inputArray[2], verticesZ.length);
}

void extrude(){
  // Calculate z positions of vertices
  float segmentWidth = extrudeLength/segments;
  for (int i=0; i<segments+1; i++){
    for (int j=0; j<4; j++){
      verticesZ[j+4*i] = -extrudeLength/2+segmentWidth*i;
    }
  }

  // render cross planes between segments
  if (isSolid){
    for (int i=0; i<segments+1; i++){
      beginShape();
      for (int j=0; j<4; j++){
        vertex(verticesX[j+4*i], verticesY[j+4*i], verticesZ[j+4*i]);
      }
      endShape(CLOSE);
    }
  }

  // render external skin
  for (int i=0; i<segments+1; i++){
    beginShape(QUAD_STRIP);
    for (int j=0; j<4; j++){
      if (i<segments){
        vertex(verticesX[j+4*i], verticesY[j+4*i], verticesZ[j+4*i]);
        vertex(verticesX[j+4*i+4], verticesY[j+4*i+4], ➡
            verticesZ[j+4*i+4]);
        if (j==3){
          // connnect last vertices back to beginning
          // to close form
          vertex(verticesX[4*i], verticesY[4*i], verticesZ[4*i]);
          vertex(verticesX[4*i+4], verticesY[4*i+4], verticesZ[4*i+4]);
```

13

653

```
        }
      }
    }
    endShape();
  }
}

/*
arrow keys control segments
 and extrusion length
*/
void keyPressed(){
  if(key == CODED) {
    // segments
    if (keyCode == UP) {
      if (segments<25){
        setSegments(1);
      }
    }
    else if (keyCode == DOWN) {
      if (segments>1){
        setSegments(-1);
      }
    }

    // extrusion length
    if (keyCode == RIGHT) {
      extrudeLength+=5;
    }
    else if (keyCode == LEFT) {
      if (extrudeLength>0){
        extrudeLength-=5;
      }
    }
  }
  if (key =='s'){
    if (isSolid){
      isSolid=false;
    } else {
      isSolid=true;
    }
  }
  if (key =='w'){
    if (isWireFrame){
      isWireFrame=false;
    } else {
      isWireFrame=true;
    }
  }
}
```

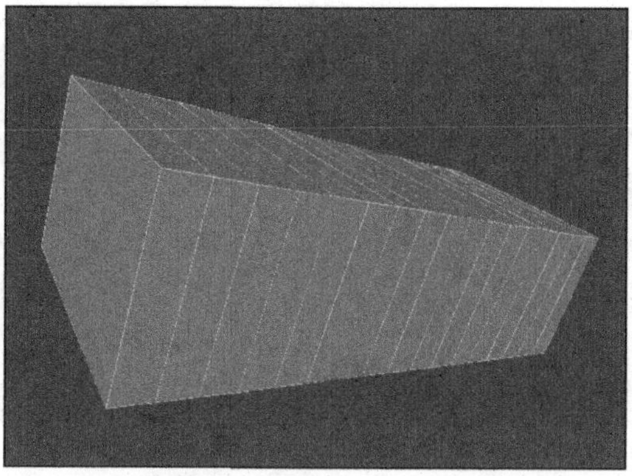

Figure 13-15. Better Extrusion Example sketch (solid box version)

Figure 13-16. Better Extrusion Example sketch (hollow box version)

13

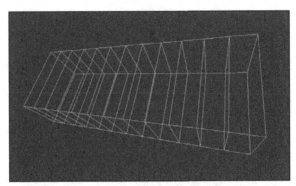

Figure 13-17. Better Extrusion Example sketch (wireframe box version)

This example is lengthy in large part because of all the interactivity. Really, the only complicated problem in the sketch is in dynamically generating the equal segementation of the solid. I also wanted the shape to remain centered as it rotated. Since the solid never actually moves (remember that the rotation is the entire drawing context) as the shape increases in width, I needed to shift the vertices negatively the same distance I increased the length of the cube; I used the following block to accomplish this:

```
// Calculate z positions of vertices
  float segmentWidth = extrudeLength/segments;
  for (int i=0; i<segments+1; i++){
    for (int j=0; j<4; j++){
      verticesZ[j+4*i] = -extrudeLength/2+segmentWidth*i;
    }
  }
```

The expression `verticesZ[j+4*i]` = `-extrudeLength/2+segmentWidth*i;` is not very friendly looking. The part inside the array brackets (j+4*i) allows the nested loops to run through all the vertices. If this doesn't make sense, run through the loops manually a couple iterations (using the supercomputer in your head). The second part of the expression, `-extrudeLength/2+segmentWidth*i;`, is what positions the vertices along the z-axis. For example, if extrudeLength is 100 and segments equals 4, then the segmentWidth would equal 25. Plugging these values into the expression would generate the following results (there's actually four copies of each value): –50, –25, 0, 25, 50. Notice how these value are symmetrical with regard to the origin.

I was able to render the segment planes as well as the external skin using two different render modes (no argument/CLOSE and QUAD_STRIP) with Processing's beginShape() and endShape(). Remember, by using no arguments in the beginShape() call and the CLOSE argument in the endShape() call, Processing creates a closed polygon. These functions are useful in 2D, but essential in 3D. The dense block that follows skins the cube, which is somewhat complicated by the need to skin between all the dynamic segments. Rather than trying to articulate what the code's doing, I recommend that you try commenting out different lines and running the sketch a couple times to see the effect. That's generally the way I build this stuff anyway—I often have little idea of what I'm actually doing until I begin to see things emerge; then I clean up the really ugly stuff (and hope for the best).

656

```
//render external skin
  for (int i=0; i<segments+1; i++){
    beginShape(QUAD_STRIP);
    for (int j=0; j<4; j++){
      if (i<segments){
        vertex(verticesX[j+4*i], verticesY[j+4*i], verticesZ[j+4*i]);
        vertex(verticesX[j+4*i+4], verticesY[j+4*i+4], ➥
            verticesZ[j+4*i+4]);
        if (j==3){
          //connnect last vertices back to beginning
          // to close form
          vertex(verticesX[4*i], verticesY[4*i], verticesZ[4*i]);
          vertex(verticesX[4*i+4], verticesY[4*i+4], ➥
              verticesZ[4*i+4]);
        }
      }
    }
  }
  endShape();
}
```

Cube to pyramid to cone to cylinder

Moving from a cube to a cylinder is very simple. In fact, you can even move from a cube to a pyramid to a cone to a cylinder quite easily (see Figures 13-18 through 13-21). Watching this transmutation reveals the interesting interrelationship between these forms. The next example allows you to interactively shift between these forms in real time. The code implementation is yet another variation on what you've already looked at the last few examples, although the form-building algorithms are slightly different. Hopefully you're beginning to see how certain implementations recur when you try to solve related problems. One of the biggest advantages of OOP is the structural abstraction it provides for handling these types of common implementations. Computer scientists refer to these common implementations as **design patterns**. This is too big a topic to cover here, but you can read more about it at www.patterndepot.com/put/8/JavaPatterns.htm.

Please note that this next sketch requires the Point3D class (not repeated following), but not the Cube class. Without further ado, here's the mutating Cube to Pyramid to Cone to Cylinder sketch:

```
/*
Cube to Pyramid to Cone to Cylinder
Point3D class required
*****************************
Instructions:
Up Arrow -- increases points
Down Arrow -- decreases points
'p' key toggles between cube/pyramid
*/
```

13

```
int pts = 4;
float angle = 0;
float radius = 115;
float cylinderLength = 100;
//vertices
Point3D vertices[][];
boolean isPyramid = false;

void setup(){
  size(400, 400, P3D);
  noStroke();
}

void draw(){
  background(170, 95, 95);
  lights();
  fill(255, 200, 200);
  translate(width/2, height/2);
  rotateX(frameCount*PI/150);
  rotateY(frameCount*PI/130);
  rotateZ(frameCount*PI/180);

  // initialize point arrays
  vertices = new Point3D[2][pts+1];

  // fill arrays
  for (int i=0; i<2; i++){
    angle = 0;
    for(int j=0; j<=pts; j++){
      vertices[i][j] = new Point3D();
      if (isPyramid){
        if (i==1){
          vertices[i][j].x = 0;
          vertices[i][j].y = 0;
        }
        else {
          vertices[i][j].x = cos(radians(angle))*radius;
          vertices[i][j].y = sin(radians(angle))*radius;
        }
      }
      else {
        vertices[i][j].x = cos(radians(angle))*radius;
        vertices[i][j].y = sin(radians(angle))*radius;
      }
      vertices[i][j].z = cylinderLength;
      // the .0 after the 360 is critical
      angle+=360.0/pts;
    }
    cylinderLength*=-1;
  }
```

```
    // draw cylinder tube
    beginShape(QUAD_STRIP);
    for(int j=0; j<=pts; j++){
      vertex(vertices[0][j].x, vertices[0][j].y, vertices[0][j].z);
      vertex(vertices[1][j].x, vertices[1][j].y, vertices[1][j].z);
    }
    endShape();

    //draw cylinder ends
    for (int i=0; i<2; i++){
      beginShape();
      for(int j=0; j<pts; j++){
        vertex(vertices[i][j].x, vertices[i][j].y, vertices[i][j].z);
      }
      endShape(CLOSE);
    }
}

/*
 up/down arrow keys control
 polygon detail.
 */
void keyPressed(){
  if(key == CODED) {
    // pts
    if (keyCode == UP) {
      if (pts<90){
        pts++;
      }
    }
    else if (keyCode == DOWN) {
      if (pts>4){
        pts--;
      }
    }
  }
  if (key =='p'){
    if (isPyramid){
      isPyramid=false;
    }
    else {
      isPyramid=true;
    }
  }
}
// Point3D class required
```

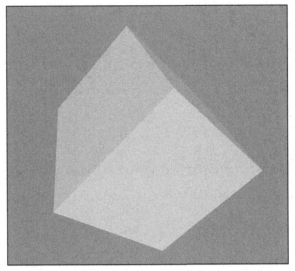

Figure 13-18. Cube to Pyramid to Cone to Cylinder sketch (in the cube form)

Figure 13-19. Cube to Pyramid to Cone to Cylinder sketch (in the pyramid form)

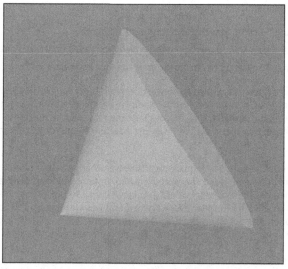

Figure 13-20. Cube to Pyramid to Cone to Cylinder sketch (in the cone form)

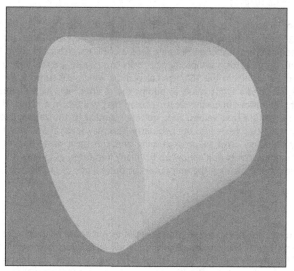

Figure 13-21. Cube to Pyramid to Cone to Cylinder sketch (in the cylinder form)

13

If you haven't figured it out by now, here's how you mutate between the four forms:

1. Press the P key to convert from a cube to a pyramid.

2. Press and hold the up arrow key to convert from a pyramid to a cone.

3. Press the P key again to convert from a cone to a cylinder.

I was surprised by how easy it was to convert between these four forms. Prior to developing this sketch, I had considered them (without really thinking much about it) as fundamental, irreducible primitives, like the primary colors. I even managed to earn two art degrees never realizing that a pyramid was just a cube with one of its faces collapsed to a point.

The sketch should be fairly self-explanatory. However, there is one subtle point worth discussing. When I first generated this sketch, it had an annoying bug. As the point count changed, sometimes the geometry would get screwed up. I found a clever but overly complicated hack to solve the problem. However, when I was cleaning up the code, I realized that the problem was actually very simple to fix, and my complicated hack was a major waste of time (sort of a pattern in my life). The problem related to the line

```
angle+=360/pts;
```

which I resolved by changing it to

```
angle+=360.0/pts;
```

You have to look closely to even notice the difference between these two lines. Adding the .0 after the 360 solved the problem. Can you tell why? Originally, I thought the problem related to needing the point count to be a factor of 360, which does solve the problem. However, that was more of a symptom, not really the cause. The real problem was that I was using two int values in the 360/pts calculation, which not surprisingly produced an int; however, I needed a float value. By adding the .0 after the 360, the value was treated as type float. Operations involving an int and a float will return a float. Thus, my angle calculations, requiring float values, were getting rounded to int values, and I was slowly losing accuracy, which screwed up the geometry. This may seem like an obscure point, but it is a pretty common error in programming and can be a nasty bug to track down. Sometimes rounding errors don't show up for many iterations, as long as the error is small enough. I recommend blaming the computer for these kinds of problems.

Toroids

Building upon the last few examples, it's possible to put some of these ideas together to build slightly more complex forms, such as toroids and related forms (shown in Figures 13-22 through 13-26). **Toroids** are ring forms (think inner tubes, bagels, or doughnuts). Toroids also have an interesting relationship to spheres and helixes, which you'll see in the following example.

The algorithm for a regular toroid, where the cross-section shape is a circle and the toroid radius is constant, might be as follows:

1. Generate a circle (actually a polygon) on the xy plane at the origin (0, 0).

2. Displace the circle on the x-axis the distance of the toroid radius.

3. Copy (lathe) the circle elliptically around the y-axis, maintaining the toroid radius distance from the origin.

Toroids have a ring thickness, which relates to the initial diameter of the lathed circle, and an inner hole diameter based on the distance of the lathed circle from the origin. The initial circle, which you'll be lathing with, will actually be a polygon with a lot of points (like in the preceding cylinder example). Finally, the lathing will be controlled by a segment level, which determines how many copies of the circle are rotated around the y-axis. The lathe segments will be evenly spaced, and will determine the smoothness of the toroid. The really cool thing is that you can easily control all these properties in real time, interactively revealing a wide range of interesting 3D forms based on your initial algorithm. The following sketch includes a bunch of key commands, which are listed at the top of the program as a code comment. The sketch requires the Point3D class, but not the Cube class.

```
/* Interactive Toroid
   Point3D class required
****************************************
key command controls
*****************
UP arrow key pts++;
DOWN arrow key pts--;
LEFT arrow key segments--;
RIGHT arrow key segments++;
'a' key toroid radius--;
's' key toroid radius++;
'z' key initial polygon radius--;
'x' key initial polygon radius++;
'w' key toggle wireframe/solid shading
'h' key toggle sphere/helix
****************************************/

//ellipse (shape to lathe)
int pts = 40;
float angle = 0;
float radius = 40.0;
// lathe segments
int segments = 60;
float latheAngle = 0;
float latheRadius = 100.0;
//vertices
Point3D vertices[], vertices2[];
// for shaded or wireframe rendering
boolean isWireFrame = false;
// for optional helix
boolean isHelix = false;
float helixOffset = 5.0;
```

13

```
void setup(){
  size(400, 400, P3D);
}

void draw(){
  background(50, 64, 42);
  // basic lighting setup
  lights();
  // 2 rendering styles
  // wireframe or solid
  if (isWireFrame){
    stroke(255, 255, 150);
    noFill();
  }
  else {
    noStroke();
    fill(150, 195, 125);
  }
  //center and spin toroid
  translate(width/2, height/2);

rotateX(frameCount*PI/150);
rotateY(frameCount*PI/170);
rotateZ(frameCount*PI/90);

  // initialize point arrays
  vertices = new Point3D[pts+1];
  vertices2 = new Point3D[pts+1];

  // fill arrays
  for(int i=0; i<=pts; i++){
    vertices[i] = new Point3D();
    vertices2[i] = new Point3D();
    vertices[i].x = latheRadius + sin(radians(angle))*radius;
    if (isHelix){
      vertices[i].z = cos(radians(angle))*radius-(helixOffset* ➡
            segments)/2;
    } else{
      vertices[i].z = cos(radians(angle))*radius;
    }
    angle+=360.0/pts;
  }

  // draw toroid
  latheAngle = 0;
  for(int i=0; i<=segments; i++){
    beginShape(QUAD_STRIP);
    for(int j=0; j<=pts; j++){
      if (i>0){
```

```
      vertex(vertices2[j].x, vertices2[j].y, vertices2[j].z);
    }
    vertices2[j].x = cos(radians(latheAngle))*vertices[j].x;
    vertices2[j].y = sin(radians(latheAngle))*vertices[j].x;
    vertices2[j].z = vertices[j].z;
    // optional helix offset
    if (isHelix){
      vertices[j].z+=helixOffset;
    }
    vertex(vertices2[j].x, vertices2[j].y, vertices2[j].z);
  }
  // create extra rotation for helix
  if (isHelix){
    latheAngle+=720.0/segments;
  }
  else {
    latheAngle+=360.0/segments;
  }
  endShape();
  }
}

/*
 left/right arrow keys control ellipse detail
 up/down arrow keys control segment detail.
 'a','s' keys control lathe radius
 'z','x' keys control ellipse radius
 'w' key toggles between wireframe and solid
 'h' key toggles between toroid and helix
*/
void keyPressed(){
  if(key == CODED) {
    // pts
    if (keyCode == UP) {
      if (pts<40){
        pts++;
      }
    }
    else if (keyCode == DOWN) {
      if (pts>3){
        pts--;
      }
    }
    // extrusion length
    if (keyCode == LEFT) {
      if (segments>3){
        segments--;
      }
    }
```

13

```
      else if (keyCode == RIGHT) {
        if (segments<80){
          segments++;
        }
      }
    }
    // lathe radius
    if (key =='a'){
      if (latheRadius>0){
        latheRadius--;
      }
    }
    else if (key == 's'){
      latheRadius++;
    }
    // ellipse radius
    if (key =='z'){
      if (radius>10){
        radius--;
      }
    }
    else if (key == 'x'){
      radius++;
    }
    // wireframe
    if (key =='w'){
      if (isWireFrame){
        isWireFrame=false;
      }
      else {
        isWireFrame=true;
      }
    }
    // helix
    if (key =='h'){
      if (isHelix){
        isHelix=false;
      }
      else {
        isHelix=true;
      }
    }
  }
  // Point3D class required
```

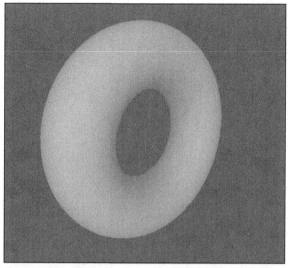

Figure 13-22. Interactive Toroid sketch (toroid variation)

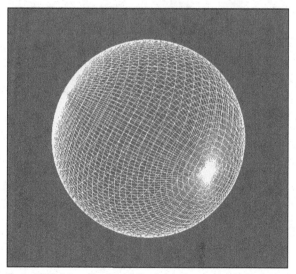

Figure 13-23. Interactive Toroid sketch (wireframe sphere variation)

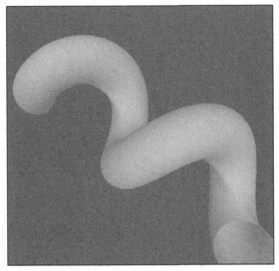

Figure 13-24. Interactive Toroid sketch (helix variation)

Figure 13-25. Interactive Toroid sketch (picture frame variation)

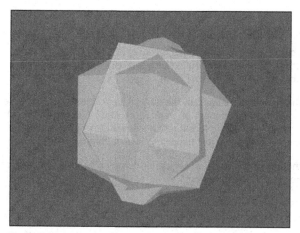

Figure 13-26. Interactive Toroid sketch (polyhedron variation)

If you haven't yet, I suggest interacting with the toroid sketch. The four arrow keys and the keys A, S, Z, and X can all be pressed and held down. The W and H keys can only be pressed and released. When playing with the sketch, you might try to make some of the following forms: a bicycle inner tube, a monster truck inner tube, a picture frame, a sawed-off pyramid, a sphere, a shell, a star, a braid, or part of a phone cord. Toggling between shaded and wireframe view (using the W key) makes it easier to see how the geometry is changing.

Here's how to make a sphere: press and hold the A key until the form stops collapsing. Make sure that you press the W key to see the wireframe. To increase the size of the sphere, press and hold the X key. Obviously, this is not the most efficient way to generate a sphere, but it's interesting to see its relationship to the toroid. A more efficient way to generate a sphere would be to create a 180-degree arc and then lathe it 360 degrees.

This sketch brings together many of the features covered earlier in this chapter. The major challenge was combining the point coordinate data used to generate the initial polygon with the lathing of that data around the toroid. I used two separate arrays, vertices[] and vertices2[], to enable me to combine the data. The initial polygon (to be lathed) was generated with the two lines of code used to plot a polygon in the xz plane:

```
vertices[i].x = latheRadius + sin(radians(angle))*radius;
vertices[i].z = cos(radians(angle))*radius;
```

13

If I had plotted this initial polygon, it would have displayed only a horizontal line on the right side of the screen, since the y values are all 0 and the z dimension of the polygon can't be seen in the xy plane.

I then took this initial polygon data and lathed it around the z-axis, on the xy plane, with the following expressions:

```
vertices2[j].x = cos(radians(latheAngle))*vertices[j].x;
vertices2[j].y = sin(radians(latheAngle))*vertices[j].x;
vertices2[j].z = vertices[j].z;
```

Notice that the equations are basically the original unit circle expressions, where the cos() function controls the x component of a point, the sin() function controls the y component, and vertices[j].x is the toroid radius value. Instead of a single point, though, I'm rotating a group of points that just happen to form a polygon on the xz plane.

The rest of the program is stuff I've gone over before. One small snippet that might raise a question, however, is the following:

```
if (isHelix){
      latheAngle+=720.0/segments;
}
```

I decided to rotate the helix version of the toroid two rotations instead of one, just to better illustrate the coil effect—that's why I used 720.0 instead of 360.0. If you want, you can change that number to see the effect. If you make it higher, you might also want to raise the 80 segment level maximum in the conditional head if (segments<80). This will allow the coil to remain smooth, if that sort of thing is important to you. Processing has a simple 3D function that does just this when creating a sphere. The function is called sphereDetail(), and it works very similarly to the arrow keys in the last toroid example. Here's a simple example (shown in Figure 13-27) to end the chapter on. Use the up and down arrow keys to see the sphereDetail() function in action:

```
// sphereDetail() Example
int detail = 10;
int depth = 100;
void setup(){
  size(400, 400, P3D);
}
void draw(){
  background(50);
  translate(width/2, height/2, depth);
  rotateY(PI*frameCount/125);
  lights();
  fill(100, 50, 175);
  stroke(150, 75, 255);
  sphereDetail(detail);
  sphere(20);
  println(depth);
}
```

```
void keyPressed(){
  if(key == CODED) {
    if (keyCode == UP) {
      if (depth<310){
        depth+=20;
        detail+=2;
      }
    }
    else if (keyCode == DOWN) {
      if (depth>70){
        depth-=20;
        detail-=2;
      }
    }
  }
}
```

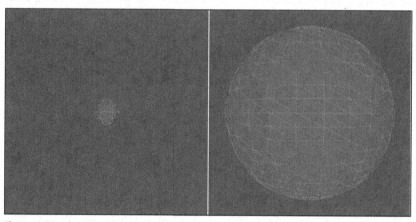

Figure 13-27. sphereDetail() Example sketch

If you play with the arrow keys, notice that the number of vertices making up the sphere increases as the sphere grows in size (it actually stays the same size, but comes closer to the screen on the z-axis), and vice versa. This represents another optimization approach used in 3D—only render the necessary resolution. Since the sphere is composed of triangles, when the sphere detail appears too low, the sphere loses its smooth, sphere-like quality. I simply changed the sphere detail based on the sphere's position on the z-axis. In the next and final chapter, I'll discuss a few other techniques for optimizing 3D, along with Processing's virtual camera and lighting functions.

13

Summary

Coding 3D, long the domain of hardcore programmers, is now accessible to the rest of us, thanks to Processing. One of the main difficulties in coding 3D has simply been getting started. Most books on the subject are geared toward computer scientists, mathematicians, and engineers, and are filled with scary diagrams and equations. Just getting a simple, static cube (a 3D primitive) on the screen can be an ordeal. This is not the case with Processing, as the simple, ten-line rotating cube sketch at the beginning of the chapter revealed. Using Processing's handy pushMatrix() and popMatrix() functions, as shown in the previous brick tower example, you can also easily construct more complex structures, combining simple 3D primitives.

This chapter went beneath the surface as well, revealing the usefulness of the same old basic trig functions you've been using throughout the book. You created your own Point3D, Cube, and SpinnyCube classes, with which you created a custom multicolored cube and even coded your own 3D rotations. Building upon these classes with some simple algorithms, you generated a larger set of 3D primitives, including a pyramid, cone, cylinder, toroid, and helix; and you explored how these forms are related through a few interactive sketches. Finally, you learned some 3D optimization techniques and looked at Processing's sphereDetail() function.

PART THREE **REFERENCE**

In Part 1 of the book, I covered general creative coding theory, and in Part 2, I demonstrated how the theory is implemented. This final part functions as sort of a Processing cheat sheet. Appendix A gives an overview of the Processing language reference; Appendix B contains some handy equations, as well as some important coding structures and concepts; and Appendix C (available online) includes information on integrating the Processing core graphics library within Java. Keep in mind that the language reference in Appendix A was designed to supplement the excellent official Processing language reference—not to replace it.

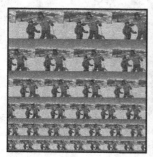  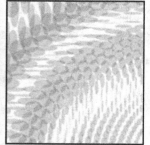

A **PROCESSING LANGUAGE API**

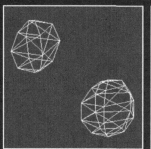

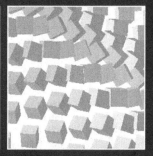

In this appendix, you will find a handy reference to all aspects of the Processing language, including many code examples to help you out and give you inspiration. This is the place to come first if you want to quickly look up anything covered throughout the rest of the book.

> Since there's already an official reference available online and within your Processing installation, you might ask why I've written this appendix. Well, my intention was to expand upon the more challenging concepts in the official reference, as well as include many additional code examples.

Introducing the Processing API

The Processing API is the reference for the core Processing language. This is the place to look up a specific Processing command. The Processing API lives online at `http://processing.org/reference/index.html`, and a copy of it is also installed within your local Processing application directory on your computer. The API is HTML-based with cross-referenced links throughout. There are also additional libraries available to Processing that extend the language. The library reference is not included in the core language API.

The Processing core API can be viewed four different ways:

- Abridged
- Abridged (A–Z)
- Complete
- Complete (A–Z)

According to a blurb on the language reference page, the abridged reference "omits description and functions for drawing in 3D and for detailed drawing and data manipulation." The abridged and complete options (bullets 1 and 3) break the language down into logical segments relating to basic command functionality. The two "A–Z" options lay the language out alphabetically. Personally, I find the segmentation of the API by function easier to work with.

When you launch the reference site, the abridged viewing option is initially loaded. However, since in this chapter I'll be discussing the complete API, you might want to select the complete option at first (before sending an angry e-mail to the publisher). To all you new coders, you don't need to work with the entire API to use Processing. A lot of really interesting things can be done with minimal amounts of code, using only a fraction of the API. As you progress, though, you'll naturally begin to use more and more of the API, so don't worry about trying to cram or memorize all this stuff.

As I mentioned, it doesn't make a lot of sense to me to re-create the entire API in this book when it is free to use, well organized, and easily accessible—both locally and at `http://processing.org/`. My main objective therefore is to briefly describe the overall organization of the API and emphasize certain key issues. The rest of the book focuses on code experiments that contextually move throughout the entire API, including some of the core code libraries, which I'll say more about at the end of this reference.

The complete (extended) API is segmented into 15 sections, which are further divided into 45 subsections, with nearly 300 separate items, including functions, operators, constants, system variables, data types, and control structures. The 15 main sections are titled as follows:

- Structure
- Environment
- Data
- Control
- Shape
- Input
- Output
- Transform
- Lights, Camera
- Color
- Image
- Rendering
- Typography
- Math
- Constants

Structure

The nearly 30 items organized within the Structure section range from basic syntactic symbols—such as comment structures (`//` and `/* */`), parentheses, semicolons, and array brackets—to reserved language keywords, such as "class," "this," "true," "super," and "extends." In addition, there are the Processing function calls `setup()`, `size()`, `noLoop()`, `delay()`, `exit()`, `draw()`, `loop()`, and `redraw()`.

Structural elements in a programming language are used to organize the process of coding—a semicolon terminates a line, a dot connects an object to its properties and methods, curly braces (`{ }`) organize a block of code, and so forth. Structure allows you to build, in a sense, sentences and stories with your code to visualize and express your ideas. I cover the concept of structure as it relates to general programming theory/practice in more detail in Chapter 3.

Environment

The Environment section contains ten entries for dealing with (getting or setting) global environment properties. Three of the entries are function calls (which include parentheses) for setting environmental properties, such as frameRate() for setting the sketch playback rate, noCursor() for hiding the cursor, and cursor() for setting the cursor's icon.

The rest of the entries are for accessing environmental properties—for example, focused gets the current focus state (true or false) of a sketch (whether the running sketch is the active application on your desktop); online accesses the sketch's online status (whether the sketch is running in a browser—note that the applet can be on your local machine or a remote server for this property to be true); and screen gets information about the resolution of your monitor (e.g., screen.width gets the width of your screen).

One somewhat confusing detail in this section is the use of the identical keywords frameRate() and frameRate. The first is a function call (you can always tell by the inclusion of the parentheses) for setting the sketch's frame rate, and the second is a variable (property) for accessing the current frame rate.

In general, environment properties are connected to what can be referred to as **object singletons**—objects representing the mouse, computer screen, Processing program, and so on—that are the only instance created from their respective class. For example, there may be a Mouse class defined in your operating system that describes the attributes and behavior of a mouse. To use the Mouse class, an object of the Mouse class is created. Since there is (usually) only one mouse connected to your computer, there is only ever one mouse object at any time—unlike, say, window objects, which are created every time you open a document. Thus, when you change an environmental variable, its effect is felt throughout the entire program.

Data

The Data section contains entries that represent the core data types within Processing, as well as utility functions that allow you to conveniently work with data (such as converting from one data type to another, manipulating strings, and transforming arrays).

At the lowest level, the computer sees all data as bits (zeros and ones), and couldn't care less what each bit stands for. In contrast, we humans, with our limited internal calculating capabilities, require more complex signs (labels) than bitstrings to be able to remember and categorize stuff. Data types add logical meaning to the process of coding, allowing us to express ourselves through programming languages—in a form somewhere between pure bits and our natural language. For example, even though the statement

```
String yourName = "Matilda";
```

is not quite English, it does tell us that the literal name Matilda is being assigned to a variable called yourName that is of data type String. This is certainly easier to understand than 1101101110000111010011010011101100110010011000001, which is Matilda converted to its binary equivalent. I used some of the commands in this section of the API to generate the Matilda bitstring. Here's the code I ran:

```
int m = int('M');
int a = int('a');
int t = int('t');
int i = int('i');
int l = int('l');
int d = int('d');
println(binary(m)+binary(a)+binary(t)+binary(i)+ ➥
    binary(l)+binary(d)+binary(a));
```

The five subsections of Data are as follows:

- Primitive
- Composite
- Conversion
- String Functions
- Array Functions

Primitive

Primitive includes data types used to store individual values—for example, int nodeCount = 6; or float speed = .5;. As discussed already, variables in Processing and Java need to be declared of a specific type. Types specify the kind of data a variable can hold and also the limit to the size of the value they can hold. Primitive variables are also assigned values directly. In the statement float speed = .5;, the real value .5 is literally assigned to the variable speed.

There are also reference variables in Processing and Java, in which a variable is not assigned a direct value, but rather the address in memory to where the value is stored. This strange-sounding arrangement is also referred to as a **pointer** in other languages. Since objects, as well as arrays (which hold multiple values), are complex structures, it makes some sense to store a reference to the data, rather than the actual data.

The Processing primitive data types are a subset of Java's primitive data types. Java has a few more subtle variations on the main ones in Processing that most beginning coders can avoid. However, you are free to use Java's extra data types in Processing if you'd like. Finally, there is a primitive data type in Processing that is not in Java: the color data type. This Processing type is really just an int type in disguise, used to deal specifically with color values. Appendix B includes detailed technical information about the inner workings of Processing's color data type.

Fortunately, actually using primitives in Processing is a lot simpler than trying to understand my theoretical, long-winded description of them. I go into greater depth about variables and data types in Chapter 3, and I also cover color in more detail toward the end of this chapter, as well as in Chapter 4.

Composite

The Composite section includes data types used to store object references (the memory addresses I mentioned in the primitive data type discussion). The three composite types Array, Object, and String can each hold multiple pieces of data.

Arrays are collections of any other data type, referenced by a single variable name. Arrays can only hold one data type at a time, but lots of it. I cover arrays in detail in Chapter 3.

Objects are the main units in object-oriented programming. An object is an instance of a class and includes copies of the properties and methods defined within the class. Objects are covered in much greater depth in Chapter 8 in the discussion of object-oriented programming (OOP).

Strings are kind of like arrays that only hold characters (e.g., letters). There are two ways to create String objects in Processing and Java (which is confusing):

```
String s1 = "hello";
```

and

```
String s2 = new String("hello");
```

The first way looks like a normal primitive declaration, like you would use to declare an int (int count = 3;), a float (float speed = .5;), and so on. The second way looks like standard object creation, called **instantiation**, which uses the standard object-oriented syntax *ClassType variableName = new ClassType();*. Based on what I've told you about data types up to this point in the book, this may not make sense. How can a string represent both a primitive data type and also a reference (composite) data type? Well, in truth, there is no primitive String data type in Java or Processing; you're always creating a String object. The shortcut approach String s1 = "hello"; internally creates a String object from the literal (the word in quotes). This is all fine and good, as well as probably a little overly technical. However, if you eventually find yourself needing to compare two strings and test them for equality, these two different string-creation approaches have some confusing (and probably annoying) differences.

As an example, run the following:

```
String s1 = "hello";
String s2 = new String("hello");
println(s1 == s2);

String s3 = "goodbye";
String s4 = "goodbye";
println(s3 == s4);
```

The output tells you that s1 and s2 are not equal, but s3 and s4 are. Even though the two values being compared in each comparison are the same (hello and hello and goodbye and goodbye), the output is different because of the different ways the strings were created. I won't bore you further with why this occurs, but you can read more about it here: http://java.about.com/library/weekly/aa_strings1.htm. Be sure to check the second part of the article as well. My suggestion when creating strings is to use the shortcut approach. If for some reason you do need to compare the values of two strings created using the object-oriented approach (using the new keyword), you can use Java's String method equals(). Here's an example:

```
String s1 = new String("hello");
String s2 = "hello";
println("s1 == s2 is " + (s1 == s2));
println("s1.equals(s2) is " + s1.equals(s2));

String s3 = new String("goodbye");
String s4 =  new String("goodbye");
println("s3 == s4 is " + (s3 == s4));
println("s3.equals(s4) is " + s3.equals(s4));
```

Conversion

The Conversion section includes ten entries, each of which is a utility function for converting between one data type and another. Since variables hold values of a specific type, there are times when, for example, you may need to use a value of type float to pass into a function that requires an integer value. Processing has a way of doing this conversion, called **type casting**. For example, to convert a float variable named gpa to an integer, you just need to write int(gpa). One issue to consider when doing conversion is truncation. In my example, the gpa float value will be truncated, or shortened, when it is converted. For example, if gpa equals 3.97, after converting it using int(gpa), the value returned will be 3 (not 4). Instead of rounding the value, it simply snips off all the values to the right of the decimal point. Thus, a simple data conversion mistake like this could keep you out of grad school. There are of course other and better ways to solve this last example (involving logical value rounding), which I'll cover later in my discussion of the Math section.

There's one final cautionary note about using Processing's int() and float() conversion functions. Currently, there is a reported and unresolved bug about their use (http://dev.processing.org/bugs/show_bug.cgi?id=4). Thus, if these functions don't seem to be working, it's recommended that you use Java's alternative syntax. Here's an example:

```
float temp = 98.64783;
//Processing conversion syntax
int pTemp = int(temp);
println(pTemp);
//Java conversion syntax
int jTemp = (int)temp;
println(jTemp);
```

String Functions

The String Functions section has seven functions that are helpful when working with strings, including join(), which combines elements in an array into a string; nf(), which formats numbers into strings; and split(), which separates a series of data within a string into separate arrays of strings. Here's a little example using the String function trim(), which removes whitespace characters around strings:

```
String s1 = "       Hi there,          ";
String s2 = "    bye now.       ";
println(s1+s2);
s1 = trim(s1);
s2 = trim(s2);
println(s1+" "+s2);
```

Array Functions

The Array Functions section includes nine functions that allow you to manipulate arrays. In Java, the size of an array can't be changed once its length has been set. Values at specific index positions within arrays can easily be changed—as in scores[3] = 23; or names[4] = "Bella";—and there are ways of easily sorting and searching though arrays (see Java's Arrays class). However, in Java, if you want to change the length of an array, you need to copy the contents of the array into a new array that has been initialized with the new desired length (too much work). I'll provide an example of this process later in this section.

There are two additional classes in Java, ArrayList and Vector, that (sort of) function as mutable arrays, in that they can dynamically change size. However, using these more complex structures necessitates converting data types (type casting, which I discussed a couple paragraphs back), and also requires some extra syntax (which I'm not going to cover here). To learn more about Java's mutable array structures, check out http://java.sun.com/j2se/1.4.2/docs/api/java/util/Vector.html.

Processing arrays, in conjunction with the array functions, are a hybrid solution—retaining the simplicity of using a standard Java array while also providing the ability to modify the array (including altering its length), similar to Java's ArrayList and Vector classes.

Processing's array functions include append() and shorten(), which respectively add or subtract data to or from the end of an array, changing the array's length by one position; splice(), which adds a single value or an entire array of values into an array at a specific index position, also changing the length of the array by the number of total values added; and subset(), which extracts an array of elements out of an array at a specific index position. The subset() function doesn't affect the initial array.

In the following sections, I've included some example implementations of an append() function. The first sketch example demonstrates the long way to append, as you might using Java arrays. The second example uses Processing's built-in append() function. Finally, the third example uses Processing's append() function again, but with an array full of object references instead of primitive values.

Example 1: A Java approach

```java
void setup(){
  // before appending
  int[]a = {2, 4, 5, 9, 13, 17, 20};
  print("before myAppend a = ");
  for (int i=0; i<a.length; i++) {
    print(a[i]+" ");
  }
  //after appending
  a = myAppend(a, 23);
  print("\nafter myAppend a = ");
  for (int i=0; i<a.length; i++) {
    print(a[i]+" ");
  }
}
/*Java append implementation -- doing it the long way.
 An array and new value are passed to the myAppend()
 function, which copies the passed in array values into a
new array, with a length 1 greater than the passed in array.
 Then the passed in valueToAdd argument is assigned
 to the added index position in the new array*/
int[] myAppend(int[]ar1, int valueToAdd){
  int length = ar1.length;
  int[]ar2 = new int[length+1];
  for (int i=0; i<length; i++){
    ar2[i] = ar1[i];
  }
  ar2[length] = valueToAdd;
  return ar2;
}
```

Example 2: Using Processing's append() function, the easy way

```java
// before appending
int[]a = {2, 4, 5, 9, 13, 17, 20};
print("before append a = ");
for (int i=0; i<a.length; i++) {
  print(a[i]+" ");
}
//after appending
a = append(a, 23);
print("\nafter append a = ");
for (int i=0; i<a.length; i++) {
  print(a[i]+" ");
}
```

683

Example 3: Using Processing's append() function on an array of objects

```
// type casting required
void setup(){
  SimpleClass[] sc = {new SimpleClass(), new SimpleClass(), ➥
      new SimpleClass()};
  println("sc length before append = " + sc.length);
  // I need to explicitly cast the returned Object array ➥
      to a SimpleClass array
  sc = ((SimpleClass[])append(sc, new SimpleClass()));
  print("sc length after append = " + sc.length);
}
class SimpleClass{}
```

This third example requires some understanding of OOP, which is covered in detail in Chapter 8.

The last line in the example is the definition for a class (which has no capabilities at all, but is a valid class nonetheless). Since a class is a legal data type, it's OK for me to declare an array of type SimpleClass, as I did in this line:

```
SimpleClass[] sc = {new SimpleClass(), new SimpleClass(), ➥
    new SimpleClass()};
```

I also filled the array with three SimpleClass objects when I declared it. Every time new SimpleClass() is called, a SimpleClass object is returned between the curly braces. Thus, the sc array holds three SimpleClass object references. The first println() statement confirms this. Next, I call Processing's append() function, which is where the type casting occurs. If I had tried to call the append() function as I did in the previous example—like this:

```
sc = append(sc, new SimpleClass());
```

I'd get an error to the effect that I can't assign an array of type Object to a variable of type SimpleClass[]. The reason that the append() function converts the original SimpleClass[] array to type Object relates to how the append() function works internally, which I won't go into. The way to fix this type mismatch is to explicitly type cast the Object array back to SimpleClass[], as I did in this line:

```
sc = ((SimpleClass[])append(sc, new SimpleClass()));
```

Control

The Control section includes 18 entries divided in four sections. Control elements in Programming are the logic constructs that control how a program flows, as well as, in the case of loops, the data processing mechanisms supplying power and iterative efficiency.

The combination of these two structures that control program flow and processing efficiency are what make most of the cool things we do with computers possible; an example might be the photorealistic effects in big-budget animated features, such as naturally moving fur on a virtual animal. To the computer, the fur is just a large array of coordinates changing over time, based on expressions and conditional logic—of course, this is a lot easier said than done. The Control section is divided into the following four subsections:

- Relational Operators
- Iteration
- Conditionals
- Logical Operators

Relational Operators

Relational operators function by Boolean logic—the condition being assessed is either true or false. These six operators include < (less than), <= (less than or equal to), == (equals), and their respective opposites. These operators are used in the heads of conditional statements, where a true condition is tested for. Based on the outcome of the conditional test, program flow continues either within the conditional block (true) or past it (false).

Iteration

The Iteration section includes just two entries, for() and while(). These are loop structures within Processing and Java that allow for efficient processing of large quantities of data. Loops are essential to programming, and programs of even modest complexity will almost always utilize them. However, loops can also be a little confusing when you are just starting out, as programming logic can get more densely packed in loops and look a little intimidating. It is also possible (and very common practice) to nest loops, in which a loop is put within another loop. This is often an efficient solution, but it adds complexity to the look and logic of the structure. Since loops are great at processing large amounts of data, they are often used in conjunction with arrays. Following, I've included three examples (shown in Figures A-1 through A-3) to help illustrate both the power and complexity of loops. The first example doesn't use a loop, but simply creates three rectangles, spacing them evenly in the display window. The second example uses a while loop to space ten rectangles evenly in the window. The third example, which is a lot more complicated, uses a bunch of for loops, including a nested for loop, to create a honeycomb structure.

Example 1: Spacing rectangles the hard way

```
// create 3 rectangles
// without loop
size(200, 200);
int rects = 3;
int w = width/rects;
int h = w;
```

685

```
int x = 0;
int y = height/2-h/2;
rect(x, y, w, h);
rect(x+w, y, w, h);
rect(x+w*2, y, w, h);
```

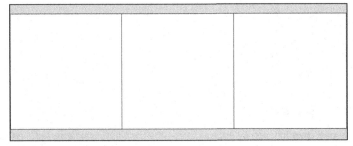

Figure A-1. Create 3 Rectangles sketch

Example 2: Spacing rectangles the easy way

```
// Use a loop to create 10 rectangles
size(200, 200);
int rects = 10;
int w = width/rects;
int h = w;
int x = 0;
int y = height/2-h/2;
int i = 0;
while (i++<rects){
  rect(x, y, w, h);
  x+=w;
}
```

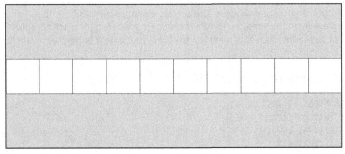

Figure A-2. Use a Loop to Create 10 Rectangles sketch

Example 3: Creating a honeycomb gradient

```
/*
HoneyComb
Ira Greenberg, November 6, 2005
*/

// total polys
int polyCount;
// poly array
Poly[]pols;
// I created 2 radii to allow asymmetry
int rad1 = 10, rad2 = 10;
// change poly orientation
float initAng = 0;

void setup(){
  size(400, 400);
  background(255);
  /* 1 extra cell is added to each row and
   column to allow the honeycomb to bleed
   off the display window */
  polyCount = (width/(rad1*2) + 1) * (height/(rad2*2) + 1);
  //create Poly array
  pols = new Poly[polyCount];

  for (int i=0; i<polyCount; i++){
    // instantiate each Poly obj in pols array
    pols[i] = new Poly(6, rad1, rad2, initAng);
  }
}

void draw(){
  background(255);
  // counter keeps track of Poly count
  int counter = 0;
  // shift creates honeycomb pattern
  // and bleed
  int shiftx = rad1/2;
  int shifty = rad2/2;
  /* create rows and columns in honeycomb,
   calling Poly drawPoly method for each
   Poly obj*/
  for (int i=shiftx; i<=width+shiftx; i+=rad1*2){
    shifty*=-1;
    for (int j=shifty; j<=height+shifty; j+=rad2*2){
      pols[counter++].drawPoly(i, j);
    }
  }
}
```

A

687

```
/*Simple Poly class, plots any
 regular polygon*/
class Poly {
  int sides;
  float r1, r2;
  float angle;

  Poly(int sides, int r1, int r2, float initAng){
    this.sides = sides;
    this.r1 = r1;
    this.r2 = r2;
    angle = initAng;
  }

  void drawPoly(int cx, int cy){
    noStroke();
    fill(cy, cx, 100);
    float  px= 0, py = 0;
    beginShape();
    for (int i=0; i<sides; i++){
      px = cx+cos(radians(angle))*r1;
      py = cy+sin(radians(angle))*r2;
      vertex(px, py);
      angle+=360/sides;
    }
    endShape(CLOSE);
  }
}
```

Figure A-3. HoneyComb sketch

Conditionals

Conditionals and the relational operators work together. The seven entries in the Conditionals section are the words/structures used in conjunction with the operators (<, >=, etc.). The two most commonly used conditionals, especially by new coders, are the if() structure and the reserved keyword else. When used together, along with the operators, this simple if...else structure become a powerful data logic tool. There are also two other structures: case, used for switch statements, and ?:, a condensed version of the if...else structure—which are variations on this important programming construct. I cover these structures, including some examples, in Chapter 3.

Logical Operators

The Logical Operators section includes just three entries: !, &&, and ||, which are "not", "and," and "or," respectively. These operators allow you to make compound conditional statements, in which more than one condition can be checked within the same structure. Using these logical operators in conjunction with the other structures in the Control section—relational operators, loops, and conditionals—you can control the world (or at least make some interesting code art).

The next example, which depicts population explosion, includes some relational and logical operators (see Figure A-4). Breeding in this simple world is caused by the bots colliding with the edges of the display window. The detectCollision() function utilizes two compound conditional expressions. Notice how I divided the sketch up into a series of functions, with each function handling a specific task; this modular approach makes the program easier to understand.

```
/* Population Explosion
 Ira Greenberg, November 6, 2005
 revised October 10, 2006 */

//declare some global variables
int botCount = 0;
int botLimit = 1000;
color worldColor = color(0, 40);
color[] botColor = new color[botCount];
float[] x = new float[botCount];
float[] y = new float[botCount];
float[] speedX = new float[botCount];
float[] speedY = new float[botCount];
float botSize = 3;

void setup(){
  size(400, 400);
  smooth();
  noStroke();
  breedBot();
}
```

689

```
void draw(){
  fill(worldColor);
  rect(0, 0, width, height);
  birthBot();
  moveBot();
  detectCollision();
}

// expand arrays
void breedBot(){
  if (botCount<1000){
    botCount++;
    // expand arrays
    x = append(x, width/2);
    y = append(y, height/2);
    speedX = append(speedX, random(-3, 3));
    speedY = append(speedY, random(-3, 3));
    botColor = append(botColor, color(random(200, 255), ➡
    random(127), random(40), random(100, 255)));
  }
}

// draw bots
void birthBot(){
  for (int i=0; i<botCount; i++){
    fill(botColor[i]);
    ellipse(x[i], y[i], botSize, botSize);
  }
}

// animate bots
void moveBot(){
  for (int i=0; i<botCount; i++){
    x[i]+=speedX[i];
    y[i]+=speedY[i];
  }
}

// check boundary collisions
void detectCollision(){
  for (int i=0; i<botCount; i++){
    // right and left boundaries
    if (x[i] >= width-botSize/2 || x[i] <= botSize/2){
      // reverse direction
      speedX[i]*=-1;
      // make new bot
      breedBot();
    }
```

```
    // top and bottom boundaries
    if (y[i] >= height-botSize/2 || y[i] <= botSize/2){
      // reverse direction
      speedY[i]*=-1;
       // make new bot
       breedBot();
    }
  }
}
```

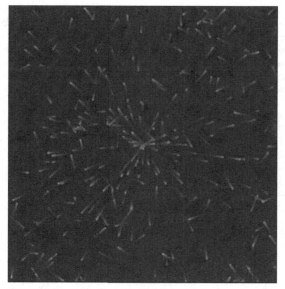

Figure A-4. Population Explosion sketch

Shape

The 30-plus entries in the Shape section are all function calls involved in drawing geometry. This section is the meat and potatoes of the API, especially with regard to the creative stuff beginning coders need to know. Most computer languages contain the other constructs I've gone over thus far—structural elements, data storage, looping, conditionals, and so forth. However, many lack extensive drawing methods, and almost none contain the ease-of-use and full-featured capabilities of Processing's drawing methods, which even include a custom 3D engine. Java does have extensive drawing capabilities, but the Java graphics APIs are complex, and something as simple as getting a rectangle to move across the screen can bring new (and even experienced) coders to their knees. Shape is divided into the following five sections:

- 2D Primitives
- Curves
- 3D Primitives
- Attributes
- Vertex

2D Primitives

2D primitives are the basic geometric building blocks. They include points, lines, triangles, rectangles, arcs, and ellipses. Shapes like squares and circles are just variations on rectangles and ellipses. These functions are incredibly easy to use and fun to experiment with. As you'll learn eventually, all shapes are really just points, or vertices connected and optionally filled. However, it makes it really convenient to encapsulate this process for the basic building block shapes into neat functions, like the ones in Processing. Here's a simple example of a point inside a triangle, inside a rectangle, inside an ellipse (see Figure A-5):

```
size(200, 200);
background(255);
smooth();
noFill();
point(width/2, height/2);
triangle(40, 160, 100, 40, 160, 160);
rect(40, 40, 120, 120);
ellipse(width/2, height/2, 120, 120);
```

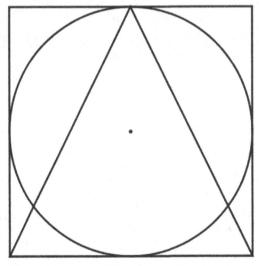

Figure A-5. Processing's 2D primitive functions

You'll notice that by default, the rectangle is drawn from its top-left corner while the ellipse is drawn from its center. If this doesn't seem to make any sense, look at the different x and y positions for these shapes (the first two arguments). You can also explicitly change how these shapes are drawn, if the default doesn't work for you, with calls to either rectMode() or ellipseMode(). These two functions can take a couple different arguments that control how the shape is drawn. For example, to reverse the default modes for both the rect() and ellipse() functions, you would write rectMode(CENTER); and ellipseMode(CORNER);, respectively. Now rectangles would be drawn from the center and ellipses would be drawn from the top-left corner.

Curves

The Curves section includes eight entries, dealing with—you guessed it—creating curves. Curves are a lot more difficult to draw than rectilinear shapes. If you don't believe me, just try drawing a circle freehand. Our brains and physical capabilities seem more equipped to deal with simple linear ratios than curvy math. Unfortunately, most really interesting forms and animations tend to deal with more organic-looking structures and dynamics. The two main curve drawing functions in Processing are bezier() and curve().

Bézier curves require two anchor points and two control points. The control points, in a sense, direct the curve between the anchor points. The common pen tools in programs like Illustrator and Photoshop employ Bézier-like curves, allowing you to interactively control both the anchor points and their control handles.

The curve() function utilizes a spline curve and also requires two extra control points. However, spline curves react quite differently from Bézier curves when these control points are manipulated. In the next code example, you can drag the control and anchor points on two different curves simultaneously to see this difference (see Figure A-6). The green path is a spline curve and the blue is a Bézier curve. Notice how the control points for the Bézier curve are off the curve, while with the spline the control points are directly on the curve. This is a pretty advanced example, which I included to illustrate how the curves work. I cover the curve functions in detail in Chapter 7.

```
/*
Curves
Ira Greenberg, November 7, 2005
revised October 9, 2006
----------------------------------------
Interact with the curves by dragging
the anchors/control points
green curve = spline
blue curve = bezier
*/

int pts = 4;
int ptSize = 6;
float[]x = new float[4];
float[]y = new float[4];
boolean[]isDragSafe = new boolean[4];
```

```
void setup(){
  size(300, 300);
  smooth();
  // fill coordinate arrays
  x[0] = x[1] =  50;
  x[2] = x[3] = width-50;
  y[0] = height/2-50;
  y[3] = height/2+50;
  y[1] = y[2] = height/2;

  //initialize dragging flags to false
  for (int i=0; i<pts; i++){
    isDragSafe[i] = false;
  }
}

void draw(){
  background(255);
  noFill();
  //draw curves and control handles
  strokeWeight(2);
  //spline curve
  stroke(0, 200, 30);
  curve (x[0], y[0],x[0], y[0], x[1], y[1], x[2], y[2]);
  curve (x[0], y[0], x[1], y[1], x[2], y[2], x[3], y[3]);
  curve (x[1], y[1], x[2], y[2], x[3], y[3], x[0], y[0]);
  //bezier curve
  stroke(0, 30, 200);
  bezier (x[1], y[1],x[0], y[0], x[3], y[3], x[2], y[2]);
  // draw bezier handles
  strokeWeight(1);
  stroke(100);
  line(x[0], y[0], x[1], y[1]);
  line(x[2], y[2], x[3], y[3]);
  // draw anchor/control points
  stroke(0);
  fill(0);
  for (int i=0; i<pts; i++){
    if (i==0 || i==3){
      fill(255, 100, 10);
      rectMode(CENTER);
      rect(x[i], y[i], ptSize, ptSize);
    }
    else {
      fill(0);
      ellipse(x[i], y[i], ptSize, ptSize);
    }
  }
```

```
  // start dragging if flag true
  for (int i=0; i<pts; i++){
    if (isDragSafe[i]){
      x[i] = mouseX;
      y[i] = mouseY;
    }
  }
}

// release any point attached to the mouse
void mouseReleased (){
  for (int i=0; i<pts; i++){
    isDragSafe[i] = false;
  }
}

// for dragg'n dem points
void mousePressed (){
  for (int i=0; i<pts; i++){
    if (mouseX>=x[i]-5 && mouseX<=x[i]+ptSize+5 &&
      mouseY>=y[i]-5 && mouseY<=y[i]+ptSize+5){
      isDragSafe[i] = true;
    }
  }
}

// show hand when over draggable points
void mouseMoved (){
  cursor(ARROW);
  for (int i=0; i<pts; i++){
    if (mouseX>=x[i]-5 && mouseX<=x[i]+ptSize+5 &&
      mouseY>=y[i]-5 && mouseY<=y[i]+ptSize+5){
      cursor(HAND);
    }
  }
}
```

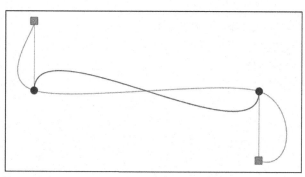

Figure A-6. Curves sketch

3D Primitives

The 3D Primitives section only includes three functions:

- box()
- sphere()
- sphereDetail()

The box() and sphere() functions generate simple 3D objects. These are not simulated 3D forms, but are actually based on 3D geometry. Thus, to use these functions, you need to specify either the P3D or OPENGL rendering mode in the size() function call. If you use OPENGL, you also need to import the OPENGL library (via the Sketch ➤ Import Library ➤ opengl menu option).

The SphereDetail() function controls the level of detail, or number of vertices, used to generate the sphere, which is constructed out of triangles that all fit together in a mosaic pattern (called tessellated triangles). Here's a little example of some spinning stuff, using all three of the 3D primitive functions (see Figure A-7). The outer ring of spheres in the example illustrates the use of the sphereDetail() function. Each of the objects in the ring is technically a sphere, but by setting the sphereDetail value very low, you get a more rigid, less sphere-like form.

```
/* Spinning 3D Stuff
Ira Greenberg, October 9, 2006 */
float px, py, angle;
void setup(){
  size(400, 400, P3D);
  noFill();
  stroke(255);
}
void draw(){
  background(0);
  translate(width/2, height/2);
  pushMatrix();
  rotateY(frameCount*PI/150);
  rotateX(frameCount*PI/150);
  box(100, 100, 100);
    pushMatrix();
      rotateY(-frameCount*PI/10);
      rotateX(PI/4);
      box(45, 15, 65);
    popMatrix();
  popMatrix();
```

```
  pushMatrix();
    rotateY(-frameCount*PI/60);
    rotateX(-frameCount*PI/70);
    for (int i=0; i<12; i++){
      px = cos(radians(angle))*150;
      py = sin(radians(angle))*150;
      pushMatrix();
        translate(px, py);
        sphereDetail(i);
        sphere(20);
      popMatrix();
      angle+=360/12;
    }
  popMatrix();
}
```

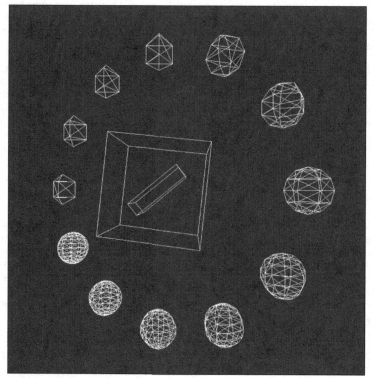

Figure A-7. Spinning 3D Stuff sketch

Attributes

The Attributes section includes seven functions:

- strokeWeight()
- smooth()
- strokeJoin()
- noSmooth()
- ellipseMode()
- rectMode()
- strokeCap()

Stroke is the term used for a line in computer graphics. The functions strokeWeight(), strokeCap(), and strokeJoin() respectively control the thickness (or weight) of lines, how the lines end (rounded, square, or extended caps), and how the lines come together at corners (mitered, beveled, or rounded). These last two line attributes are details we tend not to focus on until we see a problem with our output, and then of course we obsess about them.

smooth() and noSmooth() control anti-aliasing. Anti-aliasing is not a political position, but a way to smooth jaggies along curved and diagonal edges. Anti-aliasing makes things look smoother, but can slow down rendering some. Please note that the smooth and stroke attribute functions do not (as of this writing) work consistently in all three supported renderers; nor do they fail consistently—the strokeWeight() attribute fails silently in P3D mode (it just won't do anything), but the other functions will generate a compiler error. For more details, please see the corresponding section of the API (www.processing.org/reference/strokeWeight_.html).

Vertex

The Vertex section includes seven functions that allow you to do some pretty amazing things. A vertex is just a point. Vertices (the plural form of *vertex*) make up lines, which make up polygons (usually triangles or quadrangles), which make up more complex geometry. In fact, most complex 3D scenes are usually just a bunch of triangles and quadrangles. To create a vertex in Processing, you use the vertex() function. Combining a series of vertex() commands allow you to create lines and shapes (both 2D and 3D). Additionally, you can use the related functions bezierVertex() and curveVertex() to specify curves, and you can also combine the three commands.

The vertex functions need to be called between the functions beginShape() and endShape(). These two functions work by first internally recording the coordinates specified by the nested vertex calls, and then plotting the coordinates. They also control how the vertices are connected by passing arguments to the two calls. For example, here's some code to generate a closed regular polygon:

```
// regular polygon
size(400, 400);
smooth();
float px, py, angle = 0, radius = 150;
int sides = 8;
beginShape();
for (int i=0; i<sides; i++){
  px = width/2+cos(radians(angle))*radius;
  py = height/2+sin(radians(angle))*radius;
  vertex(px, py);
  angle+=360.0/sides;
}
endShape(CLOSE);
```

By default, beginShape() and endShape() will fill the shape created by the vertices. However, the shape will not actually be closed unless the CLOSE argument is included in the endShape(CLOSE) call. Try removing the CLOSE argument from the last sketch and also adding the call noFill() above beginShape(). If you run the sketch, you should see a partial polygon drawn, with one of its sides missing. If you now remove noFill(), the fill of the shape will return, but the stroke outline surrounding the polygon will remain unclosed. There are a number of arguments that can be added to the beginShape() call, including POINTS, LINES, TRIANGLES, TRIANGLE_FAN, TRIANGLE_STRIP, QUADS, and QUAD_STRIP.

In addition, using the P3D and OPENGL rendering modes, it's possible to map an image onto a shape's surface (really the shape's vertices) using extra coordinate arguments passed into the individual vertex() commands. It's also necessary to include two additional function calls: textureMode() and texture(). This is an advanced feature called **UV mapping**. The *U* and *V* represent two extra coordinates for the image mapping space on the surface. Even though it's an advanced feature, it's also pretty cool, so I decided to include an example.

The sketch is of a rotating cube mapped with six images that rotate with the cube (see Figure A-8). To try this example, you'll need to create a data directory within your sketch folder that contains six images named img1.jpg through img6.jpg. The data directory will be created automatically when you import your images (by selecting Add File from the Sketch menu). I suggest making the images each 250 by 250 pixels, but other sizes will work as well.

```
/*
ImageMap
Ira Greenberg, November 4, 2005
revised, October 10, 2006
*/

/* IMPORTANT- to run this, you need
6 images in your data directory named
img1.jpg - img6.jpg. Images should each
be 250 x 250 pixels */
```

```
PImage[] images = new PImage[6];

void setup(){
  size(400, 400, P3D);
  noStroke();
  //load images
  for (int i=1; i<7; i++){
    images[i-1] = loadImage("img"+i+".jpg");
  }
  // map images using 0.0-1.0
  textureMode(NORMALIZED);
}

void draw(){
  background(255);
  //*center geometry in display windwow.
  translate(width/2, height/2);
  //rotate around y and x axes
  rotateY(frameCount*PI/100);
  rotateX(frameCount*PI/75);
  createCube(100, 100, 100);
}

void createCube(float w, float h, float d){
  //front face
  beginShape(QUADS);
  texture(images[0]);
  vertex(-w/2, -h/2, -d/2, 0, 0);
  vertex(w, -h/2, -d/2, 1, 0);
  vertex(w, h, -d/2, 1, 1);
  vertex(-w/2, h, -d/2, 0, 1);
  endShape();
  //back face
  beginShape(QUADS);
  texture(images[1]);
  vertex(-w/2, -h/2, d,  0, 0);
  vertex(w, -h/2, d,  1, 0);
  vertex(w, h, d, 1, 1);
  vertex(-w/2, h, d, 0, 1);
  endShape();
  //left face
  beginShape(QUADS);
  texture(images[2]);
  vertex(-w/2, -h/2, -d/2, 0, 0);
  vertex(-w/2, -h/2, d, 1, 0);
  vertex(-w/2, h, d, 1, 1);
  vertex(-w/2, h, -d/2, 0, 1);
  endShape();
  //right face
  beginShape(QUADS);
```

```
        texture(images[3]);
        vertex(w, -h/2, -d/2, 0, 0);
        vertex(w, -h/2, d, 1, 0);
        vertex(w, h, d, 1, 1);
        vertex(w, h, -d/2, 0, 1);
        endShape();
        //top face
        beginShape(QUADS);
        texture(images[4]);
        vertex(-w/2, -h/2, -d/2, 0, 0);
        vertex(w, -h/2, -d/2, 1, 0);
        vertex(w, -h/2, d, 1, 1);
        vertex(-w/2, -h/2, d, 0, 1);
        endShape();
        //bottom face
        beginShape(QUADS);
        texture(images[5]);
        vertex(-w/2, h, -d/2, 0, 0);
        vertex(w, h, -d/2, 1, 0);
        vertex(w, h, d, 1, 1);
        vertex(-w/2, h, d, 0, 1);
        endShape();
}
```

Figure A-8. ImageMap sketch

Input

This is another large section in the API, generally involved in receiving or inputting data. Some of these processes are relatively low level, like reading bytes. However, Processing, as you've probably come to expect by now, encapsulates and simplifies these processes. The Input section includes 22 functions and 9 system variables, divided into five categories. The categories are as follows:

- Mouse
- Keyboard
- Files
- Web
- Time & Date

Mouse

The Mouse section includes six properties and five functions, used to evaluate when, where, and how mouse input is received by your running sketch. Variables such as mouseX and mousePressed provide live information about the mouse state; mouseX provides the current x position of the mouse and mousePressed returns true or false depending if the mouse button is pressed. Often, you can use this data creatively—for example, in a drawing program that colors pixels as the mouse moves over them.

The mouse functions, such as mouseMoved() or mouseDragged(), put code within separate function blocks (between the curly braces), allowing other functions or commands to be called when the mouse motion event is detected. Following is a mouseMoved() example that illustrates some of the interesting things you can do via mouse detection (see Figure A-9). There are a bunch of significant concepts within this example, and in spite of it being a bit dense, the sketch is a good base for other experiments. When the sketch loads, move your mouse over the rectangle.

```
/*
Box Springs
Ira Greenberg, November 13, 2005
revised October 11, 2006
move mouse over white rectangle
*/

// you can change block count
int blocks = 40;
float margin = 50;
float boxHeight = 75;
```

A

```
//lots of arrays
float[]x = new float[blocks];
float[]y = new float[blocks];
float[]w = new float[blocks];
float[]h = new float[blocks];
float[]py1 = new float[blocks];
float[]py2 = new float[blocks];
float[]radius = new float[blocks];
float[]amplitude = new float[blocks];
float[]frequency = new float[blocks];
float[]ang = new float[blocks];
float[]drag = new float[blocks];
float[]gravity = new float[blocks];
boolean[]isOver = new boolean[blocks];

void setup(){
  size(400, 300);
  background(0);
  noStroke();
  frameRate(30);
  /* amplitude, gravity, and frequency
  can be messed with. Also, if you remove
  the random functions, you can get more
  standard wave patterns
  */
  for (int i=0; i<blocks; i++){
    w[i] = (width-margin)/blocks;
    h[i] = boxHeight;
    x[i] = margin/2+w[i]*i;
    y[i] = height/2-h[i]/2;

    amplitude[i] = random(20)+height/4;
    radius[i] = amplitude[i];
    gravity[i] = .85+random(.13);
    drag[i] =  gravity[i];
    drawBlocks(x[i], y[i], w[i], h[i]);
    frequency[i] = 12+random(-5, 5);
    //flags let us know which box
    //we're over
    isOver[i] = false;
  }
}
```

```
//main loop
void draw(){
  fill(0, 50);
  rect(0, 0, width, height);
  fill(255, 255, 0);
  for (int i=0; i<blocks; i++){
  //you can add/subtract py1, py2 to x
  //and width arguments as well
    drawBlocks(x[i], y[i]-py1[i], w[i], h[i]+py2[i]);
    // flags set in mouseMoved function
    if (isOver[i]){
     //trig controls spring effect
      py1[i] = sin(radians(ang[i]))*radius[i];
      py2[i] = cos(radians(ang[i]))*radius[i];
      // spring values affect color shift
      fill(255, 255-radius[i], radius[i]*2);
      ang[i]+=frequency[i];
      radius[i]*=drag[i];
    }
  }
}

/*While mosue is moving, detect what
box the mouse is over and change flag.
Also, need to reset radius, which is
decremented by drag - causing blocks to
stop */
void mouseMoved(){
  for (int i=0; i<blocks; i++){
    if (mouseX>x[i] && mouseX<x[i]+w[i] &&
      mouseY>y[i] && mouseY<y[i]+h[i]){
      radius[i] = amplitude[i];
      isOver[i] = true;
    }
  }
}

//function to draw rectangles, called initially by
//setup and then repeatedly in draw loop
void drawBlocks(float x, float y, float w, float h){
  rect(x, y, w, h);
}
```

704

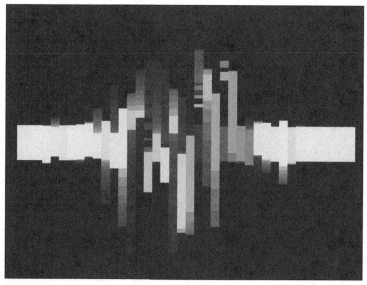

Figure A-9. Box Springs sketch

Keyboard

The Keyboard section is similar to the Mouse section in that it combines both system variables and functions that allow you to communicate with the keyboard. The difference between the mouse and the keyboard is the amount and type of data input and output. The mouse can have multiple buttons, like a small keyboard, but it also has coordinate data. The keyboard (at least mine) remains stationary, but has to translate between many possible input values, for all the letters, numbers, and special keys that it uses. The keys on your keyboard have integer values associated with them, commonly referred to as ASCII code. For example, the *a* key equals 65. There are also constant values for the special keys, such as UP, DOWN, LEFT, RIGHT, ALT/OPTION, CONTROL, SHIFT, BACKSPACE, TAB, ENTER, RETURN, ESC, and DELETE. The following simple example allows you to control a rectangle with the arrow keys. Notice in the code the use of the if (key == CODED) { } structure around the specific key detection code.

```
int x, y;
void setup(){
  size(200, 200);
}
void draw() {
  stroke(0, 50);
  fill(255, 50);
  rect(width/2+x, height/2+y, 4+x, 4+y);
}
void keyPressed() {
```

```
        if(key == CODED) {
          if (keyCode == UP) {
            y--;
          } else if (keyCode == DOWN) {
            y++;
          } else if (keyCode == LEFT) {
            x--;
          } else if (keyCode == RIGHT) {
            x++;
          }
        }
      }
```

Files

The Files section includes four functions:

- •openStream()
- •open()
- •loadStrings()
- •loadBytes()

loadStrings() and loadBytes() allow you to load the contents of a file or URL as a string array or byte array, respectively. A byte array of a text file will include all the individual characters converted into their ASCII equivalents. If only a file name is specified as an argument with either of these functions, the file needs to reside within the sketch's data directory. It's also possible to specify a URL, assuming you use a valid path. Relative paths should be specified in relation to the data directory in the current sketch directory. For example, if your file (file.txt) is outside the data directory, in another directory called docs (also located within the sketch (parent) directory), it can be accessed (using UNIX/OS X path syntax) as: ../docs/file.txt, or on Windows: ..\docs\file.txt. The double dot syntax (..) refers to the parent directory; (single dot syntax(.) refers to the current directory). There is some general information about paths at http://en.wikipedia.org/wiki/Path_(computing).

The openStream() function provides a simplified way of using Java's InputStream class. The InputStream class provides you with more control when inputting data. To learn more about Java's InputStream class, check out http://java.sun.com/j2se/1.4.2/docs/api/java/io/InputStream.html.

Here's what the Processing reference says about the open() function: "Attempts to open a file or process using the platform's shell." A shell is just an interface to your operating system. There are GUI (graphical user interface) shells, such as the Finder (OS X) or Windows Explorer, where you simply click to launch an application. There are also command-line shells, which is the type of shell the Processing reference is referring to. To communicate with your system via a command-line shell, you type text-based commands in a terminal (emulator) program, such as the Terminal application in OS X. (On Windows, you can access the command shell by selecting the Run command in the Start menu and then entering **CMD**). When using a command-line shell instead of a GUI shell, you need to be explicit when issuing commands. It is common for modern GUI shells to hide the suffixes of files. In OS X, to launch the Calculator application using the Finder (GUI shell), you double-click the calculator icon, named simply "Calculator." In contrast, from the Terminal application (command-line shell), you need to type: **open Calculator.app**. In addition, you need to be explicit as to where files reside (the path) to access/launch them. When using relative paths with Processing's open() command, you need to provide path addresses in relation to the Processing application. For example, the Processing application on my computer lives within a Processing directory, which lives in the Applications directory. The Calculator application also lives within the Applications directory. To launch the Calculator on a mouse press, I can use the following Processing sketch:

```
void draw(){
}

void mousePressed(){
  open("../Calculator.app");
}
```

The open() command also allows to you pass a String argument. You can read more about open() at http://processing.org/reference/open_.html.

Web

The Web section includes the functions link(), param(), and status(). Stating the obvious, these functions involve web-based features and are used within a browser environment. link() allows you to load a web page, as well as specify which browser window to use (the existing one or a new one). param() reads the value of a parameter, specified within the HTML of a web page. For example, if you have the following HTML in the page holding an applet, created from a sketch named SimpleBall:

```
<applet code="SimpleBall" archive=" SimpleBall jar">
<param name="ballradius" value="50"> </applet>
```

you can use the param value ballradius in your SimpleBall sketch:

```
// SimpleBall sketch
String strgRadius = param("ballradius");
int radius = Integer.parseInt(strgRadius);
size(200, 200);
ellipse(width/2, height/2, radius, radius);
```

You'll notice that the param value comes back as a String, so it needs to be converted to a number. Integer.parseInt() is a static method of Java's Integer class that converts strings to integers. (Remember, in Processing, you can use Java code along with Processing code.)

status() allows you to display messages in the browser's status area—normally in the lower-left corner of the browser.

Time & Date

Time & Date is the last subsection of the Input section of the API. The functions `second()`, `minute()`, `hour()`, `day()`, `month()`, and `year()` return a component of the time, based off your system clock. The function `millis()` tells you how long, in milliseconds (thousandths of a second), your sketch has been running since you started it. Here's an analog clock example (see Figure A-10):

```
/* Analog Clock
Ira Greenberg, October 9, 2006 */

PFont font;
float x, y, r = 100;
float textH = 12;

void setup(){
  size(400, 400);
  font = createFont("Arial", textH);
  textFont(font);
  x = width/2;
  y = height/2;
  smooth();
}

void draw(){
  background(75);
  drawClock();
}

void drawClock(){
  float px, py, angle = -60;
  fill(200);
  strokeWeight(4);
  ellipse(x, y, r*2, r*2);
  for (int i=1; i<13; i++){
    px = x+cos(radians(angle))*(r*.8);
    py = y+sin(radians(angle))*(r*.8);
    fill(0);
    // need to subtract 1/2 text width/height
    // to align center
    float textW = textWidth(str(i));
    text(i, px-textW/2, py+textH/2);
    angle+=360/12;
  }
  /*Subtract 90 degs. from each trig function, since 12
   is at top of clock (not at 0 postion on unit circle).
   Other numeric value is calculated by 360/number of units.*/
```

```
//hour hand
strokeWeight(2);
stroke(50);
float h = hour();
float hourHandX = x+cos(radians(30*h-90))*(r*.5);
float hourHandY = y+sin(radians(30*h-90))*(r*.5);
line(x, y, hourHandX, hourHandY);

//minute hand
strokeWeight(1);
stroke(150);
float m = minute();
float minuteHandX = x+cos(radians(6*m-90))*(r*.7);
float minuteHandY = y+sin(radians(6*m-90))*(r*.7);
line(x, y, minuteHandX, minuteHandY);

//second hand
strokeWeight(1);
stroke(200, 100, 30);
float s = second();
float secondHandX = x+cos(radians(6*s-90))*(r*.9);
float secondHandY = y+sin(radians(6*s-90))*(r*.9);
line(x, y, secondHandX, secondHandY);
}
```

Figure A-10. Analog Clock sketch

Output

This section involves outputting data, both to the screen and to a file. As in the Input section, Processing makes these relatively low-level processes really easy to perform. This section is divided into three subsections:

- Text Area
- Image
- Files

Text Area

Text Area is a simple category that includes the two functions print() and println(). Both output to the text area in the Processing window, but println() adds line returns between each call to the function. You can use the string concatenator + within the argument string, passed to the print() or println() function. For example, the following code outputs I love Processing:

```
String name = "Processing";
print("I love "+name);
```

Image

Image includes two very cool functions that allow you to save screen image data to the sketch directory. saveFrame() will actually save a sequence of images in TIF, TGA, JPG, or PNG format. You can then import these sequenced images into video editing software and produce movies of your Processing animations. save() just saves the current screen image. Please note that neither of these functions will work when running your sketches from within a web browser. This is a limitation of Java applets in general, imposed by Sun to "keep applets from compromising system security," as mentioned in the article "What Applets Can and Can't Do" (see http://java.sun.com/docs/books/tutorial/deployment/applet/security.html). To learn more about Java applets, check out http://java.sun.com/docs/books/tutorial/deployment/applet/index.html.

Files

The Files subsection of the Output section is similar to the Files subsection of Input, except things work in reverse. The two functions saveStrings() and saveBytes()—as you might guess—save strings and bytes, respectively, to files within the current sketch directory. There are also two more general-purpose output functions, beginRecord() and endRecord(), which can be used to write out drawing functions as well as the contents of the display window (just be sure to call beginRecord() before the drawing calls you want recorded). To use these functions, you need to explicitly specify a renderer and file name as arguments in the beginRecord(renderer, filename) call.

In the next example, I use beginRecord() and endRecord() as part of a simple drawing program (see Figure A-11). When you want to output your drawing, simply press any key on the keyboard; this will cause your sketch to close and your drawing to be saved to your sketch directory in PDF format.

```
/*
Hairy Brush Drawing
Ira Greenberg, October 9, 2006
outputs to PDF
*/

import processing.pdf.*;

void setup() {
  size(400, 400);
  background(255);
  smooth();
  String id = str(hour())+"_"+str(minute())+"_"+str(second());
  beginRecord(PDF, "img"+id+".pdf");
}

void draw() {
  stroke(0);
  strokeWeight(4);
  if (mousePressed){
    line(pmouseX, pmouseY, mouseX, mouseY);
    bleed(pmouseX, pmouseY);
  }
}

void bleed(float x, float y){
  float px = 0, py = 0, angle = 0, radius=10;
  float brushDetail = 36;
  stroke(0, 100);
  strokeWeight(.5);
  for (int i=0; i<brushDetail; i++){
    px = x+cos(radians(angle))*random(radius);
    py = y+sin(radians(angle))*random(radius);
    line(x, y, px, py);
    angle+=360/brushDetail;
  }
}

// press any key on the keyboard to
// output a pdf of your drawing
void keyPressed() {
  endRecord();
  exit();
}
```

711

Notice the following statement at the top of the example:

```
import processing.pdf.*;
```

This imports Processing's PDF library, one of Processing's core libraries. Finally, note that the file functions will not work from a web browser.

Figure A-11. Hairy Brush Drawing sketch

Transform

This is a very cool part of the API, and one of the feature sets that makes Processing a truly unique and powerful creative tool. However, all this coolness does come at a small price. The transform functions are a little complex and take some time to get your head around. While beginning to use them isn't all that difficult, using them well can be a challenge. At the core of these functions is a mysterious mathematical structure called a matrix. A **matrix** is just a table-like structure for organizing values. Matrices (plural) are central to linear algebra (which I'm not going to go into), and they're also central to computer graphics. What makes them so significant is the ease with which geometric transformations can be done by using them.

Transformations include moving, scaling, skewing, and rotating vertices. Remember, vertices (points) are the foundation for all the other geometry you see on the screen. The simplest way to show how the transform functions work is through some examples. First, I'll give you a (rather dull) example that transforms 2D geometry (see Figure A-12). Then I'll apply the concepts from the 2D example to a more interesting (albeit more complicated) 3D example.

```
//Example 1:
noStroke();
rect(10, 10, 25, 25);
printMatrix();

pushMatrix();
translate(20, 20);
scale (1.5);
rect(10, 10, 25, 25);
printMatrix();
popMatrix();

pushMatrix();
translate(70, 70);
scale (.5);
rect(10, 10, 25, 25);
printMatrix();
popMatrix();
printMatrix();
```

Figure A-12. Transform Example 1 sketch

713

This example isn't too exciting, but it does illustrate the power and simplicity of doing matrix transformations in Processing. In the example, I used the rect() command three times, using the same four arguments; yet I got three rectangles with different sizes and positions. If you run this example, you should notice four tables of numbers output in the Processing console. Each table is composed of two rows and three columns. These mysterious numbers are the actual matrices at different states in the program. You'll notice that the first and last table of numbers are identical:

```
1.0000   0.0000   0.0000
0.0000   1.0000   0.0000
```

These tables represent the base, or identity, matrix, without any transformation applied. The first rectangle I created used this matrix, before I called the first translate() function, and that's why what I input with regard to the arguments is what I got out. The other two rectangles have different transforms, and thus look different. In going over this sketch, you should take the time to see what parts of the matrix get changed after each transformation.

Another strange concept to deal with is the **matrix stack**. A stack is a temporary data structure that operates following the last in, first out (LIFO) principal. Stacks are utilized in many areas of computing, including managing transformation matrices. The pushMatrix() and popMatrix() functions alter the matrix stack, allowing different transformations to happen in a seemingly independent fashion. When you want to create a localized transformation (not affecting everything following the transformation call), you first call pushMatrix(), which adds any transformations that follow it onto the matrix stack. Then, when you're done, you call popMatrix(), which restores the matrix to its previous form. This is the reason that the first and last tables of values shown previously were identical— the first table represented the untransformed matrix and the last table represented the matrix after popMatrix() was called—which removed the last transformation pushed onto the stack.

This next example (shown in Figure A-13) is much more interesting than the last, and really illustrates the power of this whole matrix business. But it's also pretty complex and long; so watch it, play with it, and don't worry about understanding all the code yet. After you get a sense of what the sketch does (visually), try messing with some of the values; it's a great way to see what's going on programatically (and don't worry about breaking the sketch, either). After you launch the example, let it run for a while, as there are some really interesting patterns that form and change in interesting and unpredictable ways over time.

```
//Example 2:
/*
 PushPop
 Ira Greenberg, November 8, 2005
 */

/*Need to import opengl library to use OPENGL
 rendering mode. You can also try running
 in P3D mode*/
import processing.opengl.*;
```

```
float ang;
int rows = 20;
int cols = 20;
int cubeCount = rows*cols;
int colSpan, rowSpan;
float rotspd = 4;
Cube[]cubes = new Cube[cubeCount];
float[]angs = new float[cubeCount];
float[]rotvals = new float[cubeCount];
void setup(){
  size(400, 400, OPENGL);
  colSpan = width/(cols-1);
  rowSpan = height/(rows-1);
  noStroke();

  // instantiate cubes
  for (int i=0; i<cubeCount; i++){
    cubes[i] = new Cube(10, 10, 10, 0, 0, 0);
    /* 3 different rotation options
    - 1st option: cubes each rotate uniformly
    - 2nd option: cubes each rotate randomly
    - 3rd option: cube columns rotate as waves
    To try the different rotations, leave one
    of the rotVals[i] lines uncommented below
    and the other 2 commented out.
    */

    //rotvals[i] = rotspd;
    //rotvals[i] = random(-rotspd*2, rotspd*2);
    rotvals[i]=rotspd+=.02;
  }
}

void draw(){
  int cubeCounter = 0;
  background(255);
  fill(200);
  //set up some different colored lights
  pointLight(51, 102, 255, width/3, height/2, 100);
  pointLight(200, 40, 60,  width/1.5, height/2, -150);

  //raise overall light in scene
  ambientLight(170, 170, 100);

  //translate, rotate, and draw cubes
  for (int i=0; i<cols; i++){
    for (int j=0; j<rows; j++){
      pushMatrix();
      /* translate each block.
```

715

```
              pushmatrix and popmatrix add each cube
              translation to matrix, but restore
              original, so each cube rotates around its
              owns center*/
          translate(i*colSpan, j*rowSpan, -20);
          //rotate each cube around y- and x-axes
          rotateY(radians(angs[cubeCounter]));
          rotateX(radians(angs[cubeCounter]));
          cubes[cubeCounter].drawCube();
          popMatrix();
          cubeCounter++;
        }
      }
      //angs used in rotate function calls above
      for (int i=0; i<cubeCount;i++){
        angs[i] += rotvals[i];
      }
    }


    //simple Cube class, based on Quads
    class Cube {

      //properties
      int w, h, d;
      int shiftX, shiftY, shiftZ;

      //constructor
      Cube(int w, int h, int d, int shiftX, int shiftY, int shiftZ){
        this.w = w;
        this.h = h;
        this.d = d;
        this.shiftX = shiftX;
        this.shiftY = shiftY;
        this.shiftZ = shiftZ;
      }

      /*main cube drawing method, which looks
       more confusing than it really is. It's
       just a bunch of rectangles drawn for
       each cube face*/
      void drawCube(){
        //front face
        beginShape(QUADS);
```

```
    vertex(-w/2 + shiftX, -h/2 + shiftY, -d/2 + shiftZ);
    vertex(w + shiftX, -h/2 + shiftY, -d/2 + shiftZ);
    vertex(w + shiftX, h + shiftY, -d/2 + shiftZ);
    vertex(-w/2 + shiftX, h + shiftY, -d/2 + shiftZ);
    endShape();
    //back face
    beginShape(QUADS);
    vertex(-w/2 + shiftX, -h/2 + shiftY, d + shiftZ);
    vertex(w + shiftX, -h/2 + shiftY, d + shiftZ);
    vertex(w + shiftX, h + shiftY, d + shiftZ);
    vertex(-w/2 + shiftX, h + shiftY, d + shiftZ);
    endShape();
    //left face
    beginShape(QUADS);
    vertex(-w/2 + shiftX, -h/2 + shiftY, -d/2 + shiftZ);
    vertex(-w/2 + shiftX, -h/2 + shiftY, d + shiftZ);
    vertex(-w/2 + shiftX, h + shiftY, d + shiftZ);
    vertex(-w/2 + shiftX, h + shiftY, -d/2 + shiftZ);
    endShape();
    //right face
    beginShape(QUADS);
    vertex(w + shiftX, -h/2 + shiftY, -d/2 + shiftZ);
    vertex(w + shiftX, -h/2 + shiftY, d + shiftZ);
    vertex(w + shiftX, h + shiftY, d + shiftZ);
    vertex(w + shiftX, h + shiftY, -d/2 + shiftZ);
    endShape();
    //top face
    beginShape(QUADS);
    vertex(-w/2 + shiftX, -h/2 + shiftY, -d/2 + shiftZ);
    vertex(w + shiftX, -h/2 + shiftY, -d/2 + shiftZ);
    vertex(w + shiftX, -h/2 + shiftY, d + shiftZ);
    vertex(-w/2 + shiftX, -h/2 + shiftY, d + shiftZ);
    endShape();
    //bottom face
    beginShape(QUADS);
    vertex(-w/2 + shiftX, h + shiftY, -d/2 + shiftZ);
    vertex(w + shiftX, h + shiftY, -d/2 + shiftZ);
    vertex(w + shiftX, h + shiftY, d + shiftZ);
    vertex(-w/2 + shiftX, h + shiftY, d + shiftZ);
    endShape();
  }
}
```

A

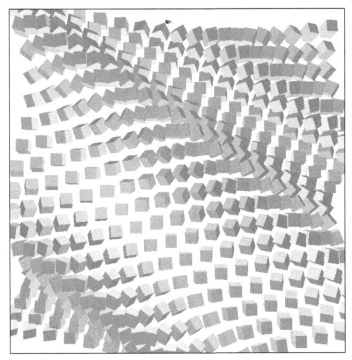

Figure A-13. Transform Example 2 sketch

Lights, Camera

This is a very cool part of the API, but it is also pretty complex. Using the near 30 functions in this section isn't all that difficult, but understanding what's happening underneath the surface, and ultimately being able to control stuff, is the complex part. There are many sophisticated concepts built into a 3D renderer, including a virtual camera, light models, surface/material properties, and matrix transformations, just to name a few. I taught 3D modeling and animation for a number of years prior to delving into the programmatic side of 3D, and I still find this stuff complicated and very challenging. If you are totally new to 3D (besides experimenting with Processing's functions), I also recommend exploring some 3D modeling and animation tools, such as LightWave, Maya, 3ds Max, or CINEMA 4D.

The Lights, Camera section is divided into four subsections:

- Lights
- Camera
- Coordinates
- Material Properties

A

Lights

The Lights section includes functions for controlling subtle, yet very important, aspects of 3D rendering. In general, lighting in 3D is modeled on the real world and the concept of placing real lights in a space. The virtual camera is a similar such construct. Of course, in Processing, all the lights are virtual, and really just a bunch of pixel color calculations. That being said, just as in the real world, virtual lights can have direction, falloff (how far and intensely they illuminate), color, cone angles (in the case of spotlights), and overall spatial illumination (in the case of ambient light). Lighting is one of the key research areas in 3D, and has an enormous impact on the overall quality of rendering.

Camera

Camera functions control the virtual camera that you view the virtual world through. This might sound like an odd concept if you haven't played with any 3D applications. A "real" 3D projection is impossible on a flat 2D monitor, so ultimately all the 3D spatial calculations need to be converted, or projected, back to the 2D Cartesian system. This translation is one of the aspects that makes 3D complicated. During this geometric flattening (which usually happens in real time), different algorithms can be applied that control how we view the implied 3D space. For example, one of the most common approaches is to try to simulate the effects of perspective, similar to how we, with our binocular vision, experience the real world.

Based on the rules of perspective, objects get smaller as they go back in space, and in a one-point perspective system, lines going into the distance converge. When objects get close to us and appear very large, distortions such as a fish-eye effect can occur. We can easily simulate these types of effects in 3D—that is, with a lot of math. Conversely, we can also create a more synthetic, or orthogonal, projection, in which there is no perspective. This is quite useful for precisely modeling geometry, where you might need to work with a set of undistorted 2D projections—for example, in an engineering application. Perspective looks good, but it is often hard to know precisely where you are (actually, where the cursor is) when working in this mode.

Virtual cameras also utilize a viewing volume and clipping planes that specify minimum and maximum values for the x-, y-, and z-axes. Normally, only stuff within the camera's viewing volume, called the **frustum**, can be seen. The boundaries of the frustum are called the **clipping planes**. If the clipping planes are not set correctly, imagery can disappear and appear unexpectedly. However, without any clipping, geometry not visible within the camera's view can get rendered, which is obviously a waste of memory. Finally, as the virtual camera is not bound by the physics of the real world, it has the ability to produce highly distorted and strange effects. This can be an interesting thing to experiment with, but also a potential source of frustration—especially when you don't want it to happen (or can't track down the problem).

Coordinates

The Coordinates section includes six (conceptually) advanced functions that return coordinate values. The six functions are modelZ(), modelX(), modelY(), screenZ(), screenX(),

719

and screenY(). The model functions return the 3D coordinates in model space, which means the coordinate values after they've been transformed (rotated, scaled, and/or moved), but before they're projected to the screen. In contrast, the screen functions return 3D coordinates in relation to screen space. If you've never worked in 3D, this may sound pretty confusing. Remember, computer-generated 3D simulates space, as everything really lives on the 2D screen surface. To simulate real space, geometry must be shifted around to give the illusion of perspective, depth layering, and so forth. The actual 3D coordinate geometry we generate ultimately has to be mapped to the space of our 2D screens, taking into account any perspective calculations. This concept is most abstract in reference to the z-axis, which doesn't really exist at all on the screen. Yet, when we work in 3D, geometry is calculated at specific locations on this illusory axis. To visualize the concept of screen coordinates vs. model coordinates, think about the classic one-point perspective image of railroad tracks receding into the distance to a point. In reality, of course, the tracks remain parallel and never actually converge—which you can think of as their model coordinates (the actual geometry). But visually, the receding tracks are no longer parallel, and these illusory coordinates can be thought of as their screen coordinates.

Material Properties

The Material Properties section includes four functions:

- shininess()
- specular()
- ambient()
- emissive()

These functions control how object surfaces interact with the light in the scene. For example, glossy and reflective surfaces have concentrated areas of light, sometimes referred to as hotspots; think about the small, intense light spots on the surface of an eyeball, or how light reflects off of a highly polished piece of chrome. This light phenomenon is referred to as **specularity**. The specular() function controls the color of these hotspots.

Ambient light, on the other hand, refers to more general and overall lighting—think about the light in a dense forest or in a room without a direct light source. The ambient() function controls the color of the ambient light. Like the other rendering attribute functions, the material functions affect the rendering state as well as the light functions. Once a material function (e.g., shininess()) is called, its influence will be felt by all future surfaces created in the scene, until another explicit call to the material function (using different rendering attributes) is made.

To give an example that involves the Lights, Camera section of the API, I developed a 3D flythrough sketch that utilizes a lot of the features I've been discussing. (This is another complex sketch that I put in more for inspiration and pleasure than your edification—but it is cool, and will still be useful for you to take apart and experiment with.)

The example (shown in Figure A-14) utilizes two images that need to be put within the sketch's data directory. The images need to be named ground2.jpg and metal2.jpg, and I recommend making them around 400 by 400 pixels. If the example runs slowly on your system, you can try lowering the resolution of the images (in an image editing program), lowering the value of the bldgCount variable in the sketch, or buying yourself a new computer. If you go with option 3, I'll take a new Mac laptop while you're at it.

```
/*
FlyThrough
Ira Greenberg, November 8, 2005
*/

/*Need to import opengl library to use OPENGL
 rendering mode. You can also try running
 in P3D mode*/
import processing.opengl.*;

// images used for mapping
PImage ground, brick;

// camera move variables
float bank=2;
float bankAngle;
float bankSpeed = .7;
float vert = -600;
float zoom;
float vertSpeed = 1.5;
float heading;
float headingSpeed = -.75;
float pitch;
float pan;
float zoomSpeed = 1.6;

//structures
int bldgCount = 300;
BLDG[]bldgs = new BLDG[bldgCount];
BLDG plane;

void setup(){
  size(600, 400, OPENGL);
  noStroke();
  textureMode(NORMALIZED);

  //load image maps
  ground = loadImage("ground2.jpg");
  brick = loadImage("metal2.jpg");

  //set up ground plane
  plane = new BLDG(width*10, 0, width*10, 0, 60, 0, ground);

  // instantiate bldgs
  for (int i=0; i<bldgCount; i++){
```

721

```
      bldgs[i] = new BLDG(10+random(30), random(100, 840), 10+random(50),
      random(-width*2, width*2), 60, random(-width*3, width*2), brick);
    }
  }

void draw(){
  background(4, 4, 20);
  // set camera and lights
  camera(width/2.0+pan, height/2+vert, ((height/2.0+1500-zoom) /
  tan(PI*60 / 360.0)), width/2.0+pan, height/2+vert, -8000, 0, 1, 0);
  fill(200);
  //set up some different colored lights
  ambientLight(90, 65, 52);
  pointLight(51, 102, 255, width/3, height/2, 100);
  pointLight(200, 40, 60,  width/1.5, height/2, -150);
  pointLight(20, 220, 25,  -200, -100, 300);
  pointLight(110, 55, 40,  width*4, height/2, 1000);

  //draw ground plane
  pushMatrix();
  translate(width/2, height/2, -20);
  rotateY(radians(heading));
  rotateX(radians(pitch));
  rotateZ(radians(bank));
  plane.drawBLDG();
  // draw buildings
  for (int i=0; i<bldgCount; i++){
    bldgs[i].drawBLDG();
  }
  popMatrix();

  //moon
  spotLight(255, 255, 10, 80, -300, -400, -1, 0, 0, PI/1.4, 2);
  pushMatrix();
  translate(-600, -1500, -100);
  fill(75, 185, 40, 255);
  sphere(75);
  popMatrix();

  //planet
  pointLight(20, 220, 25,  2000, -4000, -2000);
  pushMatrix();
  translate(2500, -4700, -2200);
  fill(100, 100, 180, 55);
  sphere(3200);
  popMatrix();

  //camera moves
  bank = sin(radians(bankAngle))*12;
```

```
    bankAngle+=bankSpeed;
    vert = -600 +zoom*.24;
    zoom+=zoomSpeed;
    if (zoom>2200 || zoom<-10) {
      zoomSpeed*=-1;
    }
    heading+=headingSpeed;
}
//simple BLDG class
class BLDG {
  //properties
  float w, h, d;
  float shiftX, shiftY, shiftZ;
  PImage img;

  //constructor
  BLDG(float w, float h, float d, float shiftX,
  float shiftY, float shiftZ, PImage img){
    this.w = w;
    this.h = h;
    this.d = d;
    this.shiftX = shiftX;
    this.shiftY = shiftY;
    this.shiftZ = shiftZ;
    this.img = img;
  }

  //main bldg drawing method
  void drawBLDG(){
    beginShape(QUADS);
    texture(img);
    //front wall
    vertex(-w/2 + shiftX, -h/2 + shiftY, -d/2 + shiftZ, 0, 0);
    vertex(w + shiftX, -h/2 + shiftY, -d/2 + shiftZ, 1, 0);
    vertex(w + shiftX, shiftY, -d/2 + shiftZ, 1, 1);
    vertex(-w/2 + shiftX, shiftY, -d/2 + shiftZ, 0, 1);

    //back wall
    vertex(-w/2 + shiftX, -h/2 + shiftY, d + shiftZ, 0, 0);
    vertex(w + shiftX, -h/2 + shiftY, d + shiftZ, 1, 0);
    vertex(w + shiftX, shiftY, d + shiftZ, 1, 1);
    vertex(-w/2 + shiftX, shiftY, d + shiftZ, 0, 1);

    //left wall
    vertex(-w/2 + shiftX, -h/2 + shiftY, -d/2 + shiftZ, 0, 0);
    vertex(-w/2 + shiftX, -h/2 + shiftY, d + shiftZ, 1, 0);
    vertex(-w/2 + shiftX, shiftY, d + shiftZ, 1, 1);
    vertex(-w/2 + shiftX, shiftY, -d/2 + shiftZ, 0, 1);
```

```
//right wall
vertex(w + shiftX, -h/2 + shiftY, -d/2 + shiftZ, 0, 0);
vertex(w + shiftX, -h/2 + shiftY, d + shiftZ, 1, 0);
vertex(w + shiftX, shiftY, d + shiftZ, 1, 1);
vertex(w + shiftX, shiftY, -d/2 + shiftZ, 0, 1);

//roof
vertex(-w/2 + shiftX, -h/2 + shiftY, -d/2 + shiftZ, 0, 0);
vertex(w + shiftX, -h/2 + shiftY, -d/2 + shiftZ, 1, 0);
vertex(w + shiftX, -h/2 + shiftY, d + shiftZ, 1, 1);
vertex(-w/2 + shiftX, -h/2 + shiftY, d + shiftZ, 0, 1);
endShape();
  }
}
```

Figure A-14. FlyThrough sketch

Color

The Color section is divided into two subsections: Setting and Creating & Reading. Although it's a relatively small section of the API, it's a very significant one. For the most part, the Color section is pretty straightforward, with simple background(), fill(), and stroke() functions that take arguments to directly change color. However, there are two issues that may be new or challenging to newbie coders, which I'll discuss in the following respective sections.

Setting

The Setting section includes the basic functions just discussed. One issue that may be new to you is the concept of a rendering state or graphics context. Graphics application software can make it seem that color is generated on a per-shape basis. If you need a blue rectangle, you grab the paint bucket tool, select a blue color, and click in your shape (or some similar procedure). What a tool like the paint bucket conceals is how color is implemented as a state change in a programming language like Java and Processing. As a comparison, I've included the code for a simple Java graphics application followed by its Processing equivalent. Both programs generate the same output, except that the Java program does it in 19 lines (not including comments or skipped lines), while Processing does it in 5. Do not try to run the Java application from within Processing; it will not work. (As an aside, for the few experienced Java readers out there—and this comes from Ben Fry directly—classes from the java.awt.* and javax.swing.* packages should not be used within Processing, as they will generate inconsistent results.) What the Java vs. Processing code comparison should show you is how much stuff Processing handles under the hood, or **encapsulates**, making our coding lives happier. Here's the Java version:

```
import java.awt.*;
import java.applet.*;

public class SimpleJavaExample extends Frame {
  //constructor
public SimpleJavaExample(){
   setSize(200, 200);
   setBackground(Color.white);
   // this program still requires window closing behavior
  }
//main method
  public static void main(String[]args){
    new SimpleJavaExample().setVisible(true);
  }
//overrides default paint method
  public void paint(Graphics g){
    g.setColor(new Color(0, 0, 200));
    g.fillRect(25, 50, 50, 50);
    g.fillOval(125, 50, 50, 50);
    g.setColor(new Color(0, 0, 0));
    g.drawRect(25, 50, 50, 50);
    g.drawOval(125, 50, 50, 50);
  }
}
```

In Processing, to get the same output, you can just write the following:

```
size(200, 200);
background(255);
fill(0, 0, 200);
rect(25, 25, 50, 50);
ellipse(150, 50, 50, 50);
```

Color, rather than being generated on a per-object basis, is part of an overall rendering state, or graphics context. In Processing and Java, this graphics context is controlled by a Graphics object, which sets properties of the rendering state, such as color and font, as well as a few others. Graphics is the base class in Java that encapsulates this process, allowing you to write relatively simple code, as in the Java example. Processing, as you'd expect, encapsulates this stuff even further, removing the need for explicitly overriding the paint() method, as in the Java example. The paint() method is the method that a Java component (a component can be thought of as a panel—like the display window) calls when it needs to paint something. What I'm actually doing in the Java example is redefining the paint() method for my component, so when paint() is called normally by the component, which happens automatically when the program starts, it will use my paint method, instead of the component's default one, to do what I want it to do—in this case, paint a simple blue rectangle and circle on the screen. This process of using one method's implementation to replace another is referred to as **method overriding**, and is a fundamental part of OOP.

If you run the Processing code, you'll notice that the sketch includes two blue shapes. This is because the state of the rendering context hasn't been changed between the two calls to the drawing functions. Thus, the fill is not really about those two shapes, but about the current rendering state of the program at that point. Until you change the rendering state color with another fill() command call, every new filled shape will be blue. I'll shut up about this now, but if you want to learn more about the Java Graphics class from Sun, check out http://java.sun.com/j2se/1.4.2/docs/api/index.html. And here's a link to some more info about how painting works in Java: http://java.sun.com/products/jfc/tsc/articles/painting/.

The next sketch is another example of the Color section's Setting functions in action (see Figure A-15). One of the functions, colorMode(), deserves a little clarification. Color can be specified as RGB (red, green, blue—the default mode) or HSB (hue, saturation, brightness). In addition, you can set the mathematical range to describe the color, or even each part of the color. In my two calls to colorMode() in the example, the first call, colorMode(RGB, 1.0), sets the mode to RGB and specifies the range of values to be set for each component between 0.0 and 1.0. Thus, (0, 0, 0) would equal black, and (.5, .5, 0) would equal yellow. The second call is pretty odd, and I only did it as an extreme example of what is possible. colorMode(HSB, 100, 10, .1) sets the mode to HSB. It specifies the hue value range from 0 to 100 (which is what you typically see with HSB values—0 to 100 percent), the saturation range from 0 to 10, and the brightness range from 0 to .1 (which is pretty odd, indeed). However, it all works, and may even impress your friends (probably not). Wikipedia has an interesting discussion on HSB (sometimes also referred to as HSV) at http://en.wikipedia.org/wiki/HSB_color_space.

```
/*
Simple Color Example
Ira Greenberg, November 10, 2005
*/
size(200, 200);
background(200, 50, 40);
stroke(45);
fill(200, 200, 0);
rect(25, 50, 50, 50);
```

```
ellipseMode(CORNER);
fill(200, 200, 0, 125);
stroke(175, 0, 255);
ellipse(125, 50, 50, 50);

noStroke();
colorMode(RGB, 1.0);
fill(0, .85, .2);
triangle(25, 175, 75, 175, 50, 125);

colorMode(HSB, 100, 10, .1);
fill(50, 9, .08);
beginShape();
vertex(125, 125);
vertex(120, 145);
vertex(140, 160);
vertex(145, 170);
vertex(175, 175);
vertex(182, 150);
vertex(155, 138);
vertex(145, 120);
endShape(CLOSE);
```

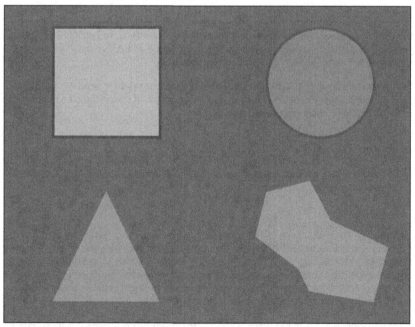

Figure A-15. Simple Color Example sketch

Creating & Reading

As discussed previously, color is specified as three components, for red, green, and blue (RGB). (You can also specify a fourth component, alpha, for controlling transparency.) Most typically on the computer, color is referred to as a hexadecimal value. The hexadecimal system uses 16 as the base, instead of 10, as in the more common decimal system. To account for 16 unique numbers, the letters A, B, C, D, E, and F are used along with the numbers 0 through 9. Also remember that 0 counts as a digit, so F is equal to 15, while B equals 11. Numbers larger than 15 are created by using additional places, just as in the decimal system. However, the values are raised by 16 instead of 10. So, the number FF would be equal to 15 * 16 + 15, which equals 255, and the number AFB would equal (10 * 16 * 16) + (15 * 16) + 11, which equals 2,811. To allow the computer to know that you want it to perform calculations using base 16 instead of base 10, you write 0x before the value. So, AFB would be specified as 0xAFB.

Try running this one-line sketch, which should output 2811:

```
println(0xAFB);
```

In Processing, you can also use also the # symbol to specify a color value, as in the following line:

```
color orange = #FF7700;
```

Each color is specified as a six-digit hexadecimal value, where the first two numbers specify the red component, the next two the green, and the final two the blue. For example, the colors red, green, and blue are specified as #FF0000, #00FF00, and #0000FF. Of course, you can any put legal hexadecimal characters (0 through 9 and A through F) in any of the six slots to create up to 16,777,215 different colors.

The seven functions red(), brightness(), blue(), saturation(), green(), hue(), and alpha() extract specific values out of a color. For example, if I want the blue component of the color 0xFFE56D, I can use this simple code:

```
color c = 0xFFE56D;
print(blue(c));
```

I can use the exact same structure for most of the functions within this section. Here's code to extract the saturation of a color:

```
color c = 0xFFE56D;
print(saturation(c));
```

Curiously, if you look at what the API has to say about the red() function, there's a mysterious blurb in the Description section: "The red() function is easy to use and understand, but is slower than another technique. To achieve the same results when working in colorMode(RGB, 255), but with greater speed, use the >> (right shift) operator with a bit mask" (see http://processing.org/reference/red_.html).

Right shift operator, bit mask—what is this stuff? Unfortunately, there's not much else to go on in the API. It seems there may be some pretty scary stuff lurking beneath the surface of this part of the API. These mysterious terms relate to **bitwise operations**. Bitwise operations are low-level operations useful for squeezing some extra performance out of a sketch, but they're also a little (actually more than a little) confusing to use. I cover bitwise operations further in Appendix B.

Processing has a convenient data type called color that encapsulates the 32 bits of information making up a color (8 bits for alpha, 8 bits for red, 8 bits for green, and 8 bits for blue). You can declare a variable of type color using the following syntax:

```
color c
```

In the Image section of the API, which I'll look at next, is a function named get(). get() returns a value as a color data type based on a specific pixel's color. Another way to create a color from scratch is to use the color() function. (I realize it gets confusing when a number of different commands/data types share common names). Finally, you can create a color by directly assigning a hexadecimal value to a color variable. Following are three statements that generate a color three different ways: through the use of get(), through the use of the color() function, and through direct assignment using hexadecimal notation. I also include a fourth direct assignment statement that includes an alpha component in the hexadecimal notation.

```
color c1 = get(50, 50);
color c2 = color(200, 100, 50);
color c3 = #FF33DD;
// this last statement explicitly specifies alpha and RGB values
color c4 = 0xFFFF33DD;
```

The Creating & Reading subsection also includes two color-blending functions: blendColor() and lerpColor(). blendColor(), the more complex of the two functions, utilizes a blending mode, declared as an argument passed to the function, along with the two colors to blend. lerpColor() uses a simpler numeric ratio for blending two colors. Here's an example that uses both functions, including blendColor()'s different blending modes (see Figure A-16):

```
/* blendColor and lerpColor
Ira Greenberg, October 12, 2006 */

size(210, 490);
background(100);
noStroke();
smooth();
color c1 = color(200, 10, 200);
color c2 = color(200, 200, 10);

//blend
color c_add = blendColor(c1, c2, ADD);
color c_subtract = blendColor(c1, c2, SUBTRACT);
color c_darkest = blendColor(c1, c2, DARKEST);
color c_lightest = blendColor(c1, c2, LIGHTEST);
```

729

```
//lerp
color c_lerp_25 = lerpColor(c1, c2, .25);
color c_lerp_5 = lerpColor(c1, c2, .5);
color c_lerp_75 = lerpColor(c1, c2, .75);

color[] cols = {
  c_add, c_subtract, c_darkest,
  c_lightest, c_lerp_25, c_lerp_5, c_lerp_75
};

for (int i=0; i<cols.length; i++){
  fill(c1);
  ellipse(35, 35+70*i, 70, 70);
  fill(cols[i]);
  ellipse(105, 35+70*i, 70, 70);
  fill(c2);
  ellipse(175, 35+70*i, 70, 70);
}
```

Figure A-16. BlendColor and LerpColor sketch

Image

The Image section relates very directly to the information I covered in the Color section, as an image after all is a just a collection of colored pixels. In general, the image functions allow you to load and alter images. In Java, loading images and altering them is real work (especially down at the pixel level). Processing, as usual, simplifies this entire process, while still giving you enough low-level access to act directly upon the pixel data. Processing also includes its own image data type, called PImage, that encapsulates many of the features, which makes working with images in Processing so easy. Yet, for all its ease of use, Processing's imaging capabilities are surprisingly powerful.

The Image section of the API is divided up into essentially two categories, with the PImage data type and createImage() function standing alone. The two categories are Loading & Displaying and Pixels. Be aware that PImage includes a bunch of methods with the same names as some of the functions in the Pixels section. For instance, following is an example that uses the PImage method get() and the function get() in the same sketch. Even though these commands are both called get(), they are fundamentally different. The get() method requires a PImage object to call it—as in myImage.get()—while the get() function works all by itself. The subtlety of this distinction requires an understanding of OOP, which is covered in Chapter 8.

You'll need an image named portrait.jpg in the data directory of this sketch to run this example. I suggest making the image 400 by 400 pixels.

```
size(400, 400);
PImage img = loadImage("portrait.jpg");
image(img, 0, 0);
println("image method before = " + img.get(50, 50));
println("function before = " + get(50, 50));
image(img, -140, -140);
println("image method after = " + img.get(50, 50));
println("function after = " + get(50, 50));
```

Here's the output generated by running the sketch:

```
image method before = -263171
function before = -263171
image method after = -263171
function after = -5686717
```

Your values will be different, since your image will be different than mine—but notice how the output changes for the function, but not for the method. What's happening is that the PImage get() method references the image data stored in the PImage object independently from its display on the screen, while the get() function returns pixel values at a specific point on the screen. Since I drew the image at two different places on the screen, the two get() function calls give two different values. However, the two get() method calls refer to the same pixel in the stored PImage object.

Pixels

The Pixels section includes functions that operate at the pixel level. In addition to functions that provide access to the entire pixel array of the display, there are two simple yet powerful functions for blending and filtering image data that provide programmatically controlled Photoshop-like capabilities. If you don't want to use these cool included functions for doing things like blurs, posterization, image masking, and compositing, you can easily spin your own, as well; just grab the image pixels using the loadPixels() function, do some bit shifting, and then just call updatePixels() to rewrite the pixel data to the screen. In addition to using the get() function or the PImage get() method to access the color of a pixel, it is also possible (and faster) to access the pixels[] array directly. Similar to the two get() commands just discussed, there are two pixels[] arrays in Processing—one represents the contents of the display window and the other is a property within the PImage class. Similar to the get() method, this pixels[] array property requires a PImage object to be accessed (e.g., myImage.pixels), and the array data only relates to the PImage object, independent of the display window. Here's an example that uses both get() commands and pixels[] arrays. This example also uses the portrait.jpg image, which should be in the sketch's data directory.

```
size(400, 400);
//create a Pimage and load an external image
PImage img = loadImage("portrait.jpg");
//PImage method get() works even without drawing image to the screen
println("PImage get() method = " + img.get(50, 50));
//PImage pixels[] array may also be accessed without drawing ➡
    the image to the screen
println("PImage pixel array = " + img.pixels[50*width+50]);
//draw the image to the screen
image(img, 0, 0);
// display window get() function works without calling loadPixels();
println("get() function = " + get(50, 50));
loadPixels();
// loadPixels() must be called prior to accessing display window ➡
    pixels[] array directly
println("pixel array = " + pixels[50*width+50]);
```

It is confusing that these two arrays have the same name but function differently. As I mentioned, you can access the pixel values of a PImage object directly, even prior to drawing the image to the screen, using object-oriented dot syntax, as in *myImage.pixels*. However, to access the pixel values of the display window, you must first call loadPixels(), as I did in the preceding example. With regard to the two get() commands, neither command requires loadPixels() to be called prior to being used. Once loadImage() has been called, the PImage get() method can access pixel values within the image. However, to access the image pixel value using the display window get() function, you need to draw the image to the screen using the image() command.

Loading & Displaying

The Loading & Displaying section includes two functions that make working with images in Processing a joy: loadImage() and image(). loadImage("*imageName*") expects a single String argument, which should be the name of the file you want to load, residing in the sketch's data directory. It is critical that you first load your image files into Processing by selecting Add File from the Sketch menu. When you select Add File, your loaded image will be placed in a data subdirectory, within the current sketch main directory. If you don't already have a data directory, it will be created for you. If you've successfully run the last few examples, you already know how to do this.

It is recommended that you do all your image loading in the setup() structure, not in draw(). After you load an image using loadImage(), you won't see it until you render it to the screen. This is another one of those things that's not so simple to do in Java, but incredibly simple to achieve in Processing—just call image(). This function can take a bunch of arguments, including a PImage object reference and the x, y, width, and height properties of the image.

This subsection also includes basic tinting functions and a simple utility function called imageMode() that gives you two options for specifying image measurements in the display window when you call the image() function. The default CORNER argument option allows you to specify x, y, width, and height properties, while the CORNERS argument makes the third and fourth measurement arguments (that were width and height) specify the position of the bottom-right point of the image. In both cases, when passing arguments that control width and height, you can scale and load the images simultaneously. Be aware that you can scale the images both proportionally and non-proportionally based on the ratio of your arguments.

As an example, I created a simple progressive tiling sketch that loads an image, and then continuously shrinks the image as it tiles it through the display window (see Figure A-17). Be aware that there is the possibility of generating an infinite loop with this example—one of **Zeno's paradoxes**, in which a float value keeps approaching a discrete value, but never reaches it. You can read about Zeno's paradoxes at http://en.wikipedia.org/wiki/Zeno%27s_paradox. If you test this, please remember to first add your image file into the data directory using the Add File command. (This sketch uses the image vail.jpg.)

```
/*
Progressive Tile
Ira Greenberg, November 12, 2005
*/

size(480, 480);
background(255);
PImage img = loadImage("vail.jpg");
float x = 0, y =0;
float w = 240*.5;
float h = w;
for (int i=0; i<height; i+=h){
  for (int j=0; j<width; j+=w){
    image(img, j, i, w, h);
```

```
  }
  // avoid infinite loop
  // Zeno's paradox waiting to happen
  if (w>5){
    w*=.81;
    h*=.81;
  }
}
```

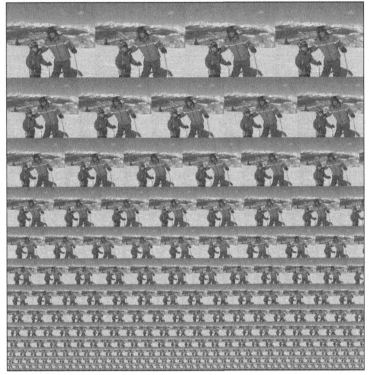

Figure A-17. Progressive Tile sketch

Rendering

This section includes the PGraphics data type and the createGraphics() function. Together, these elements provide low-level access into Processing's graphics and rendering context—sort of the meat (or tempeh, for vegan readers) and potatoes of the Processing API. PGraphics is one of Processing's core, base classes, and it has a rich set of properties and methods, which you can learn more about at http://dev.processing.org/reference/core/javadoc/processing/core/PGraphics.html. One of the main uses for these elements is the creation of an off-screen image, also sometimes referred to as an **image buffer**. Beyond drawing to the display window, you can also use the createGraphics() function to generate a PGraphics object that you can draw directly into. You can then output this off-screen image to the screen, or even save it to a file.

The next example uses these two structures to generate an off-screen image that will eventually be turned into a tiled background (see Figure A-18). The sketch allows a user to draw within the display window. The drawing is simultaneously output to the screen (using Processing's built-in graphics context) and written to an off-screen buffer (using a PGraphics object created with the createGraphics() function). When the user releases the mouse, the off-screen image is scaled, positioned, and drawn to the screen as a tiled fill pattern. Notice in the sketch code that the two PGraphics methods beginDraw() and endDraw() are used, in a sense, as entry and exit portals for drawing to the off-screen PGraphics object.

```
/* Tile Designer
 Ira Greenberg, October 11, 2006
 draw to off-screen buffer
 to create a tiled background */

PGraphics p;
int tiles = 10;
float strokeWt = 2.75;
float scaleFactor;
boolean isRecordable = false;

void setup() {
  size(400, 400);
  background(0);
  smooth();
  float tileWidth = width/tiles;
  scaleFactor = tileWidth/width;
}

void draw() {
  // write to off-screen buffer
  if (isRecordable){
    p.line(pmouseX, pmouseY, mouseX, mouseY);
  }
  // preview drawing of tile
  if (mousePressed){
    stroke(255);
    line(pmouseX, pmouseY, mouseX, mouseY);
  }
}

void mousePressed(){
  p = createGraphics(width, height, JAVA2D);
  noStroke();
```

```
    fill(0);
    rect(0, 0, width, height);
    isRecordable = true;
    p.beginDraw();
    p.background(0);
    p.stroke(255);
    p.strokeWeight(strokeWt/scaleFactor);
}

void mouseReleased(){
  p.endDraw();
  isRecordable = false;
  // scale tile
  scale(scaleFactor);
  for (int i=0; i<tiles; i++){
    for (int j=0; j<tiles; j++){
      // draw off-screen image
      image(p, i*width, j*height);
    }
  }
}
```

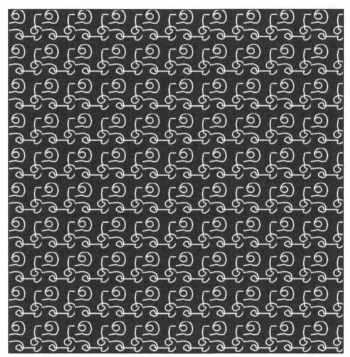

Figure A-18. Tile Designer sketch

Typography

Processing utilizes multiple approaches to rendering typography in your sketches, including both raster- and vector-based solutions. Historically for graphic designers, typography on the Web has required a cost-benefit analysis between using common but ubiquitous fonts (i.e., native fonts, which are likely to be installed on most users' systems) and using more involved, memory-intensive, or unpredictable solutions. Processing sketches are widely distributed as applets on the Web, so there are some similar trade-offs when using typography in your sketches.

The Typography section is divided into four sections:

- PFont
- Loading & Displaying
- Attributes
- Metrics

PFont

PFont is Processing's custom font data type. When using type in Processing, you first need to declare a PFont object. This object is then assigned a reference to a specific font. For example, assuming you have a font named Verdana-24.vlw in the data directory of your current sketch, you can render type in Processing using the following:

```
PFont f = loadFont("Verdana-24.vlw");
textFont(f);
text("Hello", 19, 55);
```

Processing's VLW format is a custom bitmapped font format, which relies on a brute-force approach to incorporating typography into sketches—characters are described as images, rather than with a scalable vector format. The benefit of this arrangement is that fonts not installed on a user's system can still be rendered in Processing, which would not be the case if Processing depended only upon installed native fonts.

Although the VLW format solves the missing typeface problem, it is not without its own challenges. When a typeface is converted to the VLW format, it should be specified at the exact point size it will be rendered at or it may not render clearly. This means that if you use the same font at varying sizes throughout your sketch, you'll want to create a number of separate VLW fonts for the different sizes (even though it's the same font). Sketch performance is also negatively impacted when the VLW fonts are not created at the specified rendering sizes in your sketch.

Before you completely write off typography in Processing, you should note that it's possible to use vector-based typography in Processing as well. You can ask Processing to use native (scalable vector) fonts, assuming the user has the specific font installed on their system, by including the following command in your sketch:

```
hint(ENABLE_NATIVE_FONTS);
```

737

Processing can also render TTF (TrueType) and OTF (OpenType) font vector formats, as long as the font is installed in your sketch's data directory. Thus, it is possible to distribute your sketch on the Web or directly to another user with the specific TTF or OTF font included in the sketch's data directory. However, there are legal/copyright issues involved in distributing fonts like this, as the Processing reference states: "Only fonts that can legally be distributed should be included with a sketch" (see http://processing.org/reference/createFont_.html).

Finally, type in Processing can also be rendered in 3D space, although there is some quality loss for this very cool capability. If quality is critical, use the textMode(SCREEN) command, which forces the type rendering to the front of the display window, increasing rendering quality.

Loading & Displaying

The Loading & Displaying subsection has four main functions that allow fonts to be displayed in Processing, as follows (please note that the Processing language reference lists text() first, but I'll discuss it last):

- text()
- createFont()
- loadFont()
- textFont()

createFont() dynamically converts a font installed on your computer to the VLW format used by Processing. This function works similarly to the Create Font command in the Tools menu. However, the createFont() function doesn't write the converted VLW font to disk the way the Create Font command does. While the createFont() function is listed in the Processing online reference as an advanced feature offering precise control, the reference states that "On most occasions you should create fonts through selecting 'Create Font . . .' from the Tools menu." For more info on this advanced feature, please refer to http://processing.org/reference/createFont_.html.

To load existing VLW fonts installed in the data directory, use the loadFont() function, which expects a string of the full font name. No path is necessary if the VLW font is installed at the root level of the data directory. textFont() allows you to set the current font, as long as it's been loaded with loadFont(). Finally, the text() function is what you call to actually add some type to the screen. text() has numerous forms with regard to arguments you can pass it, including x, y, z, width, and height.

The following typography example I created rotates two text strings in 3D space (see Figure A-19). I created one of the fonts dynamically and loaded the other out of the sketch's data directory. In creating the font dynamically, I needed to make sure that I used a font installed on my computer (I specified Helvetica). If you're not sure what fonts you currently have installed, run the following line of code in Processing:

```
println(PFont.list());
```

This will output a list of all the fonts currently installed on your computer. In the line of the sketch that reads font2 = createFont("Helvetica", 32);, you can replace Helvetica with any font you have installed.

In addition to createFont(), I also used the loadFont() command:

```
font = loadFont("Garamond-32.vlw");
```

Before I could use loadFont(), I needed to first use the CreateFont command from the Tools menu. I selected Garamond and a size of 32, and left the smooth box checked and the All Characters box unchecked. If you don't have the font Garamond, pick another font, but be sure to change the name in the following sketch. The Tools ➤ CreateFont command automatically creates and installs the VLW font in your current sketch's data directory.

```
/*
Orbiting Text
Ira Greenberg, November 14, 2005
*/
PFont font;
String s = "Spinning Word";
PFont font2;
String s2 = "flipping Word";
float ang = 0, ang2 =0;
void setup(){
  size(400, 400, P3D);
  //load text from data directory
  font = loadFont("Garamond-32.vlw");
  //dynamically create text and specify size as the second argument
  font2 = createFont("Helvetica", 32);
}

//rotates text in 3D space
void draw(){
  background(255);
  translate(width/2, height/2, 50);
  pushMatrix();
  rotateY(radians(ang));
  textFont(font, 32);
  fill(45, 78, 28);
  text(s, -textWidth(s)/2, 0, 100);
  popMatrix();

  pushMatrix();
  rotateX(radians(ang2));
  textFont(font2, 24);
  fill(250, 125, 28);
  text(s2, -textWidth(s2)/2, 0, 0);
  popMatrix();
  ang+=3;
  ang2-=10;
}
```

739

Figure A-19. Orbiting Text sketch

Attributes

The Attributes subsection includes five functions, textMode(), textSize(), textAlign(), textLeading(), and textWidth(), which respectively refer to model or screen mode (for 3D), font size, alignment (left, center, or right), leading (the distance between lines of text), and a function for returning the width of a character or text string.

Metrics

The Metrics subsection includes two functions for returning the actual height of a line of text. textDescent() returns the distance of any descending parts of the fonts below the baseline, and textAscent() does the same for any parts above the baseline. Adding these two values together gives you the total height of the line.

Math

This section is one of the largest in the API and perhaps the scariest one for creative coders. However, you've used large parts of it in this book already, as math is (unavoidably) the underlying language of coding. Also, many of the functions within this section are actually designed to simplify the mathematical demands of programming. So, I'll cruise through most of this stuff pretty swiftly. The Math section is divided into the following five subsections:

- Operators
- Bitwise Operators
- Calculation
- Trigonometry
- Random

"Operators" will hopefully sound pretty familiar by now. Operators are the basic math symbols used to do mathematical operations. I've been using the most common four (+, -, +, and /) throughout the book, so I'll assume you know what these basic operators do. If not, you can always refer to the "Operators" section of Chapter 3. These symbols can be used in conjunction with = for assignment operations, as in speed+=.5. I also cover assignment operations in detail in Chapter 3. % is a strange operator to many people, so it may need a little more clarification. You might remember that % is called the modulus operator, and it used to find the remainder of a division operation. For example, **5 % 3 = 2** and **6 % 2 = 0**. In the first example, 2 is the remainder of the division; in the second expression, there is no remainder, so it equals 0. Two other operators that may need a little further clarification are the increment and decrement operators (++ and --). I've used these throughout the book as well, so you are probably familiar with how they basically work. What I haven't covered are the pre and post options when using them. I've mostly been using them on the right side of the operand, as in speed++, but it is perfectly valid to write the statement as ++speed. However, there is a subtle difference in how these two forms work. For example, in the following code snippets, the pre increment expression outputs a 7 and the post increment a 6. Why?

Here's the pre increment code:

```
int val = 6;
print(++val);    //outputs 7
```

And here's the post increment version:

```
int val = 6;
print(val++);    //outputs 6
```

The pre increment performs the incrementation before the print function returns a value, and the post version does it afterward. If you run a second print statement on the variable, as follows, you'll see that it now says 7:

```
int val = 6;
println(val++);    //outputs 6
print(val);    //outputs 7
```

Bitwise Operators

Bitwise operators act at the bit level (down at the zeros and ones), and are especially useful for efficiently manipulating the individual RGBA color components of pixels. The four bitwise operators included in Processing are: >> (right shift), << (left shift), & (bitwise AND), and | (bitwise OR). In addition, there are a few more bitwise operators in Java that you can use in Processing but that are not covered within the Processing API. I cover bitwise operations in detail in Appendix B.

Calculation

The Calculation section includes 15 very handy functions. Some of the functions round values based on different rules. For example, ceil() always rounds up, floor() always rounds down, and round() rounds the normal way—to whichever value is closer. There is a function to calculate distance (dist()), square roots (sqrt()), maximums (max()), and minimums (min()). Many of these functions can be considered convenience functions, in the sense that it's possible to use other existing code structures in Processing to derive your own routines for these functions. That said, it really doesn't make a whole lot of sense to re-create perfectly fine (and very likely more efficient) existing code.

Trigonometry

Trigonometry rocks! I know this might sound like a shocking and absurd statement to many of you (or you've already written me off as a major geek and have come to expect it). Trig allows you to do very cool things with code that would be a major pain without it. Some of these things include wave generation, firing projectiles/aiming, 2D and 3D rotations, and any type of organic motion. I cover trig in Chapter 4, in the section entitled "The Joy of Math," as well as in Appendix B; and (in case you haven't noticed), I've also been using it in many of the code examples throughout the book.

The Trigonometry section includes nine functions: the basic three and their inverses (sin(), cos(), tan(), asin(), acos(), and atan()); two useful utility functions (degrees() and radians(), which convert between these different units of measure); and atan2(), a variation on atan(). Remember that trig functions expect angles in radians, not degrees. Without the radians() function, you'd have to take all your angles, multiply them by pi, and then divide by 180 to convert to radians; it's much simpler to write radians(*angle in degrees*). The atan2() function is really handy for aiming and shooting stuff on the computer—two things my seven-year-old son can't seem to get enough of (in spite of his peacenik, granola-eating parents' best intentions).

Random

The Random section includes five functions involved in random number generation. In practically every piece of software art I create, I include some random processes. Randomization brings an organic quality to the coding process, as well as a sense of continuous discovery. Processing has two random generators: random() and noise(). random() is the far simpler function, and the one I use most often. It works by receiving either one or two arguments, as in

```
random(1)
```

or

```
random(1, 10);
```

The first case generates a random float value between 0 and the argument (in this case, 1). The second version generates a random float value between the two arguments (1 and 10). If you need the returned value to be an integer, you'll need to convert the result using a statement such as the following:

```
round(random(1, 10));
```

The noise() function is an advanced function based on Perlin noise, developed by Ken Perlin. Ken Perlin is a professor at NYU's Media Research Laboratory (within the Department of Computer Science) who actually won an academy award for his development of Perlin noise. The problem with using pure random numbers for generating textures, motion, or any type of organic effect is the overly even distribution of the randomness. It's a paradox, but pure randomness is not quite random enough in a sense. Perlin addressed this issue by creating more harmonically structured and pleasing noise that utilizes controllable, semi-random number generation in combined octaves of varying frequencies, generating noise patterns that have both high and low peaks within the random distribution (it sounds complicated because it is). Perlin's breakthrough allowed for all kinds of procedural textures and fractal-like structures to be developed, including virtual clouds, oceans, and mountains.

There are also two seed functions within the Random section: noiseSeed() and randomSeed()—one for each generator. The seed functions, when passed a constant, allow the generators to produce repeatable random patterns. For example, when you run the following sketch, the first loop utilizes a seed to generate a repeating value, while the second loop generates a random value each iteration of the loop:

```
println("using a seed");
for (int i=0; i<5; i++){
  randomSeed(0);
  println(random(1, 10));
}
println("without a seed");
for (int i=0; i<5; i++){
  println(random(1, 10));
}
```

Constants

The Constants section includes three constants: HALF_PI, TWO_PI, and PI. If you haven't realized it by now, pi is a very significant number, especially in trigonometry; enough said. And that concludes the core API.

Processing libraries

In addition to the core language, there are seven core Processing libraries. These libraries extend Processing's capabilities into more specific areas, such as video, networking, serial communication, and JavaScript. In addition to the core libraries, there are (as of this writing) over 40 user-contributed libraries, each with its own API. These libraries extend Processing in areas including sound control, physics, motion detection, and database connectivity, just to name a few.

A detailed description of Processing's libraries are beyond the scope of this book, which focuses on the core language. It is likely that in future releases of Processing, only minor new functionality will be added directly to the core. Instead, Processing's growth will happen externally, through user-contributed libraries. The most up-to-date information about Processing's libraries, including their respective APIs, can be found at `http://processing.org/reference/libraries/index.html`. Information on how to go about creating a library (which requires a working knowledge of Java) can be found in the `howto.txt` document located in the `libraries` subdirectory within your Processing application directory. Please note that libraries cannot be created from within Processing itself.

Finally, as you progress in coding, there are times you'll want to refer to the Java API directly, or even take a look under the hood at Processing's source code. The Java API (Standard Edition, version 1.4.2) can be found at `http://java.sun.com/j2se/1.4.2/docs/api/`. The Processing source code, as well as information relating to Processing's overall development, is at `http://dev.processing.org`.

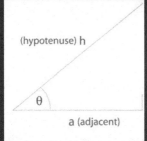

(hypotenuse) h

θ

a (adjacent)

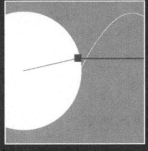

B MATH REFERENCE

Appendix B includes mathematical concepts and code examples that didn't quite fit within earlier sections of the book, but nonetheless could be useful and hopefully interesting for creative coding.

Algebra

We use the term *literate* to describe a person fluent in the use of a natural language. The term *numerate* describes a similar fluency with math, and algebra is first and foremost at the core of that fluency. Programming and algebra have a close relationship, as they both utilize expressions composed of symbols. Following are some handy rules and procedures fundamental to algebra and programming.

Adding negative numbers

Adding two negatives results in a larger negative:

$$-3+(-6)=-9$$

Here's another (simpler) way to write the previous expression:

$$-3-6=-9$$

Subtracting negative numbers

Subtracting by a negative is like adding:

$$3-(-4)=3+4=7$$

Multiplying negative numbers

Multiplying two negatives creates a positive:

$$-3\times(-5)=15$$

Dividing by zero

You can't do it!

Multiplying fractions

Multiply the two numerators and two denominators:

$$\frac{x}{y}+\frac{y}{x}=\frac{xy}{yx}$$

After multiplying, you can reduce the fraction to its lowest terms:

$$\frac{5}{8} \times \frac{2}{3} = \frac{10}{24} = \frac{5}{12}$$

Adding fractions

The following gives an example of adding two fractions.

$$\frac{2}{3} + \frac{3}{4}$$

First, find the least common multiple of the denominator. In this case, 12 is the lowest common multiple of 3 and 4. Then, multiply the numerators by the same factor needed to make the denominators 12:

$$\frac{2(3)}{4(3)} + \frac{3(2)}{6(2)}$$

Finally, add the numerators, put the sum over the common denominator, and reduce:

$$\frac{2(3)}{4(3)} + \frac{3(2)}{6(2)} = \frac{6+6}{12} = 1$$

Dividing fractions

Flip the numerator and denominator in the bottom fraction (which is called its reciprocal) and then multiply the original fraction in the numerator by this reciprocal.

Here's a general form of the process:

$$\frac{\frac{x}{y}}{\frac{y}{x}} = \frac{x}{y} \times \frac{x}{y} = \frac{x^2}{y^2}$$

And here's a concrete example:

$$\frac{\frac{7}{4}}{\frac{2}{9}} = \frac{7}{4} \times \frac{9}{2} = \frac{63}{8} = 7\frac{7}{8}$$

Working with negative exponents

Make the negative exponents positive by moving them to the other side of the fraction. Here's a general form of the process:

$$y^{-x} = \frac{y^{-x}}{1} = \frac{1}{y^x}$$

Here's an example:

$$2^{-3} = \frac{2^{-3}}{1} = \frac{1}{2^3} = \frac{1}{8}$$

Understanding the exponential-logarithm relationship (they're inverse)

Here's an exponential statement in a general form:

$$x = b^n$$

This last expression is equivalent to the following logarithmic statement (also in a general form):

$$n = \log_b(x)$$

Here's an example:

$$16 = 2^4$$

$$4 = \log_2(16)$$

Understanding the relationship between radicals and fractional exponents

The square root of a value and that value raised to the 1/2 power are equivalent. Here's the relationship in a general form:

$$\sqrt{x} = x^{\frac{1}{2}}$$

Here's an example:

$$\sqrt{25} = 25^{\frac{1}{2}} = 5$$

The relationship holds for a radical to any root. Here's the relationship expressed in a general form:

$$\sqrt[n]{x} = x^{\frac{1}{n}}$$

Here's an example:

$$\sqrt[3]{27} = 27^{\frac{1}{3}} = 3$$

Multiplying and dividing exponents

When multiplying, if the bases are the same and the exponents are different, add the exponents. Here's the rule in a general form:

$$x^a \times x^b = x^{a+b}$$

Here's an example:

$$5^2 \times 5^4 = 5^6 = 15625$$

When dividing, if the bases are the same and the exponents are different, subtract the exponents. Here's the rule in a general form:

$$x^a \div x^b = x^{a-b}$$

Here's an example:

$$5^4 \div 5^2 = 5^2 = 25$$

When multiplying, if the bases are different and the exponents are the same, raise the product of the two bases to the exponent. Here's the rule in a general form:

$$x^a \times y^a = (xy)^a$$

Here's an example:

$$3^2 \times 4^2 = (3 \times 4)^2 = 144$$

When dividing, if the bases are different and the exponents are the same, raise the product of the two bases to the exponent. Here's the rule in a general form:

$$x^a \div y^a = \left(\frac{x}{y}\right)^a$$

Here's an example:

$$5^2 \div 2^2 = \left(\frac{5}{2}\right)^2 = 6.25$$

When raising a base to two powers, raise the base to the product of the two powers. Here's the process in a general form:

$$\left(x^a\right)^b = x^{(a \times b)}$$

Here's an example:

$$\left(4^2\right)^3 = 4^6 = 4096$$

Raising a base to a power of 0 equals one.

$$x^0 = 1$$

Geometry

Drawing anything on the computer ultimately comes down to working with points, lines, curves, shapes, and so forth, so dealing with geometry is unavoidable. However, unlike the vague memories (perhaps nightmares) you may have of perplexing geometry proofs, for the purpose of basic creative coding, you really just need some simple rules and a list of handy formulae.

Pythagorean theorem

I suspect most of you remember something about the Pythagorean theorem. It is a simple equation for figuring the lengths of sides of a right triangle. The side opposite the right angle is the hypotenuse, which we commonly refer to as c, and the other sides are labeled a and b. The way the sides relate is as follows:

$$c^2 = a^2 + b^2$$

Although the Pythagorean theorem is relatively simple, it is crucially important to our work in computer graphics, so it's worth memorizing.

Distance formula

The distance formula relates directly to the Pythagorean theorem, and we use it to find the length of any line on the Cartesian coordinate system. Finding the length of vertical and horizontal lines is easy, as their distance is just the difference between either the x (horizontal line) or y (vertical line) components of the two points at either end of the line ($x_2 - x1$ or $y_2 - y1$). Diagonal lines are harder to measure and require the distance formula. The distance formula is the following:

$$\sqrt{(x_2 - x_1)^2 + (y_2 - y_1)^2}$$

x_2 and x_1 are the two x components of the two points at either end of the line you're trying to measure, and y_2 and y_1 are obviously the y components. The trick is to put the line in a form you can easily solve for—and that is as part of a right triangle (as shown in Figure B-1). Make the line you're attempting to measure the hypotenuse of a right triangle, with one of its legs parallel to the x-axis and the other leg parallel to the y-axis. Now, if you know the distance of the two new sides you added to the triangle, you can easily solve for c, the hypotenuse. The distances of a and b respectively are simply the values $x_2 - x_1$ and $y_2 - y_1$. Thus, just stick these expressions in the hypotenuse theorem, solving for c, and you get the distance formula.

Area of a triangle

The area of a triangle equals one half times the length of a base times the corresponding height:

$$A = \frac{1}{2} \times b \times h$$

Area of a rectangle

The area of a rectangle equals its length times its width:

$$A = l \times w$$

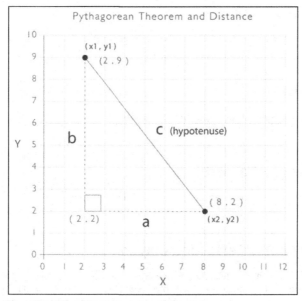

Figure B-1. Using a right triangle to solve for distance

Area of a parallelogram

The area of a parallelogram equals its base times its height:

$A = b \times h$

Area of a trapezoid

The area of a trapezoid equals 1/2 times its height, times the sum of its bottom base and its top base (Figure B-2 shows an example):

$$A = \frac{1}{2} \times h \times (a + b)$$

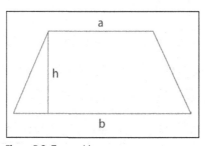

Figure B-2. Trapezoid

753

Perimeter of a rectangle

The perimeter of a rectangle equals two times its length plus two times its width:

$P = 2 \times l + 2 \times w$

Area of a circle

The area of a circle equals pi times the radius squared:

$A = \pi \times r^2$

Circumference of a circle

The circumference of a circle equals two times pi times its radius:

$C = 2 \times \pi \times r$

Area of any non-intersecting polygon

There are times when you need to find the area of a shape (an irregular polygon) that's not a rectangle, circle, triangle, or other polygon with a handy area formula. One approach is to break the shape into smaller triangles and sum up their combined areas. However, there's an easier solution that works for all non-intersecting polygons, using the shape's vertices. This approach, shown in Figure B-3, also lends itself very well to programming.

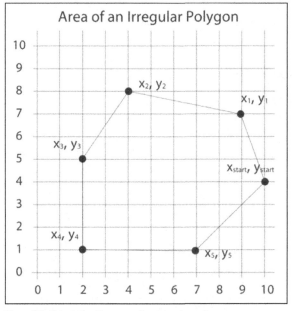

Figure B-3. Calculating the area of an irregular polygon

Here's how the process works: pick a point on the polygon and begin moving in a counterclockwise fashion around the shape. Assuming the first point you choose is (x_{start}, y_{start}) and the last point before you close the shape is (x_n, y_n), you multiply the start x value with the next vertex's y value and subtract that same vertex's x value multiplied by the start y value. You continue this process all the way around the shape. Obviously, the last point will be the first point (x_{start}, y_{start}), since you're dealing with a closed shape. Finally, you take half of the entire value to get the area. Here's the process in a generalized equation form:

$$\frac{1}{2}\left[\left(x_{start} \times y_1 - x_1 \times y_{start}\right) + \left(x_1 \times y_2 - x_2 \times y_1\right) + \ldots + \left(x_{n-1} \times y_n - x_n \times y_{n-1}\right) + \left(x_n \times y_{start} - x_{start} \times y_n\right)\right]$$

> Please note that if you happen to do the rotation in the wrong direction, and move in a clockwise fashion around the polygon, you'll get the same area, but as a negative value.

Trigonometry

The trig functions are central to graphics programming. However, if you're anything like me, you probably have a hazy memory of how and why they are used. Perhaps you remember the mnemonic device **soh-cah-toa**, used to remember the relationships between the trig functions and a right triangle (illustrated in Figure B-4).

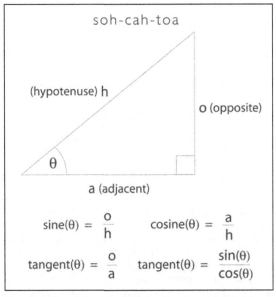

Figure B-4. The relationship of trig functions to a right triangle

- **soh** stands for "sine equals opposite over hypotenuse." "Opposite" refers to the side opposite the angle.

- **cah** stands for "cosine equals adjacent over hypotenuse." "Adjacent" is the side next to the angle.

- **toa** refers to "tangent equals opposite over adjacent."

You should also notice in the figure that tangent equals sine(θ) over cosine(θ). You may also remember that sine and cosine are similar when you graph them, both forming periodic waves—only the cosine wave is shifted a bit (90° or pi/2) on the graph, which is technically called a phase shift. I fully realize that it is a difficult to deal with this stuff in the abstract. Fortunately, there is another model used to visualize and study the trig functions: the **unit circle** (shown in Figure B-5).

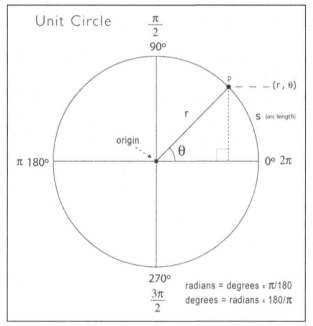

Figure B-5. The unit circle

The unit circle is a circle with a radius of 1 unit in length—hence its imaginative name. When you work with the unit circle, you don't use the regular and trusted Cartesian coordinate system; instead you use a polar coordinate system. The Cartesian system works great in a rectangular grid space, where a point can be located by a coordinate, such as (x, y). In a polar coordinate system, in contrast, location is specified by (r, θ), where r is the radius and θ (the Greek letter *theta*) is the angle of rotation. The unit circle has its origin at its center, and you measure angles of rotation beginning at the right-middle edge of the unit circle (facing 3 o'clock) and moving in a counterclockwise direction around it.

In Figure B-5, the point p is at 45° or pi/4. You can use pi also to measure around the unit circle, as illustrated in the figure. Halfway around the circle (180°) is equal to pi radians, and all the way around the circle is equal to 2pi radians and also 0 radians, since a circle is continuous and ends where it begins. The number pi is a constant that is equal to the circumference of a circle divided by its diameter, and is approximately 3.142. Pi is probably most famous for its non-repeating decimal expression, as it is an irrational number. Irrational numbers, as opposed to rational numbers, can't be put into an exact fractional form. If you divide a circle's circumference by its diameter, you'll never get the remainder to 0, nor will the number after the decimal point ever repeat.

B

> *Expressing pi, or at least trying to understand its irrational nature, has fascinated people for a long time. An extreme example of this fascination is the work of Japanese scientist Yasumasa Kanada (http://en.wikipedia.org/wiki/Yasumasa_Kanada), who in 2002 calculated pi out to over 1.24 trillion places. Check out also the work of the Chudnovsky brothers (http://en.wikipedia.org/wiki/Chudnovsky_brothers), who not only previously held the pi-crunching world record, but also applied their mathematical prowess in the service of art, on a complex restoration project of the Hunt of the Unicorn tapestries (http://en.wikipedia.org/wiki/The_Hunt_of_the_Unicorn), hanging in the Cloisters, in New York City.*

In the polar system, you use radians to measure angles, instead of degrees. The angle of rotation in radians is commonly referred to as θ (the Greek letter *theta*). The arc length of this rotation is calculated by r*θ where r is the radius. In a unit circle, with a radius of 1, θ is equal to the arc length of rotation (arc s in Figure B-5). It's nice to know the arc length, but most of the time (in computer graphics), you really just want to know the location of a point in relation to the unit circle. For example, if I wanted to rotate a point around the unit circle, I'd need to know how to place and move the point in a circle. With the unit circle, this is an incredibly easy task and precisely the kind of thing trig is used for.

There is a really simple relationship between the trig functions and the unit circle. Notice in Figure B-5 that from point p on the ellipse, a right triangle is formed within the unit circle. This should immediately make you think of good old Pythagoras. Notice also that r (the radius) is the hypotenuse of the right triangle. In addition, you now also know that with the trig functions, you can use theta and any one side (opposite, adjacent, or hypotenuse) to solve the rest of the triangle. The big payoff of these relationships, for our purposes, is that to translate point p in the polar coordinate system to the Cartesian coordinate system (the system used by our monitors), you would use these simple expressions:

$x = cosine(θ) \times radius$

$y = sine(θ) \times radius$

These seemingly humble little expressions are very powerful and can be exploited for all sorts of expressive and organic purposes.

Here's how you actually use the trig functions in Processing:

```
float x = cos(radians(angle)) * radius;
float y = sin(radians(angle)) * radius;
```

Notice that there is a function call (radians(angle)) inside each of the trig function calls. Remember that theta is measured in radians, in the polar coordinate system. However, in the Cartesian coordinate system, you work in degrees. To convert between radians and degrees and vice versa, you can use the following expressions:

$radians = angle \times \pi \div 180$

$degrees = \theta \times 180 \div \pi$

Or better yet, just use Processing's handy conversion functions:

```
theta = radians(angle)
angle = degrees(theta)
```

Lastly, I include an example that clearly demonstrates how the unit circle and sine function relate. A while back I came across a Java applet on the Web that showed this relationship (sorry, but I don't remember the link), and I thought it was interesting, so I created my own version in Processing (shown in Figure B-6):

```
/* Sine Console
 Ira Greenberg, October 23, 2005 */

float px, py, px2, py2;
float angle, angle2;
float radius = 100;
float frequency = 2;
float frequency2 = 2;
float x, x2;

// used to create font
PFont myFont;

void setup(){
  size(600, 200);
  background (127);
  // generate processing font from system font
  myFont = createFont("verdana", 12);
  textFont(myFont);
}

void draw(){
  background (127);
  noStroke();
  fill(255);
  ellipse(width/8, 75, radius, radius);
  // rotates rectangle around circle
  px = width/8 + cos(radians(angle))*(radius/2);
  py = 75 + sin(radians(angle))*(radius/2);
  rectMode(CENTER);
  fill(0);
  //draw rectangle
```

```
  rect (px, py, 5, 5);
  stroke(100);
  line(width/8, 75, px, py);
  stroke(200);

  // keep reinitializing to 0, to avoid
  // flashing during redrawing
  angle2 = 0;

  // draw static curve - y = sin(x)
  for (int i=0; i<width; i++){
    px2 = width/8 + cos(radians(angle2))*(radius/2);
    py2 = 75 + sin(radians(angle2))*(radius/2);
    point(width/8+radius/2+i, py2);
    angle2 -= frequency2;
  }

  // send small ellipse along sine curve
  // to illustrate relationship of circle to wave
  noStroke();
  ellipse(width/8+radius/2+x, py, 5, 5);
  angle -= frequency;
  x+=1;

  // when little ellipse reaches end of window
  // reinitialize some variables
  if (x>=width-60) {
    x = 0;
    angle = 0;
  }

  // draw dynamic line connecting circular
  // path with wave
  stroke(50);
  line(px, py, width/8+radius/2+x, py);

  // output some calculations
  text("y = sin x", 35, 185);
  text("px = " + px, 105, 185);
  text("py = " + py, 215, 185);
}
```

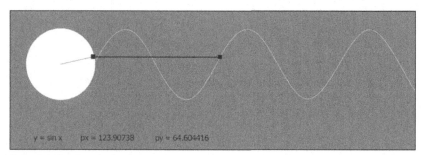

Figure B-6. Sine Console sketch

Bitwise Operations

If you look at what the Processing language reference has to say about the red() function, there's a mysterious blurb under the description section:

"The red() function is easy to use and understand, but is slower than another technique. To achieve the same results when working in colorMode(RGB, 255), but with greater speed, use the >> (right shift) operator with a bit mask."

The terms *right shift operator* and *bit mask* can be generally grouped under the heading of bitwise operations. I briefly mentioned bitwise operations in Chapter 10 and in Appendix A, but next I'll provide a detailed account of how they work and why you might want to learn them.

> *A word of caution: Bitwise operations can be daunting for beginners (actually even experienced coders) and are an advanced topic. Though they can be difficult to get your head around, bitwise operators are also powerful and highly efficient processing tools and certainly worth (eventually) learning about.*

As part of my research for the book, I did a web search on bitwise operations, and was surprised at how poorly they were explained—including in my trusted Wikipedia. There are plenty of bitwise operation examples, but I had trouble finding a really clear elucidation—especially for new programmers. Thus, I have taken this challenge on, as a personal mission, to demystify the mass confusion and escalating anxiety over bitwise operations (at least in their relation to Processing and color).

First of all, what the heck are bitwise operations, and why are they in Processing in the first place, especially if they're not easy to use? Bitwise operations are super-low-level mathematical operations, down at the binary or bit level. Rather than dividing 4 by 2 like 4/2, I could get the same answer (2) using a bitwise operation, which would look like 4>>1, or even 4^6. Yikes, why would I want to do that?! Well, most of the time I wouldn't. However, there are some good reasons to break out bitwise operations (as well as some really geeky low-level reasons that most of us Processing types are not gonna want/need to do). Color manipulation is one area in which bitwise operations are pretty handy, and why I believe they were included in Processing.

OK, but I still haven't really told you anything about bitwise operations. To begin to understand them, you need to think a little about how numbers are represented on the computer, and to do that you need to go all the way down to the periodic table and the element silicon. (Oh boy.)

Semiconductors

I suspect by now, most of you realize computers groove on zeros and ones. Why? Well, this is actually a pretty interesting story (that I will very highly abridge). The brain of the computer, or the CPU, is made up of a lot of little data processing units called transistors; you can actually buy CPUs now that have over 1 billion transistors etched onto a 1-inch-square silicon chip, with wiring over a thousand times thinner than a human hair. (Which maybe offers some insight into the famous question, "How many angels can fit on the head of a pin?") Angels aside, transistors are like little switches that open and close, controlling how electricity flows.

Silicon, a really common and cheap element (think sand on the beach), has one very significant property. Its outer shell (we're on the periodic table now, down at the atomic level) has four measly electrons that all bond with other nearby silicon atoms, forming crystal lattice structures.

> *A somewhat valuable by-product of this tendency to form crystal lattice structures is the diamond, made from carbon, which is right above silicon on the periodic table, and has a similar property.*

Because all four of silicon's outer electrons form these perfect bonds, there are no free electrons roaming around, which is not a good thing in regard to electricity, as electricity requires these free electrons to flow. So silicon, unlike a metal such as copper, is not considered a conductor. However, it's not considered an insulator either (like rubber, for instance). Instead, silicon is classified as a semiconductor. You've probably heard the term *semiconductor* before, as the entire computer industry is built on semiconductors. So if silicon can't conduct electricity, why do we use it, and what the heck does this all have to do with color?

There is a process called doping (no, I'm not contesting Lance Armstrong's seventh Tour de France win) that allows silicon to be developed into a controllable conductive material. The controllable part is what is key here. Using doping, it's possible, applying the right amount of current to the silicon transistors, to cause them to conduct electricity; you can think of the process almost like pushing on a hinged gate—the gate stays shut until enough force is exerted on it. These relatively simple and inexpensive gates are the basis of computing, and ultimately why we have bitwise operations.

Since the gates can only either be open or closed, you can use just two values to represent the different possible states of the gate: 1 for open and 0 for closed. A single transistor being either open or closed wouldn't give us much logic to work with, but if you take all the transistors on a CPU, and begin coding logic based on series of these gates being open or closed, well, the possibilities are limitless. And since the core processing logic at the chip level is based on this binary (zeros and ones) system, bitwise operations (also based on a binary system) are really efficient, which means large amounts of data can be processed more quickly. This speed benefit is the main reason it's worth learning to directly manipulate bits with regard to graphics computing.

Color data structure

Besides the silicon story, there is another practical reason why bitwise operations work well with color, and it relates to how color is stored and structured in memory.

Color information is stored in what's referred to as a packed 32-bit integer, representing alpha, red, green, and blue. The reason the integer is referred to as "packed" is because the components—alpha (A), red (R), green (G), and blue (B)—are divided up into distinct, delineated 8-bit sections. The following line shows how the color is actually stored as an integer (the letter of the color is used to show the place in the integer):

AAAAAAAARRRRRRRRGGGGGGGGBBBBBBBB

In actuality, of course, the values of each of the bits can only be 0 or 1. Remember, a 32-bit integer is just a binary (base 2) number to 32 places. Also, alpha by default is set to 100% when you create a color (which equals all ones for its eight bits). So, for example, the color purple at 100 percent alpha would be represented like this: 11111111 11111111 00000000 11111111. (I separated the 32 bits into four 8-bit groups just to help you visualize where each of the components is stored in the continuous 32-bit string). Likewise, the color red would be 11111111 11111111 00000000 00000000, and blue would be 11111111 00000000 00000000 11111111. If this still isn't clear, maybe this list will help (please note that the bits are counted from right to left):

- **Alpha**: Bits 25 through 32
- **Red**: Bits 17 through 24
- **Green**: Bits 9 through 16
- **Blue**: Bits 1 through 8

What is confusing about the color integer (at first glance) is that the 8 bits controlling alpha seem to be on the wrong side of the bit string, since alpha is normally specified as the fourth argument when you create an (RGBA) color, as in color c = color(255, 127, 0, 255). However, in the integer, alpha is specified in the first 8 bits. I'm also using the default value for alpha, which is 100 percent, which is why all the places (where alpha is specified) are 1.

OK, but that still doesn't explain why the value of eight ones is equal to 100 percent alpha? The trick to converting a binary value (like eight ones) back to our more familiar decimal (base 10) system is to think about how numbers are represented, which is easiest for us to do in our base 10 system. For example, what's the difference between the numbers 52, 479, and 100,000? The key to answering this question is found in the number of places in the number, as shown in the following equations—remember that any number raised to the 0 power is equal to 1—that is, $n^0 = 1$):

$52 = 5 \times 10^1 + 2 \times 10^0$

$52 = 50 + 2$

$479 = 4 \times 10^2 + 7 \times 10^1 + 9 \times 10^0$

$479 = 400 + 70 + 9$

$100,000 = 1 \times 10^5 + 0 \times 10^4 + 0 \times 10^3 + 0 \times 10^2 + 0 \times 10^1 + 0 \times 10^0$

$100,000 = 100,000 + 0 + 0 + 0 + 0 + 0$

Now let's go back to the alpha setting in base 2:

$11111111 = 1 \times 2^7 + 1 \times 2^6 + 1 \times 2^5 + 1 \times 2^4 + 1 \times 2^3 + 1 \times 2^2 + 1 \times 2^1 + 1 \times 2^0$

$11111111 = 128 + 64 + 32 + 16 + 8 + 4 + 2 + 1$

$11111111 = 255$

The 255 probably rings a bell, as it's the highest value any of the individual RGBA components can have.

Bitwise operations to the rescue

Referring back to the Processing reference, if you call the function float r = red(myColor); by passing in a color argument (which I'm calling myColor), the red value is pulled out of the color and returned as a float value, which I'm assigning to the float variable r. Well, a faster way to get the red value is to perform a bitwise operation on the color. Now you may say, big deal, computers are fast. This is way too confusing to warrant the little savings in time. However, imagine now you have an image that is 1,500 pixels times 1,000 pixels (or a total of 1,500,000 pixels) and you want to do a series of manipulations to all the pixels in the image, and maybe you even want to animate it—well, processing time is now a huge deal, and the bitwise operators may very well save the day.

Again, here's the expression float r = red(myColor); handled as a bitwise operation:

```
float r = myColor >> 16 & 0xFF;
```

I know this expression must look odd (and maybe even scary) to many of you—it totally did to me. There are two distinct processes occurring on the integer in this little line of code. The first process involves the bits of the integer being shifted 16 places to the right (using >> 16), and after that, a bitwise AND operation (using & 0xFF) is performed, yielding the isolated red value. I'll look at each process separately.

Shifting bits

Shifting bits 16 places to the right literally means moving all the bits over 16 places. There are two different bitwise shift operators in Processing: >> and <<. The first (>>) shifts bits to the right and the second (<<) shifts them to the left. So for example, if the number 64 (expressed as 1000000 in binary) has its bits shifted 1 place to the right, using the expression 64 >> 1, then the binary result will be 100000, which equals 32 in decimal (2^6).

It's no coincidence that shifting to the right 1 bit halved the number. In fact, this is an excellent use for bit shifting. As you might suspect, shifting to the left 1 bit doubles the number. Here's a simple example in Processing that outputs some results verifying this:

```
int val1 = 1000;
int val2 = 32044;
int val3 = -2275686;
println("val1 = " + val1);
println("val1 >> 1 = " + (val1>>1));
println("val1 << 1 = " + (val1<<1));
println("--------------------");
println("val2 = " + val2);
println("val2 >> 1 = " + (val2>>1));
println("val2 << 1 = " + (val2<<1));
println("--------------------");
println("val3 = " + val3);
println("val3 >> 1 = " + (val3>>1));
println("val3 << 1 = " + (val3<<1));
```

The sketch outputs the following:

```
val1 = 1000
val1 >> 1 = 500
val1 << 1 = 2000
--------------------
val2 = 32044
val2 >> 1 = 16022
val2 << 1 = 64088
--------------------
val3 = -2275686
val3 >> 1 = -1137843
val3 << 1 = -4551372
```

Working with Processing's color data type (which as I described earlier is a packed 32-bit integer) is a little trickier. Most of the complexity involves how the 32-bit integer evaluates to a decimal value. For example, run the following sketch, the output of which may surprise many of you:

```
color c1 = color(255, 255, 255, 128);
color c2 = color(255, 255, 255, 127);

println ("c1 in binary = " + binary(c1));
println ("c1 in decimal = " + c1);
println ("-----------------------------------------------");
println ("c2 in binary = " + binary(c2));
println ("c2 in decimal = " + c2);
```

Here's the output:

```
c1 in binary = 10000000111111111111111111111111
c1 in decimal = -2130706433
-------------------------------------------------------------------------
c2 in binary = 1111111111111111111111111111111
c2 in decimal = 2147483647
```

Look at the output closely. Notice that c1's binary bit string (32 digits) is actually 1 digit longer than c2's (31 digits). (If you don't feel like counting all the ones, just take my word for it.) Also, and more bewildering, c1's decimal value is negative while c2's is positive. Why?

Both c1 and c2 have identical RGB values. However, their alpha values are 128 and 127, respectively. So all the variations between their binary bit strings and decimal values are somehow caused by this slight variation (probably not even visibly noticeable) in their alpha values. Why again? The long answer is not simple, so I'll give a "good enough" answer (and of course provide a link to a more detailed explanation).

Processing's (and Java's) 32-bit integer type needs to account for positive and negative values (and 0). There are various ways of coding these values as a binary bit string. The most efficient and common approach is using what's referred to as a **two's complement** system. The very basic way the two's complement system works is as follows: to create a positive number, you simply encode the value using standard binary conversion, as you looked at earlier. So for example, the number 8 in decimal becomes 2^3, or 1000 in binary. To create a negative number, you need to first create a positive binary equivalent of the number, and then invert all the bits (zeros become ones and ones become zeros), and then add 1. So to express –8 in a two's complement system, first you need to specify 8 as a positive binary number, which you know is 1000. However, 1000 is not the full 32-bit representation of 8, as Processing discarded the 28 zeros to the left of the number. Normally this would be fine, as these zeros on the left side of the number don't change its actual value. But to understand the two's complement system, you need to account for these bits. Here's the full 32-bit binary representation of 8 (with the 28 zeros added on):

```
00000000000000000000000000001000
```

So to calculate –8, first you invert all the bits:

```
11111111111111111111111111110111
```

And then you add 1:

```
11111111111111111111111111111000
```

Simple, right? OK, I know this stuff is pretty confusing. If the two's complement stuff isn't doing it for you, just remember one final rule about it: if the leftmost digit of the entire bit string (referred to as the signed bit) is a zero, the value will be positive, and if the signed bit is a one, the number will be negative. To confirm this, try looking at the binary equivalent of some positive and negative numbers in Processing (or just take my word for it).

If this exciting two's complement discussion really did it for you, check out http://en.wikipedia.org/wiki/Two's_complement.

Let's now return to the initial expression listed in the Processing reference that sparked this discussion:

```
float r = myColor >> 16 & 0xFF;
```

You'll remember that this expression is a way of getting just the red component of the color and a faster alternative to Processing's red() function. Let's assume myColor is #FF00FF (purple) and 100 percent alpha (which you'll remember is the default). The bit string of this color integer is as follows:

```
11111111 11111111 00000000 11111111
(alpha)  (red)    (green)  (blue)
```

Again, I divided the 32-bit string into 4 bytes, just to show how the packed integer represents the different color components. As I specified, the four 8-bit groups, from left to right, represent the alpha, red, green, and blue components, respectively. Remembering what I discussed a few paragraphs back, can you guess whether this integer would evaluate to a positive or negative value? The answer is negative, since the signed (leftmost) bit is a one. To test this, run println(#FF00FF);, which should output -65281. This specific value is not terribly useful. (I remember being pretty confused the first time I ran a println() on one of my colors and it came up with this huge negative value.) What is worth remembering is that the sign of the number is based on the leftmost bit (1 is negative and 0 is positive).

Next, let's shift the bits of the original purple color 16 places to the right. Here is the original bit string:

```
11111111  11111111  00000000  11111111
```

Shifting the bits 16 places to the right, it becomes the following:

```
11111111  11111111  11111111  11111111
```

The 16 bits on the left side of the number move to the right 16 places. The original 16 bits on the right side move over as well, but since there are no places to their right, they are discarded. You may be wondering then why the original 16 places on the left, after the shifting takes place, remain ones instead of becoming zeros. This is a good question, which originally confused me as well. The reason for this relates to the signed bit (the leftmost bit), which you'll remember was a one in the original purple color. When bits are shifted to the right in a two's complement system, any empty positions on the left side, where the bits were shifted away from, as in this example, are filled with the value of the signed bit. That's why in the last example, the left 16 bits were replaced with ones instead of zeros. Here's one more example in Processing:

```
color c1 = color(255, 255, 0, 127);
println("c1 = " + c1);
println("binary(c1)    = " + binary(c1));
println("show 32 bits  = 0" + binary(c1));
println("binary(c1>>16) =                   " + binary(c1>>16));
println("show 32 bits  = 0000000000000000" + binary(c1>>16));
```

This sketch outputs the following:

```
c1 = 2147483392
binary(c1)      =   11111111111111111111111100000000
show 32 bits    = 01111111111111111111111100000000
binary(c1>>16)  =                   111111111111111
show 32 bits    = 00000000000000000111111111111111
```

Notice that I explicitly added zeros to the left of two of the binary outputs (labeled show 32 bits) just to reveal the actual 32 bits of data. Again, the zeros on the left of the number don't change the number's value (and thus normally aren't output when you call println()), but seeing them does make it easier to visually compare the different binary bit strings. The color I began with, c1, had an alpha of 127, giving the color integer a positive value (2147483392) since the signed bit was a zero. Thus, when I shifted all the bits 16 places to the right, the 16 places emptied on the left side of the number were filled with zeros—again following the rule that the signed bit controls what these values should be.

> Please note, when shifting to the left, places emptied on the right (due to the shifting) are always filled with zeros.

Bitwise operators

In addition to bit shifting, the original expression float r = myColor >> 16 & 0xFF; contains a bitwise operator (&) as well as what's referred to as a bit mask (0xFF).

Bitwise operators are similar to other operators you know about (+, *, -, etc.), only bitwise operators work directly on binary numbers. There are four bitwise logical operators in Java, two of which are included in Processing. However, as Processing really is Java, you can use all four in Processing, even though the Processing language reference only covers two of them. As I mentioned, these operators work on binary values (directly with the bits). So if I write 4 | 6, using the bitwise OR operator (which I'll explain shortly), the numbers 4 and 6 will be evaluated as their binary equivalents (100 and 110, respectively). This is great for the computer, which loves (assuming it could actually feel) dealing at the bit level, but kind of lousy for us squishy bio-forms, who are not used to doing fast base 2 calculations. It helps to see the bitwise operators in action to get a better sense of how they work.

The four logical bitwise operators are &, |, ^, and ~.

& is the bitwise AND operator; it works by evaluating the parallel bits of two binary numbers. If the two parallel bits are both 1, then the result for that place is a 1. All other results evaluate out to 0 for that bit position.

The following example compares the parallel bits of the binary values of 4 and 6 (which are listed next) using the bitwise AND operator:

4&6=4

Here is the operation expressed in base 2 (remember, only when both parallel bits are 1 is the result 1; otherwise it's 0):

```
    100
&   110
    100
```

Surprisingly, this result is still 4 when you convert it back to base 10. Pretty odd, huh?

Here's an example that compares the parallel bits of the binary values of 126 and 3498, again using the bitwise AND operator:

126 & 3498 = 42

And here's the operation expressed in base 2:

```
    000001111110
&   110110101010
    000000101010
```

The simplifies to 101010 if zeros on the left are removed.

> *While adding zeros to the left of the number has no effect, adding zeros to the right of a binary number will change the value, so don't do it.*

| is the bitwise OR operator, also called inclusive OR. It operates by evaluating whether either of the two parallel bits is a one, in which case it evaluates to a one; otherwise the result is a zero. (You can also think about this as two parallel zeros equals a zero.)

This next example compares the parallel bits of 4 and 6 using the OR operator:

4|6 = 4

And here's the operation expressed in base 2:

```
    100
|   110
    110  = 6
```

This example compares the parallel bits of the binary values of 126 and 3498, again using the bitwise OR operator:

126|3498 = 3582

And here's the operation expressed in base 2:

```
    000001111110
|   110110101010
    110111111110
```

I'm not going to provide examples for the other two operators, but I'll tell you about them.

^ is the XOR, or exclusive OR, operator. It works by comparing parallel bits, as with the first two operators. However, XOR is looking for differences. If the parallel bits are different, then the result is a one; otherwise the result is a zero.

~ is the bitwise complement and is a unary operator, meaning it works like a binary minus sign on a single operand, inverting zeros to ones and vice versa.

B

Putting it all together

Finally returning to the original bitwise color expression, float r = myColor >> 16 & 0xFF;, you should now have some sense of what is happening in the expression. The last mystery to solve is the bit mask 0xFF. A **bit mask** is just a pattern of bits used to perform some type of operation on another binary value, using one of the bitwise operators you just looked at. The bit mask value itself (0xFF) hopefully looks familiar to you, as it's just a number expressed in hexadecimal notation (base 16). Remember, colors are commonly represented as hexadecimal values. The 0x part of 0xFF tells the compiler that the characters FF should be evaluated in base 16. Since F is the highest value in base 16 (equal to 15 in decimal), FF evaluates to $15 * 16^1 + 15 * 16^0 = 255$, which you'll remember is the same thing as 11111111 (in base 2).

> For those of you who actually like this bit-mathy stuff, break the binary value 11111111 into two even groups of four bits and then evaluate each separately in base 2. Compare the results to the hexadecimal value 0xFF. Do you see the relationship between the binary and hexadecimal values?

Finishing up this long discussion, you now have all the ingredients to understand the bitwise color expression myColor >> 16 & 0xFF. Next is a description of how the expression actually returns the red component of a color.

I'll begin by creating a new color:

    color myColor = color(200, 190, 75, 255);

This color looks like this in binary (please note that I divided the continuous 32-bit string into byte-sized components, for readability):

    11111111   11001000   10111110   01001011

Performing the 16-bit right shift on the number yields the following:

    11111111111111111111111111001000

Next I'll use the bitwise AND operator and bit mask 0xFF (11111111 in binary). Remember, the & operator works by comparing the parallel bits. If the bits are both 1, then the result for that place is a one. All other results evaluate out to zero.

```
  111111111111111111111111111001000
& 00000000000000000000000011111111
  00000000000000000000000011001000
```

Removing the extra zeros on the left of the number, we're left with 11001000, which in decimal notation is equal to 200—the value of the red component.

You can (of course) also use bitwise operations to extract the green, blue, and alpha values from the color, using the following expressions:

```
int g = myColor >> 8 & 0xFF;
int b = myColor & 0xFF;
int a = myColor >> 24 & 0xFF;
```

Finally, to put the individual color component values back together into a packed 32-bit integer, you'd use the left shift operator and the bitwise OR operator, which can be done in multiple lines of code, like this:

```
color newColor = a << 24;
newColor |= r << 16;
newColor |= g << 8;
newColor |= b;
```

Better yet, it can be done as one line of code, like this:

```
color newColor = (a << 24) | (r << 16) | (g << 8) | b;
```

Here's a simple Processing example you can run that confirms all this:

```
// create original myColor
color myColor = color(200, 175, 100, 200);
println("myColor   = " + myColor);
println("myColor in binary = " + binary(myColor));

// extract myColor ARGB components
int a = myColor >> 24 & 0xFF;
println("alpha = " + a);
int r = myColor >> 16 & 0xFF;
println("red = " + r);
int g = myColor >> 8 & 0xFF;
println("green = " + g);
int b = myColor & 0xFF;
println("blue = " + b);

// build newColor from myColor components
color newColor = (a << 24) | (r << 16) | (g << 8) | b;
println("newColor   = " + newColor);
println("newColor in binary = " + binary(newColor));
```

Well, I imagine for some of you this whole bitwise discussion has been rather unpleasant. Hopefully, you now have a better sense about what lurks behind the deceptively simple-looking paint bucket tool in your favorite paint program. You don't need to use bit-wise operations, as Processing has the component property functions red(), green(), blue(), and alpha(); but there may be times when the bitwise operations will really come in handy. Here's a final Processing sketch that illustrates one of the things you can do with bitwise operations (shown in Figure B-7). (Please note this example requires the use of an external image, which needs to be added to the sketch's data directory.)

```
/*
Color Variations Filter Using
Bitwise Operations
Ira Greenberg, November 11, 2005
revised: April 3, 2007
*/

/*change display size to accommodate
 the size of your image */
size(360, 600);

/*remember to add an image into
 the sketch data directory before
 using loadImage() and also to update
 the name of the image below. */
PImage img = loadImage("robin_and_sophie.jpg");
image(img, 0, 0);
// pixel array
int[]pxls = new int[width*height];
// holds shifted colors
color[]newCol = new int[width*height];
// keep track of pixels
int pxlCounter = 0;

/* loop gets color components out
 of color integer using bitwise operators
 and shifts color components before
 rebuilding pixel array- effect is similar
 to Photoshop's variations filter */
for (int i=0; i<width; i++){
  for (int j=0; j<height; j++){
    pxls[pxlCounter] = get(i, j);
    int r = pxls[pxlCounter] >> 16 & 0xFF;
    int g = pxls[pxlCounter] >> 8 & 0xFF;
    int b = pxls[pxlCounter] & 0xFF;
    int a = pxls[pxlCounter] >> 24 & 0xFF;
    /* conditionals check where we are in the image
     min() functions keep color component values in
     range 0-255 to avoid psychadelic artifacting */
    //left column, top row(red+)
    if (i<=width/3 && j<=height/3){
      r = min(r*2, 255);
```

```
    } //left column, middle row(green+)
    else if (i<=width/3 && j> height/3 && j<=height*.667){
      g = min(g*2, 255);
    } //left column, bottom row(blue+)
    else if (i<=width/3 && j>height*.667 && j<height){
      b = min(b*2, 255);
    }
    //middle column, top row(value-)
    if (i>width/3 && i<=width*.667 && j<=height/3){
      r*=.4;
      g*=.4;
      b*=.4;
    } //middle column, middle row(normal)
    else if (i>width/3 && i<=width*.667 && j>height/3 && ➥
            j<=height*.667){
      // leave pixels alone in middle box
    } //middle column, bottom row(value+)
    else if (i>width/3 && i<=width*.667 && j<height){
      r = min(r*2, 255);
      g = min(g*2, 255);
      b = min(b*2, 255);
    }
    //right column, top row(yellow+)
    if (i>width*.667 && j<=height/3){
      r = min(r*2, 255);
      g = min(g*2, 255);

    } //right column, middle row(purple+)
    else if (i>width*.667 && j>height/3 && j<=height*.667){
      r = min(r*2, 255);
      b = min(b*2, 255);
    } //right column, bottom row(orange+)
    else if (i>width*.667 && j<height){
      r = min(r*2, 255);
      g = min(int(g*1.5), 255);
    }
    // put colors back together
    newCol[pxlCounter] = (a << 24) | (r << 16) | (g << 8) | b;
    /*The counter needs to be incremented each
     iteration of the loop, and I'm doing it
     within the array brackets. Since that's the last
     place it's used in the loop, it's ok to do this*/
    set(i, j, newCol[pxlCounter++]);
  }
}
```

Figure B-7. Color variations filter using bitwise operations

INDEX

Printed in the United States
By Bookmasters